Comrades and Enemies

Comrades and Enemies

Arab and Jewish Workers in Palestine, 1906–1948

ZACHARY LOCKMAN

University of California Press

BERKELEY   LOS ANGELES   LONDON

This book is a print-on-demand volume. It is manufactured using toner in place of ink. Type and images may be less sharp than the same material seen in traditionally printed University of California Press editions.

University of California Press
Berkeley and Los Angeles, California

University of California Press, Ltd.
London, England

Parts of the Introduction, the Conclusion, and Chapters 2, 3, and 4 were published in earlier versions in Z. Lockman, "Railway Workers and Relational History: Arabs and Jews in British-Ruled Palestine," *Comparative Studies in Society and History* 35, no. 3 (July 1993), 601–627, © 1993 by the Society for the Comparative Study of Society and History, reprinted by permission of Cambridge University Press; and in Z. Lockman, "Exclusion and Solidarity: Labor Zionism and Arab Workers in Palestine, 1897–1929," in Gyan Prakash, ed., *After Colonialism: Imperial Histories and Postcolonial Displacements* (Princeton, N.J., 1995), 211–240, © 1995 by Princeton University Press.

Library of Congress Cataloging-in-Publication Data

Lockman, Zachary.
    Comrades and enemies : Arab and Jewish workers in Palestine,
  1906–1948 / Zachary Lockman.
        p.   cm.
    Includes bibliographical references and index.
    ISBN 0-520-20259-7 (alk. paper).—ISBN 0-520-20419-0 (pbk. :
  alk. paper)
    1. Working class—Palestine—History.   2. Labor Zionism—
  Palestine—History.   3. Jews—Employment—Palestine—History.
  4. Palestinian Arabs—Employment—History.   5. Labor movement—
  Palestine—History.   6. Railroads—Palestine—Employees—History.   7. Histadrut ha-kelalit shel ha-'ovdim be-Erets-Yiśra'el—History.   I. Title.
  HD8660.L63   1996
  331.6'992—dc20   95-22264
                                                            CIP

Printed in the United States of America

For my father, Michael Lockman (1912–1994),
and my daughter, Talya Mara Lockman-Fine

Contents

Acknowledgments

Many people and institutions contributed in different ways to the research, thinking, and writing that went into this book. Though I cannot hope to thank all of them properly, I would like at least to mention those who contributed most significantly and directly, though none of them bears any responsibility for my analyses or judgments in this book, or for any errors it may contain.

I carried out the bulk of the archival and library research for this book in Israel. A preliminary trip was funded by a faculty research support grant from the Harvard Graduate Society, while an extended stay in 1987 was made possible by a fellowship from the Fulbright Scholar Program. A fellowship from the Social Science Research Council supported research in the United Kingdom.

In Israel I spent a great deal of time at the Histadrut archives, known formally as Arkhiyon Ha'avoda Vehehalutz, at the Makhon Lavon Leheker Tnu'at Ha'avoda in Tel Aviv. The Lavon Institute's staff were always helpful and efficient; I thank them, though I suspect that not all of them will be entirely happy with the fruits of my labors. The same applies to the staff of the Hashomer Hatza'ir archives (Merkaz Te'ud Veheker shel Hashomer Hatza'ir) at Giv'at Haviva, recently renamed Yad Me'ir Ya'ari in honor of the movement's founder and longtime leader. Yad Izhak Ben-Zvi Archives in Jerusalem very kindly gave me permission to use the photograph which appears on the cover of this book. Me'ir Lamm granted me permission to use the MAKI papers at the Hakibbutz Hame'uhad archives at Yad Tabenkin.

While in Israel and the occupied Palestinian territories my thinking about what I was doing benefited from conversations with many people, among them Musa Budeiri, David De Vries, Lev Luis Grinberg, Reuven

Kaminer, Michael Shalev, and Salim Tamari. Simha Tzabari was particularly supportive of (and perhaps even excited about) my project, probably because I was studying a piece of the history she had lived through (and sought to shape) as a communist activist. Yosef Vashitz kindly provided me with a copy of his unpublished manuscript on Jews and Arabs in Haifa during the mandate period. I am grateful to all of them, as well as to the veterans of some of the political and social struggles discussed in this book who consented to be interviewed.

A fellowship at Princeton University's Shelby Cullom Davis Center for Historical Studies in 1991–92 enabled me to make many leaps forward, great and small, in the conceptualization and writing of this book. Not only was I freed of teaching responsibilities for a year, I was also immersed in an environment that was simultaneously intellectually stimulating and socially pleasant. The focus of the Center's inquiry in that period, "Colonialism, Imperialism and the Colonial Aftermath," fit in very nicely with my own project, and I learned a lot from (and enjoyed the company of) the other fellows, the scholars who came through each week to present their work, and the many Princeton University faculty and graduate students whom I got to know (or know better). I would particularly like to thank the Center's director at the time, Natalie Zemon Davis, whose intellectual and personal example, leadership skills, and moral support helped make my year in Princeton especially productive and happy.

A year's fellowship at the Woodrow Wilson International Center for Scholars in Washington, D.C., enabled me to finish a first draft of this book and get a lot of other work done as well. Virtually all of my time in Washington was devoted either to writing or to caring for my daughter, and as a result I did not get to know many of my colleagues there as well as I would have liked. I regret that, but I would anyway like to thank them, the institution, and its friendly staff. I must also thank the John Simon Guggenheim Memorial Foundation for a fellowship which enabled me to revise this book for publication and begin or continue work on various other projects.

David Abraham, Joel Beinin, Juan Cole, Beshara Doumani, Stephen Humphreys, Rashid Khalidi, Joel Migdal, Timothy Mitchell, and Gyan Prakash were among those who read and offered useful comments on papers or articles that (after much revision) eventually became part of this book, or on the manuscript as a whole. I owe special thanks to Joel Beinin, for his friendship, his consistent support through difficult times, and his intellectual and political insights, but also because he understands perhaps better than anyone how my personal history intersects with the history this book explores. David Landes and the late Albert Hourani were always encouraging. I would also like to thank everyone at the University of California Press who worked on this book, especially Lynne Withey, Tony Hicks, and Douglas Abrams Arava, as well as my copy editor, Usha Sanyal, whose touch was both light and deft.

I met Melinda Fine, who would eventually do me the honor of marrying me, at an early stage of the process that culminated in this book. She has thus accompanied it through most of its long gestation and deserves credit for helping to bring it to birth. In our years together we have experienced not a few trials and tribulations and lived in far too many different places. Melinda has had to put up with a lot for my sake; I hope she knows that I have always been, and remain, deeply grateful for her abiding love, her patience, and her faith in me and in us.

This book is dedicated to two members of my family, one recently departed and the other a recent addition. My father, Michael Lockman, died in February 1994, as the manuscript of this book was approaching completion. In his eighty-one years he experienced some of the most terrible things that human beings can inflict on one another, but also much joy and satisfaction. Had he lived to read this book he might well have disagreed with much of it, but I believe that his love for me, and his faith in me, were such that he would have made the effort to understand what it was I was trying to do, and why.

One of the blessings which my father received toward the very end of his life was the birth of his first granddaughter (and my first child), Talya Mara Lockman-Fine. Though that was surely not the intention of the granting institutions, various fellowships allowed me to spend a great deal of time with Talya during her first two years of life. That certainly slowed completion of this book, but I am and will always be thankful for that extraordinary experience, and for her presence in my life. Perhaps by the time she is an adult the two peoples of Palestine/Israel will live in peace and justice.

Abbreviations

Bibliographical Citations

AA	Arkhiyon Ha'avoda Vehehalutz, Makhon Lavon Leheker Tnu'at Ha'avoda (Histadrut archives), Tel Aviv
AH	Arkhiyon Abba Hushi, Haifa University Library
CC	Central Committee (*hamerkaz, hava'ad hamerkazi, al-lajna al-markaziyya, al-hay'a al-markaziyya*)
CID	Criminal Investigations Division, Palestine Police
CO	Colonial Office papers, Public Records Office, London
CoC	Coordinating Committee (*hava'ada hamerakezet*) of EC/H, minutes and correspondence at AA
CZA	Central Zionist Archives, Jerusalem
EC/H	Executive Committee of the Histadrut (*hava'ad hapo'el*), minutes and correspondence at AA
EC/KA	Executive Committee of Hakibbutz Ha'artzi, minutes and correspondence at HH
FO	Foreign Office papers, Public Records Office, London
HH	Arkhiyon Hashomer Hatza'ir, Merkaz Te'ud Veheker shel Hashomer Hatza'ir (Hashomer Hatza'ir archives), Giv'at Haviva
HH/AC	Aharon Cohen papers, at Hashomer Hatza'ir archives
ISA	Israel State Archives (Ganzakh Hamedina), Jerusalem
S/EC/H	Secretariat of the Executive Committee of the Histadrut (*mazkirut hava'ad hapo'el*), minutes and correspondence at AA
TUC	Trades Union Congress archives, London

Organizations and Other Terms

AHC	Arab Higher Committee
AURW	Arab Union of Railway Workers
AWC	Arab Workers' Congress
AWS	Arab Workers' Society
COLA	cost of living allowance (added to basic wage)
CRL	Consolidated Refineries, Limited (Haifa)
ETZEL	Irgun Tzva'i Le'umi (National Military Organization)
IPC	Iraq Petroleum Company
IU	International Union of Railway, Postal and Telegraph Workers
MAPAI	Mifleget Po'alei Eretz Yisra'el (Party of the Workers of the Land of Israel)
MAPAM	Mifleget Hapo'alim Hame'uhedet (United Worker's Party)
NLL	National Liberation League
NURPTW	National Union of Railway, Postal and Telegraph Workers
PAWS	Palestinian Arab Workers' Society (Jam'iyyat al-'Ummal al-'Arabiyya al-Filastiniyya)
PCP	Palestine Communist Party
PLL	Palestine Labor League (Ittihad 'Ummal Filastin, Brit Po'alei Eretz Yisra'el)
RWA	Railway Workers' Association
SWP	Socialist Workers' Party
URPTW	Union of Railway, Postal and Telegraph Workers

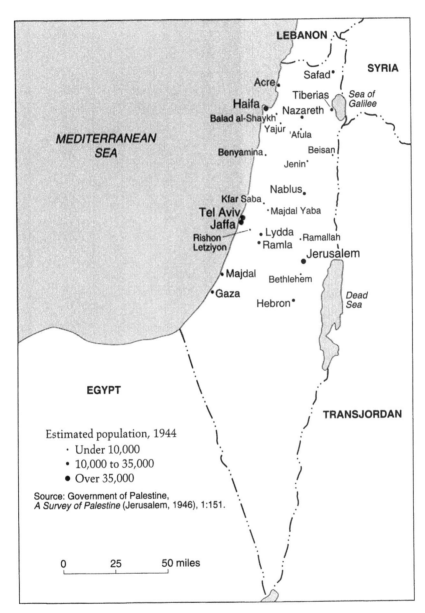

MEDITERRANEAN
SEA

LEBANON

SYRIA

Acre

Safad

Haifa
Balad al-Shaykh

Tiberias

Sea of
Galilee

Nazareth

Yajur

Afula

Benyamina

Beisan

Jenin

Nablus

Kfar Saba

Majdal Yaba

Tel Aviv
Jaffa

Rishon
Letziyon

Lydda

Ramallah

Ramla

Jerusalem

Majdal

Bethlehem

Gaza

Dead
Sea

Hebron

EGYPT

TRANSJORDAN

Estimated population, 1944
· Under 10,000
• 10,000 to 35,000
● Over 35,000

Source: Government of Palestine,
A Survey of Palestine (Jerusalem, 1946), 1:151.

0   25   50 miles

Palestine in the British Mandate period (1920–48): places mentioned in the book.

Introduction

The modern history of Palestine, and especially the fateful encounter between Arabs and Jews in that land from the late nineteenth century onward, has been the subject of numerous studies by scholars and non-scholars alike. Yet despite its size, the literature on Palestine is very uneven in both coverage and quality. In this book I seek to redress some of the shortcomings of that literature and offer new perspectives on the history of Palestine in the twentieth century, and particularly the period of British rule that stretched from the end of the First World War until 1948, when the new State of Israel was established in most of that territory, with the remainder falling under the control of two neighboring states, Transjordan (later renamed Jordan) and Egypt. I do so by exploring certain aspects of Palestine's history in a way that, in terms both of subject matter and of approach, tries to break with the framework within which that history has conventionally been interpreted.

To put it most broadly, this book, drawing mainly on sources in Arabic or Hebrew, explores the interactions among Arab and Jewish workers, trade unions, labor movements, and labor-oriented political parties in Palestine during the British mandate period. That exploration proceeds along several distinct but overlapping and often intertwined paths. Some of these paths venture into territory that has hitherto received little or no scholarly attention; others cover somewhat more familiar ground, though from a different angle and in a way which I hope will enhance our understanding of this historical period.

To begin with, this book explores the thought and practice of the left wing of the Zionist movement, and particularly how it conceived of, and related to, Palestine's indigenous Arab population, especially Arab workers. It seeks to situate this particular variant of Zionism, in all its diversity

1

and specificity, in relation to other strains within Zionism as they emerged in the late nineteenth and twentieth centuries, to contemporary socialism and to contemporary European conceptions of the world and its peoples. At the same time, I argue that any interpretation of Zionism which restricts itself to the European arena is inadequate, for it is one of the central premises of this book that the Zionist movement and the Jewish society it helped create in Palestine were shaped in crucial ways by their interactions with the Arab society they encountered "on the ground" in Palestine itself. As a result, though Chapter 1 takes us as far back as the 1880s and the bulk of the book deals with the mandate years, its subtitle specifies 1906 as the beginning of the period it covers, because it was around then that Jewish socialists newly arrived in Palestine (as opposed to socialist-Zionist theoreticians in Europe) first began to address the issue of relations with Arab workers. This dimension of the book can perhaps best be characterized as a contribution to the social, political, and cultural history of modern Palestine, and especially to the study of Zionist ideology and culture, broadly defined to include Zionists' perceptions of themselves, their project, and the Arabs of Palestine as well as the practices in which those perceptions were manifested.

The complex interactions between Palestine's Arab working class and labor Zionism—by which I mean all the organizations, institutions, parties, and ideologies which were part of, connected with, or oriented toward the Jewish working class and labor movement in Palestine while also seeing themselves as very much part of the broader Zionist project—provide particularly interesting and important terrain for scholarly investigation and will receive considerable attention in this book. Under that rubric I reconstruct the long and complex history of the labor-Zionist movement's efforts to organize Arab workers under its tutelage, the debates which accompanied that project and the contradictions it often entailed, as well as the largely unknown record of its relations with Arab workers and the Arab labor movement. I also discuss the involvement in this arena of the anti-Zionist communist movement in Palestine, at first exclusively Jewish and later comprising both Jews and Arabs. This aspect of the book involves a blend of political, intellectual, institutional, and social history, as well as some biography.

Throughout this book I have tried to ensure that the voices and actions of Arab workers and labor activists, often neglected, are taken into account and incorporated into the narrative I am presenting here. For the historical record as I have reconstructed it demonstrates quite clearly that Arab workers in Palestine were not passive objects of propaganda or organizing efforts by either Zionists or upper-class Arab nationalists, but historical actors in their own right. Moreover, in keeping with the paradigm of historical interpretation which informs this work and on which I will elaborate shortly, I insist that the complex relationship between Arab workers and labor Zionism must be seen as interactive and mutually formative, though perhaps not always in ways which are immediately obvious. I believe that this aspect of the book in particular breaks some new ground in the study of modern Palestine's social, political, and economic history.

A substantial portion of this book is devoted to an in-depth reconstruction of the history of one specific group of Arabs and Jews in Palestine: the workers who operated Palestine's railway system during the mandate period, whose interactions and relationships I explore in great detail. This book is thus also a study in Palestinian working-class history, a field which is still sadly underdeveloped. Other groups of Arab and Jewish workers in Palestine also figure in this book, if in less detail than the railway workers, who enjoy pride of place for reasons which I will explain.

To make clear how these seemingly disparate elements fit together in the framework of a single book, what it is I have tried to do here, and how I have gone about it, I must first discuss the paradigm of historical interpretation which has conventionally been applied to Palestine in the twentieth century and what I see as its defects.[1]

THE "DUAL SOCIETY" PARADIGM

During the period of Ottoman rule over the Arab East, from 1516 until the end of the First World War, the term "Palestine" (in Arabic, *Filastin*) denoted a geographic region, part of what the Arabs called *al-Sham* (historic Syria), rather than a specific Ottoman province or administrative district. By contrast, from 1920 to 1948 Palestine existed as a distinct and unified political (and to a considerable extent economic) entity with well-defined boundaries. Ruled by Britain under a "mandate" obtained from the League of Nations—in essence, a new and somewhat disguised form of colonial rule—Palestine in that period encompassed an Arab majority and a Jewish minority.

By now a substantial historical and sociological literature on Palestine during the mandate period has accumulated. Broadly speaking, several features can be said to characterize this literature.[2] For one, it gives greatly disproportionate attention to elites and to diplomatic, political, and military history, to the disadvantage of other social groups and of the social, economic, and cultural dimensions of the histories of the Arab and Jewish communities in Palestine. There is also, for a variety of reasons, a great quantitative (and to some extent qualitative) disparity between the published research on the policies and activities of the Zionist movement and its component parties and institutions in Palestine, and more broadly the development of the *Yishuv*, the pre-state Jewish community in Palestine, on the one hand, and the literature on the political, social, economic, and cultural history of Palestine's Arab community on the other. I would also argue that many, if not most, of the historians, sociologists, and others who have contributed to this literature have worked from within (and implicitly accepted the premises of) either Zionist or Arab/Palestinian nationalist historical narratives. As a result, much of the published research, while often valuable and important in its own right, nonetheless fails to adopt a sufficiently critical stance toward the categories of historical analysis which it deploys.

These characteristics are to varying degrees related to another historiographical issue, one which is central to the way in which the modern history of Palestine has been framed but which has only recently begun to be subjected to a serious critique. The paradigm of historical interpretation which informs much of the literature has been premised on the implicit or explicit representation of the Arab and Jewish communities in Palestine as primordial, self-contained, and largely monolithic entities. The Yishuv, and to a lesser extent the Palestinian Arab community, are thereby treated as coherent, cohesive, and internally unconflicted objects which developed along entirely separate paths in accordance with dynamics, and as the result of factors, which were largely unique and internal to each. The paradigm thus assumes that the Arab and Jewish communities in Palestine interacted only in very limited ways and only *en bloc* and certainly did not exert a formative influence on one another, as whole communities or through interrelations and dynamics that affected certain segments of each. By extension, this paradigm defines communal identities as natural and pregiven, rather than as constructed within a larger field of relations and forces that differentially affected (or even constituted) subgroups among both Arabs and Jews.

We may call this the "dual society" model, because it posits the existence in mandatory Palestine of two essentially separate societies with distinct and disconnected historical trajectories. This model manifests itself most clearly, perhaps, in the work of leading Israeli scholars, who start from the premise that the history of the Yishuv (and later of Israel) can be adequately understood in terms of the Yishuv's own internal social, political, economic, and cultural dynamics, interacting with the dynamics of world Jewish history. The influence of the largely Arab environment within which the Zionist project and the Yishuv developed, and of the matrix of Arab-Jewish relations and interactions in Palestine, is defined *a priori* not as constitutive but as marginal, and is therefore largely excluded from consideration. This paradigm's conception of the Yishuv as well as of Arab society in Palestine is also rooted in a rather crude version of modernization theory.

A classic example is S. N. Eisenstadt's widely cited 1967 study, *Israeli Society*, which at the outset promises to provide "a systematic analysis of the development of the Jewish community in Palestine from its beginnings in the late 1880s up to the present day."[3] As Talal Asad (among others) has pointed out, Palestinian Arabs play virtually no role whatsoever in Eisenstadt's analysis: the Yishuv appears to have developed in a vacuum, entirely disconnected from and uninfluenced by the Arab society in whose midst it was situated. Instead, for Eisenstadt and many other sociologists and historians, the contours and dynamics of Jewish society in Palestine, and of the future Israeli society, were decisively shaped early in the century by the generation of Zionist "pioneers" who brought with them from eastern Europe those values most conducive to successful institution-building and launched the Yishuv on its own distinct trajectory toward statehood.[4] Eisenstadt's students Dan Horowitz and Moshe Lissak embrace the dual society model even more explicitly in their influential *Origins of the Israeli Polity: Palestine under the Mandate*, which has helped shape the way many historians and sociologists have conceptualized this period:

> In Mandatory Palestine two separate and parallel economic and stratification systems of different levels of modernization emerged which maintained only limited mutual relations. Our contention is that this phenomenon arose due to the influence of ideological and political pressures exerted within each of the two national communities.[5]

As Michael Shalev has noted, the narrative of Yishuv and Israeli history which this paradigm yields is "profoundly conservative."

> It echoes the official version of history and the self-image of the founding fathers. It presents an evolutionary view of history that resonates well with the functionalist theoretical perspective of its proponents. It erects a firm dividing line between the "utopian" and "revolutionary" prehistory of Israeli society and the mundane and disappointing realities of more recent times. It places enormous weight on ideology and leadership as sources of social transformation, leaving little room for economic conflicts and constraints. It conceives of ethnic tensions as reflecting cultural divi-

sions rather than distributive struggles and views the national conflict between Arabs and Jews as a challenge to Israeli society from beyond its
walls, rather than as an endogenous dynamic deeply implicated in the very
constitution of that society.[6]

The dual society model also informs most work on the mandate period
by Palestinian and other Arab scholars, though it is usually not explicitly
theorized. No Arab historian or sociologist could plausibly suggest that
the Zionist project did not, in the long run, have a tremendous impact
on Palestinian Arab society. But that society is usually represented as a
preexisting, already-formed entity which was then threatened, encroached
upon, and, in 1947–49, largely destroyed by an aggressively expanding
Yishuv. Interaction between Arabs and Jews is largely limited to the
sphere of political and military conflict, rather than seen as having had a
significant impact on the development of Palestinian Arab society in other
spheres as well.[7] Many of the foreign scholars who have published research
on the modern history of Palestine have also shared this exclusive focus on
one or the other of the two communities and implicitly or explicitly depicted them as entirely separate, self-contained, and primordial entities.[8]

The dual society paradigm does allow for a single significant mode of
interaction between Arabs and Jews in Palestine: conflict, violent or otherwise. This is one reason for the disproportionate attention in the literature
to the political, diplomatic, and military dimensions of Arab-Jewish relations. However, even as regards conflict one can extend to many historians of modern Palestine the criticism which Avishai Ehrlich put forward
with regard to Israeli sociologists. Arab-Jewish conflict, Ehrlich argued,

> is not integrated analytically into the theoretical framework of the sociolog-
> ical discourse. . . . [It] is not perceived as a continuous formative process
> which shaped the institutional structure and the mentality of the Israeli so-
> cial formation (as well as that of the Palestinian Arab society). At best, if
> at all, the Arabs and conflict are regarded as an external addendum, an ap-
> pendix to an internally self-explanatory structure: an appendix which
> erupts from time to time in a temporary inflammation.[9]

Several factors may explain why the dual society paradigm has been
dominant for so long and why its premises went largely unquestioned.
Very few of the historians, sociologists, and other scholars who have
worked on modern Palestine have had a knowledge of both Arabic and
Hebrew, the most widely spoken languages in Palestine during the mandate period (and after). As a result most of the historical and sociological
literature has been based on source materials in only one of these languages, usually Hebrew, supplemented by material in various European

languages. This willingness to ignore sources written in the language of the "other side" certainly contributed to the prevalence and persistence of the dual society model, even as that model itself provided theoretical justification for this one-sided approach.

But at least as important, and probably more so, are the insularity, self-absorption, and reluctance to challenge the prevailing consensus and dominant nationalist historical narratives characteristic of (but of course not unique to) societies which perceive themselves as still engaged in a life-or-death struggle to realize their national(ist) project and secure their collective existence against grave threats. Without suggesting perfect symmetry between the two sides, it is nonetheless the case that the grip of mythologized national pasts on both Israeli Jews and Palestinian Arabs has until very recently been quite strong, making it difficult even for those historians who regarded themselves as fully committed to the norms of objective scholarship to transcend, or even perceive, the nationalist filters through which they understood the past. Moreover, on both sides perceptions of day-to-day experience, especially the threat or reality of hostility and violence by members of the other group, have served to constantly reconfirm and give new strength to the dominant nationalist narratives, adherence to which thereby becomes a matter of both common sense and survival.

However one explains it, the dominance of the dual society paradigm has manifested (and reproduced) itself in the way in which most scholars have implicitly or explicitly conceptualized their object of study. The result has been a historiography which has hardly questioned the representation of the two communities as self-evidently coherent entities largely or entirely uninfluenced by one another. This approach has rendered their mutually constitutive impact virtually invisible, tended to downplay both intracommunal divisions and intercommunal linkages, and focused attention on episodes of violent conflict, implicitly assumed to be the only normal, significant, or even possible form of interaction. It has also helped divert attention away from exploration of the processes whereby communal identities and nationalist discourses in Palestine were constructed (and contested), including the ways in which boundaries between (and within) communities were drawn and reproduced, and practices of separation, exclusion, and conflict articulated. The glaring lack of attention to the ways in which those identities, discourses, and practices have been thoroughly gendered can be seen as yet another effect of the dominance of the dual society paradigm.

THE EMERGENCE OF A RELATIONAL PARADIGM

In recent years the utility of this paradigm has been increasingly challenged by Israeli, Palestinian, and foreign scholars who have consciously sought to problematize and transcend, or at least to render more complex, both Zionist and Palestinian nationalist historical narratives and categories. This project of critique and reconceptualization has involved a move beyond the narrowly political to explore the social, economic, and cultural histories of each community. In theoretical terms, it has reflected a new commitment to what I will here term relational history, rooted in an understanding that the histories of Arabs and Jews in modern (and especially mandatory) Palestine can only be grasped by studying the ways in which both these communities were to a significant extent constituted and shaped within a complex matrix of economic, political, social, and cultural interactions.[10] This project has also sought to explore how each was shaped by the larger processes by which both were affected, for example the specific form of capitalist development which Palestine underwent from the mid-nineteenth century onward, markets for labor and land, Ottoman patterns of law and administration, and British colonial social and economic policies.

Several factors contributed to this turn to relational history, but the most important was probably the new forms of interaction between Israeli and Palestinian societies that developed in the aftermath of Israel's 1967 conquest of the remainder of mandatory Palestine and the extension of its rule to encompass fully one half of the Palestinian people. The subsequent decades of occupation, conflict, and crisis have made it increasingly clear to all that at the core of the Arab-Israeli conflict lies the Zionist-Palestinian conflict. This has led Israeli Jewish intellectuals in particular to seek a new, demythologized understanding of their past as a way of making sense of the political, social, and cultural changes their own society has undergone as a result of this historic encounter. For their part, since 1967 Palestinian intellectuals and scholars in the occupied West Bank and Gaza and elsewhere have acquired a much deeper and more nuanced understanding of Israeli politics, society, and culture, which has opened the way to a better understanding of Zionist and Israeli history. Foreign scholars have also contributed innovative new work in recent years, influenced in part by developments in a variety of disciplines and fields which they have sought to apply to the study of modern Palestine.[11]

I envision this book as a contribution to the collective scholarly effort currently under way to critique and go beyond the conventional approach to the modern history of Palestine, and particularly relations between Arabs and Jews. This book therefore adopts a conceptual framework that does not focus exclusively on either the Arab or the Jewish community or treat them as if they were entirely self-contained and isolated entities. Instead, it explores their mutually formative interactions, how they shaped one another in complex ways and at many levels. On that basis, building on but also hoping to broaden and deepen the work of other scholars who have worked along similar lines, I have tried to fill in one of the many blank spots in our knowledge of modern Palestine's history, through painstaking empirical research aimed at retrieving the kinds of materials for which the conventional paradigm and the narrative it yielded had little or no use, and then by assembling those materials into a new and different narrative. In so doing my goal is not to altogether replace the old narrative, with its focus on elite politics and diplomacy; it is rather to complement, extend, and complicate it, and more broadly to raise new questions which may help open up fruitful new avenues of research.

Having argued for the utility of a relational approach, I must also acknowledge that adopting such an approach incurs certain risks which must be taken seriously. The most important of these is that by trying to focus not on one or the other of the two communities in Palestine but rather on their mutually formative interactions, the very real specificity of their histories may be lost sight of. It was this—or perhaps more precisely, a concern that the history of the Palestinians would continue to be largely subsumed within a Zionist historical narrative, thereby denying them an independent identity and agency—that Palestinian political scientist Ibrahim Abu-Lughod seems to have been warning against more than a decade ago when he rebuked historians of Palestine for assuming that it is impossible to "study the historical development of the Palestinian Arab community at any particular point in modern times without taking immediate cognizance of the presence—effective or fictitious—of the Jewish community as represented by the Zionist movement." While admitting that it is "difficult to disentangle Palestinian history and culture from the endemic conflict between Palestinian and Zionist and Palestinian and British imperialist," Abu-Lughod insisted that "the Palestine of 1948 was a very different Palestine from that of 1917 and the difference is not solely the result of the impact of either imperialist or Zionist."[12] The subsumption of Palestinian identity, agency, and history to which Abu-Lughod points is obviously related to the long-standing disparity of power and status between Israeli Jews and Palestinians: while the former are citizens of an established and strong nation-state, most of the latter live under alien (and often repressive) rule whether within or outside their historic homeland, and as a people are still denied national self-determination in any part of Palestine.

Abu-Lughod is certainly right to argue that the very disproportionate attention paid to Zionism and the Yishuv, and the not unrelated neglect (and implicit marginalization) of Palestine's Arab majority, have had a distorting effect on our overall understanding of the modern history of Palestine. His assertion that "the social and cultural evolution of the Palestinians in modern times is in desperate need of study" is also entirely justified. Without question, more (and better) research on the history of the Palestinian Arab community as a distinct (though of course not homogeneous or internally unconflicted) entity is urgently needed. There is no question, for example, that the Palestinian Arab national identity that emerged in the course of the mandate period had important (if not yet adequately understood) roots in older forms of identity, social relations, and practices prevalent among the country's indigenous Arab population. At the same time, however, it seems to me that historians cannot avoid seeking to grasp how the development of Palestine's Arab community (including even its distinctive national identity) was shaped by a complex set of economic, social, cultural, and political forces, including those generated by the Zionist project and British colonialism. The same principle applies, of course, to historians of Zionism and the Yishuv. We must certainly recognize, though, that there will inevitably be some tension between the effort to achieve a relational perspective and respect for the historical specificity of each community.

DISCOURSE, WORKERS, AND NARRATIVE

The particular domain of interaction which I have chosen to delve into in this book encompasses Arab and Jewish workers, trade unions, labor movements, and labor-oriented political parties. This book thus explores a broad range of interactions between Arab and Jewish workers during the mandate period, including competition within overlapping labor markets, the experiences of and relations among Arab and Jewish workers employed in "mixed" workplaces, debates and dissension within Arab and Jewish unions and labor movements over the question of how to relate to fellow workers belonging to a different national group, and efforts by various segments of the Jewish labor movement to organize Arab workers. I also analyze the different (and always contested) discourses within which various elements within the Arab and Jewish working classes and labor movements in Palestine defined their own identities, aspirations, and policies, and formulated various representations of those with whom they interacted—in short, the systems of meaning within which they made sense of who they were (and were not) and what they were doing.

It is my hope that this book's attention to discourse, to structured systems of meaning embodied in language as well as in nonlinguistic signs and practices, will help enrich the relational paradigm of the history of modern Palestine. Some of the scholars who have adopted what I term a relational approach, especially in Israel, have given primary emphasis to the structural economic relationships between Arabs and Jews in Palestine, notably the markets for labor and land in which Jewish immigrants found themselves when they arrived in the country before the First World War and through the interwar period. This turn to political economy and historical sociology has been very salutary as a corrective to conventional Israeli historiography's functionalism, its inability to recognize, much less transcend, nationalist mythologies, and its failure to achieve critical distance by putting Zionism in comparative perspective. But this approach has perhaps also tended to marginalize questions of meaning and may conduce to an economistic reductionism, whereas I would argue that we should treat the realm of meaning (or more broadly put, of culture) and the realm of the economic as inextricably bound up with one another.

From this standpoint, it seems to me that neither the evolution nor the character of a distinctly Palestinian Arab culture, identity, and national movement can be adequately understood except in relation to the specific character of the Palestinians' confrontation not only with Zionist practices of exclusion but also with Zionist discourses about Arabs and the land of Palestine. Nor can one make full sense of what the labor-Zionist movement in Palestine was doing, and what it thought it was doing, without taking into account not only its labor market strategies but also the ways in which "the Arab worker" and the Arab working class in Palestine were represented, and the roles they were made to play, in left-Zionist discourse. As we will see, at a crucial stage it was to a significant extent in relation to a certain representation of Arab workers that the dominant current within labor Zionism articulated its own identity, its sense of mission, and its strategy to achieve hegemony within the Yishuv and realize its version of Zionism. In this sense, the modes of interaction between the Arab and Jewish communities in Palestine, and their mutually constitutive impact on one another, must be seen as simultaneously discursive and material. I have therefore paid attention both to structural economic relations, which certainly imposed constraints on what was feasible and imaginable, and to the representations and practices through which people understood, justified, and articulated their identities, beliefs, and actions.

Two full chapters of this book, and short segments of other chapters, are devoted to the railway workers of Palestine. Several factors make exploration of this group especially important, and especially relevant to a study which seeks to study Arabs and Jews relationally. Unlike nearly all Arab-owned enterprises and most Jewish-owned enterprises in Palestine, the Palestine Railways (an agency of the mandatory government of Palestine) employed both Arabs and Jews. It was therefore one of the few enterprises in which Arabs and Jews worked side by side, encountering similar conditions and being compelled to interact in the search for solutions to their problems. The Palestine Railways was also one of the country's largest employers, with a workforce that numbered about 2,400 in 1924 and reached a war-swollen peak of 7,800 in 1943. This workforce comprised numerous unskilled Arab peasants hired to build and maintain roadbed and track, but it also included substantial numbers of skilled personnel in the running and traffic departments and at stations across the country and (in 1943) some 1,200 Arab and Jewish workers employed at the Haifa repair and maintenance workshops. Indeed, until the establishment of an oil refinery in Haifa at the start of the Second World War and then the proliferation of British military bases during the war, the Haifa workshops constituted Palestine's largest concentration of industrial wage workers.

In addition, the railwaymen were among the first industrial workers in Palestine to organize themselves: an organization of Jewish railway workers was established as early as 1919, while Arab railway workers began to evince interest in trade unionism soon thereafter and would go on to play a key role in founding and leading the Palestinian Arab labor movement. It was, moreover, in large part the interaction of Jewish and Arab railway workers that first compelled the Zionist labor movement and the various left-Zionist political parties, as well as the largely Jewish but anti-Zionist communists, on the one hand, and various forces in the Arab community on the other, to confront, both theoretically and practically, the question of relations between the Jewish and Arab working classes. Last (but to a historian, not least), the sources available on the railway workers are relatively extensive and rich. Study of the ways in which the intersection of class, nationalist, and cultural politics shaped the interactions between the Jewish and Arab railway workers in this specific historical conjuncture may therefore make a particularly useful contribution to a rereading of the history of the Zionist-Palestinian conflict.

This book is not a study of either the Arab or the Jewish working classes or labor movements in Palestine. A number of such studies have been published, and though I have made use of them I believe that for the most part they share the flaws of the conventional historiography, in that they are deeply embedded in Arab or Jewish nationalist historical narratives. Though critical distance and objective scholarship are in short supply on all sides, the standard histories of the Jewish labor movement in the Yishuv and then Israel unfortunately take partisanship and tendentiousness to an extreme: they loyally reflect the perspectives of one or another of the left-Zionist parties and seem fixated on the task of "proving" that whichever party they favor was invariably correct. My goal here is to explore how these two working classes and labor movements interacted and helped shape one another, at a variety of levels and in a variety of ways. Nonetheless, much of the material I have unearthed along the way and present here may contribute to a better understanding of the Jewish and Arab working classes and labor movements in Palestine even considered separately.

I did not choose to focus on workers and labor movements in this book because I think that workers enjoy an ontological or epistemological status that is *a priori* superior to all other social groups. While I certainly believe that working-class history is important and have done quite a bit of it myself, I do not think that it is inherently more important than the study of social groups defined by some criterion other than class. Indeed, I think that just as the social relation we call class is deeply imbricated in, for example, race and gender relations, so gender and race and many other things are inextricably bound up with class, which cannot be usefully understood (or deployed as a concept) as if it were an entity unto itself. In a sense, the relational principle which underpins this study of Palestine applies to class as well: it is best understood not as a self-contained and objective category but rather as a relation which is itself constituted by many other social relations and practices. We must therefore try to develop an understanding of class that breaks with the essentialism and teleology found in certain readings of Marx and instead sees class as an effect of historically specific material and discursive practices.[13] I believe that my analysis in this book of Jewish working-class formation in Palestine effectively illustrates this contention.

First and foremost, this book focuses on working classes and labor movements because in the particular case of Palestine there is a very concrete and historically specific reason to do so. As I will discuss in great detail, one of the features which distinguishes Zionism from other nationalist movements is that for a lengthy historical period—roughly from the early 1930s to the mid-1970s—the international Zionist movement, the Yishuv, and from 1948 the State of Israel were to a large extent dominated by parties and institutions which saw themselves as part of the left wing of the Zionist movement. Though internally divided and always contentious, the labor-Zionist camp broadly defined was in that period usually able to exercise effective control over most of the key levers of political and economic power in the Yishuv and later Israel, and to exert a dominant ideological-cultural influence as well, though it often had to work with other Zionist parties, secular-centrist or religious, as junior partners. For a crucial phase of its history, then, especially in Palestine itself, Zionism was a nationalist movement which, while in principle appealing to all Jews across class lines and upholding the nation as the central category of identity, was largely led by political forces which professed a commitment to socialism and saw themselves as guiding a working class and labor movement whose role it was to act as the vanguard of the broader Zionist movement.

Because Jews who defined themselves as socialists as well as Zionists played such a central role in the Yishuv and the Zionist movement, and also because (as we will see) they came to adopt a strategy which saw in a particular mode of Jewish working-class formation the key to the achievement of Zionism's goals, the issue of how the Jewish labor movement in Palestine should relate to Arab workers and the Arab labor movement surfaced early on. In fact, socialist-Zionist ideologists and activists in Europe and Palestine were compelled to grapple with the question of relations between Arab and Jewish workers and working classes well before the First World War. Later, some Jews in Palestine found themselves working alongside Arabs and this reality, along with the growth of an Arab working class and labor movement, raised difficult issues to which the contending left-wing Jewish parties offered different solutions. As time went on, Arab workers employed alongside Jews, and Arab unionists and labor leaders confronted with the reality of an increasingly powerful Jewish labor movement whose actions and strategies directly impinged on Arab workers, were also compelled to address the issue of relations between Arab and Jewish workers in Palestine. As a result this domain of Arab-Jewish interaction is a particularly fertile one for historical exploration. In it we can see in microcosm many of the issues which were central to the struggle over Palestine, but also many episodes and forms of Arab-Jewish interaction which have been left out of the conventional historical narratives.

This book is largely narrative and chronological in form, and these days that requires some explanation. I am quite sympathetic to recent poststructuralist critiques of narrative and of the premises and categories of positivist history, and I believe that those critiques must be taken seriously. I have no problem accepting that what we as historians are really up to is not so much the retrieval of some transcendentally objective truth about the past "as it actually was" as the inevitably selective use of materials from the past to construct stories whose form and content are influenced by present-day concerns and categories and which could also perhaps be told quite differently. At the same time, however, it is crucial that there be some agreed-upon criteria for evaluating the many different stories that could be told about the past and determining which is most plausible or reliable, most "true" in at least some consensual sense. We should also remember that human beings make sense of their lives and identities through the stories which they tell about themselves and which others tell about them.

As historians we must therefore attempt to do two rather contradictory things at the same time. In keeping with an antiessentialist epistemological stance, we need to make the categories of analysis we deploy and the historical narratives we produce complex, contingent, and provisional, and their underlying premises (and our own perspectives) as transparent as possible. At the same time, we have to act as if we can in fact produce reliable knowledge by adhering scrupulously to scholarly standards and procedures and using them to fashion relatively coherent and meaningful stories that people can understand, accept, and use. It is hard, perhaps impossible, to achieve these goals simultaneously, but I would like to think that the tension between them could be productive rather than debilitating.

In this book I have chosen to deal with this issue by offering, as a complement to the usual scholarly and nationalist narratives, what amounts to a long and very detailed counternarrative. I have taken this tack in part because I am unaware of any work on Palestine that does what I have attempted to do here and in part because I wanted to show what might be achieved by taking a different approach. I think that the history I present here adds to and improves on previous versions by taking into account more of the available evidence, by bringing into the picture aspects and dimensions of history that have hitherto been largely neglected, and by resting on premises, and deploying categories of analysis, that I believe are more useful and productive. Obviously, readers will have to judge the success or failure of this enterprise for themselves.

SOURCES, TERMINOLOGY, AND POLITICS

The catastrophic disruption of Palestinian Arab society in 1947–49 resulted in the loss or destruction of many of the archives, libraries, personal papers, and other source materials from which many aspects of Palestinian social, cultural, political, and economic history might have been reconstructed. In addition, the dispersions of 1948 and 1967 scattered many of the individuals whom historians might have interviewed as part of their research into the country's pre-1948 history. The research institutions under Palestinian control have generally had limited resources and had to confront heavy burdens of many kinds, which have impeded their ability to study their people's history. In contrast, the Yishuv, the Zionist movement, and the various institutions and organizations they comprised tended to maintain well-organized archives from an early date, and these have survived and remain accessible to researchers. The Jews in Palestine also had a much higher rate of literacy than the Arabs as well as a higher propensity to produce written material, much of which was actually published. Israel also possesses numerous (and relatively well-funded) research centers and institutions of higher education which have supported extensive research on the history of Zionism and the Yishuv. In addition, though the generations which played important roles in the affairs of the Yishuv and Zionist movement during the mandate period are now rapidly aging and many of their members have already died, those who survive with their mental faculties and memories reasonably intact are not too hard to locate and interview.

The upshot of all this is that the history of the Yishuv and Zionism in Palestine is much better documented than the history of the Palestinian Arab community, especially its poorer and less educated segments; we simply know much more about most aspects of Jewish life in Palestine than we do about the corresponding aspects of Arab life. This makes it very difficult for historians trying to bring both Arabs and Jews into the picture to avoid privileging the history and perspectives of the Yishuv. This is, alas, a difficulty which my own research presented here has not escaped. Despite my best efforts to locate Arabic-language source materials, the version of any particular interaction, relationship, or episode related by Jewish individuals or organizations is almost invariably much fuller and better documented (though not necessarily more reliable) than the Arab version. I can therefore analyze what went on on the Jewish side in much greater depth and relate it as a much more complex and nuanced story. As a result, this book devotes much more time and space to analysis and discussion of left-Zionist thought and practice than it does to the thought and practice of Arab labor activists and leftists.

Further research into Palestinian Arab history may alleviate this imbalance somewhat, but it is unlikely to rectify it completely. It is something that we will have to live with and try to compensate for. The relational approach I advocate and have tried to implement here may be of some help in this regard. For example, most of the archives and records of the Arab trade union movement in mandate-era Palestine appear to have been lost or destroyed during 1948, compelling most historians of that movement to rely on press accounts, other published material, some government records, and interviews with a handful of surviving veterans. Paradoxically, however, a great deal of material generated by or bearing on the Arab workers' movement in Palestine has survived in the archives of the Jewish labor movement, including original leaflets, other ephemeral publications, and correspondence. Those archives also contain numerous reports on the doings of the Arab unions by Jews who were in frequent contact with them. This makes it possible not only to reconstruct interactions between Arab and Jewish workers and labor organizations in considerable detail but also to learn much that was previously unknown about the structure, politics, and activities of Arab unions and labor movements in Palestine. This may be scant compensation for all that was lost in 1948, a loss which historians can never fully overcome, but it is very much better than nothing.

A few words about some of the terms I will be using in this book may be in order. As noted earlier, I use "labor Zionism" to refer very broadly to all worker-oriented but also Zionist organizations, institutions, parties, and ideologies in Palestine. I therefore include under this rubric not only parties like Po'alei Tziyon, Ahdut Ha'avoda, Hapo'el Hatza'ir and their successor MAPAI, but also Po'alei Tziyon Smol and Hashomer Hatza'ir. I realize that in the course of the mandate period the English term "labor Zionism" came to be associated mainly with the social-democratic MAPAI, rather than with its explicitly Marxist rivals on the left, which preferred stronger terms like "socialist Zionism" or "proletarian Zionism." Yet for all their often bitter disagreements on many issues of principle, strategy, and tactics, these parties shared substantial ideological common ground and saw themselves as components of one and the same Jewish (and Zionist) labor movement in Palestine. I therefore feel justified in using "labor Zionism" as a general rubric in this broad sense, while of course also delineating and analyzing the very real and important differences among these parties and their distinct trajectories.

I generally use the terms "Palestinian Arab," "the Arabs of Palestine," or (where the meaning is clear) simply "Arab" to refer to the Arab community in Palestine during the mandate period. Adding the term "Arab" when referring to the people whom we would today simply call "the Palestinians" may seem redundant, but in fact it avoids an anachronism, for it was really only after 1948 that the Palestinian Arab people came to call themselves, and be called by others, simply Palestinians. During the mandate period most Palestinian organizations and institutions (in today's sense) officially called themselves "Arab," sometimes with "Palestinian" as a modifier; hence the Arab Executive, the Arab Higher Committee, the Arab Workers' Congress, the Palestinian Arab Workers' Society, and so forth. Moreover, I want to be sure to distinguish between the Arab and Jewish communities in Palestine, and use of the term "Palestinian" with reference to a period in which Palestine was still undivided might cause confusion. However, this choice of usage has nothing in common with the bizarre claim advanced by some Zionists that there can today be no authentic Palestinian people or nationalism because in mandate-era Palestine, Jews as well as Arabs were officially designated as "Palestinians." However they referred to themselves, a distinctly *Palestinian* Arab national identity began to emerge during the mandate period, in significant measure precisely because of the Palestinian Arab people's confrontation with Zionism, a challenge other Arab peoples were not compelled to face in the same very direct way.

Before 1948, in Hebrew but also in Yiddish, the language of the eastern European Jewish masses, Jews usually referred to Palestine by one of its ancient Hebrew names, *Eretz Yisra'el* ("the Land of Israel"). Because Hebrew was (along with English and Arabic) one of Palestine's official languages during the mandate period, the term by which the country would be officially denoted in that language became a political issue: Zionists demanded adoption of Eretz Yisra'el, in order to stress Jewish claims to the land, while the British authorities, anti-Zionist Jews (e.g., communists), and the Arabs preferred *Palestina*, a Hebraicized version of Palestine. When quoting from Hebrew-language sources in this book I will normally leave the Hebrew term Eretz Yisra'el untranslated. I do this because we know that to name something is in large measure to define it, to situate it within some larger system of meaning; and as I will show, Zionists' use of this particular name, rich with evocative associations from Jewish history and culture, was bound up with a certain conception of the land and its Arab inhabitants.

I feel it necessary to be so careful about explaining how and why I have used these terms in part because writing on the history of Palestine has been rife with polemic masquerading as historical analysis, and also because efforts at serious scholarship have frequently been attacked on essentially political grounds. This is perhaps not surprising, given the intensity of many people's emotional involvement with, and commitment to, Zionism or Palestinian nationalism, the longevity and bitterness of the conflict between them, and the perception that what is at stake is not just political power or territory but a people's survival. But the intrusion of emotionally charged political agendas has made life hard for scholars committed to studying Palestine just as they would any other part of the world, or to studying Zionism and Palestinian nationalism as they would similar movements elsewhere. Some of the analyses and arguments in this book may displease or even anger committed partisans of Zionism or Palestinian nationalism who do not want to hear (or see published) anything that may contradict their cherished beliefs or complicate the historical narratives which they regard as unchallengeably true. There is not much I can do to assuage them, except to say that while I certainly have my own opinions about the question of Palestine, opinions which I have expressed in the appropriate circumstances, my chief purpose in this book is not to judge but to understand.

It is for that reason that I repeatedly insist that however difficult it may be for those who have suffered the consequences of the attitudes, policies, or actions of one side or the other, it is essential to distinguish between subjective motives or intentions and historical outcomes. We must not altogether lose sight of the latter, for all of us are ultimately responsible for our actions and their consequences, and historians are no less entitled to discuss morality than anyone else. But if we truly want to understand why these or any other historical actors did what they did, we need first and foremost to understand what it was they believed they were doing, and why. Only then can we critically probe the belief systems which shaped their attitudes and actions, analyze their premises, contradictions, and consequences, and begin to talk about right and wrong, good and bad, what was and what might have been. Unfortunately, not all those who have written about modern Palestine, and particularly the Zionist-Palestinian conflict, have shared this attitude. As a result the literature includes a lot of rather crude Zionist-bashing and a lot of equally crude Arab-bashing. I must hope that those who read this book will approach it with an open mind and judge it on its merits, as they would a work of scholarship that focused on some less controversial and emotionally sensitive aspect of history.

Finally, though I will return to this issue in the Conclusion, I would like to make it clear at the outset that it is not my intention here to argue that things might have turned out differently, and better, if only there had been more cooperation between Arabs and Jews, or less ethnic and more class solidarity. That "if only" contains so many untenable assumptions and leaps of faith that it is of very little use for historical analysis. The outcome of the struggle between Zionism and Palestinian nationalism was not preordained, and it is certainly important to remember the alternative visions of the future for which people and parties fought, to maintain a sense of history as always contingent and open-ended—indeed, that is one of the purposes of this book. And it is not a sin to consider what our understanding of the past may tell us about the present and even the future. That is not the same, however, as arguing that all would have been well "if only" certain people and groups had thought and acted differently. Perhaps, but they did not, so we must resist the temptation to deploy our perfectly sharp moral hindsight and instead try to understand why the people we are concerned with saw themselves and the world they lived in as they did and behaved as they did. As I suggested earlier, we may ultimately come to believe that what they did was right or wrong, farsighted or misguided, unavoidable or disastrous for themselves and for others, but first of all we need to understand. That is what I have tried to do here.

1 Zionism and Palestine before the First World War

In this chapter I set the stage for my study of the mandate period by exploring how pre–First World War Zionists in Europe and Palestine, and especially socialist Zionists, perceived Palestine and its Arab inhabitants. In keeping with the relational paradigm I outlined in the Introduction, I argue that from a very early stage of the Zionist project's historical trajectory, Zionist thought and practice were significantly shaped by the need to come to terms with the fact that Palestine had a substantial Arab population, whether or not Zionists explicitly acknowledged or addressed that Arab presence. I also show how early Zionist perceptions of, and attitudes toward, the land and its indigenous Arab majority were profoundly influenced not only by a radically new nationalist appropriation of Jewish history and culture but also by the specific historical conjuncture within which Zionism emerged in Europe—the heyday of colonialism.

As I noted earlier, during the four centuries of Ottoman rule the term "Filastin" referred not to a specific Ottoman province or district with clearly defined boundaries but to a vaguely defined geographic region within al-Sham, the Syrian lands broadly conceived. The term was in use among Arab geographers and not unknown in official, scholarly, and perhaps even popular discourse, but those who resided within what would after the First World War become Palestine thought of themselves not as "Palestinians" in a modern national sense but rather in terms of the confessional, ethnic, kinship, and professional groups to which they belonged, as residents of a particular town, urban neighborhood, village, or region, and as subjects of the Ottoman sultan and his local agents. Moreover, the future Palestine was divided into a number of districts which were under the jurisdiction of provincial governments based in Damascus, Sidon, or elsewhere.

From the nineteenth century onward, however, the term "Palestine" became more widely used and took on greater significance, not least because it was a term often used by Europeans (and by powerful European states) who were exerting growing economic, political, and cultural influence in the region as a whole, while displaying special interest in this particular part of the Ottoman empire. This process, together with various local transformations and later the conquest of this territory by a European colonial power and its constitution as a distinct political entity, would interact to open the way for the emergence of a new form of identity among the indigenous majority of this country's population, finally manifesting itself in Palestinian Arab nationalism.

That nationalism will obviously be central to my concerns in this study, but in this chapter I focus on another nationalism which emerged in roughly the same period and also oriented itself toward this particular part of the Ottoman empire. Among the Europeans who in the nineteenth century began to take a special interest in Palestine—an interest which, as I will argue shortly, cannot be separated from the contemporaneous establishment of European world hegemony—were a number of Jews, whose long-standing religious attachment to this territory now began to be transformed into something quite new and different. For centuries Jews had referred to this land as "the Land of Israel" (in Hebrew, *Eretz Yisra'el*) or "the Holy Land" (*Eretz Hakodesh*). This land, and especially Jerusalem, where the First and Second Temples had stood and which Jews still faced during prayer, occupied a special place in premodern Jewish culture, a place preserved and reproduced in historical memory and the imagination through ritual practices, sacred and legal texts, stories and legends, metaphors, and figures of speech. Messianic strains in Judaism even envisioned restoration of the ancient homeland, under the rule of a descendant of King David, at the end of days.

Yet before the nineteenth century, this territory was for Jews not only sacred but also largely outside of history. It was a far-off place that was often imagined, idealized, and invoked but that had little to do with the daily life of Jews in the Diaspora or any conceivable future they might have, at least until the coming of the messiah. Though small Jewish communities continued to exist in Palestine, for many centuries the great centers of Jewish cultural life, as well as the vast majority of the world's Jews, had been elsewhere. Nor was the trickle of Jews who migrated to and settled in Palestine before the late nineteenth century motivated by anything remotely resembling a state-building project. To reside in the Holy Land, to die and be buried in its soil, were in religious terms meritorious acts, but they had no political significance for the few Jews who chose to fulfill this commandment; and it was far more often ignored than fulfilled. Indeed, the idea of creating a sovereign Jewish state, in Palestine or anywhere else, was virtually unimaginable within the framework of traditional normative Judaism. For the few Jews who lived in Palestine, as for virtually all Jews before the modern era, only the end of history as manifested in the coming of the messiah could bring about the termination of "exile" and its attendant sufferings, the redemption of the Jews, and their restoration to the land which God had promised to their ancestors but from which they had—also by divine decree—been uprooted.

Despite its claims of ancient roots, unbroken continuities, and essential identities, then, Jewish nationalism—like Palestinian Arab and all other nationalisms—is a thoroughly modern phenomenon, a product of the nineteenth and twentieth centuries. Though it is possible to point to earlier precursors, modern Jewish nationalism, which came to be known as Zionism—a term which surfaced only in the 1890s, derived from the Hebrew *Tziyon*, a synonym for Jerusalem—emerged in a more or less recognizable form only in the last third of the nineteenth century. Some of its foremost early articulators and leaders were relatively assimilated Jews from central Europe. But Zionism found its chief base of support among the Jewish masses of eastern Europe, where by that time the great majority of the world's Jews lived.

THE EMERGENCE OF ZIONISM

For Jews in the cities, towns, villages, and hamlets of eastern Europe, and especially of the Tsarist empire, Zionism was only one of several responses to deepening socioeconomic crisis and virulent antisemitism, both official and popular. The hope that Jews in the Tsarist empire might eventually attain the legal equality and opportunity for social integration and advancement which their coreligionists increasingly enjoyed in western and central Europe was frustrated by persistent, even intensified, oppression. This oppression had long been manifested in a subordinate legal status, restrictions on residence and occupation, and widespread official and popular antisemitism. But it took on a much more virulent and dramatic form in the waves of officially sponsored (or at the very least officially tolerated) anti-Jewish pogroms that erupted in 1871 and then again in 1881, after the assassination of Tsar Alexander II. The poverty and relative economic backwardness of eastern Europe, exacerbated by major shifts in the global economy in the later nineteenth century and rapid population growth, also contributed to an apparent worsening of the situation of the Jewish masses there.

Jews responded to their deteriorating plight in a number of ways. Many remained loyal to what they regarded as the faith of their ancestors, rejecting the new secular forms of Jewish identity and practice which emerged in the nineteenth century while adjusting as best they could to changing conditions. Others hoped for assimilation into the societies in which they lived, to be achieved through economic success, education, and political reform, though this was not a route even potentially available to the masses. Substantial numbers of eastern European Jews turned to socialism, which promised the eradication of antisemitism and full equality through radical social transformation. Still others were attracted by the new Jewish nationalism which surfaced in the last two decades of the nineteenth century, though at first these were relatively few in number. A great many "voted with their feet" by emigrating westward in search of greater freedom and a better life.

The rise of nationalist movements among other European peoples in this same period certainly played an important role in preparing the way for, and stimulating, the emergence of a specifically Jewish nationalism. By the middle of the nineteenth century it was becoming plausible (as it had not really been even a generation earlier) to ask why Jews should not emulate the example of the Greeks, Serbs, Italians, Hungarians, Poles, and others by seeking an independent nation-state of their own. As with other peoples, cultural movements—including first a Yiddish and then a mid-century Hebrew-language cultural revival pioneered by the new secular Jewish intelligentsia in eastern Europe—also facilitated the reimagining of Jewish identity in a new national sense.

The first organized political manifestation of this new nationalism was the small and loose knit Hibbat Tziyon ("Love of Zion") movement, which crystallized after the pogroms of 1881 and took the form of a network of local associations established to promote Jewish immigration to and settlement in Palestine, and the reconstitution there of Jewish national life. The Lovers of Zion understood migration to Palestine as ontologically different from migration to any other place. It was not just one more movement across the face of the globe in search of safety, tolerance, and opportunity. Rather, it was seen as a return through both time and space to the ancestral homeland, where the Jews had become a people and which remained the only place on earth where they could, through their commitment, their love, and their labor, achieve personal and collective regeneration by tapping into the wellsprings of the nation's eternal spirit.

But relatively few Jews responded to the call of Zion. Hibbat Tziyon's proto-Zionism (and later Herzl's political Zionism) remained minority movements in eastern Europe itself, overshadowed by the other tendencies contending for support in the Jewish communities of eastern Europe. This reality was perhaps most dramatically manifested in the fact that very few of the millions of Jews who between 1881 and the First World War sought to escape the oppression and poverty of Tsarist Russia (and of eastern Europe in general) by emigrating from the lands in which their ancestors had lived for centuries chose to go to Palestine. Of the approximately 2.4 million Jews who left eastern Europe in this period, some 85 percent went to the United States, and another 12 percent to other countries of the western hemisphere (mainly Canada and Argentina), to western Europe, or to South Africa. In so doing they helped swell the great stream of impoverished and uprooted Christian peasants and laborers who in this same period left their homelands in eastern and southern Europe and sought a new life in the west. By contrast, less than 3 percent of this vast outflow of Jews went to Palestine, and for a high proportion of those Palestine proved only a temporary way station on the road westward.[1]

Despite its slender human and material resources, the Hibbat Tziyon movement managed to establish a number of new Jewish agricultural settlements in Palestine, referred to in Hebrew as *moshavot* ("colonies" or "settlements"). It soon became evident, however, that Hibbat Tziyon was incapable of sustaining a settlement project on this scale, and within a few years many of the new settlements were on the verge of bankruptcy and collapse. They were rescued by the generosity of Baron Edmond de Rothschild, an assimilated French Jew who had little interest in Hibbat Tziyon's romantic nationalism but was aroused by the plight of the east European Jewish masses and favored their resettlement—though preferably not in France, where an influx of poor Jews from the east might fan the flames of antisemitism and undermine the tenuous place which the Rothschilds and other assimilated Jews had secured in French society. Rothschild, and later other European Jewish philanthropists, assumed control of many of the settlements and provided them with large-scale financial support, along with technical assistance and a large dose of paternalistic supervision.

By 1900 there were twenty-two moshavot with a total population of about 5,000. Most of these settlements had come to be organized on the Algerian colonial model preferred by Baron Rothschild and his agents, with European Jewish farmers employing local Arab peasants to cultivate their vineyards, citrus groves, and fields. Zionist historiography has tended to focus on this segment of the growing Yishuv, seeing in these struggling farmers the forerunners of Zionism's settlement and state-building project. Yet the great majority of Jews in Palestine, including most of those who arrived in what would later be dubbed the First *Aliya*, the 1881–1903 wave of Jewish immigration, preferred to live in towns, and much of the Yishuv was still quite distant from the vision of Jewish national-cultural rebirth in Palestine put forward by Hibbat Tziyon, much less the vision of Jewish statehood which Herzl's new and explicitly political Zionist movement would articulate.

Neither the proto-Zionism of Hibbat Tziyon nor the new Zionist Organization founded in 1897 by Theodor Herzl (1860–1904) were unitary or monolithic movements. They encompassed a variety of tendencies which shared certain broadly defined premises and goals but differed—often sharply and bitterly—about many other things. Thus Zionism, like all nationalist movements, has to be disaggregated in order to be properly understood. In general terms, Zionism as an ideology rested on the premise that the plight of the Jews was most directly and significantly attributable to their lack of political power, a consequence of their dispersion among the peoples of the earth without a land of their own in which they could be masters of their own fate. Most (though not all) Zionists agreed that only the Jews' achievement of sovereign political power in their own land could resolve "the Jewish problem" once and for all, could make the Jews a "normal" people able to take its rightful place as an equal member of the community of nations, rather than a weak, persecuted, and rootless minority. Yet beyond this Zionists could and did disagree about many things, including the means by which the future Jewish homeland or state could be secured, its social, political, and cultural character, and even (for a time, at least) its location.

ZIONISM, PALESTINE, AND COLONIAL DISCOURSE

As it coalesced into a coherent ideology and movement, Zionism was strongly influenced, for good and ill, by the other nationalisms which had emerged somewhat earlier in southern, central, and eastern Europe.[2] Yet despite the strong family resemblance, there was also a very important difference, one which powerfully distinguished Zionism and shaped much of its specific character and historical trajectory. Most European national groups aspiring to independence constituted the majority of the population in the territory in which they hoped to achieve national sovereignty. But the Jews of Europe were everywhere dispersed among non-Jewish majority populations, and this ineradicable reality made it impossible for Jewish nationalists to imagine emulating the Poles, Ukrainians, Hungarians, or other European peoples by seeking to establish a Jewish state in eastern Europe, where the Jewish masses actually lived. As a result, Zionism was—had to be—not simply a conventional nationalist movement but a colonizing and settlement movement as well, a project whose goals were to find some territory outside Europe suitable for Jewish settlement, organize the migration thereto of a large number of Jews, and therein establish some form of Jewish self-rule or sovereignty.

Had the Zionist movement located some completely uninhabited and isolated territory, organized the immigration of a substantial number of Jews to it, and there established a Jewish state, the troublesome question of how to relate to an existing non-Jewish population would not have arisen. But it is virtually impossible to imagine how such a scenario might have become a reality, and not merely because in the late nineteenth century completely uninhabited lands suitable for large-scale European settlement were in rather short supply, if not nonexistent. More important is the fact that, not surprisingly, the Zionist movement quickly fixed on Palestine as the site of its settlement and state-building project. Those early Zionists (including, for a time, Herzl himself) who were willing to consider some other territory, either temporarily until Palestine "became available" or permanently, were soon marginalized. Palestine, Eretz Yisra'el, had simply played too great a role in Jewish history, especially as the site of ancient Jewish statehood, and still occupied too important a place in the Jewish imagination, to allow any alternative to gain significant and durable support.

Some early Zionists may initially have believed that Palestine was an empty land, in the sense of being completely or virtually uninhabited. There is the well-known (but perhaps apocryphal) episode, dated to the last years of the nineteenth century, in which Max Nordau, friend and colleague of Theodor Herzl, is said to have one day "discovered" that Palestine was already inhabited and exclaimed to Herzl, "But then we are committing an injustice!" It quickly became obvious, however, that Palestine was not completely devoid of inhabitants, so the more interesting and important question is how Zionist leaders, ideologists, activists, and sympathizers handled the fact that Palestine already had a substantial non-Jewish population. There were in fact cultural tools readily available from both Jewish and general European sources with which a way of coming to terms with this reality could be forged, and early Zionists were quick to make use of them.

Zionism did not have to formulate its representations of the indigenous population of Palestine *ex nihilo*. It could and did draw on the vast repository of Jewish texts and stories about, images of, and associations with this land. Jews (or more precisely, their ancient ancestors the Hebrews) were obviously the central actors in these stories and images, not a few of which concerned the establishment and loss of Jewish hegemony in part or all of the Land of Israel. Given the rich raw materials at their disposal, it was not too difficult for Zionist thinkers, educators, and propagandists to selectively appropriate various elements of Jewish history and culture and mold them into a new nationalist vision of the Jewish past and the Jewish future. Not surprisingly, this process entailed the relegation of the non-Jews who had lived in this land, and those who happened to live there now, to marginal status.[3]

But European Jews also had at their disposal another set of representations which neatly complemented and reinforced images and attitudes developed from Jewish sources. The historical moment in which the Zionist project was launched was also the heyday of European colonial expansion and rule. In this era the global superiority of European civilization was widely taken to be self-evident, as was the right of Europeans to rule over (and settle among as a privileged caste) non-European peoples deemed to be less advanced. These assumptions formed the backdrop, the often invisible and taken-for-granted ground, not only of nineteenth-century European politics but also of much of popular and high European culture, and later of mass culture as well.[4]

The Jews who embraced the Zionist vision of Jewish redemption were also Europeans, albeit marginalized and often victimized Europeans, and very much part of European culture as both creators and consumers. Educated middle-class Jews living relatively freely in western and central Europe probably absorbed prevalent European images of, and attitudes toward, non-Europeans through the same channels as the rest of the population. Though we know little about how these images were conveyed to the Jewish masses in eastern Europe, or the specific ways in which they were adopted and adapted, we have no reason to believe that they were not absorbed.[5]

Zionism shared the propensity of all nationalisms to ignore the rights, needs, and aspirations of those excluded from the national "family." But it also partook of an available contemporary European discourse that delineated a certain set of perceptions of, attitudes toward, and relations with the African and Asian lands and peoples subject to, or now falling under, the economic and political domination of Europeans. That broader colonial discourse also drew on, and overlapped with, older European images and representations of "the Orient."[6] With appropriate modifications, these systems of representation could be made to fit the specific situation of the Jews and of Zionism and could be applied to Palestine, just as they were at that same moment being applied elsewhere by other projects of European colonization and settlement that altogether lacked Zionism's origin as a response to a very real (and worsening) oppression in Europe itself.

The assertion that early Zionists were profoundly influenced by the political, social, and cultural environment in which they formulated and articulated their project should be self-evident, as should my insistence that Zionist conceptions of Palestine and its indigenous non-Jewish inhabitants cannot be adequately understood except in the context of contemporary European colonial discourse and practice, including the models provided by other projects of European overseas settlement. After all, as an ideology and a movement, Zionism emerged at the very historical moment when the European imperialist powers (and the United States) were engaged in the territorial division of the globe, subjugating and imposing their rule on non-European peoples on an unprecedented scale. Zionism was, inevitably, strongly influenced by that conjuncture; it is hard to imagine how it could have been otherwise.

It is worth recalling in this connection that at the turn of the century, Zionism's similarities to other projects of colonization were not a source of embarrassment or shame for most of the movement's adherents; indeed, they often saw them as a selling point. Zionist leaders studied and sought to learn from the experience of European colonial-settlement enterprises in places like Algeria, Rhodesia, and Kenya, and many imagined their own endeavor as similar in certain ways.[7] Moreover, the Zionist movement readily used such terms as "colony," "colonial," and "colonization" to refer to its activities; thus, for example, the original name of its financial arm was the Jewish Colonial Trust. It was only later, after the First World War, that colonialism came to have strongly pejorative connotations for many Europeans. As a consequence the Zionist movement sought to dissociate itself from other European projects of colonization and settlement, began to stress the uniqueness and noncolonial character of its mission and methods, and stopped using such terms, at least in languages other than Hebrew.

EARLY ZIONISM, PALESTINE, AND ITS INHABITANTS

This study focuses on the perceptions and practices of the left wing of the Zionist movement, to which I will turn shortly. But many of the Zionist left's most durable conceptions of, and attitudes toward, Palestine's indigenous Arab population drew on themes and images already manifested in the public and private writings and pronouncements of earlier nonsocialist Zionists, including the founder and first leader of modern political Zionism, Theodor Herzl. Though Herzl and many of his colleagues initially knew very little about Palestine, their ideas about that land and its inhabitants should be understood not primarily as a matter of ignorance, of a lack of adequate information, easily enough remedied, but rather as the product of a coherent discourse which rendered certain things invisible or marginal.

Until relatively recently, students of Zionism and of the history of Palestine often took it for granted that before the First World War, the proto-Zionist and Zionist movements were simply unaware that Palestine was inhabited and thus did not realize that they had an "Arab problem"—their way of denoting the fact that the land in which Jewish national rebirth was to take place was already populated by another people.[8] As illustration they have cited remarks like that of Max Nordau, quoted earlier, and the dearth of discussion about this issue at Zionist meetings and in Zionist publications. This way of posing the problem misses the point, however. There was undoubtedly a great deal of ignorance and misinformation about Palestine and its Arab inhabitants among early Zionists. But whether or not they explicitly addressed the issue of a substantial non-Jewish presence in Palestine or even acknowledged that it was an issue, that presence nonetheless constituted an important part of the context, the horizon, the background, in relation to which Zionism took shape, especially in Palestine itself. As such it certainly helped shape Zionist discourse, through the silences and exclusions it generated and through the ways in which it was represented (and acted upon). Though a great deal of research remains to be done on this question, it is nonetheless possible to isolate two persistent and interrelated themes that appear in much of Zionist discourse on the Arabs of Palestine.

Early on, Zionist discourse often simply rendered the country's indigenous Arab population invisible. From most early Zionist writing—including, for example, Herzl's *The Jewish State*, published in 1896—it is difficult, if not impossible, to learn that Palestine was at the time anything other than empty. The Arabs were simply not mentioned, as if they did not exist. But another, ultimately more durable and important theme emerged almost simultaneously, one which did not so much displace as supplement the representation of Palestine as empty and its inhabitants as invisible. Once it was beyond question that the country in which Zionism sought to establish a Jewish state was not empty in the literal sense, the Arabs of Palestine came to be represented as essentially, ontologically, marginal to the land and its destiny. Their physical presence in large numbers, closely settled in hundreds of villages and towns, was perhaps no longer disputable, but the character of their relationship to the country was represented as fundamentally different from, and inferior to, that of the Jews, regardless of where most of the latter had actually lived for centuries.

Palestine was represented in Zionist discourse as by definition a Jewish land, whose eternal essence was Jewish. Therefore no other people could have an equally authentic historical or contemporary presence in it, or an equally valid claim or organic link to it. At the same time, the dominant Zionist representation of Palestine's non-Jewish inhabitants asserted that they lacked the requisite characteristics which might entitle them to national rights in the country; they were not, and by their very essence could not be, a distinct or coherent people or nation. For most (though, as we will see, not all) Zionists, Palestine was inhabited not by a more or less coherent *ethnos*, nor even by a group in the process of becoming a distinct people or national entity, but rather by a heterogeneous and incoherent amalgam with no definite national characteristics. This motley assemblage of many different races and peoples had only shallow roots in the land and could therefore just as easily and happily be resettled somewhere else, or be reduced to a residual minority living alongside (and in subordination to) the land's new Jewish majority.

In contrast, it was taken as self-evident that despite their geographical dispersion, their cultural and social diversity, and their small numbers in Palestine itself, Jews everywhere constituted a single nation with permanent and exclusive rights in the country. Indeed, this was a core premise of Zionism. It is within this discursive context that we can make sense of the early Zionist slogan, "A land without a people for a people without a land." It was not so much that Palestine was deemed to be literally empty, though some Zionists may initially have imagined this to be the case; it was that the Arabs who were the majority of the population did not constitute a distinct people with a legitimate claim to the land, whereas the Jews did. The land lacked not people, in the sense of inhabitants, but *a* people, a nation organically linked to this particular territory, that is, the Jewish people. It was this lack which Zionism saw itself as remedying: by returning the Jews to this land, the land would be restored to its rightful owners.

As I will discuss shortly, not all Zionists shared these conceptions of the land and its inhabitants, and some would offer different representations which suggested alternative strategies for realizing the goals of Zionism. But with few exceptions these too presumed the heterogeneity of Palestine's Arab population (and thus their lack of national rights in it), represented the Arabs as newcomers to the land (and thus without any historic claim to it), recognized their rootedness but denied that Palestinian Arabs constituted a distinct and coherent national entity, or merely stressed the superiority of the Jewish connection with (and therefore claim to) the land. They were thus also rooted in a discourse, a distinct system of meaning, that took the alleged marginality of the Arabs in Palestine as their defining characteristic.[9]

It is not difficult to discern these images and attitudes embedded in the writings and pronouncements, public and private, of early Zionist thinkers and leaders. Even while visiting Palestine in 1898, Herzl could see its non-Jewish inhabitants as no more than a "mixed multitude," a motley assortment of different ethnic and racial types which obviously lacked any of the characteristics of a nation.[10] That Palestine's Arab population was hardly visible to Herzl made it all the easier to imagine moving it elsewhere, or submerging it in a Jewish majority. In his diary Herzl could envision—without any apparent moral qualms—the dispossession of the indigenous peasant population: the land they worked would be discreetly bought by Jews and never resold to non-Jews, while the landless peasants would be "spirited" across the border through the provision of employment outside Palestine.[11]

The invisibility, or at best marginality, of Palestine's Arab population is also evident in Herzl's utopian novel *Altneuland* (Old-New Land), first published in 1902. Set twenty years in the future, the novel depicts Palestine as having an overwhelmingly Jewish population, while its former Arab inhabitants are virtually absent from the scene. At the same time, Herzl insists that the Arabs have actually benefited from Zionism, that their economic prosperity more than compensates for—indeed, renders utterly irrelevant, hardly worthy of mention—their transformation into a small minority living in a predominantly Jewish society. The Arabs of *Altneuland* are apparently content with their new marginal status, their virtual invisibility in the land where twenty years earlier—at the time Herzl was actually writing—they had been demographically and culturally dominant.

That Herzl's attitudes were less the product of ignorance or misinformation than of a certain way of grasping reality is also confirmed by an episode that took place in 1899, a year after Herzl's first visit to Palestine. The chief rabbi of France passed on to Herzl a letter he had received from Yusuf al-Khalidi (1842–1906), a prominent notable of Jerusalem who had served as the city's mayor and a member of the Ottoman parliament of 1876–78 and held various posts in the local Ottoman administration.[12] In his letter al-Khalidi expressed sympathy for the professed aim of Zionism, the relief of Jewish suffering. But, he insisted, large-scale Jewish settlement in, and ultimately Jewish sovereignty over, Palestine could only be achieved by force and violence, in the face of strong resistance by the local population, and he implored the Zionists to find some other territory in which to settle Jews and seek a Jewish state.[13]

It is significant, and characteristic, that Herzl's reply to this plea, which might have impressed upon him the existence of an "Arab question" or at least a "native problem," focused on the economic benefits Zionism would bring to the local population. Herzl insisted that the Jews had only peaceful intentions and emphasized the wealth which would accrue to the country's Arab landowners as Jewish immigration led to rising land prices. "That is what the indigenous population must realize, that they will gain excellent brothers as the Sultan will gain faithful and good subjects who will make this province flourish—this province which is their historic homeland."[14] For Herzl as for most Zionists, Palestine was the "historic homeland" only of the Jews, pointing up their conception of the indigenous population as lacking national characteristics or any genuine attachment to its land and culture—or at least of an attachment that was of the same order as the Jews', which brought with it political-national rights the Arabs were to be denied. The Arabs would and should be content with the prosperity which Zionism would bring to (some of) them as individuals. Of course, even as Herzl was reassuring al-Khalidi of his movement's peaceful and benevolent intentions, he was laying siege to the chancelleries of Europe, seeking the backing of a European power for Zionism if, as seemed likely, the Ottoman sultan proved reluctant to concede Palestine.

By contrast, Herzl was quite capable of understanding (and even sympathizing with) indigenous aspirations when they concerned places other than Palestine. For example, he was impressed by the educated young Egyptians he encountered while passing through Cairo in 1902, referring to them as the "coming masters" of the country and wondering why the British officials who controlled Egypt did not grasp this: "They think they are going to deal with Fellahin [peasants] forever."[15] Palestine was for

Herzl a different matter altogether: there neither the peasants nor the emerging Arab intelligentsia merited mention, much less serious attention.

For Herzl and others, the subordination, dispossession, and even displacement of Palestine's indigenous population were implicitly or explicitly made thinkable and legitimate by the fact that those inhabitants were non-European, perhaps even nonwhite according to the typology of colonial discourse (and of contemporary "scientific racism"). Herzl explicitly located his project within a powerful contemporary European conception of the world when, in *The Jewish State,* he assured his readers—Jews and non-Jews, but certainly Europeans—that the future Jewish state in Palestine would form "a portion of the rampart of Europe against Asia, an outpost of civilization against barbarism."[16] For Zionists, the new Jewish nation they sought to create might not be located *in* Europe but it would certainly be *of* Europe. Indeed, the attainment of Jewish sovereignty would for the first time allow Jews to participate in the great project of Western civilization on an equal footing. Except for a few marginal romantics, Zionists rejected any form of cultural integration into the Middle East, and when after 1948 Israel's Jewish population came to consist heavily of immigrants from Arab lands and their descendants, the state's political and cultural elites would denounce "levantinization" as a grave danger to Israel's essentially European cultural character. In a sense, then, Zionists were seeking a way to ensure that non-Jewish Europeans would treat the Jews not like inferior non-Europeans but like fellow Europeans with equal status and rights. Underpinning this perspective was a shared hierarchical conception of Europe and non-Europe and of the relations between them, which Zionists found it perfectly natural to apply to Palestine and its Arab inhabitants.

None of this should be taken to suggest that Herzl and his colleagues did not think of themselves as liberal humanists, as men who adhered to universalist values of reason and progress. They most certainly did, which is precisely my point (though one that many historians of Zionism seem unable to grasp): they were, inevitably, men of their time, and as such they were able without too much difficulty to reconcile their liberal and universalist humanism with confidence in the superiority of European civilization and an ability to ignore the aspirations, concerns, and rights of the non-Europeans whom their project affected.[17] In this the early Zionists were not at all unique: the system of inclusions and exclusions, of superiority and subordination, which largely governed relations between Europeans and other peoples defined as less advanced was a powerful component of the culture in which they (and most other Europeans) were imbricated in this period. Many elements of Zionist discourse about Palestine and its Arab inhabitants—the conception of the land as empty and available for European settlement or exploitation, the depiction of the indigenous population as marginal, incoherent, backward, rootless, and therefore movable, the legitimization of coercion as a means of achieving European purposes, the denial of equal human, civil, or national rights, and so on—show up in other contemporary colonial-settler projects, and more broadly in a widespread and deeply rooted contemporary European discourse on non-European peoples and lands.[18]

As with slavery in an earlier period, it would be some time before significant numbers of western Europeans would be brought to feel that the Asians and Africans subject to European control were entitled to the purportedly universal human rights which Europeans regarded as their birthright and a mark of the genius of their civilization. Anticolonial resistance by Asians and Africans themselves played an important role in bringing about this change, as did political, social, and cultural shifts within Europe. Until that time, however, colonialism, broadly defined as not simply a system of European political domination over non-Europeans but also as a relatively coherent set of perceptions and attitudes, was a central component of much of European culture. As such, it inevitably helped shape the perceptions and attitudes of adherents of Zionism, a European nationalism which regarded an already inhabited extra-European territory as the site of its realization.

Ironically, in this period and later many Europeans applied this same system of classifying human groups to the Jews, defining them as essentially non-European and therefore as undeserving of equal rights. Some would go even further and, drawing on the same "scientific" principles used to justify racist attitudes toward nonwhite colonial subjects, and oppressive and exploitative rule over them, would define Jews as less than fully human, with horrific consequences. It is also important to remember that Zionism won support among Jews (and many non-Jews as well) largely because it could portray itself as a solution to a very real and pressing crisis: the "Jewish problem" in Europe. By contrast, the non-Jewish "poor whites" who migrated to and settled in various European colonies overseas were largely motivated by a desire to improve their lot in life, rather than (as with Jewish immigrants to Palestine) by a nationalist project or (later) by the need to escape persecution. Though one may perhaps understand why members of Palestine's indigenous Arab population might not feel it particularly important to distinguish between the objective consequences of Jewish immigration to Palestine and the immigrants' subjective motivations, that distinction is certainly crucial to understanding how the Zionist movement, under whose auspices many of those Jews came to Palestine, understood what it was doing and why.

We must of course always be careful to avoid analyzing discourses, ideologies, and movements as if they were monolithic or immutable, and this caveat applies to Zionism as well. The representation of Palestine and its Arab population that characterized Herzl and Herzlian Zionism did not go entirely unchallenged. Among Herzl's contemporaries and successors there were individuals who, for various reasons, articulated perspectives that implicitly or explicitly acknowledged the presence in Palestine of a coherent Arab community with which the Zionist movement would have to reckon. However, I argue that the ultimate marginality of such voices to mainstream Zionist thought and practice demonstrates that the representation of Palestinian Arabs prevalent within the Zionist movement had less to do with ignorance than with a particular way of knowing and a particular kind of knowledge, one that served certain needs and furthered certain goals.

Asher Ginsberg (1856–1927), far better known by his pen name Ahad Ha'am ("One of the People"), is a case in point. He was the preeminent Hebrew essayist of his day and the leading literary light and publicist of Hibbat Tziyon. After visiting Palestine in 1891, he published a scathing article (provocatively entitled "Truth from Eretz Yisra'el") in which he told his readers that Palestine was not empty and desolate but densely settled and cultivated by Arabs, who were not ignorant savages but a people of intellect and cunning. While some Ottoman officials were doubtless corrupt and incompetent, the empire's rulers were patriots and would never give Palestine up without a struggle. Ahad Ha'am went on to accuse many Jewish colonists in Palestine of treating Arabs in an unjust, cruel, and hostile manner. After another visit in 1911 he warned his readers that a national consciousness was beginning to develop among many Arabs in Palestine, which would only make Jewish immigration and land acquisition even more difficult.[19]

In the 1890s Ahad Ha'am criticized Hibbat Tziyon's model of settlement, and later he would criticize Herzl's vision of a sovereign Jewish state comprising all or most of the world's Jews, to be secured through the intervention of one or more of the European powers. Not only was Herzl's vision grandiose and unrealistic, he argued, but the Jewish state Herzl imagined (in *Altneuland* and elsewhere) lacked any authentic Jewish content, and Herzl also failed to take Arab opposition seriously.[20] As an alternative, Ahad Ha'am advocated a program of small-scale and gradual Jewish immigration and settlement, leading to the firm rooting in Palestine of a relatively small but viable and vigorous Jewish community which would serve as a "spiritual center" for the regeneration of Jewish national culture in the Diaspora.[21]

Ahad Ha'am was certainly one of the first major Zionist thinkers to acknowledge that Arabs were a collective presence in Palestine and to insist publicly that Zionism must recognize them as an important factor, even as a potential adversary. Yet few Zionists took his warnings seriously. Nor did they heed others who tried to raise the issue, and the mainstream of the Zionist movement continued to deny the existence of an "Arab problem."[22] During Herzl's tenure as president of the Zionist Organization (1897–1904), the movement focused on a primarily "political" Zionism whose main goal was to obtain a "charter" for Jewish settlement and autonomy in Palestine from the Ottoman government or one of the European imperialist powers. But no charter was forthcoming. After Herzl's death immigration, land acquisition, and settlement work in Palestine itself—an approach known as "practical Zionism" and supported by most Zionist activists in Russia, where the movement had its mass base—again began to assume pride of place in Zionist strategy, especially during the 1903–14 wave of Jewish immigration, the Second Aliya.

Yet the search for a European big-power sponsor was never really abandoned. Nor could it be, since as Herzl and his successors understood, without a powerful patron there was little likelihood that the Zionist project could succeed in the face of Ottoman restrictions on immigration and land acquisition, and the increasingly vigorous and coherent opposition of Palestine's Arab majority. This quest would eventually be crowned with success when, during the First World War, the British government decided that support for Zionism would serve its war aims and was compatible with its plans for the postwar disposition of the former Arab provinces of the Ottoman empire.

The new synthesis of "political" and "practical" Zionism which took shape during the Second Aliya also tended to ignore or reject Ahad Ha'am's view of the Arabs of Palestine as an authentic and significant factor. That synthesis instead absorbed and reproduced the prevailing Zionist representation of the Arabs as essentially marginal and irrelevant. But this representation was now conditioned by two new factors: on the one hand, the need to reconcile Zionism with the universalistic moral claims of socialism, which had made its appearance as an organized ideological and political force within the Zionist movement as well as in the Yishuv, and on the other the concrete circumstances and problems encountered by Jewish immigrants who arrived in Palestine in the decade or so preceding the First World War. The representations of the Palestinian Arabs produced within socialist-Zionist discourse, and the attitudes and practices in which that discourse was manifested, would play a decisive role in determining the course of Zionist-Palestinian relations during the many decades during which labor Zionism played a prominent, and for a time hegemonic, role within the broader Zionist movement and the Yishuv.

SOCIALIST ZIONISM AND THE ARABS OF PALESTINE

As a distinct tendency, socialist Zionism was almost contemporaneous with Herzl's liberal political Zionism, although it could lay claim to such forerunners as Moses Hess (1812–75), an associate of Karl Marx in the 1840s and later the author of the proto-Zionist essay *Rome and Jerusalem* (1862). The first major theoretician of socialist Zionism, Nahman Syrkin (1868–1924), published his essay "The Jewish Question and the Socialist Jewish State" only a year after the First Zionist Congress, to which he was a delegate.[23] Syrkin sought to synthesize his conception of socialism—ethical and utopian rather than Marxist—and his strong commitment to Zionism, arguing against bourgeois Zionists like Herzl that only the proletarianized Jewish masses could realize Zionism (which therefore had to be socialist in content), and against anti-Zionist Jewish socialists that there could be no solution to the Jewish problem without the creation of a Jewish state.

Syrkin was not always convinced that that state had to be located in Palestine: for a few years after the Seventh Zionist Congress (1905) Syrkin quit the Zionist Organization and headed the Russian socialist wing of the Territorialist movement, which regarded Palestine as only one of several possible sites for Jewish settlement and autonomy. By 1909, however, he had returned to the Palestine-oriented Zionist mainstream by joining Po'alei Tziyon ("Workers of Zion"), the strongest socialist-Zionist tendency within the Zionist movement. In time, Syrkin would come to be regarded as the intellectual godfather of labor Zionism in the non-Marxist, social-democratic form embodied in MAPAI ("Party of the Workers of the Land of Israel") from 1930 onward.[24]

It is therefore worthy of note that Syrkin apparently did not feel it necessary to justify Zionism's claims to Palestine or its likely impact on the country's indigenous population in terms of socialist principles. In fact, none of his pre–First World War theoretical or programmatic works

makes any implicit or explicit mention of Arabs or of an "Arab problem."
In "The Jewish Question and the Socialist Jewish State" Syrkin proposes
that Zionism acquire Palestine from the Ottoman government by purchase, by diplomacy, or by mobilizing European democratic and proletarian opinion to pressure the Ottomans into conceding the country to the
Jews. The best option, Syrkin argued, was for Zionism to aid the oppressed
Christian peoples of the Ottoman empire—he mentions the Macedonians,
the Armenians, and the Greeks—in their struggles for independence.
After victory, each people would have its own state in the former Ottoman
territories in which it constituted a majority, while in territories with
mixed populations partition and peaceful exchanges of population would
ensue. For their role in the anti-Ottoman struggle the Jews would get
Palestine: "Eretz Yisra'el, which is very sparsely populated and in which
Jews are even today 10 percent of the population, should be turned over
to the Jews."[25]

Syrkin's ability to ignore the fact that Palestine had a substantial Arab
population and his failure to see anything problematic in the transformation of a small Jewish minority into an exclusively Jewish (albeit socialist)
state and society, apparently by the removal of the indigenous population,
suggest that, despite his sharp differences with Herzl over the social character of the future Jewish state, he shared the dominant Zionist representation of Palestine's Arabs as invisible or marginal. For Syrkin as for
Herzl, Palestine's indigenous population was to be the object of power
politics, to be moved elsewhere to satisfy the needs and aspirations of
Europeans, and it was certainly not entitled to national rights in Palestine
equivalent to those which Jews were presumed to possess.

BOROKHOV, BOROKHOVISM, AND PALESTINE

The work of the other preeminent early socialist-Zionist thinker, Ber Borokhov (1881–1917), exhibits a more complex but not essentially dissimi-
lar attitude. It was Borokhov who laid the theoretical foundations for the
synthesis of Marxism and Zionism espoused by Po'alei Tziyon, the largest
of the prewar socialist-Zionist parties in eastern Europe and Palestine. In
"The National Question and the Class Struggle" (1905) Borokhov sought
to elaborate a Marxist theory of the nation and nationalism.[26] Borokhov
supplemented the Marxian concepts of "relations of production" and
"forces of production" with his own "conditions of production," which
included national territory and other factors. He sought to demonstrate
that the achievement by oppressed nationalities of "normal" conditions of

production—that is, their own independent nation-state—was a prerequisite for, rather than a hindrance to, the successful waging of the class struggle and, ultimately, socialist revolution.

In this theoretical project Borokhov's methods and models were steeped in the strongly positivist, economistic, and mechanistic Marxism characteristic of the parties and ideologists of the Second International, with their faith in "iron laws" and inexorable historical processes operating independently of human agency or will. The utility of Borokhov's theoretical work was immediately obvious to his disciples: it provided a seemingly rigorous Marxist rationale for dissolving the apparent—and, to many eastern European socialist-Zionists, deeply troubling—contradiction between socialism and Zionism by making the latter an essential precondition for the realization of the former, a necessary and unavoidable means to an end, rather than a dangerous diversion. Borokhov's analysis helped socialist-Zionists fend off criticism from fellow socialists who were strongly anti-Zionist, including almost all factions of the Russian social-democratic movement but also the Bund, the independent Jewish socialist party which had strong support among the impoverished Jewish masses of eastern Europe. Both the all-Russian social democrats and the Bundists denounced Zionism in all its forms as reactionary, since by calling on the Jews to emigrate to Palestine it diverted the attention of the Jewish workers from the struggle against capitalism and antisemitism in the countries where they actually lived, implicitly or explicitly accepted the antisemitic premise that Jews and non-Jews could never live together in harmony as equals, and promised what they saw as an illusory and utopian solution to the very real problems of the Jewish masses.

In 1906 Borokhov published "Our Platform," which applied his general analysis of nationalism to the Jewish question and provided the fledgling Po'alei Tziyon movement with a distinctive theoretical perspective and political program.[27] In Borokhov's view, the Jews were unassimilable and persecuted wherever they lived in the Diaspora because of their "abnormal" social structure: they were overwhelmingly concentrated in the interstices and on the margins of national economic life, in petty trade, small-scale service enterprises, moneylending, and the like rather than in agriculture and primary industry. Unable to compete successfully in economies dominated by non-Jews and arousing antisemitism wherever they went, the petit bourgeois Jewish masses would ultimately—inexorably—be compelled to migrate to Palestine, the only territory in which they could successfully achieve economic normalcy by becoming workers and farmers. Here this new normal Jewish proletariat would finally be able to wage the class struggle and ultimately achieve a Jewish socialist society.

But why was Palestine the territory to which the Jewish masses would inevitably make their way and in which they would ultimately achieve both socialism and statehood? Borokhov made a signal contribution to socialist Zionism by providing a purportedly objective rationale cast in Marxist terms for the choice of Palestine as the site of this project, as opposed to the emotional, religious, or historical justifications advanced by other Zionists. For Borokhov, Palestine was unique in one crucial respect: only there could the Jewish immigrants crisscrossing the globe in search of a permanent haven

> not encounter organized and united resistance and displacement. In all the other lands legal restrictions and prohibitions on entry are an expression of the needs of the local population, which does not want foreign competitors. As a result no democratization of the regime or of international relations in bourgeois society can remove these restrictions. By contrast, prohibitions on the entry of Jews from Russia and Austria to Eretz Yisra'el are only a manifestation of the [Ottoman] sultan's arbitrariness, without any connection to the real needs of the population of Eretz Yisra'el itself.[28]

Borokhov thus understood that Palestine was not unpopulated. But like most early Zionists he was certain that the country's inhabitants presently did not, and for the foreseeable future would not, constitute a coherent or distinct community which might rationally oppose Jewish immigration. In fact, his analysis and prognosis were rendered plausible only by this rather dubious premise. That premise was in turn supported by Borokhov's conception of Palestine's population. Although the ignorant might call them "Arabs" or "Turks," he wrote, "they in fact have nothing in common with Arabs or Turks, and their attitude toward both of these is cold and even hostile."[29] He argued that

> The natives of Eretz Yisra'el have no independent economic or cultural character; they are divided and disintegrated not only by the structure of the country's territory and by the diversity of its religions, but also by virtue of its character as an international hostel [i.e., a land whose inhabitants were a mixture of races and types, the remnants of numerous peoples who had passed through without striking roots, and thus lacked a common national culture or character]. The natives of Eretz Yisra'el are not a single nation, nor will they constitute a single nation for a long time. They very easily and quickly adapt themselves to every cultural model higher than theirs brought from abroad; they are unable to unite in an organized act of resistance to external influences; they are unsuited for national competition, and their competition has an individualistic and anarchic character.

In the long run, Borokhov predicted, "the inhabitants of Eretz Yisra'el will adapt themselves to the economic and cultural type that seizes a dominant economic position in the country. The natives of Eretz Yisra'el will assimilate economically and culturally with whoever brings order to the country, whoever undertakes the development of the forces of production of Eretz Yisra'el." His conclusion: "It is the Jewish immigrants who will undertake the development of the forces of production of Eretz Yisra'el, and the local population of Eretz Yisra'el will soon assimilate economically and culturally to the Jews."[30]

To bolster his argument Borokhov could also draw on contemporary European racial typologies. "The local population in Eretz Yisra'el," he asserted, "is closer to the Jews in racial composition even than any other of the 'Semitic' peoples. . . . In any event, all the travellers-tourists confirm that except for their use of Arabic it is impossible to distinguish in any respect between a Sefardi porter and a simple [Arab] worker or peasant." Borokhov had to rely on travelers' accounts to support this assertion because he himself never actually set foot in Palestine.[31]

Curiously, despite a poor grasp of the region's geography, culture, and history, Borokhov did have some notion that an Arab nationalist movement had appeared. In a footnote to "Our Platform," he acknowledged that Arab nationalists included Palestine in their future patrimony and that "our haters of Zion [i.e., outright anti-Zionists but also the 'Territorialists' who were willing to consider lands other than Palestine for Jewish settlement and self-rule] see the Arab movement as a terrible threat to Zionism." But he dismissed Arab nationalism as irrelevant because he was certain that despite a shared language and religion, the peasants of Palestine had nothing in common with the Arabs.[32]

The precondition for the massive influx of Jewish immigrants into Palestine and their eventual absorption of the indigenous population was, of course, the removal of the Ottoman government's restrictions on the free entry of Jews. But how was this to be achieved? Like Syrkin, Borokhov believed that the antisemitic governments of the European countries in which the Jewish masses presently lived would pressure the Ottoman government to allow the Jews free entry, in order to facilitate their emigration and thereby get rid of this unwanted element. In the longer run, the class struggle of the Jewish proletariat in eastern Europe would contribute to the overthrow of those reactionary regimes, and the new democratic governments which the Jewish workers would help install would reward them by forcing the Ottoman sultan to allow the Jews into Palestine without restriction.[33]

The wishes of the indigenous population of Palestine did not enter into Borokhov's vision of the present or the future. In fact, his whole theoretical edifice rested on the nonexistence of anything resembling a coherent Arab society in Palestine, on an image of the indigenous population as no more than a heterogeneous and rootless mass of backward peasants. In this sense, the socialist-Zionist theoretician was very much a man of his times. There was certainly much debate within the contemporary European social-democratic movement about the relationship between proletarian internationalism and the national rights of, and nationalist movements among, the oppressed peoples (including the Jews) within the multiethnic empires of Europe, especially Tsarist Russia and Hapsburg-ruled Austria-Hungary. European social democrats were also generally committed to mitigating the harsher aspects of European colonial rule and rendering it more benign, while opposing the militarism and chauvinism which they well knew imperialism bred and which were exploited by reactionary forces in Europe itself to weaken the social-democratic movement. Yet before the First World War, relatively few socialists opposed colonialism in principle or rejected its underlying premises, and most shared with their avowed class enemies a firm belief in the superiority of European civilization and the consequent right (if not duty) of Europeans to rule over less advanced peoples. The principle of national self-determination which many European socialists were prepared to accept with respect to European peoples was not deemed to apply to most if not all non-European peoples, who were seen as more or less childlike tutelaries of more or less beneficent Europeans. They imagined that future socialist governments in Europe would certainly exercise a more benign form of tutelage than did the present-day bourgeois regimes, and they would not exploit colonial rivalries to fan the flames of national hatred at home. But the right of Europeans to dominate non-Europeans and share or impose their superior ways, including socialism itself, was largely taken for granted.

This was as true of socialist Zionists as it was of anti-Zionist socialists, with few exceptions. Both Syrkin and Borokhov believed that eventually Palestine would be given to the Jews by the European powers, whether their governments were reactionary and antisemitic or democratic, even socialist. The wishes of the country's indigenous population were simply not something that even socialist Zionists had to take into account. Where Syrkin envisioned that population's emigration so as to make room for Jewish immigrants, Borokhov imagined that the Arab inhabitants of Palestine would simply disappear through assimilation with the economically and culturally more advanced Jews. In Borokhov's prognosis we can discern the intersection of conceptions of non-European peoples that were central to contemporary colonial discourse with a version of Marxism that was little more than crude economic determinism.

In the years that followed the publication of his most important theoretical and programmatic statements, Borokhov would make only passing reference in his published essays and articles to the indigenous population of Palestine. In his later writings he did occasionally use the term "Arabs," but he never abandoned his belief that they did not constitute a distinct national entity, much less possess any legitimate rights in Palestine. Despite some expressions of respect for Ottoman resistance to foreign encroachment in the years leading up to the outbreak of the First World War, he and the movement he helped lead could attribute Arab and Ottoman opposition to Zionism only to antisemitism. Thus the third congress of the World Union of Po'alei Tziyon, which grouped the socialist-Zionist parties in various countries, noted in the summer of 1911 that "there have recently been manifestations of antisemitism among certain segments of the Arab community in Eretz Yisra'el and also among some elements of Turkish society, manifestations which cause conflicts and clashes and create political-legal obstacles to Jewish immigration and settlement in Eretz Yisra'el." [34]

This resolution also contains several other elements which would be central to labor-Zionist discourse about Palestine and its indigenous population. First, while it proclaimed Po'alei Tziyon's support for the territorial integrity of the Ottoman empire and its solidarity with the empire's progressive and democratic forces, it also declared that "our [Zionist] aspirations run parallel to the course of development of the productive forces in Eretz Yisra'el and to the interests of Ottoman democracy." This formulation reflects Borokhovism's image of itself as simply implementing the stern decrees of historical necessity, an image rooted in its rigidly mechanistic understanding of Marxism. Though Borokhov sometimes wavered on this issue, allowing greater importance to human agency, he generally insisted that inexorable "stychic" processes would inevitably channel Jewish capital and then Jewish immigrants into Palestine, leading to the development of capitalism there. As the productive forces developed the Jewish proletariat would grow in size and strength, waging its own class struggle which would also contribute to the broader struggle for Ottoman democracy. Hence the beneficial and necessary character of Zionism, as grasped from within Borokhovist discourse. There was little room in that discourse for the wishes or aspirations of Palestine's Arab population, who as we have seen had been more or less defined out of existence.

This formulation also resonated with what was to be a central justification deployed by defenders of labor Zionism in response to criticism that the national rights of the indigenous majority were being violated. This was the argument that, in effect, the land belonged to those who made it productive. Jewish immigrants had settled in what had been a barren land, had through their loving labors made the land fertile and productive, and this almost sacred act of redemption gave the Jews superior rights to the land. Implicit in this representation was an indictment of the Arab population, who were depicted as having abandoned, neglected, and abused the land, and therefore not to really deserve it or be entitled to it.

Another segment of this resolution foreshadows yet another theme that would play a key role in labor Zionism's thinking about relations with Palestinian Arabs in general and Palestinian Arab workers in particular. On the one hand it depicted Arab opposition to Zionism as antisemitism pure and simple, implicitly likening the peasants of Palestine to the vodka-besotted Russian or Ukrainian pogromists with whom eastern European Jews were all too familiar. On the other hand the resolution called for rapprochement and mutual understanding with "the popular elements among the Arab inhabitants dwelling in Eretz Yisra'el." As we will see, the distinction which this formulation drew between potentially friendly "popular elements" within the Arab population of Palestine and other, presumably hostile, elite elements would later be developed along lines that would serve important discursive and political purposes. Labor Zionism's distinction between the good (if backward) Arab working masses and the pernicious (because nationalist and anti-Zionist) Arab elite would buttress not only a certain conviction about the objectively pro-Zionist interests of Arab workers but also a long-standing rejection of the authenticity, legitimacy, and mass base of Palestinian Arab nationalism.

THE ENCOUNTER IN PALESTINE

That Zionist leaders, ideologists, and activists based in Europe who (like Borokhov) had never set foot in Palestine, or who (like Herzl) had paid only hurried visits, should develop such images of the land and its Arab inhabitants may perhaps not seem so surprising. These people were often preoccupied with matters directly concerning the Jews of Europe and had little time for the situation in Palestine itself. However, the record of the nascent Jewish workers' movement in Palestine makes it impossible to sustain the argument that these distorted perceptions were simply or primarily a result of distance and ignorance. Members of that movement actually in Palestine generally continued to accept and propagate the prevailing Zionist discourse which represented Palestine's Arabs as a motley amalgam with only a marginal presence in the country and no legitimate national claim to it. This is not to suggest that socialist-Zionist views did not change over time; they certainly did, especially as it became evident that what these self-proclaimed "pioneers" (*halutzim*) actually experienced in Palestine did not coincide with what their ideology had led them to expect. As we will see, however, there was a great deal of continuity as well, especially when it came to attitudes toward the Arabs of Palestine.

For a time, Borokhov's comrades and disciples who actually left their homes in the Tsarist and Hapsburg empires and went to Palestine during the Second Aliya remained loyal to his vision and to the conception of Palestine's indigenous Arab population which it entailed. In 1906 a handful of activists of the new Po'alei Tziyon branch in Palestine itself, officially dubbed the "Jewish Social-Democratic Workers' Party in the Land of Israel," met in the Arab town of Ramla to draw up a program for their party. That program opened with a Borokhovist paraphrase of the first lines of *The Communist Manifesto:* "All human history is a history of national and class struggles." The only reference to the indigenous population appeared in the context of a reiteration of Borokhovist orthodoxy: since the capitalism developing in Palestine required "educated, energetic workers, and since the local worker is still in a lowly state (*natun beshefel madrega*), capitalist development in Palestine depends on the immigration of more developed workers from abroad"—that is, Jews. Here the Palestinian Arab worker makes an early appearance, though not explicitly denoted as such and only as a figure whose backwardness requires another more advanced kind of worker, the immigrating Jewish proletarian, to take center stage. Neither this document, nor a second program drafted a few months later at a party meeting in the coastal city of Jaffa, also overwhelmingly Arab, made any specific reference to Arabs or to a Zionist policy toward them. The second draft program did have something to say about Palestine's future, however: it declared the party's goal to be "political autonomy for the Jewish people in this country."[35]

This is not to say, however, that the issue did not surface at all. As early as 1906, at a Po'alei Tziyon meeting in Jaffa, some party members called on their leaders to begin organizing Arab workers. One participant recalled that the discussion was "heated to the point of a split, which was avoided only by the majority's proposal to postpone a party effort to organize Arab workers but to permit individuals to take action in this area." A few months later, at the party's second congress, some delegates demanded that a Jewish-Arab workers' organization be established, but nothing came of the idea.[36]

In the aftermath of the Ottoman constitutional ("Young Turk") revolution of 1908, the intensification of Arab-Jewish conflict in Palestine and the appearance of a movement for Arab autonomy within (and later independence from) the Ottoman empire compelled the Yishuv and the Zionist movement to pay greater attention to the question of political relations with the Arabs of Palestine. Arab protests against Jewish immigration and land purchases, and explicitly anti-Zionist sentiments, were now voiced more frequently and vigorously, indicating that Arab opposition might pose a serious threat to the Zionist project; hence, for example, Ahad Ha'am's warnings after his 1911 visit.[37] However, though some Zionists now began to perceive relations with Palestine's Arab majority as an actual or potential problem, the issue did not at this stage attain a significant place on the agenda of the Zionist movement, and no explicit or coherent policy was formulated to address it.

These early debates do, however, provide support for the argument which scholars attempting to rethink the history of Zionism and the Yishuv have advanced and which I set forth in the Introduction: to understand the development of the Yishuv, and especially of labor Zionism, which by the 1930s would be the dominant sociopolitical force in the Yishuv and the world Zionist movement, one must focus not so much on the socialist ideology which the generation of "founders," the self-proclaimed pioneers of Zionist settlement, brought with them from Europe in the decade before the First World War, but rather on the environment in Palestine itself and Arab-Jewish interaction there. The utility of a relational approach which situates the Zionist project in relation to its Arab context can be demonstrated by analysis of one aspect of the "Arab problem" which was now already of serious concern to socialist Zionists in particular and had become the subject of extensive discussion within the fledgling Jewish labor movement in Palestine.

THE "CONQUEST OF LABOR"

This issue was not explicitly political, nor did it at this stage directly impinge upon the prevailing Zionist discourse about Arabs and their relationship to Palestine. Rather, it reflected the circumstances surrounding the encounter of Jews and Arabs in Palestine itself, and specifically their encounter in the labor market. For socialist Zionism, this issue was encapsulated in the related concepts of the "conquest of labor" (*kibbush ha-ʿavoda*) and "Hebrew labor" (*ʿavoda ʿivrit*). These concepts would come to occupy a central place in labor-Zionist discourse and practice, and would play an important role in shaping relations between Arab and Jewish workers in Palestine throughout the period explored in this book.[38]

The syntheses of Zionism and socialism elaborated by Syrkin, Borokhov, and others in the early years of the twentieth century were soon put to the test in Palestine itself. A majority of the Jews who came to Palestine during the Second Aliya settled in towns and cities (including the new exclusively Jewish town of Tel Aviv, founded in 1909 on the outskirts of Jaffa), but this wave of immigration also included several thousand young men and women, mostly of eastern European middle-class origin, who saw themselves as the vanguard of the social transformation of the Jewish people. Some, adherents or sympathizers of Poʿalei Tziyon, wanted to implement the Borokhovian synthesis of class struggle and Zionist settlement by transforming themselves into agricultural or industrial wage workers, thereby constituting a Jewish proletariat in Palestine which could then wage its class struggle in the country's developing capitalist economy. Others belonged to or inclined toward another left-Zionist party, Hapoʿel Hatzaʿir ("The Young Worker"), which rejected both Marxian socialism and class struggle and instead, influenced by Tolstoyan principles, expounded a commitment to physical labor, self-sacrifice, and settlement on the land as the means by which Zion would be "redeemed." All of them shared the belief that only the establishment in Palestine of a large and solidly rooted class of Jewish agricultural workers subsisting by the sweat of their brow, and as capitalism developed of industrial workers as well, would allow the Zionist project to succeed and avoid the reproduction in the Yishuv of the Diaspora "abnormalities" denounced by Syrkin, Borokhov, and others.

Even before they arrived in Palestine, these socialist Zionists had already begun to conceive of themselves as workers charged with a unique mission. They thus discursively transformed themselves into the nucleus of a Jewish working class in Palestine long before they actually managed to find jobs as wage workers. Once in Palestine they naturally placed great emphasis on "productivizing" themselves by means of what they called the "conquest of labor." This term could be used in a personal sense to denote an individual's struggle to overcome his or her bourgeois or petit bourgeois class background and lack of experience with manual labor by transforming oneself, through physical labor in Palestine, into an authentic Jewish proletarian. It was also used in a more general and collective sense to denote socialist Zionism's vision that in Palestine Jews would master the kinds of work (especially heavy physical labor in agriculture) which relatively few performed in the Diaspora. They would thereby prove that the Jews as a people were capable of escaping their past and returning to their authentic national selves, of becoming once again a working people tilling the soil of their ancestral homeland. As we will see, "conquest of labor" would increasingly come to be used in a third sense, one which much more directly involved Arabs.

However, these new arrivals soon encountered obstacles which had not been foreseen by the theoreticians of labor Zionism. In particular, Borokhov's prognosis for capitalist development in Palestine was quickly proven inaccurate. Borokhov had predicted that both Jewish capital and Jewish wage labor would inexorably be channeled into Palestine by what he called (in the manner of Second International Marxism) "stychic" processes, resulting in the creation of a growing capitalist economy which would provide Jewish immigrants with jobs and make class struggle both possible and necessary. It soon became obvious, however, that the process would be neither rapid nor automatic. Neither Jewish nor non-Jewish private capital rushed to invest in Palestine, a poor and underdeveloped land with apparently limited economic prospects. Nor did "national capital"— the funds collected worldwide by the financial, land-purchasing, and settlement institutions of the Zionist Organization—even begin to suffice for the large-scale settlement of new immigrants, at least along the lines followed up to that point in the moshavot.

At the same time, agricultural employment in the moshavot—precisely the kind of jobs to which these would-be workers aspired—was largely monopolized by Arab peasants working as wage laborers. The Jewish newcomers, with no capital of their own, thus found themselves competing with an abundant supply of cheaper Arab labor, which was naturally preferred even by Jewish employers, especially the citrus plantation owners and other farmers. The new Jewish immigrants could not subsist on the wages paid to Arabs, and were in addition unaccustomed to heavy physical labor, resentful of their employers' efforts to discipline and control them, and prone to vociferating loudly about class struggle and socialist revolution—traits which did not endear them to prospective Jewish employers. They thus found themselves with few prospects either for settlement on land acquired by the Zionist movement or for employment on land owned by private Jewish farmers. In this bleak situation, exacerbated by disease and Arab hostility, many (perhaps most) of these Second Aliya immigrants soon left Palestine, either returning to Europe or (more often) continuing on to a wealthier and more attractive "promised land"—the United States.

THE STRUGGLE FOR "HEBREW LABOR"

It was in this specific context—the inability of these immigrants to compete effectively in Palestine's labor market and the resulting prospect that the Zionist project would founder because neither jobs nor resources for settlement were available to maintain those who had come or attract others to follow—that the struggle for the "conquest of labor" was transformed from a struggle for individual and collective proletarianization into an active campaign to replace Arab workers employed in the Jewish sector of Palestine's economy with Jewish workers. Hence the doctrine of "Hebrew labor," which in the decade preceding the First World War came to occupy a central place in labor-Zionist discourse and practice. The fate of the Zionist project in Palestine came to be seen as depending on the success of this campaign of "conquest," on the achievement of "Hebrew labor"—that is, exclusively Jewish employment—in every enterprise of the Jewish sector of the Palestinian economy.[39]

For adherents of Hapo'el Hatza'ir, adoption of the Hebrew labor strategy—I will henceforth dispense with quotation marks to distinguish this term, and conquest of labor as well—was relatively easy, given their lack of interest in, if not outright rejection of, the principle of proletarian internationalism and their insistence that priority always be given to the needs of Jews and of Zionism. If the implantation of a Jewish working class in Palestine, seen as an essential prerequisite for the success of Zionism, required a struggle to force Jewish farmers to dismiss their Arab workers and hire Jews in their place, so be it. Their conception of Zionism had little room for, indeed explicitly rejected, too much concern for the needs and rights of others. In fact, a lack of anxiety about what the *goyim* (non-Jews) thought and the unabashed prioritization of Jewish national needs was regarded as a sign of labor Zionism's decisive break with what they depicted as a cringing and subservient "*galut* [exile] mentality."

Members and sympathizers of Po'alei Tziyon, who took their Marxism rather seriously, found this a much more difficult and anxiety-provoking issue. How could socialists endorse a struggle to deprive fellow workers of their livelihoods simply because they were Arabs rather than Jews? Was this not precisely the kind of discrimination of which Jews them-

selves had been victims in the Diaspora? How could the principle of proletarian solidarity across ethnic and national lines be reconciled with the
Jewish workers' urgent need to find work?

It was Yitzhak Ben-Tzvi (1884–1963) who most carefully and fully
formulated the ideological rationale which helped Po'alei Tziyon embrace
a policy it had initially denounced as unprincipled. A childhood friend and
early disciple of Ber Borokhov, Ben-Tzvi had arrived in Palestine in 1907
with several years of both legal and underground work in the service of
Po'alei Tziyon in Russia already behind him. He soon became one of the
leaders of the fledgling Jewish labor movement in Palestine. As we will
see, after the First World War he would be a leading figure in the labor-
Zionist movement and in the broader Yishuv and would play a significant
role in labor Zionism's early interactions with Arab workers. His career
of public service would culminate in his election in 1952 to the presidency
of the State of Israel, a largely ceremonial post he would hold until his
death in 1963.

In a two-part essay published in 1912, Ben-Tzvi sought to ease his
comrades' consciences by demonstrating that in certain historical circumstances, national interests must take precedence over class solidarity. At
the present time, he argued, the organized and class-conscious Jewish
workers in Palestine had the right to demand that cheap and unorganized
Arab labor be excluded from jobs in the moshavot and elsewhere in the
Jewish sector. Indeed, this was a question of life or death for the Jewish
working class in Palestine. Only later, when capitalist development had
proceeded further and employment opportunities became abundant for
all, would a material basis be created for solidarity between Jewish and
Arab workers.[40]

Not a few Po'alei Tziyon members were initially dismayed at the prospect of their avowedly socialist party giving priority to depriving fellow
workers of their livelihoods simply because they were Arabs rather than
Jews. At the party's second congress, one delegate proposed that "instead
of the slogan of the conquest of labor by displacing Arab workers—the
task of the Jewish worker is to organize the Arab worker and reduce the
[Arab landowners'] influence over him." No explicit policy was adopted,
but party members acting on their own are said to have organized a strike
of Arab workers employed in the citrus groves of the moshava of Petah
Tikva in 1907. The strike was broken by the Ottoman police, who arrested
and beat the strikers, while the Jewish employers threatened to import
workers from Egypt.[41] As time passed and the unemployment crisis grew
ever more desperate, however, doubts and qualms subsided and the em-

phasis on Hebrew labor won widespread acceptance. Gradually, opposition within the party to this doctrine was silenced, though as we will see it remained a live question because other segments of the Jewish labor movement in Palestine would continue to take issue with it.

In theory, the Jewish workers' movement in Palestine might have sought another way out of its dilemma. Instead of trying to exclude Arab workers from jobs with Jewish employers so as to secure those jobs for Jewish immigrants, it might have sought to reduce the wage differential between Jews and Arabs by encouraging and assisting Arab workers to organize and win higher wages. As the wages of Arab workers rose toward Jewish levels, Jews would have found it easier to compete with Arabs for the available jobs. This strategy had its supporters within the Zionist labor movement, though they were always in the minority. To the extent that it later gained significant support among Jewish workers and union activists, it was mainly in workplaces where Arab-Jewish solidarity and joint organization seemed the only way to improve the desperate situation of the Jewish employees and preserve a foothold for Jews.

By contrast, the great majority of labor Zionists dismissed the idea that Jewish-Arab class solidarity could ease the plight of Jewish workers as a delusion, at least for the foreseeable future. In this they were probably quite right: the abundance of low-wage Arab labor, from within Palestine and from neighboring lands, made it unlikely that even determined efforts by Jews to organize Arab workers could have raised general wage levels enough to open a significant number of unskilled or low-skill jobs to Jewish immigrants. More importantly, such a strategy was generally perceived as incompatible with the goals of Zionism, which included the establishment of a more or less homogeneous Jewish society and state in Palestine. Devoting a significant proportion of the very slender resources which the Zionist labor movement had at its disposal to the improvement of Arab wages and living standards seemed absurd as well as futile.

The exclusion of Arab workers from employment in the Jewish sector of Palestine's economy would come to be seen by the labor-Zionist movement as absolutely crucial to the formation of a Jewish working class in Palestine, at least for the short and medium terms. However, this exclusionary strategy was not depicted or understood as such by those who engaged in it, or as constituting the kind of discrimination from which many of these Jewish immigrants had themselves suffered in their countries of origin. Nor was the conflict this practice entailed seen as ethnic or national in essence. Rather, the Jewish workers saw themselves (or more precisely, were encouraged to see themselves) as the innocent victims of a vicious "boycott" of Jewish labor on the part of Jewish employers. Rather than taking the offensive in an effort to displace Arab workers, they were engaged in an essentially defensive battle to protect the rights and gains of "organized" (Jewish) labor against the threat posed by "unorganized" (Arab) labor.

ECONOMIC SEPARATISM AND WORKING-CLASS FORMATION

The labor-Zionist movement would wage a long-term struggle to secure jobs for Jews by excluding Arab workers from privately owned Jewish enterprises. Various means were used to induce Jewish employers, especially farmers but also urban construction contractors and others, to put the "national" (i.e., Zionist) interest ahead of their class interest by excluding cheaper Arab labor and instead hiring more expensive Jewish labor. As we will see, after the establishment of the British mandate in Palestine efforts were also made to induce the mandatory government and its agencies, and private employers who were neither Jewish nor Arab, to hire more Jews.[42]

However, the Zionist labor movement's efforts to achieve Hebrew labor enjoyed only limited success. Before the First World War that movement was much too weak to enforce its demands on private employers, and in the interwar period it would be only sporadically successful, for reasons to be discussed in subsequent chapters. Moreover, the strategy of replacing Arab with Jewish workers was in and of itself unlikely to resolve Zionism's problems on the ground in Palestine. For it was clear that given the weakness of the Yishuv's economy and the low level of investment by private capital, even the achievement of a relatively high level of Hebrew labor in the Jewish private sector could not possibly provide enough jobs for the large numbers of immigrants needed to make the Zionist project feasible. Nor was private capital likely to invest in ways that efficiently facilitated the absorption of immigrants or enhanced the infrastructural development and self-sufficiency of the Yishuv. The struggle for Hebrew labor had therefore to be supplemented by job creation, through the development of an exclusively Jewish, high-wage enclave within the Palestinian economy. This in turn required the labor-Zionist movement to establish its own industrial, financial, construction, transport, and service enterprises. Some of the capital which that movement used to launch these enterprises and enable them to pay relatively high wages was mobilized from within the movement. But much of it was "national capital," funds donated by the wealthier nonworker elements which at that time still dominated the Zionist movement and channeled through the institutions of the Zionist Organization.

Much of the Zionist leadership was initially unsympathetic or even hostile to socialist Zionism and to the labor movement's vision of itself as the vanguard of the Zionist movement. But along with substantial segments of the Yishuv, it eventually came around to the view that it was the labor-Zionist movement which was most effective at actually getting immigrants to Palestine, settling them, and mobilizing their energies in ways that enhanced the development of the Yishuv. The initiatives and enterprises of the labor movement therefore merited financial and ultimately political support, since without the labor movement's numbers, energies, and capacity for commitment and self-sacrifice, it seemed unlikely that the Zionist project would make much headway. For its part, the labor-Zionist movement, though initially intent on waging class warfare and building a socialist Jewish Palestine by its own forces, was driven by circumstances to seek the support of bourgeois Zionists so as to realize its goal of creating a Jewish working class in Palestine. It needed the funds controlled by the Zionist Organization and its institutions, and by private capital as well, to create jobs, subsidize meager wages, and strengthen the labor movement. Israeli sociologist Michael Shalev has aptly characterized the resulting relationship, which developed gradually over a period of several decades and was never free of tensions and conflicts, as a "practical alliance between a settlement movement without settlers and a workers' movement without work."[43]

It was really only after the First World War that the labor-Zionist movement—unified from 1920 within the framework of the "General Organization of Hebrew Workers in the Land of Israel" (known as the Histadrut, the Hebrew word for "organization")—was able to embark on the creation of its own economic sector, with support and subsidies from the Zionist movement. This new sector expanded slowly at first, and with many failures and setbacks, but eventually the Histadrut would become one of the Yishuv's (and Israel's) largest employers, monopolizing or dominating whole sectors of the economy while providing a broad range of social and cultural services as well as many new jobs. New sources of Histadrut-controlled urban employment were complemented by new forms of agricultural settlement, also heavily subsidized in many ways by the institutions of the Zionist movement. These were the *kibbutz,* a collective farm whose first prototypes were established a few years before the First World War, and the cooperative smallholders' village (*moshav*), the first of which was established in 1920. These new types of settlement seemed to overcome the problems inherent in the moshava model of Zionist agricultural settlement which had characterized the First Aliya by allowing for more cost-effective absorption of immigrants and more efficient use of their labor.[44]

The drive to create a separate high-wage economic sector dominated by the labor movement, coupled with that movement's emphasis on the struggle for Hebrew labor, amounted to an abandonment of orthodox Borokhovism, though this was fully acknowledged only in the 1920s, when the old schema was supplanted by a new doctrine sometimes referred to as "constructivism." This further development of socialist-Zionist ideology cast the organized Jewish working class in Palestine—and not Borokhov's "stychic" processes—as the historic agent which would realize the Zionist project. Since "normal" capitalist development seemed unlikely to create a substantial Jewish working class in Palestine, as Borokhov had predicted, this task would have to be accomplished by the fledgling labor movement itself, through direct involvement in the development of the Yishuv's economy and through the conquest of labor in other sectors. The emphasis thus shifted from waging the class struggle within the framework of an economy dominated by Jewish capitalists to the task of constructing a self-sufficient and largely labor-controlled Jewish economy in Palestine, with the support of nonworker elements in the Zionist movement and even private capitalists, whether Zionist or not. This task required the mobilization of the energies of the working class through the creation of a highly centralized (and bureaucratized) apparatus, incessant appeals for self-sacrifice, hard work, and discipline, and a steady focus on the tasks of national construction. Human agency, the voluntary commitment of the Jewish workers to self-sacrifice for the sake of the nation, was now depicted as the central factor in the struggle for the realization of Zionism.

Backed by the resources of the world Zionist movement (and thereby entailing an alliance with the bourgeois forces within that movement), the labor-Zionist movement in Palestine would create relatively high-wage employment for its members and for the immigrants to come, both by securing as many existing jobs as possible for Jews and by creating an economic sector which, though subsidized by others, would remain largely under its control. This sector would become the dynamic motor propelling the development of a self-sufficient Yishuv, and would also strengthen the Zionist labor movement's political influence, in the Yishuv and beyond. In ideological and political but also material terms, this strategy put the Jewish working class in Palestine, the Histadrut into which it was largely organized after 1920 and the labor-Zionist parties which led it, at the very center of the Zionist project rather than constituting just one of many sociopolitical forces within a diverse movement.

It was on the basis of this strategy, which seemed to offer a way out of the problems which the Zionist project had encountered in Palestine, that the labor-Zionist movement would enhance its economic, political, and cultural power to the point where it could effectively assert its leadership of the Yishuv and the Zionist movement. Building on its control of a large and increasingly powerful network of political, economic, social, and cultural institutions which encompassed a large proportion of the Yishuv's population, labor Zionism (from 1930 dominated by a single party, MAPAI) would ultimately achieve a position of hegemony within the Zionist movement, signaled by the elevation in 1935 of party and Histadrut leader David Ben-Gurion to the chairmanship of the Jewish Agency executive— that is, to the effective political leadership of the Yishuv. On its own, MAPAI never attained an absolute majority in the deliberative bodies of the Zionist Organization or the Yishuv (or, later, in Israel's parliament), but in alliance with its bourgeois-Zionist and religious-Zionist junior partners it could exercise a large measure of control, dominate policy making, and largely shape the ethos of the Yishuv and the Zionist movement.

Adoption of this model of settlement and development helped make Zionism significantly different from other initially similar projects of European overseas settlement. A Jewish society developed in Palestine that, though never hermetically sealed off from the surrounding Arab society, did not crucially depend on the exploitation of Arab wage labor. Instead, a substantial class of Jewish industrial, construction, and transport workers was successfully created and implanted, and agricultural settlement took forms that excluded or displaced rather than exploited Arab labor. This specific path of development, largely shaped by local conditions and especially by the specific form and consequences of Zionism's encounter in Palestine itself with the country's Arab majority, helped shape many of the social, economic, political, and cultural institutions and patterns that would later come to be seen as unique to Yishuv and later Israeli society. This is why I argue that interpretations which explain the Yishuv's (and later Israel's) distinctive course mainly in terms of the values and ideology which the "pioneers" of the Second Aliya brought with them to Palestine are inadequate. They simply fail to take proper account of the ways in which Zionism's interactions with the existing Arab society in Palestine played a crucial part in shaping the Yishuv as a society.

Nonetheless, though it is essential to remain focused on the ways in which Arab and Jewish societies in Palestine were mutually formative, we must also remember that the Zionist project's specific pattern of development was ultimately made possible by world-historical events over which the Zionist movement had little influence. In November 1917, even as its armed forces were conquering Palestine from the Ottoman empire, the British government proclaimed its commitment to the creation in Palestine of a "national home" for the Jewish people (the "Balfour Declaration"). That decision certainly owed something to Zionist lobbying, but other factors were at least as important, among them the British government's desire to garner Jewish support for the Allied cause in Russia and the United States, and imperial planning for the postwar Middle East. Zionism had finally secured the big-power sponsor it had been seeking since Herzl's time. After the war, Britain constituted Palestine as a distinct political entity, established its own rule (in the form of a League of Nations "mandate"), and implemented its wartime pledge by facilitating the Zionist project in a variety of ways.[45]

The British-Zionist alliance was never free of tensions and would break down just before the Second World War as the two parties' interests diverged. It is nonetheless clear that it was British colonial rule over Palestine which, in the face of growing Palestinian Arab nationalist opposition to Zionism and demands for self-determination, opened the way to Jewish immigration, land acquisition, and development of the Yishuv's infrastructure on a scale which would have been unimaginable had Palestine either remained under Ottoman rule or achieved independence under an Arab government. The relative success of labor Zionism's strategy of pursuing Hebrew labor and building up a relatively self-sufficient Jewish high-wage sector, and the labor-Zionist camp's attainment of hegemony within the Yishuv and world Zionism, would in this sense have been inconceivable in the absence of a sympathetic colonial regime which could hold the indigenous majority (still two-thirds of the country's population in 1947) in check until the Yishuv was strong enough to stand on its own.

2 Labor Zionism and the Arab Working Class, 1920–1929

Although the Second Aliya period had witnessed episodes of Arab-Jewish tension and conflict, it was still possible in that period for many Zionists to ignore the question of Arab-Jewish relations in Palestine or consider it an issue of only marginal importance. A few years later such an attitude had become altogether impossible. Palestine's conquest by the British during the First World War, the rise under Hashemite leadership of an Arab nationalist movement whose goal was the establishment of an independent Arab state including Palestine, the issuance in November 1917 of the Balfour Declaration, the establishment of the British mandate, the increasingly unmistakable emergence in Palestine of organized Arab nationalist opposition to Zionism and British rule—all these developments required the labor-Zionist movement to address the Arab question much more seriously and directly. The urgency of the issue was further underscored by outbreaks of Arab violence against Jews, in Jerusalem (1920) and Jaffa (1921).

Numerous attempts to come to grips with the ideological and practical dilemmas that Arab (and specifically Palestinian Arab) demands for self-determination posed for left-wing Zionism were made in the early mandate period. These often incorporated elements of prewar socialist-Zionist discourse while developing them into a more theoretically coherent and systematic position that also reflected immediate political exigencies. One of the most serious and authoritative of these early mandate-era texts was a 1921 essay entitled *The Arab Movement*, by Yitzhak Ben-Tzvi. This essay contains many of the constituent elements out of which labor Zionism's discourse on the Arabs would be constructed for decades to come and therefore merits a close reading.

THE ARABS OF PALESTINE IN LABOR-ZIONIST DISCOURSE

Already a prominent leader of the socialist-Zionist Po'alei Tziyon party in Palestine before the war, in 1919 Yitzhak Ben-Tzvi was one of the founders of a new successor party, Ahdut Ha'avoda ("Unity of Labor"). In the immediate postwar period the international Po'alei Tziyon movement and its local affiliates underwent a bitter split over the question of membership in the new Communist International and participation in the Zionist Organization. Ahdut Ha'avoda was the affiliate in Palestine of the world Po'alei Tziyon movement's right wing, which rejected Comintern membership and favored continued cooperation with the bourgeois Zionists who controlled the Zionist Organization. (I will discuss the path followed by those in Palestine who supported world Po'alei Tziyon's left wing later in this chapter.) In the 1920s and beyond, Ben-Tzvi would play a central role in the recasting of the prewar Po'alei Tziyon's Borokhovist synthesis of Zionism and Marxism into the non-Marxist, social-democratic ideology espoused by MAPAI, formed by the merger in 1930 of Ahdut Ha'avoda with Hapo'el Hatza'ir, its smaller, nonsocialist rival within the Zionist labor movement. Ben-Tzvi was also, from its establishment in 1920, a member of (and labor Zionism's chief representative on) the Va'ad Le'umi ("National Committee"), the executive organ of the Yishuv's elected assembly. Ben-Tzvi was in addition a prolific journalist and a respected scholar. His seniority within the labor-Zionist movement and his knowledge of Arabic, quite rare among Zionist leaders even in Palestine, gave his 1921 essay on the Arab question significant weight for many left-wing Zionists.

Ben-Tzvi began his essay by admitting that only a few years earlier the subject under discussion had been a "hidden question," while today the Jewish press in Palestine and abroad was full of sensational stories about it and everyone was discussing it.

> And if one judges from these [press] accounts it would seem that there is a strong Arab movement in Palestine directed forcefully against us [i.e., Zionism]. And by means of comparison and analogy with other national movements known to us from other peoples and countries, there easily arises the illusory and misleading impression that this Arab movement rests on solid popular foundations, that its demands stem from the interests of the Arab working masses, and that it therefore possesses the character of a movement for liberation and human progress. And not only this, but we already have some Jews with an "Arab orientation," just as we have more than enough Jews with Polish, Ukrainian, Russian, etc. orientations. These types smear the Jewish national liberation movement, and Zi-

onism generally, with false accusations that it exists only as an agent of European imperialism in order to suppress the liberation movement of the Arab people, and that its whole purpose is to exploit and enslave the Arab working masses.

It was necessary, then, to demonstrate explicitly that there was no contradiction between Zionism and the objective interests of the indigenous population of Palestine. A decade or two earlier the whole issue had played a minor role in socialist-Zionist thinking and practice; now it assumed a central place and had to be addressed directly and forcefully.

Ben-Tzvi argued at the outset that it was incorrect to speak of a single Arab nation, given the absence of any real social, economic, or political basis for unity among the Arabic-speaking peoples. As for Palestinian Arab nationalism, it too was essentially inauthentic. Its demands—opposition to Jewish immigration and settlement and to the Balfour Declaration—were entirely negative, a reflection of the fact that it was not a genuinely popular movement with roots in the indigenous working masses. Rather, it was an artificial creation designed to serve the interests of the Palestinian Arab large landowners, moneylenders, and clerics, who wanted to perpetuate their domination and exploitation of the Arab peasants and workers.[1]

In Ben-Tzvi's analysis, rooted in the economistic Marxism he shared with his late friend and mentor Borokhov, it was the economic interests of the Arab landowning elite that made it hostile to Zionism. The landowners and their lackeys feared that "the [Jewish] immigrants will come and settle on [unused state lands] and forever deprive the *effendis* (big landlords) of any hope of grabbing the empty lands for exploitation and speculation, thereby placing in danger the entire future of this class." These landlords also opposed Zionism because they knew that Jewish immigration and settlement undermined their domination of the peasantry, which actually benefited from the growing Jewish presence and the enhanced opportunities for prosperity and employment it brought. Ben-Tzvi insisted that the Arab peasant in Palestine

> does not suffer from Jewish immigration, but from the pressure of his effendi and from exploitation by the city dweller, who is of the same race and religion and mediates between him and the effendi. . . . [The peasant] is interested in the new [British] regime which ensures peace and security from bandits and thieves, especially the bedouin who used to come out of the desert into the settled lands and lay the country waste without interference; the peasant is interested in a regime which raises the cultural level and ensures justice and defense against extortion. The peasant is also interested in the expansion of employment and industry in the country and the

improvement of the workers' lot, which of necessity results from Jewish settlement and immigration. Thus the peasant is not opposed to immigration. . . .

Zionism was thus deemed to serve the objective interests—defined strictly in economic terms—of most of the population of Palestine. This was already an old theme in Zionist discourse, going back to Herzl. But since the existence of an explicitly anti-Zionist Palestinian nationalist movement was by this time undeniable, Ben-Tzvi had to extend his argument to reject the legitimacy of indigenous anti-Zionism and nationalism by depicting them as the instruments, indeed the entirely artificial creations, of a reactionary elite anxious to preserve its wealth and power. This was a relatively new theme, designed to resolve the moral dilemmas of socialist Zionism in particular and equip its ideological arsenal with arguments more adequate to refuting doubts and criticism within the Yishuv as well as abroad.

However, the circumstances in which Ben-Tzvi and his movement operated also required the further extension of the argument by means of the revival of another old theme and its elaboration in socialist terms. The kinds of socialist and bourgeois-liberal audiences at which Ben-Tzvi's arguments were mainly directed tended to accept the principle that national groups were entitled to political rights, including the right of self-determination. A central task facing Zionism, and particularly a socialist Zionism which sought to distance itself ideologically from colonialism, which many Europeans were coming to see as morally questionable and economically burdensome, was therefore to resolve the apparent contradiction between the long-term goal of Zionism—the creation in Palestine of a Jewish majority and state—and the fact that at present the overwhelming majority of Palestine's population was Arab. To many observers, and even to some Zionists, it was disturbing that the ultimate success of Zionism was predicated on the denial of self-determination and self-rule to Palestine's indigenous population pending its transformation, under the auspices of the British colonial state, into a minority. It was therefore necessary to demonstrate, in "objective" terms and in a progressive vocabulary, that no violation of the principle of self-determination was in fact involved.

To accomplish this Ben-Tzvi drew on an element of Zionist discourse already manifest in Herzl's references to the indigenous inhabitants of Palestine as a "mixed multitude" and in Borokhov's prognosis of assimilation. Ben-Tzvi, and following him most labor Zionists, transformed these rather crude characterizations into a coherent denial of the very existence of a distinct Palestinian Arab people. Only the bedouins were of pure Arab racial stock, Ben-Tzvi insisted; the remainder of the non-Jewish population consisted of peasants and urban dwellers who are

> Arabs in language and culture but by origin and race are mixed and composed of different elements. . . . As is proven by its national, religious and racial composition, the population of this country is not of one national character and do not constitute a single nation, an enemy to Israel [i.e., the Jews] as a new nation in the country. On the contrary, this population is composed of different religious and national groups each of which has a more or less definite national character.[2]

Using what he asserted were purely objective criteria, Ben-Tzvi determined that the inhabitants of Palestine were divided by religion and ethnicity into eleven distinct communities. The largest of these, the Sunni Muslims, comprised a majority of the country's population and might one day come to constitute a distinct national group, but it was not one today because of its internal racial, economic, and class divisions, and also because nationality was not a legitimate category of identity for Islam. The other components of the population were much smaller, and only the non-Muslim sects were deemed to possess any national characteristics.

Besides eliminating any possible basis for an authentic Palestinian Arab nationalism, Ben-Tzvi's representation of Palestine's population as essentially heterogeneous and disaggregated had the additional virtue of enhancing the relative demographic weight and political importance of the Yishuv. At the time he wrote, Jews constituted perhaps 10 percent of the country's total population. But by denying that most of the remaining 90 percent formed a more or less coherent Arab community and by breaking that overwhelming majority down into a mosaic of much smaller units, Ben-Tzvi could make the Jews of Palestine—presumed to constitute a monolithic bloc with self-evident national characteristics—suddenly appear as the country's second largest group. The Jews were, moreover, the most active, energetic, and constructive community in the country.[3]

The conclusion drawn from this analysis was that "there is as yet no place for a single Arab national movement among all the inhabitants of Eretz Yisra'el. The 'Arab movement' which pretends to be national is nothing but a movement that arose among certain strata of the owners of property and land, the notable families of the former [Ottoman] regime. This movement is directed not against the Jews, but rather against the workers among their own people and among all the [country's] other peoples and communities." What then, Ben-Tzvi asked, should be the attitude of the Jewish working people, "not toward today's 'Arab movement,' which is not national and has no social content, but toward the various non-Jewish elements living in Zion?" Ben-Tzvi acknowledged that many mistakes had been made in the past and that the question had until now not received the attention it merited, but he failed to offer any clear policy. He concluded rather vaguely:

> If we take as a starting-point the common interests of the workers and keep in mind the common interests of our country and its future, on the basis of labor, progress and social justice, then we will easily find the path which will lead us to the solution of our national question in our land, and together with this to the solution to the question of international relations in the interests of the working class in Eretz Yisra'el. What the concrete form of the solution will be, and what is the practical program for achieving the desired relations between the Jewish working people and the workers of the other peoples living in our country—this is material for another topic, beyond the bounds of this essay.

DELEGITIMIZING PALESTINIAN ARAB NATIONALISM

These themes would persist in labor-Zionist discourse on the Arabs of Palestine for decades, and some are still current in Israel and elsewhere. For Ben-Tzvi and many of his comrades, the only way to reconcile their commitment to Zionism with their socialist principles was to deny the existence of a Palestinian Arab people, to define Palestinian nationalism as essentially inauthentic, and to attribute all opposition to Zionism to the machinations of a reactionary and antisemitic elite. At the same time, socialist Zionism adopted from an existing Zionist discourse (and directly or indirectly from colonial discourse) the representation of the Zionist project as the chief (or even sole) force for progress in Palestine, a force which was self-evidently bringing great benefits to the indigenous population through economic development and by opening their minds to new ideas and ways of life. Since there was thus no legitimate basis for Palestinian rejection of or resistance to Zionism, whose benefits for the country and the bulk of its indigenous population were deemed self-evident, it followed that the apparent failure of all too many Arab peasants and workers to understand that Zionism (in its left-wing variant, at least) was entirely in their interest could only be explained by the lies and base appeals to hatred and fanaticism generated by the pseudonationalist effendis and their agents. All manifestations of opposition to Zionism on the part of Arabs were attributed to the insidious effect on the ignorant, unconscious, and gullible masses of "outside agitators"—self-promoting politicians, greedy landowners, obscurantist clerics, antisemitic British officials, even anti-Zionist Jewish communists.

Underlying and reinforcing this explanation of Arab behavior was a representation common in colonial discourse, of colonized peoples as passive, largely incapable of rational thought, and susceptible to control or manipulation: in short, as essentially the eternal objects of the actions of others. Of course, passivity was always in a strange discursive tension with, and always threatening to turn into, its apparent opposite, unreasoned violent action, so that even the apparently docile masses were somehow menacing, capable of exploding into irrational and bloody action at virtually any moment. This only heightened the perceived danger from outside agitators, who might be able to push the right buttons and turn docility into rebellion. Such a discourse left little or no space for a middle ground of rational, self-motivated, self-activated opposition on the part of the "other." Acknowledgment of the possibility that Arab opposition to Zionism was perhaps not totally irrational or unjustified might have threatened to unravel the whole fabric out of which the discourse was fashioned, with potentially dangerous results for a movement mindful of the need for internal unity, maximal mobilization in the face of enormous obstacles, and the support of Jews and non-Jews abroad.

As we will see, there would be moments in which Zionist leaders explicitly recognized the existence in Palestine of an Arab community deserving of at least some national rights, and the last decade of the mandate would witness the emergence of groups, especially but not exclusively on the Zionist left, calling for a binational, Jewish-Arab state in Palestine. But the central thrust of Zionist discourse and practice, especially of the increasingly influential labor-Zionist movement, was to deny the existence of a distinct Palestinian Arab people with a legitimate claim to the country. This was implicit in the Zionist movement's key demands: the right of unlimited Jewish immigration to Palestine and land acquisition in it, and (explicitly from 1942) a Jewish state in all or most of Palestine. Achievement of these goals would inevitably consign the country's indigenous Arab population to either submersion in a Jewish majority or departure from the scene, voluntarily or otherwise.

It is in this context that the following examination of relations between Jewish and Arab workers must be situated. At bottom, the debate that ensued among the various Zionist workers' parties about the importance of Arab-Jewish workers' solidarity and the means to achieve it was framed by a left-Zionist discourse which represented Arab workers as potential allies of the Jewish working class in Palestine while simultaneously assuming that any such alliance should first and foremost serve the interests of the Zionist project. Perhaps not surprisingly, this engendered contradictions which frustrated efforts to achieve cooperation among Arab and Jewish workers. At the same time, so pervasive and powerful was this discourse, so necessary was it to the realization of the Zionist project, that there was very little ground from which Jews advocating a different perspective could operate. As we will see, those Palestinian trade unionists and leftists who sought common ground with Jewish workers often encountered similar problems. The result was a complex series of interactions, a pattern of cooperation and conflict deeply enmeshed within, but always seeking to transcend, its larger political context, the Zionist-Palestinian struggle for control of the country.

THE HISTADRUT AND THE "ARAB QUESTION"

In the 1920s, as the labor-Zionist movement struggled to achieve hegemony within the Yishuv and world Zionism on the basis of the strategy I discussed in Chapter 1, the issue of its relationship with Palestine's Arab majority, and especially its working class, not only persisted but grew more complex, both as a theoretical problem in labor-Zionist ideology and as a pressing practical issue. The question evoked considerable discussion and debate within and among the different parties contending for the allegiance of Jewish workers in Palestine, and in fact surfaced as early as December 1920, at the founding congress of what would become the central institution of the Zionist labor movement in Palestine, the Histadrut.

After the war Zionist labor leaders in Palestine had come to see the establishment of a unified organizational framework for Jewish workers in Palestine that would stand above the existing parties and enhance the movement's political and social weight in the Yishuv as an urgent necessity. After lengthy negotiations and several abortive initiatives, elections were held in November 1920 for delegates to a congress of the Jewish workers in Palestine. Less than 4,500 voters participated, out of a total Jewish population of some 80,000—an accurate gauge of the weakness of the Jewish labor movement which the creation of the new organization was designed to remedy.[4] Ahdut Ha'avoda was the strongest single force at the congress that met in Haifa a month after the elections, and though it lacked a majority on its own it largely dominated the proceedings by cooperating with Hapo'el Hatza'ir.

These two labor-Zionist parties envisioned the new Histadrut not as a trade union federation on the European model, but rather as an instrument whose primary purpose was to foster the settlement of Palestine by Jewish workers and build a Jewish commonwealth. The Histadrut would thus embody the labor-Zionist synthesis in its emerging "constructivist" form by acting as the vanguard of the Zionist project in Palestine even as it enhanced the power of the Jewish labor movement within the Yishuv and Zionism. This naturally required that the Histadrut be an exclusively Jewish organization rather than one open to all workers in Palestine, for otherwise it could not carry out its Zionist tasks. Hence the presence of an adjective modifying "workers" in the new organization's official title: the General Organization of Hebrew Workers in the Land of Israel.[5]

The conception of the Histadrut's membership, structure, and mission advanced by Ahdut Ha'avoda and Hapo'el Hatza'ir was opposed at the organization's founding congress by a small but vocal contingent from the Socialist Workers' Party (SWP), who also insisted that the question of relations with Arab workers be addressed.[6] The SWP had coalesced in the fall of 1919 as the affiliate in Palestine of the left wing of the Po'alei Tziyon movement, then in the throes of the split between left and right, just as the much larger and more powerful Ahdut Ha'avoda was the Palestinian affiliate of world Po'alei Tziyon's right wing. The SWP comprised elements which continued to espouse the orthodox Borokhovism of the prewar unified Po'alei Tziyon, but also a more radical group which was already moving in the direction of a break with Zionism.

Members of both tendencies had been radicalized by the Bolshevik revolution and saw themselves as the Jewish section of the new Communist International, founded in Moscow the previous year. At this stage it was still possible for SWP leaders and activists to insist that there was no contradiction between enthusiastic support for the Bolshevik revolution and the Comintern on the one hand, and their commitment to creating a Jewish homeland in Palestine on the other. The SWP denounced Ahdut Ha'avoda for what it saw as that party's abandonment of class struggle, its links to the revived Socialist International, its cooperation with British imperialism, and its alliance with the Jewish bourgeoisie, manifested in its participation in the Zionist Organization. In contrast, the SWP saw itself as providing a revolutionary socialist but also Jewish and still Palestine-oriented alternative to the reformism of Ahdut Ha'avoda, a position that might be described as "Bolshevik-Zionist." This position would soon become untenable, and within a year of the Histadrut's founding the SWP would splinter into a number of mutually hostile factions. But in the unique conjuncture of 1919–21, when world socialist revolution seemed imminent, the new Soviet regime enjoyed widespread support among Jews (including Jewish workers in Palestine), and the Comintern was still engaged in a dialogue with left-wing Zionists, these tensions could still

seem manageable. It was even possible for some party members to imagine the triumphant Red Army marching on Palestine to liberate it from
British imperialism and transform it into a Jewish soviet republic.[7]

In the period just before and after the founding of the Histadrut, the
SWP's stance attracted significant support among Jewish workers in Palestine, and especially recent arrivals from eastern Europe for whom the
radicalizing impact of the Bolshevik revolution was still fresh and powerful. The influence of SWP activists in several of the small Jewish trade
unions that sprang up in Palestine after the war was also enhanced by
their strong commitment to class struggle and worker militancy. Their
resistance to what not a few workers regarded as the domineering and
centralizing tendencies of Ahdut Ha'avoda, and later of the new Histadrut's bureaucratic apparatus, also won them sympathy.[8]

The struggle for support was also fought out in the domain of culture,
over the question of language. Yiddish was the mother tongue of the Jewish masses in eastern Europe, and many new immigrants arriving in Palestine remained attached to it even as they increasingly came to use Hebrew. This benefited SWP activists, who used Yiddish proudly in their
oral and written agitation and propaganda. By contrast, Ahdut Ha'avoda
supporters saw Yiddish as a language of the rejected Diaspora and tried to
avoid speaking anything but Hebrew, whose revival and dominance in the
Yishuv were considered essential to the Zionist project of building a new
Jewish society. Along with many other nonsocialist but strongly Hebraist
Zionists, they regarded Yiddish as a threat and actively sought to suppress
its use, especially in public discourse. Those who attempted to speak in
Yiddish—to make a political point or because they did not yet have a
sufficient command of Hebrew—were frequently shouted down at public
meetings. Yet in the very early 1920s this hard-line "Hebrew only" policy
hampered Ahdut Ha'avoda's efforts to communicate with and win over
new Jewish immigrants and gave SWP militants opportunities for organizing which they were quick to seize.[9]

In the debates at the founding congress, SWP delegates criticized the
proposal put forward by Ahdut Ha'avoda and Hapo'el Hatza'ir that the
new Histadrut be an explicitly Zionist and exclusively Jewish workers'
organization. They proposed instead that two separate organizations be
established: "a nonparty trade union federation of all the workers of Eretz
Yisra'el without regard to national affiliation or political opinions," and a
"settlement organization of all the Jewish workers engaged in building
the Jewish socialist center in Eretz Yisra'el." Complementing these two
bodies would be an "international [i.e., Jewish-Arab] workers' council as

the political organ of the country's entire working class whose task it would be to seize the reins of government"—that is, a soviet. The SWP thus did not reject immigration and settlement work, the establishment of kibbutzim and cooperatives, or more broadly the goal of creating a Jewish homeland in Palestine. But it demanded that these tasks be handled by a separate organization of Jewish workers, while the class struggle (to which it gave much higher priority than did Ahdut Ha'avoda) would be led by an organization that included both Jews and Arabs, though in separate national sections.

Not surprisingly, the SWP's proposals received very little support. The other parties had no great desire to discuss, much less resolve, these issues, and in the end they were referred for further consideration to the Histadrut council (*mo'etza*), which was to guide the organization's work between congresses. The new organization's constitution made no explicit mention of Arab workers, and when the founding congress resolved that the new Histadrut would "unite all the workers and laborers in the country who live by their own labor without exploiting the labor of others, in order to arrange for all the settlement, economic and also cultural affairs of all the workers in the country, so as to build a society of Jewish labor in Eretz Yisra'el," it was obvious that "all the workers in the country" actually meant the Jewish workers alone.

"IT IS CLEAR THAT WE MUST ORGANIZE THEM, BUT . . ."

The issue of relations between Arab and Jewish workers could not be put aside so easily, however, and it reappeared on the Histadrut's agenda almost immediately. As I discuss in Chapter 3, through the mid-1920s it was the specific situation of the Jewish railway workers in Palestine that was primarily responsible for compelling the Zionist labor movement to confront the issue, and it was among the Arab and Jewish railwaymen that the various perspectives and approaches advocated by different parties were first put to the test. A discussion of the railway workers' situation at a meeting of the Histadrut executive committee on December 30, 1920, just a few weeks after the founding congress, illustrates the dilemma which labor Zionism faced in grappling with this issue.[10]

The specific item on the agenda was the upcoming congress of the exclusively Jewish Railway Workers' Association (RWA), but because the railway workforce was overwhelmingly Arab a more substantive discussion of the larger question of relations with Arab workers was inevitable. Berl Katznelson (1887–1944), one of the leading figures in Ahdut Ha-

ʿAvoda (and later MAPAI), opened by stating that he saw no danger in the Arab railway workers organizing themselves and cooperating with their Jewish coworkers. Clearly mindful of the SWP's proposal at the recent Histadrut congress that Arabs be allowed or even encouraged to join hitherto exclusively Jewish trade unions, he also expressed concern that the Arab railway workers might want to join the RWA, which would thereby lose its Jewish and Zionist character. Other executive committee members agreed with Katznelson that Jewish and Arab workers should belong to separate organizations.

But some went beyond insistence on maintaining separate organizations to express grave doubts about the whole idea of helping Arab workers organize, for fear that organized Arab workers would inevitably turn against Zionism. "From the humanitarian standpoint, it is clear that we must organize them," said Eliezer Shohat of Hapoʿel Hatzaʿir, "but from the national standpoint, when we organize them we will be arousing them against us. They will receive the good that is in organization and use it against us." Another member noted that the trade unions in Egypt were under the influence of the nationalists. It was also well understood, even in this early discussion, that organizing Arab workers might conflict with the goal of achieving Hebrew labor on the railroad: higher pay and better conditions might attract more Jews to railroad work and keep them there, but it might have the same effect on Arabs, thereby making it more difficult for Jews to secure a larger percentage of railroad jobs.

In the end the executive committee decided to procrastinate, affirming the principle of Arab-Jewish solidarity but avoiding any practical decisions pending clarification of the question by a special Histadrut committee. Nonetheless, the issue was now firmly on the Histadrut's agenda, and in subsequent years it would be the subject of considerable debate, publicly in Histadrut and party forums and publications and privately at closed meetings of the leadership. The most immediate problem was what left-wing Zionists referred to as the question of "joint organization" (*irgun meshutaf*): in what framework should Arab and Jewish workers employed in "mixed" workplaces (i.e., those employing both Arabs and Jews) be organized and seek to cooperate? The railway workers and their specific circumstances were usually at the center of debates about this issue, but before 1948 the mixed sector of Palestine's economy also included other government enterprises and agencies like the telephone and telegraph systems, the Public Works Department and the port authorities, as well as municipal government in cities with mixed populations. Later, the British and Allied military bases and installations in Palestine would become a key arena of interaction between Arab and Jewish workers. There were also a number of privately owned enterprises which employed both Jewish and Arab workers, including several large foreign-owned companies like the Iraq Petroleum Company with its terminal at Haifa, the oil refinery in that city, the Dead Sea potash works, and the Nesher quarry and cement factory. The issue of joint organization was thus potentially relevant to substantial numbers of Arab and Jewish workers.

The question of joint organization overlapped with the question of Hebrew labor, which was by the 1920s the firm policy of the two largest labor-Zionist parties and of the Histadrut which they jointly dominated.[11] It was clear from the outset that Histadrut support for Arab-Jewish cooperation in mixed workplaces, intended to improve the lot of Jews already employed in them and enable them to stay at their jobs, might have the contradictory effect of undermining Jewish employment in those same workplaces by also raising Arab wages. As we will see, the goal of maximizing Jewish employment in mixed enterprises was never absent from the calculations of Zionist labor leaders of various stripes when they approached the question of joint organization, and it played a significant role in the form and character of the Histadrut's initiatives in this field.

More generally, most Histadrut leaders understood that unskilled and semiskilled Arab and Jewish workers were often competing for jobs within a single labor market. Although the wages of these Jewish workers were generally higher than those of Arab workers at similar skill levels, the two wage structures were linked such that low Arab wages helped keep down wages for Jews. As a result, in addition to ensuring that Jewish employers hired only Jews and grappling with the issue of joint organization in mixed workplaces, the Jewish labor movement had to explore other means of keeping Jewish wages high, whether by subsidizing the wages of Jewish workers (an expensive proposition), by trying to raise Arab wages, by replacing Arabs with Jews in jobs with non-Jewish employers (private or public), or by some combination of these. This exigency made the issue of relations between Arab and Jewish workers of broader importance than it might otherwise have been.[12]

The question of relations between Arab and Jewish workers and working classes in Palestine had other dimensions as well, raising wider theoretical, political, and moral issues central to labor-Zionist ideology and practice. Socialist Zionists in Palestine felt it necessary to work out a clear position on this question which they could believe was consonant with their commitments to both the principle of class solidarity across ethnic lines and the goals of Zionism. At issue was not only the potential for joint organization of Arab and Jewish workers in mixed workplaces, but also the possibility of the Histadrut's encouraging and supporting the efforts of Arabs in public or private employment to organize. As the existence of an Arab working class became more evident in the early 1920s and as Palestine's economic development seemed to presage the further growth of that class, these issues seemed to become increasingly urgent.

While Palestinian Arab society was still overwhelmingly rural, a high rate of natural increase, a deepening agrarian crisis, and new employment opportunities in the towns resulted in substantial migration from the countryside to urban areas, and especially the booming coastal towns of Jaffa and Haifa. Between the censuses of 1922 and 1931 Palestine's Arab population grew by some 40 percent, but the Arab population of Jaffa grew by 63 percent (from 27,429 to 44,638) and of Haifa by 87 percent (from 18,240 to 34,148).[13] Some of the migrants were seasonal or temporary, while others became permanent urban dwellers. In both cases, many retained strong links to their home villages and to rural life. These new arrivals swelled the ranks of the urban poor and competed with them for jobs as wage laborers in construction, in public works, on the docks, on the railways, in small-scale manufacturing and service enterprises, and elsewhere. A stratum of skilled and semiskilled workers was also emerging, especially in Haifa, which as we will see was in this period on the verge of becoming Palestine's main port and industrial center.[14] Moreover, some of the members of this stratum were already beginning to take an interest in trade unionism.[15]

The formation of a distinct urban Arab working class was only in its early stages in the 1920s, but it had already begun to impinge on the consciousness of Histadrut leaders, and especially those in contact with such relatively advanced groups as the railway workers. As we will see, while their identity as socialists made them inclined to look out for (and take a special interest in) this development, their evaluation of it, and their efforts to formulate a policy to deal with it, were primarily framed by their concern over its potential significance and consequences for the Zionist project. In fact, the positions on relations between Arab and Jewish workers adopted by all the Jewish leftist parties, whether Zionist or non-Zionist, were closely bound up with their broader perspectives on the future of Palestine and of its Arab inhabitants. For one, the question of cooperation between Arab and Jewish workers could not ultimately be separated from the larger Zionist-Palestinian conflict, though this linkage took a variety of specific forms. Moreover, some of the Jewish parties in Palestine now gave the Arab worker and the Arab working class important new roles to play in their scenarios for the future. That the new communist movement in Palestine, in the 1920s still overwhelmingly Jewish, should designate the Arab working class as the force which would spearhead the struggle for national independence and socialism is not surprising. As we will see, however, in the early 1920s many labor Zionists would also embrace a new conception of the Palestinian Arab worker, one which coexisted in uneasy tension with the earlier image of that worker as a competitor for scarce jobs, a dire threat to the Jewish worker and to Zionism. This new conception portrayed the Arab working class in Palestine as labor Zionism's natural ally and was accompanied by a proposed strategy of Arab-Jewish working-class solidarity, a strategy which it was believed would actually enhance Zionism's prospects for success.

Increasingly, too, what had been largely a monologue, entirely unidirectional—Zionists of various kinds discoursing about Arabs, whether workers or not—became increasingly multidirectional and complex, more of a dialogue, as Palestinian workers and unionists made themselves heard. This is not to suggest that lower-class Palestinians had not been social and political actors even earlier, though we still know very little about their perceptions, aspirations, and actions. In the 1920s, however, it becomes easier to hear their voices more clearly. Palestinian workers and unionists would be compelled to confront the issue of cooperation with Jewish workers from their own perspectives and in light of the needs and interests of their own constituencies within the emerging Arab working class in Palestine. Whatever the extent to which their Jewish counterparts explicitly heeded them, their words and deeds affected the course of events and had to be taken into account.

BEN-GURION AND THE ARAB WORKING CLASS

The policy on joint organization which Ahdut Ha'avoda, and with it the Histadrut, would ultimately adopt was first outlined by David Ben-Gurion in the summer of 1921. Ben-Gurion (1886–1973) had emigrated from Russia to Palestine in 1906 and soon emerged as a leading figure in the prewar Po'alei Tziyon and then in its postwar successor, Ahdut Ha-'avoda. He was abroad on a mission for his party when the Histadrut was founded, but upon his return at the end of 1921 he was elected the organization's secretary and quickly established himself as the preeminent leader of the labor-Zionist movement in Palestine. Under his guidance the Histadrut became a highly centralized and powerful institution, and the platform from which Ben-Gurion's party MAPAI would ultimately achieve a hegemonic position in the Yishuv and in the world Zionist movement. As chairman of the executive of the Jewish Agency, Ben-Gurion was the de facto leader of the Yishuv from 1935 to 1948, and he served as Israel's prime minister from 1948 to 1953 and again from 1955 to 1963. He possessed tremendous willpower, first-rate organizational ability, and a great capacity for combining tactical flexibility with an unwavering determination to achieve the long-term goals of Zionism. His critics on both left and right not inaccurately saw him as overbearing, self-righteous, and stubborn, but those very traits often enhanced rather than diminished his effectiveness as a leader.

Ben-Gurion first set forth his theses on the question of relations between Arab and Jewish workers in August 1921, in a proposal to Ahdut Ha'avoda's upcoming party congress. He began by stating that the basis for these relations must be "joint economic, political, and cultural work, which is the necessary prerequisite for our redemption as a free working people and for the emancipation of the Arab working people from enslavement by its oppressors and exploiters, the dominant landowners and propertyowners." It was "the conscious and cultured Jewish worker, whose historic mission is the building of a free community of labor in Eretz Yisra'el, who must lead the movement of liberation and rebirth of the peoples of the Near East" and "educate the Arab worker to live an orderly and cooperative life of labor, discipline, and mutual responsibility."

Starting from these premises, which suggest a sort of socialist-Zionist *mission civilatrice* toward Arab workers in Palestine, Ben-Gurion proposed that "in all the trades which employ Jewish and Arab workers (such as the railways, metalworking, and so forth) the Jewish trade unions should organize the Arab workers in trade unions linked to the Jewish unions. The united unions will together implement activities to improve working conditions and arrange for cultural activities and medical assistance for the Arab workers." He also suggested that the Histadrut employ Arab as well as Jewish workers, on equal terms, to carry out public works contracts obtained from the government, and called for the establishment of a number of joint workers' clubs which would provide lectures, social activities, and language lessons in Hebrew and Arabic. The kibbutzim should, he proposed, strive to establish contact with the neighboring Arab villages for mutual assistance, including protection against "bandits."[16]

As noted earlier, Ben-Gurion and his colleagues felt compelled to take up this issue mainly as a result of developments among the railway workers. But the issue had also surfaced, if in a small way, in other sectors as well. For example, in 1921 the new Jewish woodworkers' union in Jaffa and Tel Aviv had sought unsuccessfully to develop ties with Arab carpenters, most of whom were employed in small workshops and were viewed by the Jews as low-wage competitors. That same year the Jewish-owned bakeries and pastry shops in Jaffa and Tel Aviv proved more fertile ground: Arab workers cooperated with their Jewish coworkers when the latter organized a union, though the Arab workers in Arab-owned bakeries remained uninvolved. The initiative for efforts to develop links with the Arab bakery workers came from radicals among the Jewish bakery workers, who in 1922 went so far as to declare their union "international," that is, open to both Jewish and Arab members, and actually registered some Arab members. The Histadrut leadership moved quickly to suppress this act of insubordination.[17]

However, such incidents were few and far between, and it was the railway sector which was of most concern to the Histadrut leadership. As I discuss in Chapter 3, since the middle of 1921 some of the Arab railwaymen had been pressing Jewish union leaders for a clear response to their offer to cooperate; some of them had reportedly even expressed interest in joining the Histadrut. Ben-Gurion and his colleagues were well aware of these developments, and of demands for action from the rank and file Jewish railwaymen. They were concerned that if the Histadrut failed to formulate a clear policy on joint organization, especially among the railway workers, the Jewish railwaymen would turn to Ahdut Ha'avoda's rivals on the left, who were advocating a fully integrated ("international") Jewish-Arab railway workers' union. But no concrete action was forthcoming.[18]

Ben-Gurion's thinking on the question of joint organization was clearly rooted in practical and political considerations, as well as in a broader sense of the good things which labor Zionism could bring the Arab masses in Palestine—what I earlier characterized as a sense of Zionist (and in this case socialist-Zionist) *mission civilatrice* in Palestine. But his conception of the relationship of the Jewish and Arab working classes in Palestine in the early and middle 1920s, and that of his party, also had other economic, political, and cultural dimensions which need to be unpacked and contextualized. For Ben-Gurion, labor Zionism's approach to joint organization was at bottom largely dictated by the concrete economic situation of the Jewish workers in Palestine. In January 1922 he told the Histadrut council:

> Until the last few years the activity of the Jewish worker in the country was almost entirely restricted to a difficult and desperate struggle for the right to work in the few enterprises of the Jewish community, which were

closed to the cultured and conscious Jewish worker as a result of the existence of unorganized and easily exploitable cheap labor. Unwillingly and unconsciously, the Arab worker, by virtue of his degraded state, his minimal needs, and his primitive culture, was undermining the Jewish worker's possibility of existence even in the only sphere of employment intended for him. In this situation there was hardly any basis for joint action and class influence. Now conditions have changed. The Jewish worker now works together with the Arab worker in government enterprises, that is in countrywide, general enterprises, on equal terms. But the extent of this "equality" is now determined by the worker with lesser culture and fewer needs; wages and working conditions are determined in accordance with the needs and demands of the Arab worker, a situation which is oppressive to the Jewish worker. Improvement in working conditions in these trades by the Jewish workers cannot be imagined without the active participation of the Arab worker. And the creation of an organized class force of Jewish and Arab workers in order to improve the workers' situation and their working conditions is a necessary condition for the survival of the cultured worker in these occupations.

Ben-Gurion concluded that "the creation of a single common front for all the country's workers to deal with their common affairs is the obligation and right of the pioneers of labor culture in Palestine—it is the mission of the Jewish workers. Not a metaphysical or theological mission, but a mission that derives from and is conditioned by the conditions of our life and work in Palestine."[19]

While insisting that cooperation was vital for both Jewish and Arab workers, Ben-Gurion was also adamant that Jews and Arabs had their own specific concerns which required some degree of separate organization. In a speech to the railway workers' union council in 1924, he argued that

Unity between workers of different nations can exist only on the basis of freedom and national equality. For the workers there are matters of common interest where there is no difference between Jew and Arab, Englishman or Frenchman. These are the things that concern work: hours, wages, relations with the employer, protection against accidents, the right of workers to organize, and so forth. In all these areas we work together. And there are interests which are specific to the workers of each nationality, specific but not contradictory interests which concern his national needs: his culture, his language, the freedom of his people, etc. In all these spheres there must be complete autonomy and equality for the workers of each nation.[20]

As Ben-Gurion and his party saw it, separate unions in mixed workplaces, or at least autonomous national sections within joint unions, were necessary to ensure that the special needs and interests of Arab and Jewish workers be attended to. The version of joint organization which they espoused would allow the Jewish workers in mixed workplaces to improve their circumstances through cooperation with their Arab coworkers while preserving the exclusively Jewish character of the Histadrut and its trade unions, which would thus remain free to carry out their Zionist ("national") tasks, including the struggle for Hebrew labor. On the same grounds Ahdut Ha'avoda insisted that Arab workers not be allowed to join the Histadrut. In economic terms, then, this conception of relations between Arab and Jewish workers was quite consonant with the broader strategy which the labor-Zionist movement was coming to embrace in these years.

That conception also had an important political dimension, however. Along with the representation of the Arab working class that underpinned it, it can be read as a response to the emergence in Palestine of a vocal Arab nationalist movement demanding the cessation of Jewish immigration and land acquisition, the termination of British rule, and the independence of Palestine as an Arab state. In various formulations of Ben-Gurion and his party in the early and middle 1920s one can discern an effort to rearticulate Zionism's rejection of the authenticity and legitimacy of Palestinian Arab nationalism in the language of class struggle and class solidarity, with the Arab workers themselves rather curiously cast as Zionism's most crucial potential allies.

In defending the struggle for Hebrew labor a decade earlier, Yitzhak Ben-Tzvi had argued that the conflict between Arab and Jewish workers in Palestine was essentially social rather than national, a struggle between organized (high-wage) and unorganized (low-wage) labor. In his influential 1921 essay, *The Arab Movement*, Ben-Tzvi had depicted Palestinian nationalism as lacking any authentic popular base or social content, as merely the artificial instrument of the Arab "effendis," labor Zionism's code word for what it saw as the reactionary large landowners, greedy moneylenders, and obscurantist clerics who wanted self-government for Palestine only so that they could more ruthlessly exploit the Arab peasants and workers. These had quickly become central themes in labor-Zionist discourse, though they did not go entirely unchallenged. Now Ben-Gurion developed this line of argument somewhat differently by insisting that the real conflict in Palestine was not between the country's Arab majority and the Zionist project of Jewish immigration, settlement, and statehood, as the Palestinian Arab nationalist movement claimed, but rather between the Arab workers and their Arab oppressors. To the false Arab nationalism espoused by those oppressors, Ben-Gurion counterposed a class alliance of Jewish and Arab workers grounded in their shared objective economic interests.

Such an alliance would, Ben-Gurion insisted, serve the interests of both Arab and Jewish workers. The more advanced Jewish workers would help their enslaved and ignorant Arab brothers liberate themselves from their real enemies, their oppressive compatriots. In the process the Arab workers would be uplifted and transformed into genuine proletarians, and would thereby come to grasp the beneficial and progressive character of the Zionist project. At the same time, Arab-Jewish class solidarity (at least in certain limited spheres) would help achieve Zionism's goal of Jewish national redemption. Indeed, in the mid-1920s Ben-Gurion was arguing that without such an alliance between Arab and Jewish workers, Zionism could not hope to succeed.

ZIONISM, DEMOCRACY, AND ARAB WORKERS

Both the economic and the political meanings built into this conception of the Arab working class and its purported relationship with Zionism were expressed very explicitly in the course of a 1924 debate within Ahdut Ha'avoda. The British Colonial Office and the mandatory government of Palestine had initiated negotiations with the Arab and Jewish leaderships about the establishment of a legislative council with limited powers. This put the Yishuv and the Zionist movement in an uncomfortable position. On the one hand, the Zionist leadership formally endorsed the principles of self-government and representative democracy and very much wanted to play a role in governing Palestine. On the other hand, it could not accept a fully representative form of self-government for Palestine, since the country had an overwhelmingly Arab population and a representative government would inevitably mean a largely Arab (and therefore anti-Zionist) legislature and administration. Zionist leaders in Palestine and abroad disagreed over how to respond to various British proposals.

The linkage between a legislative council for Palestine on the one hand, and relations between Arab and Jewish workers on the other came to the fore at the third congress of Ahdut Ha'avoda, held at Ein Harod in May 1924.[21] Shlomo Kaplansky, a prominent veteran of the Second Aliya who had emerged as leader of the party's left wing, proposed that Ahdut Ha-'avoda demand the immediate establishment of a democratically elected parliament with broad powers. Kaplansky acknowledged that this parliament would inevitably have an Arab majority, but he argued that the vital interests of the Yishuv could be safeguarded, and the long-term goals of Zionism achieved, through an agreement with the Palestinian Arab nationalist leadership.

Ben-Gurion strongly opposed Kaplansky's proposal. Insisting that Zionism was essentially a state-building project, he demanded that all proposals for representative government, however democratic in the abstract, be judged by the extent to which they advanced that project. Any system of government based on the current demographic and political balance of forces in Palestine could only damage Zionism's long-term prospects. In this debate, Ben-Gurion again depicted the Palestinian Arab national movement as an inauthentic tool of the effendis. He told his party's congress: "We must not be afraid to proclaim openly that between us, the Jewish workers, and the leaders of today's Arab movement, the effendis, there is no common language." "Certainly," Ben-Gurion went on,

> the Arab community in the country has the right of self-determination, of self-rule. It would never occur to us to restrict or minimize that right. The national autonomy which we demand for ourselves we demand for the Arabs as well. But we do not admit their right to rule over the country to the extent that the country is not built up by them and still awaits those who will work it. They do not have any right or claim to prohibit or control the construction of the country, the restoration of its ruins, the productivization of its resources, the expansion of its cultivated area, the development of its culture, the growth of its laboring community.

But then, Ben-Gurion asked rhetorically, with whom could Zionism come to an agreement, if not with the Arab leadership? "We must take the longer and more difficult path—the path toward the Arab worker. There is no common platform between us and the ruling class among the Arab people. But there is a common platform between us and the Arab workers, even if this platform still exists only potentially and not yet in reality." The Arab worker, he continued, is "an inseparable, organic part of the country, just like one of its mountains or valleys." It was the historic mission of the Jewish workers to raise their Arab brothers from poverty and ignorance, not out of charity but out of self-interest.

> The fate of the Jewish worker is linked with the fate of the Arab worker. Together we will rise, or together we will fall. The Jewish worker will not work 8 hours a day if the Arab worker will be forced to work 10–12 hours. The Jewish worker will not get 30 piastres a day if the Arab sells his labor for 15 piastres or less. . . . We must seek agreement and understanding with the Arab people only through the Arab worker, and only an alliance of Jewish and Arab workers will establish and maintain an alliance of the Jewish and Arab peoples in Palestine.

The Arab working class in Palestine was thus made to play a significant role in Ben-Gurion's political vision of this period. By representing it as Zionism's potential ally, Ben-Gurion could overcome the apparent contradiction between his unwavering commitment to a Jewish majority and (ultimately) a Jewish state in Palestine on the one hand, and on the other his formal commitment to democracy and to the right of the Palestinian Arabs to self-determination. Denied any voice of its own or capacity for self-motivated action, the Arab working class could be cast as a *deus ex machina* in labor-Zionist thinking at this time: it compensated for the objective weakness of the Jewish labor movement in Palestine and in effect guaranteed the ultimate success of the labor-Zionist project at a time when a Jewish majority and Jewish sovereignty in Palestine seemed a very long way off and the path to their attainment highly uncertain. This vision affirmed the Arab workers' deep roots, their elemental authenticity ("just like one of [Palestine's] mountains or valleys"), but mainly in order to be able to contrast their rootedness and authenticity with the purported inauthenticity and illegitimacy of the Palestinian nationalist movement. Concomitantly, the Arabs' right to self-rule was recognized in principle, only to be immediately subordinated to the rights, needs, and interests in Palestine of the Jews, who were developing the land and therefore had a stronger right to possess and rule it. Arab objections on nationalist grounds to Jewish immigration, and to Zionism more generally, were by definition invalid, and the whole Arab national movement no more than a fraud which had to be fought, not merely for the sake of the Jews but also for the sake of the guileless and oppressed Arab masses themselves.

The Ahdut Ha'avoda congress at Ein Harod overwhelmingly endorsed Ben-Gurion's stance rather than Kaplansky's. The Histadrut had already endorsed Ben-Gurion's conception of joint organization among the railway workers, where the issue was most urgent, though debate on the question would continue for years to come: in January 1922 the Histadrut council had adopted a resolution which declared the basic principles of joint organization among the railwaymen to be "organization of the workers on the basis of national sections" and "preservation of the Jewish Railway Workers' Association as part of the Histadrut."[22] From the standpoint of labor-Zionist ideology, this "separate but equal" policy had the apparent virtue of reconciling what seemed to be the conflicting demands of Zionism and proletarian internationalism. The Histadrut would thereby demonstrate its commitment to helping Arab workers unionize and improve their lot, which in mixed workplaces would presumably also benefit the Jewish employees. At the same time, this approach eliminated the threat that integrated Jewish-Arab unions and Arab membership in the Histadrut might dilute the Zionist character of these organizations and undermine the struggle for Hebrew labor as well as the achievement of the long-term goals of Zionism. To Histadrut officials it also seemed that organizing Arab workers employed in mixed workplaces or in purely Arab workplaces under the tutelage of the Jewish labor movement would insulate those workers from the pernicious influence of Arab nationalist activists seeking to mobilize them against Zionism. As we have seen, this concern had surfaced early on, and it would persist for decades to come.[23]

THE CONTROVERSY OVER JOINT ORGANIZATION

Though the Histadrut had now formally adopted a policy on joint organization among the railway workers, concrete action was another matter. Through 1922 and into 1923, the Histadrut executive committee sporadically discussed finding someone who could take charge of organizing Arab workers, especially at the Palestine Railways. But effective organizers who were both politically reliable—that is, members of Ahdut Ha'avoda—and had a command of Arabic were extremely rare, funding was scarce, and many Histadrut leaders were in any case dubious about devoting scarce resources to the project of organizing Arab workers. Some felt that other tasks deserved priority, while others had ideological objections to the whole idea. Ben-Gurion continued to urge his colleagues not to neglect the issue, but apart from passing vague resolutions the Histadrut failed to take action.[24]

As before, it was developments among the railway workers that compelled the Histadrut leadership, preoccupied with other matters, to once again pay serious attention to the question of joint organization. As I discuss in more detail in Chapter 3, toward the end of 1923 members of a small but vigorous party to Ahdut Ha'avoda's left won effective control of the still exclusively Jewish railway workers' union, now called the Union of Railway, Postal and Telegraph Workers (URPTW). That party was Po'alei Tziyon Smol, which may be translated as "Workers of Zion (Left)," not to be confused with the pre-1919 unified Po'alei Tziyon. Po'alei Tziyon Smol had emerged largely from the disintegration during 1921 of the SWP, which I mentioned in connection with the founding congress of the Histadrut.

Between 1919 and 1921, leaders of the Po'alei Tziyon left in Europe, with which the SWP in Palestine was affiliated, engaged in lengthy negotiations with the Communist International over the terms under which socialist-Zionist parties might be admitted. The chief obstacle was of course Po'alei Tziyon's commitment to Zionism, which the Comintern (like most of the prewar social-democratic movements) strongly rejected. Until the question of admission was definitively resolved, it was possible for those who saw themselves as Zionists first and foremost to remain in the SWP alongside those who were coming to see themselves primarily as Bolsheviks. But once the Comintern declared in 1921 that communism and Zionism were utterly incompatible and insisted on total acceptance of its stringent conditions for admission, including renunciation of Zionism and dissolution of local Po'alei Tziyon parties into territorial communist parties, the SWP in Palestine splintered into several factions.

Out of the wreckage, and a series of further mergers and splits, there emerged distinct political tendencies which ultimately cohered into two parties. One was the Palestine Communist Party (PCP), which in 1924 received Comintern recognition as its section in Palestine. Through the 1920s the PCP's membership and leadership were overwhelmingly Jewish. In this period the party was often referred to as "Hafraktziyya," from Fraktziyyat Hapo'alim ("Workers' Faction"), the name under which it operated in the Jewish labor movement; but to avoid confusion I will always refer to the party and its adherents as "communist," even when discussing the period before the emergence of a unified PCP recognized as such by the Comintern.[25] The communists will appear often in this narrative, but for the moment I will focus on the second tendency which emerged from the disintegration of the SWP. This was Po'alei Tziyon Smol, heir to the Zionist segments of the defunct SWP and the affiliate in Palestine of the left wing of the world Po'alei Tziyon movement.[26]

Po'alei Tziyon Smol occupied the far left end of the Zionist spectrum. Despite rejection by Moscow, it continued to regard itself as an authentic communist party, committed to world socialist revolution and profoundly loyal to Bolshevism, the Soviet Union, and the Comintern—except when it came to the question of Zionism, about which it deemed Moscow sadly misguided (though perhaps not irredeemably so). Until the late 1930s Po'alei Tziyon Smol refused to participate in the institutions of the Zionist Organization, since it regarded that organization as an instrument of the Jewish bourgeoisie, with which it could never collaborate. It held fast to a pristine Borokhovist orthodoxy, arguing that the Jewish workers in Palestine must organize themselves and wage their class struggle independently. Like Borokhov, party ideologists were convinced that capitalism was inexorably developing in Palestine, leading to the growth of the working class and preparing the way for the ultimate triumph of socialism.

They therefore rejected Ahdut Ha'avoda's strategy of building up a separate Jewish workers' economy under the auspices of the Histadrut. Not only was such a course foolhardy and a dangerous diversion of workers' energies from class struggle to economic construction, but it also entailed collaboration with (and therefore submission to) the Jewish bourgeoisie, which through the Zionist Organization and its institutions subsidized the Histadrut's enterprises and settlements. At the same time, Po'alei Tziyon Smol regarded itself as thoroughly Zionist: it encouraged Jewish immigration to Palestine and envisioned that land as the site of the future Jewish socialist state.

Po'alei Tziyon Smol never succeeded in gaining a strong and durable base in Palestine. In the early 1920s most of its members and sympathizers were recently arrived urban workers. As time went on, even left-wing Jews in Palestine came to see the party as rigid, doctrinaire, and sectarian, disconnected from much of what went on in the Yishuv and embarrassingly eastern European in ethos and political style. By the 1930s its place at the left end of the Zionist spectrum would be taken by a new socialist-Zionist political formation with deeper roots in the Yishuv, while Po'alei Tziyon Smol would decline into marginality. Paradoxically, however, at least in the 1920s, its sister parties in eastern Europe were often stronger than Ahdut Ha'avoda's sister parties, since the left wing of Po'alei Tziyon initially won the support of a larger segment of the movement's mass base than did the right wing, though of course the latter was much stronger among Jews in Palestine itself.

As a party, Po'alei Tziyon Smol initially had little to say about the fate of Palestine's Arab majority. This silence was in part a product of its adherence to orthodox Borokhovism, since as I discussed in Chapter 1 Borokhov himself (who died in Russia at the end of 1917) had envisioned the disappearance of the indigenous population through assimilation into the immigrating Jewish population. As we will see, Po'alei Tziyon Smol partook of much of mainstream labor-Zionist discourse on the Arab question, though always filtered through its own unique brand of Marxist-Zionist dialectics. In some ways the party was even less willing than Ahdut Ha'avoda to acknowledge that the Arabs might have national rights in Palestine, insisting that capitalist development and class struggle would make the problem go away.

However, in the workplaces where party militants agitated, things were different. Whatever the party's line on Arab national rights, it was strongly committed to working-class unity across communal lines.[27] More significantly, as I discuss at greater length in Chapter 3, Po'alei

Tziyon Smol garnered considerable support among the Jewish railway workers in 1923–24, largely because its opposition to separate national sections for Arabs and Jews seemed to open the way for the establishment of a single (and presumably more effective) union encompassing all the railway workers in Palestine. When Po'alei Tziyon Smol activists secured the leadership of the Jewish railway workers' union in 1924, they went even further in order to win over Arab workers already suspicious of the Histadrut's Zionist character. To the Histadrut leadership's horror, they not only declared the union international (i.e., open to both Arabs and Jews) but also launched an effort to induce the Histadrut to turn its settlement and cooperative functions over to a separate entity and transform itself into a territorial trade union center open to Arabs as well as Jews— a proposal that came to be known as "separation of functions." This development intensified the debate over joint organization, and over relations between Jewish and Arab workers, that had long been simmering among left Zionists.

Ben-Gurion and other Ahdut Ha'avoda leaders were extremely distressed that the key railway workers' union had fallen into the hands of Po'alei Tziyon Smol, whose commitment to Zionism they mistrusted. They were also concerned because their party's control over the labor movement seemed to be slipping, putting it on the defensive.[28] This was also a period in which a wave of Jewish immigration (the Fourth Aliya, 1924–26), largely from Poland and including many middle-class immigrants with some capital of their own, brought economic prosperity to the Yishuv but simultaneously strengthened the social and political weight of nonworker forces, to the detriment of the labor movement.[29] Ahdut Ha'avoda leaders tried various means to reassert their party's influence, including an effort to improve relations with Hapo'el Hatza'ir. Efforts were also made to reassert control over the railway workers' union, and as I discuss in Chapters 3 and 4 these were ultimately successful. To thwart Po'alei Tziyon Smol's demand for the restructuring of the Histadrut, which won some support elsewhere in the Zionist labor movement, Ben-Gurion proposed that the next Histadrut congress, still some years off, establish an all-Palestine workers' alliance, in essence an umbrella organization that would include both the Histadrut (which would continue to be autonomous) and its as-yet-nonexistent Arab counterpart. Unions in mixed workplaces would have separate national sections affiliated with their respective national organization.[30] Facing persistent criticism from Po'alei Tziyon Smol that Ahdut Ha'avoda had neglected joint organization, party leaders defended their record, largely through articles in Ahdut Ha'avoda's weekly organ *Kuntres.* They insisted that Ahdut Ha'avoda had always taken the issue seriously and suggested that the Histadrut's failures in this arena were largely due to Arab workers' backwardness and incapacity for organization.[31]

The terms in which this debate was cast well illustrate the contours of left-Zionist thinking on the question of relations with Arab workers. The supporters of the Ahdut Ha'avoda line accused the railwaymen's union leadership, now under the influence of Po'alei Tziyon Smol, of neglecting or downplaying its national responsibilities. To even think of divesting the Histadrut of its responsibilities for immigration, settlement, and economic development amounted to "liquidationism," that is, the abandonment of Zionism. Arab workers should be organized under Histadrut tutelage, but separately, in their own organizations and sections; this was, Ahdut Ha-'avoda supporters insisted, what the Arab workers themselves really wanted. In contrast, the partisans of Po'alei Tziyon Smol argued that separate national sections were a barrier to joint organization: many Arab workers were ready to join the Histadrut and its trade unions, and the only thing preventing the rapid realization of Jewish-Arab class solidarity was the obstructionism of the Histadrut leadership and its misguided policy.

Yet despite their differences, both sides in this debate shared a common premise: the nonexistence or illegitimacy of Palestinian Arab nationalism, especially as far as Arab workers were concerned. For Ahdut Ha'avoda, the Jewish national sections in mixed unions would be affiliated to the Histadrut and be part of the Jewish national movement; but the corresponding Arab sections, and an Arab labor federation if and when established, were to be resolutely non-national, indeed even antinational, in the sense that the Arab workers and their unions were to be under the tutelage of the Histadrut and allied to the Zionist movement rather than to the Arab nationalist movement. Po'alei Tziyon Smol's demand that the Histadrut be open to both Arabs and Jews was also not neutral in national terms. Other exclusively Jewish institutions would carry on the "national" tasks taken over from the Histadrut, while the Arab workers were to have no such institutions, since their interests were defined as purely social rather than national. In fact, as I suggested earlier, it can be argued that Po'alei Tziyon Smol's unreconstructed Borokhovism more completely delegitimized Palestinian Arab nationalism than Ahdut Ha'avoda's (and later MAPAI's) social-democratic pragmatism. But in this period both these parties largely excluded from thought the possibility that Arab workers in Palestine might in any legitimate way see themselves as members of a national community with interests and needs in conflict with those of the Jewish workers, whose Zionist commitments were simply taken for granted.

THE STRUGGLES AT NESHER, 1924–25

Though the railway workers still held center stage in labor-Zionist debates about relations between Arab and Jewish workers, by the middle of the decade relations among Arab and Jewish workers in other workplaces were also raising complex issues. This period witnessed the first significant manifestations of organization and action by Arab wage workers, for the most part in and around Haifa. Haifa was at this time experiencing rapid growth: its population (one-quarter of which consisted of Jews) was almost 25,000 in 1922 and would double by 1931.[32] In the interwar period the city would become not only Palestine's main port but also its leading industrial center. The Palestine Railways built its main repair and maintenance workshops there, a new deepwater harbor was developed, the Iraq Petroleum Company completed pipeline facilities in 1934, an oil refinery began to function soon after the outbreak of the Second World War, and a substantial number of industrial enterprises (most but not all of them Jewish-owned) were established in or near the city. Haifa would become not only "Red Haifa," a bastion of the Jewish workers' movement and a base for its most radical elements, but also the cradle of the emerging Palestinian Arab working class and of its trade union movement.

The new Nesher cement factory, located not far from Haifa, was the site of several of this period's most important and controversial struggles. Nesher was established in 1924–25 by Michael Pollack, a Jew who was born in Russian-ruled Georgia, made a fortune in Baku oil, and fled Russia after the revolution, eventually settling in Paris. The site chosen for the factory was close to the Arab village of Yajur, on the eastern slopes of Mount Carmel. In 1872 the Ottoman government had sold Yajur village lands to the Sursuq brothers and Salim al-Khuri, Lebanese businessmen who later sold them to Zionist land-acquisition institutions. The Jewish settlement of Yagur was established on a portion of these lands in 1922, but the new cement factory itself seems to have been located on land traditionally belonging to the nearby (and larger) village of Balad al-Shaykh, just to the north. Another Jewish settlement, named Nesher like the factory itself, was established nearby in 1925.[33]

Construction work for the Nesher factory was carried out by both Jewish workers supplied by the Histadrut and Egyptian workers brought in by a local Arab contractor. The former, Histadrut members, received 20 piastres for an eight-hour workday, while the Egyptians received only 10 piastres for a nine- or ten-hour day. (Egyptian currency was used in Palestine from the end of the war until 1927, when it was replaced by a separate Palestinian currency. Both the Egyptian and Palestinian pounds, close in value to the pound sterling, were divided into one hundred piastres and one thousand milliemes.) Such differentials in Jewish and Arab wage rates for both skilled and unskilled labor were to be typical in Palestine through most of the mandate period. This was the first time these Jewish workers had worked alongside Arabs, if not their first experience of direct contact. Though Haifa was still a largely Arab city, it was already possible for Jewish immigrants to have only minimal contact with Arabs, and very easy to have no ongoing day-to-day engagement. Given that few if any of the Jewish workers at Nesher knew Arabic, and none of the Egyptians were likely to have spoken either Yiddish or Hebrew, the possibility of conversation was probably limited. But decent relations seem to have prevailed nonetheless among the 200 Jewish workers and the 80 Egyptians engaged in building the Nesher factory by 1924.

Nothing is known about the Egyptian workers, but the Jewish contingent seems to have consisted in large part of recent arrivals. The great majority were likely to have inclined toward one of the labor-Zionist parties (Ahdut Ha'avoda, Hapo'el Hatza'ir, and Po'alei Tziyon Smol) or to have been apolitical Zionists, but a handful of members or sympathizers of the Palestine Communist Party were also employed at the Nesher site. Unlike many labor Zionists, who were usually prepared to set aside worker grievances and preserve labor peace in the interests of developing the Yishuv, the communists had no hesitation about taking militant stands on workplace issues. At Nesher as elsewhere, the communists also attacked the Zionist movement for displacing Palestinian peasants, claiming that the very land on which the Nesher factory was being built had been expropriated. The communists may not have been correct in this instance, since the factory site seems to have been uninhabited wasteland, but the nearby village of Yajur and the Jewish settlement of Yagur certainly provided an example of one means by which Palestinian villagers had been deprived of land which ended up permanently in Jewish hands.

As the factory approached completion, tensions rose between management and the Jewish workers. The latter resented management's adamant refusal to recognize or negotiate with either their own elected committee or the Histadrut to which they belonged. They also wanted an increase in wages to 25 piastres and a one-hour reduction in the workday. Ultimately the Jewish construction workers went on strike. They quickly realized that to win they needed the support of the Egyptian workers. Histadrut and Haifa Workers' Council officials opposed trying to get the Egyptians to join the strike, for fear that their participation might undermine the Histadrut's long-range goal of achieving exclusively Jewish employment at the site, in keeping with the Hebrew labor doctrine. But the Jewish workers decided to seek their support anyway, and the Egyptians, whose wages, working conditions, and treatment by foremen were much worse than those of the Jewish workers, quickly responded by joining the strike, to the astonishment of the contractor who had employed them. The strike dragged on for two months until finally Pollack himself sent a message ordering his agents in Palestine to reach a settlement. An agreement was quickly concluded between Nesher and the Haifa Workers' Council which won for the Jewish workers some of their demands. The agreement said nothing about the Egyptian workers, however, and the Histadrut insisted that it had no responsibility for them. Defying their leaders, the Jewish workers voted 170 to 30 not to return to work unless the Egyptians were also rehired, which Nesher management refused to do. The Histadrut ignored the vote and successfully pressured the Jewish construction workers to abandon the struggle and resume work. Most of the Egyptians were deported to their homeland by the mandatory authorities.

After Nesher actually began production in 1925, another struggle ensued which pitted Jewish against Egyptian workers. While only Jews were employed as production workers at the cement factory itself, Nesher's owner had given the contract for work at the quarry which supplied the factory with its raw materials to Musbah al-Shaqifi, a Palestinian Arab contractor who employed Egyptian workers. Michael Pollack resisted pressure from the Histadrut to replace the Arab quarry workers with Jews, insisting that because Nesher was Palestine's only cement factory and sold its output to Arabs as well as Jews, he was obligated to employ some Arab workers. In protest the Histadrut ordered its members to go on strike against this use of what it called "coolie" labor, and they complied. The contrast with the solidarity the Jewish workers had displayed the previous year is striking. It may well be that the disobedient Jewish workers who had been employed to help build the factory were not taken on as production workers when the factory went into operation, or perhaps the Histadrut had managed to tighten its control over the workforce by some other means. Whatever the case, this strike—a classic manifestation of the Hebrew labor doctrine in practice—was unsuccessful, and until the revolt of 1936–39 the company's quarrying work remained the preserve of Arabs, though over time Egyptians were replaced by Palestinians, mainly villagers from the vicinity.[34]

Curiously, even as the Histadrut and the Jewish workers at Nesher were seeking to force that company to get rid of its non-Jewish employees, they were supporting a strike for higher wages initiated by twenty-five Egyptian, two Palestinian, and seven Jewish workers employed at another quarry in Yajur, run by a Belgian contractor connected with Nesher. In the latter case the Jewish workers at Nesher provided the strikers with material and moral support, and the Histadrut intervened with the authorities when the Egyptian workers were threatened with deportation. That the Histadrut could simultaneously launch a struggle to deprive non-Jewish workers of their jobs while supporting another strike nearby by non-Jewish workers demanding higher wages might seem contradictory. But the contradiction is only apparent. For the Histadrut, the issue at Nesher was Hebrew labor: jobs in the Jewish sector of the Palestinian economy should go exclusively to Jews. The Jewish labor movement, it was argued, was engaged in a life-and-death struggle with cheaper Arab labor and had the right to defend its standard of living, indeed its very existence.

Commenting on the Nesher strike, David Ben-Gurion was prepared to admit that the Histadrut's struggle to displace Arab workers might "contradict the *personal* interest of that number of Arab workers engaged in cement quarrying." But he insisted that the Jewish workers' struggle to secure jobs and increase their wages in the face of cheap local labor would ultimately improve the economic situation of Palestine as a whole, create new and better jobs in the Arab sector as well, and thereby benefit the Arab workers. The Nesher strike was therefore justified, Ben-Gurion argued, since "this struggle completely conforms to the *class* interest of the Arab worker in Palestine no less than to the class interest of the Jewish worker." In any event, Ben-Gurion insisted, there was no ethnic or national discrimination involved: "It is not by virtue of his being an Arab that the Arab worker endangers the Jewish worker's employment opportunities, but by virtue of his being unorganized and competing with others." What better proof could there be of this than the fact that the Histadrut supported strikes by non-Jewish workers when the question of Hebrew labor was not involved? Hence the proud publication in *Kuntres* of a letter signed by two of the striking Egyptian workers at the Belgian contracting company in Yajur, thanking the Histadrut and the Nesher workers for their support.[35]

ORGANIZING ARAB WORKERS

The events at Nesher, a number of other incidents elsewhere, and signs that the embryonic Palestinian Arab working class was beginning to stir, finally pushed the Histadrut to take action in the spring of 1925, after years of procrastination. In large measure its initiative was intended to preempt other projects and developments already under way. Some local unions (for example, the woodworkers' union in Haifa) had on their own already begun to informally admit Arabs, who thereby also became members of the Histadrut itself. From both Haifa and Tel Aviv came reports of Arab workers, attracted by the Histadrut's size, wealth, and apparent effectiveness, seeking admission to the organization—which also meant access to its various institutions, including its employment office, loan fund, and the Kupat Holim health clinics. Histadrut leaders were also concerned that their political enemies on the left might capitalize on this issue. They were well aware that Po'alei Tziyon Smol, which was demanding that Arabs be allowed to join the Histadrut and whose members now led the railway workers' union, had already initiated an organizing committee in Haifa to develop links with Arab workers outside the railways. This initiative had made some headway: party activists had begun to work with a group of some two dozen Arabs who frequented the railway workers' club. The party had also established ties with a small group of Arab workers in Jaffa.

There were also fears that the communists were gaining ground among Arab workers. The communists already enjoyed some support among the Jewish railway workers in Haifa, from which base they were reaching out to Arab railway workers involved in complex negotiations over the establishment of a joint union (see Chapter 3). In the fall of 1924 the party had begun to publish its own Arabic-language journal, under the name *Haifa*. Its efforts to win support in the Arab community were enhanced by a much stronger and clearer anti-Zionist stance, one of whose first manifestations was a campaign to support Arab peasants resisting eviction from lands near 'Afula, in the Jezreel Valley, which Arab landlords had sold to the Jewish National Fund. The party was also trying to win over Jewish workers through a "workers' unity" movement (known in Hebrew as "Ihud"), in keeping with recent Comintern directives instructing communist parties worldwide to overcome their isolation by seeking cooperation with left social-democrats within the trade union movement. Though the communists had been expelled from the Histadrut the previous year, the party's strong advocacy of class struggle and trade union autonomy allowed it to retain some support among Jewish workers. In the December 1925 elections to the Yishuv's representative assembly, the party's list won some 8 percent of the vote, and more than 10 percent in the big cities—an electoral success which communists in Palestine (or later in Israel) would never equal.[36]

At the same time, an independent Palestinian Arab labor movement had begun to emerge, in the form of the Palestinian Arab Workers' Society (PAWS), established in Haifa in the spring of 1925. As I discuss in Chapter 3, the PAWS emerged in the context of the secession of most of the Arabs who had joined the short-lived Arab-Jewish railway workers' union. For a decade and a half its core and most stable component would consist of Haifa-area railway workers, but from the outset it aspired to become the Arab counterpart of the Histadrut, a truly national labor organization encompassing all the Arab workers of Palestine. The emergence of the PAWS, whose leaders were rather conservative but clearly unsympathetic to Zionism and supportive of the Arab national cause, was yet another indication to the Histadrut leadership that the issue of organizing Arab workers could no longer be ignored.

These developments took place in a changed economic climate, which also had an impact on events. In the middle of 1924, the Jewish population of Palestine was estimated at 94,945; a year later it had reached 121,725 and by the middle of 1926 149,500.[37] This Fourth Aliya, the largest wave of Jewish immigration which Palestine had yet experienced, helped set off an economic boom in the Yishuv, both because of its size and because unlike earlier waves many of the new immigrants brought some capital with them. The immigrants settled overwhelmingly in the cities, especially Tel Aviv, whose population increased from 22,000 in 1924 to 40,000 at the end of the following year. The Jewish construction sector flourished as a result, opening up many new jobs. Jewish unemployment eased dramatically, creating a climate in which Jewish workers were better positioned to try to improve their wages and working conditions. The positive impact on Arab workers was much smaller, if at all palpable, but the period nonetheless witnessed unprecedented labor activism among Arabs as well as among Jews.

By March 1925 the Haifa Workers' Council, on which Ahdut Ha'avoda was still the strongest party, had grown alarmed by Po'alei Tziyon Smol's effort to use its base among the railway workers in order to develop contacts with other Arab workers. To preempt that initiative, the Council created a committee to recruit Arab workers into a separate organization which was to have its own employment bureau, so as not to compromise the principle of Hebrew labor. When Histadrut officials in Haifa appealed to headquarters in Tel Aviv for the funds necessary to implement this effort they received a positive response, for the Histadrut leadership was now finally convinced that the time had come to begin organizing Arab workers.[38] During 1925, with funds from its own budget and from the Zionist Executive, the Histadrut launched two initiatives aimed at developing links with the Arab working class: an Arabic-language newspaper (the Zionist movement's first) and a "club" in Haifa whose mission was to make contact with and then organize Arab workers.

Zionist leaders had talked of starting an Arabic-language newspaper for years, as a means of propagandizing in favor of Zionism among the literate Arab public in Palestine and beyond, as well as of countering the strongly anti-Zionist stance of most of the country's Arabic press. Little progress was achieved, however, until Yitzhak Ben-Tzvi finally convinced the Zionist Executive not only to subsidize the project but to allow the Histadrut to run it. The new newspaper, which began to appear in April 1925, was called *Ittihad al-'Ummal* (Workers' unity), which (perhaps coincidentally) had also been the name of a workers' newspaper published the previous year by the short-lived Egyptian labor federation aligned with the nationalist Wafd party. At first Ben-Tzvi edited *Ittihad al-'Ummal* (which initially appeared biweekly and later weekly, with some gaps) himself; later Dr. Nissim Malul, the Jerusalem-based publisher and journalist, took over. When Malul moved to Baghdad his wife and later yet another Arabic-speaking Jew took charge.

Ittihad al-'Ummal had a clear political purpose: as one official Histadrut source put it, it sought "to impart to the Arab proletarian reader general concepts from the international workers' movement and an understanding of the activities and position of the Histadrut in Palestine, and to develop his class consciousness."[39] There were therefore numerous articles setting forth the history, ideology, and achievements of the labor-Zionist movement and explaining the structure and functions of the Histadrut and its various components. The newspaper also sought to introduce its readers to socialism by publishing in serial form classic texts by Ferdinand Lasalle and others, and to European literature through translations from such writers as Maxim Gorky and Oscar Wilde. It also featured extensive news of the Histadrut, its subsidiaries and trade unions, and the international labor movement, along with general political, economic, and social news and commentary.

The impact of *Ittihad al-'Ummal* on Arab workers seems likely to have been slight, given that most of its target audience was illiterate and that those who could read were also probably most likely to be hostile toward Zionism on nationalist grounds. In any event the newspaper's pressrun was usually only about 500 copies, most of which seem to have been distributed free of charge to Arab railway workers. *Ittihad al-ʿUmmal* was never a moneymaking proposition: it survived thanks only to subsidies from the Histadrut and the Zionist Executive. The crucial funding which the latter institution provided eventually allowed the centrist and middle-class "General Zionists" who still dominated the Zionist leadership to insist that their sociopolitical perspectives be better represented in the newspaper. Consequently from the summer of 1926 it began to devote less attention to the labor-Zionist movement and more to the Yishuv as a whole. This reorientation may also have reflected a desire to reach a broader section of the Arab reading public.

At about the same time as it launched *Ittihad al-ʿUmmal*, the Histadrut hired both a part-time Jewish organizer for Arab workers in Haifa and a full-time Arab assistant, both of whom would work under the supervision of the Haifa Workers' Council. The scarcity of suitable candidates made it obvious from the start who would occupy these posts. Avraham Khalfon was born in Tiberias in 1900, into a Jewish family long established in Palestine. He grew up in Haifa, spoke fluent Arabic, and had extensive contacts with Arabs in that mixed city. In 1923 he was elected to the city's Jewish community council and soon thereafter, at the request of local Histadrut officials, began to devote several hours a week to assisting the railway workers' union make contact with and recruit Arab railway workers (see Chapter 3). A trusted labor Zionist and well known to Ben-Tzvi, who was responsible for Arab affairs in the Histadrut secretariat, Khalfon was the logical choice to take charge of the Histadrut's efforts to organize Arab workers outside the railways as well.

Khalfon worked closely with his assistant, a young Arab tailor named Philip Hassun, said to be originally from Transjordan and the son of a Protestant minister. Hassun is reported to have sought to organize Haifa workers, especially porters, even before he began to frequent the railway workers' union club and developed close ties with local Poʿalei Tziyon Smol activists. An effective speaker with a good sense of humor, Hassun agreed to work as Khalfon's assistant at the substantial salary of £E8 a month. Over the years, Hassun's enthusiasm for socialist Zionism would make him seem somewhat ridiculous even to his Jewish colleagues. In his memoirs Berl Repetur, who would decades later serve as general secretary of the Histadrut but who at the time was a young man working at the port of Haifa, recounted inviting Hassun to a meeting with two Jewish visitors from the Soviet Union in the later 1920s. Hassun embarrassed Repetur and his colleagues with his exaggerated praise for all Zionism had done for the Arabs of Palestine. Repetur recalled that among Jews Hassun was jokingly referred to as "the Histadrut's *goy*."[40]

In July 1925, with a small budget from the Histadrut, Khalfon and Hassun opened the "General Workers' Club" in a busy, Arab, and largely Christian section of the "old city" of Haifa. The club seems to have met a need among Haifa's Arab working class, for it quickly attracted the attention and interest of a substantial number of skilled craftsmen, mainly tailors and carpenters. It offered evening classes in the Hebrew language and in Arabic literacy, lectures by members of various left-wing Zionist parties, and Arabic newspapers from Palestine and elsewhere. Through the club a number of Haifa workers also gained access to a special vocational training course at the Technion, the Jewish technical institute which had been founded in Haifa shortly before the war. But the club's chief mission was labor organizing, which it pursued through the creation of new unions for tailors and carpenters.

THE CARPENTERS' AND TAILORS' STRIKE

Discontent among both groups over meager wages, long working days, and abusive employers predated contact with the Histadrut, and it was the workers themselves who pressed Khalfon and Hassun to help them organize a strike if their employers would not agree to raise wages and institute the eight-hour day. Khalfon resisted this pressure at first because he did not think the carpenters and tailors were ready for a strike. In October 1925, however, with the support of the Histadrut executive committee, he decided that the time for action had arrived. In the name of the General Workers' Club Khalfon sent letters to the owners of the twelve workshops in which the one hundred or so unionized carpenters were employed, setting forth the workers' demands and requesting a response within ten days. The employers, never before faced with this kind of organized action on the part of their workers, simply ignored the letters. The carpenters, along with some thirty tailors, then went on strike, under the leadership of Khalfon and Hassun and with the backing of the Histadrut.

The strike was peaceful at first, but clashes ensued when the employers tried to bring in strikebreakers from the nearby town of Acre. The police intervened and arrested a number of the strikers, but the well-connected Khalfon was able to free them, by posting bail for them and by sending the alcoholic English police inspector in charge a case of his favorite brand of whiskey. Nonetheless, as the strike went on, it became increasingly clear that despite financial support from the Histadrut and the railway workers' union the clashes and arrests were exhausting the meager resources at the workers' disposal. There was also growing pressure on the workers from the local Arab press and local church officials. Haifa's oldest Arabic newspaper, *al-Karmil*, was strongly anti-Zionist, and while expressing sympathy for the workers' demands it also voiced its fear that the strike would serve Zionist rather than Palestinian Arab interests. "We fear," *al-Karmil* declared, "that the purpose of inducing the Arab workers to strike is (1) to incite them to rebellion; (2) to cause a disturbance in the business activity of Arab enterprises; (3) to raise prices so that it will be easier for Jewish goods to combat and compete with the Arabs and take jobs from them. We warn the leaders of this movement against falling into a trap, even as we acclaim the workers' awakening, for we are disgusted that someone should enrich themself from the sweat of the worker's brow."[41]

Local Christian clerics echoed *al-Karmil* and other Arab newspapers. The spiritual leader of Haifa's Maronite community, Father Francis, called in twenty of the strikers to warn them against cooperating with the Jews, who were spreading Bolshevism in Palestine, and appealed to them to form their own Muslim-Christian union which would be free of Jewish influence. According to the Histadrut's account of the meeting, the Arab workers replied that the Socialist International had delegated the task of organizing workers in the Middle East to the Histadrut and they must therefore affiliate with it. The International had of course done no such thing, but the claim does convey the sense of proletarian *mission civilatrice* with which socialist Zionists in Palestine were often imbued. The strikers were also said to have told the cleric that there was nothing to fear from the Jewish workers because the latter would not accept the meager wages paid to Arab workers.[42] This was probably true in tailoring and carpentry, but of course one of the Histadrut's motives in helping Arab workers organize was to open up more jobs for Jews by raising wage levels.

After meeting with a delegation of strikers, Najib Nassar, the editor of *al-Karmil*, invited the two sides to meet at his newspaper's offices and resolve their conflict. The strikers insisted that Khalfon and Hassun accompany them to the meeting. Nassar was unhappy that the two officials of what his newspaper referred to as the "Zionist workers' association" had come, but they were ultimately allowed to remain as observers. After several hours of negotiations an agreement was reached by which, after two weeks, the strike was brought to an end. The workers achieved gains that, given the miserable conditions that had prevailed until then, were not insubstantial: a nine-hour workday, a half-hour lunch break, and seven paid sick days a year.[43]

In its account of the strike's settlement, *al-Karmil* expressed the hope that in every trade a "guild" of employers and workers could be established to deal with the workers' grievances and thereby "block the involvement of Zionists in the affairs of Arab workers."[44] Nassar and his associates in the Arab bourgeoisie of Haifa were quite conservative on social issues and did not initially have much interest in the needs or interests of the emerging Palestinian working class. But events like the October 1925 strike pushed them toward greater awareness of, and interest in, labor affairs, mainly out of concern that the Zionists (whom they believed were also spreading the virus of Bolshevism) might promote and capitalize on class conflict within the Arab community. It was thus probably *al-Karmil*'s strongly anti-Zionist stance, rather than a newfound concern for social justice and worker empowerment, that led it and other conservative but nationalist newspapers to publish news of the new Palestinian Arab Workers' Society formed in Haifa a few months earlier, and more generally to take an interest in Arab workers and even to support the formation of labor unions. By the summer of 1927 *Filastin*, based in Jaffa, was expressing pleasure that Arab workers finally seemed to be heeding its frequent warnings that "the Jewish unions got involved in [Arab] workers' affairs only when it was in their own interest, in the interest of the Jewish workers, while the Arab worker was in their view only an instrument with which to threaten the government if it did not submit to demands to provide jobs for Jewish workers at high wages." The newspaper went on to call on Arab workers to quit Jewish unions and form their own labor organizations.[45]

The Histadrut leadership was still not without misgivings about the idea of organizing Arab workers. On a visit to Haifa during the carpenters' and tailors' strike, Ben-Gurion congratulated Khalfon: the strike was a big achievement for which labor Zionism had been striving for many years. It would allow the Histadrut to prove to the international socialist movement that it was not only seeking to build an advanced Jewish society in Palestine but also looking after the Arab workers. But, Ben-Gurion warned Khalfon, "Do not go too far. You are their teacher, and you have taught them to strike. They have already made some large steps. [But] the day will come, and it is not far off, when [the Palestinian nationalist leader] Hajj Amin al-Husayni will come and collect these same workers whom you have led like laid eggs, in order to use them to fight against us with the same means you have taught them." Ben-Gurion urged Khalfon to accept Najib Nassar's proposal for negotiations with the employers and seek a compromise which would end the strike quickly.[46] Despite his rhetorical support for organizing Arab workers, the Histadrut secretary was clearly uneasy about the long-term political consequences of such a course, from an entirely realistic assessment that as they became more organized and class-conscious Arab workers would also probably incline more strongly toward nationalism and against Zionism.

As it happened, the October 1925 strike led by Khalfon, Hassun, and their General Workers' Club marked not the beginning but the high point of the Histadrut's first attempt to organize Arab workers in Haifa. While some Arab workers are said to have attended the traditional May Day strike and rally organized by the Haifa Workers' Council the following spring, the influence of the General Workers' Club was in fact already on the wane. In part this was due to a deteriorating economic climate. The last months of 1925 witnessed the beginning of a severe economic downturn in Palestine that would last until 1929, resulting in high unemployment and depressed wages for both Arabs and Jews in many trades. The grim situation in the Haifa building trades, particularly hard-hit, was exacerbated by an influx of carpenters and other craftsmen from Syria, where a nationalist uprising and massive repression by that country's French colonial rulers had disrupted normal economic life. In these circumstances workers were less willing to take risks and the General Workers' Club found it impossible to repeat the success it had achieved with the carpenters and tailors in October 1925. Its involvement in subsequent workers' struggles was restricted to a few isolated instances.[47]

The decline of the Haifa club was certainly also hastened by the barrage of criticism and hostility to which it was subjected from both Arab nationalists and Jewish communists. These groups were united in seeing the club as essentially an instrument by which the Zionists were surreptitiously and illegitimately seeking to infiltrate and dominate the Arab working class. As an Arab directly employed by the Histadrut and doing its work, Philip Hassun was a prime target of nationalist invective, denounced as a lackey of the Jews and a traitor to his people.[48] By 1927 the club was virtually moribund: its organizing efforts had petered out, few workers frequented its premises, and the activities of Khalfon and Hassun were largely restricted to arranging lectures and evening classes. Elsewhere in

Palestine, the Histadrut's efforts to develop links with Arab workers never even approached the level briefly attained in Haifa.

After two years of effort, the Histadrut leadership could point to few successes that might justify the continued allocation of funds and staff to the project of organizing Arab workers. At the same time, it was increasingly preoccupied with other problems. The economic crisis had hurt the Yishuv badly: the unemployment rate in Tel Aviv reached 40 percent in February 1927, the Histadrut's Solel Boneh contracting company went bankrupt four months later, and that year more Jews left Palestine than entered it. Both the Histadrut and the Zionist Executive were forced to cut their budgets, with the result that funding for organizing Arab workers was sharply reduced. One consequence of these cuts, which can also be taken as an indication of the Histadrut's changing priorities, was the end of Avraham Khalfon's career as a labor organizer. In the spring of 1927, at the urging of Ben-Gurion and Ben-Tzvi, Khalfon left the General Workers' Club and moved on to a new job as the Jewish secretary at the Haifa municipality, from which post Histadrut leaders hoped that he would be able to get the municipality to hire more Jews. Over the following quarter-century Khalfon would ascend through the ranks of the local administration and ultimately attain the post of secretary of the municipality. Philip Hassun remained in charge of the General Workers' Club after Khalfon left, but the club had accumulated large debts and Hassun's job was itself precarious. *Ittihad al-'Ummal* no longer appeared with regularity and after several hiatuses it ceased publication altogether at the beginning of 1928, largely because the Zionist Executive, facing its own budget shortfalls, cut the subsidy it had been providing the Histadrut for the newspaper.[49]

"WE CANNOT BE YOUR SLAVES"

Though the Histadrut's first effort to develop a base among Arab workers had been unsuccessful and its leaders' interest in the project was waning, the question of relations with Arab workers did not completely disappear from the agenda of the labor-Zionist movement. In fact, even as practical activity virtually ceased the issue continued to garner attention, especially during the period leading up to the Histadrut's third congress, scheduled for the summer of 1927, at which the question would be discussed and policy set. In the process Ahdut Ha'avoda was compelled to fend off criticism from its rivals on the left and right while clarifying its own position on the issue.

Po'alei Tziyon Smol was the chief source of criticism from the left, since the openly anti-Zionist communists were altogether beyond the pale. Po'alei Tziyon Smol could by this point claim that it had living proof that Jewish-Arab solidarity was possible, in the form of a small group of Arab workers in Jaffa with which it had developed close ties. The leader of the group was a carpenter, George Nassar, who had become an enthusiastic and loyal adherent of Po'alei Tziyon Smol and a protégé of one of the party's top leaders, Moshe Erem. Once, when asked why he supported Zionism and whether that support did not make him a traitor to his people, Nassar responded that he supported Zionism "precisely because I am a good Arab. I know and see with my own eyes that Jewish immigration improves the situation of the Arab masses, it contributes to raising the [Arab] worker's wages in Palestine and his standing in society. And since I seek the welfare of the Arab worker, I am ready to support Jewish immigration to Palestine." [50]

Very few Arabs in Palestine were prepared to embrace this logic, and it is not even clear that any of the Jaffa workers in Nassar's group shared his political vision. There is room for suspicion that the Po'alei Tziyon Smol activists with whom these workers were in contact tended to emphasize the party's refusal to join the Zionist Organization and its proletarian internationalist ideology rather than its strong Zionist commitments. Nonetheless, it does seem that in this period there were in fact Arab workers who sincerely wished to join the Histadrut, which they perceived as a powerful and wealthy organization, provided that it dissociate itself from Zionism. Po'alei Tziyon Smol used this sentiment to bolster its demand for "separation of functions" in the Histadrut and its transformation into an Arab-Jewish trade union center, with Arab workers as full and equal members.

In December 1925 Po'alei Tziyon Smol leaders arranged a meeting between Histadrut secretary David Ben-Gurion and George Nassar, accompanied by several of his coworkers. The meeting was not a success: the Arab workers heard the Histadrut leader reject their demand for admission, which Ahdut Ha'avoda regarded as a threat to the labor-Zionist project and a provocation on the part of Po'alei Tziyon Smol. In response Nassar told Ben-Gurion that he and his comrades wanted to join the Histadrut as "loyal members" and rejected the proposal that they join a separate club, as in Haifa. "We cannot be your slaves," he told the Histadrut leader. "We want to be members and subject to [Histadrut] discipline. . . . All our comrades want to be members of one organization with you, they will pay dues and organize meetings everywhere." But Ben-Gurion stood firm: "We will not decide here. The members of the Jaffa Workers' Council will consult with other workers and inform you of their decision. We will not argue about [Histadrut] membership cards. This is our rule, and until the next congress we can decide nothing." [51]

In the run-up to the 1927 Histadrut congress Po'alei Tziyon Smol sought to step up pressure on the organization's leadership by circulating petitions to be signed by Arab workers demanding admission. Among those who signed were a group of several dozen workers at a building site in Nazareth, who had sent one of their number to Haifa to seek Histadrut support upon launching a strike. Local Histadrut officials promised help but failed to act. The Nazareth workers then linked up with Po'alei Tziyon Smol activists in Haifa, and George Nassar traveled to Nazareth where he was apparently able to convince the workers still at their jobs to join the strike. With Po'alei Tziyon Smol's encouragement (and perhaps guidance), the Nazareth workers subsequently wrote to the Histadrut to demand that they be allowed to join. All told, Po'alei Tziyon Smol leaders claimed that some 700 Arab workers had signed petitions asking to be allowed to join the Histadrut. [52]

PALESTINE, SOUTH AFRICA, AND NATIVE LABOR

Criticism from the left was, however, less politically significant to Ahdut Ha'avoda than criticism from its rival (and junior partner) on the right, Hapo'el Hatza'ir. That party was much more straightforwardly nationalist than Ahdut Ha'avoda. Because it was not explicitly socialist, much less avowedly Marxist, had never professed allegiance to the principle of proletarian internationalism, and was able to concede the nationalist character of Arab opposition to Zionism, Hapo'el Hatza'ir did not need to resort to the tortured dialectics to which Ahdut Ha'avoda (and Po'alei Tziyon Smol as well) had recourse when called upon to justify their positions. From Hapo'el Hatza'ir's standpoint, the central task of the Histadrut was to realize the Zionist project through the construction in Palestine of a separate Jewish society and economy, and this alone was sufficient justification for such policies as Hebrew labor. As a party Hapo'el Hatza'ir was thus at best profoundly skeptical about, and at worst hostile to, what it regarded as utopian pipe dreams like joint organization in mixed workplaces and the organization of Arab workers elsewhere. In fact, it saw such projects as potentially dangerous, in that they diverted scarce resources better devoted to meeting Jewish needs and aroused false hopes. From Hapo'el Hatza'ir's standpoint, too much concern for the well-being of the

Arabs or guilt and self-doubt over possible violations of their rights were manifestations of an unhealthy *"galut* mentality" inappropriate to the project of Jewish national reconstruction.

Hapo'el Hatza'ir's analysis of the problem was articulated by Hayyim Arlosoroff in a 1927 essay entitled "On the Question of Joint Organization," published as an intervention in the debates on the question that preceded the Histadrut's third congress. Born in the Ukraine in 1899 and raised in Germany, where he studied economics, Arlosoroff settled in Palestine in 1924 and became a prominent leader of Hapo'el Hatza'ir. When MAPAI was founded through the merger of Ahdut Ha'avoda and Hapo'el Hatza'ir in 1930, he became one of the new party's top leaders. A year later he was chosen to direct the Political Department of the Jewish Agency, which had been established in 1929 to bring together Zionist and non-Zionist Jews in the project of developing the Jewish "national home" in Palestine. Though not formally a Zionist institution, the Jewish Agency was soon dominated by Zionists and became the institution through which resources were channeled to the Yishuv from Jewish communities worldwide. The Jewish Agency executive would come to function as the de facto leadership of the Yishuv, and Arlosoroff's appointment to direct its Political Department, like Ben-Gurion's elevation to the executive and then to its chairmanship, signaled the ascendancy of labor Zionism in the Yishuv and the Zionist Organization. Arlosoroff's assassination on Tel Aviv's beachfront in 1933, a crime which most labor Zionists blamed on Jewish extremists linked to Vladimir Jabotinsky's right-wing Revisionist Zionist party, ignited a bitter conflict between the left and right wings of the Zionist movement whose legacy is still discernible in Israeli politics today.

In his essay Arlosoroff claimed to be undertaking a strictly realistic and rational economic analysis, unencumbered by the ideological considerations which, he argued, had distorted the thinking of Ahdut Ha'avoda leaders like Ben-Gurion. Arlosoroff accused the latter of trying to theorize out of existence the real, everyday, and essentially national conflict between expensive Jewish and inexpensive Arab labor. He rejected the notion that joint organization could significantly raise the general wage level in Palestine and thus facilitate the struggle for Hebrew labor by making Jewish workers more competitive with Arab workers. He was also convinced that Ben-Gurion's portrayal of the nascent Palestinian Arab working class as Zionism's potential ally was nothing but a fantasy. Even in the form envisioned by Ahdut Ha'avoda, joint organization would lead to disaster for the Zionist project, for it would result in the deterioration of

Jewish wages to the Arab level, making it impossible for European Jewish workers to survive in Palestine.

To support his argument Arlosoroff cited the case of South Africa, where as he saw it conditions most closely paralleled those which confronted the Jewish workers in Palestine. The white workers there were unable to compete in a labor market dominated by abundant and cheap African and Indian labor. They had therefore organized and used their political clout to secure the imposition of a "color bar" which excluded nonwhites from supervisory, skilled, and well-paid jobs. Similarly, if Jewish and Arab workers in Palestine competed within the same labor market, the result would be not only the cessation of Jewish immigration—for Jews would not come to or stay in Palestine if they could not find decently paid jobs there—but also substantial Jewish emigration, making realization of a Jewish majority unlikely. Joint organization could never overcome the dynamics of the capitalist labor market. The only way out of this dilemma, Arlosoroff insisted, was for the Zionist labor movement to devote its resources and energies to developing a separate high-wage, high-productivity, and exclusively Jewish economic sector, which would coexist with an unproductive and low-wage Arab sector for decades to come. This was in fact already happening, but Arlosoroff wanted the movement to be much clearer about its goals and methods, and above all to give up on what he saw as the dangerous delusion of joint organization.

In addition to building up a separate Jewish economic enclave, the labor-Zionist movement was also using political means to try to escape the constraints of a local labor market in which, as Arlosoroff had demonstrated, its members found it difficult to compete successfully. For example, during the middle and later 1920s, the Histadrut pressed the Colonial Office and the government of Palestine to set a minimum wage for unskilled labor. This would have the effect of reducing the competition which Arab labor could offer Jewish labor, thereby preserving jobs for Jews and perhaps also opening new ones to them. The British authorities were not receptive to this demand, however, in keeping with their general policy of avoiding direct regulation of the labor market insofar as possible.[53] The Zionist Organization and the Histadrut also sought to ensure that wage rates for unskilled Jewish workers employed on relief projects by the Public Works Department during the post-1925 economic crisis were higher than those paid to Arab workers. British officials resisted this demand, too, because it favored Jewish labor over Arab labor and because it would increase their labor costs. Nonetheless, in 1928 a government wages commission reported that four wage levels for unskilled labor were in effect:

rural Arab labor received 12–15 piastres a day, urban Arab labor 14–17 piastres, unionized Jewish labor (i.e., Histadrut members) 28–30 piastres, and nonunion Jewish labor 15–30 piastres.[54]

At the same time, as I will discuss later, Histadrut and Zionist officials incessantly lobbied the British authorities in both Jerusalem and London to ensure that Jews received as large a proportion as possible of public works jobs and contracts. For example, the Zionist Organization demanded that Jewish workers be given 50 percent of the unskilled jobs created by the construction of the new deepwater port at Haifa and paid at standard Histadrut rates. Zionist leaders argued that this demand, and many similar demands raised with regard to other spheres of employment, were justified by the fact that the Jewish contribution to the government's tax revenues was proportionally much larger than the Jews' share in Palestine's population. Labor Zionists contributed to this lobbying campaign by utilizing their close connections with Trades Union Congress and Labor Party leaders in Britain to step up the pressure on the Colonial Office. British officials, especially in Palestine, opposed Zionist demands, on the grounds that it constituted favoritism toward Jews and because it would substantially increase the costs of the Haifa harbor project.[55]

FROM "HISTORIC MISSION" TO BENIGN NEGLECT

By the second half of the 1920s, then, the mainstream of the labor-Zionist movement was in practice firmly committed to a strategy based on both the struggle for Hebrew labor and the development of a separate Jewish economic enclave. Yet Ben-Gurion and his party found it difficult to accept this reality, which implied giving up on the vision of joint organization and Arab-Jewish working-class solidarity as a solution to labor Zionism's dilemmas. In October 1926, at Ahdut Ha'avoda's fifth party congress, Ben-Gurion acknowledged that the difficult situation in which the labor-Zionist movement currently found itself was not conducive to a correct assessment of the question of joint organization. But, he insisted, both moral and other considerations required that the party and the movement it led continue to understand that the fate of the Jewish working class in Palestine was inextricably linked to the fate of the Arab working class. "It is inconceivable," Ben-Gurion declared, "that we should succeed in entrenching ourselves in Palestine, in creating a large Jewish working class, in putting masses of Jews to work, and in building a lasting Jewish economy if, alongside the Jewish worker and the Jewish economy, there will remain the downtrodden and unorganized Arab worker, who will compete with us and see us as his enemy." Ben-Gurion reiterated his call for a Jewish-Arab workers' alliance, based on autonomous national organizations and separate national sections for mixed workplaces.[56]

Ben-Gurion made his remarks in the context of a discussion about the general policy on joint organization and relations between Arab and Jewish workers which the forthcoming Histadrut congress would adopt. Besides his own proposal, the party had before it a more complex scheme for an "international Eretz Yisra'el workers' alliance" (*brit po'alim beinle'umit eretz-yisra'elit*) put forward by Yitzhak Ben-Tzvi, to be composed of the Histadrut, such purely Arab unions or labor federations as might be established, and "international" unions with separate national sections in mixed enterprises like the railways.[57] Ben-Tzvi's proposal was (like Ben-Gurion's) designed to deflect criticism from the left by demonstrating Ahdut Ha'avoda's commitment to creating a framework for Arab-Jewish workers' solidarity, while at the same time protecting the party's right flank by barring Arabs from Histadrut membership, preserving the Histadrut's Zionist character, and ensuring that even Jewish workers in mixed unions would be able (through their separate national sections) to participate in the effort to construct a separate Jewish society in Palestine.

While more detailed than any previous proposal, Ben-Tzvi's scheme can also be seen as a manifestation of Ahdut Ha'avoda's declining interest in organizing Arab workers. When Ben-Tzvi had first outlined his scheme for an Arab-Jewish workers' alliance two years earlier, it had been implicitly understood that the Histadrut should play a key role in organizing its sister organization for Arab workers.[58] By contrast, his proposal to the fifth party congress made no mention of what Ben-Gurion had once called the Histadrut's "historic mission." Nor, for that matter, did Ben-Gurion's own remarks at the congress: they were rather vague and general, and though not without passion they seemed to imply that the Histadrut's responsibility was restricted to allying itself with the Arab working class once the latter had succeeded in organizing itself, rather than actively assisting it to do so.

In effect, the leaders of Ahdut Ha'avoda were moving away from their earlier emphasis on the importance of an alliance between the Jewish and Arab working classes in Palestine and toward Hapo'el Hatza'ir's relegation of joint organization, and more generally of the question of Arab-Jewish relations, to the margins. This shift reflected the gradual ideological convergence of the two parties which a few years later would result in their merger and the creation of MAPAI. Ahdut Ha'avoda's drift in this direction was manifested in a much more modest notion of what joint organization might achieve for both Jewish and Arab workers, and greater emphasis on labor Zionism's own constructive efforts as the determining factor in Zionism's ultimate success.[59]

The Histadrut's declining interest in organizing Arab workers and its move toward what might be called a policy of "benign neglect" also coincided with (and was probably bolstered by) the launching of a campaign to compel Jewish citrus farmers in the moshavot to dismiss their Arab workers and hire Jews instead. Most immediately, the Histadrut's rationale for renewing the struggle for Hebrew labor in the moshavot was the urgent need to relieve very high urban unemployment in a period of severe economic crisis. But the campaign also served to deflect Jewish workers' anger and frustration about their plight onto Arab workers, with whom they were competing for scarce jobs and who could be depicted as taking the bread out of their (and their families') mouths. In launching this campaign the labor-Zionist movement also gained an opportunity to assert its self-proclaimed role as vanguard of Zionism and the Yishuv, since it could cast itself as the defender of poor Jewish immigrants fighting for jobs and survival against the greed of the unpatriotic farmers, who preferred to employ cheap Arab labor even if that undermined the Zionist enterprise. This campaign dramatically heightened intra-Yishuv tensions but it thereby also enhanced the power, moral authority, and vanguard status of the labor-Zionist leadership and the institutions it controlled in relation to competing Jewish sociopolitical forces.

Ahdut Ha'avoda's new orientation also reflected the growing strength and social weight of the Jewish labor movement in Palestine. The Histadrut had grown from 4,433 members at its inception in 1920 to some 25,000 members by 1928. Despite the economic downturn that had set in by 1926, the Yishuv seemed to be developing and labor-Zionist leaders could envision continued slow but steady growth. Arab opposition to Zionism persisted, but in the later 1920s the national movement was factionalized and ineffective, and British support for the establishment of the Jewish national home seemed secure. In the second half of the 1920s Ahdut Ha'avoda gradually abandoned the radicalism that had sometimes characterized its rhetoric earlier in the decade and gave up on the idea of building a socialist Jewish community in Palestine through the workers' efforts alone. Instead it more wholeheartedly embraced the idea of an alliance with Jewish (private and Zionist) capital, and sought (successfully) to exploit that alliance in ways that would enhance its own strength and that of the institutions it controlled. These trends and developments interacted with one another and contributed to the party's retreat from its earlier emphasis on the importance of Arab-Jewish working-class solidarity.

The shift emerged clearly at the Histadrut's third congress, held in July 1927. Among other things, the congress was to finally decide what form joint organization of Arab and Jewish workers in mixed workplaces should take. Po'alei Tziyon Smol had submitted draft resolutions calling for the radical restructuring of the Histadrut into a trade union federation open to all workers in Palestine, along with petitions signed by hundreds of Arab workers requesting membership in the organization.[60] But the party was a small minority in a congress dominated by Ahdut Ha'avoda and its ally Hapo'el Hatza'ir, and the question of joint organization no longer enjoyed a very prominent position on the Histadrut's agenda.

Nonetheless, the issue surfaced right at the outset, as various observers and guests rose to present their greetings to the delegates. One of these was Philip Hassun, who claimed to speak on behalf of the Arab workers organized by the Histadrut in Haifa. Hassun praised the Histadrut in rather obsequious terms for the selfless assistance it had extended to Arab workers and declared that "the Arab worker has no one to depend on except the Hebrew worker." This kind of rhetoric was predictable, since Hassun was a Histadrut employee. However, the speaker who followed Hassun struck a very different tone. This was Ahmad Hamdi, who said he was greeting the congress as representative of a group of some 600 Arab workers. We know nothing about Hamdi, but it would seem that his appearance at the Histadrut congress was sponsored by Po'alei Tziyon Smol, that he had acquired his knowledge of the Jewish labor movement largely through that party, and that the Arab workers he claimed to represent were those who had, at that party's urging, indicated their interest in joining the Histadrut. Hamdi called on the Jewish workers to help the Arab workers liberate themselves from their degraded state. But why, he wondered, did the Jewish workers want to isolate themselves in their own separate organization?

> Such separate organizations are dangerous. Let not [distinctions between] East and West, Zionism and Arabism, Torah and Qur'an, cause divisions among us. When the Arab workers approach the Jewish workers, their enemies say to them, "You are Zionists!" And others say, "You are communists!" And so the Arab worker is confused. We must unite and present common demands to the government, which ignores its obligations to the worker and instead sends in the police and puts him in jail.

As Hamdi saw it, the Jewish workers' movement as such was not Zionist, and that distinction should be made clear to all so that there would be no divisions between Arab and Jewish workers.[61]

These remarks seem to have aroused Ben-Gurion's ire, for he immediately rose to respond. The Histadrut secretary declared that while he welcomed any sign of awakening among the Arab workers, he wanted the Arab workers and intellectuals—at least those few who, Ben-Gurion said, had so far freed themselves from "the enmity which the effendis were sowing around the Zionist enterprise"—to understand that "the Jewish workers in Palestine *are* the Zionists," a remark which the delegates greeted with applause. Ben-Gurion went on:

> They came to Palestine only thanks to Zionism. Had it not been for Zionism there would not be 30,000 organized workers in Palestine, there wouldn't be this congress, nor the Histadrut nor the movement which will raise the [Arab] worker from his degradation. And I want to tell you, Comrade Hamdi, what the workers' Zionism is. You say that the Arab worker is oppressed and his situation is degraded. But our situation is even worse. If the Arab worker works in difficult conditions, the Jewish masses don't even have the opportunity to work. And Zionism aspires to bring the Jewish masses to Eretz Yisra'el and to labor, to transform here the Jewish masses into workers, and they will also bring about the strengthening of the workers and Arab masses in Eretz Yisra'el and the neighboring lands. . . . This is Zionism: the return of the Jewish masses to Eretz Yisra'el and their transformation into a productive workforce on which the country's future regime will be based.

That is why, Ben-Gurion argued, the effendis were fighting Zionism: this new force would put an end to their plundering and exploitation. "You, the Arab workers, must not harness yourselves to the cart of the effendis in their war against Zionism," he warned. "We believe that to the extent that our strength in the country grows, so will grow the strength of the working class which Hamdi and his comrades hope will liberate this country."[62]

The main presentation on joint organization was given by Ben-Tzvi, who criticized both Hapo'el Hatza'ir's insistence on a complete separation between Jewish and Arab workers and Po'alei Tziyon Smol's demand that Arabs be allowed to join the Histadrut, arguing instead for his rather complex scheme for an "international workers' alliance" in Palestine. There was also another resolution put forward by the "Kibbutz Faction," representing new political forces based in the Third Aliya (1918–23) which, in the form of Hashomer Hatza'ir, would eventually supplant Po'alei Tziyon Smol as the main party on the Zionist left (see Chapters 4 and 5).[63] In the end, the congress adopted what amounted to a rather vague statement of principles, apparently the result of a compromise worked out behind the scenes between Ahdut Ha'avoda and Hapo'el Hatza'ir. The resolution stated that the congress saw the need for "cooperation between Jewish and Arab workers in the vital matters common to them," but immediately qualified this by stating that "the basis for common action is recognition of the essential value and rights of Jewish immigration to Palestine." It went on to proclaim the establishment of an "international alliance of the workers of Palestine" on the basis of autonomous national units, but appended a clause making it absolutely clear that this decision would entail no change whatsoever in the structure or mission of the Histadrut.

With this resolution the Histadrut's highest body put the organization on record as favoring the creation of some framework within which Arab and Jewish workers might cooperate. It was clear, however, that this was to be done in a manner consistent with Ahdut Ha'avoda's vision of the Zionist project. The Histadrut left's demand for the admission of Arabs was decisively rejected, while the congress strongly endorsed the Histadrut's independence, gave Jewish immigration priority over Arab-Jewish cooperation, and ensured that even in mixed workplaces Jewish workers would have their separate organizations. Perhaps as important as what the resolution said, however, was what it did not say. The resolution dealt only with the organizational structure within which Arab-Jewish workers' cooperation was to occur, with no mention whatsoever of any commitment on the part of the Jewish working class to assist Arab workers to organize. The sense of labor-Zionist mission, a frequent theme in Ahdut Ha'avoda rhetoric only a few years earlier, was absent from the resolution.

This silence, and the tone and content of remarks on the question by Histadrut leaders, underscore the change that had taken place in Ahdut Ha'avoda's perception of the linkage between the fate of the Zionist project and Arab-Jewish working-class relations. The equation which Ben-Gurion had set forth a few years earlier had now been reversed: the organization of Palestinian Arab workers and Arab-Jewish working-class solidarity were no longer seen as the guarantor of the success of Zionism, an essential element in the struggle to secure the basis for a large and powerful Jewish working class in Palestine and defeat the effendis' opposition to Zionism. Instead, it was the success of the Histadrut, the development under its guidance of the Yishuv's economy, the construction of a strong and exclusively Jewish enclave, that would enhance the ability of Arab workers to win higher wages, improve their working conditions and living standards, and by organizing themselves become a significant force in their own community. From this perspective, the Jewish working class would still play a leading role in "awakening" the Arab workers, but it would be a much less direct role than initially envisioned. It would entail not so much the commitment of significant human and material resources to the organization of Arab workers as the provision of an attractive model of a well-organized and powerful labor movement which Arab workers could emulate, along with the creation of a high-wage sector which would eventually help raise wages throughout the Palestinian economy.

In fact, from this point on Arab workers largely ceased to occupy a key place in mainstream labor-Zionist discourse, and the movement's script for the drama of Jewish redemption in Palestine was rewritten so as to eliminate the central role they had earlier been assigned. However, this is not to say that the question of relations between Arab and Jewish workers disappeared from the agenda of the labor-Zionist movement in Palestine: it did not, though the ways in which that question was posed, as both a practical and an ideological issue, would change considerably. But for much of the labor-Zionist movement, realization of Arab-Jewish class solidarity and joint organization had lost their perceived urgency and centrality. It was mainly the smaller left-Zionist parties (and of course the communists as well) which, along with a few dedicated but isolated individuals within MAPAI, continued to regard them as vital missions. For Ahdut Ha'avoda and then for MAPAI, this whole arena would come to be seen as a sideshow.

As a result, though they were the culmination of years of debate within the Zionist labor movement in Palestine, the resolutions adopted at the Histadrut's third congress had virtually no immediate impact. Given their limited scope, the difficult economic situation, and the preoccupation of the Histadrut leadership with other problems, no new resources were devoted to organizing Arab workers. As I noted earlier, *Ittihad al-'Ummal* was allowed to fade out of existence in the half year that followed the third congress, while the General Workers' Club in Haifa closed its doors sometime in 1928 or 1929. There is evidence of only one strike by Arab workers in which the Histadrut was involved in this period, and it is symptomatic that this was a spontaneous walkout which the Histadrut supported only after it erupted.[64] Po'alei Tziyon Smol maintained its links with George Nassar's circle in Jaffa, but this remained a very small and isolated group which exercised no influence on the growing Arab working class in that city. Other relationships which that party had sought to develop with groups of Arab workers failed to survive, much less thrive.[65]

During 1928 and into 1929 there was sporadic talk of reviving *Ittihad al-'Ummal*, reopening the Haifa club, and devoting greater attention and resources to organizing Arab workers. Several factors helped keep the issue alive, including explicitly economic considerations. In May 1929 David Hacohen, a leading figure in the Histadrut's economic enterprises, warned the secretariat that the government's Public Works Department was inclined to hire cheap contracted Arab labor, which would make it impossible for Histadrut enterprises to win contracts which provided jobs for Jewish workers at good wages. He proposed that the Histadrut begin organizing Arab workers, in order to show the Public Works Department that "the path of pushing down wages for Arabs is not strewn with roses." While there was no immediate follow-up on Hacohen's proposal, the idea of securing more jobs for Jews by raising Arab wages through labor organizing would continue to influence Histadrut policy-making in this arena for many years.[66]

Histadrut officials also saw a need to counter the communists' ongoing efforts to organize Arab workers in Haifa, as well as to refute continuing criticism from the Zionist left.[67] At the same time, individual Arab workers were still approaching the Histadrut and seeking admission, suggesting that some framework was needed within which such people could be absorbed. There was also an international dimension which helped prevent the Histadrut from abandoning this sphere of activity altogether. The Histadrut and the parties of the labor-Zionist movement in Palestine were active participants in the international trade union and social-democratic movements, and they very much wanted to secure those movements' support for the Zionist cause. Many European leftists, Jews and non-Jews alike, were critical of labor Zionism's refusal to admit Arabs to the Histadrut and its policy of Hebrew labor, as well as its rejection of immediate independence for Palestine. To counter such criticism and bolster labor Zionism's internationalist credentials, it helped to be able to point to ongoing efforts to establish contact, and develop friendly relations, with the Arab working class in Palestine. This led at least some Histadrut leaders to feel that continued activity in this sphere was worthwhile.

Although Histadrut officials were somewhat skeptical about Philip Hassun's capabilities and suspicious of his links with Po'alei Tziyon Smol leaders, it was clear that he was the only candidate available to take this work on. Hassun had repeatedly proven his loyalty to the Histadrut and had sacrificed much on its behalf, including his tailoring business and the financial well-being of his family, and he had considerable experience in this field. In the spring of 1929 the Histadrut secretariat resolved to look seriously for funds, from the Zionist Executive and other sources, with which to clear up Hassun's debts and resume the Histadrut's work among Arabs. This decision was not, however, followed by action, in large part because it came during a period when Histadrut and Yishuv leaders were increasingly preoccupied by rising tensions between Arabs and Jews, rooted in growing Arab popular resentment of perceived Zionist encroachment and fueled by an increasingly politicized dispute over rights of access and worship at the Western Wall/Temple Mount complex (*al-Haram al-Sharif*) in Jerusalem.

In August 1929 these tensions suddenly exploded into a week of countrywide violence on an unprecedented scale: 133 Jews lost their lives at the hands of Arab mobs, 116 Arabs were killed (mostly by British police and soldiers), and many hundreds were wounded. The heavy loss of life and the ferocity of the violence, after years of relative calm, came as a tremendous shock to the Yishuv and the Zionist movement and produced a variety of responses. The violence led Ben-Gurion to reevaluate his attitude toward Palestinian Arab nationalism, which he had hitherto dismissed as a fraud on the part of the effendis. Displaying his characteristic tactical flexibility, Ben-Gurion now began to tell his colleagues that it was a mistake to ignore or downplay the depth and strength of Arab nationalist sentiment in Palestine. Zionism had to come to some agreement with the Arab national movement, indeed with the very effendis he had denounced for much of the previous decade as bloodsucking exploiters with whom the Jewish workers had nothing in common and could never compromise.

This was something of a departure from labor Zionism's traditional denial of the authenticity of Arab nationalist sentiment, though not (as future events would show) an irreversible one. However, this shift also implied abandonment of the notion, advanced by Ben-Gurion and his comrades earlier in the decade, that the Arab working class was the Zionist project's natural (if not only) ally in the Arab community, and hence the loss of a prime ideological and strategic rationale for investing resources in organizing Arab workers under the Histadrut's tutelage. As a result, while the 1930s were to witness the intensification of labor-Zionist efforts to organize Arab workers, these would be motivated by different goals, take place within a different organizational framework, and be informed by a different ethos than had been the case during the previous decade.

3 The Railway Workers of Palestine (I): The Struggle for Arab-Jewish Unity, 1919–1925

A visitor to Israel, or to the West Bank and Gaza, might be forgiven for completely failing to notice the existence of a railway system. Some of the oldest and historically most important lines today operate on a minimal schedule and carry few passengers and little freight, while others no longer function at all. In truth, motorized road transport won its lengthy struggle with the railroad as the preferred means of moving goods and people several decades ago. Despite sporadic discussion in Israel of reviving the existing rail system and even of building new lines, the railways are moribund and seem likely to continue to decline for lack of investment and interest.

Yet the railways of Palestine have a long and memorable history. Proposals to construct a railroad in Palestine, a relatively underdeveloped region of the Ottoman empire but one which was already attracting the special interest of Europeans, were put forward as early as the 1850s. But it was only in 1888 that Yosef Navon (1858–1934), a wealthy Jewish notable from Jerusalem, acquired from the government of Sultan 'Abd al-Hamid a concession to build and operate a railway line between Jaffa, Palestine's largest town and main port, and Jerusalem high up in the hill country. Navon Bey then sold the concession to a new company formed in France to raise the necessary capital and implement the project. The Jaffa-Jerusalem railroad was completed in the summer of 1892, and in the years that followed it helped stimulate the economic growth of Palestine by facilitating the export of citrus and encouraging the tourist trade.[1]

The Ottoman government also developed Palestine's railway system on its own, in connection with the Hijaz Railway. That project, implemented in 1900–1908 with German technical and financial support, was intended to strengthen Ottoman control of the Hijaz and its holy cities and facilitate the annual pilgrimage by linking Damascus with Mecca, but the line reached only as far south as Medina. In 1905 a branch line was completed which linked the Hijaz Railway in southern Syria with Haifa on the Mediterranean, via Dara'a, Samakh (at the southern tip of the Sea of Galilee), Beisan, and 'Afula, and a spur connecting Haifa with Acre to the north was opened in 1913.

The First World War witnessed the rapid extension of Palestine's railway system, largely for military purposes. With German technical assistance and local conscript labor, mainly Arab peasants but also Jewish artisans and others, the Ottomans built narrow-gauge rail lines through the central hill country of Palestine, connecting the Haifa-Samakh line at 'Afula with Jenin, Nablus, and Tulkarm, ultimately reaching the town of Lydda, on the coastal plain southeast of Jaffa. Military railroads also extended on to Gaza and across the Sinai, to facilitate an Ottoman invasion of Egypt. The British forces which conquered Palestine from the Ottomans contributed several lines of their own which were abandoned once their military usefulness had ended, but the British also built a permanent new line along the Mediterranean coast of Sinai and Palestine, running from al-Qantara on the Suez Canal (where it connected with the Egyptian railway system) to Haifa, via Gaza and Lydda. This latter town, which was also on the Jaffa-Jerusalem line, thus became the country's main rail junction.

After the war's end, control of the country's railways—as well as of the Sinai and Hijaz railways—was transferred to the Palestine Railways, Telegraph and Telephone, an agency of the mandatory government of Palestine. The new management shut down many of the little-used lines, but over the years it also upgraded several existing lines to standard gauge and constructed some new ones. Perhaps the most important of these was the extension in 1942 of the al-Qantara–Haifa coastal line northward to Beirut and Tripoli in Lebanon, which Allied forces had just conquered from the forces of Vichy France. By the end of the British mandate period there were 290 miles of railroad in Palestine, which in 1946–47 carried 1.9 million tons of freight and some 900,000 passengers.[2]

Throughout the mandate period, the Palestine Railways was one of the largest employers of wage labor in the country. The size of its workforce fluctuated, but at its wartime height in 1943 there were nearly 7,800 railway workers in Palestine. Most of these were unskilled Arab peasants hired to build and maintain roadbed and track, but a substantial minority—more than 1,200 in 1943—were relatively skilled and permanent industrial workers concentrated in the railway workshops on the northern outskirts of Haifa, while many others worked elsewhere in Palestine operating and maintaining railroad equipment, stations, and depots.[3]

THE EARLY RAILWAY WORKFORCE

We know very little about the railway workers in Palestine before or during the First World War. At least initially, Europeans probably held a substantial number of the more highly-skilled jobs on both the Jaffa-Jerusalem route and on the Hijaz Railway's lines in Palestine, as well as at railroad repair and maintenance facilities. A small number of Jews, whether long-time residents or recent arrivals, were also employed on the railroads of Palestine, especially during the war when railway employment seemed a relatively safe and easy way of performing obligatory military service. But the majority of the permanent workforce certainly consisted of Muslim and Christian Arabs, along with some Turks in supervisory and clerical positions and some members of indigenous but non-Arab minority groups like the Armenians. Not all the Arab railway workers originated from within the territory that would later become Palestine: before the collapse of the Ottoman empire, Palestine was a purely geographic term and there was considerable labor migration across Ottoman provincial and district boundaries. So, for example, the extension of the Hijaz Railway to Haifa in 1905 and the establishment in that town of its operational offices and other installations led to the settlement of some Syrian Muslim railway workers in the Wadi Salib neighborhood of Haifa. As we will see, several of the railway workers who in the mid-1920s would emerge as the founders of the Palestinian Arab trade union movement were Syrian-born veterans of the Hijaz Railway.[4]

Considerably more information is available about the railway workforce in the period immediately after the end of the war, though major gaps remain. In these years the railways were transferred from military to civilian control, and both skilled and unskilled workers were needed to replace the departing soldiers who had helped operate the system during the war. A small number of non-Jewish Europeans were kept on or hired to fill skilled and supervisory positions; not a few of the foremen at the workshops, for example, were Greeks, possibly from the large Greek community settled in Egypt, while senior officials were all British. But the great bulk of the railway workforce, then and through the mandate period, continued to consist of Arabs, mainly from Palestine itself but also from Syria and Egypt, where there were more workers with experience in railroad work. A considerable portion of the railroad's unskilled manual labor was initially performed by Egyptians, large numbers of whom had been conscripted by the British and brought to Palestine for labor service.

A rudimentary mutual aid society seems to have emerged among the Arab railway workers as early as 1920, when a small group in Haifa began collecting funds with which to assist sick workers and the families of deceased workers. By 1923 this seems to have evolved into a somewhat more organized benevolent society for railway workers, formally registered with the government. As we will see, among those most actively involved in this society were a number of skilled workers and foremen who in 1925 would help organize the first purely Arab labor union in Palestine. Until then, however, they seem to have kept largely to themselves, refraining from any kind of overt trade union activity and from seeking any contact with Jewish railway workers. They will therefore not resurface in this narrative until we come to the events of 1925.[5]

From 1919 on, the railway workforce also included a small but growing number of Jews who had recently arrived in Palestine. Some were demobilized soldiers who had served with the British forces, but most were immigrants who came to Palestine as part of the Third Aliya (1918–23). They were initially channeled into railroad jobs by the Zionist Commission, sent to Palestine by the Zionist Organization in April 1918 to help restore the Yishuv, which had been impoverished and partially dispersed by the war, and to prepare the way for the large-scale Jewish immigration which the Balfour Declaration had finally made possible. Jews were also recruited for railroad work through the employment offices run by the two rival labor-Zionist parties, Ahdut Ha'avoda and Hapo'el Hatza'ir. Later these modes of recruitment were supplemented by personal connections, as newly hired Jewish supervisors, foremen, and workers got other Jews taken on.[6]

For the Zionist Commission and the labor-Zionist parties, placing the new immigrants in jobs on the railroads was of course a way of securing their individual livelihoods, since jobs were in short supply. As I discussed in Chapters 1 and 2, however, it was also part of the broader campaign for the conquest of labor and the achievement of Hebrew labor. The creation of a strong cadre of Jewish railway workers was seen as a means of transforming those individuals into proletarians and of demonstrating that in Palestine Jews could successfully perform even the most strenuous kinds of physical labor. But it was also regarded as a way of securing for the Jewish working class a foothold in this important sector of Palestine's economy. It is not surprising, then, that labor-Zionist leaders regarded the main task of the Railway Workers' Association (Agudat Po'alei Harakevet, RWA) established by the Jewish railway workers in 1919 to be the conquest of labor on the railways.[7] The usual purpose of trade unionism, the improvement of workers' wages and working conditions, was not deemed unimportant, but in accordance with the ideology of labor Zionism it was considered to be secondary to broader national interests, a means to an end. By securing higher wages and better conditions for their members, unions would serve to strengthen Hebrew labor and further the goals of the Zionist project in Palestine. As we will see, however, not all the Jewish railway workers would always share this conception.

The first wave of Jewish immigrants channeled into work on the railroad did not last long. Looking back on this period from the vantage point of January 1921, the union leadership commented that the Zionist officials in charge of employment apparently intended mainly to

> provide work for the newly arrived young men, who had been looking in vain for jobs. They wanted to get rid of them, and so they sent them to the railroad. But in truth, this was not the human material needed to accomplish this great conquest of labor, and those who sent them did not take an interest in creating for these young people the conditions which would facilitate their entry into this work. And so from all those who were hired to work on the railroad, a few hundred in number, only a few remained, those who—solely because of their aspiration to win for Jews a place in railroad work—possessed enough patience to endure and suffer through the difficult conditions.[8]

This problem was to plague the labor-Zionist leadership throughout the mandate period. Few Jews were willing to endure for long the low wages, long hours, harsh conditions, and abusive treatment characteristic of railway work in Palestine, and whenever better jobs were available elsewhere they left. The leadership was thus continually confronted with a conflict between the material interests of individual workers and the strategic goal of strengthening Hebrew labor in this vital enterprise. Only by significantly improving wages and working conditions could they hope to keep a significant number of Jews working as railwaymen. But the Jewish workers could only win such improvements by cooperating with the Arab railway workers who constituted the great majority of the railroad workforce. Yet the gains which such cooperation might achieve were likely to strengthen the position of the Arab workers and make the achievement of Hebrew labor even more difficult.

This was a contradiction which labor Zionism never successfully resolved. In an effort to circumvent the problem, the Zionist Executive lobbied the British authorities to dispense with the many Egyptians who were employed by the Palestine Railways and on public works projects and replace them with Jews, or if not with Jews at least with local Arabs. It was hoped that this measure might open up more jobs for Jews; at worst it would mean that Palestinian Arabs would replace the Egyptians, whose wages were extremely low. British government and army officials initially resisted this demand, since replacing Egyptians with Jews or even with Palestinian Arabs would mean substantially higher wage bills, but by 1922 the government of Palestine was committed to phasing out Egyptian labor. This did not, however, open up any significant number of new jobs for Jews, since few Jews were interested in, or capable of, doing the kinds of work the Egyptians had done.[9]

THE ARAB AND JEWISH RAILWAY WORKERS: FIRST CONTACTS

It was from the ranks of those few Jews who remained in railway work for more than a few weeks or months that the organizers of the first Jewish railwaymen's union were drawn. The RWA, whose first congress was held in Jaffa in November–December 1919—a year before the founding congress of the Histadrut—got off to a rocky start. In part this was a result of the instability caused by high turnover in membership as new immigrants entered and then quickly quit the railway workforce, but the fledging organization was also weakened by struggles for control waged by the various parties. In 1919–21 the Socialist Workers' Party, still straddling the boundary between Zionism and Bolshevism, found considerable support among the Jewish railway workers, which led to conflict with Ahdut Ha'avoda. There were also conflicts between the union's central committee, elected by the workers themselves, and the official appointed by the Zionist Commission to supervise the union and get more Jews hired as railway workers, in keeping with the campaign for the conquest of labor in this sector. In its early years the union was financially dependent on the Zionist Commission, which supplemented the wages of Jewish railway workers and gave the union money with which to provide them with such services as workers' kitchens (to compensate for the inadequate nutrition their meager wages allowed them), classes in Hebrew and English (the latter so that they could upgrade their technical skills and qualify for better jobs), and books and magazines.

Even after factional infighting diminished and the union's leadership managed to convince the Zionist Commission to remove the supervisor it had appointed, the organization remained weak. Contact with its branches, especially those in distant stations such as al-Qantara at the far end of the Sinai line, was irregular, and the union's main preoccupation seems to have been directing new immigrants to job opportunities on the railroad. A memorandum setting forth the grievances and demands of the Jewish railwaymen was drawn up and sent to the newly arrived High Commissioner, who headed the mandatory government of Palestine, but there was no response.[10]

Even at this early stage, the question arose of how the Jewish railway workers should relate to their Arab coworkers. On the one hand, it was obvious to labor-Zionist leaders that the Jewish railway workers—a few hundred out of a workforce of several thousand—could not hope, however well organized they may be, to improve their lot without the cooperation of their unorganized Arab fellow workers, and that only by achieving such improvements could the way be opened to strengthening Hebrew labor on the railroad. At the same time, there was considerable anxiety about the possible consequences of organizing Arab workers and the extent to which these might hinder achievement of Zionist goals. As I discussed in Chapter 2, this issue surfaced at one of the very first meetings of the Histadrut's executive committee, on December 30, 1920, only a few weeks after the organization's founding congress. While some Histadrut leaders at the meeting argued that the Jewish workers must help their Arab co-workers organize themselves, they also expressed fears about the potential implications of such assistance for the Zionist project. It was also well understood, even at this early stage, that organizing Arab workers might conflict with the goal of achieving Hebrew labor on the railroad. At the same time, many felt that the Histadrut could not remain uninvolved. In part this was for political reasons: if the Histadrut did not organize the Arab workers, anti-Zionist leftists or Arab nationalists might, with poten-tially dangerous consequences. But it should also be said that many of the labor Zionists took their internationalist and socialist principles seriously and felt a moral obligation to help those they perceived as their less class-conscious and unorganized Arab brothers. This obligation could often take the form of paternalism, and ultimately it cannot be separated from the broader issue of the Zionist project in Palestine and its implications for the country's Arab majority. It would nonetheless be a mistake to lose sight of the subjective moral impulse involved, and of the humanitarian and socialist terms in which many left Zionists understood what they were doing.

In the end, as we have seen, the Histadrut executive committee decided to procrastinate: it instructed its representatives to the Jewish railway workers' union congress to affirm the principle of Arab-Jewish solidarity but avoid any practical decisions pending further clarification of the issue.[11] As a result the thirty or so delegates to the RWA's third congress, representing some 600 Jewish railway workers, devoted little or no attention to the question of relations with their Arab coworkers. Apart from deciding that the RWA would join the new Histadrut as a unit, their discussions focused on how to get more Jews hired and how to improve the lot of those already employed on the railroad. As a result, in the months that followed the Histadrut's interventions with the mandatory government were exclusively on behalf of the Jewish railwaymen. In this period and through much of the 1920s, it was generally Yitzhak Ben-Tzvi who served as the Histadrut official with primary responsibility for overseeing the railway workers and representing them in contacts with Palestine Railways management and government officials. His mediation was necessary because both railway and government officials refused to grant the RWA official recognition or deal directly with it as the workers' bargaining agent.[12]

However, the question of relations with Arab workers soon surfaced again, and this time as a much more pressing issue. In the summer of 1921 Arab railway workers in Haifa, to which the main maintenance and repair workshops of the Palestine Railways were gradually being transferred from Lydda, along with many Jewish and Arab skilled workers, began approaching their unionized Jewish coworkers about the possibility of cooperation. That the Haifa workshops were the scene of these initial contacts was no coincidence. At the time these shops constituted the largest single concentration of industrial wage labor in Palestine, employing side by side hundreds of Arab, Jewish, and other workers, skilled, semiskilled, and unskilled. In this hothouse atmosphere numerous ideas, political tendencies, and organizations contended for the workers' allegiance.

Bulus Farah, who came to work in the Haifa railway workshops in 1925 as a fifteen-year-old apprentice and would later become a leader of the communist and labor movements in Palestine, has provided a vivid description of this unique environment:

> The railway workshops were a mixture of every nationality, but the Arab and Jewish workers were the overwhelming majority. A kind of mutual understanding prevailed among them, despite the differences in language, customs, traditions, and level of civilization. The majority of the Jewish workers had come from eastern Europe, mostly from Poland, and they would try to learn Arabic from their colleagues the Arab workers. The common

language among them was Arabic. There was also a scattering of European workers, some of whom had participated in labor or socialist movements. And while Zionism interfered directly in the affairs of the Jewish workers, through its agents, there also came a response to this interference from leftist elements among the Jewish workers, regardless of whether these leftists were Bolsheviks or social-democrats who inclined toward the Second International. I would notice that violent arguments and discussions would go on between the left generally and the partisans of the Histadrut, who supported the Second International. These arguments did not take place in a vacuum, they were not about this or that abstract theory; for the Jewish right and left the key question was their attitude toward the Zionist movement, British imperialism, the Arab national movement, the communist revolution in Soviet Russia, the revolutionary line on the workers, socialism, imperialism. . . . The Jewish workers regarded their Arab coworkers with considerable respect, for they understood that the Arab workers possessed a great deal of professional skill, even if they were not on the level of the Jewish workers in terms of culture.[13]

Farah's portrait of relations between Arabs and Jews in the Haifa workshops is too rosy, but it does seem that a unique atmosphere prevailed in this workplace. That atmosphere helped make possible a matrix of interactions between Arab and Jewish workers that existed nowhere else in Palestine. Just as important, however, was the emergence in the 1920s of a new stratum of relatively skilled and educated Arab workers receptive to trade unionism. Some of them were no doubt influenced by the activities of the Jewish union and conversations with Jewish unionists. But others may have gained awareness of labor organization in their countries of origin (e.g., those from Syria or Egypt) or through contacts with non-Jewish European railway workers, mainly Greeks and Italians, who had their own mutual aid societies.

In the summer and autumn of 1921 a series of meetings was held at the homes of Arab railway workers at which the Arabs expressed to Jewish union leaders their interest in participating in a joint union of all railway workers in Palestine, and even in joining the Histadrut, which offered its members a variety of services such as health care, loan funds, and consumer cooperatives. These initiatives induced considerable anxiety and confusion among the leaders of the RWA, who at first sought to dampen Arab interest by avoiding their questions and exaggerating the burdens of union membership. When the Arabs persisted and pressed for an unequivocal response, the RWA again turned to the Histadrut for guidance.[14] As I discussed in Chapter 2, the issue of relations between Arab and Jewish workers in mixed workplaces, usually referred to as the problem of "joint organization" (*irgun meshutaf*), thus forced its way onto the agenda of the Histadrut leadership late in 1921 and became the subject of controversy and debate among the labor-Zionist parties. In January 1922, spurred on by the need to provide guidance for the railway workers, the Histadrut council endorsed Ben-Gurion's proposal that among the railway workers joint organization would entail "organization of the workers on the basis of national sections" and "preservation of the Jewish Railway Workers' Association as part of the Histadrut."[15] Any Arab railway workers who joined the RWA would thus be consigned to a separate section, while the Jewish workers and their organization would remain tightly linked to the Histadrut.

This conception of joint organization came under fire from left forces in the Histadrut and among the Jewish railway workers, countrywide but especially among those employed at the Haifa workshops, where both Po'alei Tziyon Smol and the communists had substantial support. In part this was due to the composition of the railway workforce, and particularly the workshop workers. Most Jewish railway workers were recent arrivals in Palestine, without deep roots in the country or strong links with the institutions of the labor-Zionist movement. At the same time, many had been profoundly affected by the revolutionary upheavals in the Europe they had just left. Impoverished and exploited but also highly politicized, many of them came to feel that they had little hope of improving conditions except through joint struggle with their Arab coworkers. The emphasis which Po'alei Tziyon Smol and communist activists and propagandists placed on class struggle and on internationalism, on unifying and mobilizing Jewish and Arab railway workers to fight for higher wages and better conditions, had considerable appeal for them. In contrast, the Histadrut leadership's constant exhortations to self-sacrifice and its insistence that the class struggle must be subordinated to the "national" tasks of immigration and settlement soon wore thin. Leftist activists accused the Histadrut of downplaying or even suppressing workers' struggles in order to accommodate the bourgeois leadership of the Zionist movement, and its preference for building up a separate labor economy—a policy leftists derided as "the socialism of poverty"—could seem misguided, even delusional, in light of the acute deprivation experienced by significant sections of the urban industrial working class in a period of low wages, widespread unemployment, and even hunger.

The circumstances of the Jewish railway workers (and again, particularly the workshop workers) also differed significantly from those of most other Histadrut members. The Histadrut included not only urban wage workers but also numerous people who, although officially classified as workers, were in fact self-employed, whether individually or collectively. These included members of kibbutzim and moshavim, members of the Gdud Ha'avoda ("Labor Brigade") who contracted themselves out collectively on public works projects, members of producers' and consumers' cooperatives, and so forth. The nonworking spouses of Histadrut members could also join and vote in elections. The railway workers were by contrast proletarians in the classic sense, urban wage workers, while the workshop workers in particular lived and worked in a large, ethnically mixed seaport city which was on its way to becoming Palestine's major industrial center. While other Histadrut members might be in conflict with their relatively small-scale Jewish employers, or might be suffering because of general economic conditions, for the railwaymen it was clearly the colonial state—the mandatory government and its agency, the Palestine Railways—which was responsible for what they experienced as starvation wages and subhuman working conditions. They therefore tended to be much more receptive to the militant message of political forces to the left of Ahdut Ha'avoda than was the bulk of the Histadrut's membership.

The railway workers also developed a strong tradition of independence. Many of them, including even some who agreed politically with Ahdut Ha'avoda, resented what they perceived as the domineering behavior and centralizing policies of the Histadrut leadership. Much of the latter consisted of veterans of the prewar Second Aliya who, though only in their mid-thirties, could now seem quite old and distant from the ethos of the younger and more radical new arrivals who made up most of the Jewish component of the railroad workforce. In the face of the Histadrut's efforts to establish its control over the trade unions, the railwaymen insisted on their organization's autonomy. At the same time, the railway workers had relatively weak ties with the rest of the Zionist labor movement. To the annoyance of the Histadrut leadership, many of them were remiss about paying their Histadrut dues, and the RWA had its own separate strike and mutual aid funds. By 1922–23 officials of the Ahdut Ha'avoda–controlled Haifa Workers' Council, the local organ of the Histadrut, had come to regard the Haifa branch of the union as a hotbed of opposition because it acted largely on its own and seemed to provide fertile ground for radicalism. However, it should also be noted that the railway workers' union was in fact dependent on the financial support of the Histadrut, which paid the salary of its full-time secretary and kept a close watch on its affairs. This enabled the Histadrut leadership to apply pressure on the union and ultimately rein it in.[16]

WORKER MILITANCY AND ARAB-JEWISH RELATIONS

The growing strength of the left among the Jewish railway workers ensured that there would be extensive debate on the question of joint organization when the RWA's fourth congress convened in Haifa in February 1922, a month or so after the Histadrut council had endorsed the policy of national sections. All the delegates agreed on the urgent necessity of joint organization with the Arab workers, which increasingly looked like the only solution to the problems faced by the Jewish railwaymen, but a substantial minority rejected the Histadrut's directives on the form it should take. The congress, dominated by supporters of Ahdut Ha'avoda and Hapo'el Hatza'ir, ultimately endorsed the Histadrut's decision to establish national sections, with the Jewish section to remain part of the Histadrut, but it added a proviso that until there were enough Arab members to create a separate Arab section the RWA would accept Arabs as full members. This already marked a departure from Histadrut policy and signaled the growing influence of the left.[17]

In the months that followed, some Arab workers in Haifa began to work closely with the union, renamed the Union of Railway, Postal and Telegraph Workers (URPTW) to reflect its broader membership, although none of them actually joined as full dues-paying members. In addition to the union's own efforts to reach out to Arab workers—in which Po'alei Tziyon Smol members in Haifa took the initiative—the impetus for growing Arab involvement seems to have been the wave of layoffs which swept the railroad in 1922 and exacerbated the resentment of workers already suffering from poor wages and working conditions. These layoffs, part of a government-wide effort to reduce expenditures by shrinking its workforce, hit the railway workers particularly hard, in part because the great majority of railway employees were officially classified as daily paid staff and therefore enjoyed no security of employment or right to compensation for dismissal. This was also a period of high unemployment, which meant that the laid-off workers had poor prospects for finding other jobs.

For the first time, the union and the Histadrut tried to intervene with management and the government on behalf of the Arab as well as the Jewish workers who had lost their jobs. Although only some of the dismissed workers were ultimately rehired, the union's efforts on their behalf enhanced its standing among Arab workers. The union also complained about harassment and persecution of workers by supervisory personnel, some of them Jewish.[18] By the autumn of 1922 there was widespread support among both Jewish and Arab workers for strike action to resist the layoffs and harassment, but the Histadrut executive committee, with which the union leadership consulted closely and to whose decisions it deferred, rejected the idea. In part this was because Ben-Tzvi and his colleagues were not convinced that the Arab workers would actually join a strike, but larger political considerations were also involved. "Let us suppose," Ben-Tzvi told a meeting of the Histadrut executive committee,

> that they succeed, that a miracle occurs and not a single Arab accepts a bribe to betray the workers, that they all strike. Let us say that we succeed in everything—then what will we demand? That Moshlin [a Jewish railway official for whose transfer to Palestine the Histadrut had fought but who was now disliked by the workers] be fired! And in his place will come an Arab or an Englishman. A few days ago the [Jewish] linemen demanded the hiring of a Jewish official, and now they will strike to demand the firing of a Jewish official? All the decisions about a strike are worthless, they cannot be considered. From every standpoint the thing is a total loss.

Ben-Tzvi told the union leaders, who were convinced that there was strong support for a strike and that they could paralyze the railways, to calm the workers down.[19]

Nonetheless, 1923 witnessed the beginning of a new phase of organizational and political activity among the railwaymen. Unrest grew as management intensified its drive to cut costs. Workers (especially union activists) were fired without notice or severance pay, the maximum allowable workday was increased to sixteen hours, the workers' old employment contracts were canceled and no new ones were issued, the right of workers to choose their weekly day of rest in accordance with their religion was revoked, and foremen and managers continued to fine, abuse, and harass workers under their control. Management ignored repeated requests by the union to discuss these and other long-standing grievances, insisting that it did not recognize the union as bargaining agent for the workers. When in January 1923 a group of dismissed Arab and Jewish workers formally authorized two Jews, presumably URPTW leaders, to appeal to management for severance pay, the General Manager of the Palestine Railways, R. B. W. Holmes, responded with sarcasm:

> As far as I know no offer was made to you by this Railway to induce you to leave your homes in Europe and seek employment in Palestine. . . .
> As presumably the workers you represent came to Palestine as emigrants [sic] under the aegis of the Zionist Commission presumably that body will look after you until such time as fresh employment can be found for you and you are, therefore, in a better position than your brother workers whose habitation has always been Palestine and who have no Society to

look after their welfare. It is regretted that it is quite impossible to consider the payment of gratuities [severance pay] to daily paid staff who
have only served the Railway for a short period.[20]

This dismissive letter, quite typical of management's attitude toward
its employees, only served to heighten their anger, which was manifested
at large meetings of railway workers organized by the union in various
parts of the country. As the months passed and the URPTW came to be
seen to be the only force trying to resist management, increasing numbers
of Arab workers participated in protest meetings sponsored by the Jewish-
led union and signed its petitions, while a few Arabs began working
closely with the union.[21] The union now wished to initiate more vigorous
and systematic efforts to develop relations with Arab workers. Very few
Jewish railway workers knew any Arabic, however, so the union turned
to the Histadrut for help in finding someone with the requisite linguistic
skills who could help it make contact with, and ultimately recruit, some
of the more educated and politically conscious Arab railwaymen. As I discussed in Chapter 2, the union finally secured the assistance of Avraham
Khalfon, a young Jew from a family long established in Palestine who had
grown up in Haifa, had extensive contacts with Arabs in this mixed city,
and now began to devote several hours a week to the union's drive to
recruit Arab workers.

As a way of establishing relations, Jewish railway workers would invite
Arab coworkers to the union club, where Khalfon could meet them and
talk to them about the union. These informal discussions might continue
at a local Arab coffeehouse. One of the first Arabs with whom contact was
made in this way was Ibrahim al-Asmar, a foreman in the freight car
("wagonage") department. Al-Asmar eventually brought along another
foreman, 'Ali al-Batal, a boilermaker by trade. The willingness of these
men to associate with Jewish unionists and to advocate unionism themselves, despite reprimands and threats by management, signaled to the
rank and file Arab workers that involvement with the union was relatively
safe, and gradually significant numbers began to frequent the club. There
the union began to offer lectures on trade unionism and talks by representatives of the various socialist-Zionist parties, translated into Arabic, as
well as language lessons in Hebrew and Arabic so that the workers could
communicate more easily. The union also sponsored social events to bring
the workers together and cultural programs that appealed to the tastes of
the Arab workers.[22]

The increasing involvement of Arab workers in the union and the upsurge of militancy among the railway workers in general, as well as wide-

spread disappointment with the Histadrut, greatly strengthened the forces to the left of Ahdut Ha'avoda—the communists and Po'alei Tziyon Smol—though the latter was still more of a loose-knit political tendency than a unified and disciplined party. As the left gained ground among the Jewish railway workers and as even some Ahdut Ha'avoda partisans among the railwaymen began to follow the left's lead, the Histadrut leadership grew increasingly nervous. In June 1923 Ben-Tzvi relayed rumors that the communists were trying to convince the railway workers to pull their union out of the Histadrut, and there were reports that the Arabs who were considering joining the union were also expressing opposition to affiliation with the Histadrut. In July Ben-Tzvi and Ben-Gurion intervened personally to delete a strike threat contained in the Arabic version of a letter of protest drawn up by railway workers in the Jaffa-Lydda area.[23] The Histadrut leadership's concern about losing control of the railway workers' union was magnified by its perception that, despite its overwhelming majority at the recent Histadrut congress, it was facing a growing threat on its left flank. For the growing strength of the left opposition among the railway workers was very much part of a general increase in support for the left among Jewish urban workers. Both the communists and left-wing Zionists were gaining ground in several of the large urban trade unions, and by organizing around the issue of unemployment, particularly acute as the Yishuv felt the effects of the economic crisis most strongly in 1923–24, they attracted support among the numerous new immigrants who earned starvation wages or could not find jobs.[24]

The confrontation between the various forces contending for the allegiance of the railway workers came to a head at the URPTW's fifth congress, held in Haifa in September 1923. The outgoing central committee was at the end of its tether, at a loss to find some way to reverse the deterioration in the situation of the Jewish railway workers and their union, and it called on the congress to resolve basic questions of organization, revitalize the union, and set strategy for the future. Twenty-one Jewish delegates represented 200–250 unionized Jewish railway workers at the congress. Of these, about 130 worked in Haifa, about 50 in Jerusalem, and the rest in Jaffa and Lydda, at smaller stations or as itinerant linemen. The total railway workforce at this time was about 2,000. The sharp drop in the number of Jewish railwaymen since 1920–21 probably strengthened the left forces in the union, because it reinforced their argument that the only way out of the desperate situation the Jewish railwaymen found themselves in was Jewish-Arab solidarity. For the first time, two Arabs—Ibrahim al-Asmar and 'Ali al-Batal—also attended the congress, as observers. Although only five Arabs had actually joined the Haifa branch of the union, these two delegates represented a much larger number of Arab workers in Haifa who were now in close contact with the union. Several top leaders of the Histadrut and of the various parties active in the Jewish labor movement, among them Ben-Tzvi, attended and participated in the debates, a reflection of the importance they attached to this union, its political orientation, and its relations with Arab workers.

The congress focused on the union's relations with the Arab railway workers and with the Histadrut. Left-wing delegates criticized the Histadrut's policy of national sections as unfeasible and a barrier to the successful organization of Arab workers. A demand by the communists to rescind the decision of the fourth congress on national sections was tabled, however, and the congress ultimately adopted a resolution calling for intensified organizational work among the Arabs without specifying the exact form it should take. The resolution was a partial victory for the left, given that it was passed in the face of appeals by Ben-Tzvi and others that the union move cautiously on this question and abide by Histadrut guidelines. On the question of relations with the Histadrut, there was much criticism of that organization's alleged failure to support the union, and especially its efforts to develop relations with Arabs. Some delegates argued that Arab workers were reluctant to join the union because it belonged to the explicitly Zionist Histadrut. But the communists' demand for withdrawal from the Histadrut won little support. Even delegates sympathetic to Po'alei Tziyon Smol were aware that their union was heavily dependent on the financial resources of the Histadrut and its access to the British authorities, and in any case they still hoped to reform the Histadrut from within. The congress ultimately adopted a Po'alei Tziyon Smol resolution that reaffirmed the union's affiliation to the Histadrut as an autonomous unit, but called on the next Histadrut congress to restructure it so as to separate its cooperative from its trade union functions and establish the latter on an "international" (i.e., Jewish-Arab) basis. If the Histadrut did not implement this separation of functions the railway workers would hold a referendum to decide on disaffiliation.[25]

All told, the results of the fifth congress amounted to a victory for the left forces in the union over Ahdut Ha'avoda. The line of Po'alei Tziyon Smol, with its emphasis on militant trade unionism, class struggle, and Jewish-Arab solidarity, was now setting the tone. This was manifested in the union's new bylaws, which made no mention of national sections but did declare that the union was "based on class struggle." But Ahdut Ha-

ʿavoda was by no means powerless. The party still had many supporters among the Jewish railwaymen, some of whom also secretly served in the Hagana ("Defense"), the clandestine Jewish military organization controlled by the Histadrut (and therefore largely by Ahdut Haʿavoda). Moreover, if the Haifa branch was a hotbed of radicalism, the Jaffa-Lydda branch tended to align itself more closely with the Histadrut leadership. The railway union was, despite its self-image as the vanguard of the radical Jewish proletariat in Palestine, still a weak organization, unrecognized by management and subject to the authority of the Histadrut executive committee, which also held the purse strings. In addition to appointing and paying the union's full-time secretary, Histadrut funding also made it possible for the union to publish its irregular journals in Hebrew and Arabic.[26] Nonetheless, in the year that followed the fifth congress, the left forces within the union would assume effective leadership, especially in Haifa, and seek salvation in joint organization.

STRUGGLING FOR UNITY

In the aftermath of the fifth congress the number of Arab workers who seemed ready to join the union rose sharply. A core group of Arab trade unionists with a substantial following were now prepared to discuss joint organization quite seriously, and for the first time the prospect of a joint Arab-Jewish union loomed large. The first manifestation of this new reality, and of the contradictions it raised for those who wanted the union to be both a model of proletarian internationalism and an integral component of the Zionist movement, surfaced at the meeting of the union's council held in March 1924. Both Ben-Gurion and Ben-Tzvi were present as representatives of the Histadrut, again indicating the crucial importance the leadership attached to this union.

Six representatives of the Arab railway workers attended the council meeting, not (as at the fifth congress) as silent observers but as active participants determined to make themselves heard. One of them, Ilyas Asad, put their perspective forward bluntly in his address to the council:

> I am striving to establish ties between the Jewish and Arab workers because I am certain that if we are connected we will help one another, without regard to religion or nationality. Many Arab workers do not want to join nationalist organizations because they understand their purpose and do not wish to abet a lie. They saw on the membership card [of the URPTW] the words "Federation of Jewish Workers" [i.e., the Histadrut] and they cannot understand what purpose this serves. I ask all the com-

rades to remove the word "Jewish," and I am sure that if they agree there will be a strong bond between us and all the Arabs will join. I would be the first who would not want to join a nationalist labor organization. There are many Arab nationalist organizations, and we do not want to join them, and they will say we have joined a Jewish nationalist organization. . . . The thousands of workers who established the Histadrut have done nothing of benefit for the workers, and the reason is that inscribed on their membership cards is the word "Jewish," and this leads to division and jealousy. If they take out this word we will unite and work together.[27]

The other Arab delegates echoed Asad's demand that the railway union sever its ties with the Zionist Histadrut and become fully independent and international. Their perspective was thus close to that of the communists, whose activists within the railway workforce had for months been working to develop their own links with Arab workers and had been warning them about the problematic character of the union's link with the Histadrut. But it was also not too distant from that of Po'alei Tziyon Smol, which was demanding that the Histadrut at least divest itself of its Zionist functions.

Many of the Jewish delegates were not unsympathetic to the Arabs' concerns: five months earlier they had threatened to disaffiliate from the Histadrut if it did not radically restructure itself, and they understood that the Arabs regarded any hint of Zionism as an insurmountable barrier to their joining the union. An alarmed and angry Ben-Gurion responded to the arguments of the Arabs and the Jewish leftists with a forthright defense of the Ahdut Ha'avoda perspective.

Unity between workers of different nations can exist only on the basis of freedom and national equality. For the workers there are matters of common interest where there is no difference between Jew or Arab, Englishman or Frenchman; these are the things that concern work: hours, wages, relations with the employer, protection against accidents, the right of workers to organize, and so forth. In all these areas we work together. And there are interests which are specific to the workers of each nationality, specific but not contradictory interests which concern his national needs: his culture, his language, the freedom of his people, etc. In all these spheres there must be complete autonomy and equality for the workers of each nation.

Comrade Ilyas said correctly that the Arab workers do not want to join nationalist organizations whose purpose would be false to the workers' interests. And we are not asking the Arab workers to join a Jewish nationalist organization, but rather to be *connected* to the Histadrut. We do not want the Arab worker to alienate himself from his people and his language. . . .

He went on to argue that deprived of the support of the Histadrut, the URPTW would be weak and without influence.[28]

The delegates were in the end unwilling to accede immediately to the demand for disaffiliation, and the resolutions they adopted reflected the contradictions in the union's position. On the one hand, the council asked the Histadrut to set up a consumers' cooperative and a loan fund for the railway workers, to fund a paid staff of organizers fluent in Hebrew, Arabic, and English, to subsidize its publications, and to find jobs for workers who had been laid off. On the other hand it demanded that the Histadrut executive convene a meeting at which its trade unions would establish a separate confederation—a variant of the Po'alei Tziyon Smol demand for the separation of functions. The council also established a special committee, consisting of members of the central committee and the Arab workers' leaders, to negotiate an agreement on joint organization.[29] From the perspective of the Histadrut leadership, the situation in the railway workers' union seemed to be going from bad to worse. After the March 1924 council meeting the secretary of the Haifa Workers' Council, concerned over the growing strength of leftist forces in the URPTW and the union's apparent determination to admit Arab members, warned headquarters in Tel Aviv that "it will likely be necessary to split the railway workers' union."[30]

By the spring of 1924 as many as forty Arab workers had formally joined the union's Jaffa-Lydda branch, and the long-dormant branch in al-Qantara, which consisted mostly of Egyptian workers, had been revived. Many Arab and Jewish railway workers participated in the traditional May Day work stoppage, despite management's threat to dock their pay. But in Haifa the crucial negotiations between Jewish unionists and the leaders of the Arab workers—better educated and more politically conscious than elsewhere—dragged on inconclusively. In a letter to their Jewish coworkers, the Arabs insisted that they could not join a union "whose purpose is not just that of labor but also has other purposes which for you are more important than the interests of the railway, postal and telegraph workers." They instead proposed the formation of a new union which would be "unconnected with any federation or other organization and whose activities, opinions, and ideas would be free from any outside influence." The URPTW leadership rejected this proposal, and the union secretary appointed by the Histadrut (an Ahdut Ha'avoda loyalist) privately argued that the union should stop trying to reach an agreement with the activist foremen with whom they were negotiating and instead bypass them by seeking to recruit Arab members directly. This approach, which as we will see the union would often adopt in later years, reflected Ahdut Ha'avoda's hostility to any form of joint organization that might involve a retreat from its conception of Zionist principles.[31]

With talks between the union and the Arab representatives at a standstill, the Jewish communists within the union apparently decided to step up pressure on the URPTW leadership to accept the Arabs' demand that the union be non-Zionist, independent, and international. Communist activists charged that by giving priority to their commitment to Zionism, the Histadrut and the union leadership were destroying any hope of Arab-Jewish class solidarity. Union leaders greatly resented these attacks, which they regarded as provocative and destructive of the union's cohesiveness, but they resisted pressure from the Histadrut leadership to purge the union of communists. Such a step would have brought the railway workers' union into line with what was going on almost everywhere else in the Histadrut, for in April 1924 the Histadrut had declared the communists to be enemies of the Jewish people and of the Jewish working class in Palestine and launched a vigorous and systematic campaign to expel them from the Histadrut, its trade unions, and the local workers' councils, and destroy their influence.[32]

In part, the anticommunist purge was triggered by the Histadrut leadership's fear that the communists would find increasing support among hungry and desperate new immigrants as the economic crisis persisted, undermining the Zionist project when it was at its most vulnerable. The expulsion of the communists was also legitimized by the increasingly explicit and vocal anti-Zionist stance adopted by the Palestine Communist Party, which had been formally accepted as the Palestinian section of the Communist International in February 1924. The communists in Palestine, still virtually all Jews, were by this point openly calling for an end to Jewish immigration to Palestine and exhorting the Jewish workers to break with Zionism and seek a revolutionary alliance with the Arab workers and peasants. As I mentioned in Chapter 2, the PCP would that autumn play a key role in supporting and publicizing the resistance of Arab peasants near 'Afula, in the Jezreel Valley, to dispossession by the Zionist land-purchase agency which had acquired their land from absentee Arab landlords. The PCP's stance was prompted in part by a vigorous anti-Zionist campaign launched that same year by the Soviet government and communist party, a campaign which culminated in the arrest of large numbers of socialist-Zionist activists and the suppression of their organizations, which had hitherto been tolerated. Both the Soviet campaign of vilification and repression and the PCP's total break with Zionism aided the Histadrut leadership's efforts to delegitimize the communists in Palestine, who found themselves increasingly isolated and reviled in the Yishuv.[33]

The Histadrut leadership's campaign to purge the communists became entangled with the URPTW's effort to achieve unity with Arab workers. In May 1924, a month after the anticommunist campaign began, communist activists in the railway workers' union invited some of the Arab workers' leaders with whom the union had been negotiating to a meeting at the PCP branch in Haifa and declared that they accepted the Arabs' proposals for unity. The union's leadership would later claim that the communists had deliberately sought to give their Arab interlocutors the impression that they were speaking for the entire union. The truth of that allegation seems doubtful, since it is unlikely that the Arabs, who had been negotiating with union leaders for months, could have been so easily misled about whom they were dealing with. But it is true that Moshe Ungerfeld, a communist who served on both the union's central committee and the special committee on joint organization, was at the meeting in question, which may have imparted to it something of an official tone. Whatever the truth of the matter, the union's leadership was outraged by this apparent breach of discipline and usurpation of its authority. For organizing this unauthorized meeting with the Arab workers, seven Jewish communist railwaymen were quickly brought before a union court and expelled from the union for one year.[34]

Nonetheless, the URPTW leadership, as always anxious to defend their union's autonomy, still steadfastly refused to take part in the Histadrut's purge of communists. However bitter their ideological conflicts with the communists and however angry they were at what they regarded as their provocations, Po'alei Tziyon Smol leaders and activists, and many unaffiliated left-wing Zionists among the railway workers, were against wholesale expulsions without due process.[35] Even after the expulsion of the seven communists charged with breach of discipline, the union continued to reject the right of the Haifa Workers' Council to expel from the Histadrut two communist activists who represented the URPTW, especially as one of them was also a member of the union's central committee. URPTW leaders persisted in this attitude despite heavy pressure from the Histadrut, protesting to Ben-Gurion and Ben-Tzvi that "We do not expel members for their opinions, we are a trade union and have members who belong to various parties. . . . We will not allow our autonomy to be reduced to nothing."[36]

Though they refused to submit to what they saw as the Histadrut leadership's dictates, many URPTW leaders in fact blamed the failure of negotiations with the Arabs on the Jewish communists, who (they were convinced) had poisoned the Arabs' minds against the union and the Histadrut and incited them to demand complete disaffiliation as the price of joining. Moshe Ungerfeld, a communist leader and URPTW central committee member, rejected this charge, as well as widespread pessimism among Jews concerning the prospects for organizing Arab workers.

> The situation is not as bad as it has been described here, and it is not the [communist] Fraktziyya that is responsible for the present situation; the Fraktziyya is more interested than others in having Arabs join the union. It was not we who told them about the Jewish Histadrut, they themselves saw what was written on the membership cards they received, and then the question of whether they could be members of a Jewish organization arose among the very first recipients. . . . There is a sickness among you and you do not know how to cure it, so you look for others to blame.[37]

A tendency to blame "outside agitators" was indeed characteristic of much labor-Zionist thinking about Arabs, serving as a convenient mechanism by which to avoid confronting real contradictions in thought and practice. The Hebrew terms often used in this regard were *mesitim* ("inciters") and *hasata* ("incitement"). Arabs were often perceived as passive subjects susceptible both to incitement and manipulation by unscrupulous outsiders (communists, Arab "effendis," clerics, etc.) and to enlightenment by labor Zionists who wanted to bring their less advanced Arab brothers class consciousness and authentic proletarian culture. (As one Jewish railway union leader put it, "We opened up the Arabs' minds" by explaining to them the virtues of cooperation, unity, and the class struggle.)[38] This conception rendered it difficult to think of Arabs as rational, thinking human beings who were capable, for example, of grasping on their own the problems involved in joining a union which belonged to the explicitly Zionist Histadrut and which was committed to strengthening Hebrew labor on the railroad. Ironically, the very meeting of the union's central committee which heard the communist activist Moshe Ungerfeld denounce the tendency to blame Arab opposition on "inciters" went on, with a complete lack of self-consciousness, to call on the Histadrut to use its influence and connections to get more Jewish workers hired.

There was also an important cultural dimension to the left-Zionist perceptions of Arabs. Very few Jews in Palestine, including even those like the railway workers who were in daily contact with Arabs, took the trouble to learn Arabic, familiarize themselves with the ways of Palestine's indigenous majority, or develop personal relationships with Arabs. Yehezkel Abramov, an Ahdut Ha'avoda loyalist who started work at the Palestine Railways in 1921 and served as the union's secretary for many years, complained that he was unable even to teach the Jewish workers to refer to Arabs by their proper names. Instead, in both private conversations and public meetings, individuals were routinely referred to, in the Yiddish which many of these recently arrived Jews still knew best, simply as "der Araber." Despite Abramov's admonitions to "go sit with the *goyim*" at lunch breaks, his Jewish coworkers usually kept to themselves.[39] These attitudes, rooted in a perception of Arabs as not only irredeemably alien but also backward and culturally, intellectually, and morally less advanced than these European Jewish immigrants, further reduced the likelihood that even those Zionists who in principle favored equality and brotherhood would be able in practice to treat their Arab coworkers with respect, confront differences openly, and eschew manipulation and dissembling.

The Histadrut leadership eventually got its way on the purge of communists. When communist activists organized a meeting of railway workers to protest the expulsion of the seven communist members, the central committee voted to suspend its one communist member.[40] This marked the end of effective communist influence in the union's leadership. However, PCP members and sympathizers continued to be active among the rank and file railway workers, agitating and propagandizing against the union leadership and the Histadrut. As relations between the communists and the labor-Zionist movement worsened, the mutual recriminations grew more virulent and sometimes degenerated into violence. Open activity by communists now carried the risk of expulsion from the union and even dismissal from their jobs, and the communists grew weaker and more isolated among the Jewish workers. This reality, and the desire to transform their organization into a binational party, stimulated the communists to redouble their efforts to develop contacts and win support among the Arab workers on the basis of their opposition to Zionism and their championing of the Arab national cause, though with little immediate success.

ARAB-JEWISH UNITY AND THE QUESTION OF ZIONISM

The removal of the communists from leadership positions in the railway union did not signal the eclipse of the left. On the contrary: in the second half of 1924, with the internal turmoil produced by the struggles with the communists largely over, the influence of Po'alei Tziyon Smol increased and the union leadership devoted more attention and energy to joint organization than ever before. At its June 1924 meeting, the union's central committee decided to dissolve the ineffective special committee on joint organization which had been formed a few months earlier and take upon itself the task of organizing Arab workers. The union's leaders now gave this project serious and sustained attention: leaflets and other propaganda material were issued in Arabic, members of the central committee visited the branches to address meetings on the question, and Jewish workers were encouraged to extend and develop their contacts with their Arab colleagues, through personal conversations as well as public assemblies. All the branches established their own committees for joint organization which took responsibility for planning and implementing systematic efforts to recruit Arab workers.

What actually seems to have opened the way to unity, however, was the leadership's abandonment of the idea of restricting Arabs to a separate national section, as Ahdut Ha'avoda and the Histadrut had long insisted, and its acceptance of the Arab demand that the union be purely unitary and territorial in structure. The Po'alei Tziyon Smol activists who now set the tone for the union had long advocated these positions, and so negotiations between Arabs and Jews, stalled for many months, could now move forward.[41] We have no evidence of an explicit written agreement between the Arab workers' leaders and the Jewish officials of the railway union. It is likely, though, that the two sides came to an understanding that the union would be formally declared international and that Arabs would be incorporated into its leadership on the basis of parity. The Arabs probably also secured assurances that the joint union would be non-Zionist, although subsequent events suggest that the Arabs and Jews had different understandings of what this meant. In light of those events, it also seems likely that the Arabs who joined considered their adherence to the railway workers' union to be conditional on the union's implementation of the decision of the fifth congress regarding relations with the Histadrut. That is, the union would demand the transformation of the Histadrut into a non-Zionist trade union federation based on mixed Arab-Jewish unions, and if that struggle proved unsuccessful it would secede from the Histadrut.

Some Arab railway workers' leaders opposed unity on this basis, instead insisting on acceptance of the proposals put forward in the spring for an entirely new and independent union. But they seem to have become inactive after the expulsion of the communists, leaving the field to those still willing to seek common ground with the Jews and join the union before the question of its relationship with the Histadrut was definitively resolved. Those Arab workers and foremen who had for several years devoted themselves to the mutual aid society for Arab railway workers mentioned earlier in this chapter simply continued to refrain from any association with Jews, though it is unlikely that they welcomed the apparent realization of Arab-Jewish unity.

On the basis of this tacit understanding between the Arab and Jewish unionists, an unprecedented influx of Arab workers into the union took place: by the end of November 1924 several hundred Arabs had joined the URPTW. The available figures are not entirely reliable, but it seems that at the end of 1924 the union comprised some 529 Jewish and Arab railway workers, out of a workforce of almost 2,400. Almost all the Jews employed on the railroad belonged to the union, but only 10 to 15 percent of the Arab employees. In the Jaffa-Lydda and Jerusalem branches, membership was more or less evenly divided between Arabs and Jews; in al-Qantara, nearly all the members were Egyptians; and in Haifa Jews outnumbered Arabs two to one. Whatever the precise numbers, a union which had since its inception been virtually all Jewish had now become roughly half Jewish and half Arab.[42]

In October 1924 the union leadership, still at this point entirely Jewish, began to fulfill another part of its bargain with its new Arab comrades: as I mentioned in Chapter 2, it launched a campaign to restructure the Histadrut. In a circular to all the branches, the central committee announced that the URPTW would lead a struggle to separate the Histadrut's Zionist settlement and cooperative functions from its trade union functions, establish the latter on a purely territorial basis, and make joint organization a key priority.

> Considering the present structure of the Histadrut, there is no possibility of the Arab worker organizing himself in an organization of "Hebrew workers" until the necessary changes have been made in it. . . . Even today a large number of Arab workers refuse to join our union as long as it is connected with the General Organization of Hebrew Workers. As long as our union did not have many Arab members who belonged to the Histadrut and were bound by all the decisions of our union, this question was not posed sharply and we did not have the right to demand changes. Now that we are confronted with the living fact of our union being truly international, it is impossible for it to be part of a General Organization of Hebrew Workers. Therefore, in order to achieve unity with the Arab workers in all branches of work, we deem it desirable that first of all the name of the Histadrut should be changed.[43]

This circular touched off a heated debate in the Histadrut on the issue of joint organization, and on separation of functions as a way of achieving that goal. Supporters of Ahdut Ha'avoda accused the URPTW leadership of being so blinded by the prospect of Jewish-Arab unity that it had forgotten its national (i.e., Zionist) tasks and obligations. One Ahdut Ha'avoda loyalist offered a sociological explanation for the strength of radical forces among the Jewish railwaymen:

> The worst thing about railroad work, as a result of which we have come to this proposal which undermines and endangers the foundations of our enterprise in this country, is that this occupation was almost entirely abandoned by elements bearing any pioneering, national, or social aspiration. The element which ended up here was influenced rather by those parties which have no support in the established workplaces and labor enterprises of the Jewish worker, because the pioneering tendency is a fatal potion for them.[44]

The union leadership and its supporters tended to respond to criticism with pragmatic arguments, insisting that "without joint organization our union cannot survive" and that the idea of national sections had simply proven unworkable.[45]

Within the union itself, the influx of Arab members led to restructuring. In November 1924 it was formally agreed that all elected union bodies would be half Arab and half Jewish, with each group choosing its own representatives, and Arabs were co-opted onto the central committee. A plan for representation at the upcoming union council was formulated which balanced the number of delegates to which each group would be entitled, with a slight majority for the Jews. The process of achieving unity was not entirely smooth, however, for the issue of Zionism soon surfaced once again. At the very first joint meeting of the central committee, one of its new Arab members, Hasanayn Fahmi, an Egyptian railway clerk, posed two questions to his Jewish colleagues. Was there, Fahmi asked, a connection between the railway workers' union and the Zionist movement, and were the Jewish members of the central committee themselves Zionists?

Fahmi's motives in asking these questions are not difficult to fathom. An Arab who joined what might be generally perceived to be a Zionist organization ran the risk of being attacked as a traitor to his people and their national cause, of allying himself with the foreigners who were seeking to take Palestine away from the Arabs and make it their own. The Arab nationalist leadership had little interest in social issues in general or the needs of the fledgling Arab working class in particular, and it would be unlikely to accept Arab participation in any organization linked to Zionism (and the Histadrut was certainly understood to be a Zionist organization) even if such participation might in some way benefit the Arabs concerned. Furthermore, for months the PCP members inside and outside the union had been warning the Arab railwaymen not to trust what the union and Histadrut leaders were saying and encouraging them to ask precisely these questions of the union leadership, in order to expose their Zionist affiliations and loyalties.

After some consultation among themselves, the Jewish central committee members responded that the union was economic in purpose and nonpolitical, with no connection with Zionism; anyone who wanted to introduce politics would be expelled. To Fahmi's second question they replied: "Just as we do not ask you who you are, to which party you belong, what are your political opinions, so you have no right to ask us about these things. . . ." The Jews felt that their response had made a good impression on their Arab colleagues, but in fact it was disingenuous and evasive and seems to have been received as such by Hasanayn Fahmi. Through its affiliation to the Histadrut, which was a key Zionist institution, the URPTW was in fact linked to the Zionist project in Palestine. And even if the more left wing of the union's Jewish leaders sincerely believed that the "proletarian Zionism" they professed eliminated any possible contradiction between the interests of Jewish and Arab workers in Palestine, from the standpoint of the indigenous Arab population they were no less involved in a settler-colonial endeavor than the Histadrut mainstream. No Arab railway worker possessing any degree of national consciousness could avoid these issues or entirely separate them from purely class considerations, for the logic of the conflict between Zionism and Palestinian Arab nationalism constantly and inevitably raised them.

A few days later Hasanayn Fahmi, apparently less than satisfied with the answers he had received, published a letter in the Arabic-language newspaper al-Nafir in which he reiterated his questions and called on the Arab railway workers to leave the union because it was in reality a Zionist organization.[46] Only a minority of the union's new Arab members seem to have followed Fahmi's advice and quit at that point, but the issue was clearly on the agenda once again and must have influenced the deliberations of the union council when it convened in January 1925.

That crucial meeting was preceded by an event which seemed to bode well for the union's future: for the first time, union representatives were granted an interview with the General Manager of the Palestine Railways. Until this point management had consistently refused any formal contact with the union, despite persistent lobbying of the mandatory government and the Colonial Office by the Histadrut, Zionist leaders, and sympathetic officials of the Trades Union Congress and the Labor Party in Britain. The formation of a Labor Party government in Britain the previous year certainly helped induce railways management to agree to the meeting; indeed, Histadrut officials commented, it had produced a "distinct improvement" in management's attitude toward the railway workers, manifested in somewhat improved working conditions. Little was accomplished at this session, but the fact that it had taken place at all was held to signify official recognition of the union. In fact, formal recognition was not to be granted for years to come, although meetings between union officials (usually accompanied by Ben-Tzvi or some other Zionist leader) and Palestine Railways managers would henceforth take place at irregular intervals. After the Labor government fell, conditions palpably worsened as management reverted to its hard-line approach.[47]

The twenty-five voting delegates who participated in the January 1925 meeting of the URPTW council, held in Haifa, comprised the nine members of the central committee along with nine Jews and seven Arabs representing the branches. Three of the Histadrut's top leaders—Ben-Gurion and Ben-Tzvi of Ahdut Ha'avoda, and Hayyim Arlosoroff of Hapo'el Hatza'ir—also attended, in the hope of countering the influence of their rival on the left, Po'alei Tziyon Smol, and its new Arab allies. The agenda was dominated by the question of the union's relations with the Histadrut, with most of the Jewish council delegates demanding the separation of functions. For many in the organization this had come to seem a question of life and death. Some number of the union's Arab members had recently heeded Hasanayn Fahmi's call and quit over the issue of Zionism. For those who remained—and for the left-wing Jewish activists—it was crucial that the railway workers' union either convince the Histadrut to transform itself into a non-Zionist entity to which the Arabs could belong as equal members or disaffiliate from it.

The Histadrut leaders were dismayed by the radicalism of some of the Jewish delegates, one of whom went so far as to dissociate the "proletarian Zionists" from the "bourgeois Zionists" who "plundered the Arabs."[48] One of the Arab delegates, Ahmad al-Nimr, declared that "the promises of the executive committee to resolve the question of joint organization are like the promises of Balfour"—a formulation which implicitly raised the issue of Zionism and must also have infuriated the Histadrut leaders. In response, Ben-Gurion directed his remarks primarily to the Arab delegates. His speech was translated into Arabic by Avraham Khalfon, who fifty years later would admit that his translation "altered Ben-Gurion's speech completely."

Because if I had translated what he said, I was sure that 90 percent of the Arabs would have fled. He spoke in a very extreme way. From a Jewish standpoint it was excellent, but whether it would have attracted or repelled [the Arab delegates] is another matter. So I changed it, I watered down the contents. I saw how long he spoke for, and then I spoke for half an hour too. During the break Ben-Tzvi [who understood Arabic] came to me and kissed me: "Bravo, thank you!" Neither Ben-Gurion nor Arlosoroff knew that I had changed anything, but Ben-Tzvi sensed that I had.[49]

Khalfon's admission raises some important questions about the character of the Jewish unionists' relationship with their Arab colleagues. Ben-Gurion's speech was not in fact particularly extreme: it was a straightforward exposition of the Histadrut's position favoring separate national sections within mixed unions and separate labor federations. As if talking to children, Ben-Gurion explained in very simple terms that beyond the common interests which all workers shared, Jews and Arabs had their own special needs which required separate organizations. Perhaps Khalfon thought that Ben-Gurion's explicit references to Jewish immigration and settlement, and the Hebrew language, as examples of the needs which made it necessary that the Histadrut remain an essentially Jewish organization were extreme; if so, one can only wonder what it was that he had been communicating to the Arab unionists for whom he had been translating over the previous year or so and how much they really understood about the aims of the Jewish labor movement in Palestine.[50] This incident, like the evasive response of the Jewish unionists to Hasanayn Fahmi's pointed questions the previous November, suggests that even left-wing Zionists were willing to deceive, or at least to mislead, the Arabs by downplaying their commitment to Zionism and using vague or even obfuscatory language. In so doing they took advantage of the fact that the Arabs knew little or no Hebrew, had only a vague grasp of the ideological differences among the parties of the Yishuv, and lacked the political sophistication and experience typical of their Jewish counterparts.

The council ignored the pleas of the Histadrut leadership and by a vote of eighteen to seven proclaimed the establishment of a territorial and international trade union open to all railway, postal, and telegraph workers regardless of race, religion, or nationality. The majority favoring this decision, as well as a second resolution demanding that the upcoming Histadrut congress require all trade unions to be international and establish a labor federation open to all the workers of Palestine, consisted of the nine Jewish members of the central committee, the seven Arab delegates, and two Jewish branch delegates. In other words, an alliance of the Arab delegates and the Jewish adherents of Poʻalei Tziyon Smol controlled a majority of the votes at this crucial meeting. To Ben-Gurion and his colleagues the council's decisions and the composition of the majority that made them were outrageous; the Histadrut leaders fumed that only Jews should have had the right to vote on the union's connection with the Histadrut and rejected the council's decisions as invalid. But Yehezkel Abramov pointed out to Ben-Gurion that it was unfair to have allowed the Arabs to vote and then denounce the council's decisions because Arabs contributed to the majority that endorsed them.[51]

Ahdut Haʻavoda still had cards to play, however, for the left lacked a firm majority among the Jewish railway workers outside Haifa and most of the Jewish delegates from the branches had voted against the resolutions that so infuriated Ben-Gurion. Moreover, many of the postal and telegraph workers who made up a significant minority of the union's Jewish membership were uneasy about the union's new course and were talking of seceding to form their own independent union. The council passed a resolution denouncing this tendency and promised to redouble efforts to incorporate them more fully into the union. On one issue, at least, there was hardly any disagreement: the delegates, including all the Arabs, voted to confirm the central committee's decision to expel Moshe Ungerfeld, the communist activist. At the end of the meeting, seven Arabs—five from Haifa, including Ibrahim al-Asmar and ʻAli al-Batal, one from Jaffa-Lydda, and one from al-Qantara—were formally elected to the union's central committee.[52]

NARRATIVES OF FAILURE

When the January 1925 meeting of the union council adjourned, it probably seemed to the participants that the way was now open for a new era of cooperation between Arab and Jewish railway workers within the framework of a joint union. In retrospect, this meeting actually marked the high point of joint organization in this sector. In the months that followed most of the Arab workers who had joined the union left it, and a new and exclusively Arab union of railway workers emerged in Haifa. The circumstances surrounding these developments are complicated and in some details unclear, but there can be little doubt that the main issue which undermined the joint union and divided Arab from Jew was the URPTW's continuing Zionist affiliations.

There are several versions of what happened in the first half of 1925, some of which tell us more about the perspective and conceptions of the narrator than about what actually took place. The Jewish union leadership blamed the communists for sabotaging the unity that had finally been achieved after overcoming so many obstacles. The union (and the Histadrut) charged that the Jewish communists had told the Arabs that the union was "Zionist-chauvinist" and that its Jewish leaders were double-dealing; the communists had sown lies and mistrust, had spread false rumors and forged embarrassing letters, and had even employed physical violence against their opponents. This campaign of slander and harassment allegedly induced the Arab workers to leave the union in large numbers in the first half of 1925. In August 1925 the union permanently expelled thirteen communist activists, arguing that its tolerant attitude toward the communists had been repaid by betrayal and subversion.[53]

There is no doubt that the PCP had been sharply critical of the union leadership and its loyalty to the Histadrut and to Zionism. Moreover, its members and publications had seized every opportunity to denounce what the communists regarded as the leadership's betrayal of the workers' interests and proletarian internationalism. It is also quite possible that the communists at times employed underhand tactics to expose and harass their enemies. It is nonetheless clear that the departure of most of the Arabs who had recently joined cannot be attributed mainly to agitation by communist activists. That agitation had been going on for many months, if not years, and communist attacks on the union leadership as Zionist cannot have come as much of a revelation to Arab workers in the first half of 1925. The communists' tactics may have become more provocative and their propaganda more virulent as they were purged from the Histadrut and its unions. Their increasingly open support for the Palestinian Arab nationalist struggle against Zionism certainly deepened their isolation from the Yishuv and made them the object of bitter hatred among most Jews. But while the union's leaders may have felt themselves under siege by the communists inside and outside the union and may have convinced themselves that everything would have been fine had the communists not "poisoned the minds" of the Arabs, this explanation says more about their perception of Arabs as guileless, passive, and easily manipulable than it does about what actually happened. It certainly exaggerates the influence of the communists and denies the Arab workers any capacity for rational reflection and self-interested decision making.

This explanation, which is fairly standard in the labor-Zionist literature on this episode, is further undermined by the fact that at the end of 1924 and through the first quarter of 1925, the communists were in fact *not* calling on Arab workers to leave the URPTW. On the contrary: the Jewish communists repeatedly and forcefully exhorted the Arab workers to re-main within (or rejoin, for those who had already quit) the union and struggle against its Zionist leadership in order to make it a truly interna-tional union oriented first and foremost toward the class struggle. For example, in December 1924, before the collapse of the joint union, articles in the PCP's Arabic-language biweekly *Haifa* noted that both Zionists and Arab nationalist effendis were upset that Arab workers had joined the railway workers' union. The two groups, *Haifa* declared, were "perfectly matched in their campaign against the workers' unity and solidarity and their splendid organization which has replaced the old enmity and divi-sion, now completely gone."[54] A month later, in January 1925, an article signed by "a railway worker" (almost certainly a Jewish communist activ-ist) specifically rejected Hasanayn Fahmi's appeal to Arab workers to leave the URPTW.

> By withdrawing from the union we strengthen the position of the Zionists within it; they welcome our withdrawal so that they will have no internal opposition to their political activities. . . . We must endeavour to take over the leadership of the union and make of it an organization which will de-fend the interests of all the workers whether Arabs or Jews. There are a large number of Jewish comrades with considerable experience in running a union who are ready to help us loyally and sincerely.[55]

A few months later, after most Arab union members had quit and after *Haifa* had reported favorably on the establishment of a separate Arab railwaymen's union, it published a letter by Moshe Ungerfeld rejecting separatism, insisting that it was incorrect to term the old union "Zionist" just because its present leadership was Zionist, and calling on the Arab workers to join progressive Jews in fighting for control of the URPTW.[56]

Some Jewish observers also blamed the management of the Palestine Railways for undermining Arab-Jewish unity. According to this explana-tion, by the end of 1924 management had realized that the joint union was gaining strength and decided to adopt a new and more sophisticated strategy to destroy it. Instead of outright and total hostility to the union and blanket rejection of the workers' demands, management agreed to meet with union representatives and for the first time acknowledged that many of the workers' grievances might be justified. At the same time, however, it made skillful use of its power to reward and punish to divide the workers and undermine the union. Instead of a general wage increase, for example, management granted selective wage increases to those work-ers favored by the foremen. The clerks as a group were granted a substan-tial increase in order to alienate them from the other employees. Arab workers who kept their distance from the union were also rewarded with higher wages and freedom from the threat of dismissal. On the punishment side, management underlined the weakness of the union by dismissing a worker who refused to work overtime and ignoring the union's appeals to rehire him. The workers cannot have missed the message management's new policy was intended to convey.[57] However, this explanation of why the joint union failed is not convincing: though Palestine Railways management was certainly likely to have desired the collapse of unity between its Arab and Jewish workers and may indeed have sought to deepen divisions within its workforce, the departure of the Arabs from the joint union cannot reasonably be attributed in any large measure to management's actions.

While communist propaganda and agitation, and management's divide-and-rule strategems, may indeed have contributed to the union's problems in 1925, they do not provide anything approaching a complete explanation of why most of its Arab members quit. For that we must pay attention, as the labor-Zionist sources generally do not, to what the Arab workers and unionists themselves were saying and doing. The Arabic-language sources are unanimous in specifying the union's persistent Zionist affiliations as the fundamental issue that induced most of the Arabs who had been elected to the union's central committee at the January 1925 council meeting to quit soon thereafter. Apparently, Hasanayn Fahmi's questioning of the Jewish unionists in November 1924 and the letter he published in *al-Nafir* had touched off a crisis in the union which the decisions of the January council meeting were ultimately not able to dispel. The scantiness of the sources makes it difficult to determine precisely how and why the Arab unionists came, at this particular moment, to conclude that the union was irretrievably Zionist and that they had no place in it. It seems that at some point most of the Arab leaders came to feel that they were not being dealt with honestly, that the Jewish unionists were in effect deceiving them about their Zionist affiliations, and that even the left-wing Jews placed their commitment to Zionism above the welfare of the railway workers. They came to believe, as one article in *Haifa* put it, that "the foundations and principles of this union were not based on the interests of the worker and the improvement of his life (*rafʿ mistawaʾhi*) but rather on the implementation among the workers of the goals of Zionism."[58]

The feeling that they had been deliberately deceived and misled, and their good faith betrayed, by their Jewish colleagues seems to have especially rankled with the Arab unionists. Arab accounts of the split make frequent reference to the "prevarications" (*murawaghat*) and "duplicity" (*khida'*) of the Jewish union leaders. An article in *Haifa* published in late April 1925 makes explicit reference to Avraham Khalfon, who as we saw had deliberately mistranslated Ben-Gurion on at least one occasion, suggesting that the Arab unionists had come to feel that were being deceived by their Jewish colleagues. The difference in language between Arabs and Jews, *Haifa* noted, had "necessitated the employment of a translator in order to solve the problem; but this employee, who was not of the working class, curried favor for Zionism in the performance of his duties and abetted the spread of its influence and introduced it into the union's affairs." More generally, the article went on, "Whenever [the Arab leaders] made even the most minor proposal to facilitate mutual understanding and unity, they encountered only opposition and contradiction from the Zionists regarding everything which might lead to success and to the establishment [of the union] on a strong basis and with a program of action capable of achieving the rights of the oppressed workers."[59]

The issue which was most likely to have convinced the Arab railwaymen of their Jewish colleagues' bad faith and which made the issue of Zionism most concrete for them was that of Hebrew labor. Getting more Jews hired on the railroad had been one of the union's chief goals since its inception, and the communists had made a point of telling the Arab workers that this was still the case, regardless of what the Jewish unionists claimed. In his memoirs, Bulus Farah quite plausibly contends that Arab workers in the Haifa workshops felt strongly about this issue. According to Farah, a supervisor named Moshlin, whom we have come across earlier as a foreman disliked by the workers but who the Histadrut wanted to keep on the job because he was a Jew, was regarded by the Arab workers as a Zionist who would give

> every job that opened up to a Jewish worker without regard for seniority or professional skill, or would hire new Jewish immigrants at high pay for jobs they were not competent to fill. . . . The Arab railway workers refrained from joining the Histadrut, and those who did join quit as a result of their bitter experience, after they observed that the Histadrut's trade unionism consisted of discrimination against Arab workers. They experienced at first hand how [the Histadrut] stole jobs from the Arab workers and gave them to the Jewish workers, and how it used them in the international labor movement to conceal its Jewishness while at the same time riding the horse of internationalism. But the Arab workers felt the need for separate trade union organization because the professed internationalism of the Histadrut had been exposed as having been exploited by Zionism.[60]

It is certainly true that in this period the Histadrut continued to use its influence with the Jewish foremen to get more Jews hired.[61]

THE PALESTINIAN ARAB WORKERS' SOCIETY

The disillusionment of the Arab unionists who had joined the joint union coincided with another development among the Arab workers which probably also contributed to their decision to quit and go their own way. Toward the beginning of 1925 a new group coalesced at the Haifa railway workshops, led by a number of skilled workers who had been involved with the mutual aid society for Arab railway workers established a few years earlier and had never displayed any interest in sharing a union with Jews. Building on their earlier experience with their benevolent society and on widespread resentment about the Hebrew labor issue, they now sought to establish an independent and purely Arab organization of railway workers.

The leaders of this group included several young men who originally came from what had become, after the First World War, the separate French-ruled state of Syria. 'Abd al-Hamid Haymur, a boilermaker by trade, was a fervent Muslim and Arab nationalist with a thin face and a wispy beard who continued to dress in the style of his native region: a long overcoat over pants and a cloak decorated in the *shami* ("Syrian") style. A man of few words who preferred to avoid the limelight, 'Abd al-Hamid Haymur worked behind the scenes for many years as one of the most important leaders of the young Palestinian Arab labor movement. His brother, 'Id Salim Haymur, worked in the Palestine Railways' wagonage department. Their colleague Sa'id Qawwas was a turner, short and slight, who wore Western-style clothing and a tarbush, in the style of the young intellectuals of those days; he was described by Bulus Farah as a man of broad culture. Both 'Abd al-Hamid Haymur and Qawwas had previously been employed on the Hijaz Railway.[62]

The Haymur brothers and Qawwas found a substantial number of other Arab workers in the Haifa workshops angry about what they perceived as discrimination in employment in favor of Jews and receptive to the idea of their own separate trade union. At the end of February 1925 they organized a meeting at which some 200 Haifa railwaymen elected a committee to represent their interests. This new movement from below, organized by skilled workers who had never joined the Jewish-led union, probably helped stimulate the departure of most of the Arabs who had joined, led by some of the foremen. The two groups, whose motives for independent organization may initially have differed but who were now brought together by circumstances, soon merged into a movement of several hundred Arab railway workers in Haifa, out of which there emerged the first purely Arab labor organization in Palestine.

Though it seems to have originally styled itself a benevolent society and may have been a continuation of the organization which the Haymur brothers and their colleagues had led for some years, by the summer of 1925 this new formation was calling itself the Palestinian Arab Workers' Society (PAWS), and it formally registered under that name with the British authorities. It consisted almost exclusively of Arab railway workers in Haifa, but its new name and its program indicated its ambition to make of itself the Arab counterpart of the Histadrut, an organization which would eventually encompass all the Arab workers in Palestine and seek to advance their interests.[63] The leadership of the new PAWS included men drawn from both the groups which had contributed to its formation: Ilyas Asad, 'Ali al-Batal, and Farid Kamil (a locomotive engineer) had long been involved in negotiations with the Jewish unionists, and Kamil and Batal had briefly been members of the joint union's central committee, while Sa'id Qawwas, 'Abd al-Hamid Haymur, and his brother 'Id Salim Haymur were skilled workers who had been involved with the old mutual aid society.[64]

Given the situation in Palestine, the emergence of a separate Arab railway workers' union was probably inevitable. Relations between Arab and Jewish railwaymen could not remain unaffected by the deepening conflict between Zionism and the Arab national movement, recently manifested in the struggle at 'Afula and other incidents. A stratum of relatively well-educated and increasingly self-confident skilled workers and foremen who had assimilated the model of trade unionism as the form of organization most appropriate to their circumstances had emerged among the Arab railway workers. When members of this stratum lost faith in the possibility of participating in a union dominated by their Jewish coworkers and tainted by its association with Zionism, the establishment of a union of their own seemed the only reasonable alternative. The Arab unionists were no longer willing to submit to what they perceived as Jewish tutelage, especially as they came to perceive that tutelage as serving goals which harmed their interests as both Arabs and workers. The survival of the URPTW as an Arab-Jewish union would have required its transformation into a completely international organization by severing its links with the Histadrut and the Zionist movement, renouncing the struggle for Hebrew labor, and accepting that the organization would be largely Arab in membership, leadership, and orientation. This was the course the Jewish communists advocated, but it went well beyond what even the most radical Po'alei Tziyon Smol activist or leader could accept. When the Arab railwaymen's leaders grasped this, most of them quit and joined up with other Arabs who had never taken any interest in the prospect of a joint Arab-Jewish union.

As a result, from 1925 until the end of the British mandate two unions were to be active among the railway workers, one exclusively Arab, the other overwhelmingly Jewish in membership and Zionist in political orientation. Nonetheless, as the next chapter will explore, not only did the conditions of the railwaymen's working lives push the two unions toward cooperation, but the dream of unity would remain very much alive among both Arab and Jewish railway workers for years to come. At the same time, various dynamics produced estrangement and conflict between the organizations and their members. Relations between the two unions would thus always be complex, in ways that tell us a great deal about the parameters and character of the matrices of interaction among Arab and Jewish workers in Palestine.

4 The Railway Workers of Palestine (II): Cooperation and Conflict, 1925–1939

Relations between the new Palestinian Arab Workers' Society, whose stable core and largest component would for many years consist of Arab railway workers in Haifa, and the older, Jewish-led Union of Railway, Postal and Telegraph Workers were never uncomplicated and rarely smooth. At times, recognition of the vital necessity of concerted action and strong pressure from the rank and file induced the two unions to cooperate. At other times relations between them were characterized by friction and conflict, as competition within the workplace and tensions stemming from the political situation in Palestine set the two organizations, and the workers they represented, against one another. Over the years, a web of personal, social, and political relations developed between some Arab and Jewish railwaymen, particularly veteran workers and union activists, and in the right circumstances this tended to promote a desire for cooperation. But even when cooperation was impossible, these relations engendered a knowledge of the other side and a high degree of political awareness which helped the railway workers avoid being sucked into the maelstrom of intercommunal hatred and violence that ultimately engulfed much of Palestine.

ONE WORKFORCE, TWO UNIONS

The events of the spring and summer of 1925 did not result in an immediate division of the railway workforce into two unions organized along exclusively ethnic lines. Instead there ensued a period of confusion characterized by further initiatives to achieve Arab-Jewish unity, competition between the unions for the allegiance of the Arab workers, and movements by those workers between the two organizations.

148

At its founding the PAWS had only about 150 members and few financial or organizational resources. Its leaders felt threatened by the larger, stronger, and more experienced URPTW which, through the backing of the Histadrut, could offer its members far greater material benefits. The new union's vulnerability and the URPTW's ability to attract Arab workers were graphically demonstrated when a number of the workers who had joined the PAWS in the spring of 1925 made their way back to the Jewish-led union a few months later.[1] To protect itself and hold onto its membership, the PAWS initially sought to emphasize its Arab and patriotic character. As a result, when several Jewish communist railway workers sought to join, insisting that they were committed anti-Zionists, they were rejected on the grounds that the organization's bylaws allowed only Arabs to become members. The PAWS also sought to offset the attractive services and benefits which the URPTW could offer by asking progressive Arab nationalist professionals in Haifa to provide its members with medical and legal services at reduced cost.[2]

Not all the PAWS' leaders agreed with this nationalist orientation. Farid Kamil, who had served on the central committee of the URPTW and was now a leader of the PAWS, continued to argue for the kind of apolitical and internationalist trade unionism which the Arab workers' leaders had originally demanded of the URPTW. He went so far as to propose that Jewish workers be accepted as full and equal members of the new organization. He failed to convince his colleagues, however, and ultimately resigned or was expelled from the PAWS. Kamil took some of his supporters with him when he left, suggesting that there was still some support among the Arab workers for the idea of bringing the Arab and Jewish railway workers together in a single organization. To achieve that end Kamil apparently rejoined the URPTW, but later he returned to the PAWS, where he remained. Despite the failure of Farid Kamil's initiative to overcome the breach between the two organizations, the PAWS would in subsequent years come to adopt his perspective: with a fair degree of consistency it expressed willingness to dissolve itself into a new unitary organization comprising all the railway workers, providing that it was truly international and unattached to the Histadrut.[3]

Even after it lost most of its Arab members, the URPTW continued to regard itself not merely as a mixed union with a commitment to joint organization but as the sole legitimate representative of all the railway workers, Arab and Jewish, and the only authentic union at the Palestine Railways. Its claim was bolstered by the fact that for a number of years it actually did retain a not insignificant number of Arab members, since not all of those who had joined in late 1924 or early 1925 quit, and others joined later. In 1926 the URPTW would claim to have 780 members, 422 of them Arabs. The number of Arab members is obviously very inflated, however, because it includes all those Arabs who had registered with the union at any point from 1922 onward but had not notified the union in writing when they quit. The number of Jewish members may well be inflated for the same reason, since we know that turnover was high in railway work and it is safe to presume that not all those who quit bothered to notify the union formally. A total membership of 300–400 in 1926, most of them Jews and not all of them actually dues-paying, seems a safer estimate. At least one of the original Arab central committee members, Ibrahim al-Asmar, also remained in the URPTW.[4]

The URPTW and the Histadrut attacked the new PAWS as a separatist and exclusionary organization and therefore subversive of the workers' unity. They also claimed that it was a trade union in name only, that it was really a tool of rich Arab nationalist effendis and reactionary Muslim clerics, a product of communist incitement, a quasi-religious organization, and so on.[5] Since they regarded the Arab organization as neither legitimate nor viable, the URPTW's Jewish leaders did not give up hope that the Arab workers who had left could be brought back into the fold. They therefore persisted in efforts to hold on to, and if possible expand, an Arab membership. This generally meant raiding the PAWS' membership or trying to attract the same unorganized Arab workers the Arab union was also trying to recruit. The URPTW was least successful at retaining and recruiting Arab members in Haifa, where the PAWS' influence and base of support was strongest. It had somewhat greater success elsewhere in Palestine, especially in the Jaffa and Lydda areas.

The URPTW's persistence in trying to recruit Arab workers engendered tremendous bitterness among Arab unionists still very much on the defensive and unsure that their new union would survive. Their resentment was clearly manifested in a lengthy article by the union's secretary, 'Id Salim Haymur, published in *Filastin* on June 4, 1926. Entitled "The Indigenous Workers between Zionism and Communism," it portrayed the Arab railwaymen's union as the target of incessant efforts to undermine it by both the "Zionist union" and the Jewish communists. Some of 'Id Salim Haymur's allegations are plausible, but others are outlandish and would seem to reflect his frustration at the union's weakness and the defection of Arab workers from it. For example, his claim that the Jewish-led union had sought (with some success) to attract Arab workers by exempting them from paying monthly dues rings true. But his claim that the "traitors" Ibrahim al-Asmar and Philip Hassun (the Histadrut's Arab organizer in Haifa) were paid 15 piastres for each Arab worker they recruited seems far-fetched. Hints of a perceived insult to conservative cultural and religious sensibilities surface in 'Id Salim Haymur's claim that the Zionists had tried to ensnare innocent Arab workers by plying them with wine at union meetings and providing them with Jewish women to dance with. As a result of these ploys, 'Id Salim complained, the PAWS had no more than ninety members a year or so after its formation.[6]

If the PAWS was in a bad way by the middle of 1926, the URPTW could hardly be described as thriving. The traumatic events of the previous year had left many Jewish railway workers without much faith in joint organization and solidarity with the Arabs as the solution to their problems. Jews now accounted for 12.7 percent of the Palestine Railways workforce, 405 out of 3,182 workers, though they made up almost 30 percent of those employed at the Haifa workshops, which had 408 Muslim workers, 264 Jews, and 228 Christians; some of the latter were probably non-Arabs. By this point the majority of the Jewish railway workers had as much as six or seven years' service behind them. These veterans had been hired as apprentices when Jews first entered railway work in 1919–20, had become "assistants" when apprentices with four years of service were promoted in 1923, and had been promoted to full-fledged "workmen" in 1925. At 28–30 piastres a day, their wages were still unsatisfactory, as were their working conditions. The Jewish workers (and the leaders of their union) also cannot have regarded the future prospects for Jewish employment in railway work as particularly promising. The new apprentices, forced to work for a six-month trial period without pay, were all Arabs, as were most of the foremen, and management was not anxious to hire more Jews, since they were seen as potential troublemakers.[7]

Some Jewish workers responded to the failure of the joint union, and to their generally demoralizing situation, by leaving railroad work altogether. This prompted the union to appeal to the Histadrut to channel additional Jewish workers into railroad jobs, and the Histadrut in turn asked the Zionist Executive to pressure the Palestine Railways to hire more Jews.[8] Disillusionment and demoralization also weakened the left forces within the union and paved the way for Ahdut Ha'avoda to reassert its influence and control. Po'alei Tziyon Smol, having finally and decisively broken with the communists and voted for their expulsion from the union in the summer of 1925, now found its own support slipping as more Jewish workers either left railroad work in despair or turned to the Ahdut Ha'avoda–dominated Histadrut to resolve their problems. This shift was manifested in various ways, including declarations of loyalty to the Histadrut in union leaflets and votes in several union branches to nominate Ahdut Ha'avoda members as candidates in the upcoming elections to the local workers' councils.[9]

The union's retreat from the radical internationalist positions it had adopted a year earlier, and Ahdut Ha'avoda's new strength, emerged clearly at the January 1926 meeting of the union council. Ibrahim Suwaylih, an Arab railway worker from Jerusalem who had remained a member of the URPTW, proposed that the union return to an organizational model based on separate national sections, as the Histadrut had long demanded. PAWS activists would denounce Suwaylih as a docile lackey of the Jews, and he does seem to have followed the lead of the Jewish union leaders; there is certainly no evidence that he had any real input into decision making. That it was Suwaylih, an Arab, who called for the restoration of national sections—at the instigation, one suspects, of his Jewish colleagues—may have been a tactic to disarm the left and counter criticism from the PAWS. Though the council rejected his proposal, instead reconfirming an earlier decision to avoid specifying the form joint organization should take for the time being, it simultaneously abandoned the union's previous claim to autonomy by agreeing that the question of its organizational structure should be decided by the Histadrut at its upcoming congress. The council then went on to essentially endorse Ahdut Ha'avoda's position on joint organization by declaring that internationalism "requires joint unionism (*ha'igud hameshutaf*) and the guaranteeing of the free development of every people on the basis of equality and autonomy." This formulation, with its implicit acknowledgment of the primacy of the Jewish labor movement's Zionist tasks, was a break with the ideas put forward by Po'alei Tziyon Smol and until recently dominant within the union.[10]

However, these victories for the Ahdut Ha'avoda line did not solve the serious problems facing the union. At a meeting with the Histadrut secretariat in July 1926, the union's leaders stressed their organization's weakness and complained that the Histadrut had not provided the funds it had promised to support the union's work and allow it to serve its members effectively. Reflecting the shift in the union's orientation over the previous year or so, they made their appeal for Histadrut support largely in terms of their organization's key role in the struggle for Hebrew labor. One union leader told Ben-Gurion and his colleagues that "the union's importance lies in the conquest of government jobs by Jews," while another attributed the union's weakness primarily to the failure to get more Jews hired. The Histadrut ultimately promised to increase its monthly subsidy to the union, which was still incapable of maintaining itself without outside financial support, and also stepped up its efforts to get more Jews hired as railway workers. The Zionist Executive also pitched in by intensifying its lobbying of British officials in Palestine and London, directly and through Zionist sympathizers in the Labor Party, on the issue of Jewish employment by government agencies, insisting that a higher percentage of jobs (and also of government contracts) should go to Jews.[11]

One aspect of that July 1926 meeting between URPTW leaders and top Histadrut officials merits special attention. For among the union leaders who sat in on the discussion of how to strengthen Hebrew labor on the railways was Ibrahim al-Asmar, an Arab who served on the URPTW's central committee. Al-Asmar does not seem to have uttered a word at the meeting; it is likely that he knew little if any Hebrew and did not understand what his Jewish colleagues were talking about. He was probably invited mainly for propaganda purposes, so that the URPTW could portray itself as including Arabs in leadership roles and thereby enhance its standing among the Arab workers. But both his presence at the meeting and his silence tell us something about the place of Arabs in the Jewish-led union.[12]

RECURRING DREAMS OF UNITY

Though the left within the URPTW had grown weaker, it remained a significant force, especially in Haifa where Jewish leftists often received backing from the branch's remaining Arab members. Moreover, the left's argument that Arab-Jewish solidarity was the only means by which the Jewish railway workers' problems could be solved was bolstered in the summer of 1926 by an upsurge of militancy among the workers, accompanied by renewed pressure for unity radiating upward from the Arab and Jewish rank and file. Frustration over long-standing grievances had been growing among the railway workers for some months, and this finally led the two unions to look for ways to overcome the bitterness between them and cooperate with one another. Early in June 1926 leaders of the PAWS and the URPTW met in Haifa and agreed to join together to press the government to issue a law to protect the workers' rights.[13] The path of cooperation was not always smooth—'Id Salim Haymur's article attacking the Jewish-led union, discussed earlier, was published shortly after this initial meeting—but many workers still felt that no progress was possible unless Arabs and Jews set aside their differences and worked together. A series of joint meetings was held, setting the stage for concerted action when two separate official decisions sparked off widespread unrest.

The URPTW had long sought official recognition as representative of the Palestine Railways workforce, but management, backed by the government of Palestine and the Colonial Office, had first equivocated and then imposed harsh conditions for recognition. In order to satisfy those conditions the union leadership overrode internal opposition and agreed even to turn over its membership lists, after extracting a promise that management would not use this information to punish union members. Nonetheless, at the end of July 1926 the Chief Secretary of the government of Palestine informed the Histadrut that the government would not recognize the URPTW as representative of the railway workers, a decision which came as a bitter blow.[14] Even more bitter, however, and even more crucial in arousing and uniting the railway workers, was a decree issued in mid-July 1926 which unilaterally revoked the workers' right to seven days of annual vacation and another eight days of vacation on official holidays.

This arbitrary act outraged the workers and touched off a campaign to resist management which, while initiated by both unions, also gave evidence of persistent tensions between them. The campaign was to have been launched at a mass meeting of Arab and Jewish railway workers at the Eden cinema in Haifa. The Arab union, apparently concerned that the stronger URPTW might exploit the situation and win over some of its members by taking sole credit for calling the meeting, insisted that the leaflet issued to publicize the event not carry the name of either union. The Arab unionists soon discovered, however, that the leaflet calling the meeting was signed by the URPTW. They took this to be a violation of their agreement and blamed the Jewish-led union for sabotaging the workers' unity. The Arab unionists' version of this incident is plausible, since we know that they were fearful of losing their membership and that the URPTW continued to insist that it alone represented all the railway workers, Arabs and Jews. Significantly, the Arab union took the trouble to argue its case in a Hebrew-language leaflet addressed to "all the workers of Palestine."[15] The Arab unionists' insistence on placing their version of the facts before the Jewish workers and arguing that the URPTW bore responsibility for disunity among the railway workers indicates a continuing concern to cultivate Jewish opinion and a continuing openness to cooperation with their Jewish coworkers.

Despite such incidents and the tensions they engendered, neither union could afford to give up all hope of cooperating. This was a period of recession and high unemployment in Palestine, and conditions were worsening for the railway workers as well. Management was threatening layoffs, and from the fall of 1926 until the spring of 1927 the Haifa workshops operated only five days a week. The two unions could not hope to defend their members unless they worked together. The railway workers' component of the PAWS had been reduced to a small and largely inactive core of loyal members, while the URPTW was also weaker than it had been a few years earlier. Only 250 dues-paying members—nearly all of them Jewish—participated in elections for the union's sixth congress, held in the summer of 1927. The previous year's tensions notwithstanding, relations between the two unions were by now good enough that 'Id Salim Haymur and 'Ali al-Batal were invited to appear at the opening session of the URPTW congress and greet the delegates on behalf of the PAWS. Al-Batal told the congress that he had joined the Arab union "in order to find an appropriate form for joint organization of all the workers. The Arab workers all seek peace, and what they promise they will carry out. . . ." [16]

This congress, like its predecessors, devoted much of its time to the question of joint organization. As I discussed in Chapter 2, in July 1927 the Histadrut's third congress had ratified Ben-Gurion's proposal on relations with Arab workers, which called for a separate Arab labor organization which would federate with the Histadrut. As usual the debate among the railway workers revolved around the question of national sections, favored by the partisans of Ahdut Ha'avoda who were especially strong in the Jaffa-Lydda branch. For their part the supporters of Po'alei Tziyon Smol still insisted that the union be unitary and international, although their arguments were not always entirely principled. For example, Naftali Panini, a leftist from the Jerusalem branch, attacked the Jaffa-Lydda branch for allegedly sabotaging the union's efforts to organize Arabs in 1924–25, but his argument against national sections evoked the very fears which Ahdut Ha'avoda played on to argue in their favor. "From the moment we create a special organization for the Arabs," Panini argued, "we no longer have control over it. The Arabs will distance themselves from us and who knows in what direction their work will develop." The Jaffa-Lydda delegates defended themselves against their left-wing critics by claiming that their efforts to recruit Arabs had succeeded but that the Arab section had disintegrated after its treasurer absconded with the funds entrusted to him.

By a small margin the sixth congress voted to adopt the principle of joint organization on the basis of national sections, signaling a triumph for Ahdut Ha'avoda and yet another defeat for Po'alei Tziyon Smol, whose influence would continue to decline. In February 1928 new bylaws formally established separate national sections, effectively reversing the

January 1925 decision to abolish them. At this time the organization also changed its name to the National Union of Railway, Post and Telegraph Workers in Palestine (NURPTW). The term "national" (*artzi* in Hebrew, *qutri* in Arabic) seems to have been chosen to emphasize the union's claim to be open to all the railway workers in Palestine, Jewish and Arab, despite its formal adoption of separate sections for members of each national group.[17]

The changes in the name, structure, and leadership of the Jewish-led union did not preclude renewed cooperation with the PAWS. In the fall of 1927, angered by management's refusal to compensate the railway workers for the reduction in their real wages caused by the issuing of a new Palestinian currency to replace the Egyptian currency used since the war, the NURPTW and the PAWS established a joint committee to mobilize the railway workers. The committee quickly garnered widespread support and began to address the whole range of issues facing the railwaymen. This time, however, to avoid at least some of the complications that had arisen when the two unions had sought to cooperate the previous year, an agreement was signed which explicitly defined the joint committee's composition and authority and prohibited either union from issuing leaflets in its own name.[18] However, this experiment in cooperation was short-lived. By May 1928 the Jewish unionists had come to the conclusion that the joint committee had outlived its usefulness and should be abolished, because it was strengthening the PAWS at the expense of the NURPTW. Still insistent that their organization was the only authentic railway workers' union in Palestine, they feared that continued recognition of, and cooperation with, the Arab union would enhance the latter's legitimacy in the eyes of the Arab rank and file—and perhaps of the government, too.[19] Instead of cooperating with the PAWS, the NURPTW now decided to recruit Arab workers directly. In its circular to the membership, however, the central committee sought to put the onus for the collapse of the joint committee on the Arabs, who were accused of violating or failing to implement the committee's decisions.

Even as the joint committee disintegrated, a group of Arab workers who had once belonged to the Jewish-led union initiated yet another effort to overcome the differences between the two unions and unite all the railwaymen in one organization. Negotiations soon foundered over the refusal of the NURPTW to merge itself into a new, all-inclusive railway workers' union without national sections. The Ahdut Ha'avoda loyalists who were now firmly in control of the NURPTW were not interested in any form of unity that might weaken their links with the Histadrut or divert them from their commitment to the Zionist project.[20] Though it failed, the fact that this initiative was launched indicates that even at this late date, after several abortive attempts to achieve unity and despite adverse political circumstances, there still remained an active nucleus of Arabs who were interested in sharing a union with their Jewish coworkers. The dream of unity thus remained alive among the railway workers and seems to have been able to endure repeated defeats and disillusionments.

Just as striking is the continued willingness of the Arab railway workers and the PAWS leadership to seek cooperation with Jewish unionists, despite pressure from the Arab nationalist movement to sever all relations with the Jewish labor movement. At the end of 1927, for example, while the joint committee was still apparently functioning smoothly, *Filastin* attacked the Jewish unions in general, and the NURPTW in particular, for allegedly seeking to exploit the Arab workers for Zionist purposes.[21] Despite their opposition to Zionism and their criticisms of the NURPTW, the PAWS leaders chose to ignore this clear warning and put the railway workers' interests first. Their stance was all the more risky because by this time the Arabs were well aware that their Jewish counterparts gave top priority to their commitment to Zionism. Even as they were discussing unity with the Arab workers, claiming to defend their interests, and heatedly denying any desire to take away their jobs, the NURPTW's leaders were privately pressing the Histadrut and the Zionist leadership to get more Jews hired on the railroad in accordance with the principle of Hebrew labor. Because low wages and poor working conditions were continually driving Jewish workers out of railroad work whenever alternative jobs became available, this was a constant preoccupation; as one veteran put it, there was an "unceasing search for new 'victims' " who could be induced to enter railroad work.[22]

For both Jews and Arabs, the situation grew even more difficult when in 1928 the Palestine Railways again reduced the workweek in Haifa to five days and began a new wave of layoffs, allegedly because of a decline in traffic. Though only a few months had passed since the dissolution of their first joint committee, the NURPTW and the PAWS were again compelled to try to work together. In September 1928 they jointly organized a mass meeting to protest the layoffs and short hours. The meeting ended in an uproar, however, with the Arab participants refusing to endorse the planned memorandum to management. The incident dramatically illustrates the bitterness and mistrust that had accumulated over the previous three years of interaction as each side blamed the other for the failure of what was supposed to have been a display of unity and solidarity among the railway workers.

In a leaflet published in both Hebrew and Arabic, the Jewish unionists claimed that their Arab counterparts had sabotaged the meeting by raising a number of issues not on the agreed-upon agenda—mainly the question of the defunct joint committee, whose scuttling by the NURPTW was still bitterly resented by the Arab union activists. In response the PAWS issued its own leaflet, also in both Arabic and Hebrew, which accused the NURPTW of bad faith. The Arab unionists cited a number of instances in which the Jewish leaders had undermined cooperation. They had, for example, allegedly issued a leaflet in the name of the joint committee without securing the approval of the Arabs, and they had failed to make serious efforts to get dismissed Arab workers reinstated. The PAWS leaflet also related an incident which to the Arabs demonstrated the disrespect with which their Jewish coworkers sometimes treated them. Some Arab railway workers had attended the funeral of a Jewish coworker who had originally come from an Arab country; the Arabic version of the leaflet referred to him as *yahudi 'arabi*, an "Arab Jew." After the funeral the Arab mourners had asked other Jewish workers why they had not been at the funeral and were told, apparently in an insulting manner, that the deceased was a Jew and therefore none of the Arabs' business. "Our extensive experience in joint work with the leadership of the NURPTW has made it clear to us that this leadership is not interested in unity between Arab and Jewish workers, because of its Zionist character . . . ," the PAWS leaflet concluded. Arguing that, unlike the NURPTW with its Histadrut and Zionist connections, the PAWS was completely independent of all political affiliations, the statement insisted that there was "no possibility of cooperation as long as the NURPTW is not a genuine workers' organization" and called upon the Jewish railway workers to choose leaders who "truthfully and sincerely favor unity between Arab and Jewish workers."[23]

The leaders of the PAWS were still careful to distinguish between the Jewish rank and file workers and their leaders, offering to cooperate with the former and their union even as they bitterly criticized the latter. That this distinction was still made, despite their accumulated mistrust and anger over what they perceived as the Jewish leaders' repeated deceptions and manipulative tactics, seems to have been a product of their relatively extensive experience of trade union work and of interaction with Jewish coworkers, and perhaps especially with the communists among them.

Both Jewish and Arab railwaymen (but particularly the veterans and union activists employed in the Haifa workshops) would prove more resistant to national and religious chauvinism than other workers in Palestine, virtually segregated as the latter usually were in separate workplaces and residential areas. This is not to say, however, that the railway workers were unaffected by the growing tension between Jews and Arabs in Palestine after 1928.

Throughout these years the NURPTW had retained a small number of Arab members, and after the breakdown in relations with the PAWS in the fall of 1928 it again tried to recruit more aggressively. The union's standing among the Arab rank and file may have been enhanced when in March 1929, for the first time in four years, the General Manager of the Palestine Railways agreed to meet with its representatives. Management still refused to grant the NURPTW the official recognition it sought, but the union was at least able to present its list of demands: a forty-eight-hour workweek, instead of the short hours in effect since the previous summer; an end to the heavy fines imposed on allegedly delinquent workers; improvements in sanitary conditions in the workshops; changes in the way medical leave was granted; and one day off a week for workers in the traffic and running departments.[24] In Haifa the presence of the PAWS made inroads among Arab workers difficult, though not impossible, but there were greater opportunities for success in Jaffa-Lydda, and in the course of 1929 the local NURPTW branch there was able to establish an Arab section which claimed one hundred dues-paying members. The section functioned for only a few months, however. According to the Jewish unionists, management deliberately sabotaged this effort at unity by transferring the leaders of the Arab section to other work sites. The other Arab workers got the message and began to abandon the union, and the eruption of countrywide bloodshed between Arabs and Jews in August 1929 dashed hopes that they could be persuaded to rejoin.[25]

COMPETITION AND COOPERATION IN THE EARLY 1930S

The explosion of violence in the late summer of 1929 marked a turning point in the interaction of Arab and Jewish railway workers. The bloodshed in the streets of Haifa did not spread to the railway workshops, where the ties that had developed over many years of working side by side stood the workers in good stead and allowed peace to be preserved.[26] But the conflict between Zionism and the Palestinian Arab national movement had entered a new and more intense phase, and the deterioration of relations between Jews and Arabs generally could not help but affect the railway workers as well. In the 1930s Jewish and Arab unionists did not cease looking for, and finding, avenues of cooperation; they could not do without one another. Moreover, despite repeated failures, the dream of uniting all the railway workers in Palestine within a single organization survived among both Arab and Jewish workers. But as the years passed, and especially from 1936 onward, the dream faded, and it became increasingly evident that if there was to be solidarity between the Arab and Jewish railway workers, it would have to take the form of cooperation between two independent and ethnically unmixed organizations.

As I will discuss in Chapter 5, in January 1930 the PAWS, hoping to lay the foundations of a more broadly based Arab labor movement, convened a congress of Arab workers in Palestine, the first of its kind. Though representatives from various parts of the country participated, half the delegates were from Haifa, where the congress was held, and many of these were railway workers.[27] The PAWS' desire to transform itself into a different kind of organization was also manifested in another way. Though the PAWS formally encompassed workers from different industries and trades, it had since its inception been largely an organization of Haifa-area Arab railway workers, and it was often difficult to distinguish between the parent organization and its railway workers' section. Now, however, as the PAWS sought to expand its geographic and occupational base, it wanted to distinguish more clearly between the railway workers and its other components, actual or potential, thereby transforming itself into something more closely resembling a federation of trade unions. As a result, the Haifa-based organization of railway workers affiliated to the PAWS would henceforth often refer to itself as the Arab Union of Railway Workers (AURW), in theory a distinct component of the larger organization. In practice, the boundaries between the AURW and the PAWS often remained vague, since many of the latter's leaders were also current or former railwaymen. In later years the Arab railway workers' union would adopt other names, at least in English; for example, by 1934 it was referring to itself in English-language correspondence as the Railway Arab Workers' Trade Union. Despite this, for clarity's sake I will henceforth always refer to the trade union of Arab railway workers as the AURW and to the broader organization of which it was a part as the PAWS.

Despite the tensions and violence of the previous year, the NURPTW managed to expand its Arab membership during 1930, establishing Arab sections in both Haifa and Jerusalem. A significant number of non-Jewish railroad clerks also joined the Jewish-led union in this period, under the leadership of a Greek, Michael Qyubik, and at the end of 1930 leaders of the new recruits were co-opted onto the NURPTW central committee. An effort was also made to reestablish links with Arab railway workers at far-off al-Qantara, on the Suez Canal, but this was frustrated by the intervention of the AURW.[28] This influx of new Arab, Greek, and other non-Jewish members soon brought to the surface the same contradictions that had plagued the union all along. While veteran Arab members like Ibrahim Suwaylih deferred to the union's Jewish leaders and played a largely ornamental role, some of the new recruits insisted on making their views known and sharing in decision making.

In the period leading up to the union's seventh congress, scheduled for May 1931, Qyubik and some of his Arab colleagues demanded that national sections be abolished, and at the congress itself they called on the union to disaffiliate from the Histadrut. They were under heavy pressure from the AURW to quit the NURPTW and join the Arab railwaymen's union; in fact, pressure from the AURW was such that the NURPTW's new Arab members insisted that the union congress be held in Tel Aviv instead of Haifa, so as to deter AURW activists from showing up to "entice" them away from the Jewish-led union and "transfer" them to the Arab union.[29] However, the demands raised by Qyubik and his colleagues found little support among the Jewish delegates, backed by both Ben-Gurion and Ben-Tzvi, whose attendance at the congress again illustrates this union's importance to the labor-Zionist leadership. After discussion the congress decided that the Jewish members of the railway union would continue to be members of the Histadrut, while the Arab and other non-Jewish members should join the "general workers' clubs" which the Histadrut was setting up for Arab workers, until such time as an "international workers' federation which will encompass the workers of Palestine without regard to religion or race" was established. In what seems to have been an effort to appease Qyubik and his allies and enhance the union's image abroad, the congress also decided to change the union's name once again, this time to the International Union of Railway, Postal and Telegraph Employees in Eretz Yisra'el (IU).[30]

Though the congress had avoided any explicit mention of national sections, Michael Qyubik and his allies understood that none of their demands had been met, and they could also not help but see the renaming of the union as a purely symbolic gesture. Immediately after the congress Michael Qyubik quit the IU, along with eighty of his fellow clerks and some of the Arab blue-collar workers. Not all the IU's Arab members left with him, however. At the beginning of 1932 the IU still claimed to have 253 Arab members, out of a total membership of 657. Of this number, 408 belonged to the Haifa branch, among them 187 Arabs; Jerusalem had 83 members (31 Arabs) and Jaffa-Lydda 108 members (9 Arabs). Like previous union membership claims, this one too was probably inflated, since the IU still continued to count as members all Arabs who had once signed up but had not bothered to submit formal resignations when they quit. In 1932 the Colonial Office estimated that the IU had 300 Jewish and 210 Arab members, which seems closer to the truth.[31]

Whatever the actual numbers, there were at this point enough Arabs still left in the Jewish-led union to induce the AURW to take a harder line when the two unions again began to discuss a joint delegation to the General Manager. Among other things, the Arab unionists were worried that the IU, which through the Histadrut had good connections with the Labor Party and trade unions in Britain, might soon win official recognition as the sole bargaining agent for all the railway workers, a status it had been seeking for many years. Recognition had seemed imminent when the Labor Party came to power in Britain in 1929, but by 1932 the Palestine Railways had come up with additional preconditions for official recognition, including a demand that the IU sever its ties with the Histadrut.[32] Even a small number of Arab members greatly enhanced the IU's claims to legitimacy and inclusiveness in the eyes of sympathizers in the British and European labor and social-democratic movements.

The Arab unionists also understood that their organization would never be entirely secure as long as the IU, which enjoyed access to the resources of the Histadrut and the Zionist movement, remained a competitor for the loyalty of the Arab railwaymen; these were the only important source of additional recruits for the IU, since it already encompassed most of the Jewish workers. The rivalry between the Arab and Jewish organizations was further exacerbated in this period by competition in other workplaces between the PAWS and the Palestine Labor League (PLL), recently established by the Histadrut to organize Arab workers (see Chapter 5). Moreover, nationalist principles made it impossible for AURW leaders to accept the right of what they deemed a Zionist organization to recruit Arab workers. These considerations taken together now led the Arab union to demand that the IU divest itself of its Arab members (i.e., hand them over to the AURW) and thereby renounce its claim to represent all the railway workers. The AURW expressed its willingness to cooperate with the IU and even to discuss unity, but only if it was recognized as the sole representative of the Arab workers, with the

IU playing the same role for the Jewish workers. Indeed, the AURW's leaders refused even to hold talks with Arabs who belonged to the IU, since it regarded them as traitors to their people and puppets of the IU's Jewish leaders.[33]

The main arena of competition between the AURW and the IU during 1932 was the running department, which included locomotive drivers, firemen, mechanics, and engine cleaners. This department had been hard hit by wage cuts of 28 percent and the transfer of many workers to lower grades. This produced widespread discontent among its mostly Arab workers, who had hitherto refrained from joining either union. The IU got the jump on its rival and organized a conference of running department workers in Jaffa. AURW representatives attended the conference, however, and succeeded in blocking a proposal put forward by the IU's secretary that the workers elect their representative committee on the basis of parity between Jews and Arabs. The IU generally insisted on parity on leadership bodies because this implied that Jews and Arabs enjoyed equal status. The Arab unionists normally rejected parity on the ground that most of the workers were Arabs and the composition of leadership bodies should reflect that fact. This struggle for influence among (and control over) the running department workers went on for some weeks, manifested in an exchange of leaflets, and ultimately led at least some of the workers to reject assistance from either union. It seems that in the end neither union was able to bring these workers fully under its wing.[34]

In any case the two organizations were soon forced to cooperate once again. In the fall of 1932 and again in the spring of 1933, the railway workers were hard hit by waves of layoffs that affected hundreds of employees. Thereafter, as I discuss in Chapter 5, a period of economic expansion got under way in Palestine and the railway workforce began to expand rapidly. The total number of "unclassified" employees rose from 2,765 in March 1933 to 3,749 a year later. Fewer unskilled laborers were hired for construction and maintenance in 1934–35, and so the total fell to 3,443 by March 1935, but over the next year it again rose to 4,138.[35] But wages and working conditions continued to be far worse than in other sectors. There had been no general increase in wages for years, and skilled workers with years of experience were still earning as little as 20–30 piastres a day. Many workers were compelled to work overtime without extra compensation, no provision for sick pay existed, and heavy fines were still being imposed for alleged infractions of work rules, with no right of appeal.

The expansion of the workforce attracted many unskilled Arab workers, for whom railway wages and conditions often surpassed those obtainable elsewhere. But the availability of better jobs in other sectors resulted in an exodus of skilled Jewish railway workers, increasingly less willing to sacrifice themselves forever on the altar of the conquest of labor. The Histadrut sought to stem the tide by such measures as the provision of loans which railway workers could use to build houses for their families.[36] Despite all its efforts, however, Jews continued to leave, and by August 1934 only 184 were left—less than 6 percent of the Palestine Railways workforce.[37] At the same time, because of budgetary constraints, the Histadrut was reducing its subsidy to the IU, making it even more difficult for that organization to retain its veteran Arab members (most of whom now slipped away) or recruit new ones. As the proportion of Jews in the railway workforce shrank and the IU grew weaker, AURW leaders came to feel that they could afford to ignore the fact that a few Arabs still remained IU members. This opened the way for renewed cooperation at the beginning of 1934. The government of Palestine had issued a circular which seemed to promise various improvements to all government employees, so yet another joint committee was established in Haifa to mobilize the railwaymen and see to it that those promises were kept.

There now began a period of unprecedentedly intense activity and mobilization among the railway workers. The joint committee, whose leading members were 'Id Salim Haymur and Michael Dana, secretaries of the AURW and the IU respectively, worked together closely, producing a stream of memoranda to the management of the Palestine Railways and to the High Commissioner setting forth the workers' grievances and demands. To mobilize the rank and file in support of these demands, Haymur and Dana organized a series of mass meetings, held in one of the large Arab coffeehouses in Haifa, and issued leaflets in both Arabic and Hebrew. In private, the IU and the Histadrut continued to seek ways to get more Jews into railway work, and there was some tension between the two unions over the AURW's insistence that its members decide on their own whether to celebrate May Day in 1934 by staying away from their jobs. But overall, relations between the two unions remained cordial and the joint committee's work proceeded smoothly.

As usual, cooperation and mobilization created renewed sentiment for greater unity with which the IU was hard-pressed to deal. By May 1934 'Id Salim Haymur was proposing a merger of the two unions, and there was also pressure for unity from the rank and file. Reporting that the Jewish locomotive mechanics supported the call for a merger, the IU's central committee told the Histadrut that "it is clear that this is the hour of decision and that we must speed up our activity, otherwise the thing [i.e., unity] will be done by other hands." Calls for a merger came not only from the (overwhelmingly Arab) rank and file and from the AURW but also from the IU's remaining Arab members, who saw unification as a way to escape their isolation and subordinate status within the Jewish-led organization. In certain situations, their symbolic importance and propaganda value to the IU and the Histadrut allowed them to exert a degree of pressure on their Jewish leaders that was highly disproportionate to their small numbers. In August 1934, after months of stalling, the IU was compelled to grudgingly accept the principle of a single union, although it continued to insist on Arab-Jewish parity in leadership positions regardless of the composition of the membership.[38]

However, relations between the two unions soon took a downward course. By the end of 1934 the joint committee was foundering, with each side blaming the other for its lack of success in winning gains for the workers, and by January 1935 the IU was ready to break it up, much as it had done in 1928. Michael Dana privately told the Histadrut leadership that "all our comrades are of the opinion that now we have the opportunity to strike at the Arab union by appearing in public [in our own right] before the Arab railway workers, which will prove with facts that all the activities of the joint committee were carried out essentially by us and that the Arab union terminated those activities out of ambition and a desire for power. . . ." Dana believed that with "a little daring" and adequate funding from the Histadrut it would be possible to split the AURW and win over many of its members, as well as the unorganized Arab workers.[39] His plan to break up the joint committee while making the AURW appear responsible was, however, delayed by an upsurge in worker militancy elsewhere in Haifa which galvanized the railway workers into action and enabled them to win significant gains.

MASS MOBILIZATION AND ITS AFTERMATH

As I will discuss in greater detail in Chapter 5, at the end of February 1935 hundreds of Arab and Jewish workers employed at the Iraq Petroleum Company's facilities in Haifa went on strike for higher wages, shorter hours, and better working conditions. Their militancy inspired other workers to emulate their example, so that the spring of 1935 witnessed an unprecedented wave of industrial unrest. Haifa-area railway workers were particularly affected, perhaps because they had long been in direct daily contact with IPC workers, most of whom reached their jobs by train. The

IU-AURW joint committee quickly put out a leaflet expressing solidarity with the IPC workers, and on March 4, 1935, a thousand exhilarated rail- waymen gathered at their usual site for mass meetings, the Café Centrale, and voted to strike unless their demands were fulfilled; in the workshops a flurry of brief partial strikes broke out. The government, surprised by this sudden upsurge of militancy and fearful of the political and economic consequences of a railroad strike, responded three days later by announc- ing the appointment of a special committee, headed by Major Campbell, the District Commissioner of Jerusalem, to investigate the workers' griev- ances and recommend improvements.[40]

Weeks passed as the committee heard testimony, investigated, deliber- ated, and then submitted its recommendations to the government in Jeru- salem and to the Colonial Office. The long delay led to growing unrest and resentment among the rank and file over the joint committee's cau- tious, even passive attitude and its refusal to initiate immediate strike action. Supporters of Hashomer Hatza'ir, a new tendency to MAPAI's left which I discuss at the end of this chapter, had gained a foothold in the Haifa branch committee of the IU, and they complained that the union leadership was failing to do all it could to pressure the government for a rapid and satisfactory response. The ongoing unrest was also expressed by the workshop workers' strong participation in the traditional May Day strike: over 700 railway workers, among them 113 Jews, struck that day, and many of them gathered at the Café Centrale for a rally which the participants concluded by singing a rousing hymn composed by a railway worker. Management's nervousness about unrest among the workers was such that it promised not to punish anyone who failed to come to work on May Day. By mid-May the joint committee had been compelled by rank and file agitation to set a strike deadline.[41]

Faced with this deadline, the High Commissioner finally issued the long-promised official communiqué specifying the improvements that were to be made in the railway workers' pay and conditions of service. The communiqué, dated May 17, 1935, came as a great disappointment to the workers because it went only a small part of the way toward resolving their long-standing grievances, and they responded with partial protest strikes at the Haifa workshops, continued unrest elsewhere, and demands for a meeting with the High Commissioner. In an effort to restore calm, the High Commissioner took the unprecedented step of agreeing to meet a delegation of railway workers. The delegation, which consisted of four Arabs (including 'Id Salim Haymur and Farid Kamil) and three Jews (in- cluding Menahem Diner, an IU leader at the Haifa workshops, and Yehezkel Abramov of Lydda), made its way to Jerusalem by train, accompanied along the way by railway workers' cheers. At their June 17, 1935 meeting with the High Commissioner, the delegates criticized the inadequacies of the communiqué. Acknowledging that the workers' demands had not been met in full, the High Commissioner announced some additional (albeit minor) concessions but insisted that he could not forget the interests of the taxpayers.[42]

The meeting with the High Commissioner marked the high point of cooperation between the two unions, and old tensions soon resurfaced. As earlier, the Histadrut's prioritization of Hebrew labor played a key role in undermining good relations between the IU and the AURW. Before, during, and after the upsurge of militancy in the spring of 1935, the IU and the Histadrut had continued to cast about for ways to get more Jews hired. At a meeting with Histadrut officials in Tel Aviv in early May 1935, just as the railway workers' mobilization was approaching its height and a strike seemed to loom, IU leaders expressed their concern that many veteran Jewish workers were on the verge of quitting railway work. The union proposed that they might be induced to stay if the Jewish Agency allocated fifty immigration certificates to railway workers so that they could get family members still in Europe into Palestine. At the same time, the IU leaders reported that "there is now an extraordinary opportunity to get many Jewish workers into the railway" because one of the Jewish foremen at the Haifa workshops stood ready to help get more Jews hired.

The real problem, however, was that there were too few Jews willing to work in this sector. In its search for recruits the Histadrut had earlier gone so far as to prepare lists of Jewish railway workers in Iraq who could be brought to Palestine if jobs were available for them, but nothing had come of this. Now it responded to the IU's complaints by issuing a circular which alerted its trade unions and the local workers' councils to the fact that Jews were leaving the railways, undermining the conquest of labor in this sector, and called on them to channel veteran workers and new immigrants into railway work. The circular also provided for sanctions: "A worker who leaves his job on the railway will not be hired anywhere else unless he can produce a letter proving that he quit with the approval of the IU."[43] In the long run the Histadrut's efforts were partially successful: overall, it managed to get some 120 to 150 Jews hired on the railway in 1934–36, although not all of them stayed. This brought the proportion of Jewish employees, which had been 12.6 percent in 1933 but had fallen to 8.2 percent in 1934, back up to just under 10 percent by 1937. At the end of 1935, the Palestine Railways employed 3,171 Palestinian Arabs,

345 Jews, and 1,307 "others," most of them Egyptians employed on the Sinai line but also a number of Turks, Greeks, Armenians, Syrians, and (in supervisory positions) British. The Jewish workers were concentrated in the workshops at Haifa and Lydda, where they held a large share of the skilled jobs. All told, 52 percent of the railway's Arab employees earned less than £P50 a year, as compared with only 5 percent of the Jews.[44]

These gains in Jewish employment seem to have strengthened the hand of those IU leaders who wanted to terminate the alliance with the AURW. Just a week after the railway workers' delegation met with the High Commissioner, IU secretary Michael Dana was again pressing for the dissolution of the joint committee. "By comparison with March 1934," he told the central committee, "the number of Jewish workers has grown. In order to carry out effective organizational work, we will have to attack the Arab union." Dana proposed that the IU insist on full freedom of action, by which he meant the right to organize Arab workers. The joint committee, he argued, should be restricted to representing the workers in talks with management, and eventually it should be abolished. But Histadrut leaders were fearful that an influx of newly recruited Arab members might "flood" the union and perhaps take it over, since there were currently no established national sections within which they could be separately organized, and they refrained from endorsing Dana's strategy.[45]

Having won limited but not insignificant gains in May-June 1935, the joint committee began to press management to translate its promises into reality and make further concessions. Ongoing talks with management, and relations between the two unions, were soon complicated by a spontaneous strike that erupted in late July among the running department workers, who had gained nothing from the May 1935 communiqué and the subsequent meeting with the High Commissioner. Both unions opposed this upsurge of militancy from below, since it threatened to undermine their authority and disrupt negotiations with management, and they quickly induced the strikers to go back to work. The leaders' rapid intervention discredited them in the eyes of many rank and file running department workers, who felt that their strike had been sabotaged. This episode also precipitated mutual recriminations between the IU and the AURW, a breakdown in relations and, finally, open competition to win over Arab workers. In the summer of 1935 the joint committee ceased functioning effectively and thereafter met only sporadically, a situation for which each union blamed the other. The IU charged that the AURW was sabotaging the committee's work, while the AURW claimed that the IU was failing to keep it informed about contacts with management, was putting out separate leaflets, and was poaching on its territory by recruiting Arab workers.[46]

Yet a complete break between the two unions was averted for another six months, mainly because neither was in a position to negotiate effectively with management on its own. In the end it was the AURW which, at the end of February 1936, took the initiative in formally declaring the joint committee dissolved. The immediate cause seems to have been the IU's refusal to stop recruiting current and former AURW members, some of whom apparently went over to the IU. But many additional reasons were set forth in a lengthy and often bitter statement which the AURW published, in Arabic, in March 1936 to explain its decision to the Arab workers. Among other things, the AURW accused the IU of bad faith, of repeatedly violating the agreement governing the functioning of the joint committee, and of sabotaging the running department workers' strike. What made the Arab unionists most bitter, however, was what they regarded as the IU's underhand efforts to take jobs away from Arabs and, with the help of sympathetic Jewish foremen, give them to Jews; its campaign to "entice" Arab workers to join by offering them loans, health care, and other benefits which the Arab union could not match; and its claim to be the sole legitimate representative of all the railway workers in Palestine. The statement explicitly attributed these actions to the IU's Zionist character, which resulted in its giving top priority to the building of the Jewish "national home" rather than to the workers' interests.[47] Some of the AURW's accusations were exaggerated or tendentious, but many were accurate. As we have seen, the IU did give priority to the goal of expanding Jewish employment; it had used its connections with Jewish foremen to get more Jews hired; it had for over a year been seeking a suitable pretext to break up the joint committee; and it had been trying to recruit Arab workers, despite the strong objections of the AURW. A day or two after the AURW informed the IU that the joint committee was dissolved, IU leaders, not at all unhappy about this development, met with the Histadrut's committee that oversaw Arab affairs to plan a renewed effort to recruit Arab railway workers.[48]

Remarkably, despite this bitter break, neither the desire for cooperation nor even the dream of unity were yet dead among the railway workers. Within a few weeks of the dissolution of the joint committee a group of Arabs and Jews from the Haifa workshops were meeting to discuss its restoration, and AURW secretary 'Id Salim Haymur, perhaps under pressure from his own rank and file, was making conciliatory statements. By April 1936 the AURW was ready to go even further: despite its recent bitter experience of joint work with the Jewish unionists, it formally proposed to the IU that both unions be dissolved and replaced by a unitary organization. Given the popularity of unity among the rank and file, and among its own Arab members, the IU could not afford to reject such a proposal out of hand. Instead it stalled for time as its leaders consulted with the Histadrut about how to respond. As previously, the Jewish unionists insisted that unity be based on Jewish-Arab parity in all institutions and the right of Jewish members to belong to the Histadrut. These were the same conditions that had frustrated earlier attempts at unity, but the IU saw them as necessary to prevent an Arab majority in a shared union from gaining control. To buy time, the IU eventually proposed that the joint committee be reconstituted in Haifa and that broader organizational questions be deferred for the time being.[49]

THE RAILWAY WORKERS DURING THE ARAB REVOLT

These efforts at reconciliation and unification came to a sudden halt when in mid-April 1936 violent clashes erupted between Arabs and Jews in various parts of Palestine. Within a matter of weeks these escalated into a six-month general strike by the Arab population against British rule and Zionism—the first stage of the Arab revolt of 1936–39. For three years Arab and Jewish railwaymen found themselves on opposite sides in the bloody conflict that now engulfed Palestine. This situation not only made overt cooperation extremely difficult but also led to serious tensions between Jewish and Arab workers as well as sporadic incidents of violence.

The IU's remaining Arab members quit, leaving it an entirely Jewish organization which would never again succeed in attracting Arab workers. Many of the key leaders of the AURW and the PAWS were arrested by the British and held in detention for long periods, leaving those organizations paralyzed and the Arab railway workers without effective representation or leadership. Yet even during this bleak period some Arab and Jewish workers remained on good terms, and some even sought to cooperate in their common interest. As late as November 1936, IU secretary Michael Dana was discussing with Histadrut officials how the union should respond to Arab workers who were still pressing for the formation of a single union for all the railway workers.[50]

Despite pressure from the Arab nationalist leadership, the Arab railway workers (like most government employees) did not join the general strike. Only in August 1936 did many of them walk off the job, and then only for ten days. Unlike other Arab workers, most of whom were employed by Arabs who were themselves participating in the general strike, the railway workers risked immediate and permanent dismissal if they failed to report for work. They knew that British security forces stood ready to help break any strike, and they also had good reason to fear that if they joined the general strike their jobs would be taken by Jews. As I discuss more fully in Chapter 6, the Zionist leadership was ready and willing to supply Jewish workers who could help keep the railways running if the Arab workers went on strike, and in fact they hoped that the general strike would lead to the hiring of more Jews. Addressing the royal commission sent to investigate the situation in Palestine, the director of the Political Department of the Jewish Agency, Moshe Shertok (later Sharett) argued that

> The presence of a substantial number of Jews would have acted as a very effective deterrent [to an Arab railway strike]. There would have been no incentive to agitation and the organisers of the disorders would not have derived so much encouragement from the prospect of being able to bring the railways to a standstill. When the crisis did occur—on the 9th August—and hundreds of Arab railwaymen walked out, there were many factors which militated against it and brought them back to reason and to work, but one of the factors was that we mobilised a few dozen Jewish engine drivers whom we placed at the disposal of the Government and they were ready to step into the breach. . . . [T]hat was one of the factors that liquidated that very dangerous situation which existed for a few days.

Shertok demanded that Jews constitute 30 to 33 percent of the workforce in all government departments. But Palestine Railways management continued to refuse to give preference to Jews, in part for fear of further alienating the already agitated Arab workers. The proportion of Jews in the railway workforce actually declined somewhat during the course of the revolt.[51]

The central concern of the IU during the revolt was security. Tensions between Arab and Jewish workers in the Haifa workshops and at stations and other installations across Palestine sometimes ran high, especially during the insurrection's more intensely violent phases, and Jews working in relatively isolated places were sometimes the target of attacks. Altogether, eight Jewish railway workers were killed in the course of the revolt. All were apparently the victims not of fellow workers but of armed Arab insurgents from outside the railway workforce. The IU and the Histadrut continually complained that the Palestine Railways was not adequately protecting its Jewish employees and demanded the assignment of more guards. When the armed revolt reached a new peak in September 1938 and two Jewish railroad clerks were killed in Lydda, the Jewish workers there refused to report to work for two weeks. Eventually the Jewish railway workers and clerks at Lydda were all transferred to Tel Aviv, as were the Jewish postal workers normally stationed in Jaffa. The British also established special units of Jewish auxiliary police to patrol railway lines and installations, frequently targeted by the Arab insurgents, and British soldiers were stationed in the Haifa workshops to supplement the Arab watchmen. To discourage Arab insurgents from mining railroad tracks and blowing up trains, British security forces adopted the practice of forcing Arab hostages to sit on a special wheeled platform attached to the front of the locomotive.[52]

Arab railway workers also suffered during the revolt. British railway officials noted in the fall of 1938 that

> [Arab] railway staff are now being brutally treated, and are working under the greatest difficulty. They are being attacked by both sides. Through their allegiance to the Government the staff are generally so unpopular that cases of refusal to sell food and necessaries to them and to help in any way are daily occurrences. On the other hand, they are being treated with the greatest suspicion by the [British and Jewish] police and troops.

The officials cited numerous instances in which security forces had without cause arrested, beaten, or shot at loyal Arab employees, simply because they were Arabs. This harassment prompted a brief protest strike in Lydda in October 1938.[53]

The revolt hurt both Arab and Jewish workers economically. Sabotage by Arab guerrillas forced reductions in service and the closing of several lines while greatly increasing costs. Revenues dropped sharply as both passenger and freight traffic fell off. As a result, management laid off some workers and imposed short hours on others. But at the urging of Ben-Tzvi, and perhaps of British security officials as well, the government sought to avoid large-scale layoffs, for fear that unemployed Arab railway workers might strengthen the ranks of the insurgents while the laid-off Jews would never return to railway work.[54] Nonetheless, circumstances in this period were not such as to allow the workers to make further gains in wages or working conditions; they were primarily concerned with getting through very difficult times and holding on to what they had.

The revolt had an important impact on the sites and forms of interaction between Arab and Jewish railway workers outside the workplace. For example, it led to greatly increased residential and social segregation in mixed cities like Haifa, as Jews moved out of predominantly Arab neighborhoods and into safer Jewish ones. Arabs and Jews became less likely to frequent markets, cafés, movie theaters, clinics, and other places located in what was now perceived as hostile and dangerous territory. As a result Arab and Jewish railway workers became less likely to have much contact outside the workplace. Nonetheless, the security situation did not completely preclude the maintenance of personal contacts between Jewish and Arab railwaymen. Their long experience of interaction and even cooperation, as well as friendly relations developed on the job, enabled at least some of the railwaymen to avoid succumbing to the hatred and estrangement between Arabs and Jews that became much more widespread in this period. Although some especially dangerous workplaces became wholly Arab as Jews were transferred to safer places, others (like the Haifa workshops) remained mixed.

There is also evidence that some Arab railway workers sought to protect their Jewish coworkers. Efrayyim Schvartzman, a locomotive engineer and longtime IU leader, reported that

> Even during the disturbances there were numerous instances of Arab railway workers saving Jews many times from very difficult situations. I was one of those who was twice saved by Arabs, when I was very close to being killed. . . . I remember one of the incidents. One day two or three Arabs entered the locomotive shed in Lydda and murdered two Jews in the office. I ran in the direction of the shots, because I didn't know where they were coming from. And an Arab saw me heading there and ran to save me—and thanks to that I was saved. . . . Many times there were instances of the Arabs warning the Jews not to travel on the workers' train, because in the village of Safariyya, which is today [1972] Kfar Habad, they were preparing to attack the train with bombs and guns. Jews were frequently saved because the Arabs warned them, out of friendship. . . . There was one Arab who was my assistant, and is today a locomotive engineer. I remember that, during the disturbances, when we were pulling trains and there were often mines on the tracks, he would travel with me as my assistant and would always check at each station if all was well, because he watched over me a lot during the disturbances.[55]

On rare occasions, cooperation between Arab and Jewish railwaymen seems to have gone even further. In the spring of 1938, for example, efforts were made in Haifa to put together a joint delegation to management, and it is likely that there were other similar initiatives. But the resumption of overt ties and a serious effort to recoup losses and gain new ground were impossible until after the end of the revolt.[56]

HASHOMER HATZAʿIR AND THE RAILWAY WORKERS

As I mentioned in passing earlier in this chapter in connection with the upsurge of militancy among the railway workers in the spring of 1935, a new political movement to MAPAI's left had begun to make its presence felt within the Jewish working class and labor movement in the early 1930s. This was Hashomer Hatza'ir ("The Young Guard"), which in the second half of that decade won significant support among Jewish railway workers, especially in Haifa, and would come to play an important role in the labor-Zionist movement, in the wider Yishuv, and in the arena of Arab-Jewish relations in Palestine.

Hashomer Hatza'ir originated as a Zionist youth movement in Hapsburg-ruled and then Polish Galicia during and immediately after the First World War. Members of the youth movement who immigrated to Palestine in the 1920s eventually founded their own kibbutzim, which in 1927 federated into the Hakibbutz Ha'artzi ("National Kibbutz") federation, with its own increasingly ramified network of economic, political, social, cultural, and educational institutions.[57] In the late 1920s and into the 1930s, Hashomer Hatza'ir and Hakibbutz Ha'artzi (in Palestine the two were in this period more or less identical for most purposes) were as a movement rather introverted, devoting itself primarily to establishing and strengthening its kibbutzim and institutions and working out its own distinctive socialist-Zionist ideology. That ideology ultimately took the form of a unique blend of "pioneering Zionism" and revolutionary socialism, situating Hashomer Hatza'ir on the labor-Zionist political spectrum between MAPAI and Po'alei Tziyon Smol. Its inward focus notwithstanding, already by the early 1930s the membership base and resources provided by its network of kibbutzim enabled Hakibbutz Ha'artzi–Hashomer Hatza'ir to emerge as the strongest force to MAPAI's left within the Histadrut, eclipsing Po'alei Tziyon Smol which gradually drifted toward marginality and ultimately, in the 1940s, absorption by other parties.

Unlike Po'alei Tziyon Smol, Hashomer Hatza'ir participated fully in the institutions and activities of the Zionist Organization and served as a kind of loyal opposition to MAPAI within the Histadrut. It rejected Po'alei Tziyon Smol's call for divesting the Histadrut of those functions which were not strictly typical of a labor federation and, abandoning orthodox Borokhovism, gave primary emphasis not to class struggle but to workers' immigration and settlement on kibbutzim, which Hashomer Hatza'ir regarded as the nuclei of the future Jewish socialist commonwealth in Palestine. At the same time, Hashomer Hatza'ir criticized MAPAI for its close working relationship with bourgeois Zionists, its virtual abandonment of class struggle in both principle and practice, its undemocratic control of a bureaucratized Histadrut, and its lack of interest in Arab-Jewish joint organization in mixed workplaces. As I discuss more fully in the next chapter, on the issue of Hebrew labor Hashomer Hatzaʻir staked out ground halfway between MAPAI and Poʻalei Tziyon Smol. Rejecting both the former's call for "100 percent Hebrew labor" in every sector and the latter's opposition to the Hebrew labor campaign, Hashomer Hatzaʻir proposed that Palestinian Arab workers permanently employed by Jews be allowed to keep their jobs.[58] As we will see, Hashomer Hatzaʻir would later develop its own distinctive approach to the question of Palestine's future, an approach which rejected exclusive sovereignty for either Arabs or Jews but also partition, and instead proposed that Arabs and Jews share the land as equals, regardless of their numbers.

Hashomer Hatzaʻir saw itself as first and foremost a kibbutz-based and kibbutz-oriented movement, and it therefore initially displayed little interest in the urban working class. So even though collectives of Hashomer Hatzaʻir members awaiting permanent settlement in kibbutzim might live and work in cities or moshavot, sometimes for years, they were primarily oriented toward their future status as kibbutz members and did not regard themselves as prospective urban proletarians. Nonetheless, by the mid-1930s the presence of Hashomer Hatzaʻir members in the cities was beginning to allow the movement to exert an influence among urban Jewish workers. Hashomer Hatzaʻir members tended to be concentrated in poorly paid and undesirable jobs, such as the railways and the ports, partly because they volunteered to put themselves on the front lines of the struggle for the conquest of labor but also because the MAPAI-controlled workers' councils tended to reserve the best jobs for party loyalists. In these workplaces Hashomer Hatzaʻir members and sympathizers constituted a vigorous new source of opposition on MAPAI's left flank, irritating party and Histadrut officials with their militancy, their criticisms of bureaucratic control, and their advocacy of Jewish-Arab solidarity. Though most Hashomer Hatzaʻir members sooner or later left for permanent settlement in the kibbutz to which they had been assigned, they often left behind them an important legacy of organizing. Moreover, a few activists remained in the cities and created urban nuclei of Hashomer Hatzaʻir supporters. In 1936 the movement finally accepted and institutionalized this development by creating the Socialist League as a political framework within which Jews who agreed with Hashomer Hatzaʻir's politics but were not current or potential kibbutz members could organize themselves. This helped enhance the movement's status as the main opposition to MAPAI within urban workplaces and within the Histadrut at large.

These developments are well illustrated by the career of Efrayyim Krisher, who would become a key leader of the left among the Jewish railway workers in Haifa. Born in the Galicia region of Poland in 1909, Krisher joined Hashomer Hatza'ir and emigrated to Palestine in 1934. He belonged to a group which was slated to settle at Kibbutz Ein Hamifratz, finally established near Haifa in 1938. Soon after his arrival in Palestine the future members of this kibbutz responded to the Histadrut's call for recruits to reverse the decline of Hebrew labor on the railroad by sending him to work at the Haifa workshops. Krisher formally remained a kibbutz member until 1941, but instead of joining his comrades when they left Haifa to establish their kibbutz he stayed in the city and remained a railway employee and union activist until his retirement in the 1970s.[59]

Krisher quickly became a popular and trusted figure in the Haifa branch of the IU. As we saw, in the 1920s this branch had been a stronghold of the left, and especially of Po'alei Tziyon Smol. That party, or more precisely the various factions into which that party was split, had long since become marginal to the political life of the Yishuv, while many of the radical railway workers had moved on to other jobs, leaving the branch and the union solidly in the hands of Ahdut Ha'avoda and then MAPAI loyalists. Now, thanks to the departure of many MAPAI members for better jobs elsewhere and an influx of young militants like Krisher, the left reestablished itself as a force in the Haifa branch of the IU. By the spring of 1935 Krisher was already a member of the branch committee in Haifa and one of those urging the IU leadership both to greater militancy and to greater receptiveness to cooperation and even unity with the Arab workers. In January 1937 he was reelected with the greatest number of votes, and the new committee, now dominated by leftists, promptly chose him as secretary of the Haifa branch.

The election of this Hashomer Hatza'ir activist greatly displeased the MAPAI loyalists who still controlled the IU's central committee. They were unwilling to surrender control of a key branch of this important union, and they were particularly alarmed by the fact that in April 1936 Krisher had apparently been willing to accept the AURW's proposal for the formation of a new joint union. MAPAI used its domination of the Histadrut bureaucracy to nullify Krisher's election, but it could not prevent the left from gaining ground in Haifa and elsewhere. Wages had been stagnant for years, working conditions had deteriorated, and the union's leadership was widely perceived as not only passive and ineffective but also unrepresentative of the rank and file, since elections had not been held since 1931. All this benefited the left, and when elections to the IU's eighth congress were finally held in the summer of 1939, MAPAI had only a three-vote edge (of 105 cast) over Hashomer Hatza'ir and its ally the Socialist League in the Haifa branch, while in the workshops Ha-shomer Hatza'ir won a solid majority. Because MAPAI remained much stronger in other branches it was able to retain control of the union, but the IU was in a parlous state on the eve of the Second World War. It had only 401 dues-paying members, of whom 186 were railway workers and 215 were postal and telegraph workers; and although it continued to style itself an "international union," it no longer had any Arab members what-soever, while Jews now constituted only 8 percent of the railway work-force.[60]

These realities enhanced the prospects of the new left opposition within the union. As I discuss in Chapters 7 and 8, during and immediately after the Second World War militants who belonged to Hashomer Hatza'ir or to its urban-based sister party would play a major role in fostering and leading workplace activism, among the railway workers and elsewhere. They would also inherit the mantle of the defunct Po'alei Tziyon Smol as the chief advocates of Arab-Jewish working-class solidarity while going even further by advocating a solution to the Palestine problem that re-jected the mainstream Zionist goal of exclusive Jewish sovereignty.

The years between the collapse of the short-lived joint union in 1925 and the outbreak of the Arab revolt against British rule and Zionism in 1936 witnessed many twists and turns in relations between the Arab and Jewish railway workers and their organizations. It seems clear that unification within a single organization was never really in the cards: though Arab unionists favored unity in principle, they insisted on terms that the Jewish unionists could never accept without compromising their Zionist commit-ments. Nonetheless, it is striking that the dream of unity remained alive as long as it did and that time and again rank and file pressure compelled the Arab and Jewish leaderships at least to go through the motions of seeking to achieve it.

The conditions in which the Arab and Jewish railwaymen found them-selves certainly seemed to provide daily lessons in the vital importance of cooperation and unity. But it would also seem that the notion of integral unity, rather than just cooperation between separate Arab and Jewish unions, was nourished by the web of personal relations that developed among these workers, who made up Palestine's oldest, largest, and most stable mixed workforce, especially at the Haifa workshops. Of all the workforces in mandatory Palestine, this one had the longest and perhaps also the densest—in the sense of most complex—experience of interaction and interrelationship. This seems to have not only helped moderate conflicts between the two unions but also to have nourished a unique sense of possibility among the workers themselves. This would continue to be the case during the war and in the final years of the mandate, which would witness unprecedented episodes of working-class militancy and Arab-Jewish cooperation, often spearheaded by Arab and Jewish railway and postal workers. In the end, of course, the Zionist-Palestinian conflict would engulf these workers too, leading to a *dénouement* in which the traumas of partition and war would culminate in the virtual elimination of Arab workers from the scene.

5 Arab Workers and the Histadrut, 1929–1936

As I discussed at the end of Chapter 2, in the late 1920s the Histadrut had essentially abandoned the notion that the success of the labor-Zionist enterprise in Palestine was closely linked to Arab-Jewish working-class solidarity. However, the bloody events of August 1929 and their aftermath compelled all Zionists to give more serious attention to the "Arab problem." Ben-Gurion and some of his colleagues now began to talk of the need for an agreement with the leaders of the Arab community, whom they had denounced through much of the 1920s as reactionaries with whom labor Zionism could never compromise. At the same time, those events and several related developments induced the Histadrut leadership to renew its attention to the question of relations with Arab workers.

That leadership was now firmly in the hands of MAPAI ("Party of the Workers of Eretz Yisra'el"), formed in 1930 by the merger of Ahdut Ha'avoda and Hapo'el Hatza'ir. MAPAI's platform addressed the question of Arab workers only by asserting that "the united party ... establishes comradely relations with the Arab worker and fosters relations of peace and understanding between the Hebrew people and the Arab people."[1] This vague and noncommittal formulation was much closer to Hapo'el Hatza'ir's line than to that of Ahdut Ha'avoda. On the other hand, when it suited its purposes MAPAI's leadership continued to use Ahdut Ha'avoda's old rationale for organizing Arab workers. For example, in a December 1929 letter to the Palestine Zionist Executive requesting funding for an Arabic-language periodical, clubs for Arab workers, and a renewed propaganda effort aimed at British and international public opinion (especially trade union movements and labor and socialist parties), the Histadrut executive committee declared that "an agreement with the Arab inhabitants cannot be effected through political compromises with those sections of the population that aspire to destroy our undertaking in Palestine, but rather through a systematic cultural-economic activity among the masses of the Arab workers in town and village, which in the course of time will bring about our desirability to the masses, on the basis of the great good that Jewish settlement showers also upon them."[2]

In January 1930 the Zionist Executive agreed in principle to subsidize the Histadrut's activities oriented toward Arab workers. But actually finding the necessary funds was a much more difficult matter, since any large sum would have to be raised outside the regular budget, from wealthy donors abroad. In the interim, the Histadrut decided to allocate a small amount of money from its own budget—£P20 a month—to reopen the Haifa club. Philip Hassun, who during the club's first incarnation, between 1925 and 1928 or 1929, had served as Avraham Khalfon's assistant and then took over the club's management when Khalfon moved on to other things, seemed the only person available to start the club up again, though Histadrut leaders had doubts about his abilities as an organizer. But in the tense political climate then prevailing, Hassun was nervous about the club being openly identified with the Histadrut and insisted that the connection be kept secret. Despite misgivings the Histadrut executive acceded to Hassun's request, because it was clear that for the moment very few if any Arab workers would be willing to join a club openly funded and run by the Histadrut. The club finally opened in the fall of 1930.[3]

THE RENEWAL OF "ARAB WORK"

Several developments prompted the Histadrut to renew and escalate what was now coming to be called "Arab activism" (*pe'ilut 'aravit*) or "Arab work" (*'avoda 'aravit*).[4] As I mentioned in Chapter 4, in January 1930, after years of inactivity, the Palestinian Arab Workers' Society had succeeded in organizing the first countrywide congress of Arab workers. Sixty-one delegates gathered in Haifa, claiming to represent some 3,000 workers. Almost half the delegates came from Haifa itself, and nearly half of those represented the railway workers there who constituted the PAWS' main base of support. But there were also smaller contingents from Jerusalem, Jaffa, and other towns representing workers in a variety of trades. Though a number of Arab unionists who belonged to or sympathized with the Palestine Communist Party helped organize the congress, it was largely under the control of the more conservative and noncommunist unionists who had originally founded the PAWS in 1925. The congress resolved to set up a nationwide labor movement which would lead

the struggle to improve the wages and working conditions of Arab workers and secure their rights. It also declared its opposition to Jewish immigration and Zionism and its support for Palestine's independence as an
Arab state. In response to Zionist efforts to secure a large percentage of
government jobs for Jews, on the grounds that Jews paid a disproportionately large share of taxes, the congress called on the government of Palestine to reserve for Arab workers a share of jobs equal to the proportion of
Arabs in the general population.[5]

Histadrut leaders were well aware of the Haifa congress and anxious
that it might signal the emergence of an active and growing Arab labor
movement aligned with the anti-Zionist nationalist movement. Before the
congress, Philip Hassun had met with some of its organizers and urged
them to avoid politics and refrain from attacking the Histadrut and Zionism. In an effort to counterbalance the impact of the congress on Haifa-
area workers, the Haifa Workers' Council issued a leaflet in Arabic, in the
name of a fictitious "Advisory Committee of Haifa Workers," welcoming
the congress but also expressing the hope that Arab workers would be
protected from "corrupting hands and misleading thoughts."[6] Po'alei Tziyon Smol tried to play a direct role in the congress: George Nassar, the
young Arab carpenter who in the 1920s had become closely connected
with the party, appeared at the congress and asked if he could deliver an
address explaining his pro-Zionist position. The organizers denied him
permission to speak, however, and had him expelled as a Zionist agent.
Increasingly isolated in his own community, Nassar found employment
at 'Etziyon, a Histadrut-owned woodworking enterprise, where he would
remain for many years while continuing to be a staunch Po'alei Tziyon
Smol loyalist.[7]

This first Arab workers' congress proved not a new beginning for the
Arab labor movement in Palestine but an isolated incident. The PAWS
was unable to follow up and lay the basis for an effective countrywide
organization, and for the next few years it remained an organization
whose base was largely restricted to Haifa and to railway workers. Nonetheless, the congress made at least some Histadrut leaders feel that a coherent program of activity among Arab workers was now an urgent necessity.

That sense of urgency was reinforced in the late spring of 1930 when
forces on MAPAI's left flank launched a new public campaign to raise the
question of Arab-Jewish workers' relations and push the Histadrut to take
action. Behind this initiative stood Po'alei Tziyon Smol, which since 1928
had been split into two contending factions: a more orthodox Borokhovist,

European-oriented, and Yiddishist faction led by Moshe Erem, and a more Palestine-oriented and Hebraist faction led by Ze'ev Abramovitch and Yitzhak Yitzhaki. On May 1, 1930, each faction, in collaboration with nonparty personalities including some prominent liberal intellectuals and academics, announced the establishment of a separate organization to promote Arab-Jewish workers' solidarity. A week later, recognizing that it made little sense to have two separate organizations pursuing almost identical aims, the two groups merged under the name which one of them had taken, Ahavat Po'alim ("Workers' Brotherhood").[8]

Over the next two months, Ahavat Po'alim sought to push the Histadrut to take a more active stance with regard to Arab workers. It insisted that the events of the past year had demonstrated the vital importance of joint organization in order to combat the efforts of both the "Arab effendis" and the Jewish bourgeoisie to incite hatred and promote discord, and to improve the lot of both Jewish and Arab workers. Ahavat Po'alim complained that the Histadrut not only remained closed to Arab workers but had done virtually nothing to help Arab workers organize themselves. Yet the new organization's insistence that Arab and Jewish workers in Palestine had completely compatible interests entangled it in some of the same contradictions which had long plagued Po'alei Tziyon Smol. For example, even as Ahavat Po'alim called on the Histadrut to admit Arab members and do more to foster joint organization, it was publicly protesting the British government's decision to restrict the immigration to Palestine of Jewish workers. The organization's first membership meeting adopted a resolution which recognized both the full right of the Arab working masses to free social and national development in Palestine and the right of unlimited Jewish immigration and Jewish social and national development. While this formulation seemed to recognize Arab national rights, its insistence on unlimited Jewish immigration inevitably infringed those rights, since such immigration would ultimately lead to a Jewish majority and the transformation of Palestine into a Jewish state. Yet without large-scale Jewish immigration the Zionist project lacked any prospect of success.[9]

The ranks of those dissatisfied with the Histadrut's failure to initiate an active program of Arab work were further swelled as Hakibbutz Ha'artzi–Hashomer Hatza'ir, which I discussed at the end of Chapter 4, emerged in the Histadrut and the Yishuv as an increasingly significant force to MAPAI's left and began to address itself to the question of joint organization. As I mentioned, Hakibbutz Ha'artzi joined Po'alei Tziyon Smol in berating MAPAI and the Histadrut it controlled for their inaction with regard to Arab workers in the cities and in calling for a much more serious commitment to joint organization. But the movement's leadership was divided over whether or not to join Ahavat Po'alim. Me'ir Ya'ari, Hakibbutz Ha'artzi's preeminent leader, argued that the new organization was too far from the socialist-Zionist mainstream, while MAPAI now seemed to be taking a greater interest in joint organization. Leaders of the left wing of Hakibbutz Ha'artzi argued that if Hashomer Hatza'ir got involved, Ahavat Po'alim could be taken out of Po'alei Tziyon Smol's control and developed into the nucleus of a broader movement to foster Arab-Jewish workers' cooperation and pressure the Histadrut into action.[10]

The question soon became moot, however: in the middle of July 1930 Ahavat Po'alim was dissolved by the mandatory government, which was never enthusiastic about initiatives to foster Arab-Jewish worker solidarity, and especially those sponsored by Po'alei Tziyon Smol, which the authorities regarded as Bolshevist and strongly anti-imperialist. There were rumors that the Histadrut leadership had secretly requested the British authorities to suppress Ahavat Po'alim, a charge the Histadrut vigorously denied and for which no evidence has surfaced.[11]

Developments in both the Arab and Jewish communities may have pushed MAPAI to devote greater attention to organizing Arab workers during 1930, but the party was adamant that this project be pursued as it saw fit. At its May 1930 meeting the Histadrut council declared that the organized Jewish workers in Palestine were obligated by class solidarity to try to help the Arab workers improve their standard of living and satisfy their "economic and cultural needs," but it added that "every step toward advancing [the organization of Arab workers] will facilitate the struggle for existence of the Hebrew worker and the Hebrew economy built on Hebrew labor in this country." At the same time, the council explicitly rejected Po'alei Tziyon Smol's long-standing demand, now taken up by Ahavat Po'alim, that the Histadrut be transformed into a territorial labor organization open to Arabs as well as Jews, and contented itself with endorsing the measures which the Histadrut had already been discussing, including the opening of clubs for Arab workers and the publication of an Arabic-language organ.[12]

At the end of 1930 the Histadrut went a bit further by formally establishing a special secretariat or department for Arab affairs, under the supervision of its executive committee. This department had one full-time staff member, Yehuda Burla, who from his office at Histadrut headquarters in Tel Aviv tried to plan and coordinate the work of a small number of other individuals attached to workers' councils in various towns and cities who had an interest in organizing Arab workers. Burla (1886–1969) was born in Jerusalem to a family that had moved from Izmir to Palestine in the seventeenth century. Trained as a teacher, he spent most of his life up to 1948 working in Hebrew-language schools in Damascus and then in Palestine. His main claim to fame, however, is as an author: he was the first modern Hebrew writer whose stories and novels focused on the lives of Jews of Middle Eastern origin, though some of his romantic fiction featured bedouin characters. After his stint at the Histadrut (1930–32) he returned to teaching, then worked for the Keren Hayesod (one of the Zionist Organization's financial arms) and after the establishment of the State of Israel served as a middle-level government official.[13]

As the Histadrut's Arab Secretary, Burla worked under the supervision of those few top leaders of the Histadrut who took an interest in Arab affairs. Among them was Yitzhak Ben-Tzvi, who as we have already seen had worked closely with the Jewish railway workers through the 1920s and had been very involved with the question of joint organization. Though preoccupied with his duties at the Va'ad Le'umi, the nominal leadership body of the Yishuv whose chair he assumed in 1931, Ben-Tzvi participated sporadically in Histadrut leadership discussions on Arab affairs. Another leading Histadrut and MAPAI official involved in this sphere was Dov Hoz (1894–1940). Hoz had arrived in Palestine in 1906 and held various senior labor-Zionist movement leadership posts until his untimely death in an automobile accident. Yet another personality who at this time began to play an increasingly important role in the Histadrut's Arab activism, mainly in Haifa but also nationally, was a young man who adopted the Hebrew name Abba Hushi (1898–1969). Born in Galicia, Hushi came to Palestine in 1920 as a member of Hashomer Hatza'ir. After a stint on a kibbutz he settled in Haifa in 1927 and worked his way up through the local Histadrut and MAPAI hierarchy, assuming the powerful post of secretary of the Haifa Workers' Council in 1931. His rather domineering and abrasive personality led many of his colleagues to find him difficult to work with. Hushi became very much the labor boss of a cosmopolitan port city, with a finger in even the most sordid of local pies; it was said, for example, that he was on good terms with members of Haifa's Jewish criminal underworld. Hushi's efforts to learn Arabic and organize Arab workers in Haifa, especially dockworkers, were in keeping with his desire to be top dog in Haifa. After nineteen years as chief of the Histadrut in Haifa, Hushi became the city's mayor in 1951, a post he retained until his death.

The new Arab Department's first and main preoccupation was funding.

The Histadrut's resources were limited, and because many of the organization's leaders were highly skeptical about, if not opposed to, efforts to organize Arab workers, the Arab Department enjoyed a rather low priority, especially in periods of austerity when the budget allocation for Arab work was often reduced. The Department was therefore always short of money and in search of additional funding, from the Palestine Zionist Executive (which also subsidized other Histadrut programs) and then from the new Jewish Agency, established in 1929 as a vehicle through which non-Zionist Jews could participate in the development of the Jewish "national home" in Palestine.[14] In their appeals to Zionist leaders for funding, Burla and his colleagues usually played on two themes. On the one hand, they argued that Arab and Jewish workers had common economic interests which could serve as a basis for building friendly relations. On the other hand, as Burla put it in January 1931, "If we do not see what is coming and take the initiative, *others* will appear and organize the [Arab] masses against us, in order to make us fail. And then, if the Arab people in their broad masses will be organized against us—our situation in Palestine will be a hundred times more difficult than it is today."[15]

As had been the case during the first phase of activity in the mid-1920s, the Histadrut's Arab activism was in this period virtually restricted to Haifa, where though desperately short of funds the Arab workers' club claimed a membership of 138 in February 1931. Almost all of these were skilled workers, mainly carpenters, stonecutters, and blacksmiths, most of whom were employed at the city's larger enterprises and earned from 15 to 40 piastres a day. The predominance of skilled workers was no accident: with the endorsement of Histadrut officials, club secretary Philip Hassun deliberately sought to exclude unskilled workers or those without steady employment, for fear that the club might acquire the reputation of an employment agency through which Arab workers could find jobs in Jewish enterprises. In addition, the club served the Arab members of the Histadrut-affiliated International Union of Railway, Postal and Telegraph Workers (see Chapter 4). Though most of the club's members possessed basic reading and writing skills, few could read books or even newspapers. The club provided language courses in Hebrew, English, and (for Jewish workers) Arabic, made books and newspapers available, sponsored lectures and discussions, and had a football team and an exercise program. But probably most attractive to its members were the services it offered: access to the Histadrut's Kupat Holim health clinics for the modest sum of 15 piastres a month, and a revolving loan fund whose initial capital had been provided by the Jewish Agency and by a Histadrut credit cooperative, and from which some fifty workers had borrowed sums ranging up to £P5 by February 1931.[16]

But the club's meager budget did not long suffice even for this level of service. Hassun repeatedly complained to his superiors at Histadrut headquarters in Tel Aviv that the club's activities had to be cut back because the money had run out, while Burla was constantly beseeching the Jewish Agency for additional funds. At the same time, Burla had to allay the suspicions of conservative Jewish Agency officials that the Histadrut might be using Zionist funds to implant socialist ideas among Arab workers. In their appeals for funding and their discussions of Arab work, Histadrut officials never lost sight of the political implications of this sphere of activity: the possibility that organizing Arab workers would benefit the Zionist project by weakening Palestinian Arab nationalism.[17]

THE DRIVERS' STRIKES

Even as the Histadrut's Arab Department was trying to get its still relatively small-scale effort off the ground, Arabs and Jews were cooperating in an unprecedented display of militant and effective action in defense of their economic interests. In July 1931 and again in November, Arab and Jewish taxi, bus, and truck drivers launched joint strikes which paralyzed motor transport in Palestine. These were not really instances of worker solidarity: most of the participants were not wage workers but petty proprietors, as a whole industry mobilized to demand redress of its grievances from the mandatory government. Nonetheless, these strikes attracted widespread public attention and sympathy, and for a moment seemed to underscore the possibility of Arab-Jewish cooperation in pursuit of common economic interests.

Drivers of motorized vehicles constituted a new social category in Palestinian society. They and their vehicles transformed local travel and transport and embodied new modes of communication that linked even remote parts of the country. As elsewhere, drivers in Palestine acquired a certain reputation as independent loners, tough guys braving life's obstacles and the dangers of the road, and were incorporated as such into Arab popular culture. This self-image and social representation may have enhanced both the drivers' solidarity and the sympathy with which much of the public regarded them.[18]

Motor transport had developed very quickly in Palestine during the late 1920s and early 1930s as the government built new roads and improved existing ones.[19] A substantial number of Arabs and Jews purchased cars, buses, or trucks and went into business carrying passengers, freight, or both. The majority of these were individuals who owned and operated only a single vehicle, but a few Arab businessmen established larger companies which employed drivers to operate more or less regular taxi and bus lines linking Palestine's cities, towns, and villages, along with buses for tourists and trucks to carry freight. Efforts had been made to reduce fierce competition among the Jewish owner-drivers by allocating fixed routes, and the Histadrut had through its Cooperatives Center sought to establish a cooperative of Jewish drivers. But these initiatives were largely unsuccessful, and motor transport remained largely unregulated, even anarchic, with too many owners and drivers competing for too few passengers and too little freight.

By 1930, all three categories of those who made a living from motor transport—owners who employed drivers for wages, those wage-earning drivers themselves, and those who owned and operated a single vehicle—had come to share a common set of grievances, largely directed at the government. The owners, drivers, and owner-drivers complained bitterly that gasoline prices, already kept high by the two companies (Shell and Vacuum Oil) which controlled the Palestinian market, were jacked up even more excessively by government taxes. A tin of gasoline, they claimed, cost 405 milliemes in Palestine (of which taxes accounted for 205 milliemes) but only 240 to 260 milliemes in Syria, Iraq, and Egypt. The government of Palestine also imposed an annual license fee of £P10–12, while licenses were free in Egypt and Syria. Customs duties on tires were also very high, as were the fines for traffic violations which the drivers claimed were being unjustly and arbitrarily imposed on them. "And as if the government were not satisfied with all these troubles and thinks that there is still some breath of life left in us that can suffer even more," declared a public statement issued in the name of the drivers and owners in June 1931, "it enacted a new law called the Road Transport Act of 1929, inserting conditions and rules which will bring ruin to us and to our trade forever and will leave us no hope in life." [20]

At the end of 1930 a group of Arab owners and drivers asked Hasan Sidqi al-Dajani, a handsome young lawyer from a prominent Palestinian Arab family, to present their demands for lower prices, taxes and fees, and relief from fines, to the petroleum companies and the government. When these talks failed to yield results, discontent among both Arab and Jewish owners and drivers grew and al-Dajani began to work closely with Shraga Gorokhovsky (later Goren), director of the Histadrut's Cooperatives Center, who claimed to speak for the Jewish drivers. By June 1931 there was growing sentiment, especially among the more militant owner-drivers, for a strike of motor transport that would compel the mandatory government to meet their demands. On June 29, 1931, al-Dajani announced the formation of a strike committee composed of both Arabs and Jews and declared that a countrywide general strike of all motorized vehicles carrying passengers and freight would begin on July 1, to be accompanied by peaceful protest caravans of vehicles in Jerusalem, Jaffa, Tel Aviv, and Haifa. The goals of the strike were a 50 percent cut in the gasoline tax and in customs duties on tires, the abolition of license fees, and revision of the Road Transport Act. The strike committee appealed to owners of private automobiles to respect the strike as well, but promised to make vehicles available in each of the major cities to transport physicians in cases of medical emergency.

In internal discussions the Histadrut leadership opposed a strike for fear that it might get out of control and result in violence, or take on political dimensions; in either case the security of Jewish settlements and the ability to get Jewish produce to market might be compromised. Some Histadrut officials professed to see the hand of the Arab nationalist movement or even the communists behind the drivers' militancy. Behind the scenes the Histadrut pressed the Jewish owners and drivers to oppose the strike, but it was unable to prevail: the Arab drivers were solidly for action and many of the Jewish drivers supported them. Unable to prevent the strike, but also fearful of the consequences of opposing it publicly and thereby breaking with the Arab drivers, the Histadrut was reluctantly compelled to endorse the proposed action.[21]

The Histadrut was not alone in regarding the drivers' militancy with unease. The Arab Executive, the nominal leadership of the Arab national movement in Palestine, cannot have been too happy about the emergence of an active Arab-Jewish alliance of this sort. For one, it tended to blur the lines that divided Arab from Jew and undermine the claims and demands of Arab nationalism. Second, this was a movement directed squarely against the policies of the British administration in Palestine, and the Arab Executive at this time still hoped that it could peacefully secure a change in British policy which would bring a quick and easy end to the Zionist project. Finally, the Arab Executive was controlled by the dominant faction within the nationalist movement, led by the Husayni family and its allies, while Hasan Sidqi al-Dajani was the scion of a prominent family opposed to the Husaynis and usually aligned with their chief rival, the Nashashibi family. The Nashashibis were regarded as pro-British and sympathetic to Britain's client 'Abd Allah, the ruler of Transjordan, who had long-standing ambitions in Palestine. It may well have appeared to the Husaynis that by organizing the drivers, their rivals for the leadership of the Arab community had acquired a new constituency of considerable economic and political importance. But like the Histadrut, the Arab Executive could not afford to defy public and press opinion, which largely sympathized with the drivers. On June 29 it issued a statement signed by its president, Musa Kazim al-Husayni, which expressed support for the drivers and hope that their grievances would be resolved without a strike. Interestingly, the statement made no reference to Arabs or Jews but spoke only of "vehicle owners and drivers."[22]

As it turned out, a last-minute concession by the government—a month's hiatus in the collection of license fees—caused the strike to be postponed. In the weeks that followed the drivers formally organized themselves into a Vehicle Owners' and Drivers' Association, with an elected executive committee comprised of equal numbers of Arabs and Jews and chaired by al-Dajani, with Gorokhovsky as vice-chair. The committee entered into negotiations with the government, which offered concessions that fell short of the drivers' demands. Though al-Dajani was hesitant and Gorokhovsky (backed by the Histadrut) strongly opposed a strike, the other members of the association's executive committee, under pressure from the rank and file, pushed for a renewal of the strike threat, and a new strike date was set for August 7. Government officials were divided over how to respond, some favoring concessions and others advocating a hard line. Among the hard-liners motives were mixed: the Director of Customs opposed any concessions that might reduce customs revenues, while the General Manager of the Palestine Railways seems to have hoped that a firm stand by the government would cause a prolonged strike, thereby enhancing the revenues of the ailing railways.[23] After urgent appeals from the Arab and Jewish chambers of commerce and the leaders of the Yishuv, anxious to avoid any disruption of motor transport, the government offered to appoint a committee which would investigate the drivers' and owners' demands and issue a report by the end of October. The Drivers' and Owners' Association accepted the offer, called off their open-ended strike, and organized a twenty-four-hour stoppage instead. The strike came off peacefully and was deemed a success by the Association.[24]

In the months that followed Hasan Sidqi al-Dajani came under strong attack in the Arab press for cooperating with Jews. Surprisingly, the attack was led by *Filastin*, a newspaper aligned with the Nashashibi-led opposition to the dominant Husayni faction. On September 18, 1931, *Filastin* published an editorial clearly directed at al-Dajani: it advised "anyone who has cooperated with the deceiving Zionists to give it up and instead strive to form an Arab association in which no non-Arab has any role, and God will forgive what has gone before." A leaflet from about the same time, signed by three Arab drivers but probably inspired by pro-Husayni activists, accused al-Dajani of being a Zionist stooge:

> There is no doubt that those who are informed about the Association's affairs know that Hasan Sidqi al-Dajani draws his power only from the Jews. He is in Tel Aviv every day, and every day he has meetings with the Jews there. Is it reasonable that he would go along with any policy that was against the interests of the Jews? And does he not do within the association what the Jews tell him to do?

The leaflet went on to call for al-Dajani's deposition and the breakup of the joint association, a demand echoed by a number of letters signed by drivers and sent to *Filastin*.[25]

Al-Dajani's response to his critics, published in *Filastin* two days later, was somewhat disingenuous. He stated that a purely Arab association of drivers and owners had been formed several years earlier. But, he went on, "we realized that we could not strike a heavy blow against the government and force it to accept our demands unless the strike was general and total in all parts of the country. As soon as word of the strike spread some of the Jewish drivers let us know that they wanted to join with us, so we met them and agreed on basic conditions—but we did not unite." Contrary to the facts, al-Dajani insisted that there was no joint association, but rather an alliance of two entirely separate organizations, one Arab and the other Jewish. In any event, these attacks do not seem to have greatly weakened al-Dajani's position or Arab-Jewish cooperation: when the drivers began to mobilize again in late October, he was still their leader and Arabs and Jews continued to work together closely. The committee of inquiry had recommended a number of concessions, including the abolition of license fees, but the government of Palestine declined to accept the recommendations and announced that it would require several more months to reach a final decision. The angry drivers organized another national congress and decided to strike as of midnight on November 2–3, 1931.[26]

This time the threat was carried out, as some 2,000 drivers struck for nine days, until midnight on November 11. The strike was highly effective: newspaper accounts indicate that apart from military and police vehicles, hardly a car, bus, or truck was to be seen on the roads of Palestine, which were taken over instead by donkey carts. For the first few days the drivers seem to have enjoyed the sympathy of Arab and Jewish public opinion; even *Filastin,* which had earlier been so hostile to al-Dajani, supported the strike. The Arab merchants' association called for a three-day sympathy strike, to pressure the authorities to accept the drivers' demands and get back to business as usual, but called it off when the government announced a one-month postponement in the collection of license fees. As the strike began to disrupt economic activity and inconvenience more people, the drivers came under increasing pressure to return to work. The Histadrut exerted pressure on the Jewish drivers, and Hasan Sidqi al-Dajani began to waver under pressure from Arab businessmen. The strikers' delegates held out for some time, but finally agreed to end the strike after the Arab chambers of commerce promised their support in achieving the drivers' demands. A few months later the drivers achieved a partial victory when the government reduced license fees, though to offset this loss of revenue the government simultaneously increased duties on spare parts.[27]

In the aftermath of the strike, al-Dajani toyed with the idea of transforming his constituency among the Arab drivers into a broader political organization. In secret talks with officials of the Jewish Agency's Political Department, he sought Zionist funding to help establish a "Palestine Arab Workers' Party," apparently envisioned as something of a cross between a political party and a trade union federation. Moshe Shertok and other Political Department officials were quite interested in the idea, and Histadrut officials went so far as to draw up a charter for the proposed organization. Nothing came of these plans, however. While remaining head of the Arab Car Owners' and Drivers' Association al-Dajani became involved in Arab politics as one of the leaders of the National Defense Party, founded in 1934 by the Nashashibis and their allies after the dissolution of the Arab Executive and the open fragmentation of Palestine's Arab elite into rival political factions, each with its own party.[28]

The motor transport strikes of 1931 thus produced no lasting Arab-Jewish organization. They did, however, lead to much more intense government regulation of motor transport in Palestine and the restructuring of the industry. New laws and regulations were issued which fixed bus routes and made licenses more difficult to obtain, thereby squeezing out small-scale owner-drivers while strengthening the fleet owners. This benefited the Arab bus company owners but also the Histadrut, which under Gorokhovsky's leadership organized the Jewish drivers into cooperatives.[29] Like other sectors of Palestine's economy, motor transport would become increasingly segregated, with several large Histadrut-affiliated bus and trucking cooperatives serving Jewish towns and settlements, and private Arab companies serving Arab towns and villages.

"ARAB ACTIVISM" IN CRISIS

The Histadrut leadership's ambivalence about the drivers' militancy was paralleled by its ambivalence about efforts to organize Arab workers employed in the Jewish sector. This was demonstrated in September 1931, when some thirty Arab workers employed by Jewish farmers in the moshava of Benyamina went on strike in response to a wage cut and approached their Jewish coworkers for support. The strike was formally endorsed by both a general meeting of the Jewish workers in the moshava and the Histadrut executive committee, which promised that Jews would not use the strike to displace the Arab workers and that Jewish workers would join the picket lines in solidarity. In private, however, officials of the Histadrut and of its local organ the Benyamina Workers' Council were quite unenthusiastic about the strike. This was a period of high unemployment in the Yishuv and MAPAI was not anxious to have the Histadrut defend Arab workers employed in moshavot when it really wanted to replace them with Jews. Unemployed Jewish workers were already venting their frustration on Arabs: in 'Afula that June a group of Jews without jobs had attacked and driven off Arabs engaged in road building work on a government contract. The MAPAI loyalists who controlled the Benyamina Workers' Council decided to refrain from any active support of the strike, which soon collapsed. While Hashomer Hatza'ir activists in the moshava denounced the Council and the Histadrut leadership for the strike's failure, MAPAI supporters blamed it on the Arab workers' alleged lack of commitment and capacity for organization.[30]

At the same time, the momentum which had seemed to characterize the Histadrut's effort to develop a constituency among urban Arab workers in late 1930 and early 1931 was faltering. In a memorandum drawn up in December 1931, Yehuda Burla stressed the urgency of expanding activities targeting Arabs as a means of overcoming the growing enmity between Arabs and Jews and called on all the institutions concerned—the Histadrut, the Jewish Agency, and the Va'ad Le'umi—to work together. He envisioned the establishment of clubs for Arab workers in all the major cities and towns, organizing work in Arab villages, a vastly expanded loan fund whose capital would be subscribed by all the Jewish-owned banks in

Palestine, and an Arabic-language newspaper.[31] But Burla's expansive vision was out of touch with reality: by the beginning of 1932 this sphere of the Histadrut's work was at a virtual standstill. Facing a budget crisis, the Histadrut suspended plans to start up clubs for Arab workers in Jaffa, Jerusalem, and Lydda, along with funding for Arabic lessons and other activities. The Haifa club continued to operate but only barely, and Histadrut leaders doubted that they would be able to provide even the modest sum hitherto allocated to sustain it. Many did not feel that the club was justifying the resources which had been put into it and wondered if it could not somehow be combined with the Arab section of the railway workers' union.[32]

Abba Hushi, the new secretary of the Haifa Workers' Council, played an increasingly active and central role in these discussions and in the Histadrut's subsequent interactions with Arab workers. Hushi believed that the Haifa club should be seen as only a transitional form, a means to an end: the ultimate goal was the mobilization of Arab workers around economic issues and their organization into trade unions linked to the Histadrut. Hushi had no use for the Haifa club in its present moribund state and saw its secretary, Philip Hassun, as an ineffective and expensive "legacy" from the club's earlier incarnation, someone who would never be capable of exercising the kind of leadership necessary to organize a substantial base among Arab workers. If the club was to be reactivated and the Histadrut, or more precisely the Haifa Workers' Council, was to undertake the strategy Hushi advocated, Hassun would have to go.[33]

By this point Hassun was in fact almost at the end of his tether. In frequent letters to the Histadrut executive committee, he complained that he had not received any funds for months and had been unable to pay the club's rent, electric bills, or caretaker's wages. Sunk in debt because he had borrowed heavily to keep the club open, Hassun pleaded with Histadrut leaders to pay off its debts and close it down so he could reopen his tailor's shop and feed his hungry family. By the spring of 1932, as his relations with Abba Hushi, never very cordial, reached the breaking point, Hassun's letters took on an increasingly desperate and bitter tone. In a letter to his old mentor Yitzhak Ben-Tzvi, Hassun charged that Hushi had publicly threatened to beat him up if he persisted in demanding to see the club's accounts. "So dear brother," he told Ben-Tzvi, "this is our reward after ten years work, and after sacrificing youth and family on the altar of the Histadruth viz;—in old age there springs up a foolish fellow from the Histadruth threatening to beat and disgrace us. Is that not a great blessing?" Hassun begged Ben-Tzvi and Ben-Gurion to come to Haifa to get the club out of the "muddle" it was in and rescue him from Hushi's abuse.[34]

But Ben-Gurion and Ben-Tzvi sided with Abba Hushi rather than with Philip Hassun, whose career with the Histadrut came to an end soon thereafter. In June 1932 he was dismissed as secretary of the Haifa club; what became of him after that is unknown. His removal from the scene was a triumph for Abba Hushi, who had already begun to implement the new approach he had been advocating and could now take full charge of the Histadrut's Arab work in Haifa. That work was bolstered by the arrival at about this time of additional funds raised in England by Israel Sieff, a wealthy Zionist who had founded a group in London which sought to foster better Jewish-Arab relations.

ON THE HAIFA WATERFRONT

The first arena in which Hushi's strategy for reviving and expanding the Histadrut's work among Arabs would bear fruit was the old port of Haifa. (A new deepwater harbor, Palestine's first, was under construction but would not be completed until the end of 1933.) Histadrut leaders had taken an interest in the port since the early 1920s, because of its obvious economic (and potential political) importance, and in keeping with the policy of Hebrew labor had sought to gain a foothold for Jewish workers there. The Zionist Executive and the Histadrut incessantly lobbied the government of Palestine and the Colonial Office to induce the port authorities and the Arab contractors who controlled most of the jobs at the port to employ Jews, both in the operation of the old harbor and the construction of the new one, but they were never very successful. The government of Palestine, backed by the Colonial Office, generally resisted these pressures for political reasons but also because Jews would have required higher wages and better working conditions. At the same time, as with railway work, it was difficult for the Histadrut to get Jews to seek and stay at jobs in the port. Except during periods of economic crisis and high unemployment, few Jews were interested in enduring the grueling working conditions and miserable wages which port work offered, even though they were paid higher wages than the Arab port workers.

At various points during the 1920s the Haifa Workers' Council had dispatched members of several kibbutzim-in-formation to work at the port, but these groups seldom stayed for very long. The number of Jews working at the old port of Haifa therefore remained small: at the end of 1929, some two dozen Jews, almost all skilled workers or supervisory personnel, were employed there, as opposed to some 450 Arabs. Of the latter, many were not from Palestine but from the Hawran region of French-ruled Syria. During the mandate period, and especially during the first half of the 1930s, thousands of desperately poor peasants came to Palestine from the Hawran, seasonally or for longer periods, in search of work in agriculture, the ports, road and railway construction and maintenance, and other sectors where low-wage manual labor was required. The term *hawrani* would in fact enter colloquial Palestinian (and later Israeli) Hebrew as a synonym for "poor" or "ragged." [35] As we will see, some left-wing Zionists would argue that Palestinian Arab and Jewish workers faced a common enemy in these Hawrani migrants and should unite to counter the threat they allegedly posed.

In the early 1930s, faced with high unemployment in the Yishuv, the Histadrut stepped up its efforts to get more Jews hired at the harbor by bringing pressure to bear on British officials, locally and through channels in Jerusalem and London, including friends in the Labor Party and the Trades Union Congress. Histadrut and Zionist leaders advanced the argument that since Jews paid some 50 percent of Palestine's taxes, they were entitled to 50 percent of the jobs in government-run enterprises, including the ports.[36] The Histadrut also sought to induce the Jewish citrus farmers, whose Pardes export company accounted for a large proportion of the goods that passed through the port, to insist on Hebrew labor at Haifa. At the same time, Abba Hushi and other officials of the Haifa Workers' Council cultivated relations with some of the Arab labor contractors at the port in order to get them to add a few Jewish workers to their work crews.

The Histadrut did manage to secure for Jews a large proportion of the jobs created by the construction of the new deepwater port at Haifa. But at the old port its lobbying yielded meager results: in May 1932 only twenty-eight Jews—mainly future kibbutz members living in Haifa temporarily and ready for any sacrifice in the struggle for Hebrew labor— were working at the old port as stevedores, porters, or lightermen. The stevedores, who loaded and unloaded ships, were the elite of the harbor workforce; the porters carried goods between the railway siding and the docks; and the lightermen worked on the boats ("lighters") that conveyed goods to and from freighters, which because of the shallowness of the water anchored about a mile offshore.[37]

In these circumstances, it was obvious that, as with the railways, Jews could be placed and kept in jobs at Haifa harbor only if wages were substantially increased and working conditions considerably improved for the

Arabs who worked there. This is why Abba Hushi moved quickly to seize the opportunity that presented itself when, in April 1932, a number of the Arab lightermen suddenly went on strike, apparently to protest the contractors' decision to employ them on a daily rather than a monthly basis and to dismiss some workers without taking seniority into account. The Jewish lightermen with whom the Arab strikers had been working side by side for a year and had developed friendly relations refused to serve as strikebreakers; many of them were Hashomer Hatzaʻir members awaiting settlement in a kibbutz, and they saw the strike as an opportunity to demonstrate the proletarian internationalism which was one of their movement's slogans. At first some of the Arab strikers suggested approaching the Haifa-based Palestinian Arab Workers' Society for assistance, but when the PAWS proved of little help the Arab workers agreed to authorize Abba Hushi to negotiate on their behalf.

Though Hushi was on good terms with the contractors, he was unable to achieve much for the strikers: after four days they returned to work with only a verbal promise that after two weeks they would again be employed on a monthly basis.[38] The Arab lightermen were nonetheless impressed by, and grateful for, the support they had received from their Jewish coworkers, the Haifa Workers' Council, and the Histadrut: the slow season had begun, and had their Jewish coworkers not joined them and the Histadrut not backed them, they probably could not have stood up to their employers. After the strike ended, the lightermen and a number of other Arab harbor workers joined a new Histadrut-sponsored Harbor Workers' Union for both Arab and Jewish workers. Though the Jewish workers who identified with Hashomer Hatzaʻir wanted a fully international union with no internal divisions, Hushi and his MAPAI colleagues insisted that the union comprise separate national sections.

The Arab members of the Harbor Workers' Union were to constitute the first cell of a new organization which was established in 1932 to recruit and organize Arab workers under the auspices of the Histadrut. In Hebrew the new organization was called Brit Poʻalei Eretz Yisraʼel, the "League of Workers of the Land of Israel," and in Arabic Ittihad ʻUmmal Filastin, the "Union of the Workers of Palestine." I will henceforth refer to it as the Palestine Labor League (PLL), its official name in English. As I discussed in Chapter 2, after years of debate on the question of joint organization the Histadrut's third congress had in July 1927 adopted a resolution calling for the establishment of an "international league (*brit beinleʼumit*) of the workers of Eretz Yisraʼel" which was to include the Histadrut and its as-yet-nonexistent Arab counterpart. No such league or

alliance had ever been formed. Instead, what was in fact a small organization created to serve as the Histadrut's auxiliary for Arab workers was
endowed with the rather grandiose name originally intended for the proposed binational labor federation. The PLL's charter was drawn up by
Histadrut officials and ratified by its executive committee in May 1932,
and though the latter claimed to be implementing the resolution of the
1927 Histadrut congress, it was obvious that this was not really what had
been envisioned five years earlier.[39]

By creating the PLL, the Histadrut leadership foreclosed any possibility
that Arab workers would be allowed to become full and equal members of
a transformed, non-Zionist Histadrut, as Po'alei Tziyon Smol and the
Arab workers aligned with it had long demanded. This step also rendered
Hashomer Hatza'ir's call for joint Arab-Jewish unions in mixed workplaces largely irrelevant, since Arab workers were now to be organized
within the exclusively Arab PLL. For the remainder of the mandate period, in fact until 1959 when the Histadrut decided to allow Arabs to become full members, the PLL (renamed the Israel Labor League after 1948)
was the organization to which Arab workers organized under the tutelage
of the Histadrut were consigned. There was never any question that the
PLL was very much an instrument of the Histadrut: it was run exclusively
by Jewish Histadrut officials, its budget came almost entirely from the
Histadrut and other Zionist sources, and it cleaved faithfully to the Histadrut line—or more precisely, the MAPAI line—on all questions. Arab
workers who joined were issued PLL membership cards, and in return for
regular payment of dues gained access to various Histadrut services, most
importantly the Kupat Holim network of health clinics and special loan
funds.

The day-to-day work of running the new PLL and recruiting Arab
workers was entrusted to a newly hired full-time organizer, Eliyahu
Agassi, who for more than four decades would play a central role in the
Histadrut's Arab work. Agassi was born in Baghdad in 1909 and followed
his family to Palestine in 1928. After graduating from the elite Herzliyya
secondary school, where he joined one of the labor-Zionist youth movements, he began studying at the Hebrew University in Jerusalem. In the
summer of 1932 he accepted an offer from Dov Hoz and Abba Hushi to
move to Haifa and work full-time organizing Arab workers there, replacing Philip Hassun. To Hoz, Hushi, and the other Histadrut leaders interested in this sphere of activity, Agassi must have seemed the perfect candidate for the job, the kind of organizer they had dreamed of for years.
Agassi was Jewish, a loyal member of MAPAI, fluent in Arabic as well as

English (essential for dealing with British officials and managers), well acquainted with Arab culture, and (unlike most MAPAI members) deeply committed to organizing Arab workers, both from socialist conviction and as a means of realizing Zionism's goals. It should be added that Agassi's personal qualities also served him well: unlike not a few of his Histadrut colleagues, who were overwhelmingly of eastern European origin, he was a gentle, soft-spoken and mild-mannered man, and also respectful of Arabs. These qualities helped endear him to many of the Arabs with whom he came into contact, including even some who vehemently rejected his politics and mission.[40]

TRAVAILS OF HEBREW LABOR

For Agassi, Hushi, and their Histadrut colleagues, organizing Arab workers was understood as inextricably bound up with the struggle for Hebrew labor. None of them saw any contradiction between the two tasks; indeed, labor-Zionist discourse posed them as entirely complementary. Decades later, when asked why Abba Hushi had felt so strongly about the need to organize Arab workers, Agassi would explain that "Haifa was a mixed city. There were workplaces in which Jews had no foothold, like the harbor. For him this was an opportunity to organize Arab workers and also to get Jewish workers into the harbor." Ben-Gurion made a similar connection at a meeting of the Histadrut executive committee immediately after the lightermen's strike: "From what the comrades in Haifa have told me, some fifty Jewish workers may be able to get work at the harbor, and thereby help the Arab workers who are there. . . . We are facing the possibility of getting Jewish workers into an important branch of activity and of organizing Arab workers."[41] When in later years Arab workers would sometimes challenge Agassi about the Histadrut's campaign for Hebrew labor, Agassi would respond with a simple metaphor. The Arabs, he argued, had three "sacks of flour"—that is, jobs in the Arab, government, and international sectors—while the Jews had only one sack, the Jewish sector. As long as this was the case, the Jews were entitled to reserve their "sack" for themselves, while also seeking their fair share of jobs in the government and international sectors.[42]

So it was that even as the Histadrut was working to secure a base among Arab workers at Haifa harbor, it was also trying to secure more jobs for Jews there, which meant the likely displacement of Arab workers. In addition to the kibbutz members who volunteered or were recruited for harbor work, Abba Hushi (with support and funding from the Histadrut) began in 1933 to organize the immigration to Palestine of groups of Jewish dockworkers from Salonika, in the hope that these tough and highly experienced men would be able to displace Arabs and gain a permanent foothold for Jews in Haifa harbor.[43] A year later Hushi worked out a deal with the Pardes company by which the latter would contract with the Histadrut to provide labor for the porterage of its citrus exports at Haifa, thereby providing more jobs for Jews, though some Arabs would be hired as well. When the new deepwater harbor opened, the Histadrut formed its own company, Manof, to supply labor, mainly Jews from Salonika, though during the busy season Manof hired Arabs as well. In April 1936, on the eve of the general strike that launched the Arab revolt, some 200 Jews had regular jobs at Haifa harbor. As we will see, that strike would create conditions in which Hebrew labor could be more securely established and considerably expanded in this vital enterprise.[44]

As the decade wore on, Hebrew labor would become an increasingly sensitive issue for labor Zionists. The Histadrut's campaign in 1929–30 to force Jewish citrus grove owners in the moshavot to employ only Jewish workers had not been a great success, despite the availability of numerous unemployed and desperate Jewish workers in the cities who could be mobilized and dispatched to the moshavot to picket, harass, and if necessary forcibly expel Arab workers. MAPAI and the Histadrut it controlled depicted this campaign as a life-or-death struggle for "the right to work" and used it as a way to enhance the Histadrut's growing power and influence within the Yishuv. But the policy elicited considerable criticism, from the parties to MAPAI's left and other sociopolitical forces in the Yishuv but also from otherwise pro-Zionist European social-democratic parties and labor organizations. Prime Minister Ramsay MacDonald browbeat Ben-Gurion about the issue at the Empire Labor Conference in July 1930, though MacDonald's concerns had less to do with socialist principle than with the security of the empire. "The Muslims of Bengal are hinting to us that we must satisfy the Arabs of Palestine," MacDonald told Ben-Gurion. "Look here, the Jewish Agency has a rule that forbids employment of Arab workers. Until now it went unnoticed, but now the business is known throughout India. I even asked to be provided with a copy of a Jewish Agency contract, to see for myself whether a rule enforcing exclusively Jewish labor does exist. . . . You are causing us tremendous problems."[45]

Such warnings did nothing to deter the Histadrut from launching several new rounds in the struggle for Hebrew labor during the first half of the 1930s, mainly in the moshavot but also in the cities. Though these aggressive campaigns aroused great resentment among Arabs and strengthened labor Zionism's preeminence in the Yishuv and world Zionism, they did not accomplish their proclaimed goal. At the beginning of 1936 Arabs constituted some 35 percent of the labor force in Jewish agriculture, 20 percent in transportation in the Jewish sector, and 12 percent in construction.[46] Moreover, as we will see, by 1934 the Histadrut's campaign had begun to engender organized Arab resistance to displacement and counterprotests. But a more significant cause of the Hebrew labor campaign's failure was the unprecedented economic expansion Palestine began to experience in 1932 and which would last into 1935.

The economic boom had several causes, one of the most important of which was the great surge in Jewish immigration into the country that began in 1932 and reached its peak in 1935. During the 1920s Jewish immigration had averaged less than 10,000 a year, below the natural increase of Palestine's Arab population. As a result, in 1931 the 174,000 Jews in Palestine still accounted for only 17 percent of the country's population; that year only 4,000 Jews had immigrated to Palestine. In 1932, however, Jewish immigration more than doubled, and the following year it more than tripled again. In 1934 over 42,000 Jews immigrated to Palestine and in 1935, the high point of this wave, almost 62,000—about equal to the net Jewish inflow (immigration minus emigration) in the entire decade from 1922 to 1931. As a result, even without counting additional thousands of immigrants who had entered the country illegally, Palestine's Jewish population roughly doubled between 1932 and the end of 1935 to reach 375,000, about 27 percent of the population. Almost 60 percent of these immigrants came from Poland and Germany, countries in which Jews faced a rising tide of antisemitism that assumed increasingly virulent and menacing forms. The new immigrants settled disproportionately in the big coastal cities, which grew very rapidly: Tel Aviv and its suburbs accounted for 26.5 percent of the Yishuv's population in 1931 and 36.7 percent in 1936, while the figures for Haifa were 9.2 percent and 13.6 percent respectively.

This influx of Jewish immigrants was accompanied by an unprecedented influx of Jewish capital, which also stimulated Palestine's economy. Some of this capital was brought by the immigrants themselves; another portion was invested by Jews who remained abroad; and some of it was channeled into Palestine through the controversial "Transfer Agreement" which the Jewish Agency negotiated with the new Nazi regime in Germany in 1933 and which remained in effect until the beginning of the Second World War. This agreement, which was vigorously denounced by many Jews and other antifascists who were trying to organize an economic boycott of Nazi Germany, permitted some of the capital of emigrating German Jews to be exported to the Yishuv in the form of German goods.[47]

Most of this new capital went into residential construction, especially in Tel Aviv and the Jewish neighborhoods of Haifa. A large fraction went into citriculture, which accounted for four-fifths of Palestine's exports and grew dramatically in these years as both Arabs and Jews expanded existing groves and planted new ones. The value of Palestine's orange exports (the great majority of which went to the United Kingdom) increased from £P727,647 in 1930–31 to more than £P3 million by 1934–35. There was also substantial growth in manufacturing, mainly for the rapidly growing local market: capital invested in Jewish-owned industrial enterprises rose from £P2.2 million in 1929 to £P5.4 million in 1933 and to £P12.7 million by 1937. All told, in the four years 1932–35 Palestine's industrial output grew by 61 percent, imports by 130 percent, exports by 77 percent, and consumption of electrical power by 335 percent.[48]

This influx of capital and immigrants, some of whom came with skills that had been in short supply, obviously benefited the Jewish sector of the Palestinian economy most. But the rapid growth of the Jewish sector stimulated growth in the Arab sector as well, and some of the Yishuv's prosperity trickled down to Arabs in the form of expanded employment opportunities and higher wages for workers, an expanding local market for merchants, manufacturers, and farmers, and growing demand for services. Large numbers of Arab peasants, desperate for some income to supplement meager livelihoods from agriculture, were attracted from the countryside of Palestine (and, as noted earlier, from the Hawran region of Syria) to jobs in the citrus groves, the ports, urban construction, and public works sites. Government statistics still classified some two-thirds of Palestinian Muslims as dependent on agriculture, but growing numbers of peasants now spent at least part of the year working for wages in the citrus groves and in the burgeoning coastal cities.[49]

The prosperity which the Yishuv enjoyed between 1932 and 1935 undermined the Histadrut's struggle for Hebrew labor. An abundant supply of Arab workers kept wages low and made it difficult for Jewish workers to compete for unskilled jobs in agriculture (especially citriculture), the railways, public works, the ports, and urban construction. At the same time, despite the Histadrut's exhortations, relatively few Jewish workers, whether newcomers or veterans, were willing to forsake relatively well-paying jobs in construction, services, or industry in the towns and cities for poorly paid and difficult work in the citrus groves, or for that matter in the ports and on the railways. As a result, Arab employment in Jewish-owned citrus groves and at urban construction sites expanded rather dramatically in the 1932–35 period. In the late 1920s high urban Jewish unemployment had provided the Histadrut with an effective weapon in the struggle for Hebrew labor. By contrast, the economic expansion of the early 1930s made the conquest of labor much more difficult. This did not stop the Histadrut from trying; but as we will see, it was not until political conditions changed dramatically in 1936 that the Histadrut would be able to achieve even partially the goals it had dreamed of for so long.

ARAB WORKERS, THE HISTADRUT, AND THE PAWS

When Agassi arrived in Haifa in the summer of 1932 to take up his new post as the Histadrut's chief organizer of Arab workers, the Haifa Workers' Council had already taken under its wing a core group of some eighty Arab port workers. Other groups of Arab workers soon began to approach Agassi and Hushi to seek their assistance in organizing and negotiating with employers. These workers were not necessarily unfamiliar with labor organizing and trade unionism; some had had previous contacts with the PAWS, which had been present (if not always very active) in Haifa since 1925. But impressed by the Histadrut's intervention on behalf of the lightermen, they hoped to benefit from the Jewish labor movement's apparent wealth, power, and effectiveness. The following case illustrates some of the circumstances in which Arab workers approached the Histadrut at this early stage, as well as some of the complexities which always characterized its interactions with Arab workers.

In July 1932, a delegation of skilled construction workers employed by the contractor 'Aziz Khayyat on a large project at the Iraq Petroleum Company installation and the nearby Customs Office appeared at the Haifa Workers' Council. The 150 skilled and unskilled workers for whom the delegates spoke worked twelve and a half hours a day, including an hour off for lunch. Unhappy with this extremely long workday, the forty or so stonecutters working at the site had consulted the PAWS, of which some of them had been or still were members, and on its advice had informed Khayyat that they would henceforth work no more than eight hours a day. To this Khayyat replied that he had no work for anyone unwilling to labor twelve and a half hours a day. The stonecutters walked off the site, in effect declaring a strike, but rather than post pickets and publicize their struggle they simply found other jobs elsewhere, so that Khayyat was able to replace them without difficulty.

The PAWS failed to take any further action, suggesting only that the remaining workers hand over membership dues and join up. The scaffold erectors employed at the site, still dissatisfied, met, announced that they too wanted an eight-hour day, and elected one of their number, a man named Jurji ("George"), as their representative. But when Khayyat fired Jurji and threatened the rest of them with dismissal, they backed down. It was at this point that the scaffold workers accepted the advice of the one Jew among them, a Histadrut member, to turn to the Haifa Workers' Council for help. Hushi told the workers that the stonecutters, the PAWS, and the scaffold workers had gone about it all wrong: one could not go on strike without proper preparations, and if one did launch a strike one didn't just find another job somewhere else. After the scolding, Hushi offered to have their one Jewish coworker approach Khayyat and threaten a strike if Jurji was not rehired. Hushi also asked the workers to contact the PAWS and convey the Haifa Workers' Council's desire for cooperation.

Three days later the delegation returned and told Hushi and Agassi that the PAWS leaders had refused to cooperate with the Histadrut, because the latter was a "Zionist organization which wants a strike so that it can remove the Arab workers from this workplace in order to replace them with Jews, just as [according to the secretary of the PAWS] the Histadrut had done after the lightermen's strike at the port of Haifa." Happily for the Histadrut, an Arab lighterman was on hand to deny this accusation, although as we have seen the allegation was in fact not entirely inaccurate. Taking the initiative, Hushi and Agassi sent two letters directly to the PAWS, suggesting that either the PAWS declare a strike, with the Histadrut's support, or that the two organizations meet and plan a strike together. There was no reply, and the refusal of the PAWS to cooperate with the Histadrut made the latter look reasonable.

However, the Histadrut was unable to take advantage of these circumstances, because just as the Arab building workers had contacted both the PAWS and the Histadrut to achieve their ends, they had also appealed for help to the British authorities, in the person of the local District Commissioner, the chief British administrator in that part of Palestine. The Commissioner rejected the workers' demand for an eight-hour day, insisting that Palestine was not like England or other European countries, but he did secure the agreement of Khayyat and other contractors to reduce the workday by one hour, to eleven and a half hours. Some of the building workers favored accepting this proposal, while others rejected it as inadequate. We do not know for certain how things ultimately turned out, but because there is no further evidence of unrest among this particular group of workers it seems likely that most if not all of them ultimately accepted Khayyat's offer or quietly found jobs elsewhere.[50]

What we do know about this incident nonetheless tells us some important things about relations among Arab workers, the Histadrut, and the Palestine Arab Workers' Society. For one, it suggests it is not at all useful or accurate to characterize Arab workers who were not unaware of the Histadrut's Zionist commitments yet nonetheless chose to cooperate with the Histadrut and its emissaries as gullible dupes. As we will see in other cases as well, Arab workers possessed a capacity for agency, for making their own sense of complex situations, and for acting to further their interests as they saw them, though their perceptions and actions did not necessarily coincide with those of middle- or upper-class nationalists. They were often willing, or more precisely compelled, to seek the help of any organization, institution, or individual that might help them in their grossly unequal battle with their employers, including even Zionists or officials of the colonial state, whose intervention they not infrequently sought when they thought it might be of some use. Hence the inadequacy of labeling such interactions simply as instances of "manipulation" or even "collaboration," as if these terms were not embedded in a particular nationalist discourse and did not themselves require elucidation and contextualization. I will return to this issue later.

This episode also helps us understand the PAWS' attitude toward the Histadrut more clearly. In Chapter 4 I showed that while the leaders of the Arab railway workers who constituted the core of the PAWS were willing to work with the Histadrut as the representative of the Jewish railway workers, they adamantly rejected the right of the Histadrut to recruit or represent Arab railway workers. The case of the building workers demonstrates that the PAWS applied the same principle in other sectors as well. Thus, in its efforts to recruit Arab workers in Haifa, the Palestine Labor League had always to contend with the hostility and rivalry of the PAWS, which though small and weak was very much part of the local labor scene. Wherever the PLL developed ties with Arab workers and sought to represent them in a labor dispute, the PAWS was sure to show up, denounce the PLL as Zionist, try to take charge of handling the dispute, and seek to recruit the workers involved. The workers themselves seem to have been aware of this rivalry and were sometimes able to take advantage of it in ways that pleased neither the Histadrut nor the PAWS.

In its rivalry with the PAWS, the PLL had some important advantages. Backed as it was by the Histadrut, whose achievements in winning higher wages for Jewish workers and building up a powerful network of economic, social, cultural, and political institutions and enterprises were plain to see, it seemed to offer Arab workers a stronger position from which to bargain with employers, useful connections, and access to a broad range of services. The PAWS sought to counter these advantages by developing its own connections with nonworker personalities, particularly locally prominent lawyers, who could bargain on the workers' behalf from a position of relative equality and impunity. One of these lawyers was Hanna 'Asfur, who served as the PAWS' legal counselor for much of the 1930s and 1940s. Born in Shafa 'Amr in 1902, 'Asfur attended schools in Palestine and Lebanon, held a clerical job at the Palestine Railways, and then served as a court translator in Haifa. He graduated from a local law school and opened his own office in Haifa in 1929.[51] Later other lawyers, linked to different factions within the Palestinian Arab elite and nationalist movement, would develop ties with various segments of the fledgling Arab labor movement.

The Histadrut frequently denounced these lawyers as self-interested and opportunistic outsiders, contrasting their role in some of the Arab unions with the purported independence of the Jewish unions, led by authentic workers. This depiction was not altogether inaccurate: some of these outsiders, like Hasan Sidqi al-Dajani in 1931 and Fakhri al-Nashashibi a few years later, did try to use the labor movement as a base from which to further their political ambitions. But from the standpoint of the rank and file Arab workers and the leaders of a weak Arab labor movement, they could often be quite useful allies, and the workers who ran the PAWS may have seen themselves as "using" these lawyers and notables every bit as much as the latter were exploiting the workers. Moreover, the Histadrut's claim to be an independent labor movement interested only in benefiting the workers was belied by an easily observable fact. The PAWS could and did point to the Histadrut's status as a central institution of the Zionist project, whose ultimate goal was the creation in Palestine of a Jewish majority and the country's transformation into a Jewish state. It also pointed out the obvious contradiction between the Histadrut's professed commitment to worker solidarity across national lines on the one hand, and on the other its unrelenting struggle for Hebrew labor, which often meant, or was taken to mean, displacing Arabs from their jobs. As the case of the building workers outlined above makes clear, attacking the Histadrut on these grounds was not automatically effective: Arab workers might choose to ignore the appeal of nationalism and work with the Histadrut, or even join the PLL, if they felt it was to their advantage. But the Zionist commitment of the Histadrut, and by extension the PLL, gave the PAWS and later other Arab labor organizations a potent weapon.

While its contacts with the building workers did not result in a sustained relationship, the PLL did in the summer and fall of 1932 develop ties with other groups of Arab workers in Haifa. The case of seven Arab workers at a Haifa bakery is typical. These workers approached their employer (a member of the city's small German community) to seek a reduction in their workweek from eighty or eighty-five hours to sixty, a wage increase (from £P3 to £P3.5 a month), and free bread, as was the custom at other bakeries; when he refused, they turned to the PLL and joined its newly formed union for Arab workers employed in European-style bakeries. Though the PLL cautioned them against hasty action, the owner's intransigence and abusiveness ultimately led the workers to strike. Hushi and Agassi saw this as a test case: in a letter to the Histadrut executive committee, they insisted that "on this occasion, the first instance of an organized strike by Arab workers connected with it, the Histadrut must demonstrate its organizational power, the solidarity of its members, and its readiness to stand by the Arab worker and help him materially and morally." The Haifa Workers' Council provided the workers with strike pay and issued a Hebrew-language leaflet to publicize their cause. But the bakery owner brought in strikebreakers, Haifa's German community supported him (rendering a consumer boycott ineffective), and the strike ended in failure. When the workers could not find new jobs, the Haifa Workers' Council helped them organize a cooperative bakery. However, within a few months internal conflicts led to the transformation of the cooperative into a private business. The small PLL-affiliated union of bakery workers survived this failure, but only barely.[52]

In October 1932, the General Workers' Club in Haifa was reopened after half a year's hiatus. It was intended to serve as a meeting place and cultural center for the workers organized into trade unions under the auspices of the PLL, and a framework within which individual workers not yet organized into unions could associate. In a report to the Histadrut leadership on activities among Arab workers in Haifa, the lack of an Arabic-language organ which would carry and reinforce the PLL's message received special emphasis. There was, the report noted, a reading room at the club which featured Egyptian illustrated weeklies and the

Cairo daily *al-Ahram;* but "the Palestinian Arab press is out of the question, because it is likely only to poison the minds of the [Arab] workers."[53] The PLL also established a cell among the workers of the Vacuum Oil Company in Haifa and made contact with various groups of workers in Jaffa and Tel Aviv. Among the latter were drivers, mostly Greek Orthodox and Armenian, who had organized independently of Hasan Sidqi al-Dajani's organization.[54]

THE NESHER QUARRY WORKERS

The most important and best publicized struggle in which the PLL was involved in this period was at the quarry attached to the Nesher cement factory at Yagur (Yajur) on the outskirts of Haifa. As I discussed in Chapter 2, Nesher had been the site of a series of important struggles in 1924–25. At the factory itself, still Palestine's only producer of Portland cement, the principle of Hebrew labor was strictly observed, with the Jewish workers earning 30 to 35 piastres for an eight-hour workday. The quarry concession, however, was in the hands of a Palestinian Arab contractor, Musbah al-Shaqifi, who employed only Arabs; by the early 1930s these were recruited mainly from villages in the area. The Histadrut had never been happy about the employment of Arabs at the quarry but had been unable to do much about it. The quarry workers received 8 to 12 piastres for a workday of twelve or thirteen hours, low even by the miserable standard for unskilled manual labor in Palestine at the time. They lived in company-owned shacks at the work site while their families remained behind in their home villages, and they were compelled to buy their groceries at inflated prices from a store owned by the contractor.

At the end of September 1932 al-Shaqifi announced a wage cut and some 150 quarry workers, pressed beyond the limits of endurance, went on strike. Their main demands were a nine-hour workday, a daily wage of 15 piastres, and the closing of the employer-owned store. The strikers immediately contacted the Nesher-Yagur Workers' Council, which not only had never previously sought to organize the Arab quarry workers but in principle opposed their employment, and asked it to negotiate on their behalf. When al-Shaqifi refused to make any concessions, local Histadrut officials, with the support of headquarters in Tel Aviv, organized picket lines, held daily meetings, and sent strikers to the villages from which they had come to spread word of the strike and warn off potential strikebreakers. Though they believed that this was a strike which had to be won, Histadrut officials at Yagur confessed that it had caused "confusion" among the Jewish workers in the factory itself. For some of the latter the quarry strike seemed a golden opportunity to introduce Jewish workers into the quarry, and it was not clear whether or not the Jewish factory workers would refuse to accept materials quarried by any strike-breakers the contractor might bring in. To Histadrut officials' relief, however, Nesher's management kept to its previously arranged schedule and shut down the cement factory for the holidays just a few days after the quarry strike began, thereby avoiding conflict between the Arab and Jewish workers.

The PAWS responded to the Histadrut's involvement by sending representatives out from Haifa to ask the strikers to sever their connection with the Jewish organization, but they were unsuccessful. When the contractor sent one of his clerks to offer a small wage increase, he was set upon by the strikers and was spared a beating thanks only to the intervention of a Histadrut official. The strikers' large numbers, their solidarity, and the support they received from the Histadrut deterred al-Shaqifi from trying to bring in strikebreakers, and after eighteen days he was compelled to offer more substantial concessions to end the strike. The workday was reduced to nine hours, the daily wage was raised to 12.5 piastres, with a further raise to 15 piastres promised after three months, and the workers would henceforth be free to spend their wages wherever they wished. Al-Shaqifi was also forced to negotiate with the workers' elected committee (but not the Histadrut) and to agree to the establishment of a committee composed of representatives of labor and management which would resolve future disputes. Out of the strike there emerged an organization of some 140 Nesher quarry workers allied with the Histadrut.[55]

This victory proved short-lived, however: al-Shaqifi had no intention of respecting the agreement he had been compelled to sign and quickly moved to regain the upper hand. In an effort to undermine the Histadrut's influence over his employees, he hired a large number of new workers and got them signed up as members of the PAWS. It is not known whether PAWS leaders were entirely happy to play this role, but they were certainly anxious to eliminate the PLL's base among the Nesher quarry workers. In the months that followed, al-Shaqifi favored the newly hired PAWS members while harassing the veteran workers who belonged to the PLL. This campaign reached its high point in April 1933: when the 130 PLL-affiliated workers at Nesher returned to work after having spent a holiday in their home villages, they found that al-Shaqifi had replaced them. He offered to take them back on condition that they purchase the implements they needed for work with their own money and submit to a medical examination at their own expense. When they refused, al-Shaqifi locked them out. Picket lines went up, but with the help of the police and the cooperation of the workers affiliated with the PAWS al-Shaqifi was able to keep the quarry operating.

The Histadrut weighed in on the PLL's side by authorizing the seventy Jewish workers employed at a department of the cement factory connected with the quarry to refuse to handle materials supplied by workers they defined as strikebreakers. In a statement defending their case published in *Filastin*, the Arab strikers denounced al-Shaqifi's many abuses and expressed their appreciation for the Jewish workers' solidarity.[56] Given the circumstances, the Histadrut's action was probably not motivated by solidarity alone. The struggle at Nesher now pitted those workers who belonged to the PLL against al-Shaqifi (and behind him Nesher's management) and the workers who supported the PAWS. The influence of the PLL and the Histadrut at this large and important workplace was at stake, and it would not bode well for the Histadrut's reputation and its ability to organize Arab workers elsewhere if an Arab employer allied with the strongest Arab labor union succeeded in driving the PLL out.

The struggle at Nesher dragged on inconclusively for some six weeks. For most of that period al-Shaqifi refused to negotiate, and for a time he even went into hiding in Nazareth in order to avoid pressure to begin talks. Nesher management initially denied that the strike was its affair, but ultimately it compelled al-Shaqifi to negotiate by threatening to cancel his contract for the quarry. The police seem to have cooperated with al-Shaqifi by protecting the nonstriking workers while harassing and arresting picketers and strike leaders. At one point the police even arrested Eliyahu Agassi after an informer swore that Agassi had given him a pistol; fortunately for Agassi, he was able to provide a credible alibi and was released. At the beginning of May 1933 the Histadrut agreed to end the strike, with all outstanding issues to be referred for arbitration to a British official. The arbitrator ordered that the contractor restore almost all of the strikers to their jobs and later ruled in favor of the strikers on some of their economic demands, but he did not require al-Shaqifi to recognize the PLL as their bargaining agent.

During the strike, the Histadrut leadership came under fire from both the Palestine Communist Party and Po'alei Tziyon Smol. The former insisted in leaflets that the Zionist Histadrut was once again betraying the Arab and Jewish workers alike and called for an independent strike committee which would lead a joint struggle to equalize Arab and Jewish wages. Po'alei Tziyon Smol publications complained that the Histadrut was not aggressive enough: instead of focusing on improving the workers' wages and working conditions, it had given priority to the more modest goal of getting the locked-out workers reinstated. It seems clear that the Histadrut very much wanted to hold on to its base at the Nesher quarry, but its commitment there also seems to have had limits beyond which it hesitated to venture. In any event, the strike of April–May 1933 marked the beginning of the end of the PLL's influence at Nesher. Over the following months harassment and firings by al-Shaqifi, who ignored most of the arbitrator's rulings, along with pressure from the PAWS, destroyed the PLL's local base, and its organization of quarry workers disintegrated.[57]

The PAWS did not fare much better. In January 1936 it led a one-week strike of Nesher quarry workers against the same oppressive contractor, Musbah al-Shaqifi, demanding that wages be raised to 16 piastres for an eight-hour day, that the system of heavy fines for infractions of work rules be abolished, that al-Shaqifi's harassment of the workers come to an end, and that the workers be allowed to live wherever they wished. This last demand reflected the workers' long-standing desire to live not in company-owned barracks but with their families, hitherto compelled to remain behind in their home villages. Al-Shaqifi signed an agreement with the PAWS but as in the past failed to honor it. Another very brief strike therefore erupted in mid-February 1936, and then yet another at the end of that month, as the 325 quarry workers tried to force al-Shaqifi to pay what was in fact still a substandard wage of 16 piastres a day and grant some reduction in their fourteen-hour workday. This last strike dragged on until mid-March, but it too ended inconclusively. As I discuss in Chapter 6, the general strike that erupted in April 1936 would finally make possible the realization of the Histadrut's long-standing goal of achieving Hebrew labor at the Nesher quarry, just as it would at Haifa harbor.[58]

THE PLL IN HAIFA

During this same period, the PLL also developed links with other groups of Arab workers in and around Haifa, including stevedores at the port and barrel makers at Shell Oil, as well as with workers in Acre and Nazareth.[59] These relationships were all short-lived, however, and neither the fledgling Harbor Workers' Union nor the other workplace-based nuclei established in 1932 succeeded in transforming themselves into stable trade union organizations. In fact, the PLL was never really able to consolidate a stable base of support among Arab workers. Apart from a very small number of loyal members in various trades, its relationships with any specific group of workers never lasted for more than a few months before fading away. The sites at which it was active were always shifting, and whatever continuity the PLL possessed as an organization in Haifa was imparted by Eliyahu Agassi and Abba Hushi.

As we have seen, the PLL's efforts in Haifa were often hindered or undermined by the PAWS, which while only sporadically capable of taking the initiative nonetheless did its best to intervene wherever the PLL was active and keep its pro-Zionist rival away from the Arab workers whom it saw as its exclusive constituency. In this struggle, sometimes (as at Nesher) waged in temporary alliance with Arab employers, the PAWS could make effective use of the argument that the Histadrut was really seeking to push Arab workers out of their jobs and replace them with Jews. Histadrut officials also blamed the Jewish communists for the PLL's lack of success, seeing them as traitors always on the lookout for opportunities to disseminate their anti-Zionist poison and mislead naive Arab workers. There is little doubt that the communists did seek to undermine the Histadrut's efforts to organize Arab workers, but the party's weakness, and the wariness with which most Arab workers regarded communism, suggest that the PLL's difficulties cannot really be accounted for by communist sabotage.[60]

Another significant factor in the PLL's inability to consolidate a stable base was the character and circumstances of the Arab working class in Palestine at the time, which of course also hindered the organizing efforts of the PAWS and other Arab unions. Many if not most of the workers with whom the PLL came into contact in 1932–33 were relatively recent recruits to the urban wage-earning workforce, peasants who found it difficult to support themselves and their families in their villages and were attracted to the rapidly growing towns by the availability of jobs there. They were largely illiterate or semiliterate, and many of them retained close ties with village life and the agrarian economy. At Haifa harbor and at Nesher, for example, much of the work was seasonal, and in the slack season workers would usually return to their home villages. Because much of the urban labor force was unskilled there was also high turnover, which made it very difficult to create stable organizations. Unskilled workers at some site who had developed a connection with the PLL (or the PAWS) might well move on after a few months, to be replaced by new workers who had no such ties. The abundance of cheap unskilled labor also made it easy for employers to dismiss troublesome workers, combat the growth of trade unions, and find strikebreakers when necessary. Moreover, while these workers were often quick to go on strike, they were much less interested in paying dues, attending meetings, or submitting to organizational discipline. As for skilled workers, as the case of ʿAziz Khayyat in June 1932 showed, during good times when their skills were in demand they might find it to their advantage simply to leave an oppressive employer and hire on elsewhere rather than assume the costs and risks of involvement with a trade union.

But the PLL's lack of success is also attributable to the low priority assigned to organizing Arab workers by the Histadrut's leadership and membership. The resources at the disposal of the PLL were miniscule; in effect, Agassi *was* the PLL, as the organization did not really exist outside Haifa before the end of 1933. Even there Abba Hushi had many other responsibilities as secretary of the Haifa Workers' Council and could devote only a small proportion of his time to Arab affairs. Scarcity of resources dictated that the PLL operate in a purely reactive manner. As a rule, Agassi and Hushi would wait until they were approached by some group of Arab workers who were already discontented and organized enough to take the initiative, and only then would the PLL and Histadrut become involved, intervene on their behalf, and try to sign them up.

It is perhaps understandable that Agassi should have felt that his time was best spent maintaining and developing links with groups of Arab workers who had already begun to organize themselves or had actually gone on strike, rather than trying to organize workers who had not yet indicated a clear interest in action. This approach maximized the limited funding and staff resources available to the PLL. However, the PLL's reactive stance, competition from the PAWS (and later other Arab trade unions), and the unfamiliarity with organization, high turnover, and vulnerability of the Arab workers it was seeking to reach, made it difficult to create a solid core of members, much less a cadre of Arab trade union organizers who could eventually work on their own. In numerous cases, Arab workers came to Agassi and Hushi after having already declared a strike, and Hushi was constantly scolding Arab strikers for what he saw as their impetuousness and their failure to prepare adequately before doing so. The Histadrut often found itself leading strikes under circumstances which did not allow much room for maneuver or much prospect of victory. But even when workers achieved some short-term gains from the Histadrut's intervention, an organizational connection with the PLL did not necessarily follow; and even when the PLL succeeded in organizing workers who approached it for help during a strike, the new PLL cell rarely lasted for long.

The parties to MAPAI's left were not hesitant about denouncing the Histadrut leadership for the PLL's rather poor showing. In March 1933 Po'alei Tziyon Smol warned of the consequences of MAPAI's failures: "Thousands of Arab workers in the government sector, in the citrus groves, in construction and crafts, in the municipal and international sector will rise up, emancipate themselves and organize despite all the obstacles. With us, if we bring them into our camp as equals; without us and against us, if we stand apart or become an obstacle to their organization."[61] While Hashomer Hatza'ir denounced Po'alei Tziyon Smol's approach as a "serious danger to the realization of proletarian Zionism," it too criticized MAPAI's insistence on total Hebrew labor, its policy zigzags, its undemocratic domination of a bureaucratized Histadrut and its failure to pursue joint organization with the seriousness it deserved.[62] Not surprisingly, the PCP went much further in its denunciation of the Histadrut:

> After strangling strikes by Arab workers, the Histadrut's leaders are trying to channel a small number of Arab workers into a Histadrut organization. The purpose of the PLL, which has been resurrected in Haifa, as well as of the International Union of Railway Workers, is to organize a certain portion of Arab workers in an organization whose function is to provide the Histadrut's efforts at conquest [of labor] an internationalist cover, and to divert the Arab worker from the path of establishing his own class organization in order to hitch him to the cart of chauvinism and Zionism.[63]

The Histadrut leadership was accustomed to such attacks, which MAPAI's domination of the Zionist labor movement allowed it to ignore for the most part. But the PLL's apparent inability to establish a durable base in Haifa, and especially its failure at Nesher, the most important struggle in which it had been engaged so far, led to a decline in its activity in that city, and the enthusiasm and sense of possibility which had characterized the PLL's work there in the summer of 1932 evaporated. By the spring of 1933 funds for Arab work were again virtually exhausted; Yehuda Burla had left his post as secretary of the Histadrut's Arab Department; and by November Abba Hushi was reduced to threatening the Histadrut executive committee that he would terminate his efforts to organize Arab workers in Haifa unless the Histadrut provided adequate funding and gave some serious attention to this project. The rent on the Haifa club was by then three months in arrears and the landlord was about to shut it down. The Histadrut seems to have come through with some money and the club remained open, but the PLL continued to stagnate through 1934, claiming no more than 200 members scattered among small workplaces in and around Haifa.[64]

ARAB WORKERS AND HEBREW LABOR IN THE MOSHAVOT

As we will see, the PLL would soon strike roots in another urban center, Jaffa. But before that a strike by Arab agricultural workers attracted widespread public attention and sparked an intense debate within the labor-Zionist movement over Hebrew labor and policies toward Arab workers, especially agricultural workers. Early in June 1934 some 250 Arab workers in the citrus groves in and around the moshava of Nes Tziyona, on the coastal plain west of Ramla, went on strike against both Arab and Jewish farmers to secure an increase in their wages from 12 to 17 piastres a day. Some of the strikers were Palestinians, but many were migrant laborers from Egypt and the Hawran, attracted to Palestine by the country's relative prosperity and higher wage levels. Po'alei Tziyon Smol activists in the moshava immediately contacted the strikers and offered their support. Anxious to head off its rival on the left, the Histadrut leadership quickly dispatched Eliyahu Agassi and other MAPAI loyalists to the scene to find out what was going on and take charge.

The Nes Tziyona strike, and a number of similar strikes that erupted at Petah Tikva and other moshavot soon thereafter, confronted the Histadrut with a dilemma. That spring the Histadrut had launched a new round in its campaign to pressure Jewish farmers to employ only Jewish workers, focused on the citrus groves in and around Kfar Saba. This campaign in the countryside was later to be supplemented by a renewed effort to enforce Hebrew labor in the cities, especially in construction. The Histadrut justified this renewed offensive by claiming that the boom in citrus cultivation had brought many more Arab workers from Palestine, Egypt, and the Hawran into this sector, but it also had roots in political struggles between MAPAI and its rivals within the Yishuv. The campaign was not, however, going very well: despite picketing, harassment, and heavy political and moral pressure the farmers were resisting the Histadrut's demand that they replace their Arab workers with Jews. Moreover, with easier and better-paying urban jobs relatively plentiful, the Histadrut found it impossible to mobilize sufficient numbers of Jews to move to the moshavot and replace Arabs in the citrus groves, even though Jewish workers earned up to twice as much as Arab workers.

In this context, Histadrut leaders feared that support for the Nes Tziyona strike might imply recognition of the right of Arab workers to employment in the Jewish sector, which would undermine the struggle for Hebrew labor. However, open opposition to the strike and a move to displace the strikers would damage the Histadrut's reputation, bolster MAPAI's opposition on the left, and strengthen the Arab nationalist movement, which made considerable political capital out of the Histadrut's Hebrew labor campaign. As a result, though the Histadrut executive committee decided (with much ambivalence) to endorse the Nes Tziyona strike, publish a leaflet supporting it, and contribute money for a strike fund, these decisions do not seem to have been implemented. This led Hashomer Hatza'ir and Po'alei Tziyon Smol members to charge that MAPAI, which controlled the Histadrut apparatus as well as the Nes Tziyona Workers' Council, had once again failed to honor its promise to support a strike by Arab workers. The strike seems to have petered out in a rather disorganized manner after a week or so, with some of the workers winning a wage increase and returning to their jobs while others found work elsewhere. A number of the Arab workers at Nes Tziyona subsequently formed their own organization which alternately approached the Histadrut and Arab labor organizations linked to the nationalist movement for support, suggesting once again that Arab workers were quite capable of maneuvering in their own perceived interest.[65]

The wave of strikes in the moshavot and its aftermath again put the question of the Histadrut's policy toward Arab agricultural workers on the organization's agenda. The question was extensively discussed when the Histadrut council convened in August 1934. Dov Hoz, speaking for the Histadrut's MAPAI majority, defended his party's position on joint organization. "We must," he argued, "refrain from activity of a missionary character."

> It is very easy to excite groups of Arabs. In their excitement, lacking knowledge and experience, they are ready to rally to any flag and later to go over to another camp. In this regard the experience of the Nes Tziyona strike is instructive. The Nes Tziyona strikers came to an agreement with us. Then they published a letter in the Arab newspapers that they had broken with us. And then they came to us again and said that the letter was only "politics." In the meantime a club linked with the Arab Executive has been formed.

Claiming that most of the strikers at Nes Tziyona were migrant laborers from outside Palestine, Hoz argued that such workers posed a threat not only to the struggle for Hebrew labor but to Palestinian Arab workers as well. He insisted that priority be given to the struggle for Hebrew labor, though he acknowledged the need to intensify the Histadrut's work among Arabs and proposed the creation of a permanent committee which would direct and develop the organization's activities in this sphere.[66]

Hashomer Hatza'ir sought to distance itself from both MAPAI's demand for "100 percent Hebrew labor" and Po'alei Tziyon Smol's outright rejection of the struggle for Hebrew labor. It proposed that the Histadrut commit itself not only to preserving the jobs of the "permanent" Arab workers in the moshavot, by which it meant workers originating from within Palestine who had worked for at least two years in one place, but also to organizing them, along with Arab workers in the cities. In its view the strikes in the moshavot marked the beginning of a new period in which the organization of Arab workers would become even more essential for the long-term success of the labor-Zionist enterprise. Po'alei Tziyon Smol's delegates to the Histadrut council ridiculed Hashomer Hatza'ir's formulaic attempt at a compromise on the question of Hebrew labor, arguing that it was impossible to impose an artificial distinction between "permanent" and "temporary" workers, organizing the former while trying to displace the latter and get Hawranis expelled from the country. This party's leaders reiterated their call for a Histadrut which would be open to, and actively seek to recruit, all the workers in Palestine, including even the migrants from the Hawran, and noted that if the Arab workers were inclining toward nationalism, they were only following MAPAI's example: "You want the Arab worker to understand why you are allowed to collaborate with the Va'ad Le'umi [which included representatives of bourgeois parties], but he is forbidden to collaborate with the Arab Executive?"

Both Po'alei Tziyon Smol and Hashomer Hatza'ir threatened that if the Histadrut did not take Arab work seriously, they themselves would take the initiative. It was in part to forestall this possibility that the resolution endorsed by the council's MAPAI majority declared that Arab work should be intensified under the guidance of a new Histadrut committee. The council also insisted that only the Histadrut had the right to organize Arab workers, though it avoided any explicit commitment to the organization of Arab workers in the moshavot. A month later, in September 1934, the Histadrut executive committee formally established a committee on Arab affairs to guide its work in this arena. Despite Hashomer Hatza'ir's objections Po'alei Tziyon Smol was excluded from participation, and only one member of Hashomer Hatza'ir (Ya'akov Riftin, a leader of the movement's left wing) was appointed. The others were all MAPAI members: Dov Hoz, Abba Hushi, David Hacohen (director of the Histadrut's Contracting Office, which carried out construction and infrastructure projects as well as public works projects on government tenders), Nataʿ Harpaz, and Reuven Zaslani, a newcomer to this sphere of activity to whom I will return shortly. In keeping with his movement's perspective, Riftin proposed an ambitious program to expand the Arab Department's work, including the organization of "permanent" Arab agricultural workers in the moshavot into the PLL. But his MAPAI colleagues on the new committee opposed organizing those workers because, as Hacohen put it, in the moshavot "I am fighting for my life against the Arab worker"—that is, to achieve Hebrew labor. It quickly became clear that the Histadrut's involvement with Arab workers was to have a strictly urban focus.[67]

THE DOCKWORKERS OF JAFFA

By the time this new committee was formed, the PLL's main arena of activity had shifted from Haifa to Jaffa, where the PLL had previously had only limited contacts with Arab workers. This began to change when a group of workers employed at a Greek-owned leather factory near Jaffa approached the Histadrut for help and Agassi began to come down from Haifa to work with them. These leather workers eventually went on strike with Histadrut support, but the employer brought in strikebreakers and the strike was defeated. Some of the workers returned to their old jobs while others found work elsewhere. Among the latter was an Egyptian who had previously worked as a stevedore at Jaffa harbor and now returned there. Through him Agassi established contacts with Arab stevedores and lightermen at the port of Jaffa who welcomed his willingness to help them seek redress of their grievances.

Jaffa's port remained important even after Haifa's new deepwater harbor opened in 1933, especially as an outlet for Palestine's booming citrus exports. The Arab stevedores and lightermen who worked there, employed through Arab labor contractors, were increasingly discontented and ripe for organization. Though paid a fixed daily wage, in the busy citrus export season the stevedores might be compelled to work up to eighteen hours a day; they were therefore interested not only in a higher daily wage but also in compensation for overtime. The lightermen received not a daily wage but a share of the receipts of the boat on which they worked, which gave the boat owner or contractor for whom they worked control over their income and plenty of opportunity to shortchange them. They wanted some reform of this system to make their

218 / Arab Workers and the Histadrut

income more predictable and enhance their control over how much they worked and earned. Both groups were engaged in dangerous work and suffered numerous accidents for which they were only rarely compensated by the employers.

At the same time, these workers, who were mostly Palestinians from Jaffa itself or from the towns and villages of the coastal plain and enjoyed some job security (though employment at the port fluctuated seasonally), saw their jobs and wages threatened by migrant workers coming from the Hawran (and to a lesser extent Egypt) who were attracted to Palestine by the country's relative prosperity and were taking over jobs at the port. The stevedores and lightermen hoped that by organizing themselves into a union they could protect their incomes from the downward pressure which the presence of these low-wage competitors posed and secure their jobs through enforcement of the principle of local preference in the allocation of work. It was not only Jaffa port workers who in this period perceived a threat from low-wage migrants: in Haifa the PAWS sent a petition to the government of Palestine protesting what it perceived as the flooding of the local labor market by Hawranis, who threatened the jobs and wages of Palestinian workers.[68]

The Histadrut shared this goal of excluding non-Palestinian Arabs, because the exclusion of migrant workers would facilitate the struggle for Hebrew labor by keeping wages within Palestine relatively high. As I discussed in relation to the debate over the Nes Tziyona strike, only Po'alei Tziyon Smol advocated extending the principle of proletarian internationalism and joint organization to encompass even the Hawranis and Egyptians, and it did not carry much weight within the labor-Zionist movement. Though MAPAI and Hashomer Hatza'ir disagreed over whether Hebrew labor should be total or should exempt "permanent Arab workers," the two parties agreed that Hawrani and Egyptian migrant workers should be displaced, barred from entry into Palestine, and whenever possible expelled. MAPAI leaders generally insisted that the Arabs of Palestine did not constitute a distinct nationality entitled to self-determination but were members of a larger Arab nation, and that it would therefore not be terribly unjust if they had to live within a Jewish state or were even resettled outside Palestine. With respect to the labor market, however, the Histadrut found it expedient to stress the distinctiveness of Palestinian Arab identity and interests so as to keep out non-Jewish immigrants whose influx might hinder the realization of Zionist goals. In fact, the Histadrut tended to exaggerate the number of Hawranis and others "infiltrating" into Palestine, and it routinely declared Arabs employed at work sites targeted for the conquest of labor to be non-Palestinians so as to justify their displacement.[69]

To attract the Jaffa stevedores and lightermen, the PLL opened a club near the port at which a Kupat Holim clinic operated; it also provided a loan fund and other services, among the most important of which was legal assistance. The government of Palestine had enacted legislation requiring employers to compensate workers for work-related injuries, but few Arab workers knew about the law or possessed the means to take advantage of it. The first cases in which Histadrut lawyers sued Arab employers on behalf of injured Arab stevedores made a strong impression on Arab workers in Jaffa and enhanced the reputation of the PLL and the Histadrut there. By the fall of 1934 the PLL was claiming about one hundred Jaffa stevedores as members of an affiliated union, and after lengthy negotiations some of the lightermen were also beginning to join. However, the fact that many port workers left Jaffa and returned to their home villages during the slack season made it difficult to sustain the Jaffa stevedores' union: it had in effect to be reestablished when the busy citrus export season began in the late fall. But for Histadrut officials the PLL's apparent success in organizing these workers made it possible to envision a situation in which, as one of them put it, "*we* will be the rulers in the port of Jaffa and will be able to do great things there, both politically and economically."[70]

Agassi began to visit Jaffa once a week to work with the lightermen and stevedores, while Histadrut leader Dov Hoz intervened on their behalf with the British officials who ran the port and sought support from dockworkers' unions in Britain. During 1934 Agassi also developed ties with cigarette workers at the Maspero factory in Jaffa and with weavers in the town of al-Majdal, on the coast north of Gaza—today the exclusively Jewish city of Ashkelon in Israel. At that time al-Majdal was a major center of textile production; one correspondent called it (with great exaggeration) the "Lancashire of Palestine." About 1,000 men and 500 women were employed in numerous small workshops owned by some sixty loom owners. In August 1933 some 800 of these workers had gone on strike for an increase in their piece rate that amounted to only one additional piastre a day. The male weavers seem to have won their demand, though at the price of abandoning the female workers whose employers rejected any concession.[71] It was during this strike that these weavers first sought to make contact with the Histadrut, rumors of whose strength and influence had apparently reached even far-off al-Majdal. A delegation was dispatched to Tel Aviv to seek the Histadrut's help but had ended up establishing contacts with Po'alei Tziyon Smol instead; it is possible that party activists conveyed to the weavers from al-Majdal that they were actually Histadrut officials. A year later, Agassi insisted on taking over these contacts and developing them on behalf of the Histadrut, which was as always nervous about Po'alei Tziyon Smol's relations with Arab workers (mainly through George Nassar and the small group he led) and determined to enforce the Histadrut's monopoly in this sphere. After a few visits to al-Majdal, Agassi and his colleagues decided that all they could offer was assistance in setting up a weavers' cooperative. Nothing came of this and contact with the al-Majdal weavers was eventually lost.

LABOR ORGANIZING AND INTELLIGENCE WORK

As the pace of PLL activity in Jaffa quickened in the summer of 1934, the Histadrut hired another staff employee to coordinate its Arab Department and work with Agassi. This was Reuven Zaslani, mentioned earlier as a member of the Histadrut's newly formed Arab Committee and perhaps better known under the name he would later adopt, Reuven Shilo'ah. He was born Reuven Zaslanski in Jerusalem in 1909, the son of a rabbi who was both orthodox and Zionist—a rare combination in Jerusalem in those days. In his teens he broke with his father's orthodoxy, studied drama, and joined the Hagana, the Yishuv's main paramilitary organization. In the late 1920s and early 1930s Zaslani was adopted into the labor-Zionist elite, developing close personal ties with Yitzhak Ben-Tzvi, his wife Rahel Yana'it, and three of their younger protégés: Dov Hoz, whom we have already encountered as a top Histadrut leader; Moshe Shertok (later Sharett), who in 1933 would succeed the murdered Hayyim Arlosoroff as director of the Jewish Agency's Political Department and would later serve as Israel's foreign minister (1948–56) and prime minister (1953–55); and Eliyahu Golomb (1893–1945), one of the founders and top commanders of the Hagana. (The three men would become relatives by marriage when Hoz and Golomb married Shertok's sisters.) In 1928 Zaslani began to study at the Hebrew University, concentrating on what in Israel is often still called *mada'ei hamizrah*—"Oriental studies"—including the Arabic language. But he remained active in the Hagana, placing his growing command of Arabic at the service of its fledgling intelligence branch.[72]

Zaslani never finished his university degree. Instead, on the recommendation of Ben-Tzvi, who had just taken over as chair of the Va'ad Le'umi following MAPAI's victory in elections to the Yishuv's representative assembly, Zaslani, not yet twenty-two years old, was sent to work as a teacher at a Jewish school in Baghdad. That at least was his cover, for while working as a teacher he also helped organize an underground Zionist youth movement and carried out propaganda and intelligence work for the Jewish Agency. In this latter capacity, under Shertok's supervision, Zaslani cultivated ties with prominent Iraqis, sought to win friends for Zionism in this key Arab country, and on at least one occasion exposed an Iraqi Jewish communist to the Iraqi authorities.

Zaslani's sojourn in Iraq between the summer of 1931 and October 1932 was one of the earliest efforts to initiate Zionist intelligence and propaganda work in the Arab world. It was also in keeping with a dimension of the Histadrut's Arab work to which I have not devoted much attention thus far. For in addition to organizing Arab workers under labor-Zionist tutelage, Histadrut and other Zionist officials were also interested in influencing Arab public opinion both within Palestine and outside it. As early as 1930 Ben-Tzvi was speaking of "committees" which had been founded in Egypt and Syria to influence the local press, a goal which the Histadrut and Jewish Agency continued to pursue. A few years later, in 1934, the Jewish Agency covertly provided funding to establish the Cairo-based Agence d'Orient news service as a means of influencing Arab public opinion. Zaslani's mission to Baghdad was part of the same project.[73]

Zaslani's effort to lay the foundations of a Zionist intelligence network in Arab countries outside Palestine was undertaken in cooperation with British intelligence. In fact, after his return from Baghdad Zaslani, with the approval of his superiors at the Hagana and the Jewish Agency, went to work as translator and secretary to the British officer in charge of the Royal Air Force's intelligence branch in Palestine. (The Royal Air Force had primary responsibility for intelligence in Palestine and the surrounding countries.) Zaslani thus served as the link between British intelligence on the one hand and the Hagana and the Yishuv's leadership on the other. In this period, despite sporadic tensions, Britain and the Zionist movement still saw each other as allies with common enemies—Arab nationalism in Palestine and elsewhere, and the communist movement, which was both anti-imperialist and anti-Zionist. Their intelligence agencies therefore sought to cooperate. It was apparently in the service of both these masters that Zaslani was again dispatched to Iraq in May 1934, ostensibly as a journalist employed by an English-language Palestinian newspaper. During this visit he traveled through Iraq's Kurdish regions. His main purpose seems to have been to survey Jewish communities in northern Iraq. But one may perhaps also discern in this trip another element which would later become a central pillar of Zionist and then Israeli

regional strategy: support for and alliances with ethnic or religious minorities disaffected from or in conflict with Arab nationalist governments or
forces, including the Kurds in Iraq, the southern Sudanese, and the Maro-
nites in Lebanon.[74]

In July 1934 the Iraqi authorities, suspicious of this peripatetic Jewish
"journalist" from Palestine, expelled Zaslani from the country. Upon his
return to Tel Aviv he was appointed coordinator of the Hagana's Arab
intelligence activities; at the same time his mentor Dov Hoz took him into
the Histadrut apparatus as secretary of its Arab Department. This is the
context in which, in the summer of 1934, Zaslani began to work with
Eliyahu Agassi in developing ties with the Arab stevedores and lightermen in Jaffa and with other groups of Arab workers in the area. Zaslani's double life as labor organizer and intelligence operative is in a sense
symptomatic of the contradiction at the heart of labor Zionism's policy
and practice toward Arab workers in Palestine. As we will see, the contacts
Zaslani and his colleagues established and the information they gathered
through their day-to-day activities as labor organizers would prove of
substantial benefit to the Zionist project, enhancing both the struggle for
Hebrew labor and the Yishuv's intelligence and military capacities. Zaslani's subsequent career was entirely in the field of intelligence: he continued to play a central role in the intelligence apparatuses of the Hagana
and the Yishuv and after 1948, under his new Hebrew name Reuven Shilo'ah, he organized and for a number of years presided over the new State
of Israel's complex of domestic and foreign intelligence and security agencies. He remained a central figure in Israeli intelligence, foreign policy,
and security circles until his death in 1959. Tel Aviv University named its
center for Middle Eastern studies in his honor, though Makhon Shilo'ah
("the Shilo'ah Institute") was later incorporated into the university's Da-
yan Center.

ARAB WORKERS AND HEBREW LABOR IN JAFFA

The PLL's successes in organizing Arab workers in Jaffa during 1934, especially the dockworkers, alarmed Arab trade unionists and their nonworker nationalist allies and stimulated much more vigorous and effective
efforts to counter the Histadrut. The summer of 1934 witnessed the emergence, initially under the patronage of a prominent politician, of a new
Arab labor organization which became quite active in Jaffa. The politician
was Fakhri al-Nashashibi, nephew and devoted assistant of Raghib al-
Nashashibi, who had been mayor of Jerusalem since 1920 and led the op-

position to the Husaynis and their allies within the Palestinian Arab elite.

As noted earlier, despite occasional tactical resorts to ultranationalist rhetoric, the Nashashibis led the pro-British and pro-Hashemite segment of that elite, while the Husaynis and their allies, led by al-Hajj Amin al-Husayni, the Mufti of Jerusalem, took a stronger anti-British, anti-Zionist, and distinctly Palestinian stance. Both factions still believed, however, that they could block the Zionist project and achieve Palestine's independence through negotiations with the British. Relations between the two camps had recently deteriorated sharply. The Arab Executive, on which all the leading Palestinian notable families were represented, had ceased to function altogether and would be formally dissolved in August 1934, opening the way for the creation of rival political parties, each linked to a particular family or faction. In the summer of 1934, moreover, Raghib al-Nashashibi was running for reelection as mayor against Dr. Husayn al-Khalidi, who was backed by both the Mufti's camp and most Jerusalem Jews, who wanted to get al-Nashashibi out of office.

It was in this context that Fakhri al-Nashashibi hit upon the idea of mobilizing local support by creating a labor organization in Jerusalem, where unlike Haifa, in which the PAWS had long been established (if not always very active), the field was wide open. At the end of July 1934 he proclaimed the establishment of an "Arab Workers' Society" (AWS), with himself as president. The AWS was generally understood to be a creation of and vehicle for the Nashashibis, though it did Raghib little good: in September he was defeated for reelection. As the Nashashibis and their allies moved toward the creation of their own political organization—the National Defense Party, formally established that December with Hasan Sidqi al-Dajani as one of its secretaries—Fakhri al-Nashashibi seems to have seen in Arab workers a potential constituency which could be organized and mobilized for the benefit of his faction. In August 1934 he therefore opened the first AWS branch outside Jerusalem, in Bayt Dajan, a substantial village some five miles southeast of Jaffa. In October an AWS branch was established in Jaffa itself, under the leadership of Michel Mitri, a young engineer who had grown up in Latin America and received his education there. The AWS was strongly supported in its efforts by the pro-Nashashibi *Filastin*, which hailed Fakhri al-Nashashibi as "protector of the workers" and began to devote unprecedented attention to labor affairs.[75]

To build support, the AWS quickly seized on an issue of concern to many Arab workers: the Histadrut's campaign for Hebrew labor. As I mentioned earlier, in the spring of 1934 the Histadrut had launched a largely unsuccessful campaign to achieve Hebrew labor in the moshavot. When that effort in the countryside yielded only meager results, MAPAI and the Histadrut it controlled decided to shift the campaign to the cities, deploying mobile bands of pickets who moved from one construction site to another and sometimes went beyond picketing by trying to forcibly expel Arab workers from their jobs. These tactics led to clashes between Jews attempting to keep out or drive out Arab workers, and Arab workers trying to get to or stay at their jobs. Employers would frequently call in the police to restore order and protect their Arab workers; this in turn led to fights between Jewish pickets and the police, and arrests of Jews for disturbing the peace. The campaign on the streets was accompanied by a very aggressive propaganda campaign waged by means of leaflets, articles, and advertisements in the Histadrut press, rallies, and the like. The propaganda campaign not only denounced the employment of Arab workers, depicted as "cheap," "unorganized," and "alien," but demanded that Jewish consumers boycott Arab produce and products and instead "buy Jewish" whenever possible.[76]

This campaign in the cities achieved only limited success. As I discussed earlier, this was a period of prosperity in the Yishuv. In the absence of a large mass of unemployed Jews desperate for jobs, the Histadrut found it almost as difficult to enforce Hebrew labor in the cities as it had in the moshavot. But its campaign did succeed in inflaming Arab-Jewish relations and heightening the anxiety and resentment with which many Arabs regarded Zionism and the Yishuv, especially in a period when Jewish immigration was surging dramatically. To alert the public to what was going on, the Arab press, along with the Palestine Communist Party's clandestine or front publications, were quick to translate and publish Histadrut calls for the imposition of Hebrew labor and the boycott of Arab produce, manufactures, and shops, and news of clashes at urban building sites spread quickly.

Fakhri al-Nashashibi and the new AWS sought to capitalize on growing concern about this issue by publicly demanding that the British authorities take forceful action against the Hebrew labor pickets. The AWS also called on Arab workers to adopt weapons from the Histadrut's arsenal by setting up their own picket lines and boycotting Jewish products and produce. In December 1934 Fakhri al-Nashashibi set up in Jerusalem what *Filastin*, his biggest booster, described as "the first Arab picket." This was in reality not so much a picket line as a march by al-Nashashibi and some of his followers through the streets of Jerusalem, in the course of which buildings being put up by Arab contractors were visited and the employment of Jews at those sites (generally as skilled craftsmen) was protested.[77] The AWS does not in fact seem to have carried out any sustained picketing in this period, though as we will see Michel Mitri would use this tactic to great effect in the spring of 1936. But the organization did take the lead in efforts to counter the Histadrut's Hebrew labor campaign, for example at the stone and gravel quarry at Majdal Yaba (also known in Arabic as Majdal al-Sadiq, and in Hebrew as Migdal Tzedek), an Arab village on the western slopes of the Nablus mountains, east of Tel Aviv. Tel Aviv was at the time experiencing a building boom, and much of the stone and gravel used for new construction came from this quarry, on Arab land leased to Jewish entrepreneurs soon after the British occupation. The quarry workforce was entirely Arab, consisting of about thirty workers from Majdal Yaba itself and an additional 400 Arab workers from other villages.

In the fall of 1934 the Tel Aviv Workers' Council, which steadfastly insisted that the quarry workers were not Palestinians but "bedouins" or Hawranis, negotiated an agreement with the quarry operators to introduce Jewish workers at the site and thereby supply Tel Aviv with what it termed "Hebrew stone." Jewish workers in the building trades were called on to refuse to handle any stone produced by non-Jewish labor, as evidenced by the absence of a special seal. To implement the agreement, the operators were to build up a large inventory of stone and gravel and then, on the pretext that supply far exceeded demand, send the Arab workers back to their home villages, whereupon they would be replaced by Jews. The AWS in Jaffa got wind of the plan, however, possibly from Jewish communist sources, and warned the Arab workers, who remained at the site and for seventeen days withstood the Histadrut's efforts to introduce Jewish workers, until the quarry's managers agreed to retain all the Arabs employed there. As we will see later, the Histadrut would make other attempts to replace Arabs with Jews at the Majdal Yaba quarry, in 1936 and again in 1947.[78]

THE JAFFA DOCKWORKERS AND THE PLL

Agassi, Zaslani, and their colleagues involved in organizing Arab workers could not avoid confronting the issue of Hebrew labor as it gained greater public attention during 1934. They were well aware of how much the Histadrut's Hebrew labor campaign alienated Arab workers and undermined the PLL's efforts. However, as loyal MAPAI members they supported Hebrew labor in principle, if not always the way the campaigns to achieve it were carried out, and they did not believe that it in any way contradicted their commitment to socialism or to the organization of Arab workers. So while Hashomer Hatza'ir activists tended to evade or downplay the issue, the MAPAI members involved in Arab work tended to confront it head-on, confident that they could make a good case for their party's position. In Jaffa at the end of 1934, however, this was less a matter of virtue than of necessity: Zaslani and Agassi could not really hope to avoid the issue, since it was being raised very openly and forcefully not only by Arab trade unionists seeking to destroy the PLL's influence and "rescue" Arab workers from Zionist influence but by rank and file workers themselves.

In November 1934, in an effort to seize the initiative from their opponents in the struggle for the support of the Jaffa dockworkers, Zaslani and Agassi went so far as to invite the secretary of the Jaffa branch of the PAWS to a meeting of some fifty Arab workers, most of them stevedores, at the PLL's club. According to Zaslani and Agassi, who submitted a report on the meeting to the Histadrut and to the Jewish Agency's Political Department, the PAWS leader denounced the Histadrut for stealing Arab jobs, reminded the stevedores of the "disaster" which had occurred at Haifa harbor (i.e., the introduction of Jewish workers after the organization of the PLL-sponsored Harbor Workers' Union there) and asked if they wanted to allow the Histadrut to bring about the same outcome in Jaffa as well. In their response, Zaslani and Agassi did not directly address the substance of their opponent's charges but instead sought to put him on the defensive and undermine his credibility by demanding that he provide proof of his allegations.

The Jewish unionists thought they had made their case, but after the PAWS secretary left the stevedores reiterated his allegation that the Histadrut was out to bring Jewish workers into the port, take it over, and deprive the Arabs of their livelihood. They pressed Agassi and Zaslani for an explicit promise that the Histadrut would not seek to bring Jewish workers into Jaffa harbor. Zaslani and Agassi could not of course make such a promise, since the Histadrut did in fact hope to achieve Hebrew labor at the harbor as elsewhere; indeed, one of the PLL's chief *raisons d'être* was to facilitate that effort. In the end the stevedores had to settle for a much vaguer promise that no Histadrut member would take a job from any permanently employed port worker. Zaslani also had to promise that the stevedores' union would remain independent even after it affiliated with the PLL.

Zaslani and Agassi concluded their report on this episode by stating that "one may say with confidence that as a result of this meeting our organization in Jaffa has been strengthened and *inoculated*."[79] This statement soon proved to be rather overconfident, as the PLL in Jaffa remained under constant pressure from Arab labor organizations. A few days after this debate, Zaslani reported to Agassi that both Michel Mitri's AWS and the Jaffa branch of the PAWS were leafleting the stevedores affiliated with the PLL and that this activity had led at least one member of the union's leadership to resign. At the same time, Ibrahim al-Sawi, who was receiving money from the PLL and acting as its main agent among the stevedores, was said to be displaying dictatorial behavior and angering union members. Moreover, the port workers were insisting on keeping some distance between their union and the PLL: they had refused to sign their names to the application of the PLL's Jaffa branch for registration as an officially recognized organization. For the same reason, the letter which the Jaffa stevedores' union sent to the various labor contractors at Jaffa port in January 1935 contained no mention whatsoever of the PLL or the Histadrut, though it was Zaslani who forwarded a translation of the letter directly to the British official who managed the port of Jaffa.[80]

The stevedores' tough questions at the meeting and their insistence on independence from the PLL indicate that they were not quite as unaware, guileless, and docile as labor-Zionist leaders tended to depict them—nor as easily duped and manipulated as Arab nationalists believed. Agassi would later speak of the effort to instill "proletarian consciousness" (*hakara po'alit*) in these workers, by which he meant labor Zionism's conception of how Arab workers should think and behave.[81] In fact the stevedores, and other groups of Arab workers elsewhere, seem to have had their own sense of who they were and what they wanted, a sense which did not necessarily coincide with what the PLL proposed. The stevedores understood that several rival labor organizations were seeking to win their support and sought to turn that rivalry to their advantage; they also knew that identifiable union members were subject to threats and harassment, and even exclusion from work, from the labor contractors through whom they were employed. They were obviously well aware of the Histadrut's commitment to Hebrew labor and that policy's implications for their own livelihood. As a result, though they were not in principle unwilling to cooperate with the Histadrut, whose clout and resources they knew to be considerably greater than those available to any Arab labor organization, they sought insofar as possible to do so on their own terms. This episode can therefore be read as reinforcing my argument that it is not useful to uncritically accept Arab nationalist depictions of cooperation between

Zionists and Arab workers as instances of either manipulation or collaboration, at least in any simple sense of those terms.

The stevedores faced extremely adverse conditions in their struggle to organize. While L. K. Pope, Port Manager at Jaffa, urged the contractors to meet with the stevedores' representatives, his main concern was to avoid any trouble and preserve the status quo until the end of the citrus export season. He and other British officials were also concerned that if the Histadrut succeeded in organizing Arab workers at Jaffa port it might achieve a stranglehold over this vital enterprise. In a letter to the Director of Customs, Excise and Trade, Pope declared that the stevedores' demands for better pay, an eight-hour day, and overtime pay—"doubtless prompted by the General Federation of Jewish Labour in Palestine"—were exaggerated. In any event, he went on, "I am not in favour of an 8 hour working day for Arab labour. Such labourers are in actual fact more contented and happier when they work than they would be were a considerable portion of their waking hours to be spent lounging in the Cafés and markets of the Town."[82]

But growing tensions and eventually open conflict at the port soon made Pope's dismissive attitude untenable. At the end of February 1935 some sixty workers employed at the port development project went on strike, originally to protest the dismissal of a comrade who had been fired after a dispute with his foreman, and then to demand an eight-hour workday, a six-day workweek, and higher wages. AWS leader Michel Mitri quickly appeared on the scene and sought to negotiate on the workers' behalf. Though the strike ended in failure after a week, it was a clear manifestation of growing discontent. The contractors' efforts early in 1935 to break the stevedores' union by harassment and, for a time, by refusing to employ union members led to persistent friction and sometimes violent conflict on the docks. To restore order, and to deflect questions being raised by Labor Party members of Parliament, the British authorities in Palestine appointed a committee to investigate labor conditions at the port of Jaffa. Since that committee was chaired by none other than L. K. Pope, it not very surprisingly reported that the stevedores had no serious grievances and that no immediate government action was called for. In fact no further action was taken before the outbreak of the 1936 general strike.[83]

During the latter part of 1935 the PLL's base of support at the port of Jaffa disappeared. With the support or acquiescence of British port officials, the contractors sought to break the dockworkers' union by various means, including the denial of work to union members and other "troublemakers." Poignant evidence of the use of this tactic has survived in the form of a petition bearing the signatures or thumbprints of fourteen Jaffa dockworkers who had been dismissed by their boss, Mahmud al-Qumbarji, at the end of June 1935.[84] Competition from the Arab unions and rising political tensions exacerbated by the Histadrut's Hebrew labor campaign also helped increase the costs of cooperation with the PLL well beyond any actual or potential benefits to Arab workers. Then, in October 1935, a barrel purportedly containing a shipment of cement accidentally broke open while being unloaded at Jaffa and was found to contain arms and ammunition being smuggled into Palestine for the Hagana. The discovery created an uproar in the Arab community and went a long way toward destroying what remained of the PLL's links with the Jaffa dockworkers. By the end of 1935 almost all the stevedores and lightermen had severed their ties with the PLL or simply allowed them to lapse, gravitating instead into the orbit of Arab trade unions. Despite this the PLL persevered in its efforts to set up a Jewish-Arab boat company at the port as a way to get Jewish workers employed there, but the anti-British and anti-Zionist general strike that began in April 1936 brought that project to an abrupt end.[85] The Jaffa dockworkers joined the general strike *en masse* when it erupted and would remain on strike until it ended.

THE "EVEN VESID" AFFAIR AND THE IPC STRIKE

Even while things were still apparently going well in Jaffa, Zaslani, Agassi, and their colleagues felt that they had not gained much if any ground. At the end of 1934 Abba Hushi was complaining that "within the Histadrut there is no psychological preparation for this work, there is a passivity which opposes it, and the work is being carried out by a small number of comrades; there is no sympathy for this work." Despite frequent appeals for a larger budget, funding for Arab work remained at very low levels from both the Histadrut and the Jewish Agency. But as Hushi saw it, the disinterest or hostility of most MAPAI members was not the only problem. The PLL's work, he felt, had been too haphazard and passive, and he called for a more active approach, one that did not depend on an individual Arab worker, or group of Arab workers, happening upon the Haifa club or approaching the Histadrut for help during a strike. "Some 1500 Arab workers have passed through the club and only a very small number of them remain today," he noted. Agassi echoed Hushi's emphasis on the importance of taking the initiative in targeting and organizing specific work sites.[86]

David Hacohen, who as director of the Histadrut's Contracting Office was one of the organization's preeminent entrepreneurs, proposed another strategy: the explicit transformation of the PLL into a labor contracting agency. The Histadrut would set up a contracting company which would bid on public works contracts and then implement them by employing only Arab workers who belonged to the PLL. Although Hacohen did not mention it, this scheme might also have brought the Histadrut extra profits by allowing it (through its PLL-linked subsidiary) to bid on and win public works contracts which stipulated that a certain percentage of those working on the project be Arabs. Hacohen also proposed that the PLL organize and supply Arab workers to Jewish-owned urban enterprises. These steps would, he argued, give the organization's membership, or at least some substantial portion of it, a clear economic stake in loyalty to it.

In fact, many Arab workers already viewed the PLL primarily as an employment agency: they approached it and sought to join only because they were under the impression that members were entitled to jobs in Jewish-owned enterprises. In October 1934, for example, three Arab workers from a village near Acre wrote to "the respected head of the Jewish workers' association" expressing their interest in joining; when someone (probably Agassi) contacted them, they asked for jobs and were refused, though Agassi did occasionally try to place loyal PLL members in jobs at various Jewish enterprises and organizations. Hacohen's proposal would have systematized this aspect of the PLL's work and used it as a way to build the organization.[87]

An incident from this period which aroused considerable debate among labor Zionists may serve to illustrate the contradictions which Hacohen's conception of the PLL's mission might have entailed. The Even Vesid stone quarry and limestone kiln, established near Haifa in 1929, was unique in that it was owned jointly by the Histadrut's Contracting Office and one of Haifa's leading Arab businessmen, Tahir Qaraman. The company employed both Arabs and Jews in roughly equal numbers, but the fact that it employed any Arabs at all was embarrassing for the Histadrut, committed as it was to Hebrew labor, especially in its own enterprises. To make matters even more embarrassing, the wages which Even Vesid paid its Arab workers were, at 12 piastres a day, not only substandard but also far below the 25 piastres a day which the Jewish workers there earned for more or less the same work. These issues, hitherto discussed only in closed Histadrut leadership forums, came to public attention in April 1935 when some of the Arab workers at Even Vesid went on strike. Their demands included a minimum daily wage of 15 piastres, an eight-hour workday, a weekly day of rest, and the removal of a foreman they disliked. Leadership of the strike was quickly assumed by the PAWS. The Histadrut denounced the strike as politically motivated, claimed the strikers were being exploited by Hanna 'Asfur and other Arab nationalist activists, and tried to keep the quarry operating with the Jewish workers and with Arab strikebreakers, apparently recruited from among quarry workers who belonged to the PLL. Despite clashes with police and arrests, the strikers held firm, and in the end an embarrassed Histadrut had to back down and grant a wage increase.

Hashomer Hatza'ir excoriated the Histadrut leadership for having failed to ensure that all the Arab employees of an enterprise of which the Histadrut was part owner were organized in the PLL. The question also arose as to why this enterprise employed Arab workers at all, to which David Hacohen responded that Even Vesid's existence depended on Tahir Qaraman's cooperation and its profitability required the use of cheap Arab labor. In other words, the jobs of the relatively well-paid Jewish workers there depended on the employment of at least some poorly paid Arab workers. To further complicate things, a Jewish quarry owner who employed only Jews filed a complaint against Even Vesid with the Yishuv committee charged with overseeing its "buy Jewish" campaign. He demanded protection from Even Vesid's competition, arguing that that quarry's use of Arab workers allowed it to sell its products for less than Hebrew-labor quarries. Histadrut leaders debated whether it was right for the Histadrut to partially own an enterprise which employed Arabs even as it demanded that other Jewish enterprises and farms employ only Jews.

This episode and the uproar it caused cannot have made MAPAI leaders enthusiastic about Hacohen's proposal. From the Histadrut's standpoint, using the PLL to supply and control Arab labor in Jewish enterprises carried significant risks. It might also present an obstacle to the ultimate realization of MAPAI's long-term goal of achieving total Hebrew labor in every such enterprise, especially those it controlled, even if that goal could not be immediately achieved.[88]

A few months before the Even Vesid affair erupted, another strike had attracted countrywide attention, especially among Arab workers, and had seemed to underscore both the potential of working-class solidarity and its complexities. As I noted earlier, February 1935 had witnessed a week-long strike among workers at the port of Jaffa. At the time, observers generally perceived that strike as having been inspired by the much larger strike (already mentioned in Chapter 4, in connection with the railway workers) which had begun a few days earlier at the Iraq Petroleum Company's facility in Haifa. The IPC workers' strike, directed against a wealthy, powerful, and highly visible transnational corporation which was also one of the country's biggest employers and whose links to British imperial interests in the Middle East were obvious, was one of the largest Palestine had yet witnessed.

Construction of the IPC's facilities, including storage tanks and an oil dock for petroleum extracted from the company's fields in northern Iraq and pumped to Haifa through a pipeline that crossed Transjordan and northern Palestine, had only recently been completed. On February 9, 1935, some fifty workers employed by one of the IPC's contractors had successfully struck for higher wages. Their example may have been fresh in the minds of the IPC's own workers, for when the company announced a few weeks later that some of its workers would be laid off and the remainder would have their wages cut, a strike erupted. The strike that began on February 22 initially encompassed some 150 skilled workers in several of the technical departments, who formed a strike committee and demanded not only the recision of the wage cut but also a minimum wage of 15 piastres a day, an eight-hour day and six-day workweek, overtime pay for extra hours, and various other gains. Within a week the strike had spread to encompass some 600 of the IPC's 800 workers, almost all of them Arabs; but even the few Americans employed at the facility, presumably skilled oil workers or engineers, are reported to have stayed away from work.

Both the PAWS and the Histadrut soon became involved in the strike. The PAWS had the support of most of the workers and called in its counsel, Hanna 'Asfur, to negotiate with the company, while the PLL represented some one hundred IPC drivers whom it had organized. Initially the PLL seems to have tried to keep the drivers separate from the rest of the IPC workers, but when this failed Eliyahu Agassi joined 'Asfur and the strike committee in talks with the company. The wave of militancy and solidarity which accompanied the first two weeks of the strike facilitated cooperation between the PAWS and the Histadrut. At one point early in the strike IPC management tried to exclude Agassi from a meeting with the strike committee and PAWS leaders, but the latter refused to permit this and the company had to back down. After some initial hesitation, the Histadrut backed the strike and appealed to its members to contribute to a strike fund.

The Histadrut and the PAWS called on the government to intervene. Under pressure from local British officials the IPC offered some concessions, but ʿAsfur was unable to convince the strikers to accept them and return to work. As the days passed, however, the leaders of the PAWS, which represented mainly the skilled workers, came to feel that their members' demands had largely been met and that the strike was now being waged mainly on behalf of the unskilled workers. They were also growing increasingly suspicious of the Histadrut, which they feared was seeking to use its base among the drivers and its control of the strike fund to take charge of the strike.

At that point, more than two weeks after the strike began, Fakhri al-Nashashibi, the self-styled "leader of the workers," suddenly appeared in Haifa and began to mediate between the company and the strike committee. It is not clear whether or not the PAWS had invited him to intervene, but once on the scene al-Nashashibi largely ignored the PAWS' leaders and conducted his own secret negotiations with IPC management. After three days of talks al-Nashashibi informed the strike committee that he had reached an agreement with the company, in whose "good intentions" he declared his trust, and persuaded the committee to endorse it. Most of the strikers returned to work on March 11; others, clearly disgruntled about the strike's outcome, held out for a few more days before reluctantly resuming work.

The Histadrut was profoundly unhappy about al-Nashashibi's intervention and denounced him as a reactionary nationalist who had sold out the workers by pressing the strikers to accept less than they might have won through greater militancy and by agreeing to the formation of what amounted to a company union. The communists agreed that al-Nashashibi was a bourgeois opportunist but held Agassi, Hushi, and the Histadrut equally responsible for "betraying" the IPC workers. By contrast the pro-Nashashibi *Filastin* hailed the outcome as a great victory for the workers, especially as it had "put an end to the Histadrut's attempts to exploit the strike." That it may have done, but in the months that followed IPC management reneged on many of its promises and largely destroyed the PAWS' organization among its workers.[89]

Though it ended in only a partial victory for the workers, the scope and duration of the IPC strike and the issues it raised aroused great interest among, and had a strong impact on, Arab workers in many parts of Palestine. Numerous Arab trade unions sent messages of solidarity, and various groups of workers were inspired by the IPC workers' militancy, including Jaffa dockworkers and the railway workers in and near Haifa, who as I mentioned in Chapter 4 were in close contact with the IPC workers. For years after, leftist and prolabor accounts of the Iraq Petroleum

Company strike of 1935 routinely attached the adjective "great" to it, and not a few contemporary observers, both Arab and Jewish, saw it as marking the beginning of a new stage in the emergence of a class-conscious Arab working class in Palestine.[90]

THE GATHERING STORM

In the aftermath of the IPC strike, the PLL seems to have lapsed into virtual quiescence. It had lost its base at Nesher and among the Haifa dockworkers, and its once promising relationship with the Jaffa dockworkers was rapidly evaporating. In both cities only small groups of workers at less important workplaces remained in its orbit, along with a number of individuals who frequented its clubs or maintained contact with Agassi. The Histadrut's Arab Committee failed to meet between May 1935 and February 1936, and the ambitious plan of action it had adopted was never implemented. There was discussion of publishing propaganda material in Arabic to put forward the labor-Zionist position on such urgent questions as Hebrew labor, but the Arab Department was desperately short of funds and nothing was done.[91]

The major reason for the PLL's virtual paralysis during the latter part of 1935 was the increasingly tense political climate in Palestine and the radicalization of the Arab community, including Arab workers, who became much less inclined to affiliate, cooperate, or even associate with a Zionist organization. The rapid growth of the Yishuv had intensified Arab fears: for the first time, a Jewish majority and Jewish statehood appeared feasible, perhaps even imminent. Reports of large-scale Zionist land purchases made the threat of dispossession ever more palpable, and the discovery that arms and ammunition were being smuggled into Palestine for the Hagana seemed to confirm long-standing Arab fears that the Zionists were preparing to seize the country by force. Government policies which Arab public opinion perceived as pro-Zionist also exacerbated Arab resentment and anger. At the same time, the Italian invasion of Ethiopia and Germany's reoccupation of the Rhineland made war among the European powers seem imminent and underscored Britain's apparent weakness.

Moreover, the years of prosperity came to an end in 1935, leading to rising unemployment and social discontent in the Arab community. Shantytowns sprang up around Haifa and Jaffa, inhabited by thousands of destitute migrants from the countryside. The residents of these shantytowns provided a constituency for recruitment by radical nationalists, notably the popular Muslim preacher Shaykh 'Izz al-Din al-Qassam of

Haifa, who called for moral renovation and denounced the factionalism and ineffectiveness of the elite politicians. Al-Qassam eventually organized a small guerrilla band that in 1935 took to the hills in the hope of sparking an armed revolt against British rule and Zionism. In November 1935 al-Qassam was killed in a gun battle with police near Jenin, but his death and funeral aroused strong nationalist and religious sentiments and dramatically increased pressure on the politicians to put aside their debilitating factional squabbles and take a much more aggressive stance toward Palestine's British overlords.

Palestinian Arabs were also well aware of nationalist upsurges in neighboring countries. In November 1935 Egypt had been swept by demonstrations demanding the restoration of the suspended constitution and full independence. These demonstrations forced the holding of new elections, the return to power of the nationalist Wafd party, and the opening of a new round of negotiations between Egypt and Britain. In French-ruled Syria rising nationalist agitation culminated in the eruption of a general strike in January 1936. The strike lasted for fifty days and compelled the French to invite a Syrian delegation to Paris to negotiate a treaty which would move Syria toward independence. Palestinian Arab nationalists were inspired by these examples of popular mobilization, especially the Syrian general strike, and contrasted them to the Palestinian nationalist leadership's weakness, disunity, and entanglement in apparently endless and fruitless negotiations for a proposed legislative council. Younger, more radical nationalist activists, convinced that further negotiations with Britain were pointless, were ready to emulate their Arab brethren outside Palestine by launching a vigorous and sustained popular struggle to put an end to what they perceived as the looming threat posed by Zionism, and to the British colonial regime which protected it.

The supercharged political climate and high unemployment among Arab workers at the end of 1935 notwithstanding, the Histadrut leadership came to the conclusion that the end of the construction boom and rising unemployment in the Yishuv justified the escalation of its Hebrew labor campaign. Given the circumstances, this escalation not surprisingly provoked an unprecedentedly vigorous and militant Arab response. Once again the AWS in Jaffa took the initiative, under the creative and effective leadership of its young president, Michel Mitri. Mitri had taken over the organization after Fakhri al-Nashashibi lost interest in labor affairs during 1935 and built it into a strong local force which claimed some 4,700 members. In some ways Mitri was a forerunner of the new kind of Arab labor leader who would emerge during and after the Second World War. An educated man with knowledge and experience of the wider world, he was a capable organizer and knew how to seize on an issue and use it to serve his movement's goals. He also understood the importance to the labor movement of building broad-based alliances. For example, he was quite willing to cooperate with radical nationalist and leftist forces in the Arab community, including members of the left wing of the pan-Arab nationalist Istiqlal ("Independence") party and even with Arab communists. Apparently impressed by Mitri's leadership abilities and potential effectiveness, the Histadrut approached him in September 1935 and offered him its organizing experience and access to funds to build up the AWS, on condition that he distance himself from the Arab nationalist movement. Mitri, a staunch nationalist, refused and instead adopted a new and effective strategy to mobilize his constituents.[92]

In December 1935 Mitri sent a letter to the District Commissioner of Jaffa claiming that more than a thousand of his members were unemployed and requesting permission to hold a protest march through the streets of Jaffa. Mitri's explanation of the purposes of the demonstration suggests that Arab unionists clearly perceived a connection between Arab unemployment, Hebrew labor, and Zionism: "to ask for the relief of unemployment, to protest against Jewish picketing, the Judaization of the Port and the policy of immigration according to the absorptive capacity of the country." The District Commissioner prohibited the march, but Mitri and his colleagues proceeded to step up their campaign against Hebrew labor. To build support the AWS convened a national conference of Arab trade unionists in Jaffa, and in February 1936, using the same arguments that the Histadrut advanced in defense of Hebrew labor, Mitri launched a campaign to protest the awarding of a government contract for three schools in Jaffa to the Histadrut's Contracting Office, which generally employed only Jews. He pointed out that the buildings were located in a predominantly Arab city, that Arabs were never given contracts for construction in Jewish areas, that the Histadrut had forcibly driven Arab workers away from Jewish building sites, and that unemployment among Arab workers was very high. When no relief was forthcoming, AWS members adopted the Histadrut's own tactics: unemployed Arab workers began picketing building sites where Hebrew labor prevailed, in particular the three schools under construction. This led to clashes in which Arab workers were arrested by the police.

The pickets seem to have been well aware of what was at stake. One of those arrested told the judge before whom he was brought that "[w]e Arab workers are unemployed. We asked the government to remove Jewish workers from Arab enterprises but it took no interest in our just demand. So we went to the site and tried to expel the Jewish workers from jobs to which we have more right than anyone else, and the police arrested us." The strategy seems to have produced results: the government eventually agreed to require that 50 percent of the jobs at the school construction sites be given to Arab workers, though it rejected the demand that Arabs also be guaranteed 50 percent of the total wage bill. But Mitri was not satisfied and, emulating MAPAI, he demanded 100 percent Arab labor. A leaflet issued by the AWS in the spring of 1936 conveys the pitch of militancy which its campaign had attained: it called for mass picketing of construction sites "until the jails are full of [Arab] workers" and designated alternative leaders for the AWS in the event Mitri and his colleagues were arrested.[93]

There was also renewed conflict at the Majdal Yaba quarry, where with the Histadrut's blessing management once again tried to fire all its Arab workers and replace them with Jews. With backing from the AWS, the Arab workers responded with picket lines. Even the MAPAI loyalists who sat on the Histadrut's Arab Committee seem to have been embarrassed by what was happening at Majdal Yaba. That the Histadrut secretariat had approved the wholesale dismissal of the Arab workers at Majdal Yaba without first consulting its own Arab Department, presumably responsible for coordinating the organization's policies toward Arab workers, was rightly taken as a sign of the low esteem in which the leadership held that department. Ya'akov Riftin, the Hashomer Hatza'ir representative on the committee, denounced the indiscriminate firing of Arab workers and the drive for total Hebrew labor which motivated it. Though uneasy, his MAPAI colleagues contented themselves with a request that the Histadrut executive committee require that all Histadrut organs check with the Arab Department before dismissing Arab workers. As had been the case in 1934, the Arab workers' vigorous response frustrated the Histadrut offensive at this site.[94]

In an article published on April 1, 1936, Riftin looked back on the preceding year and saw nothing but missed opportunities. MAPAI, which controlled the Histadrut, had never really tried to implement Histadrut decisions with regard to organizing Arab workers, and the PLL was weak and ineffective. While the Arab pickets in Jaffa were misguided, Riftin argued, it was MAPAI which had given Michel Mitri the weapon he needed to mount his campaign by insisting on total Hebrew labor and firing Arab workers wholesale. Riftin reiterated Hashomer Hatza'ir's vision of an alliance between Jewish and Arab workers, which he counterposed to MAPAI's tendency to see the entire Palestinian Arab community as a monolithic bloc with which Zionism would have either to compromise or fight. Riftin feared that unless the labor-Zionist movement changed course, difficult times lay ahead: the nationalist tide was rising in Syria and Egypt, and in Palestine "the legend of [al-Qassam's] 'heroic struggle' near Jenin is growing." [95]

Had Riftin written his article a few weeks later, he might have cited another development which he would surely have seen as ominous. On April 10, even as public opinion was demanding that the Arab politicians set aside their differences and close ranks, representatives of the various segments of the Arab labor movement in Palestine gathered again, this time in Haifa, to lay the foundations of an all-Palestine Arab labor federation. Among those attending were 'Abd al-Hamid Haymur, the veteran Haifa railway worker who was secretary of the PAWS; Sami Taha, who would later emerge as that organization's preeminent leader; Michel Mitri and George Mansur, leaders of the AWS in Jaffa; Khalil Shanir, one of the Palestine Communist Party's top Arab leaders; Hamdi al-Husayni of Gaza, a radical young journalist who belonged to the Istiqlal party and had links with clandestine Arab nationalist groups preparing for armed revolt; and Akram Zu'aytar of Nablus, another radical Istiqlalist in contact with members of al-Qassam's guerrilla band holed up in the hills around Nablus.[96] This gathering manifested the convergence of the fledgling Arab trade union movement with the most radical segment of the nationalist movement and with the Arab communists, signaling not just a desire for labor unity but also a sense that the Arab labor movement must play an important role in the more militant phase of the national struggle that seemed about to begin.

The Haifa conference, and the convergence of sociopolitical forces that it manifested, suggest that accounts which depict the outbreak of mass popular opposition to Zionism and British rule in April 1936 as entirely spontaneous and unexpected are inadequate, since they fail to take into account the kinds of grievances, struggles, and developments discussed here which prepared the ground for that explosion of popular energy and helped shape the historical conjuncture within which it emerged. The uprising which began in the spring of 1936 had antecedents, for example, in the rising tide of worker militancy which the AWS campaign against Hebrew labor both built on and stimulated. At the same time, that campaign strengthened the links between worker grievances and militancy on the one hand and the national question on the other, links which were further reinforced by the labor movement's new ties with radical nationalists anxious to mobilize the populace at large. The tide of worker unrest had itself been fueled by al-Qassam's resort to arms the previous fall and the popular sentiments it unleashed, and more generally by the poverty and despair in the shantytowns and working-class neighborhoods of Haifa and Jaffa, which had in turn nourished al-Qassam's movement.[97]

Though tensions in Palestine were clearly rising in the spring of 1936, the storm broke earlier than anyone expected, and long before efforts to establish a new Arab labor federation linked to the more radical wing of the nationalist movement could bear fruit. The Arab general strike, and then the revolt against British rule and Zionism, would have complex and paradoxical consequences for both Arab and Jewish workers and labor movements in Palestine. While it unmistakably demonstrated the Arab community's rejection of Zionism, it resulted in the paralysis of the Arab labor movement and allowed the Histadrut's Hebrew labor campaign to achieve unprecedented gains, though it also undermined whatever prospects the PLL may have had of taking on some life of its own. At another level, the character and consequences of the revolt, and especially its defeat, contributed significantly to determining the ultimate outcome of the struggle for Palestine a decade later.

6 The Arab Revolt and Labor Zionism, 1936–1939

On April 15, 1936, members of the guerrilla band founded by Shaykh 'Izz al-Din al-Qassam held up cars and buses near Nablus, killing two Jewish passengers. Two days later a right-wing Jewish paramilitary group retaliated by killing two Arabs. Arab protests soon erupted throughout the country, gradually taking on the character of a broad-based anticolonial and anti-Zionist popular uprising. To contain the violence and channel the upsurge from below, Arab nationalist activists quickly called for a countrywide general strike. The strike spread rapidly, as did new "national committees" which sprang up to lead the struggle in all the major towns. Taken by surprise, the elite politicians tried to catch up with and ride the wave of popular energy by endorsing the strike call and forming a new Arab Higher Committee (AHC) on which all the major parties were represented, with Amin al-Husayni as its president.

The general strike would continue for six months, until October 1936, making it one of the longest general strikes in history. It constituted the first stage of a countrywide Arab nationalist revolt against both British rule and Zionism which would end only in the summer of 1939. The strike was accompanied by numerous attacks on Jews and Jewish property as well as on British installations, transport, communications, and personnel, carried out mainly by the numerous village-based guerrilla bands that sprang up in the countryside during the spring and summer of 1936 and gave the revolt an increasingly violent and openly insurrectional character.[1]

Most segments of Palestine's urban Arab population participated in the general strike, with urban workers playing a key role. Hasan Sidqi al-Dajani's drivers' union paralyzed Arab motor transport and the Jaffa port workers shut down Jaffa harbor. To sustain the strike, the national committees collected donations from wealthy Palestinians and from sympathizers in neighboring countries, and distributed strike pay to those idled by the strike, including the Jaffa dockworkers. Except in Haifa, which as I will discuss later was something of a special case, the general strike destroyed most of what remained of the PLL's visible influence and made open PLL activity among Arab workers impossible. In this respect it is noteworthy that the Jaffa stevedores and lightermen, who at the end of 1934 had cooperated with the PLL and whose organization seemed about to place control of Jaffa port in the Histadrut's hand, were now at the forefront of the general strike. Arab trade unions which had previously cooperated with Jewish labor were quick to rally to the national cause. The 1936 May Day rally organized by the PAWS in Haifa and consisting largely of railway workers sent a message to the High Commissioner denouncing the government for tolerating the "judaization of this Arab country, depriving the worker of his job and the peasant of his land." Rather defensively, the statement went on to declare that Zionist propaganda about cooperation between Arab and Jewish workers was "a baldfaced lie of which we are innocent."[2]

THE GENERAL STRIKE AND HEBREW LABOR

Despite the success of the general strike in many parts of Palestine it was never total, and the nationalist movement's inability to make it so undermined its effectiveness. This failure can be attributed in part to specific local factors, such as the pro-Zionist and pro-British stance of Haifa mayor Hasan Shukri and his local allies, who opposed the general strike, and later deep (and eventually violent) factional divisions within the Palestinian Arab leadership. But at least at certain sites, it is also attributable to the years of patient and persistent work which the Histadrut had invested in trying to introduce Jewish workers into economically and politically strategic workplaces which had once been almost exclusively Arab, a project to which the PLL's efforts in 1932–35 to organize Arab workers at those same workplaces certainly contributed. The footholds which the Histadrut had thereby gained in these workplaces greatly facilitated the British authorities' ability to block Arab nationalist efforts to spread the general strike and fully paralyze the country's economy. At the same time, forceful British military and police intervention now made it possible for the Histadrut to expand some of those footholds into more secure bastions of Hebrew labor.

Events at the port of Haifa provide the most telling example. The local National Committee and the Arab nationalist leadership as a whole very much wanted to shut down Palestine's largest port. Some 100 of the 250 porters there did strike in late April, but unlike Jaffa, where all the port workers had quickly joined the strike, the great majority of the Arab labor contractors and port workers at Haifa remained at their jobs, despite offers of generous strike pay and intense pressure from the National Committee. Amin al-Husayni and other prominent nationalist leaders came to Haifa on several occasions and tried to persuade 'Abd Allah Abu Zayid, the contractor who largely controlled the port labor force, to shut the harbor down. But Abu Zayid insisted that circumstances in Haifa were very different from those in Jaffa. In the latter city all the port workers were Arabs, but at Haifa port some 200 Jews were employed through labor contractors. The porters who had stopped work in April had quickly been replaced by Jews and Hawranis, and the nonstriking porters were lodged at the port itself under close official supervision. If his workers joined the strike, Abu Zayid argued, their jobs would immediately be taken over by the Jewish workers already at the port, by other Jews who would be brought in, and by Arab migrant laborers from the Hawran, whereupon Haifa harbor would be forever lost to the Arabs of Palestine. This was certainly not Abu Zayid's only consideration, however: he had long-standing personal and business links with Jews, especially local Histadrut officials, and there is evidence that the Jewish Agency was secretly disbursing considerable sums to him (and presumably to others as well) to keep Haifa harbor open.[3]

In August, after a sustained campaign of pressure and threats, some of the Arab port workers in Haifa finally did go on strike, along with workers at the Palestine Railways, the Iraq Petroleum Company, Shell, the municipality, and the Public Works Department. Abu Zayid fled to Lebanon to escape nationalist threats on his life. Determined to prevent these vital enterprises from being shut down, however, the British authorities promptly dispatched military forces to protect strikebreakers at the port and the other affected sites, and used Royal Navy engineers to keep the trains running. The Haifa Workers' Council pitched in by mobilizing kibbutz members and others to take the place of striking Arab harbor workers, while Agassi's PLL did its part by readying a group of Arab strikebreakers from among its members and contacts. This forceful intervention by both the British authorities and the Histadrut kept the port and railways in Haifa functioning, while the strikers' fear that their jobs would be permanently lost to Jews induced almost all of them to return to work after ten days. Neither the port nor the other important workplaces in Haifa witnessed any further disruptions for the duration of the revolt.

This unprecedented conjuncture allowed the Histadrut to achieve other long-sought gains. For example, at the end of 1936 the Jewish Agency persuaded the Haifa port authorities to employ Jews directly, rather than through labor contractors as had previously been the case, thereby displacing Arab workers and further strengthening Hebrew labor there. In 1933 some MAPAI leaders had worried that Abba Hushi was spending too much time and effort organizing Arab workers: "He should remember," they cautioned him, "that he is the secretary of the *Jewish* Haifa Workers' Council." To the extent that the Histadrut's successes in 1936 owed something to Hushi's commitment to both Hebrew labor and the organization of Arab workers, it would seem that they need not have worried.[4]

Before the revolt, the government of Palestine had been generally unsympathetic or even hostile to the Histadrut's aggressive Hebrew labor campaign, for fear that it might inflame Arab-Jewish relations, threaten public order, enhance the Zionist movement's power, and cost the government money by driving up its wage bill and the cost of public works contracts. Now, however, the Arab revolt created circumstances in which the government had a strong political and security interest in backing the Histadrut's drive for Hebrew labor, in order to keep vital enterprises functioning and weaken the nationalist revolt. At Haifa the British authorities and the Zionist movement had a clear common interest in breaking the August strike, and they succeeded in doing so through a combination of military force (supplied by the British) and highly motivated strikebreakers (supplied by the Histadrut).

At the Nesher quarry, too, the general strike and the government's interest in breaking it made it possible for the Histadrut to realize an old dream: the introduction of Jewish workers. As I discussed in Chapter 5, in March 1936 the quarry workers at Nesher, now represented exclusively by the PAWS, had concluded the last of several unsuccessful strikes against the quarry operator, the same notorious Musbah al-Shaqifi who over the previous years had routinely signed agreements and then promptly broken them. When the general strike began in April, nationalist threats on his life prompted al-Shaqifi to flee to Lebanon. The quarry workers joined the strike and nearby villages became hotbeds of nationalist activity. The British authorities and the Zionist movement shared a common interest in breaking the strike at Nesher; as Moshe Shertok, director of the Jewish Agency's Political Department, put it, if the strike at the quarry went on and the cement plant it supplied had to shut down for lack of raw materials, "the Arab leaders would be in a position to boast that they had succeeded in paralysing the largest Jewish factory in the country and this would greatly strengthen their standing in the Arab public."[5] Nesher's management was also finally convinced that production and discipline could be restored only if Jews took over at least part of the work at the quarry, and therefore acceded to a long-standing Histadrut demand by canceling al-Shaqifi's contract and transferring the quarry concession to the Histadrut's Contracting Office, directed by David Hacohen.

Hacohen and his colleagues feared that the Arab quarry workers would violently resist the employment of Jews. They therefore planned their moves in close consultation with British officials, who welcomed this effort to undermine the general strike, start up the quarry, discipline an apparently pronationalist workforce, and reassert the government's authority in a largely hostile area. Hacohen also consulted with Sami Taha, secretary of the PAWS, which represented most of the quarry workers. Taha was willing to cooperate with Hacohen, apparently because he wanted to preserve at least some of his members' jobs, and perhaps also because he was politically aligned with the anti-Husayni faction within the national movement. On May 4, 1936, Hacohen, accompanied by Taha and police officials, brought some fifty Jewish workers, members of nearby Kibbutz Yagur, to the quarry. After receiving Hacohen's promise that their jobs would be secure and their wages increased, the Arab workers there accepted the introduction of Jews without resistance. The PAWS' influence at the quarry was soon eliminated and the Arab workers were recruited into the PLL, with the approval of Solel Boneh, which had been reestablished in 1935. (In 1937 Solel Boneh absorbed the Contracting Office to become the Histadrut's road-building, construction, and general contracting company.) This made the Jewish quarry workers unhappy, because they feared that PLL membership would ensure that Arab workers could keep jobs Jewish workers might eventually want. Over the following years, as the quarry shifted to more intensive methods of production (including the introduction of more machinery, a quota system, and piecework), the workforce shrank and became more Jewish: by 1939 it comprised sixty Jews and fifty Arabs, with the former earning base pay of 37 piastres a day and the latter 16 piastres. Eventually the Nesher factory and quarry were sold to a new company owned jointly by the Histadrut and a group of Jewish cement dealers.[6]

The revolt also allowed the Histadrut to achieve victory in its battle to impose Hebrew labor at the Majdal Yaba (Migdal Tzedek) quarry, where as I discussed in Chapter 5 earlier efforts, in 1934 and again in April 1936, had been thwarted by the Arab workers' vigorous resistance. As at Haifa harbor and Nesher, it was official British support that made the difference this time around. At the end of 1936, at the Histadrut's insistence, all the Arab workers at Majdal Yaba were fired and Jewish workers brought in. As they had done twice before, the displaced Arab workers mounted a strong protest, but this time the British authorities stood squarely behind the Histadrut and a large contingent of police and numerous arrests broke Arab resistance. This defeat, which meant the loss of some 400 jobs, left a legacy of bitterness. "It is not surprising," an Arab observer wrote the following year, "that villagers from this neighborhood participated in the derailment of a train near Ras-el-Ain Station on October 14th 1937. . . . [The perpetrators] came from . . . villages which had had personal experience of what Zionists mean by the 'conquest of labor'."[7]

Yet the Histadrut's success at Majdal Yaba was only temporary: during the war Jewish workers left for better jobs elsewhere and by war's end the quarry workforce was again at least partially Arab, prompting yet another effort to impose Hebrew labor in 1947. Something similar happened in the citrus groves of the moshavot. During the strike nearly all Arab workers stayed away and their places were taken by Jewish workers mobilized and dispatched by the Histadrut. Once the strike ended, however, Arab workers returned and recaptured much of the ground they had lost. The tide turned again in the summer and fall of 1938, when the revolt reached its height and Jewish workers once again monopolized employment in Jewish-owned groves. However, after the revolt was suppressed in the summer of 1939, and especially once the war began and better jobs became available elsewhere, Jews abandoned the moshavot *en masse* and Arab workers resumed their role in the Jewish citrus sector. Thereafter the issue was largely shelved until 1948, after which the flight or expulsion of most of the Arabs who lived within the part of Palestine that became Israel "solved" the problem. That solution would of course prove temporary as well: after 1967 the labor force in Israel's citrus groves would come to consist largely of Palestinian workers from Gaza.[8]

To win the sympathy of British officials and secure more jobs for Jews, Zionist leaders did their best to highlight the key role Jewish workers had played in weakening the general strike. In his December 1936 testimony before the royal commission appointed to investigate the causes of the "disturbances" in Palestine and headed by Lord Peel, Moshe Shertok asserted that

This is a country of two races and it is a very important question to make the public services proof against racial unrest. [Interjection by a commission member: "Immune against the bacillus, shall we say?"] Yes, against dislocation in the event of racial trouble and in this respect the experience of the last disturbances, disturbances which were based on a racial strike, has taught us a good lesson. We have found that where the service was exclusively in Arab hands, as in the port of Jaffa, the service was paralysed completely, and that contributed to the spread of the strike and disorders, but the two remained organically connected and the strengthening of the one led to the spread of the other. Where Jews were present the service remained intact and we submit that it is, therefore, essential, as a matter of policy, that the racial composition of the population should be reflected in the personnel of the state services in this country.

By way of example, Shertok told the commission that when in August a strike had erupted at Haifa port, "Jewish labour stepped in and the strike was nipped in the bud, because Jewish labour was able to maintain the lighterage and stevedoring services. They were there and could do it. In Jaffa they were not there and could not do it."[9]

THE PLL DURING THE REVOLT

The ability of the PLL to mobilize Arab strikebreakers for work at Haifa harbor in August 1936 was less a sign of its strength in that city than of the desperate plight of unemployed Arab workers there. At a meeting of MAPAI's central committee in January 1937, Agassi told his colleagues that since 1932 the PLL had been in contact with some 2,500 Arab workers, issued 1,100 membership cards, organized thirteen trade unions, and led several strikes. Now, Agassi said, there were no more than fifteen Arab workers still completely loyal to the PLL and in close contact with it in Haifa and Jaffa combined, and another fifty or sixty on its periphery, while all the trade unions the PLL had sponsored were defunct. Its club in Haifa remained open, however, thanks in part to the continuing loyalty of one Mahmud Abu Dabus, whose local reputation as a tough guy offered some protection to the handful of Arabs publicly identified with the PLL.[10] That the PLL continued to exist at all testifies to the relative weakness of the Arab nationalist movement in Haifa as well as to the years of patient and persistent work which Eliyahu Agassi had invested in developing good relations with Arab workers in the city. But something else brought Arab workers to the PLL as well, even in this period: the organization's reputation as a source of jobs for Arab workers, for whom the revolt had brought increased unemployment. Agassi's notebooks from 1936 and 1937 record numerous instances in which Arab workers from

Haifa and from villages near and far approached him during his travels or appeared at the Haifa club and asked to join the organization, in the conviction that membership brought with it secure and well-paid employment at some Jewish enterprise.[11]

As a rule Agassi turned individual applicants away, holding to the PLL's policy of accepting only groups of workers employed at the same workplace. But the PLL did in fact come to function as an employment agency during the revolt years, supplying Arab workers deemed reliable from a security and political standpoint to the Histadrut's Contracting Office (and later Solel Boneh) for various public works projects in Haifa and to the Even Vesid quarry and limekiln, still jointly owned by the Histadrut and Haifa businessman Tahir Qaraman, which experienced only a few strike days during 1936.[12] Employing Arab workers who were also PLL members sometimes entangled the Histadrut in problems, however. In 1937, for example, Solel Boneh won a tender for the construction of a new government hospital in Haifa. Since the contract specified that 50 percent of the wage bill should go to Arabs, the Histadrut turned to an Arab labor contractor and required that his workers be members of the PLL. The contractor recruited workers from the countryside and from outside Palestine and compelled them to join the PLL. However, the relationship between Solel Boneh and this labor contractor soon deteriorated, his contract was canceled, and his workers were dismissed, putting the Histadrut and PLL in an embarrassing position when the fired workers asked, apparently in vain, for the return of their PLL membership dues. The hospital project also aroused considerable public controversy: Arab unionists denounced the awarding of the contract to Solel Boneh, charged that Arab labor was not receiving its fair share of the wage bill, and complained that skilled Arab workers were not receiving the same pay as their Jewish counterparts.[13]

Wage differentials between Jewish and Arab workers, even workers with special skills, remained large and continued to be a source of irritation to Arab workers and unionists. A study published in 1938 by the Economic Research Institute of the Jewish Agency found large gaps between Arab and Jewish wages. For example, in 1936–37 Jewish carpenters averaged 37 piastres a day, while Arab carpenters earned 27 piastres. For turners the figures were 39 and 35 piastres, respectively; for bricklayers 54 and 43; for plasterers 53 and 33; for floor-tilers 54 and 38. Some of the differential may have resulted from differences in skill levels and productivity, but this was certainly not true in all cases. The Jewish Agency study also found that the wages earned by some skilled Arab workers, in the building trades for example, and perhaps even by unskilled workers, were often higher than wages in surrounding Arab countries or even in some of the poorer and less developed countries of Europe. In this sense, the Zionist argument that the influx of Jewish immigrants and capital had helped to raise wage rates in Palestine was not groundless. But the comparison which Arab workers in Palestine deemed important was not with even more impoverished Egyptian or Hawrani workers but with local Jewish workers who were being paid more for performing the same jobs and whose organization, the Histadrut, also seemed to covet the Arabs' jobs.[14]

In addition to supplying labor, the PLL contributed to the Yishuv's struggle against the Arab revolt in other ways. Money provided by the Jewish Agency was secretly passed on to Arab port workers and labor contractors to keep Haifa harbor open, and Shmu'el Alafiya, a Damascus-born Jew who had replaced Agassi as PLL organizer in Haifa when the latter began to spend most of his time in Tel Aviv and Jaffa, paid off Arab taxi drivers there to keep them from joining the general strike.[15] The first boats for the new Jewish port at Tel Aviv were bought from Arabs in Haifa through PLL contacts. The PLL was also an important source of intelligence for the Hagana and the Jewish authorities. Reuven Zaslani had left his job at the Histadrut's Arab Department just before the general strike began and gone to work in the Jewish Agency's Political Department; assigned the task of setting up an effective countrywide intelligence network, he also continued to serve as the go-between linking Zionist and British intelligence. But he attended meetings of the Histadrut's Arab Committee at least through the end of 1936, and in 1938 he was still receiving copies of the Arab Department's reports on its activities.

Even after Zaslani moved on to bigger and better things, the Histadrut's involvement with Arab workers continued to have an important intelligence and security dimension. Agassi and Alafiya regularly passed on information they received from their Arab contacts about conditions in various Arab towns and villages and the doings of specific individuals and organizations. George Nassar seems to have done the same: Histadrut files contain numerous letters which he sent to his mentor Moshe Erem and other Po'alei Tziyon Smol leaders reporting in broken Hebrew on the situation in Jaffa during the general strike. So complete was Nassar's identification with his Jewish friends that he could in his letters unselfconsciously report what "the Arabs" were up to, as if he were not an Arab himself.[16]

Agassi and Alafiya also used their knowledge of Arabic—still a rather rare commodity in the Yishuv—to conduct antinationalist propaganda. During 1936 the PLL issued its own leaflets denouncing the strike and also distributed others prepared by the Jewish Agency's Arab Department.[17] The PLL also paid ʿAbd al-Rahman ʿUthman al-Husayni, a Syrian from Damascus who had recently retired from his post as a Syrian government clerk and settled in Haifa, to write a pamphlet (*An Appeal to Suffering Humanity*) espousing the author's blend of socialist and pacifist principles and then distributed it. Given the context, al-Husayni's pamphlet could only be understood as a denunciation of the revolt. Al-Husayni initially insisted on keeping his connection with the PLL secret, but he was quite willing to work as a Zionist agent of influence. In 1937 the PLL sent him to the village of Wadi ʿAra to follow up on a friendly letter which a village resident had written to the PLL, in the hope that this contact could be developed into a PLL branch. This initiative had a clear security dimension: Wadi ʿAra, situated in the long narrow valley which connected the coastal plain with the Jezreel Valley, was of considerable strategic importance. More generally, the Histadrut hoped that by establishing links with villages through the PLL, it could combat Arab nationalist influence in the countryside and capitalize on resentment of the Arab Higher Committee's ineffective leadership and weariness with the revolt. The moment seemed auspicious for initiatives of this kind: during the spring and summer of 1937 the revolt was more or less on hold as the Peel Commission investigated the situation in Palestine and considered its future. The PLL was able to outfit the Wadi ʿAra club (and later one in the nearby village of ʿArʿara) with a radio and reading material, and it maintained regular contacts with sympathizers in the two villages through 1937.[18]

Later in 1937 the PLL's relationship with al-Husayni deepened when it secretly hired him to organize a network of pro-Zionist intellectuals and clubs in various towns and villages and rented an office for him, at a total cost of some £P250—a sum whose size reflected the political importance of this project in the eyes of Histadrut and Jewish Agency officials. British security officials got wind of the plan, however, invited al-Husayni in for a talk, and tried to induce him to work for them as an informer who would infiltrate one of the Arab nationalist parties. This rather diminished al-Husayni's utility to the Histadrut, but he was nonetheless able to perform various services for his new friends. Among other things, he was the anonymous author of *Kashf al-Qinaʿ* (Removing the mask), a pamphlet published by the PLL in January 1937 which denounced the general strike and the nationalist revolt while praising the Histadrut for its concern for Arab workers.

Al-Husayni and a handful of other pro-Zionist Arabs were also extremely useful to Zionism's public relations efforts. They could be depended on to sing the praises of labor Zionism and explain its benefits for the Arabs of Palestine when foreign visitors and delegations passed through. Indeed, they seemed the living embodiment of labor Zionism's practical commitment to Arab-Jewish friendship and worker solidarity, and living proof that Arab nationalist fears of displacement and domination by Jews were unjustified. The claim of al-Husayni (who was not even a Palestinian) and others like him that their pro-Zionist line represented the true sentiments and real interests of the Arab working masses infuriated pronationalist Arab trade unionists. They lacked the Histadrut's strong connections with the international trade union movement and with European (especially British) labor and socialist parties, and they were extremely frustrated by their inability to put their case before world public opinion. When, for example, two members of Parliament from the Independent Labor Party (ILP) visited Palestine in January 1937 on a tour sponsored by the Yitzhaki-Abramovitch faction of Po'alei Tziyon Smol, with which the ILP had developed close ties, they met exclusively with Jews and with Arabs selected by the Histadrut, including al-Husayni, whose performance Alafiya deemed very effective. George Mansur, who tried unsuccessfully to keep the AWS operating after Michel Mitri was assassinated by an unknown assailant in December 1936, made repeated requests for a meeting with the ILP leaders but was turned down.[19]

Hashomer Hatza'ir did not have any loyal Arab cadre available for exhibition to foreign audiences, but it too sought to win support among European leftists for its version of socialist Zionism and its vision of a binational Palestine.[20] This period also witnessed Hashomer Hatza'ir's first efforts to conduct propaganda directly targeting Arabs. In honor of May Day 1937 the movement published what seems to have been its first Arabic-language pamphlet, entitled *The Path of Agreement between the Jews and the Arabs of Palestine*. The pamphlet argued that both Arab and Jewish workers would benefit from solidarity and explicitly differentiated Hashomer Hatza'ir from the Zionist majority by advocating the establishment of a binational Arab-Jewish state in Palestine. It also sought to place the Palestine question in a proletarian internationalist framework: the Arab and Jewish workers of Palestine, it declared, could give no greater gift to the workers of the world, to the victims of Hitler and Mussolini, to the workers of Spain fighting for liberty, democracy, and socialism, than fraternal concord and solidarity among themselves. On the other hand, the pamphlet strongly denounced the Arab nationalist leadership while avoiding any explicit discussion of Arab nationalism or Zionism. It also made no explicit mention of the question of Hebrew labor or of Hashomer Hatza'ir's differences with MAPAI, though in Histadrut forums and in the Hebrew-language press the movement rarely refrained from airing those differences. Moreover, despite Hashomer Hatza'ir's frequent criticisms of the PLL's inaction and failures, the pamphlet endorsed it as the proper framework for the organization of Arab workers.

Jewish PLL officials also contributed to weakening the Arab revolt in Palestine by helping to develop the first links between the Zionist movement and the Druze communities in Palestine and Syria. In 1936 leaders of the largely Druze village of 'Usufiyya, on Mount Carmel, asked the Haifa Workers' Council for help in getting the British authorities to provide protection against the nationalist guerrillas who were harassing the village because of its refusal to support the revolt. These contacts, which Hushi, Agassi, and Alafiya facilitated, eventually led to meetings between leaders of the Yishuv and of the Druze community, including some of the Syrian Druze leaders in exile in Palestine and Transjordan. In October 1937 Abba Hushi and Shmu'el Alafiya, accompanied by Shaykh Hasan Abu Rukn, a Druze leader from 'Usufiyya, traveled to Lebanon and then to Jabal al-Duruz ("the Mountain of the Druze," a center of the Druze population in southern Syria) on a secret mission for the Jewish Agency. As Agassi put it in a report, their goal was to "sign an official (though for the present covert) agreement between us and the residents of the Mountain so that their leaders influence the people of the Mountain not to be dragged in by the inciters from Palestine, and so that they will serve as a source of information. In all these areas some extremely beneficial things were accomplished."[21] Some Palestinian Druze were in fact supportive of and active in the anti-Zionist movement, and Zionist leaders hoped that an agreement with Syrian Druze leaders would weaken Palestinian Druze involvement in the revolt. A month later a second mission took place, to Beirut and Damascus.

These contacts and secret missions marked the beginning of a de facto alliance between the Yishuv and significant segments of the Druze community in Palestine and beyond, who saw in this alliance a way of providing the Druze with a counterweight to the Muslim-led Arab nationalist movements in Palestine, Lebanon, and Syria. During the 1936–39 revolt good relations with these Druze enhanced the security of Jewish settlements and enterprises in the Mount Carmel area, notably Kibbutz Yagur and the Nesher cement factory and quarry, and weakened the nationalist insurrection in the countryside. They also paved the way for the neutral or pro-Zionist stance which most Palestinian Druze took during the battles of 1947–49. Like Zaslani's interest in the Kurds of Iraq in 1934, this budding relationship pointed toward what would become a central element in Zionist and then Israeli strategy: the search for non-Arab and non-Sunni Muslim communities within the region who could be brought into an alliance directed against Arab nationalism.[22]

THE ROYAL COMMISSION AND LABOR IN PALESTINE

The hearings held by the Peel Commission allowed both Jewish and Arab unionists to air their views before a wider public. Labor-Zionist leaders who testified insisted on the benefits which Jewish immigration and settlement had brought to the Arabs of Palestine, citing the higher wages which prevailed there by comparison with neighboring countries. A memorandum submitted by the Histadrut insisted that "the workers of both communities, the Jews, consciously, and the Arabs, instinctively, realised that there exists a real and organic basis for the establishment of friendly relations between them." The distinction which this passage drew between the Jewish workers' conscious understanding and the Arab workers' instinctive understanding seems to have been a way of explaining why so few Arab workers had openly articulated their recognition of a "real and organic basis" for friendship with the Jews. Be that as it may, it was, the Histadrut declared, the Jewish workers who had taken the initiative:

> . . . the Jewish workers considered it their bounden duty to raise the Arab worker from his exploited and degraded position, for which his employers, backed by the Government and the [Muslim] clergy, were responsible. They felt themselves ethically bound to assist in the abolition of conditions which led to poverty and oppression wherever they existed in the country; and also they wished to make impossible the existence in Palestine of a large group of workers whose poor conditions of living and of work constituted a permanent danger to their own standing as workers and to their standards of living.

Despite its centrality to relations between Arab and Jewish workers, the memorandum never mentioned or even alluded to the issue of Hebrew labor, though it did explicitly defend the policy of excluding Arabs from the Histadrut. It also attacked the leadership of the Arab community in Palestine, which allegedly objected "to the very attempt to raise the standard of living of the Arab labourer, and also to the possibility of an understanding between Jewish and Arab workers."

But the real culprit, the Histadrut implied, was the government of Palestine, which had blocked efforts to achieve Jewish-Arab workers' cooperation. Although this allegation seems to have annoyed Lord Peel, in his testimony Dov Hoz, speaking for the Histadrut, defended the claim. Hoz rejected any suggestion that Arab and Jewish workers might have conflicting interests; rather, he stated, "there are matters in which we do not think Arabs or the Arab unions would be interested," such as Jewish immigration and settlement as well as Jewish educational and cultural work. Commission members pressed Histadrut leaders for clear and unevasive answers about whether the organization's Hebrew labor policy did not mean the displacement of Arab workers, without much success.[23]

By contrast, when George Mansur of the AWS appeared before the Royal Commission in January 1937 to testify about the conditions and grievances of Arab workers in Palestine, he emphasized the issue of Hebrew labor, which he argued had contributed greatly to Arab unemployment.[24] However, pro-Zionists in Britain refused to take him seriously: when the Peel Commission's report was debated in Parliament in July 1937, one of the Independent Labor Party members who had failed to meet Mansur during his visit in January insisted that "Mansour [sic] represents nobody but himself." Obviously frustrated by Arab unionists' lack of success in reaching and influencing British public opinion, Mansur published a booklet in English "to give the English reader some idea of *why* Arab labour is at one with the rest of the Arab population in its opposition to Zionist immigration . . . and to call attention to the inadequacy of the Royal Commission's treatment of the relationship of Jewish and Arab labour in Palestine." Though a clearly written and well-argued piece of work, *The Arab Worker under the Palestine Mandate* did not have the impact its author hoped for. The labor-Zionist movement had close ties with the Labor Party and the support of many Labor members of Parliament, while anti-Zionist Conservatives were unlikely to have much interest in, or sympathy for, Arab workers or labor unions. To the extent that there was even a battle for left-of-center but noncommunist British public opinion, the Zionists and their sympathizers had the upper hand.

"THE TRUTH OF THE MATTER"

The general strike and the full-scale insurrection into which it developed made the Zionist movement's lack of an Arabic-language propaganda organ more glaring than ever. There had been sporadic efforts to surreptitiously buy influence with some Arab newspapers in Palestine, but neither the Histadrut nor any other Zionist institution had put out a regular Arabic-language publication since the demise of *Ittihad al-'Ummal* in 1928. Since 1935 Histadrut leaders had repeatedly declared that there should be no further delay in launching such a publication, but nothing had happened, largely because it took the Histadrut a long time to secure the funding needed to launch the project, from the Jewish Agency, wealthy donors abroad, and its own budget. In addition, MAPAI's political committee, which made all important decisions affecting the Histadrut before they were discussed and ratified by that organization's own leadership bodies, was uncertain whether there was any suitable candidate to take charge of the enterprise. Many MAPAI leaders were dubious about the whole idea: for example, both Moshe Shertok and Berl Katznelson felt that an Arabic newspaper was likely to contribute more to Jewish self-satisfaction than to enhancing Zionism's image among the Arabs. There was also continuing disagreement about the newspaper's content and sociopolitical orientation.[25]

Hashomer Hatza'ir leaders kept nagging MAPAI about the issue. "I do not know why the Histadrut cannot publish an Arabic newspaper," Ya'akov Hazan asked at a meeting of the Histadrut executive committee in the autumn of 1936. "I cannot believe that among the 10,000 members of MAPAI there aren't three editors for an Arabic newspaper." MAPAI's Eliyahu Golomb responded by admitting that the party's nominee for editor, Michael Assaf, was incapable of writing an article in Arabic; in fact, he added, "there aren't among us even ten comrades who know Arabic."[26] MAPAI's choice of Assaf as editor in fact indicates the low priority the party assigned to this project. Born in the Polish city of Lodz in 1906, Assaf immigrated to Palestine in the early 1920s and quickly won a place in the second tier of the Ahdut Ha'avoda leadership. However, he proved uninterested in, or incapable of, building a power base within the party, and by the mid-1920s he had been shunted off into cultural work, ending up as a journalist for the Histadrut's daily newspaper *Davar*, founded in 1925. Despite his limited knowledge of Arabic, by the early 1930s Assaf had acquired a reputation as MAPAI's preeminent expert on Arab affairs.[27] Unable to come up with anyone better, MAPAI's leaders appointed Assaf to edit the Histadrut's projected Arabic weekly and assigned Eliyahu Agassi, who knew Arabic well, to work with him. This left the Histadrut's Arab Department without a single full-time employee in Tel Aviv and the inexperienced (and, some suggested, not overly competent) Alafiya on his own in Haifa, but it finally got things moving on the newspaper.

The first issue of *Haqiqat al-Amr* (The truth of the matter) was published in March 1937. Though *Haqiqat al-Amr* was officially designated the organ of the PLL and usually featured a column on labor affairs, its focus was much broader, in keeping with its openly proclaimed goal of combating anti-Zionist propaganda. *Haqiqat al-Amr* carried numerous articles discussing Zionism (especially but not exclusively labor Zionism) and trying to show how the Zionist enterprise benefited rather than harmed Palestine's Arabs. The first issue began with an assertion (in a rather ornate Arabic) that would be repeated in one form or another almost weekly:

> Every discerning and unbiased person must acknowledge the Jewish people's dedication to their eternal and sole homeland whose virtues the centuries had extinguished. For the Jews have established great civilizational (*'umraniyya*) projects in Palestine which have improved the lot of the country and the situation of all its inhabitants. . . . The Jewish workers' movement organized in the Histadrut—the backbone of the Zionist movement—has been and will always be in the vanguard of those calling and pressing for the development and peace and progress of the country, for the benefit of the Jewish people and for the benefit of the Arabs who dwell in it. That is "the truth of the matter."[28]

This depiction of Palestine as the land of both "the Jewish people" and "the Arabs who dwell in it" did not constitute a break with labor-Zionist discourse as it had been articulated over the previous decade and a half, but only a shift in emphasis. MAPAI leaders continued to believe in an eternal and superior Jewish right to Palestine, as evidenced by the contrast this statement implicitly drew between "the Jewish people" whose "eternal and sole homeland" Palestine was, and "the Arabs" who happened to "dwell" in the country. Zionism's settlement and development activity in Palestine had further strengthened the Jewish claim to the land. This formulation embodied labor Zionism's conception of the Arabs of Palestine not as a distinct nationality in their own right but rather as members of a larger entity, the Arabs, some of whom happened to dwell in Palestine but who could (and perhaps should) achieve their national self-fulfillment elsewhere, since that country was destined to be the site of the realization of Jewish sovereignty.[29]

During 1936–39, the obvious strength and popularity of the Arab revolt led some MAPAI leaders to acknowledge (usually in closed party forums) that the Arabs of Palestine had comprehensible grievances, were imbued with an authentic nationalist spirit, and might even possess certain national rights in the country. In February 1937, for example, Ben-Gurion declared that "The right which the Arabs in Palestine have is one owed to the inhabitants of any country . . . because they live here, and not because they are Arabs. . . . The Arab inhabitants of Palestine should enjoy all the rights of citizens and all political rights, not only as individuals, but as a national community, just like the Jews." [30] This formulation too was tellingly vague and ambiguous: the rights of Palestine's Arab majority were still understood as not quite of the same order as the Jewish people's rights in Palestine and certainly did not include the right of self-determination, while no compromise was possible on the key question of Jewish immigration.

In any case such statements did not reflect any fundamental reevaluation of Zionism's goals; rather they manifested Ben-Gurion's pragmatism, his capacity to adapt his tactics and strategy to changing circumstances. When the Peel Commission recommended in July 1937 that Palestine be partitioned into a small Jewish state, an Arab state that would encompass Transjordan as well, and a British-ruled enclave including Jerusalem, Bethlehem, and a corridor to the sea, Ben-Gurion (together with Hayyim Weizmann, president of the Zionist Organization) were able to convince the Zionist movement to refrain from any outright rejection of the principle of partition. This was not out of concern for Arab rights but because Ben-Gurion believed that even a small Jewish state in Palestine could provide a haven for European Jews, while changing circumstances might allow its expansion in the future. In private Ben-Gurion continued to envision a Jewish state in all of Palestine and regarded the "transfer" of the Arabs living on that state's territory as both advisable and just. Weizmann too saw partition as a temporary solution, viable for a generation or so; ultimately, he believed, the Jewish state would encompass all of Palestine. [31]

It was the milder, more flexible version of labor Zionism's understanding of Arab rights in Palestine which was presented to the Arab public through the pages of *Haqiqat al-Amr*. The weekly also devoted considerable space to denouncing the Arab revolt, refuting anti-Zionist allegations in the Arab press and trying to demonstrate the strength and permanence of the Jewish presence in Palestine. Arab nationalist leaders were taken to task for allegedly exploiting Arab workers for base political ends. At the same time *Haqiqat al-Amr* provided international news, though with special emphasis on Jewish and labor topics, along with accounts of PLL and

Histadrut activities and literature in translation. The latter included stories by the Hebrew writer (and former Histadrut employee) Yehuda Burla as well as Maxim Gorky and other noted European writers. In 1940 *Haqiqat al-Amr* began providing Hebrew lessons for its readers. Its press run of 2,000 copies was almost entirely distributed free of charge through various channels, including Jewish institutions and settlements (for example, the International Union of Railway, Postal and Telegraph Workers and various kibbutzim), which passed copies on to Arabs with whom they were in touch; the mail, through which copies were sent to government schools in the hope of influencing Arab teachers and students; and the network of personal contacts Agassi and his colleagues had developed over the years.

It is difficult to determine what impact *Haqiqat al-Amr* actually exerted on its intended audience, but it is likely to have been minimal. It reached relatively few Arab readers and could not really hope to compete with the Arab press, especially during a period of popular upsurge and nationalist revolt. Though Histadrut and Zionist officials were very proud of it and touted *Haqiqat al-Amr* both in the Yishuv and abroad as proof of their commitment to Arab-Jewish understanding, most of the Arabs who came across it saw it for what it was: a Zionist propaganda organ. Almost all the Arab schoolteachers to whom it was sent by mail, and many others besides, returned it, spurning the offer of a free subscription.[32] Nonetheless, with subsidies from the Jewish Agency and other Yishuv institutions, the Histadrut continued to publish and distribute *Haqiqat al-Amr* right up to 1948 and beyond; indeed, it continued to appear until 1960, when the Histadrut finally closed it down.

THE REVOLT AND ITS SUPPRESSION

Though the Histadrut's Arabic newspaper had finally been launched, the organization's efforts to organize Arab workers languished during the years of the revolt. Agassi and his colleagues attributed the PLL's failures to both the Arab workers' backwardness and their own party's lack of interest in the project, manifested in the meager resources the Histadrut had devoted to it.[33] But other MAPAI members rejected Agassi's criticism. David Hacohen, a top manager of the Histadrut's burgeoning business empire, insisted that given the conditions prevailing in Palestine, no effort to organize Arab workers was likely to succeed. Work among Arabs should continue, of course, but without constant complaining and breast-beating by people like Agassi over the Histadrut's alleged neglect. Hacohen claimed that he had once "proved" to an Arab leader that it was in the Palestinian Arabs' own objective economic interest that only Jews be employed at Nesher, because Hebrew labor raised wage levels for Arabs as well. But economics was beside the point: it was a question of nationalism. The Arab worker "will not abandon his religious and political leaders," Hacohen insisted; "the Arab masses talk of defending the homeland," and the Histadrut must therefore be realistic about its prospects in this arena.[34]

Early in 1937 Ben-Gurion told the Histadrut council that he had been in error when, at the Ahdut Ha'avoda congress at Ein Harod thirteen years earlier, he had declared that Zionism could never reach an agreement with the effendis but only with the Arab working masses. "We must," he now declared, "find a way to the whole Arab people . . . by contact and negotiations with its representatives, whoever they may be."[35] Ben-Gurion's new line implicitly underscored the low priority which efforts to organize Arab workers enjoyed among MAPAI's leadership. It would be continued but only at a low level, and the lion's share of the Arab Department's budget would go to *Haqiqat al-Amr*, whose publication could be seen as useful for general Zionist propaganda purposes.[36]

Yet despite MAPAI's distinct lack of enthusiasm for the PLL's work, a minimal budget and the commitment and dedication of a handful of individuals kept the organization and the Arab Department going and for a time even allowed sporadic worker-oriented activity. During the year of relative quiescence between October 1936, when the general strike ended, and October 1937, when the revolt again exploded in a wave of violence that the British quickly met with heightened repression, contacts were made with porters at the Jaffa customs house. The PLL provided the porters with some money and helped them formulate and deliver their petitions to British officials. As always, organizing Arab workers had an ulterior motive: in one of his many letters to the Jewish Agency requesting financial support for the Histadrut's Arab Department, Agassi emphasized that "we see in the turn to us for help by the customs porters employed in the port of Jaffa an easy and never-to-be-repeated opportunity to undermine the position of the contractor of the customs [labor force], Salim al-Khuri, who despite all of your efforts [with the government] and all of our efforts we have never been able to compel to agree to Hebrew labor to the extent we deserve." With the PLL's support the customs porters eventually went on strike, but they were defeated and their incipient organization was destroyed.[37]

In sharp contrast to 1934–36, when the AWS and the Arab press had fought the PLL in Jaffa vigorously, the PLL's more or less overt relationship with the porters in 1938 aroused no reaction. Government censorship and preoccupation with political affairs may account for the silence of the press, but the lack of response on the part of the Arab labor movement is an indication of the virtual paralysis into which it had fallen. After Michel Mitri's assassination at the end of 1936, rival factions fought for control of the AWS, resulting in its disintegration. The small communist-led Transport Workers' Union in Jaffa also ceased to function, and even the PAWS in Haifa was largely dormant. High unemployment certainly contributed to the weakness of the labor movement, but so did repression: many of the movement's leaders and key activists were imprisoned as the British cracked down hard on all manifestations of organized activity linked with the nationalist movement. For example, Sami Taha, who a few years later would emerge as the preeminent leader of the PAWS, was held in detention without trial for six months during 1937, under the Emergency Regulations which the British promulgated to crush the revolt, for alleged possession of "an apparatus used in the construction of landmines." Francis Sayigh, a communist active in the labor movement during the 1940s, was also detained for six months during the revolt as an "active terrorist." [38] Many of the nationalist professionals and intellectuals who had links with labor unions were preoccupied with the revolt during 1936 and 1937, and after the armed struggle resumed in the fall of 1937 a large number of them were detained or forced into exile.

The Palestine Communist Party, which had hoped to build and lead the Arab labor movement, was also paralyzed and divided as a result of the revolt. Some of its Arab leaders and activists tried to take an active part in the armed struggle, but in so doing they lost their specifically communist identity without gaining any significant influence on the course, character, or leadership of the revolt. The party's support for the revolt led many of its Jewish members to quit, while most of those who remained organized themselves into a largely autonomous "Jewish section" which grew increasingly alienated from the party's predominantly Arab leadership and increasingly anxious to overcome its isolation from the Yishuv by moving toward a less unequivocally anti-Zionist stance. By the end of the revolt the PCP's Arab and Jewish components had become deeply estranged, resulting in a number of splits and ultimately (as I discuss in Chapter 7) the collapse of the PCP as a unified Arab-Jewish party.

For a brief period, then, the competition which the PLL had faced on the ground in 1935 was absent. But the PLL's limited resources, and more importantly the upsurge of the revolt in a much more violent and widespread form during 1938, made headway impossible. By the summer of 1938, rebel bands controlled much of the hill country and many towns throughout Palestine; as one British official put it, by September 1938 "the situation was such that civil administration and control of the country was, to all practical purposes, non-existent."[39] The British government, preoccupied with the Sudetenland crisis, did not feel it could heavily reinforce its garrison in Palestine as long as a European war threatened.

At Nesher, where both Jewish and Arab workers were on short hours and experienced numerous "vacations" because of the depressed economic situation, the armed groups operating in the vicinity made their presence increasingly felt. One of the members of the PLL's committee at Nesher was kidnapped and held for two weeks by guerrillas as a warning to the workers there. The tactic succeeded: the workers begged management to tell Alafiya to stop visiting the site. Workers at other sites who were suspected of collaboration with the Histadrut were also harassed and, in a few instances, killed; among them was the PLL's chief contact in the village of Wadi 'Ara, who was executed by the guerrillas as a suspected police informant.[40] During 1937 and into 1938 Arab workers would still show up at the PLL club in Haifa in the hope of finding work, but by the fall of 1938 the Histadrut Arab Department's organizing work had come to a complete halt; as Agassi put it, "in this situation of terrorist political tension, economic decline and spiritual depression, there is nothing harder than to find some possibility for activity on the part of the PLL."[41]

The agreement which the European powers reached at Munich in September 1938 allowed the British government to dispatch large numbers of troops to Palestine to crush the Arab rebellion; eventually British military forces would outnumber the rebels by a ratio of ten to one.[42] Massive repression, including collective punishment and aerial and artillery bombardment of insurgent villages, allowed the gradual restoration of British control. Dissension and division within the Palestinian Arab community also weakened the revolt. The rebel bands were rarely able to coordinate their efforts, most of the nationalist leadership was in prison or in exile after the fall of 1938, and significant segments of the population grew weary of the revolt and alienated from the rebels. Moreover, the Nashashibis and some of their allies came out openly against the revolt and with British support organized armed "Peace Bands" which attacked the rebels and the villages which supported them. As the rebels were pushed onto the defensive, internecine killings multiplied as all sides seized the opportunity to settle scores old and new. Among those assassinated was Hasan

Sidqi al-Dajani, a leader of the Nashashibi faction, who was gunned down in Ramallah in October 1938. Fakhri al-Nashashibi, who had founded the AWS in Jerusalem in 1934, would be assassinated in Baghdad in 1941.

By the spring of 1939 the revolt was dying out. Having gained the upper hand militarily, the British sponsored yet another round of Arab-Jewish negotiations. When these failed, the British government issued a new statement of policy for Palestine, the White Paper of May 1939. The White Paper met at least partially a number of long-standing Arab demands by providing for the establishment of an independent Palestinian state within ten years, restrictions on further Jewish land purchases, and a ceiling of 75,000 Jewish immigrants over the following five years, after which additional immigration would require Arab consent. With a European war in the offing, British officials hoped that the White Paper would conciliate Arab opinion and secure for Britain the support and allegiance of Arabs in Palestine and neighboring lands.

The Zionist movement charged that the White Paper was a repudiation of Britain's commitment, embodied in the Balfour Declaration of 1917 and the mandate itself, to foster the establishment of a Jewish "national home" in Palestine. Its promulgation did in fact mark the end of the alliance between Britain and the Zionist movement. That alliance had given the Zionist movement the time, protection, and support it needed to lay the demographic, economic, military, and political foundations of a strong and increasingly self-sufficient Yishuv, despite mounting and often violent (if not always very effective) resistance by Palestine's Arab majority. As a result, by 1939 the Yishuv was nearly at the point where it could stand on its own even without British support, while the Palestinian Arab nationalist movement had suffered a devastating defeat, leaving the Arab community demoralized, disorganized, and without effective leadership.

Outraged Zionist leaders initially called for resistance to, and defiance of, the policies set forth in the White Paper. But a few months after it was issued war broke out in Europe, and the Yishuv and the Zionist movement put their opposition to the White Paper on hold and allied themselves with Britain in order to fight and defeat Nazi Germany, obviously a much greater enemy of the Jewish people. The confrontation between Zionism and its erstwhile ally and protector, Britain, was thus put off until the end of the war, by which time the Zionist movement and the Yishuv would be in a stronger position not only to frustrate the policies outlined in the White Paper but to launch a successful drive for Jewish statehood in Palestine.

THE 1930S IN RETROSPECT

In the years 1932–35 the Histadrut's project of organizing Arab workers achieved some notable successes. The PLL developed organizational connections with Arab workers in several important workplaces, notably the ports of Haifa and Jaffa, and for the first time recruited significant numbers of unskilled and semiskilled wage workers, quite different from the skilled crafts workers employed in small workshops with whom the Histadrut had developed ties in the mid-1920s. But the PLL's successes were all short-lived: it proved unable to create stable unions or a cadre of Arab unionists willing to openly identify with the PLL, nor did it ever develop a sizable or stable membership base. As Histadrut officials themselves acknowledged, by 1937 it retained only a few dozen members and sympathizers in and around Haifa and had come to be seen by Arab workers as less a labor organization than an employment agency.

Although the Histadrut leadership was always rather ambivalent about this sphere of activity and never devoted great human or material resources to it, it is hard to argue that it justified even the limited investment made in it. But meager resources were not the chief cause of the PLL's failure during the 1930s, though some of its Jewish activists certainly saw it that way. What they were unable to grasp was that the reasons for this effort's failure were largely inherent in the way it was conceived, a conception rooted in labor-Zionist discourse about Arabs in general and Arab workers in particular. That discourse presumed, even insisted, that an initiative to organize Arab workers undertaken by the Histadrut, a central institution of the Zionist project in Palestine, could be perceived by Arabs as nonpolitical and unconnected with the larger issue of Zionism and its implications for Palestine's future. As we have seen, there were in fact not a few instances in which Arab workers turned to the PLL and the Histadrut, for a variety of reasons: to get help in workplace struggles, to gain access to health care and loans, to find jobs, because they believed in working-class solidarity, and so forth. But as the Palestinian Arab working class grew in size and social weight and as a stratum of better-educated and more politically sophisticated workers emerged, as Arab trade unionism developed, and as the Arab nationalist movement began to take an interest in labor issues, these kinds of links between Arab workers and the Histadrut came to seem increasingly less innocent, less unproblematic. This was especially true as the extent to which the labor-Zionist project of organizing Arab workers was bound up (if in complex ways) with the campaign to achieve Hebrew labor became not only evident but a public issue, as was certainly the case from 1934 onward, when the Arab Workers' Society in Jaffa placed it at the top of its agenda.

This kind of Arab response is not something that Histadrut officials or PLL activists anticipated or found easy to comprehend. Their lack of comprehension stemmed in part from their conception of Arab workers as a largely inert mass, a raw material available for molding by one or another outside force but generally lacking a capacity for independent thought or agency, at least beyond a certain basic level. This is borne out by the striking fact that in the great mass of material generated by the labor-Zionist movement's effort to develop some relationship with the Arab working class during the 1930s—reports on organizing activities, internal correspondence among Histadrut departments and officials, minutes of debates in party, union, and Histadrut forums, published leaflets, and so on—it is quite rare to hear an Arab voice, especially a rank and file voice or one which in some sense says no, which does not mutely go along but actively challenges the premises of this project. Thus incidents like Zaslani and Agassi's November 1934 confrontation with the Jaffa dockworkers, at which the latter pressed the Jewish unionists for clear and unevasive answers about the Histadrut's ulterior motive in helping them organize and its commitment to Hebrew labor at the port of Jaffa, have few if any antecedents in this literature.

There must in fact have been many such encounters, but they rarely surface, at least in part because there was little room for them in the conceptual framework of those who drafted the reports, sent the correspondence, and participated in the debates. Zaslani, Agassi, Hushi, and their colleagues found it hard to grasp such responses as manifestations of rational self-interest, since they (and the Zionist movement in general) tended to attribute all expressions of rejection and opposition to the nefarious manipulation of the innocent rank and file workers by self-interested outside agitators, in this case Arab unionists imbued with nationalism. This too manifested a perception of Arab workers as passive and largely incapable of self-motivated rational action, who therefore had to be acted upon, whether benignly by Zionists or malevolently by anti-Zionist Arab nationalists with selfish ulterior motives. Though labor Zionism saw itself as a movement which would give the Jewish people its own voice again, allowing them to overcome their powerlessness and take control of their destiny, it found it difficult to envision Arabs, and especially working-class Arabs, as having their own distinct voices, identities, and agency.

It is undeniably true that, at least into the 1930s, Jewish unionists in Palestine had much more experience of organizing and maintaining labor organizations than did most Arab workers, and also that the Jews were often steeped in a broad international labor movement culture which might have been useful to Arab workers. However, Jewish unionists grasped that experience and that culture through the filter of the premises and conceptions of labor Zionism. As a consequence the meaning of the labor organizing which the Histadrut undertook among Arab workers in the 1930s could ultimately not be separated from the larger issue of Zionist aims in Palestine and Zionism's conflict with Palestinian Arab nationalism. The Histadrut's efforts therefore increasingly engendered, and were increasingly frustrated by, opposition and counterorganizing by Arab unionists who, much like the labor Zionists, saw their national and labor commitments as complementary.

As we have seen, through the 1930s the Histadrut's activity (or inactivity) in this sphere was sharply criticized by other left-Zionist forces, especially Hashomer Hatza'ir. Yet it is highly unlikely that that movement's conceptions of joint organization and Arab-Jewish working-class solidarity would have proven any more successful than MAPAI's, for they were rooted in premises which were probably even less realistic. Nor was Hashomer Hatza'ir really any better than MAPAI at translating its rhetoric of Arab-Jewish friendship and solidarity into practice, even in its own kibbutzim. Moshe Shamir, the noted Israeli novelist who began as a partisan of Hashomer Hatza'ir but after 1967 gravitated toward the right end of the Israeli political spectrum, went to school in the 1930s at Kibbutz Mishmar Ha'emek, one of the movement's kibbutzim in the Jezreel Valley. In his book *Hayyai 'im Yishma'el* (My life with Ishmael) Shamir addressed this gap between rhetoric and reality.

> . . . in the [kibbutz] dining room the [Hashomer Hatza'ir] leaders spoke of "brotherhood among peoples." None of them knew a word of Arabic, they never spoke [with Arabs] as a man speaks with his friends. They had no friends among the villages in the area, they never once paid even a simple visit to their neighbors in the nearby villages. In the [kibbutz's] excellent modern school—for a long time perhaps the most advanced educational institution in the country—Arabic was not taught. . . . So we just simply lived with our nice theories to one side and the bitter reality to the other, and we saved ourselves any unpleasantness and the burden of thinking simply by never trying to look at the theories and reality side by side, for a first, elementary, basic examination of the extent to which they coincided or differed. . . . We organized ourselves behind the fence, we prepared to defend ourselves, we spoke of "brotherhood among peoples" and we never in fact fulfilled a single serious obligation of [the principle of] brotherhood among peoples.[43]

This is no doubt a harsh judgment, but it contains a large measure of truth. In fact, one might go even further and suggest that for Hashomer Hatza'ir, and for labor Zionism in general, achievement of their goals in fact required a substantial gap between ideology and reality, between principled commitments and clear recognition of the implications of one's actions, between subjective intentions and objective consequences. Such gaps are probably characteristic of all political and social movements, but in this particular time and place they were perhaps especially wide, and they ultimately frustrated labor Zionism's project of developing relations with Arab workers, at least as that project was conceived and implemented during the 1930s.

As I noted in Chapter 4 with reference to the railway workers, the Arab revolt of 1936–39 led to increased residential and social as well as workplace segregation, as Jews moved out of predominantly Arab neighborhoods and into safer Jewish neighborhoods. Arabs and Jews also became less likely to frequent the same public spaces, whether for business, shopping, or recreation, and the fears and hatreds evoked on both sides by acts of terrorist violence targeting civilians were not easily erased. At the same time, the revolt, and its political, social, and economic consequences, left the Arab national movement in Palestine severely weakened while setting the Yishuv more firmly than ever before on the road to statehood. Yet as the following chapters will show, developments during the war and the immediate postwar period unleashed significant new forces and generated important new dynamics that affected many spheres of life in Palestine. These forces and dynamics would create new arenas and forms of interaction between Arab and Jewish workers and labor movements, shaping not only the relationships among them but also the ways in which those relationships were conceived.

7 Workers, Labor Movements, and the Left during the Second World War

The promulgation of the White Paper of May 1939, the end of the Arab revolt a few months later, and then the outbreak of the Second World War in September 1939 set the stage for the beginning of a new period in the history of mandatory Palestine. The hothouse atmosphere engendered by the war brought about rapid social, economic, and political changes, profoundly affecting the scope and character of interaction among Arab and Jewish workers. Though the overt political struggle over Palestine's fate was largely in abeyance while the war lasted, developments during the war years had an important, perhaps even decisive, impact on the final phase of that struggle which began when the war came to an end.

THE WAR YEARS: ECONOMIC AND POLITICAL CHANGE

The war affected Palestine's economy in important ways. In its first months, the closing of the Mediterranean shipping lanes badly hurt the country's export-oriented citrus industry. The civilian construction industry, a very important sector of the Yishuv's economy in particular, also suffered, both because Jewish immigration fell off and because the imported materials on which the industry was heavily dependent were less available, and most of what did reach Palestine was diverted for military use. Unemployment remained relatively high among both Arabs and Jews through 1940. As the war went on, however, the decline in imports of foreign-made finished goods created new opportunities for local manufacturers. More importantly, Palestine became a major base and staging ground for British and other Allied military forces, which enormously stimulated demand for manufactured goods as well as agricultural produce. To help meet this demand, the British authorities took steps to encourage local industry in Palestine and surrounding countries, coordinated after April 1941 by the Cairo-based Middle East Supply Center. The construction sector also began to flourish as the War Office and the government put out numerous contracts for military-related projects.

A few figures will suffice to illustrate the scale of the war-induced economic boom. Between 1940 and 1946, some £P12 million were invested in Jewish-owned industrial enterprises in Palestine, almost double the total for the entire 1930s. British and Allied military expenditures in Palestine for goods ranging from clothing to processed food products to ammunition, for construction and for maintenance and repair services amounted to about £P1 million in 1940; they quadrupled the following year, more than doubled again the following year, and reached some £P12 million in 1943. Military orders in 1942 equaled Palestine's entire industrial output in 1939. During the war Palestine came to export significant quantities of various manufactured goods, mainly to Allied forces and neighboring countries: industrial exports rose from £P470,000 in 1940 to £P11 million in 1945.

As a result tens of thousands of Arabs and Jews found employment in new and newly expanded factories and workshops, and in the scores of British and Allied military bases, repair, maintenance, and storage facilities, and other installations which sprouted the length and breadth of the country. The war also led to the creation of many new jobs in construction, ground transport, the ports, and shipping, to serve both military and civilian needs. The widespread unemployment and underemployment that had afflicted the Arab sector of the Palestinian economy for much of the second half of the 1930s were replaced by labor shortages, despite government efforts to expand and channel the country's labor force and regulations which prohibited workers in essential industries (including the railways) from leaving their jobs. Employment in both Arab and Jewish agriculture declined during the war years as many people sought better-paying and less onerous work in industry and services.

The extent and speed of war-induced proletarianization within the Arab community was particularly striking. By 1944, Palestine's wage labor force is estimated to have encompassed some 100,000 Arab wage workers employed full-time outside agriculture—approximately one-third of the entire Arab male population of working age.[1] More than a third of these were employed at British army camps and installations, alongside some 15,000 Jewish workers, while thousands of others were employed by contractors working on military-related projects. The camps thus constituted a new and important social space which came into existence very quickly and in which unprecedentedly large numbers of Arabs and Jews worked side by side, producing new forms and dynamics of interaction.

Wartime economic expansion was accompanied by a surge of inflation, after a long period of price stability. By one calculation, the cost of living index rose only from 100 in 1936 to 103 in 1939, but then surged to 153 in 1941 and to 222 in 1942. By 1943 the index had reached 269, rising to 274 the following year, and to 295 in 1945. As a result real wages declined sharply in the first part of the war. To this both Arab and Jewish workers responded with widespread activism and organization. Many of their struggles were successful, and by war's end real wages in Palestine had risen considerably. This was true not only in industry, construction, and services but also in agriculture: the war brought considerable prosperity to the Arab rural economy as wage rates for agricultural labor rose, the government paid high prices for produce, and rural indebtedness declined somewhat.[2]

The war years also witnessed important changes in the political arena, creating space for the emergence of new political forces among both Arabs and Jews. The defeat of the Arab revolt had left the Palestinian Arab nationalist movement much weakened and in disarray. Its top leaders were in exile, as were many key activists who were not dead or in prison. It was clear that the end of the war would bring a renewal of the struggle over Palestine's fate, but in the interim the old guard nationalist politicians still in Palestine were largely quiescent. The weakening of the control which the powerful elite factions had exercised over the Arab community, together with growing social differentiation in urban and rural communities, widespread proletarianization, and the hothouse political climate of the war years made possible the emergence of a new Arab left, embodied in the National Liberation League (NLL), which developed out of the disintegration of the Palestine Communist Party in 1943. This organization, which included veteran Arab communists but also members of a new generation of progressive intellectuals and many working-class activists, developed a strong base in the rapidly expanding and unprecedentedly active Arab trade union movement. As we will see, the NLL advocated Arab-Jewish working-class solidarity, for its own sake but also as a way of achieving what it regarded as a "democratic" solution to the Palestine problem.

The war years brought significant shifts in the politics of the Zionist movement and the Yishuv as well. The Zionist movement's struggle against the 1939 White Paper was largely put on hold as the Yishuv mobilized in support of the Allied war effort, though efforts to get Jewish immigrants—refugees from persecution, and then from extermination, in Nazi-controlled Europe—into Palestine despite British restrictions continued, as did Jewish land acquisition and settlement. The war years witnessed the consolidation of the gains that the Yishuv had made during the 1930s, when it first approached the demographic weight, military capacity, social development, economic base, and political unity necessary to launch a viable bid for statehood. This emerging reality in Palestine itself, along with growing awareness of the unprecedented persecution to which the Jews of Europe were being subjected, prompted a Zionist conference held in New York City in 1942 (known as the "Biltmore conference" after the hotel at which it convened) to openly declare, for the first time, that Zionism's goal was the establishment of a Jewish "commonwealth" in all of Palestine.

Though the demand for statehood enjoyed majority support within the Zionist movement and the Yishuv, it was not unopposed. In 1939 a group of liberal professionals and intellectuals, together with several Poʻalei Tziyon Smol leaders, had formed the League for Jewish-Arab Rapprochement and Cooperation to promote mutual understanding and political compromise. In 1942 Hashomer Hatzaʻir formally joined the League, adding the weight of its Hakibbutz Haʼartzi federation (which now encompassed over forty kibbutzim in various stages of settlement with more than 7,500 members) and of its urban sister party, the Socialist League. Hashomer Hatzaʻir had developed into an increasingly significant force in the Yishuv: in the elections to the Histadrut's fifth congress, held in April 1942, Hashomer Hatzaʻir and the Socialist League together garnered 19 percent of the vote (mostly from cities and moshavot) on a platform advocating worker militancy, nonviolent mass opposition to the 1939 White Paper, and Arab-Jewish compromise. During the war years and until the end of 1947, Hashomer Hatzaʻir vigorously opposed both the Zionist leadership's demand for Jewish statehood in all of Palestine and any form of partition, advocating instead the establishment in an undivided Palestine of a binational state in which Arabs and Jews would have political parity regardless of their relative numbers. This was very much a minority position within the Yishuv, but as Joel Beinin has pointed out, binationalism was at the time still within the bounds of legitimate political discourse in the Yishuv.[3]

Political change in the Yishuv was facilitated by factional infighting within MAPAI, culminating in a bitter split in 1944 and the secession of its left wing, which established itself as a new party under the name of

Ahdut Ha'avoda. In so doing it claimed the mantle of the old Ahdut Ha'avoda, which had been the larger and more explicitly socialist of the two parties that had merged to form MAPAI fourteen years earlier. Though MAPAI remained the single largest party in the Histadrut, the Yishuv, and the Zionist movement, the split weakened MAPAI's hegemonic grip and opened up new political space within which other forces could expand and demand a share in decision making. The changing wartime political climate benefited even the Jewish communists. The Jewish communist organizations that emerged from the breakup of the Palestine Communist Party in 1943 remained small and weak, but their efforts to seek common ground with Zionism won them greater legitimacy in the Yishuv, as did the reflected glory of the Soviet Union, which enjoyed great prestige and popularity among Jews in wartime Palestine as the Red Army blocked the Nazi onslaught and then began to destroy the German war machine as it fought its way toward Berlin.

THE RAILWAY WORKERS: FROM ESTRANGEMENT TO JOINT STRUGGLE

It was within this rapidly changing economic, social, and political context that interactions between Arab and Jewish workers unfolded during the war years. The new atmosphere, already palpable from the beginning of 1940, was manifested in the restoration of Arab-Jewish links that had been severed, or at least dormant, during the Arab revolt. In January 1940, for example, Arab and Jewish citrus grove owners in the Petah Tikva area met to choose a joint delegation to present their demands for relief to the government. Later that year Jewish and Arab building owners, merchants, and other propertied groups also began to work together to further their common economic interests, in a manner that would not have been possible a year earlier.[4] Not surprisingly, the Arab and Jewish railway workers were also among the first groups to resume contact after the end of the revolt, as the restoration of tranquillity and the sharp decline in real wages caused by wartime inflation facilitated the resumption of organizing activities on both sides and renewed interaction between them. The war and immediate postwar years would witness not only an unprecedented degree of cooperation between the Arab and Jewish railway unions but also unprecedented militancy, highlighting trends manifested by other segments of the Arab and Jewish working classes in Palestine as well.

In addition to higher wages, the railwaymen wanted an end to the short hours in effect during most of the revolt years as well as implementation of all the promises made by management and the government in 1935 but never fulfilled. By the beginning of 1940 the International Union of Railway, Postal and Telegraph Workers, now exclusively Jewish in membership, had renewed contacts with some of the veteran leaders of the Arab railwaymen, especially in Haifa. Progress was slow, however, because the Arab unionists were still reluctant to be publicly associated with Jews. Nonetheless, Arabs and Jews at the Haifa workshops were able to formulate a joint memorandum setting forth their demands. When in March 1940 management rejected these demands, interest in renewed activism and cooperation spread from Haifa to other parts of Palestine. As the Arab Union of Railway Workers, which had virtually ceased to function during the revolt, resumed activity and began recruiting new members, talks involving activists from both unions as well as unaffiliated Arab workers got under way in Haifa, Lydda, and elsewhere. As in previous years, the AURW demanded that any joint delegation to management be constituted not on the basis of parity—as the IU insisted—but in accordance with the relative proportions of Arabs and Jews among the railwaymen. Under pressure from the rank and file to find some way to cooperate with the IU, the AURW ultimately conceded on this issue, and in August a joint delegation met with the General Manager of the Palestine Railways for the first time in more than four years.[5]

The new opportunities for mobilizing workers which the war opened up once again compelled the two unions to grapple with the question of their mutual relations. The IU leadership understood that the situation of the Jewish railwaymen could be improved only through cooperation with the Arabs and the encouragement of worker activism. But they also understood that the renewal of activism would stimulate many of the Arab workers to seek trade union organization, an impulse which would primarily benefit the AURW. They had not entirely given up the hope that the IU might be able to recruit Arab workers, but under the circumstances this seemed an unrealistic prospect. In practice, therefore, the IU generally accepted that it had to cooperate with the AURW as representative of the Arab workers. For its part, the AURW had abandoned the idea of uniting all the railway workers into one organization, although it had made such proposals up to the very eve of the revolt. Still fragile and cautious, and anxious to avoid any action which might subject it to criticism on nationalist grounds, the AURW was ready to cooperate with the IU in drawing up memoranda and forming delegations but still refused to forge any public or formal links with the Jewish union. So while its leaders did in fact work with the IU, they did not do so as official representatives of their organization but as individual activists.[6]

The two unions continued to work together on this informal basis through 1940 and 1941, jointly pressing their common demands in meetings with management officials. In this period the Palestine Railways expanded rapidly to serve the British and Allied military forces stationed in and passing through the country. Total tonnage carried rose from 858,995 in 1940–41 to 2,194,848 in 1943–44, the chronic deficits of previous years were replaced by budget surpluses, and the railway workforce rose to an all-time high of 7,778 in 1943.[7] As a result short hours were abolished and the workers no longer faced any threat of layoffs. Indeed, skilled labor was in short supply, leading to a great deal of overtime (but also to speed-ups), and thousands of Arab peasants acquired their first experience of wage labor as unskilled railway workers. The key issue confronting the railwaymen (and most other workers as well) was now higher wages, since the cost of living allowance (COLA) granted by the government as a supplement to their basic wage late in 1941 had failed to offset steadily rising prices. The wage gap between the railway workers and private-sector workers rose to 50 percent or more, a differential which was made even more burdensome by the promulgation of military regulations which prohibited railway workers from leaving their poorly paid jobs because they were deemed essential to the war effort and labor was in short supply.

Under pressure from the rank and file, AURW leaders finally agreed in January 1942 to make their links with the IU public and official and participate in a joint campaign to win the railway workers' demands. A countrywide petition drive was launched, and early in February 1942 the two unions convened a meeting of representatives of the railway workers at the PAWS union hall in Haifa. This well-attended and highly spirited event reminded observers of the heyday of solidarity among the railwaymen in 1935.[8] Over the months that followed worker discontent was further exacerbated by shortages of basic commodities: by August 1942 flour was altogether unavailable in some urban areas and bread could be found only with difficulty, and then at such a high price that it accounted for nearly half of a railway worker's wages. In meetings with management and Labor Department officials, railway workers' representatives demanded that the workers be provided with regular rations of flour, rice, sugar, clarified butter, and other basic commodities, and also that the government establish a consumer cooperative for them to reduce prices. The Palestine Railways, apprehensive about growing unrest and anxious to prevent a decline in the efficiency of its workforce due to inadequate nutrition, did in fact arrange for the sale of essential foodstuffs to railway personnel at controlled prices.[9] But negotiations over higher wages and the COLA dragged on without result, until workers' frustrations finally erupted in the form of a three-day strike of all the Haifa workshops workers in December 1942, in defiance of an official prohibition of strikes in essential industries.

Palestine Railways management at first refused to respond to the workers' wage demands, insisting that it could not act until a government committee on wages had made its decisions. But a few days later General Manager A. H. Kirby, fearful of further disruptions and more sympathetic to the workers' demands than his predecessors, made a number of important concessions, including the institution of annual wage increases for all workers, a wage scale based on seniority, and the introduction of regular overtime pay. Kirby was himself a veteran railwayman and former union member (in Britain) who had worked his way up through the ranks. The Jews with whom he dealt also regarded him as quite sympathetic to Zionism, unlike many other British officials in Palestine. Kirby was aware of changing official attitudes toward unions and had come to feel that the high-handed and repressive methods which had previously characterized management's dealings with the railway workforce were outdated. He therefore sought to institutionalize management's hitherto rather sporadic and informal contacts with the workers through the establishment of a "standing staff committee" consisting of representatives of management, labor, and the government's Labor Department. The establishment of this committee amounted to unofficial recognition of the workers' trade unions, since the General Manager agreed to allow the two unions to nominate the workers' representatives to it.[10]

Some months passed before the IU and AURW were able to reach agreement over who would represent the railway workers on the committee. Once again, a key sticking point seems to have been the question of parity: the AURW demanded at least a symbolic majority on the joint committee which would choose the workers' representatives on the staff committee. At the same time, the IU leadership seems to have hoped that it could take advantage of the AURW's weakness outside Haifa by organizing Arab railway workers under its own auspices. In Lydda, for example, the IU branch developed ties with a substantial number of Arab workers early in 1943. But lack of organizational resources, especially someone who knew Arabic and could work with this group on an ongoing basis, prevented the IU from consolidating its links with these workers.

As 1943 wore on the AURW established an increasingly effective presence outside Haifa, rendering the IU's hopes unrealistic, though a few Arab workers retained ties with the IU even in Haifa. In the end each union appointed one member to the staff committee, though a proposed joint committee representing all the railway workers never came into being. As we will see later in this chapter, as well as in Chapter 8, the railway workers' discontent and their readiness for action would assume even more dramatic forms in the months and years ahead.[11]

THE HISTADRUT, HASHOMER HATZAʿIR, AND "ARAB WORK"

During the first year of the war Histadrut officials gradually became aware that the hostility and tensions unleashed by the revolt had diminished greatly and that new opportunities for developing relations with Arab workers had opened up. In July 1940, for example, Eliyahu Agassi visited the town of Safad, in the Galilee, where a group of some fifty Arab workers had contacted the local Workers' Council and asked its help in organizing themselves. Agassi was struck by the changed atmosphere, less than a year after the end of the revolt: though the Arabs of Safad were, he reported, known to be no less "fanatical" than the residents of Nablus—by reputation one of the most strongly nationalist towns in the country—he found Arabs and Jews again mixing in the streets and cafés.

However, it soon became clear to Agassi and his colleagues that in one crucial respect little had changed: as had been the case before and during the revolt, Arab workers approached the Histadrut and took an interest in the PLL largely in the hope of finding jobs. In this instance, Solel Boneh, the Histadrut's construction and road-building company, had won a tender to build a new police station near Safad, on condition that it employ some Arab workers from the vicinity. This police station was one of many fortlike structures which the government had built to garrison and control the countryside of Palestine during and after the revolt; they were nicknamed "Tegarts," after Sir Charles Tegart, one of the government's chief counterinsurgency experts and the man who had recommended their construction. The Arab workers who had approached the Histadrut wanted Solel Boneh to hire them in place of the workers already employed through the local Arab subcontractors to whom Solel Boneh had given some of the work. Cautious as always, Agassi was hesitant about the PLL taking on the role of a labor contractor for Histadrut enterprises, mainly because organizing these Arab workers might interfere with the employment of as many Jewish workers as possible on the project. Agassi also feared that any Arab union he helped organize might later get out of control and start demanding not only more jobs but also the same wages and hours as the Jewish workers. Nonetheless, he concluded, it was important for political reasons to organize them and place them in jobs with Solel Boneh: demonstrating the benefits that good relations with the Jews could yield might shake things up a bit in Safad.[12]

However, the Histadrut's Arab Department was hardly prepared to take advantage of the new circumstances. Its funds were depleted, the PLL did not exist outside Haifa, and even its branch there was barely functioning. After three years of publication *Haqiqat al-Amr* remained a hand-to-mouth operation, kept going by a subsidy from the Jewish Agency and by such meager supplemental funding as Agassi, Michael Assaf, and their colleagues could induce Histadrut officials to allocate. The Histadrut committee charged with overseeing Arab work rarely met and its decisions were never implemented.[13] Perhaps most importantly, despite a sense that new opportunities had arisen, Histadrut officials remained wary. "We must do our work with caution," Dov Hoz told his colleagues early in 1940. "We must not be swept away by the enthusiasm for linking up with us which the Arabs are displaying in the present conjuncture, because it may cause us and them many disappointments and failures. We must try to form among the Arab workers a stable nucleus which will benefit both them and us."[14] The death of Dov Hoz in an automobile accident a few months later removed from the scene one of the few top-ranking Histadrut leaders who had taken a serious interest in Arab work.

As I discussed in Chapters 5 and 6, Hashomer Hatza'ir had been criticizing the Histadrut's cautious, reluctant, and pessimistic approach toward organizing Arab workers for many years. Yet despite its denunciations of MAPAI, numerous internal discussions of the issue, and repeated resolutions on the need for Arab-Jewish working-class solidarity, through the 1930s Hashomer Hatza'ir had done very little in this sphere. Movement members working in the cities and moshavot had in certain instances pressed for vigorous support for strikes by Arab coworkers; among the railway workers Hashomer Hatza'ir members and sympathizers strongly advocated cooperation and even unity with the Arab railway workers; and on some Hakibbutz Ha'artzi–affiliated kibbutzim there were individuals or small groups who tried to foster friendly relations with neighboring Arab villages. But Hashomer Hatza'ir had been largely preoccupied with immigration, the establishment and consolidation of its kibbutzim, and its crystallization as a unified and stable movement with a coherent and distinctive ideology, and so its ringing resolutions on relations with Palestine's Arab majority remained without practical effect. Once a year, as May Day approached, the secretary of Hashomer Hatza'ir's political committee would draw up a leaflet exhorting Arab workers to solidarity with their Jewish comrades, have it translated into Arabic, and send it off to the kibbutzim, which were supposed to distribute it to neighboring Arab villages. Thus for all its criticisms of MAPAI's and the PLL's shortcomings and failures, in practice Hashomer Hatza'ir left concrete organizing work to the Histadrut, which it continued to see as bearing primary responsibility for dealing with Arab affairs.

By the end of the 1930s, however, there was growing agreement within the movement about the need to act independently in this arena. The revolt had not only made the depth of Arab opposition to Zionism unmistakably clear but had also raised the specter of partition, to which Hashomer Hatza'ir was strongly opposed. Yet in order to be able to "sell" its binationalist alternative to the Jewish labor movement, the Yishuv, and the Zionist movement as a whole, Hashomer Hatza'ir needed to show that it had actual or potential allies within the Arab community who might be amenable to such a solution. Moreover, the Histadrut's hesitant and small-scale efforts to organize Arab workers seemed unlikely ever to yield significant results, despite the new opportunities which the changed political and economic climate in the country seemed to offer. It therefore seemed increasingly clear that Hashomer Hatza'ir would have to act on its own.

By 1940 this realization had culminated in an explicit decision that Arab activism (pe'ilut 'aravit), as Hashomer Hatza'ir generally called it, was too important to be left to the Histadrut's lackadaisical Arab Department, the inactive PLL, and a Histadrut largely uninterested in (if not disdainful of) the whole enterprise. The leadership of Hashomer Hatza'ir, by now a well-established, self-confident, and highly disciplined movement, in fact the second-strongest force within the labor-Zionist movement in Palestine, decided to form a trained cadre of activists drawn from within the movement which would formulate and implement a systematic program of Arab work. Primary responsibility for this initiative was entrusted to Aharon Cohen, who would play a central role in Hashomer Hatza'ir's efforts in this field through the 1940s.

Cohen was born in Bessarabia (then within the Tsarist empire but later part of Romania) in 1910; he had come to Palestine in 1929 already a dedicated member of Hashomer Hatza'ir and joined Kibbutz Sha'ar Ha'amakim, not far from Haifa. Four years after his arrival in Palestine, his movement sent him back to Romania as a youth movement organizer and

Zionist emissary. After his return in 1936 Cohen rose quickly within the ranks of his movement: he was elected to the executive committee of Hakibbutz Ha'artzi the following year and would remain a member of that body until 1954. In 1937–38 he coordinated Hashomer Hatza'ir's political work in Haifa, while continuing to undertake missions abroad for his movement and helping organize illegal Jewish immigration into Palestine. A talented and highly efficient organizer—it was said that he kept a record of every work-related conversation he ever had—he was a logical choice when the movement leadership looked around for an energetic and proven activist who could launch Hashomer Hatza'ir's program of Arab activism.[15]

With characteristic energy, Cohen laid the foundations of the Hashomer Hatza'ir–Hakibbutz Ha'artzi Arab Department, which he would head for the next decade. While recognizing the growing importance of the urban intelligentsia and working class, Cohen initially proposed a strategic focus on the countryside. This approach was in keeping with both Hashomer Hatza'ir's character and self-image as a kibbutz movement and the fact that many of its kibbutzim interacted with neighboring Arab villages and their residents on a daily basis. Such an approach would also clash less directly with the Histadrut, since that organization's Arab Department had a predominantly urban focus, except for efforts to develop ties with specific villages for security reasons—as with the Druze in 'Usufiyya on Mount Carmel, or with Wadi 'Ara and neighboring villages during the revolt.

Cohen's conception of how to go about developing relations with Arabs was, at least on paper, much more systematic and proactive than the rather haphazard and reactive style which characterized MAPAI's work in this field. Cohen also went well beyond his MAPAI counterparts by proposing not only new organizational initiatives but also the production of a new and comprehensive kind of knowledge about the Arabs of Palestine. Cohen insisted that to successfully develop ties with the Arabs, with whom he believed the Jews would one day share an undivided and socialist Palestine as equals, one had first to understand them thoroughly. He therefore envisioned the establishment of a centralized set of files packed with data on Arab villages and the state of the Arab community, to be achieved through systematic information gathering. While Abba Hushi, Agassi, and their MAPAI colleagues had certainly developed a wide network of contacts and informants in Arab towns and villages, the idea of setting up what today we might call a comprehensive database never seems to have occurred to them. The research which Cohen and his Hashomer Hatzaʿir colleagues carried out during and after the war years, and the relationships they developed, resulted in the publication of some of the most substantial and relatively objective studies on the Arabs of Palestine produced by avowed Zionists up to that time.[16] As Aharon Cohen probably knew, the Hagana's intelligence service was engaged in a database project of its own: looking ahead to future battles, it was systematically gathering and cross-indexing information on every Arab town and village in Palestine. Cohen's conception of the relationship between knowledge about Arabs and Zionism's power relations with them was certainly much more benign than that of the mainstream Zionists, for he saw that knowledge as a way of building bridges of friendship with the Arab community. But of course the knowledge he and his colleagues produced could be, and in the event would be, put to use in ways they might not have intended or approved of.

Cohen began by trying to educate his own movement's members about the importance of good relations with Arabs. In numerous lectures to kibbutz members he exhorted them to build bridges with their own Arab neighbors, for example by establishing clinics and sports clubs which would serve nearby villages. He also sought to identify individuals in kibbutzim and in the towns and cities who were interested in this sphere of activity and could form local cells of activists linked into an ever growing network guided by the movement's Arab Department. To build that network, Cohen began publishing an information bulletin which covered the doings of activists in various kibbutzim, publicized the work of the Arab Department, and discussed Hashomer Hatzaʿir's programs and policies in this arena. He also sought, with some success, to have the movement's various periodicals devote greater attention to Arab affairs, both to raise members' consciousness about the issue and to propagandize the movement's line in the wider Yishuv. At the same time he built up his department by recruiting additional staff members, all of whom learned Arabic thoroughly.[17]

Cohen pressed his movement's leadership to have Hashomer Hatzaʿir formally join the League for Jewish-Arab Rapprochement and Cooperation, which he saw as the vehicle through which those forces within the Yishuv which opposed MAPAI's demand for Jewish statehood could coalesce into an effective counterweight and develop alliances with like-minded elements within the Arab community. When Hashomer Hatzaʿir finally did join the League in June 1942, Cohen became its most vigorous and outspoken activist. At the same time, he and his colleagues continued to urge the Histadrut to activate the PLL, and more generally to take advantage of what they saw as the great new opportunities which now existed for furthering Arab-Jewish cooperation. In this respect Cohen was carrying on the long tradition of the left wing of labor Zionism, which had always insisted that Arab-Jewish understanding, and ultimately cooperation and compromise, was essential to the realization of Zionism.[18]

Hashomer Hatza'ir's independent initiatives were accompanied by stronger criticism of MAPAI's (and therefore the Histadrut's) inactivity with regard to organizing Arab workers. However, MAPAI leaders, more focused than ever before on the goal of Jewish statehood and skeptical about the possibility of compromise with the Arabs, resisted demands that the Histadrut revive the PLL and take the offensive. In a letter to the League for Jewish-Arab Rapprochement and Cooperation Moshe Shertok, director of the Jewish Agency's Political Department, declared:

> The most crucial time for Zionism is the period of transition from a Jewish minority to a majority. In this period not the Arabs but the British and the Americans will be the decisive factors. It is not the Arabs who will have the final word, neither in the world nor here; let us not adopt the view that one has to go to the Arabs and agree with them.[19]

Eliyahu Sasson, head of the Political Department's Arab Bureau, expressed the leadership's attitude clearly in an April 1941 letter to Aharon Cohen, responding sarcastically to a recent article in which Cohen had argued that new opportunities for political compromise had arisen which should not be neglected as they had been in the past.

> I would be very grateful if you would be good enough to explain to me, in a personal letter and not in the pages of the newspapers, what are the newly-opened possibilities for political negotiations and who are the "certain circles" [among the Arabs] who are ready at this time to discuss a Jewish-Arab political agreement which will permit the realization of Zionism.

As in the past, MAPAI loyalists blamed the PLL's failures on Arab workers' lack of discipline and their reluctance or inability to organize themselves properly.[20]

Despite profound disinterest at the top, the handful of Histadrut officials still committed to the project of organizing Arab workers desperately sought some way of reviving the PLL. One option, which had already been considered in years past, was to focus on the PLL's function as a supplier of reliable Arab labor to Jewish contractors. After all, it was not the PLL's trade union activity (minimal in any case) but its ability to place members in jobs at Jewish enterprises that gave those workers some incentive to remain loyal. Eliyahu Agassi and his colleagues naturally looked to the Histadrut's own contracting company, Solel Boneh, as a potential source of jobs for PLL members, especially as that company's contracts with the government and the military generally stipulated that it employ at least some Arab labor. However, Solel Boneh was completely uninterested in turning to the PLL for the Arab workers it needed, to the extent that Agassi accused it of deliberately boycotting PLL members. At the same time, the very fact that Solel Boneh employed Arab workers at construction projects and elsewhere, in apparent violation of the principle of Hebrew labor, was a source of distress to the Histadrut leadership and the subject of repeated discussions.[21]

At the end of 1941, after many months of drift, Abba Hushi, the powerful secretary of the Haifa Workers' Council, intervened to get the Histadrut's program of Arab work back on track and moving forward. In 1932, when the Histadrut's effort to organize Arab workers had foundered, it was Hushi who had breathed new life into the Arab Department and launched the PLL, with the help of Agassi and a handful of others. Now, a decade later, after having devoted only sporadic attention to the question during the intervening years, Hushi stepped in once again and, with the blessing of the Histadrut's top leadership, took charge. As the Jewish labor boss of Haifa, Hushi was well positioned to see what was going on: a rapid expansion of the Arab working class in and around Haifa as elsewhere, and especially the burgeoning of British military bases and facilities in which unprecedented numbers of Jews and Arabs were employed side by side. Hushi was anxious to take advantage of the new situation by launching a renewed effort to organize Arab workers (including camp workers) into the PLL through workplace-oriented trade union activism, and he asked the Histadrut for an increased budget and the appointment of additional personnel.[22]

Some Histadrut executive committee members were dubious: one of them told Hushi that in the past "the question was not about an unwillingness to give money, it was the recognition that [Arab activism] was a waste. . . . For me the essence of the PLL was first of all something for tourists." Hushi nonetheless went ahead and prepared a plan of action which provided for the hiring of several new organizers and staff members, to be funded jointly by the Histadrut and the Jewish Agency. Much of 1942 went by, however, before Hushi obtained the commitment of resources he wanted. In the interim the PLL signed up Arab workers at several army bases but then failed to follow up because the Histadrut still refused to commit to any serious initiative.[23]

THE REVIVAL OF THE ARAB LABOR MOVEMENT

Two factors finally induced the Histadrut leadership to address seriously the question of organizing Arab workers at the end of 1942 and to launch a major new initiative during 1943. On the one hand, after many months of prodding by Abba Hushi and others, MAPAI officials became seriously concerned that Hashomer Hatza'ir, now their party's major ideological and political rival within the labor-Zionist movement in Palestine, had initiated its own organizing effort in this politically and economically sensitive sphere.[24] But of even greater concern to the Histadrut leadership, and much more important in stimulating it to take action, was the reemergence and rapid expansion, after years of dormancy, of the Arab trade union movement in Palestine, along with the fact that much of that movement was now led by leftists.

As I discussed in Chapter 6, after an upsurge in 1934–36 the Arab trade union movement became all but paralyzed during the revolt years. Widespread unemployment undermined organization, energies were diverted to the struggle against British rule and Zionism, and massive repression, including the detention of many unionists, made overt activity all but impossible. During the first year of the war high unemployment and the aftereffects of the revolt's defeat hindered the resumption of trade union activity. But as we have seen, the AURW had gradually resumed activity during 1940 and 1941, and by the end of 1941 the PAWS with which it was affiliated was also beginning to expand its membership base and influence. The PAWS' core still consisted largely of Arab railway workers in Haifa, and several of the railway workers who had founded it in 1925 still played key leadership roles, among them 'Abd al-Hamid Haymur, his brother 'Id Salim Haymur, and Sa'id Qawwas. However, these veterans, men of working-class origin who had little formal education, preferred to remain in the background. As a result, from this time onward the organization's best-known public figure was Sami Taha. Born in 1915 in the village of 'Arraba, Taha had begun his career in labor in the early 1930s as a young clerk at the PAWS headquarters. As I noted in Chapter 6, he was detained without trial for six months during the revolt. Though still only in his late twenties, Sami Taha now came to see himself as Palestine's preeminent spokesman for Arab labor and worked to enhance the PAWS' size and stature.[25]

Although Sami Taha and the veteran leaders backing him exercised considerable influence in Haifa itself, the PAWS was a rather loose-knit organization and the authority of its national leadership was limited outside Haifa. As a result it was possible for leftists (including veteran Palestine Communist Party activists) to assume the leadership of many of the rapidly growing new PAWS branches which sprang up in 1942. Thus although, for example, the vigorous new labor organization in Jaffa was formally a branch of the PAWS, it was in fact headed by Khalil Shanir, a longtime PCP leader. These leftists regarded Sami Taha and the old guard in Haifa as conservative, cautious, and ineffective, but they preferred to remain within the PAWS, Palestine's oldest and most established labor organization, in the hope of transforming it, first in the branches they controlled and then at the national level as well, and eventually taking it over.

A leaflet issued during this period by the Jaffa branch sheds some light on the attitude of PAWS activists there, and especially the leftists among them. The leaflet appeals to Arab workers to unite in defense of their common economic interests, outlines the purposes of the PAWS, and explains the benefits organization could yield for those who join. The leaflet is devoid of any specific political, much less explicitly nationalist, content. The Jews do receive mention; however, they are not castigated as an alien element scheming to seize Palestine or deprive Arab workers of their jobs, themes popular up to 1936. Rather, the Jewish workers are upheld as a model worthy of emulation. "Here are the Jewish workers before you," the leaflet declared.

> You can see that every one of them works no more than eight hours a day, earns a high wage, more than the Arab worker gets, and receives free medical treatment for themselves and their families. What is it that has brought them to this situation? Do you think that the Jewish employer is more beneficent than the Arab employer? No, my brothers! The Jewish workers know how to defend their rights, they established a union and all of them joined it, and that is what brought them to the state that you see them in.[26]

The PAWS, and soon rival trade union formations as well, benefited greatly from an unprecedentedly favorable attitude on the part of the government of Palestine. In the late 1930s the Colonial Office had begun to rethink its traditionally hostile attitude toward trade unionism and labor movements in Britain's colonial empire. Episodes of worker unrest in various countries led British officials to realize that trade unions in Asia, Africa, and the Caribbean could no longer be ignored or suppressed but must instead be accommodated or even co-opted. In part this revised strategy was the result of a growing understanding that capitalist development in the colonies had given rise to a permanent new class of wage workers in relatively large and modern industrial and transport enterprises whose needs and demands would have to be taken into account. But this shift in attitude and policy also had a political dimension, in that British officials hoped that the appearance of solicitude for labor, official recognition of trade unions, the promulgation of labor and social legislation, and the establishment of labor departments in colonial administrations would help channel trade unionism in safely apolitical directions and insulate it from radicalism and anticolonial nationalism. The entry of the Labor Party into the wartime coalition cabinet gave further impetus to this new turn.[27]

In keeping with this policy shift, in 1940 the government of Palestine appointed its first Labor Advisor, R. M. Graves. Brother of the poet and novelist Robert Graves, he had begun his career in the British-run security apparatus in Egypt. When a Labor Office was created within the Egyptian Ministry of the Interior in 1930, Graves was appointed to direct it, and he remained at the head of that department until 1939, when Egyptianization of the upper levels of the government bureaucracy made his position untenable. He thus came to Palestine with considerable experience in colonial labor policy and administration.[28] Graves' recommendation that the government of Palestine create a full-fledged Labor Department was accepted in 1942, and the new department was charged with the investigation of labor conditions, preparation of labor legislation, and regulation of trade unions. A number of British, Arab, and Jewish inspectors and subinspectors were appointed to staff the department, signaling the government's intention to play an active role in labor affairs. Since the Histadrut was already a well-established and powerful organization, Labor Department officials devoted themselves largely to the encouragement of trade unions for Arab workers.

In this endeavor one of the Labor Department's British inspectors, H. E. Chudleigh, played a key role. Chudleigh, a veteran of the English trade union movement, devoted much of his time and energy in 1942–43 to urging and overseeing the establishment of Arab unions in many parts of Palestine. Some observers, especially Histadrut officials, felt that Chudleigh was particularly supportive of labor organizing by communists or those close to them. This may well have been the case, in part because Chudleigh thought that communists were the most effective organizers and in part because, as I will discuss shortly, in 1942–43 the Arab communists in Palestine were strongly supportive of the Allied war effort.[29]

Government solicitude and support for trade union organization undoubtedly stimulated the process of unionization. But the main impetus, and much of the leadership for unions old and new, came from a cadre of experienced communist activists and radical intellectuals who helped create and lead a militant new left wing within the Arab labor movement. As I noted earlier, some of these leftists operated within the framework of the PAWS, where they nominally acknowledged the national leadership of Sami Taha and the old guard in Haifa while building up their own largely autonomous local branches in Jaffa, Jerusalem, al-Majdal, and elsewhere. At the same time, another group of communist and leftist intellectuals and unionists led by Bulus Farah was organizing an entirely independent labor organization in Haifa itself.

Farah had gone to work in the Haifa railway workshops in 1925, at the age of 15. By the early 1930s he had joined the Palestine Communist Party and in 1934 was sent by the party to the University of Toilers of the East in Moscow, where communist activists from the colonial world received training. Farah returned to Palestine in 1938 and soon became a figure around whom Arab communists disgruntled with the party's longtime secretary, Radwan al-Hilw (usually referred to by his party name, Musa) gathered. Farah made it clear that he had little respect for Musa and considered himself more capable of leading the party.

But Bulus Farah's conflict with the party leadership did not mainly concern personalities; there were important political differences as well. Farah was more inclined toward Arab nationalism than some of his comrades and played a key role in the struggle which the party's largely Arab leadership waged to restore control over the autonomous Jewish Section established during the revolt. While some of the Jewish Section's former leaders and members ultimately submitted to the authority of the central committee, others broke away from the PCP in 1940 and formed a separate, exclusively Jewish communist group under the name Emet ("Truth"). But Farah was himself expelled from the PCP central committee that same year, after the leadership claimed he had informed on the party while briefly in police custody. Farah insisted that his enemies within the party had not only turned him in but also besmirched his good name.[30]

Farah was now on the fringes of the party and openly contemptuous of its leadership, which he argued was not only ineffectual but also infected with Zionist deviationism; among other things, he was outraged that the PCP leadership had readmitted the dissident (and largely unrepentent) Emet group in 1942. Farah struck out on his own and during 1941–42 built up a strong following in Haifa. The group he led included both PCP members and a growing circle of left-leaning educated young men, mainly secondary school graduates now employed in white-collar jobs. Farah and his colleagues also developed close ties with members of an emerging stratum of militant working-class unionists who were frustrated by the PAWS' failure to respond aggressively to the new circumstances and opportunities created by the war, and receptive to Farah's emphasis on trade union organization and worker militancy. In 1942 Farah's group established a club in Haifa under the name "Rays of Hope" (Shu'a' al-Amal) to serve as a center for its activities, which initially had a democratic and antifascist focus. The PCP leadership responded by setting up its own rival "People's Club" (Nadi al-Sha'b), but it failed to significantly undermine the appeal and influence of Farah's dissident group.

That these organizations, in which known communists played key roles, could function more or less openly without fear of the kind of police repression with which every manifestation of communist activity had been met in the 1920s and 1930s was largely due to the fact that since the German invasion of the Soviet Union in June 1941, the communists and their allies were among the strongest and most vocal supporters of the Allied war effort within the Palestinian Arab community. The British authorities knew full well that, at least until the tide of war began to turn in the Allies' favor, many Palestinian Arabs were at best ambivalent about the Allied cause and at worst hopeful of an Axis victory, which would mean the end of British rule and the Zionist project. Some of the leaders of the nationalist movement, including its preeminent leader Amin al-Husayni, had gone so far as to openly embrace the Axis cause from exile. The British were therefore ready to tolerate, and even encourage, the Arab communists' activities, because a key component of communist propaganda and organizing work in Palestine was building Arab support for the antifascist cause and the Allied war effort, which the communists saw as a contribution to the defense of the Soviet Union.

In November 1942 the coalition of young radical intellectuals and working-class activists organized around the Rays of Hope Club took the leap into labor organizing by establishing the Federation of Arab Trade Unions and Labor Societies (FATULS). This new organization quickly won the allegiance of unionists at several large Haifa-area workplaces long neglected by the conservative and unenergetic PAWS, including the Iraq Petroleum Company, the just-completed Consolidated Refineries, and the Shell Oil Company's installation, and it later organized port and camp workers as well. At the end of 1942 the Labor Department estimated that the FATULS had some 1,000–1,500 members, compared with the PAWS' countrywide membership of about 5,000 and a dues-paying PLL membership generously estimated at 500.[31] The rivalry between the PAWS and the FATULS, and later between both of them and the PLL, stimulated all of them to escalate their efforts to organize unorganized workers and win the allegiance of those in unions. It should be kept in mind, however, that a significant portion of the PAWS' membership belonged to branches under the leadership of communists and their allies, so that from 1943 onward a sizable segment of the organized Arab working class in Palestine was effectively communist-led. Relations between the PAWS' Haifa-based conservative leadership, headed by Sami Taha, and its left wing were characterized by sporadic conflicts and jockeying for power within the organization, so that the Arab labor scene was complicated by internal tensions as well as interorganizational rivalries.

HASHOMER HATZA'IR IN SEARCH OF THE ARAB LEFT

Aharon Cohen and his comrades in Hashomer Hatza'ir were quick to grasp the significance of these developments. "We are witnessing important developments among the Arabs which open new horizons and encourage intensification of our activity," wrote Eli'ezer Bauer in July 1942. "A workers' movement is awakening, trade unions are emerging, groups of socialist intellectuals are taking shape, and the socialist intellectuals and the workers' movement are growing closer together."[32] Not surprisingly, their frustration over what they regarded as the Histadrut's abject failure to rise to the occasion and take the initiative grew more intense, and they vented their feelings in their movement's press and at Histadrut meetings.[33] But these developments also prompted Cohen and his colleagues to rethink and then reorient their strategy, by shifting their focus away from the countryside (which in any case seemed unpromising) and toward what they saw as "progressive Arab forces" in the cities, especially socialist and left-leaning workers and intellectuals. They hoped that by developing close ties with these forces, Hashomer Hatza'ir could counteract the influence of both bourgeois Arab nationalism and anti-Zionist communism while fostering the emergence of an Arab left which would be Hashomer Hatza'ir's partner in fighting for a binational and socialist Palestine.[34]

This reorientation prompted Cohen and other members of the Hashomer Hatza'ir Arab Department staff to devote considerable time and effort to cultivating relations with left-wing Arab circles. During 1942 they made contact with the group around the PCP's People's Club in Haifa, and especially with 'Abd Allah al-Bandaq. It was no secret to Cohen that al-Bandaq, who came from a prominent Bethlehem Christian family, was a leftist with close and long-standing connections with the PCP, and he also knew full well that al-Bandaq was widely believed to be a member of the still illegal party's top leadership. Yet Cohen not only accepted al-Bandaq's assurances that he was not currently a party member but vigorously promoted him to his colleagues in Hashomer Hatzaʻir, the League for Jewish-Arab Rapprochement and Cooperation, and the Histadrut's Arab Department as the prototype of a new breed of leftist but noncommunist Arab activist with whom left-wing Zionism could find common ground. In fact, because Cohen saw al-Bandaq and his circle as the key to establishing a long-term relationship with the emerging vanguard of the Palestinian Arab radical intelligentsia and workers' movement, he went even further: he discussed with al-Bandaq the idea of using funds provided by Hashomer Hatzaʻir to launch a new newspaper which would conduct antifascist propaganda in the Arab community and promote Arab-Jewish cooperation on the basis of political equality. He also convinced his movement's leaders to agree to help al-Bandaq establish an Arab socialist party which would promote Arab-Jewish cooperation. By February 1944 Cohen and al-Bandaq had together formulated a draft program for the new party which, among other things, seemed to recognize Jewish rights and interests in Palestine.[35]

In retrospect, the relationship between Cohen and al-Bandaq seems quite bizarre, because despite al-Bandaq's denials he was not only a member of the PCP but had been a leading member of the party's central committee since 1936. In 1944 he would surface as a member of the central committee of the newly formed National Liberation League, a quasi-communist and unequivocally anti-Zionist organization. Al-Bandaq's motives in pretending to Cohen and other Jewish contacts that he was not a communist, and thus not fundamentally hostile to Zionism, even in Hashomer Hatzaʻir's socialist and binationalist version, are perhaps comprehensible. He seems to have hoped that this kind of Stalinist double-dealing would enable him to extract from his Jewish interlocutors material resources which his party could put to good use. What is less easily understandable is how Cohen could not have known that al-Bandaq and his associates were committed communists and as such unlikely to be suitable partners for Hashomer Hatzaʻir; or if he did know, why he concealed that fact and tried so hard to "sell" al-Bandaq to his own movement and to the Histadrut as a potential ally.

An Israeli historian of the communist movement in Palestine has recently depicted Cohen as a deceiver who simply lied about al-Bandaq, even to his own comrades.[36] Yet one might more reasonably suggest that Cohen's friendship with al-Bandaq, his passionate commitment to the cause of Arab-Jewish cooperation and compromise, and his conviction that there existed authentic Arab socialists ready to ally themselves with socialist Zionists impelled him not only to convince himself of al-Bandaq's veracity but to try to convince others. This would then be an instance not so much of deliberate prevarication for political ends as of unconscious self-delusion, of an inability to "see" certain things or to admit them to oneself, even long after the relevant political conjuncture had passed. Indeed, Cohen seems to have gone to his grave unable to fully acknowledge that in the 1940s there were no significant left-wing forces within the Arab community ready to compromise with Zionism, of whatever variant. To fully acknowledge this truth would have been to admit the futility, or at least the failure, of his vision of Palestine's future and his life's work.[37]

THE RESURRECTION OF THE PLL

Confronted toward the end of 1942 by the rapid expansion of a reinvigorated Arab labor movement with a strong communist-led component and by Hashomer Hatza'ir's overtures toward the new Arab left, the Histadrut leadership finally began to devote greater attention and funds to its Arab Department and to the PLL. A number of high-ranking MAPAI leaders were appointed to guide the work of the Histadrut's Arab Department, along with Aharon Cohen representing Hashomer Hatza'ir and Moshe Erem representing Po'alei Tziyon Smol, and the department's budget was greatly increased. This made it possible, for the first time in years, to hire additional Arab and Jewish organizers, revive dormant PLL branches, and establish new ones. At long last, the Histadrut seemed to be sending a clear signal that it was launching a serious effort to organize Arab workers.[38]

The Histadrut's conception of what it was undertaking and why was set forth in a pamphlet on the PLL which it published in April 1943, under the signature of Abba Hushi.[39] The pamphlet opened with an epigraph, attributed to "an old Arab worker," which very nicely captures the way that labor Zionists wanted to believe they and their enterprise were seen by Arab workers: "Just as the sun, unbidden, spreads light and warmth, so the Histadrut has spread light and warmth to the Arab workers by the very fact of its existence." Hushi's pamphlet reviewed the history of the Histadrut's efforts to organize Arab workers and the work of the PLL up to the present time, paying special tribute to the contribution which the PLL's activities in Haifa had made to preventing Arab "terrorists" from closing the port there during the revolt. Like other MAPAI loyalists, Hushi attributed the PLL's failure over the previous decade to the difficulties inherent in organizing Arab workers, who belonged to "a poor, largely under-nourished, semi-feudal people, living in a part of the world where fatalistic resignation is consciously inculcated, a subject people faithful to a patriarchal religious tradition which has continued virtually unchanged for more than thirteen centuries." As for the Arab labor unions established during the war, Hushi asserted that they were organized by "sons of wealthy Effendis, whose political past is somewhat questionable, and by Communists who participate either openly or covertly," and claimed that they did not have the workers' true interests at heart. The pamphlet called on the Histadrut to rededicate itself to the task of organizing Arab workers into trade unions under its auspices (i.e., into the PLL) so as to facilitate realization of the labor-Zionist project. An English-language version of the pamphlet, obviously targeting audiences in Europe and the United States, also rebuked the government of Palestine for allegedly hindering efforts to develop closer relations between Arab and Jewish workers—a veiled reference to the Labor Department's encouragement of Arab unions and its disinterest in the PLL.[40]

It was clear to the Histadrut leadership that reviving the PLL and aggressively seeking to recruit Arab workers meant destroying any basis for cooperation with the PAWS and (in Haifa) the FATULS, which would regard these steps as provocative and threatening. But as Abba Hushi put it at a meeting of the Histadrut's Arab Affairs Department, reiterating MAPAI's long-standing position, "the Histadrut must act on behalf of the Arab workers as if the Arab unions did not exist . . . we want the Arab worker to be organized by us alone." Others associated with the Arab Department, especially Aharon Cohen and Moshe Erem, were doubtful about this strategy, partly because they understood why Arab workers were attracted to the Arab unions rather than to the PLL. Erem quoted an Arab he knew in Haifa who had told him that he was going to join the FATULS "because there the Arabs themselves run everything, it is a lively, bustling club and not just an employment agency like the PLL." But as usual, MAPAI's domination of the Histadrut ensured that the course of action it preferred would prevail.[41]

The strategy advocated by Hushi and endorsed by the Histadrut was soon put into effect in Jerusalem and then Jaffa, sabotaging initially promising efforts at cooperation between the Histadrut and Arab unions. At the beginning of 1943 the Jerusalem branch of the PAWS and the Histadrut's Jerusalem Workers' Council were negotiating jointly with city officials on behalf of some 340 employees of the Jerusalem municipality, including sanitation workers, road crews, and drivers, of whom 250 were Arabs and 90 were Jews. Like almost all workers in Palestine, the Jerusalem municipal employees had suffered a sharp decline in their real wages because of inflation; they also lacked many basic benefits, including paid sick days or vacations and compensation for work injuries. These negotiations failed to yield results, and in February 1943 the Histadrut and the PAWS together led a six-day strike which compelled the municipality and British officials to grant the workers a cost of living allowance and some of their other demands. The basis seemed to have been laid for fruitful cooperation along the lines which the PAWS had long advocated and which the Histadrut seemed to have tacitly accepted: the PAWS would represent the Arab workers and the Histadrut would represent the Jewish workers. A Histadrut official involved in the February 1943 strike summed up the spirit of a joint meeting by expressing the hope that "this is the beginning of joint action and that we will continue to work together to improve the working conditions of the laborer in this country, Jew and Arab."[42]

Within a few weeks, however, it had become evident that the Histadrut had instead decided to exploit the prestige which the municipal workers' victory had given it by establishing a PLL branch in Jerusalem which would directly recruit Arab workers, a policy which Hushi's soon-to-be-published pamphlet would set forth explicitly. This shift outraged the Arab unionists, who insisted that Arab workers should belong exclusively to Arab unions rather than to a subsidiary of the Jewish Histadrut and who could not regard the launching of a PLL branch in Jerusalem as anything but a hostile act intended to undermine and perhaps destroy the PAWS in that city. Their anger was certainly magnified by the fact that the nucleus of the new PLL branch (consisting largely of workers recruited at Jerusalem-area army bases) included some PAWS members, one of them a former branch secretary who as recently as January 1943 had been a delegate to the PAWS' national congress. Histadrut officials in Jerusalem had secretly been cultivating ties with anticommunists struggling for control of the PAWS in Jerusalem as far back as September 1942, and when the PLL branch was established the following spring some of them were induced to defect from the PAWS and join the PLL. (Perhaps partly as a consequence of this, by the fall of 1943 the Jerusalem PAWS branch was firmly in the hands of the left.) However, the Histadrut's control of the new PLL branch in Jerusalem was not absolute: branch members blocked the Histadrut's attempt to impose the most prominent PAWS defector as branch leader, leaving Histadrut officials without a well-known local figure around whom to build the organization.[43]

The same confrontational strategy was soon thereafter implemented in Jaffa, where the Histadrut also sought to establish a PLL branch. In this city the PAWS had a solid base and was headed by a veteran communist, Khalil Shanir. In Jaffa as elsewhere, PAWS leaders expressed willingness to cooperate with the Histadrut as representative of the Jewish workers but vehemently rejected the Histadrut's right to organize Arab workers through its subsidiary the PLL. The PAWS particularly resented PLL efforts to win over its current, former, or potential members. Aware of the difficulties of securing a foothold in Jaffa, the Histadrut secretly hired Adib al-Disuqi, who had been a member of the defunct Arab Workers' Society and was now involved in Jaffa-area sports activities, as its local organizer. Al-Disuqi began by opening a sports club which he used as a means of making contacts with local workers. Eliyahu Agassi helped out by exploiting the contacts he had made in his many years as the PLL's moving spirit.

By the summer of 1943 al-Disuqi and Agassi had signed up over one hundred Arab sanitation workers, some of them former PAWS members, who had been aroused by the victory of their counterparts in Jerusalem but were disappointed by the PAWS' failure to act vigorously on their behalf. Now the PLL, with the backing of the powerful and prestigious Histadrut, offered to fight for them if they joined the PLL, and many of them responded positively despite harassment from the PAWS. By July Agassi and al-Disuqi were openly negotiating with the Jaffa municipality on behalf of both the Arab and Jewish sanitation workers, and by August they felt strong enough to call the sanitation workers out on strike for four days. Despite threats by management and PAWS efforts to convince them to leave the PLL, the strikers remained steadfast and won higher wages. This victory allowed the PLL to consolidate a branch in Jaffa which by September 1943 claimed some 200 members, most of them municipal employees. By that time the PLL had also expanded its presence in Haifa, where it claimed (with great exaggeration) 1,200 members, and had established new branches in Acre, Tiberias, and the village of Qalunya, near Jerusalem.[44]

Nineteen forty-three thus witnessed the reentry of the Histadrut onto the Arab labor scene as a well-financed and determined contender for the support of Arab workers. This led to conflict with the Arab unions while further complicating struggles within the expanding Arab trade union movement and affecting political struggles within the Arab community. The Histadrut's efforts in Jerusalem and Jaffa signaled a new aggressiveness and yielded significant short-term successes, but it was the 50,000 Arab and Jewish workers employed at British and Allied military bases and installations throughout Palestine who would constitute the most important battleground in this struggle for power.

THE CAMPS AND THE CAMP WORKERS

The British military bases and installations that sprang up across the landscape of Palestine during the first years of the war created a new social space in which unprecedentedly large numbers of Arab and Jewish wage workers interacted. By 1943 about 35,000 Arabs (most of them manual laborers) and 15,000 Jews (two-thirds of them skilled or semiskilled, or engaged in clerical work) were employed directly by the British military authorities in well over a hundred installations large and small; thousands more were employed by Arab and Jewish contractors, including the Histadrut's own Solel Boneh, to build bases, Tegart police forts, roads, railways, and other projects. In everyday and even official usage, Jews in Palestine generally referred to these bases as *hakampim*, "the camps," a Hebraicization of the English word for camp. In Arabic they were referred to as *al-muʿaskarat*, the military camps.

Many of the Arab camp workers were peasants, often from villages located near the camp in which they worked, drawn into wage labor for the first time or now dependent on nonagricultural income as never before; others came from the ranks of the prewar urban unemployed. Many of their Jewish coworkers were recent immigrants, young people, Jews of Middle Eastern origin, individuals who for a variety of reasons had not found better and more secure jobs in other sectors, and even some people seeking to evade the mobilization for the war effort decreed by the Yishuv leadership. Wages and working conditions in the camps were generally poor. Though Jewish workers were better paid than Arab workers, camp pay scales in general were well below those which Jewish industrial workers enjoyed, and the British authorities refused to grant camp workers the cost of living allowance which the Histadrut had won for industrial workers. While some of the larger camps were located on the outskirts of cities and towns, many of the smaller ones were situated in remote areas where living conditions were often substandard, health and recreational facilities were meager, and workers were under the control of British army officers whose management style was often highly authoritarian and who treated their workers as if they were soldiers. Camp workers enjoyed little protection against exploitation, arbitrary dismissal, or military-style discipline, they were exempted from legislation providing compensation for work-related injuries, and their hours of work tended to exceed norms in other sectors.

As early as 1940, Histadrut leaders had appealed to the Trades Union Congress in Britain for help in improving the low wages paid to camp workers. The following year *Haqiqat al-Amr* reported that Arab and Jewish camp workers had asked the Histadrut for help in winning higher wages, and after lengthy negotiations with the British authorities the Histadrut did in fact secure a wage increase for all camp workers, which was however soon eroded by inflation.[45] But the Histadrut made relatively little effort to establish a strong organizational presence in the camps during the first two and a half years of the war, so that at the end of 1942 only about one-quarter of the Jewish camp workers were dues-paying Histadrut members, a proportion far below that which prevailed in most other sectors in which Jewish workers were employed. Several factors seem to have contributed to this neglect. For one, the camp workers' dispersion in numerous sites throughout the country, some of them in remote and largely uninhabited areas, made organization difficult. Moreover, it was obvious that these were temporary workplaces: as soon as the war was over most of the camps would be dismantled and those employed in them would lose their jobs. The Histadrut leadership also seems to have been reluctant to confront the British military authorities over the camp workers' situation as long as Egypt and Palestine seemed imminently threatened with invasion by Axis forces; neglect of the camp workers was in this sense a manifestation of the Yishuv's strong commitment to the Allied war effort.

However, Histadrut documents from this period suggest that other factors were also involved. Labor officials tended to perceive the camp workers as a rootless, volatile, and motley group, as "human material" of rather poor quality who were largely beyond the influence (much less control) of labor Zionism's economic, social, cultural, and political institutions and who were not really doing their part to realize the Zionist project. They were seen as not measuring up to the widespread (though of course highly idealized) labor-Zionist image of the authentic Jewish proletarian in Palestine, the experienced, ascetic, and self-disciplined industrial or construction worker or kibbutz member who was also an obedient member of the Histadrut and, by extension, a MAPAI loyalist. This image had a distinct ethnic component, since a significant proportion of the Jewish camp workers were of *Mizrahi* ("Oriental," i.e., Middle Eastern) rather than *Ashkenazi* (eastern and central European) origin, which cannot have enhanced their status in the eyes of the almost exclusively Ashkenazi Histadrut (and Zionist) leadership. One report from 1942 sneered that the Jewish camp workers "were gathered from among the peddlers of Shuk Hakarmel [the Jewish market] in Tel Aviv. Itinerant shoe-repairers from the streets of Tel Aviv have elevated themselves to the rank of expert builders." Reports that some Jewish camp workers were stealing and selling government property also imparted to this workforce a whiff of criminality, or at least of immorality and lack of Zionist and proletarian discipline—though it should be noted that the Hagana also exploited the camps as a source of weapons and other useful materials. The Histadrut leadership regarded this relatively unorganized, undisciplined, and transient workforce as especially vulnerable to "penetration" and influence by its political enemies, including the communists and Hashomer Hatza'ir on the left and the Revisionists on the right.[46]

The Histadrut did seek to maintain contact with Jewish workers at remote sites by sending emissaries on sporadic visits, but this was hardly sufficient to integrate them firmly into the embrace of the labor-Zionist movement. As a result the Histadrut had little effective presence in many of the camps in the early war years, and many Jewish camp workers displayed little interest in or enthusiasm for the Histadrut; some members even refused to pay Histadrut dues, prompting official concerns about lost revenue. Many Jewish camp workers expressed bitterness toward the Histadrut for what they perceived as its failure to defend their interests. The Histadrut's organizational weakness in many camps made it possible for activists from parties to the left of MAPAI—Hashomer Hatza'ir and the PCP—to win support among Jewish camp workers, whose low wages, oppressive working conditions, and isolation from the Yishuv mainstream tended to make them receptive to an oppositional perspective. Both communist and Hashomer Hatza'ir activists in the camps also made strenuous efforts to establish friendly relations with Arab coworkers and lay the basis for cooperation.[47]

Even though Jewish and Arab camp workers were brought together by common concerns—mainly a sharp decline in real wages through 1940 and 1941—cooperation was often impeded by a legacy of mistrust. One incident from the summer of 1941 may serve to illustrate both the potential for militancy and the complexities of relations among the Arab and Jewish camp workers in the first years of the war. Some 150 Arabs and 100 Jews were employed at a site known as Wadi Sara, for daily wages of

12 and 20 piastres respectively—a not untypical wage differential, related only in part to differing skill levels. Unrest erupted when the commandant announced that the workday would be increased from nine to twelve hours. At least some of the Arab and Jewish workers agreed to protest this decree by showing up for work an hour later than usual. However, the protest failed, in part because the Arab workers believed that they were being manipulated by their Jewish coworkers, who they thought were out to get their jobs. In the end some forty Jewish workers involved in the protest movement were fired, and Histadrut efforts to get them reinstated were unavailing.[48]

In the long run, the camp workers were too large and potentially important a group for either the Histadrut or the resurgent Arab labor movement to ignore. Histadrut officials worried that unless camp workers' wages could be improved, primarily by compelling the British to extend the COLA to cover workers in this sector, Jews would be forced out of camp jobs which would then be taken by Arabs who were more willing to accept the substandard wages offered by the military. The low wages and poor working conditions in the camps were also a drag on Jewish wages elsewhere in the Palestinian economy. As a result, in the camps as on the railways, the Histadrut's desire to secure high wages and jobs for Jewish workers eventually compelled it to pay attention to the plight of Arab workers as well, for here too Jews formed a minority of the labor force. In addition, Histadrut officials had become concerned that if they did not seek to organize and improve conditions for the Jewish camp workers, forces hostile to MAPAI (the communists and Hashomer Hatza'ir) might seize the initiative and gain a solid base in this sector. There was also growing awareness that both the PAWS (especially the communist-led branch in Jaffa) and the FATULS (in Haifa) were making efforts to contact and organize Arab camp workers.[49]

In the summer of 1942 the Histadrut launched a more serious effort to establish committees to represent the Jewish workers in camps where these did not already exist and to link these committees into an effective network under the control of a new Histadrut department coordinated by Berl Repetur. Some of the local urban workers' councils also established new departments for workers in nearby camps. Given that the Histadrut was dominated by MAPAI, this also meant an effort to ensure that MAPAI loyalists, and not Hashomer Hatza'ir members or communists, controlled both the newly established and the existing committees, even if undemocratic means were necessary to ensure the desired outcome. The Histadrut's campaign to organize the camps also had a security dimension, in that Histadrut officials helped the Hagana set up channels through which Jewish camp workers could smuggle out stolen weapons.[50] At the same time, the PAWS and the FATULS were intensifying their efforts to organize Arab camp workers in various parts of the country. Both the Arab and Jewish labor movements were in part responding to grassroots demands by camp workers for support and assistance as well as to independent local efforts to organize.

Neither the Arab unions nor the Histadrut achieved total success. While the PAWS (and to a lesser extent the FATULS) did sign up new members in various camps, the great majority of the Arab workers remained unorganized. Similarly, as late as March 1943 only about 8,000 of the 15,000 Jewish camp workers were Histadrut members, while an additional 1,200 belonged to other Jewish labor organizations, probably those affiliated with the right-wing Revisionist and religious-Zionist parties. A small number of Arab camp workers were recruited into the PLL, but in general the Histadrut remained quite reluctant to organize Arab camp workers directly, for fear of having to find employment for them when the camps were dismantled at the war's end. Instead the Histadrut sought to build strong local Jewish workers' committees through which it could exercise influence over Arab workers too, though at some sites it had to contend with existing joint Arab-Jewish committees.[51]

By the beginning of 1943 there were already signs of growing unrest among the camp workers, including a flurry of brief protest strikes and other actions.[52] Though the daily wage for unskilled camp labor had risen to about 21 piastres for Arabs and 28 piastres for Jews, prices had increased much more rapidly. Discontent was also fueled by the military authorities' increasing reluctance to recognize or negotiate with local committees, or even with the Histadrut, as well as what seems to have been an attempt to strengthen management's control over the camp workforce. This harder line may have had something to do with a more abundant labor supply: the British military no longer needed the cooperation of the Histadrut to channel workers into the camps and military industry, and it was also increasingly anxious to keep labor costs down. At the end of March 1943 a government committee on wages approved a substantial cost of living allowance for industrial and service workers, but despite numerous appeals from delegations of Arab and Jewish camp workers the military authorities refused to extend it to the camp workers. Those workers now displayed a new readiness to organize and fight with which both the PAWS and the Histadrut had to reckon. It was clear that the time for action had come, requiring both organizations to decide what means of struggle were appropriate and how to relate to one another in an effort to improve the lot of this mixed Arab-Jewish workforce.

THE STRUGGLE FOR THE CAMPS

The PAWS responded to the upsurge of unrest in the camps by convening a meeting of some one hundred branch leaders and delegates in Jaffa early in April 1943. The camp workers' situation was the main issue discussed at the conference, which approved resolutions calling on the government to grant the camp workers large wage increases, along with the COLA, overtime pay, and pay for religious holidays, to soften the harsh discipline imposed in the camps, and to negotiate with the Arab workers' representatives. A number of the delegates also denounced what they saw as official discrimination in favor of Jewish camp workers, manifested mainly in higher wages for Jews, and the meeting demanded the equalization of Arab and "non-Arab" (i.e., Jewish) wages in the camps. But though speakers criticized the Histadrut's attempts to organize Arab camp workers, accused it of trying to take jobs away from Arabs, and insisted that only Arab unions could speak for Arab workers, the PAWS remained willing to cooperate with the Histadrut in negotiations with the British authorities, on condition that the Jewish organization desist from recruiting Arabs and restrict itself to representing the Jewish camp workers alone. PAWS leaders made no mention of strike action: aware of their limited resources and somewhat fearful of directly confronting the British authorities, they seem to have hoped that their demands could be achieved through negotiations, provided that a common front could be formed with the Histadrut. It is likely too that in Palestine as elsewhere, the communists who controlled the FATULS and played a major role within the PAWS opposed any work stoppage as detrimental to the war effort, or more precisely to the defense of the Soviet Union, a duty to which all other considerations were to be subordinated.[53]

The Histadrut was now faced with a decision over whether to cooperate with the PAWS, which had a substantial base among the Arab camp workers, or to go it alone by claiming the right to represent both Jewish and Arab camp workers. During the first two years of the war the Histadrut had in effect been negotiating with the British authorities on behalf of all the camp workers. The PAWS had lacked the capacity to bargain with the British civil and military authorities on a national scale, nor did it have anything approaching the Histadrut's close and long-standing connections with government officials in Jerusalem or with Colonial Office, Labor

Party, and Trades Union Congress officials in London. By the spring of 1943 the Histadrut had revived the PLL and committed itself to an aggressive effort to recruit Arab workers in Jaffa, Jerusalem, and other towns, in direct confrontation with the Arab unions. Yet the camp workers constituted something of a special case: insistence on the Histadrut's right to organize and speak for at least some of the Arab camp workers would inevitably provoke a very open and public clash with the PAWS and might sabotage efforts to mount an effective campaign on behalf of the camp workers.

When the Histadrut secretariat met on April 13, 1943 to discuss the situation, there was general agreement that if the army did not agree within ten days to extend the COLA to the camp workers, the Histadrut would follow the PAWS' example and convene its own national conference of camp workers, and also stage a one-day protest strike. The question of how the Histadrut should relate to the PAWS—whether meetings in the camps, and the projected national delegate conference, should be sponsored by the Histadrut alone, or jointly with the PAWS—was delegated to the organization's newly established Merkaz Ha'avoda ("Labor Center"), responsible for the Jewish camp workers, and to its Arab Department. At a joint meeting two days later the decision was taken: the Histadrut would not cooperate with the PAWS in the struggle to win the COLA. A national conference of camp workers was scheduled for May 2 in Tel Aviv, to be followed by a one-day strike.[54]

The PAWS responded angrily to this unilateral initiative and to the Histadrut's efforts in the weeks that followed to organize mass meetings in the camps in order to mobilize the workers and choose both Jewish and Arab delegates to the May 2 conference. A PAWS leaflet dated April 26 denounced the Histadrut's attempts to recruit Arabs to attend that meeting and warned Arab workers against participating in what it described as an effort to destroy what the PAWS' own April 4 conference had sought to build.[55] The Histadrut nonetheless went ahead with its conference, which was attended by some 147 delegates from ninety work sites throughout Palestine. The official report on the meeting does not specify exactly how many Arab delegates attended but, apparently in order to convey a sense that the meeting brought Arabs and Jews together on an equal footing, claimed that equal numbers of Arabs and Jews had spoken during the discussion. After concluding remarks by Berl Repetur and Golda Meirson (later Meir), then head of the Jewish Agency's Political Department and a top Histadrut leader, the delegates, claiming to speak for all 50,000 camp workers, called for a one-day strike if the COLA was not granted, with the exact date to be set by the Histadrut leadership. A telegram sent by the PAWS declaring that the conference represented only the Jewish camp workers, that any Arabs attending represented only themselves and that the Arab workers recognized only the decisions of its own April 4 conference in Jaffa, was apparently not read to the delegates. A few days later the Histadrut announced that the strike would take place on May 10.[56]

The PAWS promptly responded with a leaflet which admitted that a few well-intentioned Arab workers had attended the Tel Aviv meeting but reiterated that the Histadrut represented only the Jewish workers. The leaflet went on to denounce as politically motivated the Histadrut's decision to organize a strike without consulting the authentic representative of the Arab camp workers. When the Histadrut officially announced a strike for May 10, the PAWS launched an intensive effort in the camps to convince Arab workers not to strike. It also issued a leaflet in Hebrew appealing to the Jewish camp workers not to join a "separatist" strike but instead to cooperate with the Arab camp workers' committees and the PAWS in order to achieve victory for all camp workers. At the same time, however, the Arab union sent the Histadrut a letter offering to discuss cooperation between the two organizations.[57] As Histadrut leaders began to realize that many of the Arab camp workers might heed the PAWS' appeal and refuse to join the strike, which as a result might end in failure, doubts began to surface about the wisdom of the decision to exclude the PAWS. Some members of the Histadrut executive committee asked why no effort had been made to secure agreement with the PAWS and wondered if there was still time to approach that organization. Those who wanted to stay the course continued to disparage the authenticity and representativeness of the PAWS while pointing out that cooperation with the Arab union was tantamount to recognizing it as the sole representative of the Arab camp workers, and by extension all Arab workers. This meant in effect giving up on the PLL as the instrument through which the Histadrut could directly recruit Arabs.

In the end the Histadrut executive committee decided to proceed with the strike. Yet doubts persisted, and on May 8 Histadrut secretary David Remez contacted a PAWS leader to see if something could be worked out. The unnamed leader held firm and insisted that there could be no cooperation as long as the Histadrut persisted in trying to organize Arab workers. Worried Histadrut officials considered postponing the strike for a week, using a recent Allied victory in Tunisia as a pretext, for fear that if the strike failed the Histadrut's prestige and bargaining position would suffer. "The strike's victory will lead to defeat," Yosef Sprintzak predicted. "We will gain no benefit from it. The Histadrut will not gain control of the Arab and Jewish workers by this means. . . . It is now irresponsible to proceed with the strike." Nonetheless, despite considerable hesitation and trepidation, the Histadrut stayed its course.[58]

As the strike date approached the PAWS stepped up its campaign to thwart Arab participation. A leaflet distributed to the camp workers denounced what it described as Histadrut propaganda to the effect that the PAWS had been consulted about, and had consented to, the strike:

> The truth is that the Histadrut has not recognized and does not recognize the Arab workers' unions. . . . The PAWS in Jaffa has decided that the date set for the strike is untimely for the Arabs and it sees the workers' interest as lying in awaiting the final results of the negotiations soon to follow. . . . The strike is the workers' only weapon, but this weapon must be used at a time when it will lead naturally to achieving our demands. . . .[59]

The Histadrut's daily newspaper *Davar* would later claim that Histadrut offers to cooperate in good faith with the PAWS had been spurned and that the PAWS had opposed the strike on purely political grounds, attacking it in leaflets as a Zionist conspiracy. But examination of leaflets issued by the PAWS in these weeks and records of the deliberations of the Histadrut leadership bear out neither of these allegations.[60] Moreover, the PAWS' appeals to Arab workers seem to have hit home, especially in the larger camps situated near major towns. A Jewish visitor to Sarafand, one of the largest British military bases in the Middle East, located a few miles northwest of Ramla, reported that Arab workers there had asked him: "How can you ask us for cooperation, when you didn't consult with us but [instead] informed us that there will be a strike tomorrow—and you want us to join it?"[61]

On the appointed day nearly all the Jewish camp workers joined the strike. The extent of Arab participation is less clear. The Arab press insisted that the Histadrut's attempt to bring the Arab workers out on strike had been a complete failure, and a British Foreign Office dispatch similarly asserted that the Arab workers had not joined in. A PAWS leaflet depicted the Arab workers' "100 percent" rejection of the strike as "decisive proof that the Histadrut has been taught a lesson, that it should refrain from claiming to represent the Arab workers because they have their own independent organization in the PAWS." By contrast, the Histadrut's organ *Davar* claimed that the great majority of Arab workers had taken part. The *Palestine Post*, which expressed the views of the Yishuv's official leadership, asserted that "solidarity between Arab and Jewish workers was complete in most camps, though some Arab workers remained at their jobs in two urban centres in compliance with the appeal of the Arab Labour Societies in Palestine." Some Histadrut officials estimated Arab participation at 17,000–20,000, about 50 to 60 percent of the Arab workforce, but a Histadrut leaflet issued a few days after the strike spoke more vaguely and modestly of "thousands" of Arab strikers.[62]

It does seem that some thousands of Arab workers joined the strike, especially those employed at sites at which the Histadrut was the only organized force and which were relatively remote from the three cities in which the PAWS exercised the most influence. But despite the Histadrut leadership's public claim that the strike had been a great success, it was understood in private to have been a failure. By far the greater part of the Arab majority of the camp labor force had refused to follow the Histadrut's lead, demonstrating that the campaign to exclude and undermine the PAWS was unviable. Since the British authorities showed no sign of granting the COLA to camp workers, the Histadrut leadership faced continuing pressure from below as both Jewish and Arab workers held protest meetings and joined brief local strikes to demand the COLA and urge their leaders to work together.[63]

In the weeks after the strike the Histadrut finally responded to outstanding invitations from PAWS leaders to begin talks. This did not, however, reflect any substantive change in the Histadrut's position. Though the strike's failure and pressure from below now compelled it to deal with the PAWS, it continued to insist that the Arab union publicly recognize the PLL and kept trying to mobilize and organize the camp workers on its own. As this was guaranteed to render cooperation with the PAWS impossible, it is not surprising that the talks did not go very well.[64] In meetings with Jaffa PAWS leaders, for example, Histadrut officials (especially Berl Repetur) took a hard line, criticizing the PAWS for opposing the strike and lecturing its leaders about their organization's numerous errors and shortcomings. Neither Khalil Shanir, leader of the PAWS in Jaffa and a veteran communist, nor any of his colleagues much appreciated this attitude, and they responded angrily. But what most effectively sabotaged the talks was the Histadrut's insistence on including PLL members, notably Adib al-Disuqi, its organizer in Jaffa. Given that al-Disuqi was just then engaged in raiding the PAWS' membership, that very few Arab camp workers actually belonged to the PLL, and that the conflict over the camp workers' strike had turned on the Histadrut's insistence on recruiting and representing Arab workers, the PAWS leaders could only see al-

Disuqi's inclusion as a deliberate provocation, if not an insult, and as proof of the Histadrut's bad faith. Shanir and his colleagues expressed willingness to cooperate with the Histadrut, but only if the PLL was excluded. One meeting broke up in an uproar after al-Disuqi spoke up to criticize the PAWS. Shanir exploded in anger: "Get out of here, you're a Zionist, a pariah, you've sold yourself to the Jews, you've rented yourself out for £P18 a month!"—a reference to al-Disuqi's salary as PLL organizer in Jaffa.[65]

Talks were also held in Haifa in early June, at the initiative of local Arab camp workers affiliated with the PAWS. Here too Histadrut representatives brought local PLL members along to the meeting and accused the PAWS of "knifing us in the back" by opposing the strike. Unlike their more militant counterparts in Jaffa, the Arab unionists in Haifa were willing to sit down with PLL members. But although these talks were less vituperative in tone, little progress was made. Nonetheless PAWS and Histadrut representatives continued sporadic negotiations through mid-June, because unrest among the rank and file camp workers compelled both sides to look as if they were genuinely seeking cooperation.[66] Soon thereafter, however, the main impetus for cooperation faded away. Early in June 1943 the government announced that government employees would be granted the COLA. Some weeks passed before it became clear that this would apply to camp workers as well, and it was not immediately certain if the COLA would be calculated in a way that came close to meeting the workers' demands. During that interval PAWS and Histadrut leaders discussed joint action, including strikes, but by late June many of the camp workers' outstanding grievances had been addressed, although the poorest-paid segment of the camp workforce had gained the least.

Though neither side now saw much point in continuing negotiations, both felt obliged to defend their own commitment to solidarity and blame the other side for the breakdown of the talks. The Histadrut claimed that the PAWS had never really been interested in unity, while the PAWS issued a long leaflet putting forth its version of relations with the Histadrut and blaming it for sabotaging efforts at cooperation. After the talks broke down, the PAWS also began to demand more forcefully than before that more Arabs be hired as foremen and clerks in the camps, jobs which were disproportionately held by Jews.[67] Both the Histadrut and the PAWS remained active among the camp workers, but as the wave of worker militancy subsided so did the intensity of the conflict between them. At the end of June 1943 the Histadrut convened another meeting of camp workers' delegates in Tel Aviv, but although some Arab delegates participated the PAWS does not seem to have responded very vigorously. In that same period Agassi, sometimes accompanied by an Arab PLL member, visited various camps and addressed meetings of Arab workers about the PLL. At some of these meetings workers asked Agassi why he was not accompanied by someone from the PAWS and how negotiations between the Histadrut and the PAWS were coming along; at other camps he was not challenged in this way.

But although Agassi, as optimistic as ever, reported to his colleagues that many Arab camp workers were ready and willing to join the PLL, the Histadrut was largely uninterested in signing them up and forming new PLL branches.[68] As earlier, the overriding consideration seems to have been the fear that recruiting Arab camp workers into the PLL would saddle the Histadrut with an obligation to provide them with jobs when their wartime employment inevitably came to an end. So even as the Histadrut continued to insist on its right to organize and represent Arab workers in general and the camp workers in particular—a stance which sabotaged cooperation with Arab labor organizations—it was not in fact very interested in actually recruiting camp workers into the PLL.

In September 1943 H. E. Chudleigh of the Labor Department summed up the state of relations between the Arab and Jewish labor movements in Palestine:

> The situation as between the Arab and Jewish Trade Unions has, if anything, hardened in recent months. Common economic interests are overridden by political considerations which dominate all discussions. "Pigheaded" would not be too strong a term to apply to the leadership on both sides. Struggle for power is a further complicating factor. Possibilities of cooperation in the army camps and workshops, the Jaffa Municipality and elsewhere have been allowed to pass. Only in the case of the Jerusalem Municipal dispute has any degree of working together been achieved.

As we saw, cooperation in Jerusalem had in fact also been short-lived.[69]

THE COLLAPSE OF THE PCP AND THE EMERGENCE OF THE NLL

The conflict between the PAWS and the Histadrut over the camp workers' strike of May 1943 had an impact in another sphere as well: it helped precipitate the crisis which led to the disintegration of the Palestine Communist Party as an Arab-Jewish organization. Tensions within the party had been building toward crisis for some time. Many of the party's Jewish members and leaders had come to believe that it should moderate its unrelenting hostility toward Zionism and take advantage of widespread sympathy for the Soviet Union in the Yishuv in order to rebuild its base among Jews. In theoretical terms, these Jewish communists argued that the party should recognize that the Yishuv had grown significantly and undergone important social changes in recent years. The Jewish community in Palestine, they argued, had to be analyzed not as an undifferentiated and uniformly reactionary bloc, an alien colonial enclave, a "Jewish Ulster" implanted in Palestine by British imperialism, but as an increasingly distinct and complex society with significant and deepening roots in the country that had acquired many of the characteristics of a nation. Some went so far as to question the PCP's opposition to Jewish immigration. Many of the Jewish communists also advocated reentry into the Histadrut, based on a distinction between that organization's Zionist leadership and the Jewish working class itself, which the communists believed could be weaned away from Zionism through a struggle carried out within the Histadrut's institutions and affiliated unions. In many arenas, these Jewish communists also argued, there was room for cooperation with progressive Zionists.[70]

Most of the PCP's Arab members, and especially those who belonged to the younger generation of Arab intellectuals and labor activists now coming to the fore, were moving in a very different direction. They believed that the party should give priority to overcoming its weakness among Palestine's Arab majority and transforming itself into a significant political force. As they saw it, Palestine was an Arab land and its communist party should therefore orient itself first and foremost toward the indigenous Arab majority and its national movement. Rejecting any accommodation with Zionism, the party should appeal to broad sections of the Arab community on a program that combined Palestinian Arab nationalism with a commitment to progressive social reform and democracy. Among Arab communists prominent within this tendency were Bulus Farah, who had built up his own following in Haifa and had long been convinced that the party leadership had already succumbed to Zionist deviationism, and 'Abd Allah al-Bandaq, a veteran party leader who was, it will be remembered, Aharon Cohen's candidate to lead a noncommunist and pro-Zionist Arab left.

The tensions within the party came to a head at the beginning of May 1943 when the central committee dissolved dissident Jewish branches and expelled several Jewish members for defying the leadership by participating in May Day celebrations organized by the Histadrut. The internal crisis this touched off was further exacerbated when it became clear that

Arab and Jewish party members were supporting different sides in the struggle between the PAWS and the Histadrut which preceded the May 10 camp workers' strike which the latter had called. Arab communists active in the PAWS naturally worked hard to convince Arab workers not to join the strike, a position endorsed by the central committee. However, though many Jewish communists agreed that the Histadrut deserved blame for trying to exclude the PAWS by calling the strike unilaterally, they very much wanted to rejoin the Histadrut fold and could not bring themselves to call on Jewish workers to break the strike.[71]

Despite efforts by some Arab and Jewish communists to hold the party together, the following months witnessed the disintegration of the PCP amidst barrages of mutual recriminations and expulsions. Stalin's dissolution of the Comintern in May 1943 as a gesture of goodwill toward his British and American allies helped deepen divisions within the party. Although the communists in Palestine had few if any direct links with Moscow, the elimination of this nominally internationalist framework strengthened those forces within the PCP which argued that it was essential to strike deeper roots by adapting to local conditions and adopting a more nationalist stance. This is the course that some of the Arab militants (among them al-Bandaq and his younger colleague Emile Habibi) seemed to be following when, at the end of May, they issued a statement in the name of the central committee declaring that the PCP had finally purged itself of those Jewish members who had succumbed to Zionist deviationism. The statement went on to define the PCP as "an Arab national party which includes in its ranks Jews who accept its national program." This constituted a decisive break with the party's historic self-definition as an Arab-Jewish and internationalist formation, though some of its proponents probably saw it (at least in part) as a response to their former Jewish comrades' apparent embrace of Zionism. Not all Arab communists immediately subscribed to this position: some, like Khalil Shanir, still hoped for a time that it would be possible to preserve an Arab-Jewish party. But efforts to find common ground failed, and the more nationalist orientation long advocated by dissident communists like Bulus Farah, whose following in Haifa now constituted the single most cohesive Arab communist group, ultimately prevailed.

Out of the wreckage of the PCP three distinct organizations would eventually emerge, two entirely Jewish and one entirely Arab in membership. One group of Jewish communists continued to move away from the PCP's traditional line and toward the Yishuv mainstream by embracing positions which the party had for many years denounced as Zionist. This group organized itself as the Communist Educational Association in Eretz Yisra'el, following the example of communists in the United States under the leadership of Earl Browder, and later renamed itself the Hebrew Communist Party. A second and larger group of Jewish communists insisted that it was the organizational and ideological continuation of the old PCP and continued to call itself the Palestine Communist Party, but it was in fact a very different party, in terms of both its exclusively Jewish membership and its ideology, which substantially abandoned many traditional communist positions in order to gain greater acceptance in the Yishuv.

However, much more important than either of these two small and weak Jewish parties was the new Arab political formation that emerged out of the wreckage of the unified PCP. In the fall of 1943 some of the leading Arab communists began holding meetings to discuss the establishment of a new, exclusively Arab organization. By the beginning of 1944 they had emerged publicly at the head of the new 'Usbat al-Taharrur al-Watani ("National Liberation League," NLL), which had as its organ *al-Ittihad* (Unity), originally established by the FATULS in Haifa and later the newspaper of the new labor federation controlled by the NLL.

Though almost all its top leaders had been PCP members, the NLL defined itself not as a communist party but as a progressive nationalist organization open to any Palestinian Arab who accepted its program, which called for the independence of Palestine as an Arab state with a democratic government as well as fundamental social transformation. The NLL sought to propagate a version of Palestinian Arab nationalism imbued with a progressive social content. It called for social reforms to benefit the Arab workers and peasants and argued that only a mass-based and democratized nationalist movement could successfully challenge British colonial rule and Zionism. The NLL leadership believed that the wartime quiescence of the traditional Palestinian Arab leadership—which had never displayed much interest in social issues and many of whose members were in exile—had created an unprecedented opportunity for the NLL to mobilize the radicalized intelligentsia and the growing working class and establish itself as a vigorous and independent left wing within the Palestinian national movement.

From its inception the NLL enjoyed a strong base within the labor movement, since it included the leaders of both the left wing within the PAWS and of the Haifa-based FATULS. It also enjoyed the support of many educated young Arabs organized in the League of Arab Intellectuals. The NLL hoped it could build on this base and ultimately capture the leadership of the national movement by combining a strong commitment to nationalism with a commitment to social reform and mass mobilization, much as communists were then doing in China, Vietnam, Yugoslavia, and elsewhere.

Like the official leadership of the national movement, the NLL opposed Zionism, Jewish immigration, and Jewish statehood, and it insisted that as the indigenous majority the Arabs of Palestine were entitled to self-determination. However, as former communists who for years had worked very closely with Jews, its leaders had a much fuller and more nuanced understanding of Zionism and the Yishuv. They therefore departed from the official nationalist stance by maintaining the time-honored communist distinction between the Jewish masses in Palestine and Zionism *per se:* while the latter was to be extirpated as a form of colonialism, the Jewish masses (and especially the Jewish working class) could and should be won over by being brought to see that their true interests lay in solidarity and unity with the Arab masses. This implied that all the Jews then in Palestine would become equal citizens, and perhaps even have the status of a distinct national-cultural minority, within the future independent Arab Palestine. More practically, it meant that unionists in those segments of the Arab labor movement under NLL leadership tended to be open to cooperation with Jewish workers and unions, and even the Histadrut, as long as the latter did not seek to organize, recruit, or speak for Arab workers. With the left gaining strength within the Arab workers' movement and with that movement experiencing both rapid expansion and internal conflicts during 1944–46, there was once again considerable room for both conflict and cooperation between Arab and Jewish unionists.

THE PLL: CONFUSION, DRIFT, AND DEFEAT

In October 1943 Histadrut officials calculated that over the course of the year some £P3,300 had been allocated for the organization of Arab workers, an unprecedentedly large sum; for 1944 the Arab Department was seeking a budget of £P12,000, over and above the cost of publishing *Haqiqat al-Amr.* This sharply increased level of funding (provided in large part by the Jewish Agency) had made possible the expansion of the Arab Department's staff in Tel Aviv, but it does not seem to have greatly enhanced the PLL's base among Arab workers. On paper, the PLL's Haifa branch remained its strongest, claiming some 400–500 dues-paying members. But the organization's membership in Haifa consisted almost entirely of individuals employed at a wide variety of small workplaces in and near the city. The PLL had not succeeded in establishing an effective or coherent presence at any of the city's major workplaces or in forming even nuclei of trade unions. One Histadrut Arab Department official likened the PLL branch in Haifa to "a sponge, absorbing and emitting members in accordance with the employment situation; the people being absorbed and emitted see the branch only as an employment office for times of need, and since dues are low it is more worthwhile than paying fees to the private Arab labor brokers operating in the market." Many of the PLL branch's core members in Haifa were employed, directly or indirectly, by the Histadrut or other Jewish enterprises.[72]

In Jaffa, the situation seemed at first glance somewhat better. The PLL branch there retained the base of support it had won among employees of the municipality earlier in 1943 and, as we will see, before the end of that year it developed what seemed a very promising connection with skilled workers at one of the city's major industrial sites, the Wagner metalworking factory, with more than 160 workers, almost all of them Arabs. The branch in Acre also seemed to be flourishing at the end of 1943, but this was largely because its Arab secretary, operating without direct day-to-day supervision by any of the Jews who ran the PLL, was signing up members (largely camp workers) by promising that the Histadrut would make sure they had jobs. When Histadrut officials discovered what he was up to he was fired and replaced by a Jew. The Acre branch subsequently disintegrated as Arab workers found their hopes of employment disappointed.[73] The Jerusalem branch had never really got off the ground: it comprised a small number of municipal employees and several dozen Arabs from the outlying village of Qalunya who worked at the Jewish-owned Steinberg tile factory nearby.

Arab Department officials were increasingly defensive about the fact that the PLL remained a Jewish-run organization, without even a provisional leadership body composed of Arab members. But they themselves had a rather low opinion of the Arabs they had elevated to local leadership positions, declaring that "when there is no Jewish worker in a branch, the Arab worker is not worth much" and that "most if not all [of the PLL's Arab activists] are greedy," requiring close supervision by Jews, especially when it came to branch funds.[74] Uncertain about how to proceed and anxious for guidance, members of the Histadrut Arab Department staff met with MAPAI's secretariat in November 1943 to discuss the future course of the Histadrut's Arab work. Present were several of the top leaders of MAPAI, the Histadrut, and the Yishuv, most of whom would later become high officials of the State of Israel, including three future prime ministers (David Ben-Gurion, Moshe Shertok/Sharett, and Levi Shkol-nik/Eshkol), a future president (Zalman Rubashov/Shazar) and at least two future ministers (Pinhas Lubianker/Lavon and Eliezer Kaplan).[75] The ensuing discussion effectively illustrates the extent to which MAPAI's leaders had relegated the PLL, and the question of relations with the Arab working class, to marginal status in their vision of Palestine's future.

The discussion was opened by Shmu'el Solomon, the senior member of the Arab Department staff, whom a visiting English trade unionist would aptly characterize as "such a nice man, a German Jew who has studied Talmadic [sic], classical and Islamic scholarship but can you imagine Laski doing a year in a Catholic University in Ireland and then organising the peasants of Salway in Erse."[76] Solomon expressed optimism about the PLL's prospects but acknowledged that Arab workers clearly regarded the Histadrut and the PLL first and foremost as sources of employment—a perception which would likely create problems after the war, when PLL members currently employed in military bases would again seek jobs in Jewish-owned enterprises and farms. "All our explanations that they are not Histadrut members, that there is a difference here [between Histadrut and PLL membership], are of as much use as the blowing of a *shofar* [the ram's horn sounded during prayers on the Jewish holidays of Rosh Hashana and Yom Kippur]." Solomon also admitted that signs of discontent had already surfaced among Arab workers over the fact that the PLL was entirely controlled by the Jewish officials of the Histadrut's Arab Department, and he noted instances in which Arab workers had told him that they wanted to pay the same dues as Histadrut members and receive equal benefits in return.

MAPAI leaders failed to give Solomon and his colleagues the support and guidance they sought. Eliyahu Sasson expressed skepticism about organizing Arab workers. Criticizing Solomon for both underestimating the strength of the Arab unions and overestimating the PLL's prospects for growth, he argued for a PLL of no more than 1,000–1,500 loyal members, just large enough to hinder the Arab labor unions and to be useful in the event of another crisis like the 1936–39 revolt. Ben-Gurion reiterated his opposition to organizing Arab workers employed by Jews but argued that Arabs employed in the government, international, and Arab sectors should be organized. However, he wanted emphasis to be placed not so much on organization as on providing social services to Arab workers, and he also raised the idea of creating a small pro-Zionist Arab party which might prove useful in the political struggles that clearly lay ahead.

On the whole, while giving the Arab Department staff a pat on the back for its efforts, the MAPAI secretariat left it to continue doing what it had been doing, despite the fact that it had little to show for the energy and money invested over the previous year. It would seem that with a few exceptions MAPAI's leaders had lost what little interest they had once had in organizing Arab workers. Having come to the conclusion that this enterprise would play little if any role in determining Palestine's fate after the war, they regarded it as little more than a side show.

But the Jewish staff of the Arab Department had not yet given up. In the first half of 1944 they tried to breathe some life into the PLL and raise the morale of its tiny cadre of active Arab members by imparting to it some semblance of autonomous organizational life. Among other things, they launched a (short-lived) internal bulletin in Arabic and convened, at Histadrut headquarters in Tel Aviv, the first meeting ever held of active Arab members of PLL branches. But none of this could alter the fact that the PLL was created and run by Jews, nor could PLL officials ever find a way to overcome the obstacles they faced as they tried to organize Arab workers. For example, Arab Department officials hoped to alter the PLL's reputation as an employment agency by recruiting Arabs who already held jobs. But they quickly discovered that the Jewish foremen at the military bases where many Arab workers were employed, as well as the Jewish officials of Solel Boneh which held contracts for numerous military and public works projects, were still at best indifferent, and at worst openly hostile, to efforts to recruit their Arab employees into the PLL. Further complicating matters was the fact that Arab workers generally saw no difference between Solel Boneh on the one hand and the Histadrut and the PLL on the other, though many believed that Solel Boneh treated Arabs worse than did most private contractors. None of this suggested that the PLL had much prospect of ever establishing a secure and substantial base in the Arab working class.[77]

The PLL's meager prospects for making permanent inroads into the Arab working class, even in a major urban center, would soon be conclusively demonstrated by the outcome of a struggle in which the organization was involved in Jaffa, at the Wagner metalworking factory, in the first months of 1944. Originally established and managed by German businessmen, when the war began the British authorities seized the enterprise as enemy property, interned its owners as enemy aliens, and closed it down. It was reopened in 1941 under the management of an Arab entrepreneur, Stilo 'Awwad. 'Awwad's harsh attitude toward his 160 or so workers, nearly all of them Arabs, and especially his refusal to pay them the full cost of living allowance decreed by the government, led a group of Wagner workers to contact the local PLL branch for assistance. Despite harassment from their employer and opposition from the PAWS, which was very anxious to prevent the PLL from gaining a foothold in this large and prominent workplace, a large majority of Wagner workers eventually signed up with the PLL, thus fulfilling the Histadrut's precondition for providing assistance. Arab Department officials felt they had achieved a major breakthrough, since the Wagner workers were not unskilled migrants from the countryside but skilled urban wage workers, just the kind of authentic proletarians they had long dreamed of organizing into a stable union.

'Awwad eventually expressed willingness to satisfy the workers' demands but adamantly refused to recognize or negotiate with the PLL. The dispute was ultimately submitted for arbitration to the Labor Department, whose officials insisted that the PAWS must also be included as a party to the discussions. Although British arbitrators eventually granted many of the workers' demands, they refused to endorse the PLL's claim to represent these Arab workers. R. M. Graves, the director of the Labor Department, told Arab Department staff members that "we want the organization of the Arab workers, but not by means of the Histadrut's method." The government favored "independent Arab trade unions, not organizations run by an alien leadership. . . . We know that the Histadrut can bring to this work knowledgeable and experienced people, but in the end this would [still] be an alien leadership." H. E. Chudleigh added that "we are interested in and support organizations of Arab workers led by [Arabs] themselves. Moreover, we are interested in unifying the [Arab labor] organizations in order to create a united Arab workers movement. The PLL creates divisions, it divides rather than unites."[78]

The PLL's base at Wagner disintegrated during the course of 1944. Wagner's management fired a number of workers identified with the PLL and harassed others, while the PAWS launched an effort to drive the PLL out, aided by denunciations in the Arab press of Wagner workers who had joined the PLL as lackeys of the Zionists. The PLL was unable to protect its supporters at the factory and by the fall of 1944 the last of its members there had severed all public connection with it. What had seemed a year earlier like a very promising beginning, a potential breakthrough to establishing a solid base in the Arab working class of Jaffa, had failed completely.[79]

During the same period pressure from the PAWS also drove the municipal workers whom the PLL had first organized to quit, and deterred other Jaffa workers from joining. That pressure, and the PAWS' struggle for the Wagner workers, were components of a more or less concerted and ultimately quite effective counteroffensive which the PAWS launched against the PLL in the spring of 1944. The high point of that campaign came when PAWS members packed the meeting organized by the PLL to celebrate both May Day 1944 and the opening of its club in the al-Manshiyya neighborhood of Jaffa. By shouting, clapping hands, and asking incessant questions of the Histadrut officials on the podium, the PAWS members succeeded in breaking up the meeting and, more importantly, in intimidating PLL members and potential recruits, who thereafter virtually ceased to visit the club and distanced themselves from the PLL. Security concerns soon compelled the PLL to move its club from al-Manshiyya to a nearby Jewish neighborhood within Tel Aviv, and by the end of 1944 the PLL hardly existed in Jaffa.[80]

We get some idea of the sentiments of the Arab workers who ruined the PLL's 1944 May Day celebration from a leaflet entitled "From Arab Workers to the Jewish Workers," signed by five Arab workers against whom the Histadrut had brought charges of disturbing the peace in connection with its abortive meeting. What is most striking about the leaflet is that it is in Hebrew, demonstrating a concern to expose Jewish workers to a version of what happened on the evening of April 30, 1944 that differed from the version propagated by the Histadrut. The leaflet rejected the Histadrut's allegations that those who had disrupted its meeting were agents of the police or of Stilo 'Awwad, manager of the Wagner factory, with whom the PLL was then engaged in a bitter struggle. The signatories insisted they were rank and file workers who "wanted to know why the Histadrut comes to them on holidays with parties and choirs, and the rest of the year—with pickets. They wanted to know why they were driven from their jobs and their bread stolen from them."

> Brother [Jewish] workers! Imagine to yourselves what *you* would say if this happened to you, if they expelled you from your job only because you were Jewish, if you saw your families hungry and your children crying for bread. Imagine to yourselves what *you* would say if these same people who yesterday expelled you from your job came to you today talking about May Day, even while declaring that tomorrow too they will put you out of work, if they can manage it. Right now, in these very days, the Histadrut has organized pickets at the [Akiva?] factory in Rishon Letziyon to drive the four Arab workers employed there from their jobs.

The leaflet went on to cite a recent article by Abba Hushi in which the Histadrut boss in Haifa had talked of stepping up the "conquest of labor" at the railroads, oil installations, and port there as a way of alleviating Jewish unemployment.[81]

It is not clear why the Histadrut chose to bring charges against these five Arab workers in particular, though one may speculate that they were known and identifiable as local PAWS activists. It is however interesting to note that although the leaflet strongly attacked the Histadrut leadership (as well as the leadership of the Yishuv, in the person of Ben-Gurion) both for pursuing Hebrew labor and demanding Jewish statehood in all of Palestine, it never condemned (or even mentioned) Zionism *per se* and stressed Arab-Jewish working-class solidarity. This may have been merely a tactical maneuver on the part of local NLL activists, but it may also have reflected an interest among leftist Arab trade unionists in seeking the support of Jewish workers on moral grounds ("Imagine to yourselves what *you* would say if this happened to you. . . .") as well as in terms of common economic interest. A Jewish witness to the Jaffa incident noted that the disrupters were quite polite toward the Jews present; their anger was directed toward the Arab PLL members, whom they regarded as traitors and abused verbally (and perhaps physically as well).[82] For these Arab leftists, the Jewish working class (and even the Histadrut) could still be envisioned as a potential ally, as long as it gave up its vision of Jewish sovereignty, its exclusionary practices, and its claim to represent and speak for Arab workers.

The PLL's fortunes in Jerusalem paralleled its fortunes in Jaffa: after some initial successes it underwent a sharp decline from which it would never really recover. Early in 1944 the PLL succeeded in recruiting more than a hundred Palestinian Arab, Egyptian, and Sudanese workers employed at the prestigious King David Hotel, and after Labor Department mediation these workers eventually secured a decent contract. However, the PLL's success prompted the PAWS to launch a campaign to induce the Arab workers at the hotel and elsewhere to sever their connection with the Histadrut. As in Jaffa, the Jerusalem PAWS branch (now led by communists) disrupted the PLL's 1944 May Day celebration, while its leaflets denounced the "hirelings of Zionism" and attacked the Histadrut for having induced the recent annual conference of the British Labor Party to adopt a resolution supporting Jewish statehood in Palestine and the "transfer" of Palestine's Arab population to neighboring Arab lands. The Arab press joined in with articles denouncing the PLL and demanding that the Arab hotel workers fulfill their obligations to the nation. The PLL managed to retain the loyalty of most of its members at the King David

Hotel. But in July 1946 the hotel (much of which had been taken over by the British civil and military authorities for office space) was closed down after a bomb planted by the right-wing Zionist military organization Irgun Tzva'i Le'umi ("National Military Organization," often referred to by its acronym ETZEL), destroyed an entire wing, killing almost a hundred people, among them Arab and Jewish civilians. Thanks to the contract which the PLL had negotiated, the hotel employees at least received some compensation when their jobs disappeared.[83]

Another struggle involving hotel workers in Jerusalem during this period more dramatically underscored the PLL's very limited prospects for establishing a cohesive and stable base among Arab workers. In September 1944 several dozen Arab men and women employed at the American Colony hotel approached the PLL for help. Originally founded in the late nineteenth century by an American Christian sect whose members came to settle in the Holy Land, the American Colony's guests now included high government officials and distinguished foreign visitors. Its management had acquired a well-deserved reputation for treating its Arab employees, many of whom came from nearby villages, very poorly. When in October management fired several employees identified as troublemakers, the workers (now PLL members) went on strike, whereupon they were summarily expelled from their lodgings at the Colony. The conflict quickly took on political dimensions, perhaps inevitably so given the PAWS' frustration at its failure to block the PLL at the King David Hotel and the rising tensions among Arabs and Jews in Palestine as the Zionist movement stepped up its drive for increased Jewish immigration and the Arab nationalist movement began to revive. The PAWS and the Arab press denounced the strike as a Zionist plot and made strenuous efforts to get the workers to abandon it. When those efforts failed, the PAWS went so far as to provide the Colony with replacements for the striking PLL members. Histadrut efforts to secure Labor Department intervention were unsuccessful, dooming the strike to failure. The Histadrut found alternative employment for some of the American Colony's workers, while others returned to their jobs on management's terms.[84]

As with the strike at Wagner in Jaffa, the defeat of the American Colony strike in Jerusalem marked the virtual end of the local PLL branch's efforts to organize Arab workers employed by non-Jews. In the years that followed the PLL in Jerusalem led a successful strike by Arab villagers from Qalunya employed at the Steinberg tile factory and represented Arab workers employed at Jewish bakeries, but these were small-scale and rather marginal efforts. The PLL's contacts with other groups of Arab workers who approached it for assistance in this period failed to develop into anything concrete. In private, Arab Department officials admitted that the disruption of their 1944 May Day celebrations in Jaffa and Jerusalem had left the PLL virtually paralyzed. Though they understood that these incidents (and a similar but less successful attempt at disruption in Haifa) were part of a campaign by the left wing of the Arab labor movement to discredit and isolate the PLL, they were unable to respond effectively. The PLL's defeats at Wagner and the American Colony confirmed that it had little prospect of overcoming its weakness and marginality, which were in striking contrast to the rapid growth which the vigorous (if fractious) Arab workers' movement was experiencing in this period.[85]

WORKER ACTIVISM AND THE ARAB LABOR MOVEMENT

Both the Arab and Jewish working classes in Palestine manifested considerable dynamism and militancy in the final two years of the war. The wage increases which substantial numbers of workers had won during 1943 did not offset rapidly rising prices for very long, ensuring that unrest would continue. This was manifested most dramatically at the Haifa railway workshops, where discontent again reached the boiling point early in 1944. A government decision to reduce the COLA produced widespread resentment, which for the Jewish workers was only made worse by the Histadrut's apparent acquiescence in the decision. Spurred on by rank and file demands for action, the Haifa branch committee of the IU—composed of two MAPAI members, two members of Hashomer Hatza'ir, and one person identified with the now entirely Jewish Palestine Communist Party, which had the support of some thirty Jewish workshop workers— approached the AURW leadership to discuss joint action. Perhaps because of the tense relations between the PAWS and the Histadrut, the Arab unionists were ambivalent about cooperation, at least until an accidental spark touched off an unanticipated explosion.

On Wednesday, February 2, 1944, an Arab worker at the workshops was seriously injured in an industrial accident. Because there was no physician stationed at the workshops and the ambulance was under repair, a physician had to be fetched from the nearby Vulcan rubber factory, owned by the Histadrut. When he arrived he was unable to suture the worker's head wound because the necessary supplies were not available. The injured man was eventually transported to a hospital, but the workers were outraged by management's failure to make adequate provision for emergency medical care. Efrayyim Krisher of Hashomer Hatza'ir and the senior MAPAI leader in the workshops immediately called for a demonstration, and within a quarter of an hour all 1,400 workers—some 200 of them Jews—had downed tools and gathered outside the main offices. They were soon joined by another 170 men in the locomotive running sheds nearby. A strike committee of three Arabs and two Jews was chosen which presented management with a list of long-standing demands, including preservation of the COLA, an increase in the base wage, compensation for workplace accidents, the extension of retirement benefits to all workers, and the permanent stationing of a physician at the workshops.

General Manager Kirby refused to negotiate until after the workers had returned to their jobs. At the end of the day the workers went home, but they returned *en masse* the next day and refused to leave the workshops until their demands were met. The workers' spirits were extremely high and Jewish-Arab solidarity was very much in evidence. The workers spent the night in the workshops compound, talking and singing around campfires. When the PAWS sent in food, the Arab workers shared it with their Jewish comrades; and when the Haifa Workers' Council belatedly sent in supplies, the Jewish workers also shared them. The food from the Jewish side arrived only after a long delay because the Histadrut leadership in Haifa, and especially Abba Hushi, were strongly opposed to the strike and wanted it ended as quickly as possible. As a rule Hushi resented, and sought to stifle, any workers' initiative from below in what he regarded as "his" city. More importantly, together with IU national secretary Yehezkel Abramov and the Histadrut leadership in Tel Aviv, Hushi feared that the strike would strengthen the AURW and the PAWS. As Abramov saw it, the Arab railwaymen would learn to organize and use the strike weapon effectively, and if another revolt broke out one day they would probably join in, unlike 1936.

Abramov did his best to end the strike. In this task he was aided by Sami Taha, the secretary of the PAWS, who as head of the more conservative wing of the Palestinian Arab trade union movement was not interested in a long, militant, and politically risky strike at a government enterprise in wartime. Under heavy pressure, the Jewish union leaders in Haifa caved in and agreed to call for an end to the strike, even though Kirby had conceded virtually nothing. The Arab unionists were more resolute, but faced with management's intransigence and pressure from Sami Taha they too eventually gave in. It took considerable effort to weaken the workers' determination to go on: at several mass meetings the rank and file expressed their readiness to hold out indefinitely. But eventually the leadership succeeded, and on Friday night, after three days on strike and two days of occupying the workshops, the workers left and went home. The next morning they reported for work as usual, having won only a minor concession over the retirement fund and a promise that the Labor Department would examine their grievances.[86]

Despite their failure to win anything substantial, the Haifa workshop workers emerged from the strike with a stronger sense of their own power and of the value of Arab-Jewish unity. This did not deter the IU leadership from looking for ways to undermine the AURW and organize Arab workers on its own,[87] but the AURW's growing strength and effectiveness frustrated its hopes, as did continued rank and file discontent manifested in a number of brief strikes during 1945. In March, for example, the Haifa workshops were shut down for an hour and a half by a protest strike which forced management to disburse wages earlier than usual, because of the upcoming Muslim and Jewish holidays. The following month some 150 Arab and Jewish postal workers in the Jaffa–Tel Aviv region, now acquiring a reputation for militancy, went on strike briefly. During the summer of 1945 the postal workers organized a national conference and elected an executive committee consisting of three Arabs and three Jews. These developments were viewed with some ambivalence by both the Histadrut and the PAWS. But the left wing of the Palestinian Arab labor movement, led by the quasi-communist National Liberation League, welcomed them. The NLL's newspaper *al-Ittihad* proclaimed that "the cooperation between the Arab and Jewish telegraph and postal workers is clear proof of the possibility of joint action in every workplace," provided the workers steered clear of interference by both Zionism and Arab reaction.[88] As we will see in Chapter 8, in the final three years of British rule in Palestine the railway and postal workers would play a leading role in mobilizing other Arab and Jewish workers across communal boundaries in defense of their common economic interests.

The rank and file militancy which characterized groups like the railway and postal workers gave impetus to efforts by Arab leftists to assume the leadership of the organized Arab working class. The breakup of the Palestine Communist Party in the middle of 1943 and the emergence early in 1944 of the NLL opened the way for a realignment of forces within the Arab labor movement in Palestine. It now became possible to envision the creation of a new NLL-led labor federation which would encompass both the Haifa-based FATULS and the PAWS branches in Jaffa, Jerusalem, and elsewhere which were under communist leadership.

At the same time, tensions between the communists operating within the PAWS and the organization's Haifa-based central leadership had been growing. The leftists increasingly resented both Sami Taha's authoritarianism and his conservatism. One British trade unionist who visited Palestine in the middle of 1945 described Taha's leadership style in these terms:

> The PAWS was founded in 1925 and have done quite a considerable amount of genuine trade union work. It has certainly managed to survive some most difficult political years and keep the flag flying.
>
> But its secretary, one Sami Taha, a snake of the first water, ran the show in a most dictatorial fashion, e.g. the organisation is on a territorial rather than a Trade basis: each branch elects an executive committee: each E.C. sends a representative to a "Supreme Workers Council" in Haifa: but the Executive Committee of the whole Society is another name for the Executive Committee of the Haifa Branch (i.e. Sami Taha) and this had not been elected for ten years. No democracy, comrade.

This observer noted, however, that though "Sami may be rather a rat . . . I do not believe he is wholly a rat." [89]

In the summer of 1944 the Nazareth branch of the PAWS, led by the communist Fu'ad Nassar, seceded from the organization and with the FATULS formed a "Supreme Arab Workers' Council," which, however, existed only on paper. But the majority of the communists within the PAWS, still anxious to preserve labor unity and hopeful that they could eventually gain control of the organization, declined to follow Nazareth's example. So although by the end of 1944 leftists led several of the most important urban branches in the PAWS, Sami Taha was able to retain control of the nominally united organization through his domination of the Haifa branch and of most of the branches in the smaller towns and large villages. But the leftists' determination to remain within the PAWS was increasingly eroded by Sami Taha's refusal to share power and his high-handed leadership. They were particularly angered when Taha succeeded in having his longtime associate Hanna 'Asfur, the Haifa lawyer and PAWS counsel, designated as the organization's official delegate to the international trade union conference scheduled to convene in London in February 1945 in order to lay the foundations of a new, unified postwar world trade union movement. Bulus Farah, preeminent leader of the FATULS in Haifa, who along with his fellow NLL members regarded 'Asfur as a reactionary and a bourgeois, was able to attend only as an observer, the same lowly status accorded George Nassar as representative of the PLL.[90]

The choice of a conservative nonworker like 'Asfur, together with the fact that the London conference had adopted a rather pro-Zionist resolution on Palestine, gave considerable ammunition to the left wing of the

PAWS in its campaign against Sami Taha and his allies. It certainly strengthened the leftists' resolve (trumpeted in the pages of *al-Ittihad*, which now spoke for the NLL, the FATULS, and the PAWS left) that the Palestinian Arab delegates to the upcoming congress at which the World Federation of Trade Unions (WFTU) was to be formally established, scheduled to convene in Paris at the end of August 1945, should be chosen democratically and should actually be workers. In the 1920s and 1930s, the kind of high-handed leadership style which Sami Taha displayed and the imposition from above of a "notable" like Hanna 'Asfur as representative of the workers had been common features of the Arab labor movement. Such practices had made it easier for the Histadrut to depict Arab unionists and unions as mere tools of scheming and self-interested nationalist effendis. By the mid-1940s, however, such things were no longer acceptable to many rank and file Arab workers and to trade union activists, especially those influenced by the left. Those who led the NLL were certainly Stalinists in terms of ideology and organizational style, but in the concrete circumstances in which they operated they constituted the more democratic, militant, and worker-oriented camp within the Palestinian Arab labor movement, in increasingly sharp contrast to the conservative, notable-linked, and authoritarian old guard which ran the PAWS in Haifa.

It was the struggle over the composition of the Palestinian Arab delegation to the Paris WFTU congress which precipitated the final split between left and right in the PAWS. After an August 1945 meeting in Nablus at which Sami Taha and Hanna 'Asfur had themselves designated the PAWS' delegates to Paris, the Jaffa, Jerusalem, and Gaza branches, along with eight others, mainly in southern and central Palestine, seceded and formed the Arab Workers' Congress (AWC), into which the FATULS soon merged itself. This new trade union federation, aligned with the NLL, chose Bulus Farah and Mukhlis al-'Amr (a leader of the PAWS branch in Jerusalem) as its delegates to Paris. There they succeeded in blocking the adoption of another pro-Zionist resolution and helped secure the election of Mustafa al-'Aris, a Lebanese communist, as Middle East representative on the executive of the newly created WFTU, defeating the candidacy of a Histadrut official. Sami Taha and Hanna 'Asfur enjoyed only observer status at the Paris congress.[91]

The struggles and realignments within the Arab labor movement had echoes even within the PLL, where the pro-Zionist resolution on Palestine adopted at the February 1945 London conference aroused discontent among the few Arab activists the organization possessed. Toward the end of the war some of those activists, constantly accused by Arab trade unionists of being Zionist agents, mere window dressing for an entirely Jewish-run organization, had begun to demand a greater role in the running of the PLL. A committee of branch representatives was eventually formed, but it never amounted to much and effective control remained firmly in the hands of the Jewish branch secretaries and the Arab Department's entirely Jewish staff. That staff had always insisted that the PLL was an apolitical organization concerned only with enhancing its members' economic, social, and cultural well-being. Resolutely ignoring the fact that the PLL was a project of, and entirely controlled by, the Zionist Histadrut, they contrasted the purported disinterestedness of the PLL's mission with what they denigrated as the explicitly political (i.e., Arab nationalist and anti-Zionist) stance of the Arab labor organizations. At the same time, MAPAI loyalists consistently rejected demands by partisans of Po'alei Tziyon Smol and Hashomer Hatza'ir that the PLL adopt a more explicitly political stance, whether the former's now rather shopworn orthodox Borokhovism or the latter's distinct blend of socialism and Zionism. These debates involved only Jews, however: rarely had Arabs within the PLL challenged their Jewish leaders, and then generally only over the immediate question of Hebrew labor rather than the broader issue of the Zionist vision of a Jewish state in some or all of Palestine.

In the increasingly tense and politicized atmosphere that prevailed in Palestine by 1945, however, such docility and deference were no longer viable. The PLL's handful of Arab activists was now more than ever on the defensive, under unrelenting pressure from Arab unionists in the PAWS and the FATULS (and later the AWC) who rarely missed an opportunity to denounce them as lackeys of the Zionists. Arabs openly identified with the PLL were no longer willing or able to remain silent when a representative of their supposedly apolitical organization took a pro-Zionist stance in a public forum. So it was that in September 1945 Muhammad al-Halabi, the Arab secretary of the PLL branch in Haifa, and three of his colleagues wrote a letter to the Chief Secretary of the government of Palestine, with copies to various international trade union organizations, dissociating themselves from the pro-Zionist stance which George Nassar had adopted in the name of the PLL at the international trade union conference in London the previous February. Probably moved to action by discussion of the Paris WFTU congress in *al-Ittihad*, which devoted considerable attention to the debate over a resolution on Palestine, they said that they had read in the newspapers that the Histadrut delegate in London had called for a Jewish state in Palestine, with the endorsement of the PLL—that is, George Nassar. Cleverly using their Jewish leaders' insistence on the apolitical character of the PLL against them and asserting the organization's autonomy from the Histadrut, they declared that "as a matter of fact the Palestine Labour League do not agree that Palestine should become a Jewish National Home, and they work on the basis of raising the Labour standard and not on the basis of exploiting their name by others from a Political point of view." They went on to "protest on [sic] the trick done by the Arab Labour section in the Histadruth to send the above mentioned [George Nassar and his colleague Muhammad al-Hajj] in the name of the Palestine Labour League" and called on the government to prevent them from traveling to Paris.[92]

The letter seems to have cost Muhammad al-Halabi his job as secretary of the PLL's Haifa branch: he was dismissed shortly thereafter, accused by the Arab Department of financial irregularities, although that charge may have been raised to deflect political embarrassment over his firing. By November al-Halabi had publicly proclaimed his allegiance to the PAWS. His protest and dismissal signaled the growing unviability of the kind of relationship between the Histadrut and the PLL that had prevailed since the latter's creation in the early 1930s. Times had changed, and the political naiveté which had allowed at least some Palestinian Arabs to take at face value the Histadrut's efforts to reach out to Arab workers was becoming increasingly rare.

The anonymous Arab teacher who wrote to *Haqiqat al-Amr* around this time to say that he read the newspaper regularly and enjoyed its style is another case in point. His letter went on to say that he had recently visited a kibbutz, where a conversation he had had with some Jewish children had left him with the impression that they believed that in the end the Arabs would be expelled from Palestine to make room for Jews.[93] By the last year of the war it was clear that the decisive struggle over Palestine's fate was fast approaching, and the always shaky ground on which the Histadrut's Arab Department had sought to build was quickly disappearing. In the postwar period it would disappear altogether, though as the next chapter will explore this actually enhanced rather than diminished the possibility of cooperation between Arab and Jewish workers—at least until the political crisis engulfing Palestine deepened to the point where cooperation of any kind became all but impossible.

8 Labor Activism and Politics, 1945–1948

The political, economic, and social changes which the war years had brought to Palestine set the stage for a renewal of the Zionist-Palestinian confrontation. The annihilation of most of Europe's Jews strengthened the resolve of the Zionist movement, backed by the great majority of the Yishuv, not only to force the British to open Palestine to Jewish immigration but also to seek Jewish statehood by any means necessary. Even before the war in Europe ended, Zionist opposition to British policy had begun to take stronger and sometimes even violent forms, eventually developing into an insurgency which the British proved unable to suppress. The Zionist campaign helped stimulate the revival of the Arab nationalist movement. Though that movement, and the Arab community in which it was rooted, had not fully recovered from the defeat of the 1936–39 revolt, they were more determined than ever not merely to stop Jewish immigration and block the Zionist project but also to achieve Palestine's independence as an undivided Arab state. It was therefore clear that once the war in Europe was over, the final and decisive phase of the long struggle for Palestine would commence.

Curiously, in one of the many ironies with which the modern history of Palestine is replete, the same years (1945–47) that witnessed rising tensions between Arabs and Jews in Palestine, tensions which would culminate in bloody civil and then interstate war, the creation of the State of Israel, and the transformation of half of Palestine's Arab population into refugees, also witnessed an unprecedented level of joint struggle among Arab and Jewish workers in pursuit of common economic goals, along with strenuous (if ultimately futile) efforts by various Arab and Jewish political forces to seek a peaceful resolution of the deepening political crisis. In retrospect it seems highly unlikely that events could have taken a different course. But for Arabs and Jews in the Palestine of those years there could be no way of knowing precisely what the future would bring; and not a few individuals and groups sought to actively shape that future by participating in the political and socioeconomic struggles of the day.

PERSPECTIVES ON COOPERATION

Unlike the official leadership of the Arab nationalist movement in Palestine, which was still dominated by Amin al-Husayni, his relatives, and his allies, and which often failed to distinguish between Zionism and the Yishuv, if not all Jews in general, the National Liberation League and its new labor front the Arab Workers' Congress continued to insist on preserving the communists' long-standing ideological distinction between Zionism and the Jewish masses in Palestine. A January 1945 article published in *al-Ittihad* declared that the representatives of Palestine's Arab workers at the international trade union conference soon to convene in London had to make clear to world public opinion that

> we distinguish between the Zionist movement as an exploitative movement and the Jews, and the Jewish workers specifically, as a minority [in Palestine]. In calling for an independent national regime, the Arab workers seek to liberate the broad masses of the people, Arab and Jewish, from the noose of exploitation and Zionism, and they declare that an independent national regime will ensure all just national rights to the Jews and the other minorities settled in Palestine.

By adopting what it termed a racist (i.e., anti-Jewish) stance and failing to make clear the Palestinian Arab national movement's essentially liberatory and democratic goals and character, another article in *al-Ittihad* charged, the reactionaries who had led that movement in the past had made it easier for the Zionist movement to maintain its control over the Jewish masses in Palestine, by frightening them with the specter of Arab rule and Arab violence.[1] Though there were disagreements within the NLL/AWC leadership over this question and some of the organizations' statements struck a more Arab nationalist tone, they generally insisted not only that the Jewish masses could be won away from their allegiance to Zionism provided the Arab national movement adopted a clear democratic and antiracist stance and offered the Jews a secure place in the future independent Arab Palestine, but also that Arab-Jewish cooperation was key to achieving the independence of an undivided Palestine.

The Arab left's insistence on both the possibility and the necessity of Arab-Jewish solidarity and cooperation, especially among workers, and its criticism of the strategic and tactical errors of the Arab nationalist leadership and its unrepresentative and undemocratic character, made it the target of attack by conservative Arab nationalists. In November 1945 the League of Arab States oversaw the reconstitution of the Arab Higher Committee, originally created in response to the outbreak of the Arab revolt in 1936 but defunct since the revolt's defeat. Early in 1946 Jamal al-Husayni returned from exile to assume its leadership, though its presidency was left vacant for his cousin, the exiled Amin al-Husayni. Determined to reassert the AHC's hegemony within the Arab community, Jamal al-Husayni publicly denounced the AWC for allegedly seeking unity with Ben-Gurion and the Jews. In his reply, NLL/AWC leader Fu'ad Nassar rejected al-Husayni's criticisms as misinformed and defended his movement's program. Reiterating the NLL's belief that it was possible to win the Jewish masses in Palestine away from Zionism, Nassar insisted that this struggle must be an essential component of the Arab national movement's overall strategy.[2]

The NLL's insistence on distinguishing between Zionism and the Yishuv was of little or no interest to the vast majority of Jews in Palestine, very few of whom would have been willing to live under any form of Arab majority rule, whatever rights they might have been promised as an officially recognized minority. Though many, perhaps most, of the Jews in Palestine had come there not so much because of Zionist conviction as because of their need to escape discrimination or persecution in their countries of origin, what they increasingly wanted, and what the Zionist movement had by 1945 launched an all-out struggle to achieve, was unrestricted Jewish immigration (to bring about a Jewish majority) and a fully sovereign Jewish state in as much of Palestine as possible. There were, however, significant forces in the Yishuv which until late in 1947 still argued that the creation of a sovereign Jewish state in Palestine was unattainable in the face of Arab opposition, would violate Arab rights in the country, or both. The most important of these were Hashomer Hatza'ir and its urban sister party, the Socialist League, which in 1946 merged into the Hashomer Hatza'ir Workers' Party.[3] As I have already discussed, Hashomer Hatza'ir (along with some liberal Zionists) rejected the official Zionist demand for Jewish statehood in part or all of Palestine and instead proposed the establishment in an undivided Palestine of a binational state in which Arabs and Jews would have political parity regardless of their numbers. At the same time, Hashomer Hatza'ir insisted that Jewish immigration must be unrestricted, or at least not so restricted as to prevent the eventual attainment of a Jewish majority. But the tide of events, and of Jewish sentiment in Palestine and elsewhere, was running against them and would render the binationalist position increasingly irrelevant. Moreover, even those forces in the Yishuv most critical of the Zionist movement's increasingly single-minded drive for statehood rejected the NLL's vision of an independent Arab Palestine in which Jews would be at best an officially recognized national minority.

Yet the NLL/AWC leadership's ideological commitment to Arab-Jewish coexistence, and especially worker solidarity, did contribute to better relations between Arab and Jewish labor organizations in Palestine. An August 1945 article in the English-language edition of *al-Ittihad*, published (somewhat sporadically) in an effort to influence public opinion within and outside Palestine, hailed the Jewish workers

> who showed willingness to coordinate their activities with organised Arab labour in spite of the taboo being observed by Histadruth [*sic*]. . . . The conditions have always existed for such co-operation and their success now depends on the policy of the Histadruth who have always wanted to promote co-operation only in so far as it furthered the political chauvinist policy of Zionism. Withall, the future is in the hands of the workers themselves who will consciously strive to build their co-operation in a manner which would bring democracy, freedom and peace to Palestine.[4]

Though less consistently, and on pragmatic rather than ideological grounds, the PAWS, which not only survived the secession of its left-led branches but experienced significant growth in the period that followed, would also cooperate with the Histadrut in certain arenas, as long as the latter did not claim to represent Arab workers and treated the PAWS as an equal.

Given Arab interest in cooperation, a shift in the Histadrut's stance was necessary to open the way to a more fruitful relationship between the Arab and Jewish labor movements. The virtually total paralysis into which the PLL had fallen by 1945 had conclusively demonstrated the futility of the Histadrut's efforts to undermine the Arab unions by organizing Arab workers under its own auspices. This led the Histadrut leadership, if grudgingly and with some lapses, to abandon that project and recognize that if it wished to protect or improve the lot of Jews employed in mixed workplaces, there was no alternative to cooperation with the Arab unions. Abba Hushi seems to have been among the prime movers behind the Histadrut's new orientation. For many months he had kept his distance from the Histadrut's Arab Department, whose staff he held in low regard, but as the war ended he resumed an active role in setting the Histadrut's policy in this arena. As the organization's top official in Palestine's main industrial center, Hushi was often more in touch with realities on the ground (and especially in the Arab community) than were many of his colleagues at Histadrut headquarters in Tel Aviv. He seems to have recognized the need to seek better relations with the Arab labor movement even if that required effectively abandoning the PLL.

In August 1945 Hushi sent an unprecedentedly polite, even comradely, letter to Sami Taha proposing cooperation in the postwar era then dawning. Taha replied that while he supported Arab-Jewish workers' cooperation in principle, the Jewish labor movement's allegiance to Zionism, manifested above all in its persistent campaign for Hebrew labor, made joint work impossible at present.[5] Given his situation at that time, with his leadership under severe challenge and his organization undergoing a bitter split, Taha was apparently reluctant to assume a more compromising stance. Sami Taha's willingness to cooperate openly with the Histadrut was probably also inhibited by the new links he was developing with the leadership of the Palestinian nationalist movement. When Jamal al-Husayni reorganized the AHC in April 1946, he appointed Sami Taha a member. Within a few months another reshuffling terminated Taha's AHC membership, but he retained close ties to the Husayni-dominated nationalist leadership through the first half of 1947. In that period he served on an AHC subcommittee charged with drafting a constitution and an election law for the future independent Arab Palestine, and he was also appointed to the AHC delegation at the abortive negotiations on Palestine held in London in 1947.[6]

The roles which the PAWS leader was called upon to assume in the nationalist leadership did not involve any real decision-making power, but they did have symbolic value. They signaled heightened public awareness of the growing social weight and potential political significance of the organized Arab working class in Palestine, as well as the leadership's desire to bring this social force more effectively and directly under its control. Moreover, by enhancing Taha's stature the Arab Higher Committee sought to weaken and isolate the AWC and the NLL, whose criticisms of the nationalist leadership's conservatism, authoritarianism, and ineffectuality were as little appreciated as their advocacy of democracy, social reform, and solidarity between Arab and Jewish workers. Taha's association with the leadership bolstered his claim to be Palestine's preeminent Arab labor leader, helping him and the PAWS recover from the traumatic schism of the left-led branches and the formation of the AWC.

These circumstances, and the deepening political crisis that began to engulf Palestine during 1946, would render cooperation between the

PAWS and the Histadrut more difficult. Nonetheless the PAWS, and the new AWC as well, would frequently demonstrate a willingness to cooperate with the Histadrut, though the interactions among the three organizations were never entirely free of conflict and suspicion. In this period three sectors of prime economic and political importance constituted the main arenas of interaction between Arab and Jewish workers: the petroleum sector, including the pipeline installations and refinery in Haifa but also facilities operated by transnational oil companies elsewhere in Palestine; government service, both white-collar and blue-collar and including the railway workers; and the British military bases.

THE PETROLEUM SECTOR, 1943–48

As I discussed in Chapter 5, a pipeline bringing crude petroleum from the oilfields of northern Iraq (exploited largely by British companies) through British-controlled Transjordan to the port of Haifa had been completed in 1934. Soon thereafter British government officials and oil company executives began discussing the construction of a refinery at Haifa, which would allow processed Iraqi crude to be used to refuel British warships in the eastern Mediterranean (for which Haifa had become a base, especially after the completion of the deepwater harbor in 1933) and enhance the position of British oil companies in the world market. Construction of the Haifa refinery, which was owned and operated by Consolidated Refineries, Limited (CRL), a subsidiary of what was then known as the Anglo-Iranian Oil Company and later became British Petroleum, began late in 1938, at a site about seven kilometers north of the center of Haifa, on the Haifa-Acre highway, not far from the railway workshops. Production of refined petroleum products began in 1940, though it was another year before the refinery reached its planned capacity of two million tons. By 1944 the refinery's capacity had been expanded to handle some four million tons of crude petroleum a year.

By the middle of 1943 the Haifa refinery employed about a thousand workers, making it one of Haifa's (and Palestine's) largest workplaces. The PAWS had a strong base among the Arab refinery workers, though its rival the communist-led FATULS also had substantial support there; only about thirty of the Arab refinery workers belonged to the PLL. Though Jews made up only about one-third of the refinery workforce, they held a much higher proportion of the skilled and clerical jobs; but only half of the Jewish refinery workers were Histadrut members, a rather low rate by the standards of the Jewish labor movement in Palestine. Like the workforce at the British military bases, the refinery workers included many new recruits to industrial wage labor. The refinery, and the petroleum sector more broadly, was one of the most capital-intensive sectors of the Palestinian economy, and its workers among the most classically proletarian. As time passed, the refinery workers and others employed by the transnational petroleum companies—especially the Arabs among them—acquired a reputation for militancy and for resistance to control by management as well as by labor leaders who failed to respect their autonomy and meet their needs.

In keeping with the Histadrut's general policy in 1942–43, the Haifa Workers' Council initially sought to convince CRL management to recognize it as the exclusive representative of all the refinery workers, Jewish and Arab. When that bid failed, the Histadrut was compelled to enter talks with the PAWS and the FATULS about the establishment of a joint committee representing all the refinery workers. Those talks foundered over the question of representation, with the Histadrut demanding Jewish-Arab parity and the Arab unions insisting that the committee's membership reflect the ethnic composition of the refinery workforce. More than ever before, this issue had come to be seen as essentially political, because the Arab unions believed that acceptance of Arab-Jewish parity implied tacit recognition of the Zionist claim to equal Jewish rights in Palestine. In the spring of 1943 the Histadrut on its own formally declared a labor dispute at the refinery, in the hope of winning improvements in the wages and working conditions of its members there, and especially of securing for them a cost of living allowance to offset skyrocketing inflation. With Labor Department mediation, the Histadrut won extension of the COLA to cover the refinery workers as well as recognition as representative of the Jewish workers, though various other issues were left unresolved pending direct negotiations between the Histadrut and company management.[7]

Continued inflation as well as the looming threat of layoffs as the war came to an end eventually created a basis for Arab-Jewish cooperation at the Haifa refinery. During the fall of 1945 the PAWS and the Histadrut negotiated jointly with CRL management and won many of the demands put forward by the refinery workers, who now numbered 1,800 and whose position was strengthened by their unprecedented unity.[8] Neither the refinery workers nor those employed by the various transnational oil companies operating in Palestine—most prominent among them the Iraq Petroleum Company, Socony Vacuum, and Shell—joined the general strike launched by government employees in April 1946; I discuss the reasons for this later in this chapter. Nonetheless, the Arab and Jewish oil workers were strongly affected by the militancy and steadfastness of the government employees, as were workers throughout Palestine, and soon after the general strike rank and file pressure compelled the leaders of the unions to which many of the oil workers belonged to become much more aggressive in seeking immediate satisfaction of the demands for higher wages and improved working conditions which they had been advancing in fruitless negotiations for some months.

However, the oil workers' newfound militancy was not accompanied by the kind of cooperation that had characterized relations between the PAWS and the Histadrut at the Haifa refinery the previous fall; indeed, an atmosphere of outright hostility now prevailed between the two organizations. The Histadrut was increasingly mindful of the economic and political importance of the transnational oil companies and wanted to strengthen its influence over their workforce by bolstering Jewish employment but also, it seemed, by once again trying to represent Arab workers. This aroused Sami Taha's suspicions and resentment, especially since he had recently come under fire from the Arab nationalist leadership and press for having cooperated with the Histadrut in the government workers' general strike. It was a politically sensitive moment as well: the Arab nationalist and Zionist movements as well as the British government were awaiting the report of the Anglo-American Committee of Inquiry, which had been established (following heavy pressure on Britain from the Truman administration) in response to Zionist demands that Palestine be opened up to Jewish immigrants, especially survivors of the Holocaust still living in displaced persons' camps in Europe.

As a result, the PAWS refused to join a countrywide strike of Socony Vacuum employees which was launched jointly by the Histadrut and the AWC in late April 1946. The Histadrut's clerical workers' union had organized many of the Jewish employees at Socony Vacuum and the other oil companies, and also had close (if covert) ties with some of the Arab clerical and other workers in this sector. Sami Taha claimed that the Histadrut had called the strike unilaterally at a time when he was still conducting negotiations with management; the Histadrut in turn denounced the PAWS as an agent of the oil companies and tried, in de facto alliance with the AWC, to shut the PAWS out of contract negotiations. Most of Socony Vacuum's Arab workers seem to have supported the strike, except in Haifa, where the PAWS was strongest and succeeded in persuading many workers to stay at their jobs. The strike lasted twelve days and resulted in some gains for the workers. The Histadrut and the AWC sought to keep

the PAWS from being a party to the new contract, but company management invited the PAWS to sign it as well, which made it possible for Sami
Taha to claim that it had been the negotiations he had conducted, rather
than the strike, which had yielded results. It was nonetheless clear that
Sami Taha had suffered a humiliating defeat, and this left a legacy of
bitterness which would for a time poison relations between the PAWS
and the Histadrut in this sector.[9]

In the aftermath of the April 1946 wave of worker militancy and the
deterioration of its relations with the PAWS, the Histadrut once again
considered trying to bypass the Arab unions and establish direct links
with Arab workers, especially clerical employees in what it called the "international sector." It was the Histadrut's links with Arab white-collar
workers at Socony Vacuum which had made possible an effective strike at
that firm in the face of the PAWS' opposition. The Haifa Workers' Council and those Histadrut officials most involved with the affairs of workers
in the state and transnational sectors urged the organization to step up
its efforts in this arena, perhaps by fostering joint Arab-Jewish workers'
committees through which the Histadrut could exert its influence at specific work sites. But the Histadrut was not in a position to implement
this strategy effectively when worker unrest again flared up in Haifa's
petroleum sector early in 1947.

At first the locus of action was the refinery, which employed about
1,800 people, almost 80 percent of them Arabs, though here too Jews held
a disproportionate share (44 percent) of the clerical jobs. As with the Socony Vacuum strike the previous spring, and as with several smaller conflicts involving oil workers, the CRL workers' struggle with management
was complicated by struggles between the PAWS and the AWC and between the PAWS and the Histadrut. Despite growing rank and file discontent over low wages and other issues, and close cooperation between the
Arab and Jewish workers at the refinery and their committees, neither the
PAWS nor the Histadrut were anxious to organize and lead a strike. But
CRL workers who belonged to the AWC or were under its influence
pressed for action, with the support of the Jewish workers' committee
dominated by Hashomer Hatza'ir activists, and in mid-January 1947 a
spontaneous strike erupted which quickly expanded to encompass hundreds of the company's workers. The PAWS sought to bring the strike to
an end as quickly as possible, in part because it was committed to an earlier
agreement with management and in part because it feared that the strike
might provide the Histadrut and the AWC with an opening to enhance
their influence at CRL. It succeeded in getting the workers back to work

after a few days, but only at the cost of angering and alienating many CRL union activists. They demonstrated their unhappiness with the PAWS leadership in various ways, among them a decision to convene several meetings of the Arab refinery workers' committee not at the PAWS' headquarters but rather at the local Hashomer Hatza'ir branch, an indication of the good relations then prevailing between Arab and Jewish worker activists at this workplace.

Left-wing Arab unionists were particularly angry about what they regarded as Sami Taha's sabotage of the strike. *Al-Ittihad* sarcastically denounced the "honorable unionists" of the PAWS who,

> compelled by their desire to save their Arab worker brothers from the clutches of the Zionist Histadrut and its many machinations and by seeing a Histadrut representative try to intervene in the strike and lead it, as the Histadrut always seeks to do, thought that the only way to frustrate the Histadrut's schemes and isolate it from the masses of workers was by demanding that the workers return to work, on the pretext that the strike had been foisted upon them by the Histadrut and its officials.

A few months later the committee representing the Arab CRL workers publicly denounced the PAWS for the high-handedness of its leaders, one of whom had told the CRL workers that he, and not the workers themselves, knew what was best for them and that they should accept his decisions without question. The committee also criticized the PAWS for its undemocratic character, its compromises with CRL management, its sabotage of efforts to unite the petroleum workers, and its unsavory tactics.[10]

The PAWS also came under fire when in early March 1947 discontent among the Iraq Petroleum Company's workers erupted into strike action. The company employed some 2,500 people, with Arabs making up 98 percent of its manual workers and 84 percent of its office workers. The AWC was the dominant force among the IPC workers and had been able to resist an attempt by the PAWS to raid its membership and set up its own union of IPC workers. A strike of some 1,600 IPC workers (including a few dozen Jewish employees) began on March 6, mainly over wages, lasted until March 19 and resulted in a new agreement between IPC and its workers, who gained some but by no means all of their demands. The strikers received moral support from Arab workers across Palestine, but the AWC accused Sami Taha (and behind him the Arab Higher Committee) of trying to bring the strike to a quick end, which indeed seems to have been the case. Taha's role in the IPC strike was apparently the last straw for the Arab refinery workers: at the end of April 1947 the CRL union formally severed its connections with the PAWS, accusing Sami

Taha of having tried to sabotage the IPC strike and of serving the interests of the oil companies rather than of those companies' workers.[11]

There were also a number of other, less dramatic, and sustained upsurges of worker activism in this sector in the postwar period. These involved Arab workers almost exclusively, since with the partial exception of the Haifa refinery, which employed a substantial number of Jewish skilled and clerical workers, the petroleum sector workforce was overwhelmingly Arab and the Histadrut's efforts to enhance its influence were largely unsuccessful. Histadrut officials in Haifa complained to headquarters in Tel Aviv about Jewish weakness in this economically and politically important sector, and in the government sector as well, and demanded more funds with which to subsidize Jewish workers' wages as well as stepped-up pressure on corporate and government officials to get more Jews hired. Abba Hushi told the Histadrut executive that it had to "place on its agenda the conquest of labor in the cities. We can over the coming years get 5000 workers hired; workers are needed in the posts, railroads, telegraph. Today it is Arabs who are hired for these jobs—and it is this which will determine the fate of Haifa."[12] But Hushi was wrong: it would in fact be the superiority of Jewish military forces that determined Haifa's fate in the spring of 1948, culminating in the flight of the great majority of its Arab inhabitants. By that time, as we will see, the Haifa refinery had achieved notoriety as the scene of the single bloodiest incident of the first month of the Arab-Jewish fighting which erupted immediately after the United Nations General Assembly voted to recommend that Palestine be partitioned.

THE APRIL 1946 GENERAL STRIKE

The largest and most dramatic episode of joint action between Arab and Jewish workers in the history of Palestine took place in April 1946. Postal, telephone, and telegraph workers were responsible for touching off what became an unprecedentedly broad strike of white- and blue-collar government employees. Postal department officials had long rejected or ignored the postal workers' demands, leading Sami Taha of the PAWS and Yehezkel Abramov, secretary of the International Union of Railway, Postal and Telegraph Workers, to plan a limited strike of mainly Jewish postal and telephone workers in Tel Aviv, scheduled to begin on April 9, 1946. Abramov had insisted that the strike be delayed until after the departure from Palestine of the Anglo-American Committee of Inquiry, for fear that it might get out of hand or that Arab nationalist activists might transform it into a protest against the Committee. In this sector Arab and Jewish unionists had many years of experience in working together, and relations were generally friendly. There is even some evidence of male bonding among them: four decades later Abramov would still remember fondly how he and his Arab colleagues would repair to the Tel Aviv beachfront after negotiating sessions and watch the Jewish women bathers.[13]

On the appointed day the workers, including thirty or forty Arabs employed at the Tel Aviv post office, went on strike. Their militancy proved infectious and by the following day all the postal workers in Palestine had stopped work. In the negotiations that ensued postal officials quickly made far-reaching concessions, and the Histadrut recommended that the workers accept the offer and end the strike. As on similar occasions, the Histadrut feared that the strike might undermine the Zionist campaign then under way to force the British government to open Palestine to Jewish immigration. However, the rank and file postal workers, who had lost all faith in official promises, were in no mood to compromise and voted overwhelmingly to reject management's offer and continue their strike. Their militancy spread quickly: on April 14 the Arab and Jewish railway workers, members of both the IU and the AURW, also went on strike, paralyzing the country's railway system.

There had never before been a general strike of Palestine's railway and postal workers, but what made this episode even more extraordinary was the fact that the middle- and lower-level white-collar government employees also joined the strike. As I noted in Chapter 7, in May 1943 desperation over sharply dropping real wages had pushed the normally docile Arab and Jewish civil servants (organized in the Second Division Civil Service Association) to the extreme measure of staging a sit-in strike. Though that action eventually won them a cost of living allowance, persistent inflation and poor working conditions ensured that unrest would continue. In the spring of 1945 the Association organized several short countrywide protest strikes; these enjoyed Histadrut support, though the Histadrut had also worked behind the scenes to ensure that these protests by civil servants, most of whom were Arabs, would not be linked in the public's mind with the protest strikes which the Palestinian Arab nationalist movement organized at the same time in solidarity with the struggle for independence in Syria and Lebanon.[14] The clerks' grievances were not redressed, however, and when the postal and railway workers stopped work *en masse* in April 1946 they too were caught up in the countrywide wave of labor militancy and joined in, as did Public Works Department and port workers.

By April 15, 1946, less than a week after the Tel Aviv postal workers had stopped work, some 23,000 employees of the government of Palestine were on strike. For a time it seemed that the tens of thousands of workers employed at British military bases, along with the petroleum workers in and near Haifa, might also join the strike. Arab and Jewish communists certainly hoped this would happen: an April 18 leaflet issued jointly by the NLL and the Palestine Communist Party called on the refinery, military base, and municipal workers to join the general strike, while castigating the "imperialist government" of Palestine for allocating more than one-fifth of its annual budget to the police and prisons but only 8 percent to health, education, and social welfare combined.[15] However, both the Histadrut and the PAWS had reason to oppose expansion of the strike by keeping the refinery and base workers at their jobs. In private, Histadrut officials expressed concern that the oil workers would be unable to stay out on strike for an extended period, weakening the government employees' ability to wage a successful long-term struggle. They were also fearful that a strike in the petroleum sector would quickly paralyze much of Palestine's economy, disrupting motor transport and the provision of food to urban areas and interfering with the Yishuv's struggle to compel the British to permit more Jewish immigration.

The Histadrut's behind-the-scenes role in keeping the oil workers at their jobs did not prevent Abba Hushi from insisting to his colleagues that it was really Sami Taha who had kept them from joining the general strike. Hushi claimed that when the government employees' strike began, Taha had received a telephone call from Arab League headquarters in Cairo telling him not to go too far in cooperating with the Jews, whereupon he tried to dampen the Arab workers' militancy and prevent the petroleum workers from joining the strike. Hushi was never renowned for his truthfulness, even to his own comrades, but it is certainly possible that Sami Taha also used his influence to keep the strike from expanding; as I noted when discussing the petroleum workers, this was a politically sensitive moment and Taha was trying to avoid overt cooperation with the Histadrut.[16]

Though neither the refinery nor the camp workers joined the strike, it effectively paralyzed the mandatory administration and compelled the government to grant its employees many of their demands, including increases in basic wages and the COLA and improvements in the pension system. By the end of April all the strikers had returned to their jobs. Leftist forces in both the Arab and Jewish communities hailed the April general strike as a victory for Arab and Jewish workers and as incontrovertible evidence of what working-class solidarity could achieve. Warning against "defeatist and reactionary elements, Arab and Jewish," the NLL and PCP declared the strike "a blow against the 'divide and rule' policy of imperialism, a slap in the face of those who hold chauvinist ideologies and propagate national division." *Mishmar*, the organ of Hashomer Hatza'ir, also acclaimed the strike and argued that it demonstrated the possibility and efficacy of Arab-Jewish cooperation. The Histadrut's *Davar*, faithful exponent of the MAPAI line, blew hot and cold, reflecting the labor-Zionist leadership's ambivalence. The more conservative newspapers were less than thrilled. *Filastin* criticized the PAWS for colluding in what it regarded as a politically motivated movement that was inspired and orchestrated by the Zionists and largely served their interests. The right-wing Hebrew daily *Ma'ariv* initially welcomed the strike but later denounced it as detrimental to the Zionist cause.[17]

Whatever various forces in the Yishuv and the Arab community made of the strike, it proved to be an isolated incident. Although there was continuing unrest among certain categories of government workers during the months that followed, there were no further dramatic upsurges, and the focus of labor activism shifted elsewhere. The hope for Arab-Jewish cooperation which the general strike had seemed to evoke soon dissipated as Palestine sank deeper into political crisis in the year that followed.

THE BRITISH MILITARY BASES, 1945-48

The British military bases, which had emerged during the war as an important site of interaction between Arab and Jewish workers, retained their significance even after the war's end. Many Arab and Jewish camp workers, and the labor organizations which sought to represent them, continued to feel that they had common interests because they faced common problems. These included the rigid work discipline which British officers sought to impose on their civilian employees, poor working conditions and lack of benefits, but perhaps most importantly the downward pressure on their real wages—both absolutely but also relative to the wages of workers employed in private industry and construction and in other sectors of the country's economy—created by persistent inflation and the British military's desire to keep labor costs down.

Increasingly, however, the camp workers also perceived a threat to their very jobs. As Allied and Soviet forces gained the upper hand in North Africa and Europe and the Axis threat to the Middle East and the eastern Mediterranean receded, the British military's needs for civilian labor in Palestine naturally diminished. In October 1943 the War Department employed some 50,000 civilians in Palestine, but by the beginning of 1944 the number had dropped to about 47,500 and by March 1944 to under 44,000. The end of the war in Europe brought much more widespread layoffs: during the first ten months of 1945 almost 20,000 camp workers lost their jobs. The wave of layoffs then subsided, and over the following half year the redeployment to Palestine of British forces stationed in Syria, the expansion of existing military facilities, and the launching of new projects resulted in the hiring of a substantial number of additional workers. In April 1946 a Histadrut official estimated that the British armed forces employed about 22,000 Arabs and 8,000–9,000 Jews in Palestine, though the actual number may well have been somewhat higher. Despite the respite, it was clear that over the longer term the number of camp workers would shrink drastically.[18]

The plight of the camp workers received increasing attention from both Arab and Jewish labor leaders from 1945 onward. *Al-Ittihad* argued that the workers of Palestine had contributed to the Allied war effort and now deserved prompt and effective government measures to offset unemployment and boost wages.[19] The Histadrut leadership was similarly concerned about both unemployment and low wages. As always, however, it was also concerned about the potential impact of low wages on Jewish employment in the military sector: officials expressed alarm that unless camp workers' wages could be increased, Jews would leave for better-paying jobs elsewhere. But since Jews constituted only a small minority of the military's civilian workforce, joint action with the Arab majority was essential. The bitter experience of the 1943 camp workers' strike had demonstrated that the Histadrut could not hope to organize significant numbers of Arab workers under its own auspices, contributing to a growing recognition that in this sector as elsewhere it would have to cooperate with the Arab unions. As in the petroleum sector, the left wing of the Arab labor movement, now organized in the new Arab Workers' Congress, was generally more amenable to working with the Histadrut than the PAWS, which was more closely linked to the Arab nationalist leadership and reluctant to be seen as overly interested in cooperation with Jews.

One of the first workplaces at which this new spirit of cooperation manifested itself was the British military workshops established on what had been the grounds of the Levant Fair, on the outskirts of Tel Aviv. In September 1945 the AWC and the Histadrut jointly planned and led a seven-day strike of some 1,300 workers there to demand official recognition of their committee, payment of the COLA, recision of a rule fining workers a full day's pay plus another day's COLA for each day of work they missed, and the reinstatement of several workers unjustly dismissed. The Arab and Jewish workers set up joint pickets at the gates of the fairgrounds and organized a joint march through the streets of Tel Aviv, chanting (in Arabic and Hebrew) such slogans as: "Long live unity between Arab and Jewish workers," "The Arab and Jewish workers are brothers," and "Long live the Histadrut and the [Jaffa] Arab Workers' Society [affiliated with the AWC]." The Hebrew-language daily *Ha'aretz* reported that "masses of people crowded both sides of the streets to watch this extraordinary sight of Jewish and Arab workers marching through the heart of Tel Aviv." Only some of the strikers' demands were met: among other things the British military authorities agreed to recognize the workers' committees and to provide a week's advance notice of layoffs.[20]

The success of this strike led the Histadrut to more explicitly endorse cooperation with the Arab labor movement. Rank and file pressure, coupled with fear of being outflanked from the left, also contributed to this shift in policy: both communist and Hashomer Hatza'ir cadres were seeking to win support among the camp workers by criticizing the Histadrut for its inaction and advocating greater militancy and closer cooperation with Arab workers.[21] Several factors rendered cooperation difficult, however. One was the division of the Arab labor movement into two competing and often hostile camps, each of which had a base among the camp workers. Having established a degree of mutual trust the previous autumn, the AWC and the Histadrut found it relatively easy during the spring of 1946 to agree on a common set of demands and plan a joint campaign of struggle which might ultimately lead to a general strike of Arab and Jewish camp workers. The AWC's largely communist leadership had no ideological qualms about cooperating with avowedly Zionist workers and unions, as long as the latter refrained from seeking to recruit Arabs and as long as that cooperation was restricted to the class struggle. By contrast, just as in the petroleum sector during this same period, the PAWS leadership was reluctant on nationalist grounds to be perceived as cooperating with the Histadrut. This presented a major problem: as Arab and Jewish unionists well understood, without the participation of the 8,000 Arab camp workers who supported Sami Taha's organization it would be very difficult, if not impossible, to wage a successful struggle on behalf of the camp workers.[22]

Another complicating issue was discontent among Arab workers over the higher wages which Jewish coworkers often received for the same jobs, as well as the disproportionate number of Jews who held better-paid and easier supervisory, skilled, and clerical jobs at British installations. Sami Taha had raised this issue in a telegram to the authorities in 1944, and *al-Ittihad* took it up early in 1946, reporting that Arab workers at the Bayt Nabala base near Lydda were demanding not only higher wages but also wage equality with their Jewish coworkers and the hiring of more Arab foremen, since the Jewish foremen were perceived as giving preference to Jews in hiring and treatment. Arab protests there culminated in clashes and even casualties. According to the AWC's organ, the Arab workers wanted more Arab foremen "not because they hate the Jewish foremen at the camp but because [those foremen] carry out Zionist plans with complete obedience; as the saying goes, 'We don't fight the wolf because of his color or shape but because he eats our ewes'." In the spring of 1947 some 1,500 Arab workers employed at military bases in the Haifa area participated in a one-hour protest strike organized by the PAWS to demand that their Jewish foremen be replaced by Arabs.[23]

Nonetheless, although wage discrimination and a desire for a larger share of the better jobs continued to be of concern to Arab workers and unionists, they were generally willing to subordinate those issues to the broader struggle to improve the camp workers' wages and working conditions and protect their jobs. By the early months of 1947 the Histadrut was discussing cooperation with both the PAWS (which had by far the strongest base among the Arab camp workers) and the AWC, though the poor relations between the two rival Arab organizations sometimes required Histadrut officials to act as mediators. Agreement was soon reached on a set of demands which included an increase in the base wage, a bonus for wartime service, severance pay, improvements in sick pay, vacations, and work regulations, and official recognition of the workers' committees and unions. When in May 1947 the British authorities began a new round of layoffs without prior warning, the Arab unionists pushed for a one-day protest strike of all camp workers, to which the Histadrut agreed.[24] The strike, which took place on May 20, 1947, encompassed some 40,000 workers and passed without incident. Its success was in sharp contrast to the debilitating failure of the May 1943 strike, which the Histadrut had called on its own and in which most of the Arab workers had refused to participate. The PAWS wanted to build on this success with further action in the form of an extended strike, but Histadrut officials were opposed, because they feared that such a strike might serve the Arab nationalist cause by touching off violent disturbances just when the

United Nations Special Commission on Palestine was due to arrive to pursue its inquiry into the country's problems and future status.

As the spring of 1947 turned into summer and talks between British officials and the camp workers' representatives failed to make much headway, the PAWS and the AWC began to push for a strike of indefinite duration. Early in July the PAWS declared that if the authorities did not meet the camp workers' demands within twenty-five days, it would call the workers out on strike. Histadrut officials had by now convinced themselves that Sami Taha and his organization were pliant instruments of the dominant nationalist faction led by Amin al-Husayni, who was still in exile, and they were certain that a camp workers' strike would serve Arab nationalist interests and harm the Zionist cause at a politically sensitive moment. As Berl Repetur later put it in a report to the Histadrut's executive committee, "we feared a strike of the Jewish and Arab workers, a strike which would be anti-Jewish in its political and security character." Consequently, the Histadrut rejected the PAWS' call and instead proposed a three-day protest strike.

For a time it seemed that both the PAWS and the AWC might adopt the Histadrut's proposal, but in early August the PAWS, acting on its own, announced that the camp workers would go out on strike on August 25, 1947. The AWC denounced this unilateral decision as destructive of the camp workers' unity and claimed that the PAWS was secretly cooperating with the Histadrut in an effort to isolate and weaken the AWC. Histadrut and PAWS officials had in fact met and decided to refrain from unilateral acts. A few days before the strike date, the British authorities agreed to satisfy several of the camp workers' demands. Though the key demand that laid-off workers be paid compensation was not met, this small victory considerably eased relations among the PAWS, the AWC, and the Histadrut. Soon thereafter the War Office finally extended formal recognition to the Arab unions and the Histadrut as representatives of the camp workers and seemed to indicate a willingness to make concessions on other issues. The way thus seemed to be open for further gains by the camp workers.[25]

THE DISINTEGRATION OF THE ARAB WORKERS' MOVEMENT

As among workers in the petroleum sector and in government service, the unprecedented cooperation that characterized relations between Arab and Jewish camp workers in the immediate postwar years was in the fall of 1947 submerged by a rising tide of intercommunal tensions. On August

31, 1947, the United Nations Special Commission on Palestine (UNSCOP) released its recommendations for resolving the Palestine problem. UN-SCOP had been established by the General Assembly the previous May, after an exhausted Britain, unable to suppress Jewish insurgency in Palestine, induce Arabs and Jews to reach agreement on the country's future, or impose a solution of its own, had turned the Palestine problem over to the United Nations. UNSCOP had visited Palestine in the summer of 1947, and after a painstaking inquiry and lengthy discussions among its members it issued a majority report which recommended that Palestine be partitioned into independent Arab and Jewish states, with Jerusalem to be placed under international control. (UNSCOP's minority report, which recommended the establishment of an Arab-Jewish federal state in all of Palestine, never received serious consideration.) According to this plan, the Jewish state would encompass some 55 percent of Palestine's territory, though Jews constituted less than one-third of the country's population at the time. The Zionist leadership welcomed the prospect of an independent Jewish state which the majority report offered, though it hoped for more territory. The Palestinian Arab nationalist movement, as well as the Arab states, vehemently rejected the recommendation as a violation of the right of the country's indigenous Arab majority to national self-determination in an undivided Palestine.

On the morrow of the report's publication, an intense diplomatic struggle began over whether the General Assembly would endorse UNSCOP's recommendations by the required two-thirds majority. In Palestine itself, with partition now a very real and imminent possibility and the country's fate hanging in the balance, the climate of Arab-Jewish relations changed abruptly. There was a hardening of political lines between and within the Arab and Jewish communities which very quickly rendered impossible the kind of cooperation among Arab and Jewish workers and labor organizations which had manifested itself so prominently during the previous two years. As a result, the momentum which the PAWS, the AWC, and the Histadrut had built up through the camp workers' struggles they had jointly led dissipated very quickly. The much more tense and crisis-ridden atmosphere that now prevailed also contributed to the virtual paralysis of the Arab labor movement. It was the PAWS which experienced the sharpest reversal in its fortunes, for in mid-September 1947 it suffered a devastating blow from which it never really recovered.

As I mentioned earlier, Histadrut officials had long been convinced that the PAWS' general secretary, Sami Taha, was a completely obedient agent of Amin al-Husayni, Mufti of Jerusalem and president of the AHC, whom

Zionists regarded as their most implacable Arab foe. In reality, tensions had been growing during 1947 between the PAWS leader and the Husayni loyalists who dominated the Arab Higher Committee. The Mufti and his allies seem to have been increasingly angered by what they saw as Sami Taha's refusal to obey the AHC's orders, as well as by his growing inclination to chart an independent course in the political arena. Taha's purported deviations included the PAWS' alleged refusal in November 1946 to endorse the AHC's call for a day-long protest strike on the anniversary of the Balfour Declaration; the PAWS' adoption that same year of a vague "socialism" as its guiding principle—a step which had to do with both its growing political ambitions and its rivalry with the communist-led AWC; Taha's talk of creating an independent Arab labor party; his denunciations of partisan and factional politics; and his pronouncements on political matters, which though often vague or naive were taken as criticisms of the Husaynis' domination of the nationalist movement. Perhaps most damning were allegations that Taha was in favor of seeking some *modus vivendi* with the Jews and might even be willing to accept partition, as well as the PAWS' secretary's ties with some of the exiled Mufti's political rivals, particularly Musa al-'Alami, who in the late summer of 1947 was regarded by the Husayni camp as the leader of those forces within the Palestinian Arab community most amenable to some compromise with Zionism.[26]

The rift between Sami Taha and the AHC emerged into public view at the end of August 1947, when the PAWS leader became the target of a barrage of defamatory attacks in newspapers identified with the Husayni camp, especially *al-Wahda*. Taha and his organization were denounced for being insufficiently anti-Zionist and anti-British, and for failing to conform to the official nationalist line; rumors were also spread that Taha was a paid agent of the Zionists. Among other things, *al-Wahda* cited a resolution adopted at the PAWS' national congress, held in Haifa in late August, which declared that "Arab Jews are our fellow citizens and brothers in nationality." The PAWS responded by issuing a series of leaflets refuting the charges against it; the last of these, dated September 9, 1947, pointed out that the Arab Higher Committee had itself recently declared that the Jews who had lived in the country before the British conquest and their descendants were welcome to remain as full citizens of the future independent Arab Palestine.

Taha's efforts to defend himself and the organization he led were unavailing. On September 12, 1947, he was assassinated outside his home in Haifa. His murderer was never apprehended, but it was generally believed that Sami Taha was killed on orders of Amin al-Husayni, as part of a campaign by the Mufti's camp to settle accounts, intimidate potential opponents, and tighten its grip on the Arab community as the final phase of the struggle for Palestine approached. It was thus probably no coincidence that Sami Taha came under public attack very soon after UNSCOP recommended that Palestine be partitioned, a recommendation whose implementation the AHC vowed to fight with all the means at its disposal.[27]

In the wake of Sami Taha's murder the PAWS' leaders publicly pledged their loyalty to the AHC. In private they assured their Histadrut counterparts that cooperation would continue, and the PAWS, AWC, and Histadrut officials responsible for camp workers' affairs soon resumed their contacts. But they were unable to follow up on the gains they had made in late summer, and as the British moved toward the complete evacuation of their military forces and installations in Palestine, the camp workers' ranks were further decimated by new waves of layoffs, though some compensation was apparently paid to dismissed workers. The PAWS never really had the opportunity to recover from the murder of its secretary and best-known public figure. In the fall and winter of 1947 and the early months of 1948, with its bases of support among camp and government workers shrinking, its organizing activity declined and then virtually ceased and it gradually fell into a state of paralysis. Early in April 1948 the Histadrut's Eliyahu Agassi met in Haifa with Sa'id Qawwas and Husayn Nasir, veteran PAWS leaders. The feisty Qawwas berated Agassi for what he saw as *Haqiqat al-Amr*'s negative portrayals of Arabs and the Arab labor movement and its lack of balance. "Why does it only expose the problems with the Mufti's policies? Are there no problems with Ben-Gurion's policies?" Qawwas asked. By that time the PAWS was barely functioning, and it seems likely that most of its historic leadership, core cadre and rank and file base was dispersed a few weeks later, in late April 1948, when Haifa's Arab neighborhoods surrendered to Jewish military forces and the great majority of their inhabitants fled the city.[28]

The AWC did not fare much better in the fall of 1947 and the winter of 1947–48. It held an apparently successful national congress (its third) in September 1947 and seemed poised to engage in a new round of vigorous activity and expansion. But in the weeks that followed, labor activism became increasingly difficult as public attention focused on the question of Palestine's fate and both Arabs and Jews closed ranks and girded themselves for the struggle ahead, a struggle in which all sides were ready to resort to violent means. At the same time the AWC and the NLL, under whose guidance it operated, were thrown into disarray, their political bearings lost, by a dramatic shift in the Soviet Union's stance on the Palestine question.

Though not formally a communist party, the NLL had become increasingly open about identifying itself with the international communist movement, most notably by participating in the conference of communist parties in the British empire, held in London in February–March 1947. Its position on the Palestine question had been identical to that long advocated by the international communist movement and by the Soviet Union. However, to the surprise and dismay of the NLL, and of Arab communists elsewhere in the Middle East, the Soviet government began moving away from its traditional position on Palestine and Zionism in the spring of 1947 and abandoned it altogether that fall, in the midst of the struggle over whether the UN General Assembly would endorse partition. In May 1947, in an address to the General Assembly on the Palestine question, Soviet representative Andrei Gromyko signaled quite clearly that his government was reconsidering its long-standing and vehement opposition to the idea of partition and Jewish statehood in Palestine. Expressing sympathy for the suffering of the Jewish people during the war and voicing understanding for the Jews' special interest in, and attachment to, Palestine, Gromyko implicitly recognized the existence of two national communities in Palestine and reluctantly concluded that if Arabs and Jews could not find a way to coexist peacefully in the framework of a single state, partition might be the only fair and viable solution.

NLL leaders did their best to avoid coming to terms with the implications of Gromyko's speech, but they could not ignore the explicit decision of the Soviet Union, in October 1947, to endorse UNSCOP's recommendation that Palestine be partitioned into independent Arab and Jewish states. The result was a split in the NLL leadership, which included many veteran communists who had loyally followed Moscow's line for many years. Some NLL leaders embraced the new Soviet line, accepted partition, and would later denounce the Arab states' military intervention to prevent the establishment of a Jewish state; others rejected the new line and would seek to participate in the struggle against the establishment of a Jewish state. As a result of the split, the suppression of the organization's newspaper *al-Ittihad* by the British authorities in February 1948, and then the uprooting and displacement of much of Palestine's Arab population in the months that followed, the NLL and the AWC fell into disarray. In the spring of 1948 AWC activists helped organize local self-defense units in Jaffa and Gaza to protect poor urban neighborhoods, but these were swept away in the chaos that was engulfing Arab Palestine. With their leaders and activists dispersed and much of their mass base transformed into refugees, the NLL and the AWC largely ceased to function, at least as coherent national organizations. The new Arab left which had emerged in Palestine during the war and which had contributed so much to the development of the Arab trade union movement was thus swamped by the rising tide of intercommunal tension—the very tension it had hoped to moderate and overcome through Arab-Jewish working-class solidarity.

THE PLL: PARALYSIS AND PATHOS

In none of the three main arenas of Arab-Jewish worker interaction during 1946–47 which I have discussed in detail in this chapter did the PLL play any role whatsoever. In fact, by the spring of 1946 internal Histadrut discussions were already taking it for granted that the PLL was no longer a particularly useful or valuable instrument. The new reality was not lost on Arab Department officials: at one meeting Shmu'el Solomon complained bitterly that the Histadrut had kept the PLL out of the strikes in the government, petroleum, and military base sectors during April and May 1946. "The PLL today is just a phrase," Solomon admitted; "neither the Arabs nor the Histadrut want it." The Histadrut leadership had in fact explicitly prohibited the PLL from trying to organize Arab camp workers, and the Histadrut's Trade Union Department, which handled labor affairs, had more or less excluded PLL representatives even from negotiations at workplaces where the PLL had some members, because it knew that if the PLL was included neither the PAWS nor the AWC would participate. Arab Department officials could not hide their feelings of betrayal and disappointment, but the decision to more or less write off the PLL, or perhaps more accurately to let it languish, had been made at the top, dictated by the exigencies of the postwar era.

Department officials now sought to preserve what they could of the project to which they had devoted so much energy, largely by trying to find jobs for loyal PLL members, even at the expense of displacing other Arab workers. Many of its branches melted away as members stopped attending meetings and paying dues. By May 1947, Arab Department officials were reduced to threatening the members of what had once seemed a flourishing PLL branch in Qalunya that the Histadrut would no longer represent them unless they paid their dues; and though the branch in Acre no longer had many members it was decided to keep it going, in hope of better times to come. It was a sign of the times that George Nassar, who under the tutelage of Moshe Erem of Po'alei Tziyon Smol had thoroughly assimilated that party's socialist-Zionist ideology and for many years had proudly served as the most prominent and publicly presentable Arab associated with the Histadrut, was now no longer able to live safely in Jaffa. As tensions rose in Palestine during 1947, Nassar's open identification with the Histadrut and Zionism raised concerns for his personal safety and that of his family and compelled him to ask for the Histadrut's help in finding a place to live in Tel Aviv.[29]

However, though the PLL was quite moribund as a labor organization, it still had its uses for propaganda purposes. The memorandum which the Histadrut submitted to the United Nations Special Commission on Palestine in the summer of 1947 included a section touting the PLL (whose membership was with great exaggeration given as 2,500) as the key vehicle of cooperation between Arab and Jewish workers and blaming the "reactionary political leadership" of the Arab community for preventing "a rising Arab proletariat [from] finding its natural ally in the Histadrut. . . ." Arab Department officials understood the useful role which those few Palestinian Arabs sympathetic to Zionism could play in the battle for world public opinion then under way. Referring to upcoming conferences of scouts in France, of youth in Prague, and of athletes in Warsaw, they noted that "it is desirable that friendly Arab delegations should appear at these conferences together with the Jewish delegations [from Palestine]. The PLL can put together such delegations from among its members."[30] The continued existence of the PLL also allowed the Histadrut to claim that it represented Arab workers and was entitled to speak for them within the international labor movement. In June 1947, the Histadrut sent George Nassar to Prague as the PLL's representative at a meeting of the WFTU General Council, accompanied by Eliyahu Agassi; Arab Department officials thought it would be useful if another Arab delegate could also be sent, preferably a Muslim, so as to give the delegation a more representative appearance.[31]

Though they still went through the motions, however, the Jewish officials who ran the Arab Department and the PLL seem to have understood that the game was up. They knew very well that in Palestine itself the PLL was discredited among Arab workers, except for those few who had secured employment through it, and that even their loyalty to the organization was extremely shallow. They also knew that leaders of the international trade union movement were becoming increasingly familiar with, and respectful of, authentic Palestinian Arab labor leaders, men like Bulus Farah who not only came from the working class but had also acquired years of experience in the communist and trade union movements. The days when the Histadrut had any chance of "selling" the PLL as the authentic representative of the Arab workers had passed forever.

The work of these Jewish officials—at least of those who sincerely believed in what they were doing—had always involved a strong dose of self-delusion, of an ability not to see what was going on around them, or more accurately to see and interpret events only through the filters imposed by the ideology they professed. Now, however, as the understanding sank in that the Histadrut's project of organizing Arab workers under its auspices had finally reached a dead end, that self-delusion was increasingly supplemented by pathos. Shmu'el Solomon, who had led the Arab Department for several years, was already sounding a note of resignation, and perhaps of self-pity, in the autumn of 1945. "We cannot be happy about what we achieved," he told his colleagues. "But we did a lot, we did our duty, without negligence. We regard the results not with pride, since there have been many failures, but not with pessimism [either], taking into consideration the circumstances. We sowed seeds which will still bear fruit—we hope—in our own day." [32]

The tone of pathos is even more evident in a letter which Eliyahu Agassi wrote to the WFTU's general secretary on the eve of the June 1947 meeting of that organization's General Council. In the letter Agassi complained about the harassment to which PLL members were being subjected by both the PAWS and the AWC. Agassi displayed no self-consciousness whatsoever about the fact that it was he, a Jew, who was writing this letter on behalf of a purportedly Arab organization, an organization which the Histadrut was still portraying (in its propaganda outside Palestine, at least) as the sole authentic voice of the Arab working class. Yet that fact, a manifestation of the PLL's inability to develop any Arab cadre or leadership or to transcend its origins as an instrument created, funded, and entirely controlled by the Histadrut, surely constituted a rather glaring admission of failure in and of itself. Just as peculiar was Agassi's insistence that now, at long last, the Arab workers were finally coming to understand "that the leaders of the [Arab] unions have misled them by warning them of imaginary disasters which are liable to strike them if they co-operate with their Jewish fellow-workers." This assertion was of course a distortion of a much more complex historical record, but it is also a sad commentary on the capacity for self-delusion of a decent and intelligent man like Agassi, who certainly believed in what he was doing, had selflessly dedicated many years of his life to organizing Arab workers, and had not a few Arab friends. [33]

By March 1948 what was left of the Histadrut's Arab Department in Tel Aviv was devoting itself to propaganda and information gathering, while the PLL was little more than a labor contracting agency through which some one hundred Arab workers in Haifa secured employment with Jewish companies at the port, especially Solel Boneh. These PLL members, whose wages were higher than those of other port workers, were now under increasing pressure from the nationalist camp, which regarded them as Zionist collaborators. In an ironic twist on the Hebrew labor issue, these workers defended themselves by arguing that if they stopped working for Jewish employers, their jobs might be taken over by Jews, or by Arab contractors using even more exploited Arab workers. But their situation took a turn for the worse when in March 1948 they became entangled in a conflict with their foreman, who was pocketing part of their wages. Some of them brought the foreman up on charges before the local National Committee. As the area in which the British still exercised control shrank, this committee had increasingly assumed responsibility for law and order among the Arab residents of Haifa. The foreman responded by charging that his accusers were helping the Hagana, which was at that moment engaged with Arab militias in a struggle for control of the city. The Committee's judges exonerated the workers, but in the days that followed the situation of the handful of Arabs still publicly associated with the PLL had become so perilous that consideration was given to having them go underground. They themselves rejected this option, since they could not afford to give up their jobs.

As the battle for control of Haifa intensified in April 1948, contact between Arab and Jewish neighborhoods became increasingly difficult. In the second half of April, after several weeks of fighting and intensive shelling of Arab neighborhoods by Jewish military forces, Arab resistance was broken. Arab Haifa surrendered on April 22, and in the days that followed the great majority of the city's remaining Arab population, panicked by the fighting and fearful of their fate under Jewish rule, was evacuated under British protection northward to Acre or Lebanon; most would eventually end up in refugee camps in Lebanon. On a visit to Haifa's Arab neighborhoods at the end of April, Eliyahu Agassi found that the formerly "teeming and noisy streets had overnight become as silent as a cemetery." But he managed to locate a few PLL members still living in their homes, arranged to get them some food, and tried to reassure them about the rights which Arab workers would enjoy in the Jewish state, whose formal establishment was now just a few weeks away.[34]

HASHOMER HATZAʿIR AND THE END OF THE
BINATIONALIST DREAM

Hashomer Hatzaʿir activists involved with Arab affairs had come to the conclusion that the PLL was not just useless but a serious obstacle to developing good relations with the Arab labor movement as early as 1945. One Hashomer Hatzaʿir activist in the Jewish railway workers' union in Haifa would later go so far as to declare that in that city, the PLL's historic base, it was regarded by the Arabs as a "quisling" organization to which no self-respecting Arab would belong.[35] However, for all its criticisms of the PLL, the Histadrut leadership and MAPAI, and its sincere efforts to develop friendly relations with Arab unionists and leftists, Hashomer Hatzaʿir shared some of labor Zionism's key premises regarding Palestine's indigenous population. It too believed in the self-evidently progressive, emancipatory, and beneficial character of the Zionist enterprise's impact on Palestine's Arab majority, and even some of Cohen's coworkers in the Hakibbutz Haʾartzi Arab Department could sometimes express skepticism about the strength and authenticity of a distinct Palestinian Arab national identity.[36] Moreover, Hashomer Hatzaʿir's political (and psychological) need to reconcile its faith in Zionism with its recognition of Arab national rights in Palestine sometimes led even those activists most passionately and sincerely concerned about Arab-Jewish relations into self-delusion.

We have already seen one instance of the self-delusion which Hashomer Hatzaʿir's ideological stance facilitated (and perhaps required) in Aharon Cohen's lengthy courtship of ʿAbd Allah al-Bandaq, the veteran communist whom Cohen—Hakibbutz Haʾartzi's leading expert on Arab affairs and a man of no small political sophistication—cast in 1942–43 as the potential leader of a pro-Zionist Palestinian Arab left. In its political struggles within the Yishuv and the world Zionist movement in 1945–47, Hashomer Hatzaʿir's advocacy of a binational state as an alternative to partition required it to find elements in the Arab community willing to take a similar stance. Though the movement and the League for Jewish-Arab Rapprochement and Cooperation in which it played a leading role devoted considerable time and energy to this search, it proved futile: such elements hardly existed, and those few Palestinian Arabs ready to break with their community's consensus in this way were quickly marginalized, if not liquidated.[37] Nonetheless, until the fall of 1947, Hashomer Hatzaʿir strove mightily to find grounds for optimism about the prospects of Arab-Jewish compromise and friendship. When, for example, units of the Arab

Legion, a force composed of Transjordanians but under British command, were stationed in Palestine in 1946 to help the authorities maintain order and suppress the Zionist insurgency, the Yishuv's leadership protested and proclaimed a policy of nonfraternization with its officers and soldiers. Some members of Hashomer Hatzaʿir kibbutzim located near Arab Legion camps defied this policy and sought to befriend the Transjordanians, who (much to the displeasure of their British commanders) were said to have responded warmly to this hospitality.[38]

The handful of Hashomer Hatzaʿir members concerned about Arab-Jewish cooperation knew that they had to overcome considerable apathy, skepticism, and hostility even within their own movement. Zyoma Ben-Artzi, a member of Kibbutz Mazraʿ, reported that when he developed friendly relations with the Arab Legionnaires stationed nearby, some of his fellow kibbutz members warned him against fraternizing with "these blacks" (*hashehorim ha'ele*), a derogatory term he was sure they would never have used to refer to Indians or Englishmen. The kibbutz youth (to whom Ben-Artzi referred by the Arabic term *shabab*) were, he went on, a rather wild bunch who were not properly educated about Arab-Jewish relations and were capable, just for the fun of it, of ganging up on "some poor Arab shepherd" and stealing a goat from him. Yosef Vashitz, who worked with Cohen in the movement's Arab Department, noted sadly (and with much idealization) that

> there is more of a simple human attitude in the Arab's attitude toward the Jew than in the Jew's attitude toward the Arab. For the Arab, the Jew is first of all a human being, and only then a Jew; for the Jew, the Arab is an Arab and only after that a human being. In our kibbutzim as well, only a few have the proper human attitude toward their Arab neighbors. We have to remove the national and political clothing from day-to-day relations and worry about normal human relations. We should not strive to be missionaries or political preacher-activists, but seek relations among people who though different from one another are nonetheless human beings.[39]

But more important than individual attitudes was the fact that rapidly changing political circumstances were eliminating the ground on which Hashomer Hatzaʿir had hoped to build Arab-Jewish friendship and develop support for a binational solution to the Palestine problem. The binational idea enjoyed only weak support in the Yishuv and the international Zionist movement, which in its great majority had embraced the demand for a sovereign Jewish state in as much of Palestine as possible, and it was coming to seem ever more unrealistic. For one, all organized political forces in the Palestinian Arab community rejected it, since it entailed political parity between Arabs and Jews even though the former outnumbered the latter two to one, and in the version Hashomer Hatza'ir espoused would also allow for continued Jewish immigration, eventually producing a Jewish majority. Like most Zionists, Arab nationalists wanted a state of their own in all of Palestine. But even those external forces on which Hashomer Hatza'ir had pinned its hopes of preventing partition and securing some sort of binational solution in an undivided Palestine now abandoned this option. As we have seen, in May 1947 the Soviet Union began moving away from its historic support for a united Palestine and toward acceptance of partition if Arabs and Jews could not find a way to live together within a single state. The formal Soviet endorsement of UNSCOP's majority report in October 1947 meant that the world communist movement, toward which Hashomer Hatza'ir oriented itself despite the obvious ideological difference over the question of Zionism, had abandoned a binational solution.

Unlike their Arab counterparts, the Jewish communists in Palestine were quick to embrace the new Soviet line. The entirely Jewish PCP not only abandoned the binational stance it had adopted after the collapse of the Arab-Jewish PCP and endorsed partition; before the end of November 1947 it went so far as to drop the word "Palestine" from its name and begin calling itself the Communist Party of Eretz Yisra'el, thereby reconciling itself to the ancient Jewish (and modern Zionist) name for this land, one which communists had always rejected.[40] And when, on November 29, 1947, after intensive lobbying and considerable arm-twisting, the General Assembly voted by the necessary two-thirds majority to endorse partition, the binational option for which Hashomer Hatza'ir and its allies had long fought was rendered entirely moot.

By that time Hashomer Hatza'ir was already moving to adapt to changing realities. In the autumn of 1947 it was conducting merger negotiations with another left-Zionist party, Ahdut Ha'avoda, which as I mentioned at the beginning of Chapter 7 split off from MAPAI in 1944 and two years later absorbed most of the remnants of Po'alei Tziyon Smol. Despite these parties' very different origins and political trajectories, they shared much common ideological ground. But Ahdut Ha'avoda strongly rejected Hashomer Hatza'ir's advocacy of a binational regime for the country, favoring instead the creation in all of Palestine of a socialist Jewish state in which Arabs would have equal rights. Ahdut Ha'avoda members played leading roles in the top ranks of the Yishuv's strongest militia, the Hagana, and of the Hagana's elite military formation, the PALMAH. Moreover, that party was infused with a rather aggressive, even militaristic ("activist") ethos, in sharp contrast to Hashomer Hatza'ir's historic aversion to violence and its emphasis on peaceful coexistence between Arabs and Jews. However, the UN's endorsement of partition allowed Hashomer Hatza'ir to abandon binationalism and opened the way for unity with Ahdut Ha'avoda. Early in 1948 the two parties merged to form MAPAM (the Hebrew acronym of "United Workers' Party"), which would serve as one of MAPAI's junior partners in the provisional government of the new State of Israel proclaimed on May 14, 1948, and which provided a highly disproportionate share of the commanders of the new Israeli army. In Israel's first parliamentary elections, held in January 1949, MAPAM emerged as the country's second-largest party, after MAPAI. By then, of course, the contours of the Palestine conflict had changed dramatically and irrevocably.[41]

THE DESCENT INTO MADNESS

It is a sad irony that the single bloodiest incident of the first month of the Arab-Jewish violence that erupted immediately after the UN General Assembly endorsed partition not only involved workers employed at a mixed workplace but occurred at a site which had a history of close cooperation between Arab and Jewish unionists. This incident, one of the first massacres of the 1947–49 period though by no means the last, contributed greatly to the dissemination of fear and hatred among both Arabs and Jews in Palestine.

The site in question was the Haifa oil refinery, which at the end of 1947 employed some 1,700 Arab and 270 Jewish manual workers, in addition to 190 Jewish, 110 Arab, and 60 British clerical workers. As I discussed earlier, the refinery workers had been involved in important struggles in 1946–47. In these struggles Arab workers and union activists had played the leading role, not surprisingly given the composition of the workforce and its high degree of organization. But the Arab unionists' relations with the Jewish refinery workers seem to have been good: the Histadrut's clerical workers' union had close ties with some of the Arab white-collar employees at the site, while the local Jewish workers' committee was dominated by Hashomer Hatza'ir members who had developed good relations with Arab leftists and labor activists at the refinery. In the summer of 1947, for example, the members of the Jewish workers' committee at CRL were invited to attend the funeral in Acre of an Arab refinery worker who had been killed in an industrial accident. The Jewish activists accepted, and at the cemetery one of them eulogized the deceased. The Jews' participation made a positive impression on the Arab refinery workers and in Acre generally. The Arab and Jewish workers' committees also cooperated in organizing a brief memorial strike in the deceased's department at the refinery, together took up a collection to help his family, and joined in pressing management for fair compensation.[42]

Whatever good feeling may have existed seems to have evaporated during the fall, and after the UN General Assembly voted to endorse partition the Jewish workers at the refinery became increasingly worried about their safety. On the morrow of the vote violence erupted in various parts of the country. At first this took the form of random attacks by Arabs against Jews and Jewish property and settlements, but Jews soon responded with attacks on Arabs. This quickly escalated into a cycle of violence and counterviolence using terrorist means, the first phase of an increasingly bitter and bloody civil war which would soon pit Arab and Jewish militias against one another in a deadly struggle for control of strategic roads, sites, and areas, and ultimately of Palestine itself. On the Jewish side the leading role in this struggle was played by the Hagana, the Yishuv's largest military force, which was closely linked to the Histadrut and was under the control of the official leadership of the Yishuv, itself largely dominated by the labor-Zionist movement from the mid-1930s onward. There were, however, other Jewish military forces which did not accept the authority of the Yishuv's leadership. The most important of these (though much smaller than the Hagana) was ETZEL, commanded by Menahem Begin and better known in the United States as the Irgun. As I mentioned in Chapter 7, it was ETZEL (linked to the right-wing Zionist Revisionist party, ancestor of today's Likud) which carried out the bombing of the King David Hotel in July 1946. And it was an operation planned and executed by this organization which at the end of 1947 touched off the orgy of bloodshed at the Haifa refinery.

During December 1947, as civil war erupted in Palestine, the Hagana focused largely on protecting Jewish lives and property and on securing key lines of communications and transportation; later it began to take the offensive by mounting a series of military operations designed to crush Arab resistance and secure territory for the future Jewish state. Although during 1948 ETZEL would also stage military operations, in December 1947 it devoted itself largely to retaliating for attacks on Jewish civilians— thereby, it insisted, deterring further such attacks—by targeting Arab civilians. On December 29, 1947, ETZEL had staged a bomb attack at the Nablus Gate of Jerusalem's Old City which killed or wounded forty-four people. On the morning of the following day, Tuesday, December 30, 1947, ETZEL operatives threw bombs from a speeding car into a crowd of several hundred Arabs standing outside the main gate of the Haifa oil refinery in the hope of finding employment as day laborers; six people were killed and forty-two wounded. ETZEL would later announce, quite unapologetically, that these acts of terrorism in Jerusalem and Haifa had been carried out in retaliation for recent attacks on Jews elsewhere in Palestine.

Within minutes of the bomb attack at the Haifa refinery gate, some of the Arabs who had been part of the crowd outside surged into the refinery compound and, along with some of the Arab refinery workers, began attacking Jewish refinery workers. An hour passed before British soldiers and police arrived to restore order, by which time forty-one Jews had been killed and forty-nine wounded. This was the largest and most brutal massacre of civilians which Palestine had witnessed since the UN vote a month earlier. A committee of inquiry appointed by Haifa's Jewish community concluded that the massacre of Jews at the refinery was unpremeditated and that it had been precipitated by the ETZEL attack on the workers outside the gate.[43] The Jewish Agency, the official leadership of the Yishuv, promptly denounced ETZEL for the "act of madness" which had brought about the catastrophe at the Haifa refinery, but it simultaneously decided to emulate ETZEL by secretly authorizing the Hagana to retaliate. A day after the refinery massacre, members of the Hagana's elite strike force, the PALMAH, attacked the village of Balad al-Shaykh not far from Haifa, where a number of Arab refinery workers lived, and nearby Hawasa as well. (The Nesher cement factory, where as we have seen the issue of Hebrew labor surfaced so contentiously in the 1920s and 1930s, was located near Balad al-Shaykh, and the village's cemetery contained the tomb of Shaykh 'Izz al-Din al-Qassam, whose death in a gunfight with police had made him a nationalist martyr and would set the stage for the outbreak of the 1936–39 revolt.) The Jewish attackers killed some sixty men, women, and children and destroyed several dozen houses. The contrast between the Yishuv leadership's official stance and its actual response to the refinery massacre was not lost on many Arabs. When Eliyahu Agassi visited Haifa early in April 1948, an Arab worker berated him: "We know you Jews: you preach one thing and practice another. What was the crime of the Arab workers at Hawasa and Balad al-Shaykh whom your people attacked at night and slaughtered?"[44]

The report of the Jewish committee investigating the refinery massacre noted that "there were isolated incidents of Arab workers and [white-collar] employees who in various ways warned and even succeeded in saving a number of Jews, their coworkers" and added that "not all the Arab workers at the enterprise participated in the rampage, and a significant number of the workers and employees did not participate in it." However, the committee also found that "some of [the Arab refinery workers] took an active part in the riot" and that "there was no effort by a group of Arab workers to prevent others from rampaging." This was, fortunately, not the case that same day at the railway workshops, located a short distance from the refinery. During December 1947 tensions between Arab and Jewish workers there had sometimes run high, despite efforts by Arab and Jewish union activists and leaders to keep the peace. When news of the bomb attack at the refinery reached the workshops, tensions soared and some of the younger and more hotheaded Arab workers there stopped work, shut down the machines, and began arming themselves with whatever makeshift weapons came to hand. For some very tense moments it seemed that the massacre at the refinery might be repeated at the railway workshops. But Arab unionists, including veteran PAWS activists like Sa'id Qawwas and AWC sympathizers as well, promptly intervened to prevent violence. At great personal risk they prevailed on the hotheads to calm down and preserved order until arrangements could be made for the Jewish workers to leave work and reach their homes safely. A Jewish unionist at the workshops declared that "without a shadow of a doubt it is thanks to [the Arab unionists'] courage that what befell the workers at the refinery was not also our lot that day."[45]

The Arab unionists' effective intervention to prevent violence against Jews at the railway workshops received little public attention. Not surprisingly, the Yishuv focused on the massacre of Jews at the refinery, while the Arab community preferred to dwell on the preceding bomb attacks by Jews and the Hagana's subsequent retaliatory raid which took an even larger number of Arab lives. The vision of Arab-Jewish worker solidarity and of peaceful coexistence which had once motivated so many people could not survive the atrocities and the mutual dehumanization which were the inevitable by-products of the ferocious intercommunal warfare which engulfed Palestine in the months that followed. Even less could it survive the actual physical displacement of much of Palestine's Arab population. By May 14, 1948, when the State of Israel was formally established, several hundred thousand Arabs had already fled or been driven from their homes, land, and places of work. Over the following half year or so the ranks of the uprooted would double again, encompassing in all some 700,000 people, half of Palestine's Arab population and some 80 percent of the Arabs who had once lived within the three-quarters of Palestine that now became Israel.

So it was that in the summer of 1948 Efrayyim Krisher, a Hashomer Hatza'ir activist employed at the Haifa railway workshops who had worked closely with Arab unionists for a decade and owed his life to their quick thinking and personal bravery on December 30, 1947, was busy trying to round up enough Jews who knew something about railway work to get what was now the Israel Railways up and running again. Some of his recruits were Jewish refugees from Europe, survivors of the Nazi campaign to exterminate European Jewry who had only recently arrived in the new Jewish state. These new arrivals, and Krisher's other recruits, filled jobs which until a few months earlier had been held by Arabs, most of whom had lost their homes and their homeland and were now beginning bitter new lives as refugees.

Conclusion

At the end of December 1947, Pinhas Lubianker (later Lavon) addressed the central committee of MAPAI on the topic of "the Arab worker in the Jewish state." A senior party official who would later serve as Israel's minister of defense and as general secretary of the Histadrut, Lubianker began by asserting that this would be the first time in the history of the Jews that they would have a non-Jewish minority population living among them, requiring them to set a good example of how a majority should behave toward a minority. It would not be easy, Lubianker warned.

> There is [already] a sediment of 20 years of education, and especially the last 10 years, which has not inculcated in us the capacity for living together with the neighboring people. There is a primitive nationalism among the *tzabarim* [young Palestine-born Jews]. There is an historical instinct for revenge among the Oriental Jewish communities. There is danger from [Jewish] terrorist groups and the [right-wing Zionist] Revisionists and their nationalist megalomania. And we must also not forget the danger from the other side: the desire to paper over contradictions and shape Jewish-Arab relations in accordance with a sentimental irrationalism imported from abroad. . . . In the past we neglected the sphere of activity among Arabs not a little. It was not just that we had a weak program, but our will to realize this weak program was also weak. Today as well, the problem is not so much a change in the program as a change in our will. In other words, in addition to sporadic activity among the Arabs by seeking connections with individuals here and there, organizing a club, etc. etc., there is a need for large-scale and comprehensive activity in the Arab sector. Let us not forget, if we neglect this sphere the communist party in all its manifestations will exploit it.

Lubianker argued that since Jews and Arabs would be equal citizens in the Jewish state, the principle of Hebrew labor should not apply to either government employment or the private sector. He also advocated the establishment of state-run employment offices open to all, the equalization of Arab and Jewish wages and, eventually, the creation of a workers' movement which would encompass both Jews and Arabs.[1]

A few months later Eli'ezer Bauer (later Be'eri), a member of the Hakibbutz Ha'artzi–Hashomer Hatza'ir Arab Department staff, put the issue even more sharply at the conclusion of a detailed report he had drawn up for the Jewish Agency's Labor Department on "The Arab Worker in the Jewish State." "The transition from a colonial regime [in Palestine] to [Israel's] independence must not be for the Arabs a transition from a colonial regime in which a people from overseas rules repressively and exploitatively to a colonial regime in which the dominant people is local. A state which seeks to realize the ideas of Herzl's *Altneuland* cannot accept the existence of conditions like those in South Africa, where the human rights of an entire subject people are denied."[2]

Bauer's reference to *Altneuland* is ironic, though that was surely not his intention. By the time he submitted his report many tens of thousands of Palestinian Arabs had already been forced from their homes, seeking refuge from the escalating warfare between Arabs and Jews or under compulsion from Jewish military forces. In the months that followed the trickle turned into a flood, and by the time the fighting ceased early in 1949 half of Palestine's Arab population had been displaced, including most of its working class, which had been concentrated in the more developed central and coastal regions which now became part of Israel. Many of these refugees found themselves outside their homeland, where they and their descendants remain today, while those Palestinians still within it, in those parts of Palestine which now became known as the West Bank and the Gaza Strip, found themselves under Arab but nonetheless alien rule, whether by the Hashemite regime based in the former Transjordan or by Egypt. The seeds were thus sown for continuing conflict, driven by the Palestinians' refusal to accept the consequences of defeat in 1948 and their apparently ineradicable drive for self-determination in some part of what had been Palestine. In his utopian novel Herzl had been vague about how Palestine's Arab majority had so quickly become a small minority amidst a sea of Jews, though he implied that the process had been peaceful and insisted that the Arabs had welcomed the influx of Jews. By contrast, the actual demographic transformation of Palestine in 1947–49 was accompanied by a great deal of force and violence and was certainly not welcomed by the country's Arabs, among whom it left scars that remain unhealed to this day.[3]

Nor did Bauer and Lubianker's vision of a Jewish state in which Arabs would enjoy equality actually come to pass. The 160,000 Arabs who remained within Israel in 1949 became citizens of the new state and had the right to vote in local and national elections. But despite the promise embodied in the eloquent language of Israel's declaration of independence, they were certainly not full and equal citizens. Most of them remained under military administration until 1966, their lives subject to the often arbitrary authority of (Jewish) army officers from whom permits were required for many of the activities of daily life. The military administration, aided by the security service, sought to control the "Israeli Arabs" (as they were now designated), ensure their docility, and garner their votes for MAPAI by manipulating village, clan, and family rivalries and by using the same extremely broad powers of administrative detention, censorship, control of associational life, and restrictions on movement which the British had used to suppress the Arab revolt of 1936–39 and then (much less successfully) against the Jewish insurgency of 1945–47. Israeli officials justified these measures by the need to protect the state's security from subversive elements within a potentially hostile minority, a dangerous fifth column aligned with the Arab states with which Israel was still at war, though in fact the Palestinians within Israel were hardly rebellious. But these broad powers also served, along with a variety of legal and administrative stratagems, to facilitate the transfer of large amounts of Arab-owned land to the control of the state, which then allocated it (as it did many other resources) for the exclusive benefit of Israel's Jewish citizens.[4]

The hope that in the Jewish state Jewish and Arab workers could finally achieve cooperation and unity as equals was also not realized. The Israeli government and the Histadrut adopted policies and practices which sought to ensure that Arab workers were largely excluded from the Jewish sector of Israel's economy—in effect, a continuation of the old Hebrew labor policy, now enforced much more effectively by the sovereign authority of the state. Arab citizens of Israel were largely restricted to jobs in their own communities, though the government sometimes turned a blind eye to their employment elsewhere. MAPAI, in control of the government as well as the Histadrut, rejected demands by the socialist-Zionist MAPAM and the Israeli Communist Party (which included both Jews and Arabs) that Arabs be allowed to join the Histadrut. Instead, the Palestine Labor League was resurrected, renamed the Israel Labor League and used as the framework within which Arab workers were to be organized, under the close supervision of the Histadrut and the security apparatus, which also prevented the establishment of an autonomous Arab labor movement within Israel.[5]

As Michael Shalev has shown, changing labor market conditions in the late 1950s, including developing labor shortages in the Jewish sector and a desire to gain access to new pools of cheap Arab labor, helped stimulate Histadrut and government officials to abandon rigidly exclusionary policies and allow Arab workers into the Israeli Jewish labor market. In 1959 the Histadrut officially resolved to admit non-Jews as full members, and they were able to vote in Histadrut elections for the first time in 1965. The Histadrut dropped the word "Hebrew" from its name and henceforth called itself simply the "General Organization of Workers in Israel." The Israel Labor League, which like its predecessor the Palestine Labor League had never achieved any autonomous organizational life, was now finally and permanently disbanded. In 1966, after a long struggle waged by both Arabs and Jews but also in order to facilitate labor mobility, the military administration of Arab areas within Israel was finally abolished. As a result of these shifts Arabs gradually replaced "Oriental" Jews—that is, Jews from Arab countries or from elsewhere in Asia or Africa—in the lower strata of the labor force, especially in agriculture and construction, allowing the latter to move up the occupational ladder and the social scale. This process was further accelerated after 1967 as the Israeli labor market was flooded by a mass of even cheaper Palestinian workers from the newly occupied West Bank and Gaza, who unlike Palestinian citizens of Israel were not permitted to join the Histadrut and enjoyed few social benefits or workplace rights. These Palestinian workers came to dominate the very bottom ranks of the Israeli labor force.[6]

The roots both of Lubianker's glowing vision of friendship and cooperation between Jewish and Arab workers in the Jewish state, and of the less pleasant realities of Arab-Jewish relations in Israel, can be traced back to the mandate period. As we have seen, the labor-Zionist movement consistently declared its adherence to the principle of friendship, solidarity, and unity between Jewish and Arab workers in Palestine. But the specific understanding of that principle evinced by the dominant force within that movement made realization of the ideal of cooperation between Arab and Jewish workers, unions, and labor organizations largely impossible. For by cooperation and solidarity Ahdut Ha'avoda and then MAPAI generally meant that Arab workers should be organized under the exclusive tutelage of the Histadrut, in keeping with their deeply ingrained conviction that neither Palestinian Arab nationalism nor the Palestinian Arab workers'

movement were authentic or legitimate. At the same time, Ahdut Ha'a-
voda and MAPAI always gave highest priority to the struggle for Hebrew
labor, which Arab workers could not help but understand as an actual or
potential threat to their livelihoods.

It was only in the years between the end of the Second World War and
the end of the mandate, when the Histadrut's Hebrew labor campaign and
its effort to organize Arab workers were largely in abeyance, that the
way was opened for fruitful cooperation between the Histadrut and the
increasingly vigorous and effective Palestinian Arab workers' movement.
As a result those years witnessed episodes of unprecedented worker activism and solidarity that transcended communal boundaries. But of course
relations between Arab and Jewish workers, complex and often conflictual
in their own right, could not be isolated from the larger conflict between
Zionism and Palestinian Arab nationalism which in that same period entered a new and decisive phase. The violent struggle for control of Palestine that ensued determined whether Jews or Arabs would dominate in
that land, and it also determined the fates of Palestine's Arab and Jewish
working classes. One was largely dispersed, while the other, though the
highly organized bulwark of Israel's dominant party, failed to achieve the
exalted status, prosperity, and security which the visionaries and propagandists of labor Zionism had promised Jewish sovereignty would bring.

"IF ONLY" HISTORY, LOST VOICES, AND WAYS OF KNOWING

There are students of the Zionist-Palestinian conflict who have pointed to
instances of Arab-Jewish cooperation in mandatory Palestine, and especially cooperation among workers, as evidence that the conflict need not
have taken the course it did, that a peaceful solution which met the basic
needs of both Arabs and Jews might have been found had the voices of
reason, compromise, and working-class solidarity on both sides prevailed.
The history of the mandate period thus becomes a story of missed opportunities focused on what might have been, a morality tale in which the
"bad guys" on both sides triumph over the peacemakers, whose weakness
and ineffectuality is somehow never really accounted for.[7] As I stated in
the Introduction, I am not making an "if only" argument here. On the
contrary, it seems clear to me that the Zionist and Palestinian nationalist
movements sought irreconcilable objectives and were on a collision course
from the very start. Moreover, while it is true that during the mandate
period various groups of Arab and Jewish workers were involved in efforts
to cooperate and in some cases (the railway workers, for example) devel-

oped a sense of solidarity that at times transcended (or at least moderated) national divisions, it is also true that relations among them were profoundly affected by the dynamics of the broader Zionist-Palestinian conflict, as the fate of much of the Arab working class in 1948 conclusively demonstrated.

Yet while rejecting this way of writing history, it is important to remember that the workers and unionists and political activists and leaders who figure in this book could not know how things would eventually turn out or what consequences their actions would have. That is why I have tried to make sense of the diverse perspectives of various Arab and Jewish individuals, labor organizations, and political formations on the question of relations between Arab and Jewish workers and labor movements, including even those which seem in retrospect to have been historical dead ends, if not nonstarters. It is easy to ridicule those Jews who in 1920 adhered to what I termed a "Bolshevik-Zionist" vision and could thus imagine Trotsky's Red Army liberating Palestine and making it into a Jewish soviet republic, or to argue that Hashomer Hatza'ir's vision of a binational and unpartitioned Palestine was never really in the cards. Nor is it difficult to see that the National Liberation League's insistence on distinguishing between Zionism and the Jews in Palestine and offering the latter the rights of a national minority in the future independent Arab Palestine never had much prospect of evoking interest in a Yishuv more determined than ever to seek a sovereign Jewish state in as much of the country as it could get. Nonetheless, a fuller understanding of the mandate era, and particularly of Arab-Jewish relations in that period, requires us to take these positions seriously, to try to grasp the spirit, the historical context, and the discursive field in which they were conceived and advanced, as well as to analyze why they failed to garner support and why other visions and strategies and policies won out. For the same reason we must (as I argued in the Introduction) make an effort to understand the subjective impulses, beliefs, and conceptions of the world which led the historical actors discussed in this book to think and act as they did, whether we ultimately judge those actions to have been right or wrong, humane or pernicious, appropriate or misguided, effective or futile.

This applies as much to faith in socialism as it does to faith in nationalism. That nationalism is by definition particularistic and in practice often divisive and exclusionary seems obvious, but in the nineteenth century and through most of the twentieth socialism seemed to many people to offer the promise of an identity and solidarity that transcended national, ethnic, religious, and racial divisions. We know of course that there has never really been a pure class identity "unsullied" by other forms of identity, other energies, other dreams; in fact, one could argue that working-class solidarity has been most effective and durable when it has also been infused by other solidarities, whether of religion, ethnicity, nationalism, gender, race, locale, or kinship. It is even plausible to argue that working-class solidarity, labor movements, and even socialism have in practice often been what we might today term a form of "identity politics" for male workers. Yet if this is an important insight, it would nonetheless be wrong to reduce socialism and worker activism to nothing but a form of identity politics. To do so would be to ignore the very diverse meanings which the socialist vision has had for different people (including many women) in different times and places, and to lose sight of some very important dimensions of human experience. As we have seen, socialism meant very different things to a variety of Arab and Jewish parties and movements in Palestine, and was related to Arab and Jewish nationalisms in complicated ways. These must be separated out and analyzed; they cannot be ignored or dismissed, however unrealistic or self-contradictory or even bizarre some of the formulations to which Arab and Jewish leftists subscribed may seem to us now.

In unpacking and analyzing the programs and actions of various individual thinkers and leaders, and of the organizations or movements within which they operated, I have argued that we must go beyond individual choice or group ideology, and beyond attributing certain attitudes to plain ignorance, to being out of touch with reality, with "the facts." I have instead tried to show how those choices, ideologies, and attitudes, indeed "ignorance" itself, are actually products of certain systems of meaning, of certain ways of knowing. The case of Zionism's (and labor Zionism's) conception of Palestine's indigenous Arab population effectively illustrates this point. As I discussed in Chapter 1, that conception is not usefully explained in terms of ignorance or even of a willful refusal to recognize reality. Rather, if we want to understand why many Zionists were unable to acknowledge the authenticity of Palestinian Arab national sentiment and opposition to Zionism, we need to examine the generation and operation of a certain Zionist discourse about the Arabs, a more or less coherent system of meanings and exclusions which constituted a field of knowledge and simultaneously embodied a specific set of power relations.

That discourse was neither self-generating nor *sui generis*. It had strong roots in Zionist appropriations of Jewish history. But it also emerged within a broader field of contemporary European conceptions of, and attitudes toward, Asians and Africans, a field which was itself shaped by (and helped reproduce) a power relationship in which Europeans (whether in Europe or settled overseas) ruled over non-Europeans—a relationship summed up under the rubric of colonialism. In this sense, despite the vigorous debates among the various Zionist parties and factions over how to deal with the "Arab question," it seems clear that "the Arabs" (and in the case of labor Zionism "the Arab workers") with whom they were grappling were a constructed representation whose characteristics and relationship to Palestine partook of a broader European colonial discourse while also reflecting the Zionist movement's own economic, political, and psychological needs and interests.

As we have seen, most of the Jews who actually settled in Palestine continued to adhere to these conceptions of Arabs, particularly the rejection of the authenticity and legitimacy of Palestinian Arab nationalism, even when confronted with strong evidence that one might have expected would cause them to question their beliefs. That they were generally able to deal with inconvenient facts in a way that left their core beliefs intact should come as no surprise. This phenomenon is hardly unique to this particular group of people or this historical encounter: all of us do it to some extent each and every day, and sociopolitical movements which must hold to a certain vision of themselves, their mission, and their opponents if they are to overcome great obstacles and achieve their goals do it all the more. This again underscores the importance of exploring the cultural systems through which people make sense of their experiences, rather than trying to explain their beliefs and actions as the unmediated products of those experiences.

SPECIFICITY AND THE RELATIONAL APPROACH

Having advanced this argument, I hasten to add that how we go about analyzing the systems of meaning which informed and helped structure the ways in which the Arabs and Jews discussed in this book saw themselves and others, and the practices in which those discourses were embodied, also makes a big difference. For it is easy, and all too tempting, to essentialize discourses, to describe and analyze them as if they were unitary, internally unconflicted, and unchanging over time. In this book I have tried to argue that although one can discern certain core beliefs and considerable continuity in each, in Palestine neither Jewish nor Arab nationalisms were unitary and static objects. They need to be disaggregated, their complex forms and contents unpacked and contextualized. They were not self-contained objects with a singular meaning, nor did they exist in any authentic, original, or pure form, an ideal against which we may measure conformity or deviation. They, and the ideologies and movements they spawned, were constructed from diverse, sometimes even contradictory, elements within a particular social, cultural, political, and economic field and a particular historical conjuncture. Indeed, what gives them their specificity is their very complexity, even contradictoriness, a product of the complex fields within which they took shape and of the diversity of the social and political forces which deployed them in different ways, as well as of the obstacles and opponents they encountered along the way and which also shaped them.

Thus, for example, I have suggested that much of labor-Zionist discourse echoes themes found in colonial discourse generally: the denial of rational agency to the indigenous population, the definition of that population as lacking the characteristics of a nation and therefore as not entitled to self-determination, the attribution of anticolonial and nationalist sentiment and action to the malign influence of a small minority of self-interested "inciters," the conception of the land as empty because not settled or utilized in familiar ways, the sense of European civilizing mission, and so forth. But labor Zionism's deployment of these themes was made distinctive, and perhaps especially complicated, because they were couched in the language of socialism, class struggle, and international working-class solidarity. As a nationalist project, labor Zionism posited ethnic/national boundaries between the Jewish and Arab working classes in Palestine, and more generally between Jews and Arabs, boundaries which also often involved elements drawn from colonial discourse. But because labor Zionism simultaneously conceived of itself as a working-class and socialist project, a component of the international labor and socialist movements, it also posited valid boundaries along class lines. It therefore had to find ways of managing the noncoincidence of those sets of boundaries.

The discursive and political contestation among the diverse forces within the labor-Zionist camp over a range of issues was bound up with the articulation over a period of several decades of a set of often exclusionary practices which shaped the Yishuv and later Israeli society in crucial ways. Those practices were themselves grasped as the basis not only for Jewish working-class formation and solidarity but for the realization of the Zionist project more broadly. These Jews in Palestine recast themselves as workers by securing or creating certain types of jobs, but also by endowing their acts with certain kinds of working-class and nationalist meaning, a process in which the economic was inextricably bound up with the cultural. As we have seen, at a certain stage in this process of self-definition Arab workers were assigned an important role: for a time the dominant tendency within labor Zionism found it useful to cast them both as an enemy to mobilize against, for economic as well as political ends, and as an ally, a passive junior partner, whose presence could be read as a guarantee of, and a justification for,the Zionist project. To put it another way, and more broadly, in Palestine as elsewhere working-class formation (indeed, all class formation) was as much a discursive as a material process, and needs to be analyzed as such.[8]

It was in this sphere of Arab-Jewish interaction, and more generally in the way in which elements of a national project, a colonial-settler project, and a socialist or working-class project interpenetrated in a unique way and a unique context, that much of Zionism's specificity can be located. Comparison of Zionism with other contemporary cases of European overseas colonization and settlement bear out this claim by showing how very different political, social, and economic outcomes can (for example) be traced back to varying labor market strategies as well as to differing discourses and practices with regard to the indigenous population, which in the case of Palestine can in turn be related to the labor-Zionist movement's struggle for hegemony within the broader Zionist project. It is of course true that the realization of labor Zionism's vision of a "normal" Jewish society could be attained only *after* the establishment of a sovereign Jewish state in Palestine, accompanied by the displacement of most of the Palestinians who lived in what became that state's territory and a massive influx of poor Jews (mainly from Arab countries) to fill the vacuum they had left. Yet labor Zionism's relative success in excluding Arab workers from the Jewish sector and constructing as self-sufficient a Jewish enclave as possible in the four decades before 1948—a strategy bound up with the articulation of certain visions of itself and of Arabs—was a key factor in making partition and Jewish statehood in most of Palestine possible. Moreover, many of the institutions most characteristic of Israeli society through the 1960s also took shape in the context of these specific practices and representations. After 1967, of course, things would change again, as Palestinians from within Israel but especially from the occupied West Bank and Gaza would come to dominate the lower ranks of Israel's working class. Yet this development too bears out my point, for it contributed in complex ways to the decline of labor-Zionist hegemony, manifested most dramatically in the defeat of the Labor Party (heir to MAPAI and its offshoots) in the 1977 elections, years of ascendancy by the Israeli right, and profound changes in Israeli politics, society, and culture.

Much of what I have said applies to Arab nationalism and the Arab workers' movement in Palestine as well. As both an ideology and a movement, Palestinian Arab nationalism encompassed a variety of interests, aspirations, visions, and sociopolitical forces, and we must be careful to avoid treating it as if it were monolithic or possessed some essential meaning. Unfortunately, most studies of this nationalism have focused on the politics of the Palestinian Arab (male) elite, while what that nationalism actually meant to the peasant and poor urban majority of Palestine's Arab community has received little attention.[9] The kinds of things I have tried to address here—such dimensions of the Palestinian Arab experience as the Arab railway workers' persistent dream of unity with their Jewish coworkers, or the hopes and concerns of the Haifa construction workers and the Jaffa dockworkers discussed in Chapter 5, or the struggle which rank and file Arab workers in Jaffa waged against Hebrew labor and which helped set the stage for the general strike against British rule and Zionism shortly thereafter—have as a consequence been sorely neglected.

By the same token, the conventional narratives of Arab nationalism in Palestine do not provide much help in understanding why it was that some Arab unionists took pains to explain their perspective to Jewish coworkers in Hebrew-language leaflets, or in understanding the attitudes toward cooperation expressed by Arab labor leaders, unionists, and leftists in the 1940s, attitudes which sometimes brought down upon them the wrath of the nationalist leadership. The Arab workers and unionists discussed in this book were virtually all nationalists, in the broad sense that they strongly opposed what they regarded as Zionist encroachment on their homeland and favored an independent Arab Palestine. Nonetheless, as we have also seen, many of them were willing to ignore or defy the official nationalist line by embracing a discourse of worker solidarity across national boundaries that justified cooperation with Jews whom they knew to be avowed Zionists, provided it was on terms they deemed fair and equal. It is of course probable that many Arab workers, such as the Haifa tailors and carpenters whose 1925 strike the Histadrut helped guide, had (at least initially) only a limited understanding of what the Zionist project meant for them as Arabs (and specifically as Arab workers). Nonetheless, as I suggested in Chapter 5, it is not helpful to attribute such actions simply to ignorance, manipulation, individual pathology, or collaboration. To do so is to uncritically adopt nationalism's own language and way of seeing the world, for neither "ignorance" nor "collaboration" (nor even, on the positive side of the ledger, "resistance") can be regarded as simple, transparent, uncomplicated, self-evident terms. All are very much embedded in nationalist discourse and must be analyzed as such.

It is not difficult to understand why nationalist movements find it necessary to condemn certain relationships between members of the national group and aliens as harmful to the national cause and try to deter or punish those involved in them; we may even deem such measures justifiable under certain circumstances. But for historians that must be where the questions about what collaboration really means to those involved in it start, not where they end—at least if we wish to avoid operating from within nationalism's conception of itself as a unitary and internally unconflicted ideal and identity that is superior to (or exclusive of) all other identities, sentiments, interests, loyalties, and aspirations. In the case at hand, the Arab nationalist perspective on cooperation between Arab and Jewish workers—or more precisely, the perspective of the nationalist movement's elite leadership—implicitly denied working-class Palestinian Arabs any capacity for agency, for making their own sense of complex (and generally adverse) circumstances and acting to further their interests as they defined them. It is not enough to label Arab workers who under certain circumstances cooperated with Zionists as "dupes" and leave it at that. We need, as I have tried to do here, to acquire a much more complex, nuanced, and historically grounded understanding of why particular people thought and acted as they did, however we ultimately judge their actions in moral or political terms. This in turn requires a more subtle and flexible conception of national identity, one that treats it as a complex of ideas, symbols, sentiments, and practices which people from various sociopolitical groups appropriate and deploy selectively and contingently, rather than some essence which is derivable from the writings and speeches of nationalist thinkers, leaders, or activists.

On both sides, then, contending sociopolitical forces put forward conflicting visions of national and class identity, and differing notions of how to relate to the other side's working class and labor movement. On both sides these conflicting definitions and strategies were influenced by Arab-Jewish interaction, in workplaces, neighborhoods, and daily life as well as in the formal political arena. More broadly, the existence in mandatory Palestine of overlapping Arab and Jewish markets for unskilled and semi-skilled labor, and even to some extent for skilled labor, especially in the large and important government and transnational sectors, helped shape perceptions, strategies, and relationships among large segments of the Jewish and Arab working classes in Palestine. In this sense we may extend the late E. P. Thompson's evocative imagery to suggest that the Arab and Jewish working classes in Palestine not only "made themselves" but also to a large extent "made each other," that each influenced the processes by which the other was formed, within a broader matrix of relations and forces. So instead of trying to characterize the sole or essential meaning of relations among Arab and Jewish workers and labor movements as either cooperation or conflict, it may make more sense to shift our focus to the ways in which intercommunal as well as intracommunal identities, boundaries, and projects were constructed and reproduced, and foreground the contestation which always characterized those processes.

However, as I suggested in the Introduction, it is not only with respect to workers that a relational approach which focuses on the mutually constitutive interactions between Arabs and Jews in Palestine may prove useful. I have argued, for example, that it was the urgent need to exit (at least partially) a labor market dominated by abundant low-wage Arab labor which prompted the labor-Zionist movement to strive to construct a relatively self-sufficient high-wage Jewish economic enclave in Palestine. This imperative also propelled the unrelenting struggle for Hebrew labor and other practices couched in the language of worker solidarity and class struggle but aimed largely at excluding or displacing Arab workers. These practices exacerbated intercommunal tensions, but they also facilitated labor Zionism's drive for hegemony over rival social and political forces *within* the Yishuv. By the mid-1930s this strategy, implemented mainly by the Histadrut (whose membership encompassed more than a quarter of the Yishuv's population in 1936) and its affiliated economic, social, cultural, and military institutions, had helped the labor-Zionist camp become the dominant force within the Yishuv and the international Zionist movement. In this sense, as I noted earlier, many of the institutions and practices which for an entire historical period—from the 1930s into the 1970s—were seen as the most distinctive features of the Yishuv and of Israeli society (the kibbutz and the moshav, the powerful state and Histadrut sectors of the economy, the cult of "pioneering," the central role of the military) can be understood as directly or indirectly the product not so much of the values brought by the immigrants of the Second Aliya, as the functionalist school of Israeli sociology would have it, as of the Zionist project's interaction with Arabs and Arab society in Palestine itself.

Similarly, while Israeli sociologists have conventionally explained the subordinate social location and status of Israel's "Oriental" Jews in terms of the failure of these culturally "traditional" people to adapt successfully to a "modern" society, recent critical scholarship has stressed their relegation upon arrival in Israel to the bottom ranks of the labor market (where they displaced or replaced Palestinian Arabs) and official denigration and suppression of their cultures, defined by the dominant groups in Israel as backward (read Arab).[10] Before the First World War some Zionist leaders had already envisioned Yemeni Jews as replacements for Palestinian Arab agricultural workers and actually sponsored Yemeni Jewish immigration to Palestine. This failed to solve the problem of Arab competition, however, and the Jewish labor movement turned instead to the struggle for Hebrew labor and economic separatism. After 1948 it was largely Jewish immigrants from Arab countries who filled the social vacuum created by the flight or expulsion of the vast majority of the Arabs who had lived within what became the borders of the new State of Israel, and as I noted earlier Oriental Jews' upward social mobility in the 1960s and 1970s was facilitated by the influx of Palestinians into the lower strata of the Israeli working class. It can thus be argued that the matrix of Jewish-Arab interactions in Palestine played a central role in shaping ethnic relations *within* Jewish society in Palestine and later Israel.

It is clear, too, that Arab society in Palestine was profoundly influenced by the Zionist project in a variety of ways. There was of course the catastrophic displacement of 1947–49, but in the preceding decades Jewish immigration, settlement, investment, and state building had already had an important impact on Arab society. That impact can be seen in the direct and indirect effects of Jewish land purchases, settlement, and agricultural practices on Arab agrarian relations, the complex effects on the Arab economy of the large-scale influx of capital that accompanied Jewish immigration and development, and the effects of the economic and social policies implemented by a British administration committed to fostering a Jewish "national home" in Palestine but also concerned about alienating the country's Arab majority. To take that impact into account does not imply downplaying other sources of social change or denigrating the Palestinians' capacity for historical agency. Rather, it broadens our frame of reference so as to include more of the complex historical field within which modern Palestinian Arab society developed.

As historians and others explore the history of modern Palestine in new ways, as the object of inquiry is reconceived and a different set of concepts and categories deployed, it will, I believe, become increasingly clear that the two communities were neither natural nor essentially monolithic entities. Nor were they hermetically sealed off from one another, as the conventional historiography assumes. Rather, they interacted in complex ways and had a mutually formative effect on one another, both as communities and through relationships that crossed communal boundaries to shape the identities and practices of various subgroups. These complex and contested processes operated at many levels and in many spheres, including markets for labor, land, agricultural produce and consumer goods, business ventures, residential patterns, manufacturing and services, municipal government, and various aspects of social and cultural life. These interactions also had an important but little-explored spatial dimension, manifested in shifts and reorientations in demographic, economic, political, and cultural relations and flows among and within different settlements, villages, urban neighborhoods, towns, cities, and regions of Palestine.

As I discussed in the Introduction to this book, a number of recently published studies already manifest new approaches to the histories of Arabs and Jews in Palestine, approaches that challenge conventional categories, cross hitherto unquestioned boundaries, and treat Palestine not as *sui generis* but as eminently suitable for comparative study. This process will be furthered as more scholars frame and explore new and different kinds of problems while drawing on both Arabic and Hebrew source materials. There is certainly a lot to be done. I have already mentioned the paucity of work on women and gender, but many other areas remain largely unexplored, among them interactions in neighborhoods and markets, the development of colloquial language, and personal (including sexual) and business relationships across communal boundaries. While many of these things do not figure, or figure only marginally, in this book, I hope that it will nonetheless help stimulate further research in new directions.

One of feminist theory's most powerful insights is that all social relations, all human interactions, are gendered; that is, they manifest, and cannot be fully understood without taking into account, the system or systems of gender relations that prevail in a given society at a given time. Similarly, in her recent book *Playing in the Dark: Whiteness and the Literary Imagination*, Toni Morrison has argued convincingly that one cannot really understand American literature, even that part of it written and largely read by whites, or by extension almost any aspect of American culture and society, without bringing race and race relations into the picture, without dealing with the way racial categories, identities, and attitudes help shape most if not all other categories, identities, and attitudes in American society. In *Culture and Imperialism* Edward W. Said has proceeded along similar lines by exploring the mutually formative relationship between nineteenth- and twentieth-century European (and

American) culture and contemporaneous European imperial expansion and domination, and later American global hegemony as well. In so doing Said seeks to break with conventional perspectives which have treated "the West" and the rest of the world as entirely distinct and largely unconnected cultural domains.

In this book I have sought to approach Arab-Jewish relations in modern Palestine in much the same way. As I argued in Chapter 1, from the very beginning of modern Jewish settlement in Palestine the presence of a substantial Arab population must be seen not as marginal to the Zionist enterprise nor simply as an extraneous obstacle to be bypassed or overcome, even though that is how many, perhaps most, Zionists thought of it at the time, if they thought about Arabs at all. That presence must instead be seen as an essential, constitutive element in the formation of the Zionist project and the Yishuv, an integral part of the story rather than just a footnote. Moreover, Palestinian Arabs must be regarded as having possessed a capacity for agency which often intruded upon and altered Zionism's conceptions of itself and its mission, and always registered itself on and helped shape the Zionist project. Similarly, though for a long time the Jewish presence in Palestine may seem to have impinged much less directly and obviously on the country's Arab majority, it nonetheless had a significant impact in many spheres well before 1948, and like it or not room must be made for that presence in the story of the Palestinians.

Though the character and circumstances of their interactions have changed over time, over the past century Arabs and Jews in Palestine have helped shape each other's society and historical trajectory, as well as the ways they have thought of themselves and each other. That this interactive relationship continues to operate is evidenced by the political, social, and cultural impact on both Palestinians and Israeli Jews of Israel's occupation of the West Bank and Gaza from 1967 onward. As I suggested earlier, the occupation and its consequences reinforced trends already operative in Israeli Jewish society, contributing to the erosion of labor Zionism's political, ideological, and socioeconomic hegemony. We can also discern the effects of that impact in (for example) the growing strength of the Israeli right during the 1970s, the new political and cultural assertiveness of Israeli's Oriental Jewish communities, the Americanization of Israeli Jewish culture and politics, chronic instability and paralysis in the political system, and the decline of the Histadrut as a political, economic, and social institution.[11] At the same time, after 1967 (and especially from the second half of the 1970s onward) the Palestinians within Israel have grown increasingly assertive in demanding both equal rights within Israel and Palestinian national rights more broadly. Their growing numbers, education, social weight, and capacity for mobilization have allowed them to take better advantage of the Israeli political system to pursue their interests as a community, while the end of their isolation from the rest of the Palestinian people has strengthened their national identity, if in complicated ways. Whatever the fate of the West Bank, Gaza, and their Arab inhabitants, the Palestinians within Israel will remain a presence with which their Jewish fellow citizens will have to reckon.

The occupation has also had profound effects on the Palestinians in the occupied territories. These include the decline of local agriculture, widespread proletarianization, the reinforcement of Palestinian national identity accompanied by a sense that the Palestinians in the West Bank and Gaza have their own particular problems and interests, the emergence of locally based organizations, a better understanding of Israeli politics, society, and culture, and a new capacity for resistance. This last effect was manifested most dramatically in the *intifada*, the Palestinian uprising against the occupation which erupted in December 1987, at a moment when most Israelis but also many Arabs and others seemed to have once again written the Palestinians off as political actors.

Though it ultimately failed to win the Palestinians statehood, the *intifada* had a significant impact on Israeli and Palestinian perceptions and on the balance of forces between them. It dramatically raised the political, economic, and moral costs of the occupation for Jewish Israelis, compelling many of them to reckon as never before with the ineradicability of Palestinian nationalism, and it eventually led Israel to negotiate directly with the Palestinians (and ultimately with the PLO itself) rather than only with Arab states. It also prompted many Israeli Jews to seek new ways of understanding Zionism's encounter with the Palestinians and how the occupation had affected their own society. At the same time, the *intifada* gave the Palestinians, and especially those within the occupied territories, a new sense of self-confidence, in their capacity to resist and confront Israel but also in their ability to live alongside it in peace, provided they too are permitted to realize their dream of self-determination. The occupation, the *intifada* and its aftermath, as well as contact with Israeli society and the bitter experience of most Arab peoples with authoritarian regimes, have also strengthened the determination of many Palestinians that the future Palestinian state be democratic and fully respect its citizens' human and civil rights and liberties.

As I write these lines, Israel and the Palestine Liberation Organization are rather fitfully striving to implement (if only partially) the agreement they signed in September 1993. That agreement provided for the gradual introduction of limited Palestinian self-rule in the West Bank and Gaza, while deferring resolution of all the difficult issues—control of land and other resources, Jerusalem, the Jewish settlements in the occupied territories, the Palestinian refugees, Palestinian statehood—to future negotiations. That deferral has allowed the Israeli government, led by the political heirs of labor Zionism, to continue to put off having to accept, once and for all, the legitimacy of the Palestinian people's national rights, including the right to national self-determination in some part of what was once Palestine. Only time will tell whether the Israel-PLO agreement marks the beginning of a process which will ultimately lead to a comprehensive and lasting peace between Israel and the Palestinian people, based on statehood for both peoples in Palestine, or whether it will turn out to be yet another dead end, another abortive attempt to reconcile Palestinian and Israeli Jewish aspirations to sovereignty and security. Given the agreement's flaws and limitations, the tragic history of this conflict, and the complex circumstances under which the current effort to bring it to an end is unfolding, a large dose of pessimism laced with a touch of hope would seem appropriate.

It is likely that many more struggles, crises and, I fear, more violence lie ahead. Beyond that it is useless to try to predict how things will develop, for the outcome of the current conjuncture will be determined by a very complex and rapidly changing mix of interacting political, social, economic, and cultural factors and forces. In that mix the effort by historians and other scholars to reinterpret the modern history of Palestine, to which this book is a contribution, may perhaps play some very modest part, by helping to undermine the hegemonic grip of nationalist mythologies on both sides and open up space for new modes of thought and action, and even new ways of imagining the future. In that sense, even if most Palestinians or Israelis do not come to see their pasts or their futures very differently as a result of scholarly reinterpretations of the history of modern Palestine, historians' efforts to understand the past may nonetheless have some bearing on current political struggles.

But historians must pursue their craft regardless of the impact of their work. I have sought here to explore some of the ways in which the histories of Arabs and Jews in modern Palestine have been inextricably and fatefully intertwined, while also attending to what makes those histories distinctive. Whatever the future may bring, the historical trajectories of

Israeli Jews and Palestinians will continue to be intertwined. We are therefore compelled to try to envision how these two peoples might one day live together in peace, for the alternatives to peace are terrible to contemplate; and we may at least hope that a better understanding of the past will help bring that day closer.

Notes

INTRODUCTION

1. Earlier versions of some of the material in this book, especially elements of the Introduction, the Conclusion, and Chapters 2, 3, and 4, originally appeared in my article "Railway Workers and Relational History: Arabs and Jews in British-Ruled Palestine," *Comparative Studies in Society and History* 35, no. 3 (July 1993): 601–27, and in my "Exclusion and Solidarity: Labor Zionism and Arab Workers in Palestine, 1897–1929," in Gyan Prakash, ed., *After Colonialism: Imperial Histories and Postcolonial Displacements* (Princeton, N.J., 1995), 211–40.

2. Much of what follows also applies to the literature on Palestine in the late Ottoman period, and to Israel and the Palestinians inside and outside what had been Palestine after 1948 as well. But it is especially relevant to the three decades during which Palestine existed as an administratively unified entity, before partition, war, Palestinian displacement, and massive Jewish immigration radically altered the terms of interaction between Arabs and Jews in Palestine. For surveys of the field, see Tarif Khalidi, "Palestinian Historiography: 1900–1948," *Journal of Palestine Studies* 10, no. 3 (spring 1981); Kenneth W. Stein, "A Historiographic Review of Literature on the Origins of the Arab-Israeli Conflict," *American Historical Review* 96, no. 5 (December 1991); and Beshara B. Doumani's important essay "Rediscovering Ottoman Palestine: Writing Palestinians into History," *Journal of Palestine Studies* 21, no. 2 (winter 1992).

3. S. N. Eisenstadt, *Israeli Society* (New York, 1967), 1.

4. Talal Asad, "Anthropological Texts and Ideological Problems: An Analysis of Cohen on Arab Villages in Israel," *Review of Middle East Studies*, no. 1 (1975), 14 n. 11; also excerpted in *MERIP Reports*, no. 53 (December 1976). See also Gershon Shafir, *Land, Labor and the Origins of the Israeli–Palestinian Conflict, 1882–1914* (Cambridge, U.K., 1989), 1–7.

5. Dan Horowitz and Moshe Lissak, *Origins of the Israeli Polity: Palestine under the Mandate* (Chicago, 1978), 13; first published in Hebrew as *Meyishuv lemedina: yehudei eretz yisra'el betkufat hamandat kekehila politit* (Tel Aviv, 1977).

6. Michael Shalev, *Labour and the Political Economy in Israel* (Oxford, 1992),

13–14. Even some of the most theoretically sophisticated work produced by Israeli scholars shares these flaws: for example, Amir Ben-Porat's *Between Class and Nation: The Formation of the Jewish Working Class in the Period before Israel's Statehood* (Westport, Conn., 1986). Ben-Porat uses what he terms a "neo-Marxist" conception of class formation to analyze Jewish working-class formation in Palestine. But he treats that process as if it were basically unconnected to the Yishuv's relations with its predominantly non-Jewish environment and therefore has very little to say about Palestinian Arabs.

7. See, for example, 'Abd al-Wahhab al-Kayyali, *Ta'rikh filastin al-hadith* (Beirut, 1970), or Muhammad Nakhla, *Tatawwur al-mujtami' fi filastin* (Kuwait, 1983).

8. I will cite just two examples. Mitchell Cohen's *Zion and State: Nation, Class and the Shaping of Modern Israel* (Oxford, 1987), an analysis of the Zionist project from what Cohen terms a "Lukacsian" perspective, more or less ignores that project's interactions with Arabs as a significant factor in class formation and state building. Virginia R. Dominguez's *People as Subject, People as Object: Selfhood and Peoplehood in Contemporary Israel* (Madison, 1989) is an interesting and in some ways enlightening study, but it has almost nothing to say about how Zionism's encounter with the Palestinians helped shape conceptions of selfhood and peoplehood among Israeli Jews. In contrast, I argue here that that encounter shaped those conceptions in crucial ways and must therefore be an integral component of any exploration of Israeli Jewish identity.

9. Avishai Ehrlich, "Israel: Conflict, War and Social Change," in Colin Creighton and Martin Shaw, eds., *The Sociology of War and Peace* (Houndmills, Hampshire, U.K., 1987), 131.

10. On relational history, see Perry Anderson, "Agendas for Radical History," *Radical History Review*, no. 36 (September 1986), though my conception of what such an approach to history entails is not identical to his. See too Joel Beinin, *Was the Red Flag Flying There? Marxist Politics and the Arab-Israeli Conflict in Egypt and Israel, 1948–1965* (Berkeley, 1990), ch. 1.

11. Readers may find useful a brief discussion of some of the work which in my opinion has contributed to a rethinking of the modern history of Palestine. I make no pretense here of being comprehensive, however, and I fully understand that the authors whom I do mention may well not share my understanding of the significance of their work.

What might be called the "revisionist" tendency in Israeli historiography encompasses several distinct but mutually interacting currents. Baruch Kimmerling can be said to have pioneered one influential approach, in his books *Zionism and Territory: The Socio-Territorial Dimensions of Zionist Politics* (Berkeley, 1982) and *Zionism and Economy* (Cambridge, Mass., 1983), his edited volume *The Israeli State and Society: Boundaries and Frontiers* (Albany, N.Y., 1989), and various articles. In his pathbreaking *Land, Labor and the Origins of the Israeli-Palestinian Conflict, 1882–1914* (Cambridge, U.K., 1989), Gershon Shafir very effectively grounded the evolution of the Zionist project in conditions in Palestine itself while expanding our understanding of its similarities with, and differences from, other projects of European overseas settlement; both the Introduction and Chapter 1 of this book draw heavily on his pioneering work. Michael Shalev drew on the "split labor market" approach pioneered by Edna Bonacich in his contribution to Kimmerling's edited volume, "Jewish Organized Labor and the Palestinians: A Study of State/Society Relations in Israel," while his book *Labour and the Political Economy in Israel* (Oxford, 1992) very usefully explored the historical development and specific character of what he called Israel's "social-democratic corporatism." Lev Luis Grinberg's *Split Corporatism in Israel* (Albany, N.Y., 1991) addressed a similar set of questions. Tamar Gozanski's *Hitpathut hakapitalizm bepalestina* (The development of capitalism in Palestine [Haifa, 1986]) is an important work of synthesis informed by a fairly orthodox Marxist perspective.

Ehrlich's essay cited earlier, "Israel: Conflict, War and Social Change," provides a useful critique of Israeli sociology, as do the opening pages of Shafir's and Shalev's books. The Israeli "new historians" have produced an extensive revisionist literature on the birth of Israel and Palestinian displacement in the 1947–49 period, including work by Benny Morris, Tom Segev, Ilan Pappé, Avi Shlaim, and the late Simha Flapan. For a discussion of some of these books and the political conjuncture within which they emerged, see my essay "Original Sin," in Zachary Lockman and Joel Beinin, eds., *Intifada: The Palestinian Uprising against Israeli Occupation* (Boston, 1989). See also Laurence J. Silberstein, ed., *New Perspectives on Israeli History: The Early Years of the State* (New York, 1991).

The studies that appeared in the now-defunct Israeli journal *Mahbarot lemehkar ulebikoret* played an important role in opening up new space for critical analysis of Israeli society and history. Ella Shohat's 1988 article "Sephardim in Israel: Zionism from the Standpoint of Its Jewish Victims" and Shlomo Swirski's *Israel: The Oriental Majority* (London, 1989) also deserve mention for breaking with Ashkenazi-centered analyses of Zionism and Israeli society. Recent years have also witnessed a dramatic improvement in the quantity and quality of published work on the culture(s) of Jews in Palestine and later Israel, including contributions by Itamar Even-Zohar, Tamar Katriel, Tsili Doleve-Gandelman, Jonathan Frankel, Ya'el Zerubavel, Nurith Gertz, and Menahem Perry.

Given the dispersion, statelessness, and subordination that characterize Palestinian life, the continuing centrality of the struggle for national self-determination and the limited resources at the disposal of most Palestinian scholars, it is perhaps not surprising that explicit revisionism has been less in evidence among Palestinians. Nonetheless, there have been a number of studies which manifest what I am calling a relational approach. One of the most important is Elia Zureik's *The Palestinians in Israel: A Study in Internal Colonialism* (London, 1979), which explicitly seeks to show that in the mandate period "the two sectors, Arab and Jewish, *did not develop separately and independently under similar conditions,* but that they were interconnected in an *asymmetrical* relationship, mediated by the British presence" (5; emphasis in the original). There have also been a number of studies which depart from the traditional nationalist narrative in approach and/or choice of subject, including work on the Palestinian communist and labor movements by Musa al-Budayri (Musa Budeiri), Mahir al-Sharif, and 'Abd al-Qadir Yasin, as well as Philip Mattar's 1988 biography of Amin al-Husayni and Muhammad Muslih's *The Origins of Palestinian Nationalism* (New York, 1988). One of the most important recent contributions to the history of Palestine is Walid Khalidi, ed., *All That Remains: The Palestinian Villages Occupied and Depopulated by Israel in 1948* (Washington, D.C., 1992), an invaluable source of information on the hundreds of Arab villages in Palestine which no longer exist. Various Palestinian research centers and institutions of higher education have also published other important work on aspects of Palestinian social and cultural history.

Among works produced by scholars who are neither Israeli nor Palestinian, pride of place belongs to Roger Owen's edited volume, *Studies in the Economic and Social History of Palestine in the Nineteenth and Twentieth Centuries* (Carbondale, Ill., 1982), and especially to Owen's introduction, which usefully discusses various conceptualizations of Palestinian history. Asad's article "Anthropological Texts and Ideological Problems," cited earlier, analyzed changes in Arab village organization in terms of "the articulation of a capitalist with a non-capitalist mode of production mediated by the British colonial state" (14). In some crucial respects Stanley Greenberg's *Race and State in Capitalist Development: Comparative Perspectives* (New Haven, Conn., 1980), a broad comparative analysis of racial and ethnic relations in South Africa, the United States, Northern Ireland, and Israel, paved the way for some of the work by Israeli sociologists which I have already cited. Derek Penslar's *Zionism and Technocracy: The Engineering of Jewish Settlement in Palestine, 1870–1918* (Bloomington, Ind., 1991) is a useful contribution to our understanding of early Zionism. Theodore Swedenburg's innovative study of the 1936–39 revolt in Palestine as constructed in popular memory is forthcoming from the University of Minnesota Press. Rachelle Taqqu's Ph.D. dissertation, "Arab Labor in Mandatory Palestine, 1920–1948" (Columbia University, 1977), which unfortunately has not been published, deserves special mention as a very useful source of information for this book. Barbara J. Smith's *The Roots of Separatism in Palestine: British Economic Policy, 1920–1929* (Syracuse, N.Y., 1993) sheds important new light on Palestine's economic development and Arab-Jewish relations. Jeff Halper's *Between Redemption and Revival: The Jewish Yishuv of Jerusalem in the Nineteenth Century* (Boulder, 1991) has helped undermine views of the "Old Yishuv" as completely insular and stagnant, if not moribund; on this topic see too Shlomo Shva and Dan Ben-Amotz, *Eretz Tziyon Yerushalayyim* (Jerusalem, 1973), an entertaining collection of clippings from the pre–First World War Jewish press in Palestine. Though Beinin's *Was the Red Flag Flying There?* deals mainly with the post-1948 period, it deserves mention here because it transcends conventional boundaries and offers a relational perspective on the trajectories of the Marxist left in both Egypt and Israel.

Recent contributions to the study of women and gender in the Zionist-Palestinian conflict include Elise G. Young, *Keepers of the History: Women and the Israeli-Palestine Conflict* (New York, 1992) and Sheila Katz's unpublished Ph.D. dissertation, "Women and Gender in Jewish and Palestinian Nationalisms before 1950: Founding and Confounding the Boundaries" (Harvard University, 1993). A great deal of work remains to be done on women and gender in Palestine, especially for the pre-1948 period.

12. Ibrahim Abu-Lughod, "The Perils of Palestiniology," *Arab Studies Quarterly* 3, no. 4 (fall 1981).

13. I discuss this question more fully in " 'Worker' and 'Working Class' in pre-1914 Egypt: A Rereading," in Zachary Lockman, ed., *Workers and Working Classes in the Middle East: Struggles, Histories, Historiographies* (Albany, N.Y., 1994), ch. 4.

CHAPTER 1. ZIONISM AND PALESTINE BEFORE
THE FIRST WORLD WAR

1. *Encyclopedia Judaica* (Jerusalem, 1972), vol. 16, 1519.

2. On nationalism generally, see Benedict Anderson, *Imagined Communities: Reflections on the Origin and Spread of Nationalism* (London, 1991), and E. J. Hobsbawm, *Nations and Nationalism since 1780: Programme, Myth, Reality* (Cambridge, U.K., 1992).

3. In this connection, see Uri Eisenzweig, *Territoires occupés de l'imaginaire juif: essai sur l'espace sioniste* (Paris, 1980), and Uri Eisenzweig, "An Imaginary Territory: The Problematic of Space in Zionist Discourse," *Dialectical Anthropology* 5, no. 4 (May 1981); and Kimmerling, *Zionism and Territory*.

4. When I use the term "European" here I also include Europe's demographic extensions overseas, namely the states which European settlers established and dominated in the Western Hemisphere, the South Pacific, and southern Africa. On colonialism and European culture, see Edward W. Said, *Culture and Imperialism* (New York, 1993). This discussion also draws on Said's *The Question of Palestine* (New York, 1979).

5. More than two decades ago the French historian Maxime Rodinson pointed out the need for research on the images of, and ideas about, Palestine, Arabs, Turks, Islam, and "the Orient" in general which were current among Jews of different classes and educational levels in Europe during the late nineteenth and early twentieth centuries, and which are likely to have colored Zionist notions of contemporary Palestine and of its inhabitants; see *Israel: A Colonial-Settler State?* (New York, 1973), 38. To my knowledge no comprehensive study of this kind, which would entail delving into Jewish literature and popular culture as well as the emerging Yiddish- and Hebrew-language mass culture taking shape in newspapers, novels, and theater, has yet been carried out, and it is obviously beyond the scope of this book as well. Nor has there yet been sufficient research on the images and attitudes of those Jews who actually went to Palestine, and how those attitudes were affected by interaction with the indigenous Arab population. Yet it seems clear that just as recent research on popular and mass culture in Europe has shed important new light on the shaping of attitudes about empire, colonialism, and race, so similar studies on the cultures of Jews in Europe may tell us something important about how early Zionists perceived Palestine, its Arab inhabitants, and its Ottoman rulers. I am thinking of such studies as John MacKenzie, ed., *Imperialism and Popular Culture* (Manchester, England, and Dover, N.H., 1986), and Malek Alloula, *The Colonial Harem* (Minneapolis, 1986). Michael Berkowitz provides some interesting material in his *Zionist Culture and West European Jewry before the First World War* (Cambridge, U.K., 1993).

6. On these representations, see Edward W. Said, *Orientalism* (New York, 1978), and Maxime Rodinson, *Europe and the Mystique of Islam* (Seattle, 1987). My discussion here draws on the analyses in both these very important works.

7. For discussions of Zionism's borrowings from various European projects of colonization, within Europe (e.g., Germans in predominantly Polish Silesia) as

well as outside it, see, for example, Shafir, *Land,* and Penslar, *Zionism and Technocracy.* This topic merits much more scholarly attention.

8. Thus even a relatively recent and critical study like Simha Flapan's *Zionism and the Palestinians* (London, 1979) takes 1917 as its starting point, without providing any rationale for that choice.

9. The notion that most of Palestine's Arabs were, as late as the British mandate period, newly arrived in the land (and hence lacked any authentic claim to it) was recently resurrected in a notorious work of pseudoscholarship by Joan Peters, *From Time Immemorial: The Origins of the Arab-Jewish Conflict over Palestine* (New York, 1984). For critiques, see the review by Yehoshua Porath, Israel's leading historian of Palestinian nationalism, in *New York Review of Books,* January 16, 1986, and Norman Finkelstein's chapter in Edward W. Said and Christopher Hitchens, eds., *Blaming the Victims: Spurious Scholarship and the Palestinian Question* (London, 1988).

10. For example, when the German Imperial Chancellor questioned him about the current owners of the land in Palestine which the Jews would purchase, Herzl described them as "Arabs, Greeks, the whole *mixed multitude* of the Orient." Entry for October 9, 1898, in *The Complete Diaries of Theodor Herzl* (New York, 1960), edited by Raphael Patai, vol. 2, 702. A little later, writing in Jerusalem, Herzl uses the same English-language phrase to describe a group of "Arab beggars, womenfolk, children, and horsemen." Entry for October 29, 1898, vol. 2, 743.

11. Entry for June 12, 1895, in ibid., vol. 1, 88–89. The Jewish National Fund, formally established in 1901 and incorporated in 1907 as the Zionist Organization's land-purchasing agency, did in fact require that its lands never be leased to or cultivated by non-Jews. In Israel this stricture was not infrequently violated, but it is nonetheless emblematic of the specific character and consequences of the Zionist project for Palestine's Arab inhabitants. For details, see Walter Lehn (in association with Uri Davis), *The Jewish National Fund* (London, 1988), especially chs. 2 and 6.

12. For a discussion of al-Khalidi and his career, see Alexander Schölch, *Palestine in Transformation, 1856–1882: Studies in Social, Economic and Political Development* (Washington, D.C., 1993), ch. 9.

13. See Neville J. Mandel, *The Arabs and Zionism before World War I* (Berkeley, 1976), 47–48.

14. Quoted in Walid Khalidi, ed., *From Haven to Conquest: Readings in Zionism and the Palestine Problem until 1948* (Washington, D.C., 1987), 91–93.

15. Quoted in Eisenzweig, "An Imaginary Territory," 281.

16. Theodor Herzl, *The Jewish State: An Attempt at a Modern Solution to the Jewish Question* (London, 1967), translated by Sylvie D'Avigdor, 30.

17. I am thinking, for example, of Yosef Gorny, who manages to read *Altneuland* as manifesting only the "universalist, humanist essence" of Herzl's thought and his "compassion and concern for human beings"; see *Zionism and the Arabs, 1882–1948: A Study of Ideology* (Oxford, 1987), 31, 33. Gorny also apparently deems his analysis of Herzl's attitudes toward Arabs complete without so much as mentioning passages from Herzl's diaries in which he envisions dispossessing and displacing Palestine's Arab peasantry. More generally, Gorny's narrow focus

on Zionist ideology obscures the broader issue of Zionism's relationship to contemporary colonial discourse and practice. In this book as in his other work, Gorny fails to transcend (or even perceive) the conceptual limits imposed by his unquestioning adherence to a Zionist framework of interpretation. In this regard, see my review of Gorny's book *The British Labour Movement and Zionism, 1917–1948* (Totowa, N.J., 1983), in *Middle East Journal* 38, no. 1 (winter 1984).

To her credit, Anita Shapira at least mentions these diary entries in her *Land and Power: The Zionist Resort to Force, 1881–1948* (New York, 1992). But she does not devote serious attention to them, or to other texts (and ways of understanding them) that do not fit her interpretative paradigm, which posits a sharp dichotomy in Zionist thinking about the use of force between an early "defensive ethos" and a later "offensive ethos." Shapira echoes Gorny when she argues that "If someone had predicted to Herzl that the state he had envisaged would ultimately be established in blood and fire and that its fate would rest on the point of a sword, the author of *The Jewish State* would undoubtedly have been repulsed and would have rejected the implications of this prophecy. His ideas about the establishment of a Jewish state were shaped by conceptions of progress in a global community of enlightened peoples, a world in which problems were solved by reason and common agreement" (354). This assertion ignores the fact that for Herzl and many of his contemporaries, the "community of enlightened peoples" was not truly global, since it excluded most of the population of the earth outside Europe and Europe's extensions overseas; consequently the "problems" of those so excluded—which often meant their resistance to European domination—could quite legitimately be "solved" not by reason but by force. As I argue here, most Zionists implicitly adopted this perspective and applied it to the Arabs of Palestine.

In other words, like Gorny, Shapira fails to situate Zionist conceptions of, and attitudes toward, Palestine and Arabs in relation to contemporary European colonial discourse and practice. She thereby ignores a significant part of the larger context within which Zionist thought and practice took shape, and outside of which it (and many of the specific texts she discusses) cannot be properly understood. More generally, while *Land and Power*'s focus on Zionist culture is welcome and the book contains much that is interesting and useful, there are many things it deals with unsatisfactorily or simply leaves out, perhaps because Shapira still remains within the confines of Zionist discourse, if on its liberal fringe.

18. See, for example, Mary Louise Pratt, *Imperial Eyes: Travel Writing and Transculturation* (London, 1992), especially ch. 3, on southern Africa.

19. Ahad Ha'am's 1891 article was originally published in the Odessa Hebrew-language journal *Hamelitz*. It was soon republished in '*Al parashat derakhim* (Odessa, 1895), a collection of his articles and essays, and later in his collected works, *Kol kitvei Ahad Ha'am* (Jerusalem, 1949). The 1911 article, "Sakh hakol," is also in *Kol kitvei Ahad Ha'am*.

20. Ahad Ha'am's scathing review of *Altneuland* is in ibid., 313–20.

21. For a discussion of these aspects of Ahad Ha'am's thought, see Jacques Kornberg, ed., *At the Crossroads: Essays on Ahad Ha-am* (Albany, N.Y., 1983), especially chs. 8 and 10.

22. Another case in point is Yitzhak Epstein, a teacher in Palestine whose 1907 article "A Hidden Question," published in the Hebrew-language periodical *Hashi-*

lo'ah, touched off debate by insisting that the Zionist movement had to come to terms with the fact that Palestine had long been settled by another people which was unlikely to leave in order to make room for Jewish immigrants. The controversy sparked by Epstein's article was short-lived, however, and the movement's attention soon turned to other issues. See Shapira, *Land and Power*, 45, 47, 49, 65–66.

23. In Nahman Syrkin, *Kitvei Nahman Syrkin* (Tel Aviv, 1938–39), vol. 1, 1–59.

24. This is certainly the way MAPAI'S leading thinker, Berl Katznelson, depicted Syrkin in his biographical preface to Syrkin's collected works; see ibid., and also Marie Syrkin, *Nachman Syrkin, Socialist Zionist* (New York, 1961).

25. *Kitvei Nahman Syrkin*, vol. 1, 53.

26. See B. Borokhov, *Ketavim* (Tel Aviv, 1955), vol. 1, 154–80.

27. Large parts of his argument had already been set forth in his 1905 essay "On the Question of Zionism and Territory." See *Ketavim*, vol. 1, 18–153.

28. "Our Platform," *Ketavim*, vol. 1, 283.

29. "Zionism and Territory," *Ketavim*, vol. 1, 148.

30. "Our Platform," *Ketavim*, vol. 1, 282–83.

31. "Zionism and Territory," *Ketavim*, vol. 1, 148.

32. In *Ketavim*, vol. 1, 290.

33. "Our Platform," *Ketavim*, vol. 1, 284–85.

34. *Ketavim*, vol. 2, 429.

35. *Ketavim*, vol. 2, 403–5.

36. See Yehuda Slutzki, "MPSI beve'idat hayesod shel hahistadrut," *Asufot 1*, no. 14 (December 1970), 135.

37. On developments in this period, see Mandel, *The Arabs and Zionism*, chs. 3–7.

38. As the "Hebrew" in "Hebrew labor" indicates, the self-styled "workers" and "pioneers" who arrived in Palestine during the Second Aliya period generally referred to themselves and their organizations not as "Jewish" (*yehudi*) but as "Hebrew" (*'ivri*). By adopting this term they expressed their denigration and rejection of Diaspora Judaism, associated in their minds primarily with statelessness, powerlessness, and passivity, and identified themselves instead with the (suitably mythologized) ancient Hebrews who had lived in their own homeland as a sovereign people. This move allowed them to link their own project with heroic episodes from the Jewish past, now reinterpreted nationalistically, such as the struggle of the Maccabees to free the land of alien rule and restore Jewish sovereignty. These Jewish immigrants newly arrived from Europe could thereby imagine themselves to be elementally connected to the land, giving them a claim to possess it stronger than that of its indigenous Arab inhabitants. At the same time, it gave them a way to see themselves as prototypes of the "new Jew" whom socialist Zionism would produce in Palestine, a person who was thoroughly modern yet deeply rooted in the national soil and intimately connected to the wellsprings of Jewish history and culture, which Zionism identified with national sovereignty. This self-image gave those who embraced it (particularly labor Zionists) a potent weapon to wield against rival forces within the Yishuv, the Zionist movement, and world Jewry.

39. For a study of early debates over this issue, see Yosef Gorny, "Ha'ideologiya shel kibbush ha'avoda," *Keshet*, nos. 37–38 (1967–68). For a much broader and more useful perspective, see Shafir, *Land*. This chapter obviously draws on Shafir's perceptive analysis, though I have sought to broaden and enrich his rather structural approach by attending to the discursive aspect of the processes and developments under discussion.

40. The second part of the essay, with which I am primarily concerned here, was entitled "Hashkafa proletarit vehagana le'umit" (Proletarian perspective and national defense). The essay as a whole, "Leshe'alot 'avodateinu ba'aretz," was published under Ben-Tzvi's pseudonym "Avner" and first appeared in the Po'alei Tziyon organ *Ha'ahdut* 3, nos. 16–17 (1912); it was soon republished in pamphlet form.

41. See Slutzki, "MPSI," 135.

42. For a discussion of these strategies from the standpoint of Bonacich's theory of split labor markets, see Michael Shalev, "Jewish Organized Labor and the Palestinians: A Study of State/Society Relations in Israel," in Kimmerling, *Israeli State and Society*, 93–133. On the struggle for Hebrew labor on the Jewish-owned citrus plantations in the late 1920s and 1930s, see Anita Shapira, *Hama'avak hanikhzav: 'avoda 'ivrit, 1929–1939* (Tel Aviv, 1977).

43. Quoted in Shafir, *Land*, 198.

44. The kibbutzim kept consumption and overhead costs low by socializing many of the costs of reproduction of labor (common kitchens, dining halls and laundries, shared living quarters, collective child rearing) as well as by promoting an ideology of asceticism and self-sacrifice. At the same time, collective labor made effective use of scarce resources and limited land. The kibbutzim also proved an efficient means of effecting the spatial extension of the Yishuv and would later play a significant military role as well.

The kibbutz soon came to occupy a unique place in the labor-Zionist imagination and in Zionist (and later Israeli) mythology, at least until the 1970s. Although kibbutz members never accounted for more than about 5 percent of the Yishuv's (and later of Israel's Jewish) population, the kibbutz was held up as the model of the Jewish commonwealth-in-the-making in Palestine. Into the 1960s, labor-Zionist politicians took pride in claiming membership in some kibbutz, even if they had in reality spent only a few months living and working there forty years earlier before going on to careers in the labor-Zionist movement's burgeoning bureaucracy. Though the Yishuv was always predominantly urban, labor Zionism cast the kibbutz member astride a tractor, rifle in hand, as the paragon of Zionist virtue and achievement, the prototype of the tough, hardworking "new Jew" which Zionism had produced in Palestine. The kibbutz became a powerful symbol not only of the "pioneering" spirit, of readiness for self-sacrifice in the national cause, but also of Zionism's authenticity and rootedness in the soil of Palestine and its ability to make the land productive, often counterposed to the Arabs' alleged failure to do so. One might usefully compare the kibbutz with the "red-roofed farmhouse" which, Jacques Berque suggests, became a central symbol of *colon* society in Algeria, even though the great majority of European settlers in Algeria actually lived in urban areas; see Jacques Berque, *French North Africa: The Maghrib between Two World Wars* (London, 1967), ch. 1.

45. For an introduction to the origins and significance of the Balfour Declaration, see my entry in Joel Krieger, ed., *The Oxford Companion to Politics of the World* (New York, 1993), 67–68.

CHAPTER 2. LABOR ZIONISM AND THE ARAB WORKING
CLASS, 1920–1929

1. This message is already suggested by the essay's title, for by calling it *The Arab Movement* (in the original Hebrew, *Hatnu'a Ha'aravit*), rather than, say, *The Arab Nationalist Movement*, Ben-Tzvi implicitly denied the authenticity of Palestinian Arab nationalism. Some sort of Arab movement apparently existed, but it was not genuinely national or nationalist in character.

2. Ben-Tzvi asserted that most of Palestine's Arab peasants were in fact descendants of the ancient Jewish rural population, who eventually adopted the language, culture, and religions of their conquerors. This would seem to contradict his argument about the ethnic incoherence of Palestine's Arab population.

3. As Ben-Tzvi put it, "The second element, after the Sunnis, is the Jewish people—second in number but first in building [up the land]." The phrase rhymes in Hebrew: *hasheni beminyan, verishon bevinyan.*

4. As Yonathan Shapiro points out, however, a few months earlier Ahdut Ha'avoda alone had received 5,600 votes (the largest total for any party) in elections to the Yishuv's representative assembly, suggesting that it had already acquired some support among broader nonworker circles in the Yishuv. See *The Formative Years of the Israeli Labour Party: The Organization of Power, 1919–1930* (London, 1976), 75. On Ahdut Ha'avoda, see also Yosef Gorny, *Ahdut Ha'avoda, 1919–1930: hayesodot hara'ayonim vehashita hamedinit* (Tel Aviv, 1963). For a lively account of the founding of the Histadrut and its early years, see Ze'ev Tzahor, *Baderekh lehanhagat hayishuv: hahistadrut bereishita* (Jerusalem, 1982).

5. As the Histadrut will henceforth play a central role in this study, it is worthwhile to discuss it further. To start with, the very Hebrew term (*'ovdim*) chosen for "workers" in its title tells us something important about labor Zionism's conception of itself and of the working class whose formation and course it saw itself as guiding. *'Ovdim* suggests all those who labor, thereby encompassing that large and politically powerful segment of the Histadrut's mass base which consisted of members of kibbutzim and moshavim, employees of Histadrut enterprises who were deemed to be members of producers' cooperatives rather than exploited proletarians, and even nonworking wives of the organization's largely male membership. (In this respect *'ovdim* may be usefully contrasted with another Hebrew term, *po'alim*, which in left-Zionist usage had the narrower connotation of wage workers conceived of as proletarians.)

The choice of term was thus rooted in a labor-Zionist discourse which saw the Histadrut not as a traditional labor movement whose goal was to defend the interests of urban wage workers, but rather as an instrument to realize the Zionist project by constructing an egalitarian-cooperative Jewish society, in effect by means of the extension of the Histadrut and its network of institutions to encompass the great majority of the Jewish population of Palestine. This vision was ultimately manifested in David Ben-Gurion's slogan of the early 1930s, *mema'a-mad le'am* ("From Class to People"), suggesting that the labor-Zionist movement had achieved hegemony within the Zionist movement, that its interests now coincided with those of virtually the entire Yishuv (and Jewish people), and that therefore the rhetoric of class solidarity and struggle could be largely put aside.

The choice of the term "organization" rather than "federation" is also discursively significant. The new Histadrut's leadership, largely in the hands of Ahdut Ha'avoda with Hapo'el Hatza'ir as junior partner, saw it not as a federation of largely autonomous trade unions, like the British Trades Union Congress or the AFL (and later the CIO and the AFL-CIO) in the United States, but rather as a highly centralized institution. Early efforts by some of the Jewish trade unions to achieve autonomy were quickly crushed by the Histadrut leadership, and thereafter top-down control was exercised through a powerful and increasingly bureaucratic apparatus based in Tel Aviv (the Histadrut's headquarters there was later nicknamed "the Kremlin") as well as through a network of "workers' councils" (*mo'etzet hapo'alim*) in every city and town whose members were largely chosen not by the trade unions but by vote of all local Histadrut members, under a system of proportional representation according to party lists. This system tended to give party officials (and especially Ahdut Ha'avoda and then MAPAI *apparatchiks*) control of the Histadrut apparatus at the local as well as at the national level.

The Histadrut was (and is) also perhaps unique among labor movements in that trade union affairs were (and to this day still are) relegated to a specific department which functioned alongside other Histadrut departments responsible for such "national" tasks as immigration, settlement, education and culture, and so forth. This again reflected the Histadrut's role as a central institution of the Zionist project, which usually overshadowed its trade union functions. By the mid-1920s, the organization's executive committee also exercised effective control over both Hevrat 'Ovdim, the holding company for many of the Histadrut's expanding network of economic enterprises, and Kupat Holim, the Histadrut's health care system.

6. The protocol of the Histadrut's founding congress has been published in *Asufot* 1, no. 14 (December 1970).

7. On the formation and evolution of the SWP, see Slutzki, "MPSI."

8. The SWP won 19.5 percent of the vote for delegates to the founding congress of the Histadrut in Jaffa and Tel Aviv and 16 percent in Haifa, reflecting the party's strength among urban workers, many of whom were recent immigrants. In contrast, the party did very poorly in the moshavot, where more conservative and veteran workers loyal to Ahdut Ha'avoda and Hapo'el Hatza'ir predominated. Overall, the SWP received 6.8 percent of the votes cast, but its influence, and especially its ability to annoy and harass the labor-Zionist leadership, was out of all proportion to its limited base of support.

9. On the language question, see the serialized memoirs of communist activist Nahman List, "Tzadak hakomintern," *Keshet*, no. 18 (1963), 139.

10. EC/H, December 30, 1920.

11. On the Hebrew labor campaigns during the 1920s and 1930s, see Shapira,

Hama'avak, and Steven Glazer, "Propaganda and the Histadrut-Sponsored Pickets for 'Hebrew Labor,' 1927–1936" (unpublished Ph.D. dissertation, Georgetown University, 1991).

12. On the linkages between Arab and Jewish wages, see Tzvi Sussman, *Pa'ar veshivayon bahistadrut: hahashpa'a shel ha'ideologiya hashivyonit veha'avoda ha'aravit 'al s'kharo shel ha'oved hayehudi be'eretz yisra'el* (Ramat Gan, 1974).

13. Government of Palestine, *A Survey of Palestine* (Jerusalem, 1946), vol. 1, 141, 148. Unfortunately, the mandatory government's censuses categorized people by religion rather than by nationality or ethnicity. As a result, the figures I cite here for Arabs are actually the combined totals for Muslims and Christians, and therefore include some non-Arab Christians, such as Armenians. But given the relatively small proportion of non-Arab Christians in the total number for Christians, my point about relative growth rates remains valid. It is perhaps also worth noting that urban growth was very uneven during the 1920s: inland towns grew much more slowly than Jaffa and Haifa, while the population of Gaza on the Mediterranean coast seems to have stagnated.

14. On labor migration, see Rachelle Taqqu, "Peasants into Workmen: Internal Labor Migration and the Arab Village Community under the Mandate," in Joel S. Migdal, ed., *Palestinian Society and Politics* (Princeton, N.J., 1980), 261–85. On Haifa specifically, see May Seikaly, "The Arab Community of Haifa, 1918–1936: A Study in Transformation" (unpublished Ph.D. dissertation, Somerville College, Oxford University, 1983).

15. On the Palestinian working class and labor movement, see *inter alia* Musa al-Budayri, *Tatawwur al-haraka al-'ummaliyya al-'arabiyya fi filastin* (Beirut, 1981); Taqqu, "Arab Labor"; Salim al-Junaydi, *al-Haraka al-'ummaliyya al-'arabiyya fi filastin, 1917–1985* (Amman, 1988); and 'Abd al-Qadir Yasin, *Ta'rikh al-tabaqa al-'amila al-filastiniyya, 1918–1948* (Beirut, 1980).

16. These theses were first published in the Ahdut Ha'avoda organ *Kuntres*, no. 91 (August 1921), and later in a collection of Ben-Gurion's essays and speeches on the Arab question, *Anahnu veshkheineinu* (Tel Aviv, 1931), 61–62.

17. As the Ahdut Ha'avoda organ *Kuntres* put it proudly some years later, "the secretariat of the [Jaffa] Workers' Council, which was composed of five members of Ahdut Ha'avoda, succeeded by means of constant and careful supervision of the union in suppressing the liquidationist [i.e., anti-Zionist] tendencies of the SWP members, and did not permit them to turn this union into a 'political' field of activity for them by bringing in Arabs whose attitude and loyalty toward trade union organization still required basic testing." In fact the Jaffa Workers' Council expelled the left-led bakery workers' union from the Histadrut, but after the unions of metalworkers and building and roads workers threatened to quit in protest the Histadrut secretariat reversed the expulsion decision, on condition that the bakers' union stop calling itself "international." See S/EC/H, July 31, 1922; ISA, Division 65 (Public Works), 2/149/1, C.I.D. report, August 9, 1922; *Kuntres*, no. 241 (November 27, 1925).

18. EC/H, October 28, 1921; S/EC/H, December 17, 1921 and January 19, 1922.

19. *Kuntres*, no. 106 (January 1922).

20. *Kuntres*, no. 165 (March 14, 1924).

21. See Ahdut Ha'avoda, *Have'ida harevi'it shel Ahdut Ha'avoda: din veheshbon* (Tel Aviv, 1924), and *Kuntres*, no. 172 (June 6, 1924).

22. Histadrut (Hava'ad Hapo'el), *Din veheshbon lave'ida hashlishit shel hahistadrut* (Tel Aviv, 1927), 155. I discuss the impact of this resolution on the railway workers' union in Chapter 3.

23. In 1921 Ben-Tzvi warned his colleagues that it was "very likely" that "agitators" from the nationalist railway and tramway unions in Egypt would come to Palestine to organize local workers. S/EC/H, December 17, 1921.

24. For example, the Histadrut's second congress, held in February 1923, called for the "establishment of comradely relations with the Arab workers in the country and the development of ties with the Jewish and international workers' movement in the world." Histadrut (Hava'ad Hapo'el), *Have'ida hashniyya shel hahistadrut* (Tel Aviv, 1923), 30, 47–48. On Histadrut discussions about organizing Arab workers, see, for example, EC/H, March 23, 1922, and AA 208/28, Ben-Tzvi to Yitzhak Shemi, January 9, 1924.

25. The acronym PKP was often used to denote the Palestine Communist Party, from its initials in Yiddish, the language which most of its early adherents knew best and made a point of using when addressing Jews, since Hebrew had Zionist connotations; Zionist anticommunists seem to have used this acronym as a way of insinuating that the party and its ideology were alien imports in the Yishuv. The most important studies of the communist movement in Palestine in this period include Musa Budeiri, *The Palestine Communist Party, 1919–1948: Arab and Jew in the Struggle for Internationalism* (London, 1979); Shmu'el Dothan, *Adumim: hamiflaga hakomunistit be'eretz yisra'el* (Kfar Saba, 1991); Alain Greilsammer, *Les Communistes Israeliens* (Paris, 1978); Samih Samara, *al-'Amal al-shuyu'i fi filastin: al-tabaqa wa'l-sha'b fi muwajahat al-koloniyaliyya* (Beirut, 1979); and Mahir al-Sharif, *al-Umumiyya al-shuyu'iyya wa-filastin, 1919–1928* (Beirut, 1980).

26. The only major study of Po'alei Tziyon Smol is Elkana Margalit, *Anatomia shel smol: Po'alei Tziyon Smol be'eretz yisra'el (1919–1946)* (Jerusalem, 1976). In the early 1920s Po'alei Tziyon Smol is perhaps better characterized as a fractious political tendency than a unified party, and it would always be plagued by factionalism and splits, but for simplicity's sake I will discuss it here as if it were already at this point a unified and coherent organization.

27. For example, one source reports that as early as the autumn of 1922, Po'alei Tziyon Smol militants in Haifa (of whom there were only a handful at this point) helped organize a strike of Arab workers employed at two carpentry workshops, one Jewish-owned and the other German-owned, which succeeded in raising wages and reducing the working day from twelve to nine hours. See Ze'ev Studni, " 'Al hayamim harishonim behaifa," in L. Tarnopoler, ed., *Ze'ev Abramovitch vemorashto* (Tel Aviv, 1971), 399. Himself a Po'alei Tziyon Smol activist in Haifa in the 1920s, Studni published a number of articles reminiscing about episodes in the history of the Jewish working class in Palestine. His accounts are not always reliable, however, as I will note later when citing him in connection with the strikes at Nesher in 1924–25.

28. Though Ahdut Ha'avoda had won only 41 and 47 percent of the votes to the first and second congresses of the Histadrut respectively, it had managed to

secure effective control of the organization's governing bodies. But in the September 1924 elections to the local workers' councils the party lost ground, and in both Haifa and Jerusalem it lost its majorities. Po'alei Tziyon Smol did especially well in Haifa, where most of its votes came from the railway workers. Moreover, after these elections Ahdut Ha'avoda perceived its rivals on left and right (Po'alei Tziyon Smol and Hapo'el Hatza'ir) as conspiring to undermine its power.

29. On this period, see Shapiro, *Formative Years*, chs. 5–6. On Po'alei Tziyon Smol in the 1924 elections, see Studni, " 'Al hayamim harishonim behaifa," 402–5.

30. *Kuntres*, no. 166 (March 28, 1924).

31. See, for example, Eliyahu Golomb's article in *Kuntres*, no. 192 (November 7, 1924), and responses in subsequent issues.

32. Government of Palestine, *Survey of Palestine*, vol. 1, 148.

33. See Khalidi, *All That Remains*, 151–54, 202–3. As I noted in the Introduction, this is an invaluable source of information on pre-1948 Palestine.

34. On events at Nesher in 1924–25, see *Kuntres*, no. 301 (April 29, 1927); David Hacohen, *Time to Tell: An Israeli Life, 1898–1984* (Cranbury, N.J., 1985), 90; Joseph Vashitz, "Jewish-Arab Relations at Haifa under the British Mandate" (unpublished manuscript), Part 3, 16–17; Ze'ev Studni, "Shvitat po'alei Nesher," *Me'asef*, no. 6 (March 1974); and Histadrut, *Din veheshbon lave'ida hashlishit*, 157, the official Histadrut account. That account somehow manages to leave out the fact that the purpose of the 1925 Nesher strike was to prevent the employment of contracted Egyptian labor, while Studni fails to mention the second strike altogether. At about the same time there also seems to have been a strike involving both Arab and Jewish workers at the Grands Moulins flour mill in Haifa, but little is known about it.

35. For Ben-Gurion's comments, see *Anahnu veshkheineinu*, 107 (emphasis in the original); the letter is in *Kuntres*, no. 211 (March 27, 1925).

36. On the communists in Palestine in the 1920s, see Nahman List, "Tzadak hakomintern," *Keshet*, nos. 18, 20, 22, 24, 27, 30, 34 (1963–67).

37. Government of Palestine, *Survey of Palestine*, vol. 1, 141.

38. S/EC/H, March 23, 1925, and EC/H, April 1, 1925; *Kuntres*, no. 301 (April 29, 1927).

39. Histadrut, *Din veheshbon lave'ida hashlishit*, 156.

40. Berl Repetur, *Lelo heref: ma'asim uma'avakim* (Tel Aviv, 1973), vol. 1, 101; AA, Center for Oral Documentation, transcript of interview with Avraham Khalfon, January 29, 1976; Ze'ev Studni, "Nitzanei ha'irgun hameshutaf behaifa beshnot ha'esrim," *Me'asef*, no. 7 (May 1975), 149–51.

41. *Al-Karmil*, October 10, 1925.

42. *Ittihad al-'Ummal*, October 21, 1925.

43. AA, interview with Khalfon, January 29, 1976.

44. *Al-Karmil*, October 21, 1925. The Arabic term which *al-Karmil* used for "guild" was *niqaba*, which was already by this time the standard term for a labor union in Egypt. But in Palestine it still apparently retained its older guild-related connotations.

45. *Filastin*, August 19, 1927.

46. AA, interview with Khalfon, January 29, 1976.

47. For examples, see Histadrut, *Din veheshbon lave'ida hashlishit*, 158.

48. For a good example of Palestinian nationalist attacks on the Histadrut's efforts to organize Arab workers, see *Filastin*, June 4, 1926, article entitled "Indigenous Workers between Zionism and Communism," and another published on August 19, 1927, entitled "Our Workers Awake . . . The Jewish Unions Exploit the Forces of the Indigenous Workers . . . Need for the Establishment of National Unions."

49. AA, interview with Khalfon, January 29, 1976; S/EC/H, May 2, December 14, 1927.

50. Quoted in Ze'ev Abramovitch, *Besheirut hatnu'a* (Tel Aviv, 1965), 263.

51. S/EC/H, December 11, 1925.

52. AA 490/1–2.

53. See Taqqu, "Arab Labor," 76–77.

54. Smith, *Roots of Separatism*, 155–59.

55. See, for example, CO 733/161/6 and 733/165/2.

56. Ben-Gurion, *Anahnu veshkheineinu*, 131–33.

57. *Kuntres*, no. 280 (October 26, 1926).

58. *Kuntres*, no. 211 (March 27, 1925).

59. See, for example, Yosef Yudelevitch's two-part essay in *Kuntres*, nos. 280 and 282 (November 1926).

60. When Po'alei Tziyon Smol leader Moshe Erem addressed the congress, he acknowledged that in Poland his party favored separate national sections for Jewish workers within the trade unions, because there Jews were an oppressed national minority. But in Palestine, he argued, there was no need to separate Jewish from Arab workers.

61. AA, minutes of the third congress of the Histadrut, 13–15.

62. Ben-Gurion, *Anahnu veshkheineinu*, 138–39; emphasis in the original.

63. One can already detect in the Kibbutz Faction's cumbersome proposal the contours of Hashomer Hatza'ir's constant battle to carve out for itself some political space within which its formal commitment to revolutionary socialism and Arab-Jewish fraternity could be reconciled with the exigencies of the Zionist project. For the wording of the proposal, see Efrayyim Krisher, "Ha'irgun hameshutaf bemivhan hahagshama," *Me'asef*, nos. 3–4 (August 1972), 168–69. Strangely, Krisher asserts that the Kibbutz Faction's position was "basically accepted" by the third congress, which was in fact not at all the case.

64. For an account of the strike at the Mabruk factory, see *Kuntres*, no. 338 (June 1, 1928). The strikers succeeded in defeating an attempt by management to extend the workday.

65. For example, the Nazareth building workers whose strike Po'alei Tziyon Smol had supported during the summer of 1927 had set up a club of their own, and Yitzhak Ben-Tzvi and Philip Hassun paid it a visit in January 1928. However, Ben-Tzvi's main concern about this fledgling organization was that the club, recently raided by the police for operating without a license, might end up under the control of the nationalists or be used to serve the interests of Po'alei Tziyon Smol rather than those of the Histadrut. There was no follow-up on the part

of the Histadrut and eventually contact was lost with this embryonic workers' organization, whose fate is unknown. S/EC/H, December 14, 1927, January 8, 1928.

66. S/EC/H, May 31, 1929.

67. For an example of the latter, see the February 10, 1929 issue of *Derekh Hapo'el* (Worker's path), published by a group which called itself the "Left Bloc" and denounced the Histadrut leadership for neglecting joint organization and sabotaging Arab-Jewish class solidarity.

CHAPTER 3. THE RAILWAY WORKERS OF PALESTINE (I):
THE STRUGGLE FOR ARAB-JEWISH UNITY, 1919–1925

1. On Navon Bey, see Joseph Glass, "The Biography in Historical-Geographical Research: Joseph Navon Bey—A Case Study," in Ruth Kark, ed., *The Land That Became Israel: Studies in Historical Geography* (New Haven and Jerusalem, 1990), 77–89. For a more general overview providing many technical details that railroad buffs will appreciate, see Paul Cotterell, *The Railways of Palestine and Israel* (Abingdon, Oxfordshire, U.K., 1984).

2. Sh. Avitzur, "Shiv'im shana lemisilot habarzel ba'aretz," *Teva' ve'aretz* 5, nos. 2–3 (1962).

3. Palestine Railways, *Report of the General Manager on the Administration of the Palestine Railways and Operated Lines for the Years 1942/43, 1943/44, 1944/45 and 1945/46* (Jerusalem, 1946), 147. Jews often referred to the Haifa workshops as the Qishon workshops, since they were located near a small river known by that name in Hebrew.

4. On Wadi Salib, see Vashitz, "Jewish-Arab Relations," Part 1, 19. Unfortunately, Vashitz cites no source for this assertion; it may have been based on the recollection of long-time Arab residents of Haifa. On the Hijaz Railway's lines in Palestine just before and during the war, see Barukh Katinke, *Me'az ve'ad heina* (Jerusalem, 1961), passim. Originally from Russian-ruled Bialystok, Katinke studied engineering in Germany and arrived in Palestine in 1908. From 1911 until the end of the war, Katinke worked in the technical service of the Hijaz Railway, which assumed control of all Palestine's railway lines in 1914.

5. See Yasin, *Ta'rikh al-tabaqa al-'amila*, 118–19, which cites the reminiscences of a veteran railway worker, and al-Junaydi, *al-Haraka al-'ummaliyya*, 15, which cites a book I have been unable to find, Fa'iq Hamdi Tahbub, *al-Haraka al-'ummaliyya w'al-niqabiyya fi filastin, 1920–1948* (Kuwait, 1982).

6. See AA, Center for Oral Documentation, transcripts of interviews with Yehezkel Abramov (April 9, 1972) and Efrayyim Shvartzman (March 20, 1972); and Bulus Farah, *Min al-'uthmaniyya ila al-dawla al-'ibriyya* (Nazareth, 1985), 40–46.

7. See, for example, AA 237/32gimmel, Zionist Commission to the RWA, January 8, 1920.

8. "Have'ida hashlishit shel histadrut po'alei harakevet (Din veheshbon shel hava'ad hamerkazi)," *Kuntres*, no. 65 (January 21, 1921).

9. On Egyptian labor and British policy, see Smith, *Roots of Separatism*, 145–47.

10. See "Have'ida hashlishit," *Kuntres*, no. 65 (January 21, 1921); AA, interview with Abramov, April 9, 1972; Tzahor, *Baderekh*, 62 n. 75; Yitzhak Ben-Tzvi, *Hehazon vehagshamato: pirkei zikhronot vereshimot 'al ba'ayot hahistadrut* (Tel Aviv, 1968), 255–58.

11. EC/H, December 30, 1920.

12. *Kuntres*, nos. 65, 66 (January 21, 28, 1921); EC/H, February 17, 1921.

13. Farah, *Min al-'uthmaniyya*, 41.

14. S/EC/H, October 28, 1921.

15. Histadrut, *Din veheshbon lave'ida hashlishit*, 155. The Jewish postal and telegraph workers, some 200 in number, were then in the process of amalgamating with the Jewish railwaymen's union. Relations between the two groups were not always smooth, and their union would always be dominated by the more numerous and better organized railway workers.

16. S/EC/H, January 19, 1922; Eliyahu Bilitzki, *Beyitzira uvema'avak: mo'etzet po'alei haifa, 1921–1981* (Tel Aviv, 1981), 66.

17. *Kuntres*, no. 114 (April 7, 1922).

18. AA 104/25alef, CC/URPTW to EC/H, June 24, 1922, and in the same file a statement by fired workers, signed by eleven Arabs and nine Jews, authorizing two Jews to approach management on their behalf, January 25, 1923, as well as the accompanying letter to the general manager of the Palestine Railways. See also Ze'ev Studni, "Nitzanei ha'irgun hameshutaf," *Me'asef*, no. 7 (May 1975), 152–55, while keeping in mind that (like Studni's other published writings) it is not altogether reliable.

19. EC/H, October 10, November 7, 1922.

20. AA 104/25alef, Holmes to Minsky and Susman, January 27, 1923. Jewish unionists also argued, in vain, that the layoffs contravened provisions of the mandate for Palestine, which required the government to create conditions conducive to Jewish immigration and settlement.

21. AA 208/14alef, CC/URPTW to EC/H, June 10, 1923; *Kuntres*, nos. 135 (July 6, 1923), 142 (September 7, 1923).

22. AA, interview with Khalfon, January 29, 1976.

23. S/EC/H, June 3, 6, July 5, 1923.

24. In the elections to the Histadrut's second congress in February 1923 the various parties and formations to Ahdut Ha'avoda's left won about 13 percent of the vote, and a larger percentage of the urban vote; in the elections to the Haifa Workers' Council in July 1923, the communist Fraktziyyat Hapo'alim won 3 of 31 seats on its own. See Tzahor, *Baderekh*, 245–46; Bilitzki, *Beyitzira uvema'avak*, 102.

25. The congress also reasserted the union's autonomy by rejecting a Histadrut demand that the URPTW refrain from establishing direct links with international trade union bodies. On this congress, see AA 208/14alef; S/EC/H, November 14, 1923; a report of the proceedings can also be found in the January 1924 issue of the union's irregular publication, *Hakatar* (The locomotive). It is worth noting that the version of the report published simultaneously in the parallel Arabic edition, *al-Qatar*, was much briefer and left out most of the contentious debates, suggesting some nervousness among the Jewish unionists about allowing their Arab comrades full access to the disagreements among the Jews. For a mock-

ing account of the proceedings written by a partisan of Ahdut Ha'avoda, see *Kuntres*, no. 144 (September 28, 1923).

26. See S/EC/H, October 22, 1923. On the Hagana and the railway workers, see Repetur, *Lelo heref*, vol. 1, 83.

27. *Kuntres*, no. 165 (March 14, 1924).

28. Ibid.

29. Ibid.

30. Bilitzki, *Beyitzira uvema'avak*, 66.

31. AA 208/14alef, "To our brothers the [Jewish] workers"; AA 208/14alef, minutes of a joint meeting of the URPTW central committee, the Haifa branch committee, and the committee on joint organization, May 27, 1924.

32. The relevant resolution can be found in Tzvi Even-Shoshan, *Toldot tnu'at hapo'alim be'eretz yisra'el* (Tel Aviv, 1966), vol. 2, 104.

33. Greilsammer, *Les communistes*, 44–45. The PCP's break with Zionism and its effort to ally itself with the Arab nationalist movement had practical consequences which further deepened the mutual hostility between Zionists and communists. For example, the Hagana had recruited sympathetic Jewish railwaymen in Haifa to steal explosives from the railway storehouses, usually on Fridays when the Muslim Arab workers had their day off. One of the Jewish communists who learned of this apparently passed the information on to Arab coworkers, who protested to railway management. The General Manager demanded of Ben-Tzvi that the thefts stop; they did not, but the Hagana had to proceed more cautiously from then on. Such incidents led many in the Yishuv to regard the communists as traitors to their own people. See Repetur, *Lelo heref*, vol. 1, 83–85.

34. On these events, see ibid.; AA 208/14alef, CC/URPTW to EC/H, June 4, 1924; AA 104/25alef, "Skira mepe'ulot hamerkaz memo'etzet 1.3.24–1.1.25"; and ISA, Chief Secretary's papers, division 149, Tidhar (of the Jerusalem police) to Divisional Inspector, June 23, 1924.

35. At the crucial April 1924 Histadrut council meeting, the sole vote against the purge of communists had been cast by a Po'alei Tziyon Smol railway workers' delegate from Jerusalem. On Po'alei Tziyon Smol's attitude toward the PCP see, for example, *Halohem*, August 1924.

36. This took place at a meeting of the union's central committee held on June 14, 1924; see AA 208/14alef. Needless to say, Ben-Gurion rejected the union's claim of autonomy and insisted that it was bound by Histadrut rules and decisions.

37. Ibid.; S/EC/H, June 16, 1924.

38. In Hebrew the phrase is *patahnu lahem et hamo'ah*. In AA, Center for Oral Documentation, transcript of interview with Michael Magen (Grobman), May 1972. On this question, see too Zachary Lockman, " 'We Opened the Arabs' Minds': Labour Zionist Discourse and the Railway Workers of Palestine (1919–1929)," *Review of Middle East Studies*, no. 5 (1992).

39. Oral interview, May 14, 1987.

40. AA 208/14, Magali to EC/H, June 19, July 4, 1924.

41. In the Jaffa-Lydda branch, however, where Ahdut Ha'avoda supporters were in control, a separate section was created for Arab workers recruited to the union. See "Have'ida hashishit shel histadrut po'alei harakevet, hado'ar vehatelegraf," supplement to *Davar*, no. 702 (September 4, 1927).

42. The union claimed at the end of November that about 350 Arabs had joined in the previous four months, but this seems too high. See AA 104/25alef, memorandum of the URPTW to the General Manager, Palestine Railways; AA 208/14alef, CC/URPTW to EC/H, November 30, 1924; AA 237/1; and also the figures given in Histadrut, *Din veheshbon lave'ida hashlishit*, 64. None of these figures include the unionized postal and telegraph workers, whose numbers were in any case much smaller.

43. AA 237/9, October 12, 1924.

44. *Kuntres*, no. 192 (November 7, 1924). As I discussed earlier, there were in fact some important differences between the Jewish railway workers and Jewish workers employed elsewhere.

45. *Kuntres*, no. 194 (November 21, 1924).

46. On this incident, see AA 208/14alef, CC/URPTW to EC/H, November 30, 1924, and *Haifa*, no. 6 (January 1, 1925), 43–44. A Po'alei Tziyon Smol publication, *Milhemet Hapo'el*, suggested in May 1925 that Fahmi's letter in *al-Nafir* was a forgery by the communists and that Fahmi himself denied having written it. This seems unlikely: there is no indication in the Arabic press that Fahmi denied the letter's authenticity, and as we will see shortly, the communists themselves treated the letter as genuine in arguing *against* Fahmi's appeal to Arabs to quit the Jewish-led union they had recently joined.

47. See AA 104/25alef, "Skira mepe'ulot hamerkaz memo'etzet 1.3.24–1.1.25"; CZA, S25/640, Labor Department of the Zionist Executive, report on the Jewish railway workers, 1926.

48. Or so the Ahdut Ha'avoda member who reported the proceedings in *Kuntres*, no. 202 (January 16, 1925), alleged. The delegate to whom he was referring later denied he had ever said such a thing and charged the reporter with libel before a Histadrut court. See *Ed hakatar*, July 1925.

49. AA, interview with Khalfon, January 29, 1976.

50. The complete text of Ben-Gurion's speech can be found in *Anahnu veshkheineinu*, 76–80.

51. Oral interview with Yehezkel Abramov, May 14, 1987.

52. See *Kuntres*, nos. 202 (January 16, 1925), 203 (January 30, 1925).

53. See the long statement jointly issued by the central committee and the branch committees, August 6, 1925, in AA 237/9, and *Ittihad al-'Ummal*, September 1, 1925.

54. *Haifa*, no. 4 (December 1, 1924), 26.

55. *Haifa*, no. 6 (January 1, 1925), 43. See also the pamphlet entitled *al-Shihab al-sati' li-inarat tariq al-'amil wa'l-sani'* (The shining meteor which lights the path of the worker and artisan), published by the PCP early in 1925, reproduced in al-Budayri, *Tatawwur*, 123–32.

56. *Haifa*, nos. 15 (April 30, 1925), 16 (May 14, 1925). Much of Ahdut Ha'avoda's propaganda against the PCP in this period distorted the communists' actual position on various questions, reflecting the intensity of the campaign to discredit and isolate them.

57. See, for example, Yitzhak Gur-Sade's article in *Kuntres*, no. 213 (April 24, 1925).

58. *Haifa*, no. 15 (April 30, 1925), 118.

59. Ibid.

60. Farah, *Min al-'uthmaniyya*, 42–43.

61. See, for example, S/EC/H, October 25, 1925.

62. Farah, *Min al-'uthmaniyya*, 44.

63. On the emergence of the PAWS, see *Haifa*, no. 15 (April 30, 1925), 117–18; *Filastin*, March 6, 1925; *al-Yarmuk*, October 22, 1925. Al-Junaydi, in *al-Haraka*, 15, seems to assert that 'Abd al-Hamid Haymur had created and sought to register the PAWS two years earlier, in 1923, but was unsuccessful until 1925. I have not found confirmation of this in other sources.

64. This information is derived from a number of documents relating to the PAWS which were left out of the Beirut edition of Musa al-Budayri's book *Tatawwur* cited above but were included in the edition apparently published in Jerusalem c. 1980.

CHAPTER 4. THE RAILWAY WORKERS OF PALESTINE (II): COOPERATION AND CONFLICT, 1925–1939

1. See *Ed hakatar*, July 1925.

2. *Al-Karmil*, October 21, 1925; *Filastin*, June 4, 1926.

3. AA 237/24, Farid Kamil to the URPTW, late October or early November 1925; *Filastin*, June 4, June 15, 1926.

4. See Histadrut, *Din veheshbon lave'ida hashlishit*, 64.

5. See, for example, *Milhemet hapo'el*, May 1925; *Kuntres*, nos. 213 (April 24, 1925) and 227 (August 7, 1925). The allegation that the Arab union was quasi-religious in character may have stemmed from its origins in a charitable society similar to numerous such societies established by members of the Muslim and Christian communities in Palestine.

6. See also Farid Kamil's letter in *Filastin*, June 15, 1926, and the response by Hassun and al-Asmar published on August 20, 1926.

7. CZA, S25/640, Labor Department of the Zionist Executive, report on the Jewish railway workers, 1926.

8. See S/EC/H, October 25, 1925.

9. Documentation of this trend can be found in AA 104/25alef; Histadrut, *Din veheshbon lave'ida hashlishit*, 75; and *Kuntres*, no. 239 (November 13, 1925). In *Formative Years*, chs. 6–7, Shapiro suggests that in this period Ahdut Ha'avoda initiated a drive to reassert and strengthen the party's control over the Histadrut and affiliated organizations and institutions. The URPTW would certainly have been a prime target of such a campaign.

10. For an account of the meeting, see *Kuntres*, no. 249 (January 29, 1926).

11. S/EC/H, July 18, 1926; AA 237/32gimmel, meeting of railway workers with the Zionist Executive, October 17, 1926; and also F. H. Kisch, *Palestine Diary* (London, 1938), 227. Arguing that Jews were discriminated against in hiring and that many of the best railway jobs were held by Arabs from outside Palestine, mainly Egyptians and Syrians, URPTW leaders asked the Zionist Executive to subsidize the wages of Jewish railwaymen, support housing projects for Jewish railway workers, and get more Jews hired, in part by pressuring the British authorities to dismiss non-Palestinian Arabs.

12. S/EC/H, July 18, 1926.

13. *Ittihad al-ʿUmmal*, August 1, 1926.

14. On this question, see CO 125/19535, inquiry from Charles Amnon, September 23, 1926, and CO 733/118/23339, Plumer to Avery, December 12, 1926.

15. AA 490/3.

16. "Haveʿida hashishit," *Davar*, September 4, 1927.

17. AA 237/21, "Gilui daʿat"; AA 237/5, "Takanot"; *Alon histadrut poʿalei harakevet*, December 16, 1927.

18. AA 237/21, "Likol hapoʿalim . . . ," November 10, 1927; *Ittihad al-ʿUmmal*, January 7, 1928; NURPTW, *Likrat hamoʿetza*, February 29, 1928.

19. When in 1930 Jewish unionists got word that the PAWS was negotiating with railway management over possible recognition for its affiliated Arab railway workers' union, they pressed the Histadrut to do what it could to prevent recognition. AA 208/280alef, NURPTW to EC/H, November 4, 1930.

20. AA 237/24, Grobman to Ben-Tzvi, May 1928; AA 208/143alef, "Skira shvuʿit," June 7–14, 15–22, 1928; Histadrut Artzit shel Poʿalei Harakevet, *Din veheshbon shel havaʿad hamerkazi laveʿida hashviʿit* (May 1931), 6.

21. *Filastin*, December 20, 1927.

22. Oral interview with Yehezkel Abramov, May 14, 1987. The Histadrut was therefore always seeking ways to maintain and even increase the percentage of Jewish workers, sometimes at the expense of Arab workers. In April 1930, for example, a Histadrut official suggested to railway management that it transfer some work to (Jewish) outside contractors, making it possible to lay off Arab workers. The Histadrut was also displeased that management had a policy of training already-employed (hence usually Arab) workers for skilled jobs, because this reduced the number of new Jewish skilled workers who might otherwise be hired. With the backing of the mandatory government and the Colonial Office, the Palestine Railways generally rejected Histadrut and Zionist pressure to hire more Jews. Management insisted that there was no policy of discrimination against Jews; Arabs were hired simply because they were cheaper. On this question see, for example, CZA, S9/1424a, NURPTW to the Zionist Executive, November 15, 1929, and Meirowitz to the Labor Department of the Jewish Agency, March 28, April 27, 1930, also S25/7208, /7209.

23. AA 237/21, September 28, 1928; AA 407/101gimmel; AA 490/3.

24. *Edim*, March 19, 1929. The grounds on which the Palestine Railways, backed by the government of Palestine and the Colonial Office, justified its refusal to recognize the NURPTW (supported by the Histadrut and its friends in the Trades Union Congress and the Labor Party) shifted rather frequently. Whenever the union satisfied management's conditions, new obstacles would be raised. There is a great deal of correspondence on this question in various archives; one can get a sense of the convoluted course of these talks by perusing CO 733/118/23339, Plumer to Avery, December 10, 1926; CO 733/190/10, Officer Administering to Passfield, July 26, 1930; AA 237/36; and CZA, S25/7208. The NURPTW was enormously frustrated by the government's refusal to grant recognition, a refusal which is probably best explained by a desire to avoid any diminution of control over the workforce of a key state enterprise.

25. *Hedim*, February 27, 1930.

26. See the account in Farah, *Min al-'uthmaniyya*, 50.

27. An account of the proceedings can be found in Jam'iyyat al-'Ummal al-'Arabiyya al-Filastiniyya (PAWS), *Mu'tamar al-'ummal al-'arab al-awwal* (Haifa, 1930); see also *Filastin*, February 4, 7, 1930, and Farah, *Min al-'uthmaniyya*, 56–61.

28. AA 208/320bet, Hushi to EC/H, February 24, 1931; NURPTW, *She'alot hasha'a*, April 22, 1931; Histadrut Artzit, *Din veheshbon lave'ida hashvi'it*.

29. AA 320bet, January 30, 1931; AA 208/280bet, NURPTW to EC/H, February 24, 1932; AA 208/280alef, CC/NURPTW to EC/H, May 3, 1931.

30. Choice of the term "international" (in Hebrew, *bein-le'umi*), attributed to Ben-Gurion himself, is curious. In North America, the term has generally been used to denote unions comprising members who live and work in more than one country, such as the International Brotherhood of Teamsters, which operates in both the United States and Canada, rather than for unions composed of workers who live in the same country but belong to different national or ethnic groups. Histadrut leaders soon realized that their use of the term "international" was somewhat peculiar but felt that it was too late to alter the organization's name once again. On the union's stationery, which bore its name in Hebrew, English, and Arabic, the adjective "international" was translated into Arabic as *'amma*, which actually means "general." The substitution of "employees" (*'ovdei mesilat habarzel*) for "workers" (*po'alei harakevet*) was intended to accommodate the white-collar employees who had recently joined. See AA 208/280bet, "Din veheshbon mekutzar"; for discussion of the term "international," see EC/H, February 1, 1932.

The communists, who rarely missed an opportunity to denounce the labor-Zionist movement, could not resist this time either, and the PCP promptly issued a leaflet attacking the Histadrut and IU leaderships in language typical of "Third Period" communism:

> The railway workers' congress just concluded in Tel Aviv was a new and dangerous maneuver by the social-imperialist leaders of the Histadrut. For 12 years these leaders have wrecked every attempt at true organization by the railway workers. For 12 years this gang of leaders, with Ben-Tzvi at their head, have served the imperialist authorities by constant betrayal of the railway workers' interests. For 12 years they have opposed unity and true brotherhood between the Arab and Jewish railway workers, by imposing Zionism, the enemy of the Arab worker, on the Jewish workers and by driving the Arab workers away from any possibility of organization. For 12 years every worker—Arab or Jewish—who stood for defending the workers' interest and for establishing a class, international, and anti-imperialist organization has been forcibly fired, kicked out of the Histadrut and turned over to the imperialist police. ... And suddenly, at the last congress, these nationalist-Zionist Histadrut leaders, these wild wolves and servants of imperialism, thanks to whose "activism" alone the railway workers are to this day in a terrible state, abandoned to every form of exploitation and repression, have changed into innocent lambs and are calling themselves an "international union." (June 1931, in AA 1272/10.)

31. AA 208/280bet, CC/IU to EC/H, February 4, 1932; CO 733/221/11.

32. On this question, see EC/H, February 1, 1932, and, more generally, AA 208/280alef, Ben-Gurion to the High Commissioner, April 26, 1932.

33. AA 237/24; AA 208/280bet, CC/IU to EC/H, February 24, 1932; AA 237/24, minutes of meeting of March 14, 1932; AA 208/280gimmel; AA 208/280dalet, IU, "Skira" (April–August 1932). For a clear statement of the Arab perspective on relations with the Jewish railway workers, see " 'Ummal al-sikka al-hadid w'al-histadrut," *Filastin*, August 3, 1932.

34. IU, *Kol Ha'oved*, August 8, 1932; CZA, S25/7208, IU, "Ila 'umum mustakhdimay da'irat al-jarr"; AA 208/280dalet, AURW, "Bayan ila 'umum 'ummal al-jarr."

35. Palestine Railways, *Report of the General Manager on the Administration of the Palestine Railways and Operated Lines for the Year[s] Ended . . . 31st December 1931, 31st March 1933, 1934, 1935* (Jerusalem, 1932, 1933, 1934, 1935).

36. The loan program was clearly designed to bolster Hebrew labor, but because that could not be said publicly the Histadrut had to address the sensitive question of whether Arab IU members should also be eligible; Histadrut leaders were certainly aware of the positive political impact that including a few Arabs might produce. See EC/H, June 12, 1933.

37. The sense of desperation which the Histadrut leadership felt at the sharp decline in Jewish employment in this strategic sector is well conveyed in AA 208/576alef, "Maskanot yeshivat hava'ad hapo'el shel hahistadrut 'im merkaz po'alei harakevet," August 29, 1934.

38. AA 208/576, 576alef.

39. AA 208/815alef, Dana to S/EC/H, January 6, 1935.

40. FO 371/18957, CID reports of February 27, March 9, 1935; ISA, Jaffa Port, 28/1/158/1935; *Filastin*, March 5, 6, 1935. A handwritten draft of the joint committee's solidarity leaflet is in AA 237/24.

41. FO 371/18957, CID report of May 31, 1935; AA 237/8, April 15, 1935; AA 237/21, joint committee's May Day leaflet; *Filastin*, May 2, 1935.

42. CZA, S25/7208; AA 237/34, delegates' conference to the High Commissioner, May 30, 1935; *Filastin*, June 18, 1935; *Hashomer Hatza'ir*, October 15, 1935.

43. AA 208/815alef, meeting of May 5, 1935; AA 250/40–5–5–7, circular of July 15, 1935; CZA, S25/7209, IU, "Din veheshbon shel hamerkaz mugash lave'ida hashminit shel hahistadrut habeinle'umit le'ovdei harakevet," August 1939.

44. CZA, S25/4618, D. G. Harris to the Palestine Royal Commission, December 30, 1936.

45. AA 208/815alef, CC/IU, June 23, 1935.

46. AA 208/815bet, IU to EC/H, August 27, 1935, and minutes of CC/IU, September 3, 11, 15, 1935; *Kol Hano'ar*, July 1935.

47. See al-Niqaba al-'Arabiyya li-'Ummal Sikak Hadid Filastin, *Bayan 'Amm* (March 1936).

48. AA 237/26alef, meeting of the Histadrut's Arab Affairs Committee, February 28, 1936.

49. AA 208/815gimmel, Zaslani to Remez, April 14, 1936, and 'Id Salim Haymur to IU, April 25, 1936.

50. AA 205/6, meeting of the Histadrut's Arab Affairs Committee, November 11, 1936.

51. Great Britain, Palestine Royal Commission, *Minutes of Evidence Heard at*

Public Sessions (London, 1937), 219 (December 29, 1936). For a slightly different version of Shertok's testimony, see CZA, S25/4618, "Precis of Evidence."

52. CZA, S25/7209, Berman to Zaslani, July 14, 1938, and IU, "Din veheshbon shel hamerkaz" (1939), 24–26. In the period April 1938–March 1939 alone, there were 690 cases of attacks on railway personnel and property, including numerous derailments. Thirteen Arab and Jewish railway workers were killed while on duty and 123 wounded. See ISA, R/16/39, Palestine Railways, *Report* for year ending March 31, 1939.

53. CZA, S25/7208, Taylor, Sargent and Willan to Chief Engineer, October 1938.

54. Oral interview with Yehezkel Abramov, May 14, 1987.

55. AA, interview with Efrayyim Schvartzman, March 20, 1972.

56. AA 237/26bet, CC/IU to Haifa Workers' Council, May 24, 1938.

57. For a study of this movement up to 1936, see Elkana Margalit, *Hashomer Hatza'ir: me'eidat ne'urim lemarksizm mahpekhani, 1913–1936* (Tel Aviv, 1971).

58. On the Hebrew labor question, see *Bulitin Hakibbutz Ha'artzi*, June 25, 1930.

59. Oral interview with Efrayyim Krisher, May 13, 1987. See also Krisher, "Ha'irgun hameshutaf," and Mordekhai Lahav, "Si'at hashomer hatza'ir behaifa beshanim 1934–1937," *Me'asef*, no. 15 (1985).

60. HH, 90/17alef (2alef); AA 208/1325; AA 237/26bet, Hakibbutz Ha'artzi to EC/H, April 20, 1937. On the 1939 elections and the struggles it generated, see *Hashomer Hatza'ir*, July 7, 28, August 11, 1939; AA 237/26bet, Histadrut central control commission to CC/IU, December 6, 1939.

CHAPTER 5. ARAB WORKERS AND THE HISTADRUT, 1929–1936

1. Quoted in Shapira, *Hama'avak*, 72.

2. CZA, S25/2961, EC/H to Zionist Executive, December 12, 1929.

3. Kisch, *Palestine Diary*, 259 (entry for September 9, 1929); EC/H, April 28, 1930.

4. In Hebrew slang, the term 'avoda 'aravit came to acquire a specific (and obviously racist) meaning: it meant work that was shoddy or inferior in quality. However, as used by labor Zionists in the context I am discussing here, the term 'avoda 'aravit meant simply work or activity *among* Arabs with the aim of organizing them under the Histadrut's tutelage.

5. The official account of the congress is in Jam'iyyat al-'Ummal, *Mu'tamar al-'ummal*. Some of the Arabic-language press was hostile to the congress, for example the conservative Muslim *al-Sirat al-mustaqim*, which alleged that the congress was a Zionist plot. This prompted PAWS leaders to insist in *Filastin* that they were strongly anti-Zionist and rejected unity with Zionist workers.

6. CZA, S9/1679, January 15, 1930; Bilitzki, *Beyitzira uvema'avak*, 222.

7. Jam'iyyat al-'Ummal, *Mu'tamar al-'ummal*, 42. In 1944 Nassar would refuse an offer to become a paid employee of the Histadrut's Arab Department because, he said, he preferred to remain a worker; see CoC/H, December 3, 1944.

8. AA 490/4; CZA, S25/30.043.

9. Not all of Ahavat Po'alim's leaders shared Po'alei Tziyon Smol's confidence that a truly socialist Zionism was entirely compatible with the interests of Arab workers in Palestine. Samuel Hugo Bergman, who was lecturer in philosophy at the Hebrew University of Jerusalem, the first director of the National and University Library, and one of the leading figures in Brit Shalom, an organization of liberal Jewish intellectuals founded in 1926 to seek Jewish-Arab reconciliation, touched off a controversy within Ahavat Po'alim when he took Moshe Erem to task for arguing that joint organization should be fostered not only because it was a manifestation of proletarian internationalism but also because it would promote class struggle and class polarization within the Arab community, thereby facilitating Jewish immigration and the Zionist project. "To use joint organization in order to realize the political aspirations of one people means destroying any possibility of joint organization," Bergman insisted. He went on to argue that

> Jewish immigration, despite all the good things that it has brought the Arab worker, weakens the political power of one of the peoples [in Palestine] and strengthens the political power of the other people, at a time of harsh struggle between the two peoples which all of Comrade Erem's class ideology cannot eliminate, at least for now, as long as no Jewish-Arab agreement has been reached. To seek joint organization at this moment in order to eliminate barriers to Jewish immigration—to this no patriotic Arab, no Arab worker with nationalist sentiments, will agree.

It is only natural, Bergman went on, that Arab workers should ally themselves with the Arab bourgeoisie; hence the only possible basis for joint organization was a purely economic one, free from politics. As events would show, this too was a delusion, since it was impossible to keep economic and political issues entirely separate.

10. EC/KA, July 14, 1930.

11. EC/H, July 14, 21, 1930.

12. AA, minutes of the Histadrut Council, May 24–26, 1930.

13. For discussions of Burla's highly romanticized depictions of Arabs, see Risa Domb's very inadequate *The Arab in Hebrew Prose, 1911–1948* (London, 1982), 49–56, and Gila Ramras-Rauch's somewhat better *The Arab in Israeli Literature* (Bloomington, Ind., 1989), 22–27. Menahem Perry has discussed modern Hebrew literature's portrayal of Arabs much more interestingly in "The Israeli-Palestinian Conflict as a Metaphor in Recent Israeli Fiction," *Poetics Today* 7, no. 4 (1986). Domb states that after 1948 Burla directed the cultural department of Israel's Ministry of Religious Affairs, while Ramras-Rauch asserts that he directed the Arab affairs department in the Ministry of Minorities; perhaps he held both posts at different times.

14. As I noted in Chapter 4, the Jewish Agency, though formally independent of the Zionist Organization, was soon effectively dominated by its Zionist members and became the *de facto* leadership body of the Yishuv. Ben-Gurion became a member of the Jewish Agency executive in 1933, after MAPAI emerged as the largest party within the Zionist movement, and its chairman in 1935.

15. See Kisch, *Palestine Diary*, 374 (entry for January 13, 1931); AA 208/320bet, Burla to Kisch, January 30, 1931 (emphasis in the original).

16. CZA, S25/3120, Burla to Kisch, February 18, 1931; EC/H, March 16, 1931.

17. Ibid; AA 208/320bet, Hassun to EC/H, February 10, 1931; CZA, S25/3120, Burla to Kisch, February 2, 9, 1931, and Jewish Agency to Histadrut, February 20, 1931; CZA, S25/2961; EC/H, March 16, 1931.

18. On drivers in Palestinian Arab popular culture, see ʿAli al-Khalili, *Aghani al-ʿamal wʾal-ʿummal fi filastin: dirasa* (Jerusalem, 1979), 127–33. Lev Luis Grinberg's unpublished seminar paper, "Shvitat irgun hanehagim hayehudi-haʿaravi, 1931," which the author kindly shared with me, contributed to my understanding of this episode, though I do not entirely agree with his analysis or his conclusions. Anita Shapira also discusses the drivers' strikes briefly (and not very satisfactorily) in *Hamaʾavak*, 83–84.

19. See Gidʿon Biger, *Moshevet keter o bayit leʾumi: hashpaʿat hashilton habriti ʿal eretz-yisraʾel, 1917–1930* (Jerusalem, 1983), 96–113.

20. AA 490/5, "Giluʾi daʿat," June 29, 1931. Though motor transport competed with the Palestine Railways and adversely affected its revenues, it provided the mandatory government with a substantial new source of revenue which exceeded expenditures on road building and repair.

21. EC/H, June 30, 1931.

22. *Filastin*, June 30, 1931.

23. EC/H, August 3, 1931.

24. See *Filastin* for August 1931.

25. The leaflet can be found in CZA, S25/10.664.

26. For an account of the congress, see *Filastin*, November 3, 1931.

27. See AA 425/13, "El hanehagim haʿaravim vehayehudim" (PCP leaflet), February 1932.

28. AA 208/321 and CZA, S25/2961. This was not the first time that members of the al-Dajani family, and perhaps Hasan Sidqi al-Dajani himself, had sought Zionist support. In 1922–23 the Zionists secretly funded a "National Muslim Society," one of whose leaders was Shukri al-Dajani, in order to undermine the strongly anti-Zionist Arab Executive; and in 1923 Hasan Sidqi al-Dajani was among the initiators (with the Nashashibis) of the anti-Husayni "Palestinian Arab Nationalist Party," which also secretly sought Zionist funding. See Ann Moseley Lesch, *Arab Politics in Palestine, 1917–1939: The Frustration of a Nationalist Movement* (Ithaca, N.Y., 1979), 93–97, and Yehoshua Porath, *The Emergence of the Palestinian-Arab National Movement, 1918–1929* (London, 1974), 215–16, 224. For a sympathetic portrait of the Nashashibis and their political role, see Nasser Eddin Nashashibi, *Jerusalem's Other Voice: Ragheb Nashashibi and Moderation in Palestinian Politics, 1920–1948* (Exeter, U.K., 1990).

29. AA, Center for Oral Documentation, transcript of interview with Shraga Goren (Gorokhovsky), May 24, 1972.

30. CO 733/206/8; *Bulitin Hashomer Hatzaʿir*, September 30, 1931; *Hashomer Hatzaʿir*, November 1931; Shapira, *Hamaʾavak*, 84–85; David Zait, *Tziyonut bedarkhei shalom: darkho haraʿayonit-politit shel Hashomer Hatzaʿir, 1927–1947* (Tel Aviv, 1985), 74–76.

31. AA 208/320alef, December 7, 1931.

32. EC/H, January 18, 1932; CZA, S25/2961, letter to Arlosoroff, March 22, 1932.

33. Hushi set forth his perspective in an article in *Davar*, December 13, 1932.

34. AA 208/321, Hassun to Ben-Tzvi, May 12, 1932; CZA S25/3120, Hassun to Ben-Tzvi, February 23, March 4, 1932.

35. See the entry in Dan Ben-Amotz and Netiva Ben-Yehuda, *Milon ʿolami leʾivrit meduberet* (Tel Aviv, 1972).

36. See, for example, the minutes of a meeting of Histadrut leaders with the High Commissioner, March 22, 1932, in AA 208/280alef; CO 733/161/6, 165/2; and the minutes of the International Committee of the TUC's General Council for 1928–30, in the TUC Archives, box T 1853.

37. On the struggle for Hebrew labor at the Haifa port, see Lina Dar, "Hanisayon leʾirgun meshutaf yehudi-ʿaravi benamal haifa be-1932," *Meʾasef*, no. 14 (1984).

38. Ibid.; Yitzhak Pesah, "Lesheʾeilat haʾirgun habeinleʾumi shel sapanei haifa," *Hashomer Hatzaʿir*, June 1932.

39. EC/H, May 29, 1932.

40. Oral interview with Eliyahu Agassi, May 6, 1987; AA, Center for Oral Documentation, transcript of interview with Eliyahu Agassi, February 22, 1972. After working in the Histadrut's Arab Department until the 1960s, Agassi set up and then directed its Arabic-language publishing house, retiring in 1975.

41. Oral interview with Agassi, May 6, 1987; EC/H, May 23, 1932.

42. Oral interview with Agassi, May 6, 1987.

43. Ben-Tzvi had already gone to Salonika to recruit Jewish dockworkers and seamen in 1914, but the outbreak of the war had frustrated his efforts. A few Salonika port workers did arrive in Haifa around 1922, however.

44. Dar, "Hanisayon," 58ff; Taqqu, "Arab Labor," 95.

45. Quoted in Shabtai Teveth, *Ben-Gurion and the Palestinian Arabs: From Peace to War* (Oxford, 1985), 110.

46. Sussman, *Paʿar veshivayon*, 40.

47. See Edwin Black, *The Transfer Agreement: The Untold Story of the Secret Agreement between the Third Reich and Jewish Palestine* (New York, 1984). On capital imports into Palestine more generally, see Rafael N. Rosenzweig, *The Economic Consequences of Zionism* (Leiden, 1989).

48. See Saʿid B. Himadeh, ed., *Economic Organization of Palestine* (Beirut, 1938); David Horowitz and Rita Hinden, *Economic Survey of Palestine* (Tel Aviv, 1938); A. Revusky, *Jews in Palestine* (New York, 1936).

49. On Palestinian agriculture, see Henry Rosenfeld, "From Peasantry to Wage Labor and Residual Peasantry: The Transformation of an Arab Village," in Robert Alan Manners, ed., *Process and Pattern in Culture* (Chicago, 1964), 211–34; Joel S. Migdal, ed., *Palestinian Society and Politics* (Princeton, 1980); Kenneth W. Stein, *The Land Question in Palestine, 1917–1939* (Chapel Hill, N.C., 1984); Ylana N. Miller, *Government and Society in Rural Palestine, 1920–1948* (Austin, Tex., 1985); and Sarah Graham-Brown, "The Political Economy of the Jabal Nablus, 1920–48," in Roger Owen, ed., *Studies in the Economic and Social History of Palestine in the Nineteenth and Twentieth Centuries* (London, 1982).

50. This episode is detailed in AA 208/321, Haifa Workers' Council to EC/H, July 1932. See too the Palestine Communist Party's Arabic-language organ *Ila al-Imam*, May 1933.

51. See *al-Shakhsiyyat al-filastiniyya hatta ʿam 1945* (Jerusalem, 1979), 99.

52. AA 208/321, letter and leaflet; AA, interview with Agassi, February 22, 1972.

53. CZA, S25/3120, Haifa Workers' Council to EC/H, undated but probably late 1932 or early 1933.

54. Moʿetzet Poʿalei Haifa, *Hahistadrut behaifa beshanim 1933–1939* (Haifa, 1939), 240–41; AA 208/321, Haifa Workers' Council, "Memorandum on the Activities of the Labour Federation among the Arab Workers at Haifa," 1932; AA 208/321, notes on meetings with Arab workers in Jaffa; AA 208/321, Dov Hoz to Tel Aviv Workers' Council, August 8, 30, 31, 1932.

55. AA 208/321, Nesher-Yagur Workers' Council to EC/H, September 28, 1932; CZA, S25/3120, Haifa Workers' Council to EC/H, c. November 1932; EC/H, October 3, 1932; AA 208/321, handwritten PCP leaflets, October 9, 10, 1932.

56. April 27, 1933.

57. AA 208/1200, "Din veheshbon memoʿetzet poʿalei Nesher"; AA, interview with Agassi, February 22, 1972; Poʿalei Tziyon Smol, *Lesheʾalot haragaʿ* (Tel Aviv, 1933).

58. AA 208/1200, Nesher, "Din veheshbon"; AA 205/6; AA 208/781bet, PAWS leaflet, March 1, 1936; S/EC/H, March 6, 1936.

59. CZA, S25/3120, "Shvitat hastevedorim haʿaravim haʿovdim behevrat Jabra, Mursi ve-Onbarji"; CZA, S25/3120, March 5, 1933, "Irgun poʿalei Shell."

60. See, for example, CZA, S25/3120, "Shvitat hastevedorim." Histadrut officials were quick to report communists to government officials and employers so that they could be fired.

61. *Halohem*, March 2, 1933. See too Poʿalei Tziyon Smol, *Meʾoraʿot oktober 1933* (Tel Aviv, 1933).

62. Hashomer Hatzaʿir, *Matzaʿ Hashomer Hatzaʾir laveʿida hareviʿit shel hahistadrut* (December 1932).

63. "Reshima maʿamadit," in MAKI (Israel Communist Party) Archive, at Hakibbutz Hameʾuhad Archive, Yad Tabenkin (Efʿal), series 35, "MAKI—shonot." Shmuel Dothan has pointed out that in the early 1930s Hashomer Hatzaʿir's membership constituted an important source of recruits for the PCP, and the leadership of that socialist-Zionist movement was preoccupied with suppressing what it saw as leftist "deviations" tending toward "liquidationism" (i.e., abandonment of Zionism) in its ranks. See *Adumim*, 165.

64. CZA, S25/2961, Kaplan to Arlosoroff, April 3, 1933, and Hoz to Shertok, December 20, 1933; CZA, S25/3120, Hushi to EC/H, November 23, 1933; CZA, S25/2961, Zaslani to Shertok and Kaplan, October 17, 1934.

65. EC/H, June 7, 13, 1934; Shapira, *Hamaʾavak*, 177–79; Zait, *Tziyonut*, 136–37.

66. AA 104/35alef-bet, minutes of council meeting.

67. EC/H, September 6, 29, 1934; CZA, S25/2961, "Kavim letokhnit hapeʿula" and meeting of the Arab Committee, December 23, 1934.

68. CZA, S25/4618, "Co-operation between Jewish and Arab Workers under the Auspices of the General Federation of Jewish Labour," memorandum submitted to the Palestine Royal Commission, 1936. On Haifa, see Vashitz, "Jewish-Arab Relations," Part 1, chs. 2, 6.

69. Hashomer Hatzaʿir managed to find in the "Hawrani threat" one more guarantee of socialist-Zionist success. The movement's second-in-command, Yaʿakov Hazan, sounded the alarm about "the uninterrupted mass entry of cheap labor from neighboring countries into Palestine." But he went on to argue that this "threat" would open the way to "a new period of development in the relations between the Palestinian Arab worker and the organized Jewish worker. This will be a period characterized by the joint struggle of the organized Jewish worker and the Arab worker against this wave of cheap labor. Such a front will pave the way to a better mutual understanding and correlation between the two peoples than any amount of diplomatic maneuvering on this field." See Yaʿakov Hazan, "Jewish Unions and Arab Labor," in Enzo Sereni and R. E. Ashery, eds., *Jews and Arabs in Palestine: Studies in a National and Colonial Problem* (New York, 1936), 244–45. Hazan's prognosis that Palestinian Arabs and Palestinian Jews would unite to defend their jobs and wages against Hawrani migrants, thereby conducing to international class solidarity, would not be borne out. Though some organized Arab workers clearly did feel threatened by migrants from outside Palestine, they felt much more threatened by the Histadrut's relentless campaign for Hebrew labor. The British authorities eventually responded to Zionist and Arab protests by encouraging Arab contractors to prefer Palestinian labor. By 1935, when about 20 percent of the stevedores and 25 percent of the porters at Jaffa harbor were non-Palestinians, no new licenses were being issued to newly arrived non-Palestinians; see Taqqu, "Arab Labor," 95.

70. CZA, S25/2961, Zaslani to Hoz, October 14, 1934 (emphasis in the original); AA, interview with Agassi, February 29, 1972; CZA, S25/3107, Zaslani to Hoz, September 24, 1934.

71. On this strike, see *Filastin*, August 18, 31, 1933.

72. On Zaslani/Shiloʾah, see Haggai Eshed, *Mosad shel ish ehad: Reuven Shiloʾah—avi hamodiʿin hayisraʾeli* (Tel Aviv, 1988), from which much of the information in this section is drawn.

73. EC/H, April 28, 1930; AA 208/320bet, "Tokhnit peʿula," 1931; Ian Black, *Zionism and the Arabs, 1936–1939* (New York, 1986), 175–85.

74. In November 1946, for example, Eliyahu Sasson, director of the Arab Bureau in the Jewish Agency's Political Department, sent a memorandum to his boss Moshe Shertok arguing that the time had come to develop a comprehensive plan to influence the course of events in the Arab world. In addition to gaining control of newspapers in the Arab states for propaganda and political purposes, Sasson proposed that the Zionist movement consider devoting resources to bringing about the partition of Lebanon between Muslims and Christians, preventing the expansion of the League of Arab States, and helping Iraq's Shiʿi community against that country's strongly anti-Zionist Sunni rulers. See CZA, S25/3016, November 20, 1946.

75. See *Filastin*, July–October 1934.

76. See Shapira, *Hamaʾavak*, 229–33; Glazer, "Propaganda and the Histadrut-Sponsored Pickets for 'Hebrew Labor.'"

77. *Filastin*, December 18, 1934.

78. A translation of the Tel Aviv Workers' Council circular and an account of the incident can be found in George Mansur, *The Arab Worker under the Pales-*

tine Mandate (Jerusalem, 1938), 29–31. George Mansur worked as a baker and then as a schoolteacher (including a year at a Jewish school in Baghdad), and later served under Michel Mitri as secretary of the AWS in Jaffa.

79. CZA, S25/2961, "Din veheshbon shel Agassi veZaslani," November 20, 1934; emphasis in the original.

80. AA 250/436, Zaslani to Agassi, November 25, 1934.

81. AA, interview with Agassi, February 29, 1972.

82. ISA, Jaffa Port, 28/1, 158/35, January 16, 1935; on political and security concerns, see FO 371/17878, CID, July 14, 1934.

83. On the strike of February–March 1935, see *Filastin*, March 5, 6, 8, 1935, and Jabra Niqula, *Harakat al-idrabat bayn al-ʿummal al-ʿarab fi filastin* (Jaffa, 1935), 10–14. Niqula was a veteran communist activist whose survey of strike activity in Palestine denounced both the "Zionist Histadrut" and the "opportunist" Michel Mitri for their "betrayals" of the workers. His accounts of strikes tend to exaggerate the role played by the Transport Workers' Union, a marginal organization controlled by the PCP. On the findings of the 1935 Jaffa labor committee, see Taqqu, "Arab Labor," 96–98, and CO 733/292/3, High Commissioner to the Colonial Secretary, April 11, 1936.

84. AA 208/4495.

85. AA 205/6, meeting of the Arab Committee, November 11, 1936; CZA, S25/2961, Agassi to the Political Department, February 15, 1937.

86. AA 250/436, minutes of meeting of the Arab Committee, December 23, 1934.

87. Ibid., and various letters in the same file; CZA, S25/2961, Hoz to Shertok, January 17, 1935.

88. Mansur, *Arab Worker*, 33; *Hashomer Hatzaʿir*, May 15, 1935; *Kol Hanoʿar*, July 1935. For an overview, see Anita Shapira, "Even Vesid—parashat shutafut yehudit-ʿaravit menekudat hareʾut shel ʿavoda ʿivrit," *Meʾasef*, no. 7 (May 1975). It is interesting to note that few of the labor-Zionist accounts of the PLL mention this strike.

89. Niqula, *Harakat al-idrabat*, 15–27; *Filastin*, February–March 1935; AA 426/16, PCP leaflet, "Lekol hapoʿalim hayehudim"; AA, interview with Agassi, February 29, 1972; Abba Hushi, *Brit poʿalei eretz yisraʾel* (Tel Aviv, 1943), 19–22.

90. For example, ibid.; Niqula, *Harakat al-idrabat*; *Hashomer Hatzaʿir*, March 15, 1935.

91. CZA, S25/2961, Hoz to Shertok, January 17, 1935; February 25, 1936, Zaslani to Shertok. The role which the PLL played in one labor struggle in this period once again pointed up the contradiction between the Histadrut's commitment to Hebrew labor and its rhetoric of solidarity with Arab workers. In October 1935 the Jewish-owned Mosaica floor-tile factory, which had employed both Jews and Arabs, was moved from Haifa to a new site north of the city on land owned by the Jewish National Fund. Because that institution required that only Jews live or be employed on land it leased out, the factory took the opportunity to fire all its Arab workers and replace them with Jews. Abba Hushi intervened, not to save the workers' jobs (he approved of the factory's transition to full Hebrew labor) but to try to secure some severance pay for them, because the fired Arab workers

were PLL members. At the same time, the factory's Jewish workers went on strike after the owner withheld their wages. A PLL leaflet urged the fired Arab workers to demand severance pay for themselves but also to support the Jewish strikers. See AA 208/781alef, Haifa Workers' Council to Histadrut Arab Secretariat, October 22, 1935, and PLL leaflet, November 1, 1935.

92. See Mansur, *Arab Worker*, 6.

93. Mansur, *Arab Worker*, 59–61; *Filastin*, February 21, 1936; *al-Difaʿ*, February 23, 1936; AA 490/2, AWS leaflet; George Mansur, testimony before the Peel Commission, in Great Britain, Palestine Royal Commission, *Minutes of Evidence*, 343.

94. AA 205/6, Arab Committee, April 2, 1936.

95. *Hashomer Hatzaʿir*, April 1, 1936.

96. *Al-Difaʿ*, April 12, 1936.

97. Curiously, Yehoshua Porath makes no mention of this politically significant convergence in either *The Palestinian Arab National Movement: From Riots to Rebellion, 1929–1939* (London, 1977) or "Social Aspects of the Emergence of the Palestinian Arab National Movement," in Menahem Milson, ed., *Society and Political Structure in the Arab World* (New York, 1973).

CHAPTER 6. THE ARAB REVOLT AND LABOR ZIONISM, 1936–1939

1. In the Yishuv, the Hebrew term most commonly used to denote the 1936–39 revolt was *hameʾoraʿot*, "the events." The same term had been used to denote earlier outbreaks of anti-Jewish or anti-Zionist violence in 1920, 1921, and 1929, along with *mehumot*, "riots." While in private many Zionist leaders were able to acknowledge the genuinely popular and nationalist character of the revolt, they never publicly characterized it as an authentic national uprising, for obvious reasons. Use of the term *meʾoraʿot* reflected and reinforced a Zionist discourse which represented the revolt as the product of manipulation and incitement by a small number of agitators who, in the interest of the "feudal" effendis, used violence and terror to intimidate and dominate the peace-loving majority of the Arab population. Far from being a genuine popular movement with a comprehensible set of goals, the events of 1936–39 were thus reduced to a series of acts of almost mindless terror perpetrated by a handful of extremists who lacked popular support.

Zionist use of the term *meʾoraʿot* paralleled official British use of the term "disturbances" to denote this anticolonial uprising in Palestine, as well as similar insurrections against British rule elsewhere. In official usage "disturbances" suggested some unnatural and undesirable disruption of the normal order of things, a troubling of the status quo by disaffected elements. By no means neutral or transparent, these Hebrew and English terms acquired their meaning and emotional power within a certain conception of relations between Europeans and their non-European subjects—i.e., the colonial discourse which I discussed in Chapter 1.

2. *Filastin*, May 2, 1936.

3. Black, *Zionism*, 34, 65. An official account of the Histadrut's activities in

Haifa in 1933–39 asserted that "the relations which were established in previous years with workers and employers at Haifa port were extremely beneficial as one of the direct factors in preventing a strike at the port of Haifa. . . ." Moʻetzet Poʻalei Haifa, *Hahistadrut behaifa*, 245.

4. Bilitzki, *Beyitzira uvemaʾavak*, 224 (emphasis added), 232–34. My account of events at Haifa port also draws on Dar, "Hanisayon," 58ff; my oral interview with Agassi, May 6, 1987; Hacohen, *Time to Tell*, 88–89; Seikaly, "Arab Community," 231–32; and Porath, *Palestinian Arab National Movement*, 167.

In May 1937 Haifa port officials acceded to Jewish Agency demands that the 200 or so Hawranis employed at the harbor be replaced with Palestinian Arabs, in part to create jobs for unemployed Palestinian Arabs in the villages of the interior and thereby alleviate the social discontent which had helped fuel the revolt. Conditions in the countryside were so bad, however, that some 1,200 desperate applicants showed up for these 200 jobs, and the government had to send a thousand of them back home at its own expense. See Mansur, *Arab Worker*, 10–11.

Ironically, the very success of the general strike in Jaffa permitted the Yishuv to secure one of its long-standing demands: a port of its own. In May 1936, as a way of undermining the strike at the port of Jaffa, the British authorities permitted the construction of a small wharf in Tel Aviv and the unloading of ships there with exclusively Jewish labor. Despite Arab protests this new facility continued to function long after the strike was over. On this episode, see Porath, *Palestinian Arab National Movement*, 175–76.

5. In ibid., 168.

6. Ibid.; Hacohen, *Time to Tell*, 89–91; AA 205/7, survey of Arab Department activities for June–December 1937.

7. Mansur, *Arab Worker*, 31.

8. On Hebrew labor in the moshavot during the revolt, see Shapira, *Hamaʾavak*.

9. Great Britain, Palestine Royal Commission, *Minutes of Evidence*, 215, 220.

10. MAPAI Archives, Beit Berl, MAPAI central committee meeting of January 16, 1937; oral interview with Agassi, May 6, 1987.

11. AA 205/5.

12. After a guerrilla attack on workers at this quarry, Tahir Qaraman sent a telegram to *Filastin* (published on June 23, 1937) in which he claimed to have severed his connections with Even Vesid at the beginning of 1937. In fact, though he had sold a larger share of the enterprise to the Histadrut, he still remained a partner.

13. Mansur, *Arab Worker*, 33; *Filastin*, July 28, 1937. But see also the version in AA 205/7, survey of Arab Department activities for June–December 1937, which portrays Solel Boneh as the innocent victim of Arab nationalist propaganda and agitation.

14. See Horowitz and Hinden, *Economic Survey of Palestine*, 194–95.

15. Hashomer Hatzaʻir activists in Haifa were not pleased about Alafiya's appointment: the local branch's discussion bulletin asserted that "the very choice [of the young and inexperienced Alafiyya as local PLL organizer] means the whole thing will be buried. . . . It is clear that strengthening the PLL is not an imperative for MAPAI. . . ." HH 90/17alef (2alef), December 6, 1936. On Jewish Agency

funding for the PLL's security and political operations during the revolt, see AA 208/2046, Agassi to S/EC/H, September 27, 1939.

16. Nassar's letters are in AA 407/605. See too AA 205/6; AA 205/7, survey of Arab Department activities for June–December 1937, 3; CZA, S25/2961, Agassi to the Jewish Agency's Political Department, February 15, 1937; and Eshed, *Mosad*, passim.

17. See, for example, "Ayyuha al-sukkan," issued in Haifa and dated July 31, 1936, in AA 208/781alef. The Erem-Nir faction of Po'alei Tziyon Smol put out at least one Arabic leaflet of its own, under the name of its front group Antifa (from "antifascist").

18. AA 298/781alef, Agassi to Harpaz and Hacohen, October 2, 1936; AA 205/6, meeting of the Arab Committee, November 11, 1936; CZA, S25/9161; AA 205/7, Agassi, report on PLL activities, May 20, 1937.

19. Mansur, *Arab Worker*, 6; for Alafiya's account of this and other meetings, see AA 205/7, survey of Arab Department activities for June–December 1937, 4. See too the comments by one of the ILP members of Parliament who had visited Palestine in Jewish Socialist Labour Party, *British Labour Policy on Palestine* (London, 1938), 114–16.

20. See, for example, Mordekhai Orenstein, *Jews, Arabs and British in Palestine: A Left Socialist View* (London, 1936).

21. AA 205/7, Agassi's report on PLL activities, May 20, 1937.

22. Ibid. See also Black, *Zionism*, 336–64.

23. The memorandum, "Co-operation between Jewish and Arab Workers under the Auspices of the General Federation of Jewish Labour," is in CZA, S25/4618; the testimony is from Great Britain, Palestine Royal Commission, *Minutes of Evidence*, 234–37.

24. Ibid., 340–43; *Filastin*, January 17, 1937.

25. MAPAI Archives, Beit Berl, minutes of MAPAI political committee meeting of May 9, 1935; S/EC/H, May–August 1936; Black, *Zionism*, 66–67.

26. EC/H, May, June, September 9, October 29, 1936.

27. On Assaf's career, see Shapiro, *Formative Years*, 82–83.

28. *Haqiqat al-Amr*, March 24, 1937.

29. Ben-Gurion expressed this perspective concisely in an address to his colleagues in the Zionist leadership in October 1936: "There is no conflict between Jewish and Palestinian [Arab] nationalism because the Jewish nation is not in Palestine and the Palestinians are not a nation." In Flapan, *Zionism*, 131. I have not seen the Hebrew original of this quotation, but I very much doubt that Ben-Gurion actually used the term "Palestinian" to refer to those whom labor Zionists usually called "the Arabs of the Land of Israel" (*'araviyei eretz yisra'el*).

30. Quoted in Teveth, *Ben-Gurion*, 170. See also Ben-Gurion's July 1938 speech to MAPAI's Political Committee, quoted in Flapan, *Zionism*, 141–42.

31. Teveth, *Ben-Gurion*, 179ff, and Flapan, *Zionism*, ch. 1.

32. EC/H, March 27, 1941. But see also AA 205/7, Agassi's report on PLL activities, May 20, 1937, which claims that *Haqiqat al-Amr* evoked some positive responses among Arab readers.

33. See, for example, Agassi's report to the MAPAI central committee, meeting of January 16, 1937, in MAPAI Archives, Beit Berl.

34. Ibid.

35. Teveth, *Ben-Gurion*, 170; Black, *Zionism*, 63–64.

36. On the continuing search for funding, see CZA, S25/2961, Agassi to the Jewish Agency's Political Department, February 15, 1937; Agassi to Shertok, May 18, 1937; Hoz to Shertok, December 17, 1937 and June 15, 1938.

37. CZA S25/2961, Agassi to the Jewish Agency's Political Department, March 22, 1938, and report on the PLL, July 1938.

38. Superintendent of Police, Lydda District, to the Acting District Commissioner, Lydda District, February 1943, reproduced in al-Budayri, *Tatawwur*.

39. Quoted in Porath, *Palestinian Arab National Movement*, 238.

40. HH/AC 4/2, from Agassi's diary.

41. Ibid.; CZA, S25/2961, PLL report for January–June 1938.

42. Lesch, *Arab Politics*, 226.

43. Quoted in Tzvi Lavi, "Hashomer Hatzaʿir–Hakibbutz Haʾartzi uvaʿayat haʿavoda haʿaravit bameshek hayehudi, 1926–1939" (unpublished M.A. thesis, Tel Aviv University, 1980), 70.

CHAPTER 7. WORKERS, LABOR MOVEMENTS, AND THE LEFT
DURING THE SECOND WORLD WAR

1. Taqqu, "Arab Labor," 159, 169–70. This figure does not include many thousands of Arabs in nonmanual occupations.

2. On the wartime economy, see Rosenzweig, *Consequences*, ch. 6; Tamar Gozanski, *Hitpathut hakapitalizm bepalestina* (Haifa, 1986), ch. 3; and Issa Khalaf, *Politics in Palestine: Arab Factionalism and Social Disintegration, 1939–1948* (Albany, 1991), ch. 2.

3. Beinin, *Was the Red Flag Flying There?* chs. 1–2.

4. Yoʾav Tadmor, "Brit Poʿalei Eretz Yisraʾel 1940–1947" (unpublished M.A. thesis, Tel Aviv University, 1981), 8–9.

5. AA 208/2109, "Skira ʿal peʿulot hamerkaz meyom 23.3.40"; AA 237/27, IU May Day leaflet; *Haqiqat al-Amr*, April 2, 1940; *Hashomer Hatzaʿir*, April 18, 1940.

6. AA 237/26bet, Berman to EC/H, May 3, 1940; AA 237/16, IU, central committee meeting of November 9, 1940.

7. Palestine Railways, *Report of the General Manager for the Years 1942/43, 1943/44, 1944/45 and 1945/46.*

8. AA 237/26bet, CC/IU to S/EC/H, January 25, 1942; *Haqiqat al-Amr*, December 9, 1941, February 17, 1942.

9. ISA, Chief Secretary, R/36/34, memorandum of August 28, 1942, minutes of meeting of August 29, 1942, and General Manager to the Chief Secretary, September 2, 1942.

10. Palestine Railways, *Report of the General Manager for 1942/43*; AA 237/26bet, AURW/IU joint leaflet, "El ʿovdei harakevet baʾaretz"; *Kol Haʿam*, January 1943.

11. AA 208/3660, IU to AURW, February 28, April 27, 1943, and AURW to

IU, April 29, 1943; *al-Difa'*, March 16, 1943; AA 250/40–5–6–5, meeting of Arab Department, May 18, 1944.

12. AA 250, 40–57–23, August 1940.

13. AA 208/2046, July 5, 1939, and Agassi to Hoz, September 27, 1939.

14. AA 208/2046, meeting of Arab Affairs Council, February 15, 1940.

15. EC/KA to Cohen, July 24, 1940.

16. Among them was the first serious attempt at a comprehensive survey of Arab labor movements in Palestine and surrounding countries, Aharon Cohen's *Tnu'at hapo'alim ha'aravit (mitzrayyim, eretz-yisra'el, halevanon, suriya, 'iraq): toldot, sikumim, ba'ayot* (Tel Aviv, 1947). For a broader discussion of Hashomer Hatza'ir's Arab experts, see Joel Beinin, "Knowing Your Enemy, Knowing Your Ally: The Arabists of Hashomer Hatza'ir (MAPAM)," *Social Text*, no. 28 (1991).

17. Cohen's earliest colleagues included Eli'ezer Bauer (later Be'eri) of Kibbutz Hazore'a and Yosef Vashitz, a member of Kibbutz Dalia.

18. HH/AC 4/2, 4/3, 6/1; *Hashomer Hatza'ir*, February 12, March 26, June 11, 1941.

19. Quoted in Flapan, *Zionism*, 283.

20. HH/AC 4/2, Sasson to Cohen, April 7, 1941; EC/H, March 27, 1941. In this period the Histadrut blocked efforts by Po'alei Tziyon Smol to induce the PLL to admit George Nassar and his small circle of Arab workers *en bloc*, for fear that they would take over the organization. See AA 208/2046, meeting of Arab Affairs Council, February 15, 1940; Moshe Erem at EC/H, May 23, 1940; AA 490/7, report of Agassi; *Davar*, September 4, 1940.

21. See AA 250/40–5–6–4, Agassi to Solel Boneh, August 26, 1942, and Hacohen to Haifa Workers' Council, September 7, 1942. On Solel Boneh's use of Arab labor, see S/EC/H, July 5, 12, 1944. The Hebrew labor principle even interfered with Agassi's efforts to reward particularly loyal Arabs with jobs at Jewish enterprises; see, for example, AA 208/2339, Agassi to Tel Aviv Workers' Council, September 1941.

22. See AA 250/40–5–6–4, January 1, 1942, for Hushi's proposed plan of action for the PLL.

23. AA 208/2341, meeting of December 21, 1941; AA 250/40–5–6–4, Hushi to EC/H, February 5, March 20, September 6, 1942; CZA, S25/3107, Hushi to the Jewish Agency, February 22, 1942. Hushi, always on the lookout for opportunities to expand his (and the Histadrut's) sphere of activity, even asked Solel Boneh officials supervising projects in Lebanon and Syria after British and Free French forces occupied those countries to try to make contact with local intellectuals and unionists. Solel Boneh dismissed the idea as impractical. AA 250/40–57–18, Hushi to Solel Boneh, August 13, 1941; Solel Boneh to Hushi, September 16, 1941.

24. See, for example, AA 250/40–5–6–4, Hushi to EC/H, February 5, 1942.

25. In his memoirs the veteran communist Bulus Farah refers to Sami Taha as 'Abd al-Hamid Haymur's *rabib*, an Arabic term which can mean foster son or stepson but also confederate or ally. Either sense of the term may be taken to suggest that 'Abd al-Hamid Haymur promoted Sami Taha as the PAWS' leader while maintaining influence from behind the scenes, where he had always preferred to operate. Farah, *Min al-'uthmaniyya*, 44.

26. AA 407/101gimmel, "Nida' wa-bayan."

27. For an introduction to this topic, see Peter Weiler, "Forming Responsible Trade Unions: The Colonial Office, Colonial Labor, and the Trades Union Congress," *Radical History Review*, nos. 28–30 (1984).

28. See Zachary Lockman, "British Policy toward Egyptian Labor Activism, 1882–1936," *International Journal of Middle East Studies* 20, no. 3 (August 1988), and Joel Beinin and Zachary Lockman, *Workers on the Nile: Nationalism, Communism, Islam, and the Egyptian Working Class, 1882–1954* (Princeton, 1987), chs. 6–7.

29. On Graves's support for organizing Arab unions, see ISA, I/LAB/31/42, Graves to the Chief Secretary, July 27, 1942. The best account of British labor policy in Palestine is in Taqqu, "Arab Labor," ch. 8.

30. My account here draws on my oral interview with Farah, May 15, 1987, on his published memoirs, and on Dothan, *Adumim*, passim.

31. Taqqu, "Arab Labor," 286–87; AA 250/40–5–4, Haifa Workers' Council, December 27, 1942.

32. HH/AC 5/3, July 31, 1942.

33. See, for example, *Hashomer Hatza'ir*, November 11, 1942, January 13, February 3, 17, 1943; AA 250/40–5–6–4, Cohen to EC/H, December 5, 1942.

34. HH/AC 5/3, July 31, 1942.

35. On Cohen's relationship with al-Bandaq, see *inter alia* HH/AC 5/6, *Yedi'ot Hamahlaka*, November 1, 1942; HH/AC 6/3, memorandum of November 16, 1943 meeting; HH/AC 6/4, Cohen to Political Committee, n.d., and Cohen to Bauer, January 7, 1944; HH/AC 6/5, draft program, February 1944.

36. Dothan, *Adumim*, 439–40.

37. Evidence for this interpretation can be found in Cohen's book *Israel and the Arab World*, published in Israel in 1964 and in an English translation in London in 1970. As proof of his claim that during the 1940s the Histadrut and the Jewish Agency had been unwilling to pursue contacts with groups of progressive Arab intellectuals who stood ready to explore Arab-Jewish compromise, Cohen presents a lengthy quotation from someone he describes as the "chief spokesman" of one such group. In this passage that unnamed "spokesman" declares that he distinguished between the "reactionary Zionism" of Ben-Gurion and the Zionist mainstream on the one hand, and a different, more progressive Zionism ready to recognize Arab rights in Palestine on the other, and even goes so far as to state that Jewish immigration is actually in the Arabs' interest. (See pages 324–27 of the English-language edition.) The Arab intellectual Cohen quotes is without doubt 'Abd Allah al-Bandaq. In other words, in a book published in Israel some two decades after al-Bandaq's communist affiliations had become public knowledge, Cohen still found it possible to depict him not as a strongly anti-Zionist communist trying to manipulate naive left-wing Zionists but rather as an "enlightened" noncommunist socialist ready to cooperate with the right kind of Zionist.

In a personal communication to me, Joel Beinin has suggested a somewhat different explanation of Cohen's behavior: so convinced was he that Hashomer Hatza'ir would eventually wean the Soviet Union and the international communist movement away from their rejection of Zionism and win their recognition as

Palestine's authentic communist party that he was sure his entanglements with al-Bandaq would turn out all right in the end.

38. HH/AC 5/6, EC/H to Cohen, October 12, 1942; HH/AC 6/2, report of March 31, 1943; AA 250/40–5–6–4, May 28, 1943. The Arab Affairs Department's budget of £P1,800 did not include an additional £P1,900 allocated for *Haqiqat al-Amr*, which was also subsidized by the Jewish Agency to the tune of £P500 a year.

39. The pamphlet was entitled *Brit po'alei eretz yisra'el* in Hebrew and *The Palestine Labour League* in English; the passages quoted here are from the English-language edition. A condensed version of Hushi's pamphlet appeared as "Organizing Arab Workers," in *Jewish Frontier*, December 1942.

40. H. E. Chudleigh of the Labor Department was moved to respond to Hushi's allegations in a private letter some months later. He described as "totally incorrect" Hushi's claim that the new Arab unions were controlled by either "sons of wealthy Effendis" or communists, insisted on their authentic working-class character and leadership, and defended the record of the Labor Department in facilitating organizing efforts by Arab workers. "The bare fact is," Chudleigh noted rather pointedly, "that some 10,000 Arabs are now organised in Unions, ten per cent being in the Palestine Labour League." AA 219/46, Chudleigh to Hushi, October 23, 1943.

41. HH/AC 6/2, report of March 31, 1943.

42. AA 208/2980, minutes of Histadrut-PAWS meeting.

43. The defector, Malih al-Kharuf, had apparently been promised leadership of the PLL branch as a reward for leaving the PAWS. On this episode, see HH/AC 5/6, Hushi to EC/H, September 25, 1942; AA 490/10, statement of Jerusalem PAWS, February 1943; *Filastin* and *Haqiqat al-Amr*, February 1943, passim; AA 219/41, A. H. Cohen (PLL organizer in Jerusalem) to Histadrut Arab Department, March 5, 1943; HH/AC 6/3, June 25, 1943.

44. AA 250/40–5–6–4, reports of A. H. Cohen, July–September 1943; *Haqiqat al-Amr*, August 1943, passim.

45. TUC archives, box 318; *Haqiqat al-Amr*, February 10, 1941.

46. AA 210/32alef. For an interesting study of Histadrut policy toward the camp workers in the context of the Histadrut's overall wartime trade union policy, see Giyora Rozen, "Ha'igud hamiktzo'i shel hahistadrut haklalit betkufat milhemet ha'olam hashniyya (1939–1945)" (unpublished M.A. thesis, Tel Aviv University, 1974).

47. See AA 250/40–5–6–4 for a report of the May 13, 1942 meeting of the Haifa Workers' Council at which left-wing Council members criticized Abba Hushi for neglecting the camp workers; Repetur, *Lelo heref*, vol. 2, 134–54, in which he recounts his visits to military bases; HH/AC 6/1, *Yedi'ot Hamahlaka*, May 31, 1942.

48. *Kol Ha'am*, August 1941. See too the PCP leaflet addressed to the workers at the Royal Engineers' Stores at Kiryat Motzkin, July 21, 1941, in AA 250/40–57–33.

49. See, for example, EC/H, January 29, March 19, 1942; AA 310/32alef, 1942; AA 250/40–5–6–4, report of meeting of Haifa Workers' Council, May 13, 1942; Repetur, *Lelo heref*, vol. 2, 98ff.

50. Ibid., vol. 2, 95ff, 151–52.

51. AA, Repetur's report to the Histadrut council, meeting of March 15–19, 1943, 32.

52. See, for example, *Kol Ha'am,* February 1943.

53. *Filastin,* March 30, April 2, 1943; *al-Difa',* *Davar,* and *Ha'aretz,* April 5, 1943.

54. S/EC/H, April 13, 1943; AA 208/2980, Arab Affairs Committee, meeting of April 15, 1943.

55. AA 407/448.

56. E. Bilitzski and M. Amster, eds., *Beshnot heirum: hakampim ba'aretz, 1937–1947* (Tel Aviv, 1956), 83–97; Ittihad 'Ummal Filastin, *'Ummal al-mu'askarat fi kifahihim* (Haifa, 1943); AA 219/56; EC/H, May 7, 1943. In an attempt to co-opt a popular demand first raised by the PAWS, Berl Repetur also called for the equalization of Jewish and Arab wages.

57. AH 1/5, May 3, 1943.

58. EC/H, May 5–7, 9, 1943.

59. AA 219/56.

60. *Davar,* May 10, 1943; *Haqiqat al-Amr,* May 18, 1943, quoting *Davar.*

61. HH/AC 5/10/4, report of September 14, 1943.

62. See AA 219/56, the PAWS leaflet of May 15, 1943, and the Histadrut's leaflet (in Hebrew and Arabic) of May 16, 1943; AA 210/32alef; FO 921/59, May 26, 1943.

63. S/EC/H, June 6, 1943.

64. S/EC/H, June 6, 1943.

65. AA 407/449, minutes of meetings in Jaffa, May 13, 16, 1943.

66. AA 208/2984, letter from the Arab army workers' committee of the PAWS in Haifa to its Jewish counterpart, May 30, 1943, and minutes of meetings, June 2, 1943; S/EC/H, June 17, 1943; AA 219/56, from Agassi's diary, June 18, 1943.

67. AA 219/56, Haifa PAWS leaflet, c. July 1943.

68. AA 208/2980, Agassi's report for June 23–28, 1943. See too AA 250/40–5–6–4, July 7, 1943, on a visit to Kibbutz Hazore'a and a meeting with Arab workers from nearby camps.

69. CO 859/93/3, September 13, 1943. As unrest among the camp workers was peaking in May 1943, another group of government employees was also resorting to collective protest. These were the middle-level civil servants of the government of Palestine, almost three-quarters of whom were Arabs. They had formed their own organization, the Second Division Civil Service Association, in 1928, and had voiced sporadic complaints about low salaries and lack of opportunity for promotion. However, they were disinclined to collective action, which conflicted with their self-image as an elite of educated and dedicated public servants, gentlemen to the core, who had little in common not only with wage workers but even with the much more numerous low-level "unclassified" government employees. Yet during the war a sharp decline in their status and salaries—both absolutely, owing to inflation, and relatively, by comparison with white-collar employees at private companies—pushed them toward militancy, though of a distinctive sort. After numerous polite petitions to the government calling attention to their grievances and many cordial but inconclusive meetings with high officials, the Arab and Jewish civil servants finally forced their reluctant leaders to take

action to win for them the COLA. On May 24, 1943, some 7,000 government employees (about 5,000 of them Arabs) reported to work but refrained from eating, drinking, and the performance of their usual duties; they also refused to shave, in defiance of official as well as self-imposed codes of appearance. They had intended to sit in at their desks for two days, but British police and soldiers expelled them on the first day, whereupon they paraded through city streets and held protest meetings in mosques, churches, and synagogues.

The Second Division Civil Service Association was resolutely apolitical, universalist, and unaffiliated to any labor organization, and its members' action in May 1943 won considerable sympathy in both the Arab and Jewish communities. Soon after their strike the COLA was extended to cover the civil servants, but as we will see persistent inflation would drive them to further protest in 1944–45 and then to participation in the general strike of government workers in the spring of 1946. The best analysis of the civil servants' situation and self-image is Taqqu, "Arab Labor," 250–69, on which my account here draws. See too EC/H, May 26–27, 1943; AH 3/54, Histadrut leaflets in Arabic and Hebrew supporting the civil servants' strike; and the Palestine press, January–May 1943, though it should be noted that coverage of the sit-in strike, and especially its suppression, was heavily censored.

70. On the history of the PCP in this period, see Dothan, *Adumim*, Part 3; Budeiri, *Palestine Communist Party*, chs. 5–6; Yehoshuʿa Porat, "Haliga leshihrur leʾumi: tekumata, mahuta vehitparkuta (1943–1948)," *Hamizrah Hehadash* 56, no. 4 (1964).

71. AA 425/30, PCP leaflet, May 6, 1943.

72. AA 208/2980, Agassi's report, March 29, 1943; AA 208/2983–4, minutes of meetings of the Arab Department, May 1943; AA 250/40-5-6-4, Agassi to Hushi, April 4, 1943; Hushi to the Arab Department, April 4, 1943; Hushi to Agassi, April 11, 1943; minutes of meeting of October 19, 1943; and Shmuʾel Solomon, report on Arab Department activities during January 1944.

73. AA 250/40-5-6-4, Solomon to Hushi, October 27, 1943, and Hushi to Solomon, November 2, 1943; Danieli, "Skira ʿal snif brit poʿalei eretz yisraʾel beʿakko," February 6, 1944.

74. AA 208/2980, minutes of Arab Department staff meeting, October 19, 1943.

75. Labor Party Archives, Beit Berl, minutes of the MAPAI secretariat.

76. TUC Archives, file 9569.

77. See the PLL's pamphlet *Kayfa tunhidu ayyuha al-ʿamil al-ʿarabi?* (How will you uplift yourself, O Arab worker?), the official account of its first "study day" (*yom ʿiyyun*) for active members; this can usefully be contrasted with the account of Hashomer Hatzaʿir's Dov Zakin on the same event, in AA 219/40.

78. AA 250/40-5-6-5, Shmuʾel Solomon, report on Arab Department activities during January 1944, and minutes of meeting of January 28, 1944; *Davar*, January 24, 1944; S/EC/H, June 7, 1944.

79. See S/EC/H, June 7, 1944; S/EC/H, September 6, 1944; AA 208/2980, meetings of Arab Department, August 17, October 17, 1944. Quite exceptionally, some of the Arab workers fired from Wagner because of their loyalty to the PLL were placed in jobs in Jewish enterprises, over the strong objections of some top

Histadrut officials who argued that this violated the principle of Hebrew labor. The issue surfaced again a year and a half later, when the Jewish building workers' union in Tel Aviv demanded the dismissal of five former Wagner workers employed as building workers at a housing project sponsored by Po'alei Tziyon Smol and named after Ber Borokhov, to whose blend of Marxism and Zionism the party (now on the verge of extinction) still avowed loyalty. It is not clear what the top leadership of the Histadrut, to which the question was referred, ultimately decided, but the episode again underscored the contradiction at the very heart of the Histadrut's relationship with Arab workers. See EC/H, March 6, 1946.

80. For an account of this incident, see S/EC/H, June 7, 1944. But it should be noted that a Labor Department official reported that he and his colleagues were not convinced that the PAWS had planned and organized the disruption beforehand. See AA 250/40–5–6–5, meeting of the Arab Department, May 18, 1944.

81. AA 425/31; emphasis in the original.

82. S/EC/H, June 7, 1944.

83. AA 219/37, report by A. H. Cohen on the PLL branch in Jerusalem, May 1943–May 1944; AA 219/3; CZA, S25/3108/819, survey of PLL activities, September 19, 1945. See too the Palestinian press for this period.

84. Davar, January 1, 1945; Tadmor, "Brit po'alei eretz yisra'el," 98.

85. AA 250/40–5–6–5, meeting of the Arab Department, July 4, 1944; AA 208/2980, meetings of the Arab Department, August 17, October 17, 1944. In 1944–45 the PLL also recruited Arab workers employed by the Jewish-owned Palestine Potash Company, which extracted potash and other mineral salts from the waters of the Dead Sea. In order to obtain a concession from the government of Palestine, granted in 1930, the company had had to promise the authorities that it would employ a "reasonable" proportion of Arab labor alongside its Jewish employees. Company management had therefore always resisted the principle of Hebrew labor and the Histadrut, understanding the value of this enterprise to the economy of the Yishuv, had not pushed too hard. (On the concession, see Smith, Roots of Separatism, 126–30.) At the same time, the Histadrut had for years refrained from any effort to organize the company's Arab workers, so as to avoid compromising the principle of Hebrew labor by formally recognizing the right of Arab workers to hold jobs at a Jewish-owned enterprise. Nor had it made much effort to ensure that the company's Arab employees enjoyed the same wages and working conditions as its Jewish employees.

However, at the end of 1944 fears that the PAWS or another Arab labor organization might act first finally propelled the Histadrut to recruit the Potash Company's Arab employees into the PLL and demand that their wages and conditions be improved, if not made equal to those of its Jewish workers. But the company's management resisted the PLL's demands and fired some of those who had joined, putting the Histadrut in a rather peculiar position. It now faced the prospect of having to wage a struggle to compel a Jewish employer to rehire Arab workers, instead of fighting (in accordance with the principle of Hebrew labor) to compel him to get rid of his Arab workers and employ only Jews. As a way out, the Histadrut ultimately decided to demand not that the fired Arab workers be rehired but only that they receive compensation for losing their jobs. In the end this effort failed and the Arab potash workers were eventually recruited by two rival Arab labor organizations. See AA 208/4217alef, Arab Workers' Department of the Histadrut to the Trade Union Department, June 5, 1947, accompanying the draft of a letter to the Palestine Potash Company dated June 8, 1947; Tadmor, "Brit po'alei eretz yisra'el," 100–101.

86. HH/AC 6 (5), " 'Al hashvita bevatei hamal'aha shel harakevet"; AA 208/3660, "Hashvita bevatei hamal'aha behaifa"; *Filastin*, February 5, 1944; *Mishmar*, February 6, 1944; *Haqiqat al-Amr*, February 8, 1944; *Palestine Post*, February 6, 1944.

87. AA 250/40–5–6–5, meeting of Arab Department, May 18, 1944.

88. *Al-Ittihad*, June 17, 1945.

89. TUC Archives, file 9569.

90. Nassar was chosen because, as the Arab Department's Shmu'el Solomon put it, "I know the PLL's members, and there is only one George who knows how he must respond when it comes to political matters." AA 208/2980, Arab Department meeting of February 3, 1944. On the selection of delegates to the London conference, see *al-Ittihad*, December 31, 1944, January 7, 1945.

91. See *al-Ittihad*, June–September 1945.

92. TUC Archives, file 9569, September 13, 1945.

93. In AA 250/40–5–6–5, Arab Department meeting of February 8, 1944.

CHAPTER 8. LABOR ACTIVISM AND POLITICS, 1945–1948

1. *Al-Ittihad*, January 14, July 8, 1945.

2. *Al-Ittihad*, June 9, 1946.

3. See Beinin, *Was the Red Flag Flying There?* ch. 2.

4. *Al-Ittihad* (English edition), August 15, 1945.

5. HH/AC 9/6, Hushi to Taha, August 7, 1945, and Taha to Hushi, August 20, 1945.

6. On Arab politics in this period, see Khalaf, *Politics in Palestine.*

7. On labor relations at the refinery through 1943, see *Kol Ha'am* (the PCP's Hebrew-language organ), February 1942; AA 250/40–3–8: Jewish welders to CRL management, January 7, 1942; Haifa Workers' Council to CRL, November 25, 1942; Arab Refinery Workers' Union to the Jewish refinery workers' committee, March 8, 1943, and reply, March 26, 1943; Army Workers' Department of the Histadrut to EC/H, June 4, 1943; *Davar*, July 1, 1943.

8. *Davar*, October 28, 1945. But *al-Ittihad* of November 25, 1945, hints at some tension between the Histadrut and the Arab unions at the refinery over the signing of the new contract.

9. *Filastin*, April 27–28, 1946; EC/H, May 23, 1946; AA 250/40–3–9, Hebrew translation of PAWS leaflet from April 1946. On Histadrut efforts to strengthen its support among Jewish clerical workers at Shell, see AA 250/40–57–83, Clerks' Union to its Jerusalem branch, November 29, 1945; the events of spring 1946 would enable the Histadrut to exert greater control over these Jewish workers.

10. *Al-Ittihad*, February 2, 1947; AA 250/40–3–9, CRL workers' committee leaflet, March 6, 1947; *Haqiqat al-Amr*, January 29, 1947; HH/AC 9/1, minutes of meeting of Hakibbutz Ha'artzi–Hashomer Hatza'ir Arab Department and activists, January 24–25, 1947.

11. See *al-Ittihad* and *Filastin* for March 1947; EC/H, April 13, 1947; AA 219/15, report on activities of the clerical workers' union, 1946–May 1947.

12. CoC/EC/H, April 13, 1947.

13. Oral interview with Abramov, May 14, 1987.

14. EC/H, May 23, 1945.

15. In AA 425/33.

16. On the Histadrut's attitude and actions, see EC/H, April 24, 1946, and HH/AC 90/25/2alef, minutes of meeting of the Histadrut's Arab Department, May 15, 1946.

17. AA 425/33 and the Palestinian press for April 1946.

18. FO 921/296, "Palestine: Employment Problems in Relation to Present Military and Political Trends (Interim Report)," (March 28, 1944); FO 921/292, 293, 296, 303, for discussions among British officials of postwar unemployment in Palestine; EC/H, April 24, 1946.

19. *Al-Ittihad*, June 17, September 30, 1945.

20. Quotation from *Ha'aretz*, September 25, 1945; see also the Hebrew and Arabic press for September 23–25, 1945. On official British responses to the demand for recognition of local workers' committees, see CO 859/97/8. The authorities later reneged on their promise to recognize the camp workers' committees and sought instead to foster docile (and unelected) "social committees" which would include a British representative; see *Haqiqat al-Amr*, December 25, 1946.

21. EC/H, April 10, 24, 1946. On Hashomer Hatza'ir's role see, for example, *Hed Hata'arukha*, a mimeographed bulletin issued in the summer of 1946 by a group of left-wing Levant Fair grounds camp workers, in AA 1272/28. On the PCP, see the MAKI Archive, Hakibbutz Hame'uhad Archive, Yad Tabenkin (Ef'al), box 35.

22. EC/H, April 24, 1946.

23. CO 733/459/5, Sami Taha to the Colonial Secretary; *al-Ittihad*, January 20, 1946; *Haqiqat al-Amr*, April 21, 1947. This same period also witnessed renewed tension at the Majdal Yaba quarry, where as I discussed in Chapters 5 and 6 the Histadrut had made repeated efforts (in 1934 and then twice in 1936) to drive the Arab quarry workers out. When the Arab workers there went on strike in the late winter of 1947, their Jewish coworkers supported them in defiance of Histadrut directives that the strikers be replaced with Jews. *Al-Ittihad* of March 9, 1947, commented that "this is the Histadrut which claims at the WFTU congress that it strives for understanding between Arabs and Jews concerning their day-to-day demands."

24. AA 219/57, minutes of Histadrut-PAWS meetings and various leaflets in Hebrew and Arabic; CoC/EC/H, May 4, 14, 26, 1947; EC/H, May 28, 1947.

25. *Al-Ittihad*, May 25, 1947; *Haqiqat al-Amr*, May 21, 28, 1947; EC/H, June 25, July 9, 30, November 19, 1947; AA 219/70, AWC leaflet, August 18, 1947; *Filastin*, July 1, August 5, 1947.

26. Hashomer Hatza'ir sources also reported that during the summer of 1947 Sami Taha had incurred the Mufti's wrath by blocking a plan to use a camp workers' strike to ignite Arab-Jewish violence on the eve of UNSCOP's arrival in the country—the exact opposite of the Histadrut's analysis at the time.

27. See *Filastin*, August 20, 21, 23, September 13, 1947; an unsigned letter

addressed to the AHC criticizing Sami Taha and the PAWS leaflet of September 9, 1947, in ISA, 65/1595; HH/AC 8/6, *Bulitin* (of the Hakibbutz Ha'artzi–Hashomer Hatza'ir Arab Department), November 15, 1947; HH/AC 9/7, "Conversation with S.H.". For a rather disparaging view of Sami Taha's admittedly naive political initiatives in 1946–47, see Yasin, *Ta'rikh*, 201–7; but see also Bulus Farah, *al-Haraka al-'ummaliyya al-'arabiyya al-filastiniyya: jadaliyyat ba'thiha wa-suqutiha* (Haifa, 1987), 203–8.

28. *Haqiqat al-Amr*, September 10, 19, 1947; CZA, S25/3107, report of Y. Lintsky to the Jewish Agency, September 1947; EC/H, November 19, 1947; AA 219/146, report by Agassi, April 4–7, 1948.

29. HH/AC 90/25 (2alef); EC/H, May 23, 1946; AA 250/40–5–4–8, decisions of the executive of the Haifa Workers' Council, June 6, 1946; AA 219/13, Solomon to Ramat Gan Workers' Council, May 22, 1946; AA 208/4217alef, meeting of Arab Department, May 8, 1947.

30. Ibid.; AA 219/15, "Co-operation between Arab and Jewish Workers," section of "Survey of Histadrut Activities" submitted to UNSCOP.

31. AA 208/4217alef, meeting of Arab Department, May 8, 1947.

32. HH/AC 9/1, *Bulitin* (of the Hakibbutz Ha'artzi–Hashomer Hatza'ir Arab Department), January 15, 1946.

33. AA 219/54, Agassi to Saillant, June 4, 1947. The heading of the Hebrew draft of this letter refers to the PLL's committee of branch delegates, which had hardly existed except on paper and was in any case now defunct. The minutes of such infrequent Arab Department meetings as were held during this period sometimes note the attendance of an Arab named 'Abbas, but he does not seem to have contributed anything to the discussions.

34. On the situation in Haifa in 1948, see AA 219/46, reports by Agassi and Alafiya.

35. HH/AC 7/5, notes for discussion at EC/KA, July 12, 1945; HH/AC 9/1, *Bulitin* (of the Hakibbutz Ha'artzi–Hashomer Hatza'ir Arab Department), March 23, 1947.

36. On Palestinian Arab nationalism, see, for example, Yosef Vashitz, *Ha'aravim be'eretz yisra'el* (Merhavia, 1947), and more generally Beinin, "Knowing Your Enemy, Knowing Your Ally."

37. In 1946 the League had at long last seemed to find an Arab counterpart in Fawzi Darwish al-Husayni and his Filastin al-Jadida ("New Palestine") society. But al-Husayni (a distant relative of the Mufti) was soon assassinated as a traitor to the Palestinian Arab national cause, and no one else stepped forward to take his place.

38. HH/AC 9/1, *Bulitin* (of the Hakibbutz Ha'artzi–Hashomer Hatza'ir Arab Department), March 23, 1947.

39. Ibid.

40. See Beinin, *Was the Red Flag Flying There?* 46.

41. On left politics in the 1947–49 period, see ibid., ch. 2.

42. HH/AC, *Bulitin* (of the Hakibbutz Ha'artzi–Hashomer Hatza'ir Arab Department), August 18, 1947.

43. The report can be found in AA 250/40–3–9.

44. See the Palestinian press for December 1947–January 1948, and AA 219/

146, Agassi's report of April 4–7, 1948. On the attack on Balad al-Shaykh, see Benny Morris, *The Birth of the Palestinian Refugee Problem, 1947–49* (Cambridge, U.K., 1987), 41–42, 156, and Khalidi, *All That Remains*, 152–54.

45. HH/AC 13/90/1, *Bulitin* (of the Hakibbutz Ha'artzi–Hashomer Hatza'ir Arab Department), April 10, 1948. The unionist quoted was almost certainly Efrayyim Krisher, Hashomer Hatza'ir's leading activist at the workshops, whose career I discussed toward the end of Chapter 4.

CONCLUSION

1. HH/AC 9/1, summary of Lubianker's address, December 28, 1947.

2. HH, "Hapo'el ha'aravi bamedina hayehudit," March 15, 1948.

3. See Morris, *Birth of the Palestinian Refugee Problem*, and Nur Masalha, *Expulsion of the Palestinians: The Concept of "Transfer" in Zionist Political Thought, 1882–1948* (Washington, D.C., 1992), which relies heavily on Morris's research but reaches somewhat different conclusions.

4. The best general studies of the Palestinians within Israel are Ian Lustick, *Arabs in the Jewish State: Israel's Control of a National Minority* (Austin, Tex., 1980); Elia Zureik, *The Palestinians in Israel: A Study in Internal Colonialism* (London, 1979); and Sabri Jiryis, *The Arabs in Israel* (New York, 1976).

5. See Beinin, *Was the Red Flag Flying There?* 139–41, which describes how the authorities hindered the Israeli Communist Party's efforts to reestablish the Arab Workers' Congress.

6. See Shalev, *Labour and the Political Economy*, ch. 2.

7. Aharon Cohen's *Israel and the Arab World* (London, 1970) and Flapan's *Zionism* are classics of this genre, though they also contain much useful information.

8. I make this point more fully in "Imagining the Working Class: Culture, Nationalism and Class Formation in Egypt, 1899–1914," *Poetics Today* 15, no. 2 (1994).

9. Exceptions include Theodore Swedenburg's forthcoming book on Palestinian peasants, the 1936–39 revolt, and historical memory, mentioned in the notes to the Introduction, and Nels Johnson, *Islam and the Politics of Meaning in Palestinian Nationalism* (London and Boston, 1982).

10. See Swirski, *Israel: The Oriental Majority*, and Shohat, "Sephardim in Israel."

11. Since the Histadrut has figured so largely in this book, it is worth noting that in 1994 a dissident slate headed by an ambitious young Labor Party defector won the organization's leadership, defeating the colorless bureaucrats who had run it for so long. It is very unlikely that this change will result in any empowerment of the Histadrut's working-class membership, but it will certainly affect the organization's (admittedly much diminished) role in Israeli society.

Bibliography

ARCHIVES

Abba Hushi archive, Haifa University Library, Haifa
Central Zionist Archives, Jerusalem
Hashomer Hatza'ir archives (Merkaz Te'ud Veheker shel Hashomer Hatza'ir),
  Giv'at Haviva
Histadrut archives (Arkhiyon Ha'avoda Vehehalutz, Makhon Lavon Leheker
  Tnu'at Ha'avoda), Tel Aviv
Israel State Archives (Ganzakh Hamedina), Jerusalem
MAKI papers at Hakibbutz Hame'uhad archives, Yad Tabenkin, Ef'al, Israel
MAPAI archives, Arkhiyon Mifleget Ha'avoda, Beit Berl, Israel
Public Records Office, London, Colonial Office and Foreign Office papers
Trades Union Congress archives, London

INTERVIEWS

Yehezkel Abramov, May 14, 1987
Eliyahu Agassi, May 6, 1987
Bulus Farah, May 15, 1987
Efrayyim Krisher, May 13, 1987
Salim al-Qasim, May 19, 1987

UNPUBLISHED PAPERS, THESES, AND DISSERTATIONS

Glazer, Steven. "Propaganda and the Histadrut-Sponsored Pickets for 'Hebrew
  Labor,' 1927–1936." Ph.D. dissertation, Georgetown University, 1991.
Grinberg, Lev Luis. "Shvitat irgun hanehagim hayehudi-ha'aravi, 1931" (The
  strike of the Jewish-Arab drivers' organization, 1931). Seminar paper, Depart-
  ment of Sociology, Tel Aviv University, 1986.
Katz, Sheila. "Women and Gender in Jewish and Palestinian Nationalisms before
  1950: Founding and Confounding the Boundaries." Ph.D. dissertation, Harvard
  University, 1993.

Kolat-Kopelovitch, Yisra'el. "Ideologiya umetziyut betnu'at ha'avoda be'eretz yisra'el, 1905–1919" (Ideology and reality in the labor movement in the land of Israel, 1905–1919). Ph.D. dissertation, Hebrew University of Jerusalem, 1964.

Lavi, Tzvi. "Hashomer Hatza'ir–Hakibbutz Ha'artzi uva'ayat ha'avoda ha'aravit bameshek hayehudi, 1926–1939" (Hashomer Hatza'ir–Hakibbutz Ha'artzi and the problem of Arab labor in the Jewish economy, 1926–1936). M.A. thesis, Tel Aviv University, 1980.

Rozen, Giyora. "Ha'igud hamiktzo'i shel hahistadrut haklalit betekufat milhemet ha'olam hashniyya (1939–1945)" (The Histadrut's trade unionism in the Second World War period). M.A. thesis, Tel Aviv University, 1974.

Seikaly, May. "The Arab Community of Haifa, 1918–1936: A Study in Transformation." Ph.D. dissertation, Somerville College, Oxford University, 1983.

Tadmor, Yo'av. "Brit po'alei eretz yisra'el 1940–1947" (The Palestine Labor League 1940–1947). M.A. thesis, Tel Aviv University, 1981.

Taqqu, Rachelle. "Arab Labor in Mandatory Palestine, 1920–1948." Ph.D. dissertation, Columbia University, 1977.

Vashitz, Joseph. "Jewish-Arab Relations at Haifa under the British Mandate." Manuscript.

PERIODICALS

al-'Amil (PLL)
Ba'avoda (NURPTW)
Bulitin (Hamahlaka Lepe'ula 'Aravit shel Hakibbutz Ha'artzi–Hashomer Hatza'ir)
Bulitin Hakibbutz Ha'artzi
Davar (Histadrut)
al-Difa' (Palestinian Arab newspaper)
Ed Hakatar (URPTW)
Edim (NURPTW)
Ehad Bemai (NURPTW)
Filastin (Palestinian Arab newspaper)
Haifa (PCP)
Hakatar/al-Qatar (URPTW)
'Al Hamishmar (NURPTW)
Haqiqat al-Amr (PLL/Histadrut)
Hashomer Hatza'ir (Hashomer Hatza'ir)
al-Ittihad (NLL/AWC)
Ittihad al-'Ummal (Histadrut)
al-Karmil (Palestinian Arab newspaper)
Kol Ha'am (PCP)
Kol Ha'oved (IU)
Kuntres (Ahdut Ha'avoda)
Mishmar (Hakibbutz Ha'artzi–Hashomer Hatza'ir)
Palestine Post
Qawl al-Haq (Po'alei Tziyon Smol)
Sawt al-'Amil

Sawt al-Haq (Po'alei Tziyon Smol)
She'eilot Hasha'a (NURPTW)
Tzror Yedi'ot (Hamahlaka Lepe'ula 'Aravit shel Hakibbutz Ha'artzi–Hashomer Hatza'ir)
Yedi'ot Hamahlaka (Hamahlaka Lepe'ula 'Aravit shel Hakibbutz Ha'artzi–Hashomer Hatza'ir)

BOOKS AND ARTICLES

Abramovitch, Ze'ev. *Besheirut hatnu'a* (In the service of the movement). Tel Aviv: Y. L. Peretz, 1965.
————, and Y. Gelfat. *Hameshek ha'aravi be'eretz yisra'el uve'artzot hamizrah hatikhon* (The Arab economy in the land of Israel and in the countries of the Middle East). Tel Aviv: Hakibbutz Hame'uhad, 1944.
Abu-Ghazaleh, Adnan Mohammed. *Arab Cultural Nationalism in Palestine during the British Mandate.* Beirut: Institute for Palestine Studies, 1973.
Abu-Lughod, Ibrahim. "The Perils of Palestiniology." *Arab Studies Quarterly* 3, no. 4 (fall 1981).
Ahad Ha'am (Asher Ginsburg). *Kol kitvei Ahad Ha'am* (Collected works of Ahad Ha'am). Jerusalem: Devir, 1949.
Ahdut Ha'avoda. *Have'ida harevi'it shel Ahdut Ha'avoda: din veheshbon* (The fourth congress of Ahdut Ha'avoda: Report). Tel Aviv: Ahdut Ha'avoda, 1924.
————. *Yalkut Ahdut Ha'avoda* (Ahdut Ha'avoda anthology). Tel Aviv: Ahdut Ha'avoda, 1929.
'Alush, Naji. *Al-Haraka al-wataniyya al-filastiniyya imam al-yahud w'al-sahyuniyya, 1882–1948* (The Palestinian national movement facing the Jews and Zionism). Beirut: Dar al-Tali'a, 1978.
al-'Amiri, 'Anan. *Al-Tatawwur al-zira'i w'al-sina'i al-filastini, 1900–1970: bahth ihsa'i* (Palestinian agricultural and industrial development, 1900–1970: A statistical study). Jerusalem: Salah al-Din, 1981.
Anderson, Benedict. *Imagined Communities: Reflections on the Origin and Spread of Nationalism.* London: Verso, 1991.
Anderson, Perry. "Agendas for Radical History." *Radical History Review,* no. 36 (September 1986).
Arlosoroff (Arlosorov), Hayyim. *Leshe'eilat ha'irgun hameshutaf* (On the question of joint organization). Tel Aviv: Hapo'el Hatza'ir, 1927.
Asad, Talal. "Anthropological Texts and Ideological Problems: An Analysis of Cohen on Arab Villages in Israel." *Review of Middle East Studies,* no. 1 (1975). Also in *MERIP Reports,* no. 53 (December 1976).
Asaf, Michael. *Hatnu'a ha'aravit be'eretz yisra'el umekoroteha: hamesh hartza'ot* (The Arab movement in the land of Israel and its sources: Five lectures). Tel Aviv: Da'arav, 1936.
————. *Hatziyonut vehasotziyalizm vehaba'aya ha'aravit* (Zionism, socialism, and the Arab problem). Tel Aviv: Hapo'el Hatza'ir, 1938.
Avitzur, Sh. "Shiv'im shana lemisilot habarzel ba'aretz" (Seventy years of railroads in Palestine). *Teva' va'aretz* 5, nos. 2–3 (1962).
Badran, Nabil Ayub. *Al-Ta'lim wa'l-tahdith fi al-mujtami' al-'arabi al-filastini,*

I: ʿahd al-intidab (Education and modernization in Palestinian Arab society, I: The mandate period). Beirut: PLO Research Center, 1979.

Bargad-Barzilai, Y. Hatragediya shel hamahpekha hasoviyetit (The tragedy of the Soviet revolution). Tel Aviv: ʿAm ʿOved, 1968.

Beinin, Joel. "Knowing Your Enemy, Knowing Your Ally: The Arabists of Hashomer Hatzaʿir (MAPAM)." Social Text, no. 28 (1991).

————. Was the Red Flag Flying There? Marxist Politics and the Arab-Israeli Conflict in Egypt and Israel, 1948–1965. Berkeley: University of California Press, 1990.

Ben-Amotz, Dan, and Netiva Ben-Yehuda. Milon ʿolami leʿivrit meduberet (World dictionary of spoken Hebrew). Tel Aviv: Leon Epstein, 1972.

Ben-Gurion, David. Anahnu veshkheineinu (We and our neighbors). Tel Aviv: Davar, 1931.

————. Jewish Labour. London: Hechalutz, c. 1932.

Ben-Nahum, Yizhar. "Hashomer Hatzaʿir veraʿayon hadu-leʾumiyut, 1942–1947" (Hashomer Hatzaʿir and the idea of binationalism, 1942–1947). Meʾasef, no. 15 (1985).

Ben-Porat, Amir. Between Class and Nation: The Formation of the Jewish Working Class in the Period before Israel's Statehood. Westport, Conn.: Greenwood Press, 1986.

Ben-Tzvi, Yitzhak. Hatnuʿa haʿaravit (The Arab movement). Jaffa: ʿAvoda, 1921.

————. Hehazon vehagshamato: pirkei zikhronot vereshimot ʿal baʿayot hahistadrut (The vision and its realization: Reminiscences and notes on the problems of the Histadrut). Tel Aviv: Histadrut, 1968.

———— ("Avner"). Lesheʾeilot ʿavodateinu baʾaretz (On questions concerning our work in the country). Jerusalem: Ahdut, 1913. First published in Haʾahdut 3, nos. 16–17 (1912).

Berkowitz, Michael. Zionist Culture and West European Jewry before the First World War. Cambridge, U.K.: Cambridge University Press, 1993.

Berque, Jacques. French North Africa: The Maghrib between Two World Wars. London: Faber, 1967.

Biger, Gidʿon. Moshevet keter o bayit leʾumi: hashpaʿat hashilton habriti ʿal eretz-yisraʾel, 1917–1930—behina geʾografit-historit (Crown colony or national home: The influence of British rule on the land of Israel, 1917–1930—A geographical-historical view). Jerusalem: Yad Yitzhak Ben-Tzvi, 1983.

Bilitzki, Eliyahu. Beyitzira uvemaʾavak: moʿetzet poʿalei haifa, 1921–1981 (In creation and struggle: The Haifa workers' council, 1921–1981). Tel Aviv: ʿAm ʿOved, 1981.

————, and Mordekhai Amster, eds. Beshnot heirum: hakampim baʾaretz, 1937–1947 (In years of emergency: The camps in Palestine, 1937–1947). Tel Aviv: Histadrut Poʿalei Habinyan, 1956.

Black, Edwin. The Transfer Agreement: The Untold Story of the Secret Agreement between the Third Reich and Jewish Palestine. New York: Macmillan, 1984.

Black, Ian. Zionism and the Arabs, 1936–1939. New York: Garland Publishing, 1986.

Bonacich, Edna. "A Theory of Ethnic Antagonism: The Split Labor Market." *American Sociological Review* 37, no. 5 (October 1972).

Borokhov, B. *Ketavim* (Writings), 3 vols. Tel Aviv: Sifriyat Poʿalim and Hakibbutz Hame'uhad, 1955.

Braslavski, Moshe. *Tnuʿat hapoʿalim beʾeretz yisraʾel* (The workers' movement in the land of Israel), 2 vols. Tel Aviv: Hakibbutz Hame'uhad, 1963.

al-Budayri, Musa. *Tatawwur al-haraka al-ʿummaliyya al-ʿarabiyya fi filastin: muqaddama taʾrikhiyya wa-majmuʿa wathaʾiq* (The development of the Arab workers' movement in Palestine: Historical introduction and collection of documents). Jerusalem: n.p., c. 1980; Beirut: Dar ibn Khaldun, 1981.

——— (Budeiri, Musa). *The Palestine Communist Party, 1919–1948: Arab and Jew in the Struggle for Internationalism.* London: Ithaca Press, 1979.

Chakrabarty, Dipesh. *Rethinking Working-Class History: Bengal 1890–1940.* Princeton: Princeton University Press, 1989.

Cohen, Aharon. *Israel and the Arab World.* London: W. H. Allen, 1970.

———. *Levaʿayot hamediniyut hatziyonit beyameinu* (On the problems of Zionist policy today). Merhavia: Hakibbutz Haʾartzi, 1943.

———. *Tnuʿat hapoʿalim haʿaravit (mitzrayyim, eretz-yisraʾel, halevanon, suriya, ʿiraq): toldot, sikumim, baʿayot* (The Arab workers' movement [Egypt, Eretz Yisraʾel, Lebanon, Syria, Iraq]: History, conclusions, problems). Tel Aviv: Histadrut, 1947.

Cohen, Mitchell. *Zion and State: Nation, Class and the Shaping of Modern Israel.* Oxford: Basil Blackwell, 1987.

Cotterell, Paul. *The Railways of Palestine and Israel.* Abingdon, Oxfordshire, U.K.: Tourret Publishing, 1984.

Dar, Lina. "Hanisayon leʾirgun meshutaf yehudi-ʿaravi benamal haifa be-1932" (The attempt at Jewish-Arab joint organization at the port of Haifa in 1932). *Meʾasef*, no. 14 (1984).

Doleve-Gandelman, Tsili. "The Symbolic Inscription of Zionist Ideology in the Space of Eretz Yisrael: Why the Native Israeli is Called Tsabar." In Harvey E. Goldberg, ed., *Judaism Viewed from Within and Without: Anthropological Studies.* Albany, N.Y.: State University of New York Press, 1987.

Domb, Risa. *The Arab in Hebrew Prose, 1911–1948.* London: Vallentine, Mitchell, 1982.

Dominguez, Virginia R. *People as Subject, People as Object: Selfhood and Peoplehood in Contemporary Israel.* Madison, Wisc.: University of Wisconsin Press, 1989.

Dothan, Shmuʾel. *Adumim: hamiflaga hakomunistit beʾeretz yisraʾel* (Reds: The Communist Party in the land of Israel). Kfar Saba: Shevna Hasofer, 1991.

Doumani, Beshara B. "Rediscovering Ottoman Palestine: Writing Palestinians into History." *Journal of Palestine Studies* 21, no. 2 (winter 1992).

Ehrlich, Avishai. "Israel: Conflict, War and Social Change." In Colin Creighton and Martin Shaw, eds., *The Sociology of War and Peace.* Houndmills, Hampshire, U.K.: MacMillan, 1987.

Eisenstadt, S. N. *Israeli Society.* New York: Basic Books, 1967.

Eisenzweig, Uri. "An Imaginary Territory: The Problematic of Space in Zionist Discourse." *Dialectical Anthropology* 5, no. 4 (May 1981).

————. *Territoires occupés de l'imaginaire juif: essai sur l'espace sioniste.* Paris: C. Bourgois, 1980.

Eshed, Haggai. *Mosad shel ish ehad: Reuven Shilo'ah—avi hamodi'in hayisra'eli* (A one-man institution: Reuven Shilo'ah—Father of Israeli intelligence). Tel Aviv: Eydanim, 1988.

Even-Shoshan, Tzvi. *Toldot tnu'at hapo'alim be'eretz yisra'el* (History of the workers' movement in the land of Israel), 2 vols. Tel Aviv: 'Am 'Oved, 1966.

Even-Zohar, Itamar. "The Emergence of a Native Hebrew Culture in Palestine, 1882–1948." *Poetics Today* 11, no. 1 (1990).

Farah, Bulus. *Al-Haraka al-'ummaliyya al-'arabiyya al-filastiniyya: jadaliyyat ba'thiha wa-suqutiha* (The Palestinian Arab workers' movement: The dialectics of its rise and fall). Haifa: Maktabat Kull Shai, 1987.

————. *Min al-'uthmaniyya ila al-dawla al-'ibriyya* (From Ottoman times to the Hebrew state). Nazareth: al-Sawt, 1985.

Flapan, Simha. *Zionism and the Palestinians.* London: Croom Helm, 1979.

Frankel, Jonathan. "The 'Yizkor' Book of 1911—A Note on National Myths in the Second Aliya." In *Religion, Ideology and Nationalism in Europe and America: Essays Presented in Honor of Yehoshua Arieli.* Jerusalem: Israeli Historical Society and Zalman Shazar Center, 1986.

General Federation of Jewish Labour in Israel. *Documents and Essays on Jewish Labour Policy in Palestine.* Tel Aviv: Histadrut, 1930; reprinted Westport, Conn.: Greenwood Press, 1975.

Gertz, Nurith. "Social Myths in Literary and Political Texts." *Poetics Today* 7, no. 4 (1986).

Gorny, Yosef (Joseph). *Ahdut Ha'avoda, 1919–1930: hayesodot hara'ayonim vehashita hamedinit* (Ahdut Ha'avoda, 1919–1930: Ideological foundations and political method). Tel Aviv: Hakibbutz Hame'uhad, 1963.

————. *The British Labour Movement and Zionism, 1917–1948.* Totowa, N.J.: Frank Cass, 1983.

————. "Ha'ideologiya shel kibbush ha'avoda" (The ideology of the conquest of labor). *Keshet,* nos. 37–38 (1967–68).

————. *Perakim be'ideologiya shel tnu'at hapo'alim ba'aliya hashniyya* (Readings in the ideology of the workers' movement in the Second Aliya). Tel Aviv: Tel Aviv University, 1966–67.

————. *Perakim nivharim betkufat ha'aliya hashniyya* (Selected readings in the period of the Second Aliya). Tel Aviv: Tel Aviv University, 1966–67.

————. *Zionism and the Arabs, 1882–1948: A Study of Ideology.* Oxford: Oxford University Press, 1987.

Gozanski, Tamar. *Hitpathut hakapitalizm bepalestina* (The development of capitalism in Palestine). Haifa: Mif'alim universita'im lehotza'a le'or, 1986.

Great Britain, Palestine Royal Commission. *Minutes of Evidence Heard at Public Sessions.* London: H. M. Stationery Office, 1937.

Greenberg, Stanley B. *Race and State in Capitalist Development: Comparative Perspectives.* New Haven: Yale University Press, 1980.

Greilsammer, Alain. *Les Communistes Israeliens.* Paris: Presses de la FNSP, 1978.

Grinberg, Lev Luis. *Split Corporatism in Israel.* Albany, N.Y.: State University of New York Press, 1991.

Hacohen, David. *Time to Tell: An Israeli Life, 1898–1984.* Cranbury, N.J.: Herzl Press, 1985. First published in Hebrew as *'Et lesaper* (Time to tell). Tel Aviv: 'Am 'Oved, 1974.

Halper, Jeff. *Between Redemption and Revival: The Jewish Yishuv of Jerusalem in the Nineteenth Century.* Boulder: Westview Press, 1991.

Harshav, Benjamin. *Language in Time of Revolution.* Berkeley: University of California Press, 1993.

Hen-Tov, Jacob. *Communism and Zionism in Palestine: The Comintern and Political Unrest in the 1920s.* Cambridge, Mass.: Schenkman Publishing, 1974.

Herzl, Theodor. *The Complete Diaries of Theodor Herzl,* edited by Raphael Patai. New York: Herzl Press, 1960.

———. *The Jewish State: An Attempt at a Modern Solution to the Jewish Question,* translated by Sylvie D'Avigdor. London: Pordes, 1967.

Himadeh, Sa'id B., ed. *Economic Organization of Palestine.* Beirut: American University of Beirut, 1938.

Histadrut (Hava'ad Hapo'el). *Din veheshbon lave'ida hashlishit shel hahistadrut* (Report to the third congress of the Histadrut). Tel Aviv: Histadrut, 1927.

———. *Have'ida hashniyya shel hahistadrut* (The second congress of the Histadrut). Tel Aviv: Histadrut, 1923.

Histadrut Artzit shel Po'alei Harakevet. *Din veheshbon shel hava'ad hamerkazi lave'ida hashvi'it* (Report of the central committee to the seventh congress [of the National Union of Railway Workers]). May 1931.

Hobsbawm, E. J. *Nations and Nationalism since 1780: Programme, Myth, Reality.* Cambridge, U.K.: Cambridge University Press, 1992.

Horowitz, Dan, and Moshe Lissak. *Origins of the Israeli Polity: Palestine under the Mandate.* Chicago: University of Chicago Press, 1978. First published in Hebrew as *Meyishuv lemedina: yehudei eretz yisra'el betkufat hamandat kekehila politit* (From Yishuv to state: The Jews of the land of Israel in the mandate period as a political community). Tel Aviv: 'Am 'Oved, 1977.

Horowitz, David. *Hakalkala ha'eretzyisra'elit behitpathuta* (The Economy of the land of Israel in its development). Tel Aviv: n.p., 1948.

———, and Rita Hinden. *Economic Survey of Palestine.* Tel Aviv: Jewish Agency, 1938.

Hushi, Abba. *Brit po'alei eretz yisra'el* (The Palestine Labor League). Tel Aviv: Histadrut, 1943.

Ittihad 'Ummal Filastin (Palestine Labor League). *Kashf al-Qina'* (Removing the mask). Haifa: Ittihad 'Ummal Filastin, 1937.

———. *Kayfa tunhidu ayyuha al-'amil al-'arabi?* (How will you uplift yourself, O Arab worker?). Tel Aviv: Ittihad 'Ummal Filastin, 1944.

———. *'Ummal al-mu'askarat fi kifahihim* (The camp workers in their struggle). Haifa: Ittihad 'Ummal Filastin, 1943.

Jam'iyyat al-'Ummal al-'Arabiyya al-Filastiniyya (Palestinian Arab Workers' Society). *Mu'tamar al-'ummal al-'arab al-awwal* (The first Arab workers' congress). Haifa: al-Matba'a al-Tijariyya al-'Arabiyya, 1930.

———. *Taqrir mu'tamar jam'iyyat al-'ummal al-'arabiyya al-filastiniyya, 29–30 ab 1946* (Report of the Congress of the PAWS, 29–30 August 1946). Haifa: PAWS, 1946.

Jewish Agency for Palestine. *Memorandum submitted to the Palestine Royal Commission on behalf of the Jewish Agency for Palestine.* First published 1936; reprinted Westport, Conn.: Greenwood Press, 1975.

Jewish Socialist Labour Party. *British Labour Policy on Palestine.* London: Poale Zion, 1938.

Jiryis, Sabri. *The Arabs in Israel.* New York: Monthly Review Press, 1976.

Johnson, Nels. *Islam and the Politics of Meaning in Palestinian Nationalism.* London and Boston: Kegan Paul International, 1982.

al-Junaydi, Salim. *Al-Haraka al-ʿummaliyya fi filastin, 1917–1985* (The workers' movement in Palestine, 1917–1985). Amman: Dar al-Jalil, 1988.

Kark, Ruth, ed. *The Land That Became Israel: Studies in Historical Geography.* New Haven and Jerusalem: Yale University Press and Magnes Press, 1990.

Katinke, Barukh. *Meʾaz veʿad heina* (From then till now). Jerusalem: Kiryat Sefer, 1961.

Katriel, Tamar. *Communal Webs: Communication and Culture in Contemporary Israel.* Albany, N.Y.: State University of New York Press, 1991.

———, and Aliza Shenhar. "Tower and Stockade: Dialogic Narrative in Israeli Settlement Ethos." *Quarterly Journal of Speech* 76, no. 4 (November 1990).

al-Kayyali, ʿAbd al-Wahhab. *Taʾrikh filastin al-hadith* (History of modern Palestine). Beirut: al-Muʾassasa al-ʿarabiyya lil-dirasat waʾl-nashr, 1970.

Kedma Mizraha. *Kovetz maʾamarim lasheʾeila haʿaravit* (A collection of articles on the Arab question). Jerusalem: Kedma Mizraha, 1936.

Khalaf, Issa. *Politics in Palestine: Arab Factionalism and Social Disintegration, 1939–1948.* Albany, N.Y.: State University of New York Press, 1991.

Khalidi, Tarif. "Palestinian Historiography: 1900–1948." *Journal of Palestine Studies* 10, no. 3 (spring 1981).

Khalidi, Walid, ed. *All That Remains: The Palestinian Villages Occupied and Depopulated by Israel in 1948.* Washington, D.C.: Institute for Palestine Studies, 1992.

———, ed. *From Haven to Conquest: Readings in Zionism and the Palestine Problem until 1948.* Washington, D.C.: Institute for Palestine Studies, 1987.

al-Khalili, ʿAli. *Aghani al-ʿamal wʾal-ʿummal fi filastin: dirasa* (Songs of work and workers in Palestine: A study). Jerusalem: Salah al-Din, 1979.

———. *Al-Turath al-filastini wʾal-tabaqat* (The Palestinian heritage and class). Jerusalem: Salah al-Din, 1977.

Kimmerling, Baruch. *The Economic Interrelationships between the Arab and Jewish Communities in Mandatory Palestine.* Cambridge, Mass.: Center for International Studies, Massachusetts Institute of Technology, September 1979.

———. *Zionism and Economy.* Cambridge, Mass.: Schenkman Publishing Company, 1983.

———. *Zionism and Territory: The Socio-Territorial Dimensions of Zionist Politics.* Berkeley: University of California Press, 1982.

———, ed. *The Israeli State and Society: Boundaries and Frontiers.* Albany, N.Y.: State University of New York Press, 1989.

———, and Joel S. Migdal. *Palestinians: The Making of a People.* New York: Free Press, 1993.

Kisch, F. H. *Palestine Diary.* London: Victor Gollancz, 1938.

Kolat, Yisra'el. "Po'alei Tziyon beyn tziyonut lekomunizm" (Po'alei Tziyon between Zionism and communism). *Asufot* 2, no. 15 (November 1971).

Kornberg, Jacques, ed. *At the Crossroads: Essays on Ahad Ha-am.* Albany, N.Y.: State University of New York Press, 1983.

Krisher, Efrayyim. "Ha'irgun hameshutaf bemivhan hahagshama" (Joint organization in the test of realization). *Me'asef,* nos. 3–4 (August 1972).

Lahav, Mordekhai. "Si'at hashomer hatza'ir behaifa beshanim 1934–1937" (The Hashomer Hatza'ir faction in Haifa in the years 1934–1937). *Me'asef,* no. 15 (1985).

Lehn, Walter, in association with Uri Davis. *The Jewish National Fund.* London: Kegan Paul, 1988.

Lesch, Ann Moseley. *Arab Politics in Palestine, 1917–1939: The Frustration of a Nationalist Movement.* Ithaca, N.Y.: Cornell University Press, 1979.

List, Nahman. "Tzadak hakomintern" (The Comintern was correct). *Keshet,* nos. 18, 20, 22, 24, 27, 30, 34 (1963–67).

Lockman, Zachary. "Exclusion and Solidarity: Labor Zionism and Arab Workers in Palestine, 1897–1929." In Gyan Prakash, ed., *After Colonialism: Imperial Histories and Postcolonial Displacements.* Princeton: Princeton University Press, 1994.

———. "Imagining the Working Class: Culture, Nationalism and Class Formation in Egypt, 1899–1914." *Poetics Today* 15, no. 2 (1994).

———. "Original Sin." In Zachary Lockman and Joel Beinin, eds., *Intifada: The Palestinian Uprising against Israeli Occupation.* Boston: South End Press, 1989.

———. "Railway Workers and Relational History: Arabs and Jews in British-Ruled Palestine." *Comparative Studies in Society and History* 35, no. 3 (July 1993).

———. " 'We Opened the Arabs' Minds': Labour Zionist Discourse and the Railway Workers of Palestine (1919–1929)." *Review of Middle East Studies,* no. 5 (1992).

———, ed. *Workers and Working Classes in the Middle East: Struggles, Histories, Historiographies.* Albany, N.Y.: State University of New York Press, 1994.

Lustick, Ian. *Arabs in the Jewish State: Israel's Control of a National Minority.* Austin: University of Texas Press, 1980.

Mandel, Neville J. *The Arabs and Zionism before World War I.* Berkeley: University of California Press, 1976.

Mansur, George. *The Arab Worker under the Palestine Mandate.* Jerusalem: Arab Cultural Company, 1938.

Margalit, Elkana. *Anatomia shel smol: Po'alei Tziyon Smol be'eretz yisra'el (1919–1946)* (Anatomy of a Left: Po'alei Tziyon Smol in the land of Israel). Jerusalem: Hebrew University, 1976.

———. *Hashomer Hatza'ir: me'eidat ne'urim lemarksizm mahpekhani, 1913–1936* (Hashomer Hatza'ir: From youth group to revolutionary Marxism, 1913–1936). Tel Aviv: Hakibbutz Hame'uhad, 1971.

Masalha, Nur. *Expulsion of the Palestinians: The Concept of "Transfer" in Zionist Political Thought, 1882–1948.* Washington, D.C.: Institute for Palestine Studies, 1992.

Mattar, Philip. *The Mufti of Jerusalem: al-Hajj Amin al-Husayni and the Palestinian National Movement*. New York: Columbia University Press, 1988.

Merhav, Peretz. *Toldot tnuʿat hapoʿalim beʾeretz yisraʾel: hahitpathut haraʿyonit-hamedinit, perakim veteʿudot (1905–1965)* (History of the workers' movement in the land of Israel: Ideological-political development, readings and documents [1905–1965]). Merhavia: Sifriyat Poʿalim, 1967.

Migdal, Joel S., ed. *Palestinian Society and Politics*. Princeton: Princeton University Press, 1980.

Miller, Ylana N. *Government and Society in Rural Palestine, 1920–1948*. Austin: University of Texas Press, 1985.

Moʿetzet Poʿalei Haifa. *Hahistadrut behaifa beshanim 1933–1939* (The Histadrut in Haifa in the years 1933–1939). Haifa: Moʿetzet Poʿalei Haifa, 1939.

Morris, Benny. *The Birth of the Palestinian Refugee Problem, 1947–49*. Cambridge, U.K.: Cambridge University Press, 1987.

Morrison, Toni. *Playing in the Dark: Whiteness and the Literary Imagination*. Cambridge, Mass.: Harvard University Press, 1992.

Muslih, Muhammad. *The Origins of Palestinian Nationalism*. New York: Columbia University Press, 1988.

Nairn, Tom. "The Modern Janus." In Tom Nairn, *The Break-Up of Britain*. London: New Left Books and Verso Editions, 1981.

Nakhla, Muhammad. *Tatawwur al-mujtamiʿ fi filastin* (The development of society in Palestine). Kuwait: Muʾassasat Dhat al-Salasil, 1983.

Nashashibi, Nasser Eddin. *Jerusalem's Other Voice: Ragheb Nashashibi and Moderation in Palestinian Politics, 1920–1948*. Exeter, U.K.: Ithaca Press, 1990.

Navarski, K. *Hamandat vemeshek haʾaretz* (The mandate and the country's economy). Merhavia: Sifriyat Poʿalim, 1946.

al-Niqaba al-ʿArabiyya li-ʿUmmal Sikak Hadid Filastin (Arab Union of Railway Workers). *Bayan ʿAmm* (Public statement). 1936.

Niqabat ʿUmmal al-Sikak al-Hadidiyya (al-Hayʾa al-Markaziyya). *Al-ʿAmil fi al-Sikak al-Hadidiyya* (The worker on the railroad). C. 1937.

Niqula, Jabra. *Harakat al-idrabat bayn al-ʿummal al-ʿarab fi filastin* (The strike movement among the Arab workers in Palestine). Jaffa: Matbaʿat al-Nur, 1935.

Orenstein, Mordekhai. *Jews, Arabs and British in Palestine: A Left Socialist View*. London: Kibbutz Artzi, 1936.

Owen, Roger, ed. *Studies in the Economic and Social History of Palestine in the Nineteenth and Twentieth Centuries*. Carbondale, Ill.: Southern Illinois University Press, 1982.

Palestine, Government of. *Memoranda Prepared by the Government of Palestine [for the Palestine Royal Commission]*. London: H. M. Stationery Office, 1937.

———. *A Survey of Palestine*, 2 vols. Jerusalem, 1946. *Supplement*. Jerusalem, 1947. Reprinted by the Institute of Palestine Studies, Washington D.C., 1991.

Palestine Railways. *Report of the General Manager on the Administration of the Palestine Railways and Operated Lines for the Year[s] Ended . . . 31st December 1931, 31st March 1933, 1934, 1935*. Jerusalem: Government of Palestine, 1932, 1933, 1934, 1935.

————. *Report of the General Manager for the Years 1942/43, 1943/44, 1944/45 and 1945/46.* Jerusalem: Government of Palestine, 1946.

Penslar, Derek J. *Zionism and Technocracy: The Engineering of Jewish Settlement in Palestine, 1870–1918.* Bloomington, Ind.: Indiana University Press, 1991.

Perry, Menahem. "The Israeli-Palestinian Conflict as a Metaphor in Recent Israeli Fiction." *Poetics Today* 7, no. 4 (1986).

Po'alei Tziyon Smol, *Leshe'eilot harega'* (On the questions of the moment). Tel Aviv: Po'alei Tziyon, 1933.

————. *Me'ora'ot oktober 1933* (The events of October 1933). Tel Aviv: Po'alei Tziyon, 1933.

Porath, Yehoshua. *The Emergence of the Palestinian-Arab National Movement, 1918–1929.* London: Frank Cass, 1974.

————. "Haliga leshihrur le'umi: tekumata, mahuta vehitparkuta (1943–1948)" (The National Liberation League: Its rise, character and disintegration [1943–1948]). *Hamizrah Hehadash* 56, no. 4 (1964).

————. *The Palestinian Arab National Movement: From Riots to Rebellion, 1929–1939.* London: Frank Cass, 1977.

————. "Social Aspects of the Emergence of the Palestinian Arab National Movement." In Menahem Milson, ed., *Society and Political Structure in the Arab World.* New York: Humanities Press, 1973.

Ramras-Rauch, Gila. *The Arab in Israeli Literature.* Bloomington, Ind.: Indiana University Press, 1989.

Repetur, Berl. *Lelo heref: ma'asim uma'avakim* (Without cease: Deeds and struggles), 3 vols. Tel Aviv: Hakibbutz Hame'uhad, 1973.

Revusky, A. *Jews in Palestine.* New York: Vanguard Press, 1936.

Rodinson, Maxime. *Europe and the Mystique of Islam.* Seattle: University of Washington Press, 1987.

————. *Israel: A Colonial-Settler State?* New York: Monad Press, 1973.

Rosenfeld, Henry. "From Peasantry to Wage Labor and Residual Peasantry: The Transformation of an Arab Village." In Robert Alan Manners, ed., *Process and Pattern in Culture.* Chicago: Aldine, 1964.

Rosenzweig, Rafael N. *The Economic Consequences of Zionism.* Leiden: E. J. Brill, 1989.

Rubenstein, Sondra Miller. *The Communist Movement in Palestine and Israel, 1919–1984.* Boulder: Westview Press, 1985.

Said, Edward W. *Culture and Imperialism.* New York: Knopf, 1993.

————. *Orientalism.* New York: Pantheon, 1978.

————. *The Question of Palestine.* New York: Times Books, 1979.

Samara, Samih. *Al-'Amal al-shuyu'i fi filastin: al-tabaqa wa'l-sha'b fi muwajahat al-koloniyaliyya* (Communist activism in Palestine: Class and people in the confrontation with colonialism). Beirut: Dar al-Farabi, 1979.

Schölch, Alexander. *Palestine in Transformation, 1856–1882: Studies in Social, Economic and Political Development.* Washington, D.C.: Institute for Palestine Studies, 1993.

Sereni, Enzo, and R. E. Ashery, eds. *Jews and Arabs in Palestine: Studies in a National and Colonial Problem.* New York: Hechalutz Press, 1936.

Shafir, Gershon. *Land, Labor and the Origins of the Israeli-Palestinian Conflict, 1882–1914.* Cambridge, U.K.: Cambridge University Press, 1989.

al-Shakhsiyyat al-filastiniyya hatta ʿam 1945 (Palestinian personalities until 1945). Jerusalem: Wakalat Abu ʿArfa, 1945 [1979].

Shalev, Michael. "Jewish Organized Labor and the Palestinians: A Study of State/ Society Relations in Israel." In Baruch Kimmerling, ed., *The Israeli State and Society: Boundaries and Frontiers.* Albany, N.Y.: State University of New York Press, 1989.

———. *Labour and the Political Economy in Israel.* Oxford: Oxford University Press, 1992.

Shapira, Anita. "Even Vesid—parashat shutafut yehudit-ʿaravit menekudat hareʾut shel ʿavoda ʾivrit" (Even Vesid—An episode of Jewish-Arab partnership from the viewpoint of Hebrew labor). *Meʾasef,* no. 7 (May 1975).

———. *Hamaʾavak hanikhzav: ʿavoda ʾivrit, 1929–1939* (The futile struggle: Hebrew labor, 1929–1939). Tel Aviv: Hakibbutz Hameʾuhad, 1977.

———. *Land and Power: The Zionist Resort to Force, 1881–1948.* New York: Oxford University Press, 1992.

Shapiro, Yonathan. *The Formative Years of the Israeli Labour Party: The Organization of Power, 1919–1930.* London: Sage Publications, 1976.

al-Sharif, Mahir. "Musahama fi dirasa aliyyat nushuʾ al-haraka al-ʿummaliyya al-ʿarabiyya fi filastin" (Contribution to the study of the mechanisms of growth of the Arab workers' movement in Palestine). *Al-Tariq,* nos. 3–4 (August 1980).

———. *Taʾrikh filastin al-iqtisadi-al-ijtimaʿi* (The socioeconomic history of Palestine). Beirut: Dar ibn Khaldun, 1985.

———. *Al-Umumiyya al-shuyuʿiyya wa-filastin, 1919–1928* (The Communist International and Palestine, 1919–1928). Beirut: Dar ibn Khaldun, 1980.

Shohat, Ella. "Sephardim in Israel: Zionism from the Standpoint of Its Jewish Victims." *Social Text,* nos. 19–20 (fall 1988).

Silberstein, Laurence J., ed. *New Perspectives on Israeli History: The Early Years of the State.* New York: New York University Press, 1991.

Slutzki, Yehuda. "Me-MPSI ʿad YKP (PKP)" (From MPSI to YKP [PKP]). *Asufot* 3, no. 16 (October 1972).

———. "MPSI beveʿidat hayesod shel hahistadrut" (The MPSI at the founding congress of the Histadrut). *Asufot* 1, no. 14 (December 1970).

———. *Poʿalei Tziyon.* Tel Aviv: Tel Aviv University, 1978.

Smith, Barbara J. *The Roots of Separatism in Palestine: British Economic Policy, 1920–1929.* Syracuse, N.Y.: Syracuse University Press, 1993.

Stein, Kenneth W. "A Historiographic Review of Literature on the Origins of the Arab-Israeli Conflict." *American Historical Review* 96, no. 5 (December 1991).

———. *The Land Question in Palestine, 1917–1939.* Chapel Hill: University of North Carolina Press, 1984.

Studni, Zeʾev. " ʿAl hayamim harishonim behaifa" (On the early days in Haifa). In L. Tarnopoler, ed., *Zeʾev Abramovitch vemorashto.* Tel Aviv: Y. L. Peretz, 1971.

———. "Nitzanei haʾirgun hameshutaf behaifa beshnot haʿesrim" (The budding of joint organization in Haifa in the 1920s). *Meʾasef,* no. 7 (May 1975).

————. "Shvitat po'alei Nesher" (The Nesher workers' strike). *Me'asef*, no. 6 (March 1974).

Sussman, Tzvi. *Pa'ar veshivayon bahistadrut: hahashpa'a shel ha'ideologiyya hashivyonit veha'avoda ha'aravit 'al s'kharo shel ha'oved hayehudi be'eretz yisra'el* (Inequality and equality in the Histadrut: The influence of egalitarian ideology and Arab labor on the wages of the Jewish worker in the land of Israel). Ramat Gan: Masada, 1974.

Swirski, Shlomo. *Israel: The Oriental Majority*. London: Zed Press, 1989.

Syrkin, Marie. *Nachman Syrkin, Socialist Zionist*. New York: Herzl Press, 1961.

Syrkin, Nahman. *Kitvei Nahman Syrkin* (The writings of Nahman Syrkin). Tel Aviv: Davar, 1938–39.

Taqqu, Rachelle. "Peasants into Workmen: Internal Labor Migration and the Arab Village Community under the Mandate." In Joel S. Migdal, ed., *Palestinian Society and Politics*. Princeton: Princeton University Press, 1980.

Teveth, Shabtai. *Ben-Gurion and the Palestinian Arabs: From Peace to War*. Oxford: Oxford University Press, 1985.

Tzahor, Ze'ev. *Baderekh lehanhagat hayishuv: hahistadrut bereishita* (On the way to the leadership of the Yishuv: The Histadrut at its beginnings). Jerusalem: Yad Yitzhak Ben-Tzvi, 1982.

Vandervelde, Emile. *Le pays d'Israel: un marxiste en Palestine*. Paris: Editions Rieder, 1929.

Vashitz, Yosef. *Ha'aravim be'eretz yisra'el* (The Arabs in the land of Israel). Merhavia: Sifriyat Po'alim, 1947.

Vilner, Me'ir. *Haderekh leshihrur* (The path to liberation). Tel Aviv: Palestine Communist Party, 1946.

Weiler, Peter. "Forming Responsible Trade Unions: The Colonial Office, Colonial Labor, and the Trades Union Congress," *Radical History Review*, nos. 28–30 (1984).

Yasin, 'Abd al-Qadir. *Ta'rikh al-tabaqa al-'amila al-filastiniyya, 1918–1948* (History of the Palestinian working class, 1918–1948). Beirut: PLO Research Center, 1980.

Young, Elise G. *Keepers of the History: Women and the Israeli-Palestinian Conflict*. New York: Teachers College Press, 1992.

Zait, David. *Tziyonut bedarkhei shalom: darkho hara'ayonit-politit shel Hashomer Hatza'ir, 1927–1947* (Zionism by peaceful means: The ideological-political path of Hashomer Hatza'ir, 1927–1947). Tel Aviv: Sifriyat Po'alim, 1985.

Zerubavel, Yael. "The Politics of Interpetation: Tel Hai in Israel's Collective Memory." *AJS Review* 16, nos. 1–2 (spring and fall 1991).

Zereik, Elia. *The Palestinians in Israel: A Study in Internal Colonialism*. London: Routledge and Kegan Paul, 1979.

Index